A GUIDE TO COMMON CAN SIZES

LABEL DESIGNATION	APPROXIMATE VOLUME	USUAL CONTENTS INCLUDE
(Tiny cans)	⅓—⅔ cup	
3 -ounces		devilled ham; pâté
4 -ounces		sardines (flat)
4½-ounces		chicken, shrimps
5 -ounces		water chesnuts, bamboo shoots
5½-ounces		tomato paste
6 -ounce can	¾ cup	lemon juice, frozen fruit juices and lemonade
7 -ounce can	¾-1 cup	salmon, tuna, chicken seafood
10 -ounce can (No. 1 can)	1¼ cups	soup, fruits, vegetables frozen soup
12 -ounce can	1½ cups	kernel corn (short) frozen orange juice (tall)
15 -ounce can	1¾ cups	vegetables, fruits, spaghetti, beans, pet food
16 -ounce can (No. 1 tall can)	2 cups	salmon, milk
19 or 20-ounce can (No. 2 can)	2½ cups	vegetables, fruits and their juices; miscellaneous products; 19-ounce designation allows for headspace (shrinkage) of 1 ounce
28 -ounce can (No. 2½ can)	3½ cups	tomatoes, pumpkin, sauerkraut, spaghetti, beans, soup
105 -ounce can (No. 10 can)	12 cups	fruits and juices; commonly called institutional or restaurant size

REPLACEMENT VALUES

1 tablespoon flour used in thickening	½ tablespoon starch (corn, rice, potato)
	1 tablespoon granular tapioca
	2 tablespoons pearl tapioca
	¼ to ½ cup dry crumbs
	2 tablespoons lightly browned flour
	2 tablespoons uncooked rice
	½ cup cooked rice
	2 tablespoons granular cereal
	1 egg
1 cup flour	⅞ cup all-purpose flour
1 cup granulated sugar	1 cup brown sugar, packed
	1½ cups molasses and ½ teaspoon baking soda (Reduce the liquid by ¼ cup.)
	1 cup corn syrup (Reduce by ¼ cup.)
	1 cup honey (Reduce the liquid by ¼ cup.)
	(It is not advisable to replace more than ½ the sugar in a recipe with syrup.)
1 pound dried eggs	36 to 40 medium fresh eggs
1 pound skim milk powder	4 quarts fresh skim milk
2 tablespoons cornstarch used to set 1 cup liquid to a soft jell	½ tablespoon gelatine
	1 large egg
	2 egg yolks
	½ junket tablet
	4 tablespoons flour
2 teaspoons regular baking powder, used to leaven 1 cup flour	1½ teaspoons double-acting baking powder.
1 egg in a batter	½ teaspoon baking powder, in leavening powder.

Nellie Lyle Pattinson's
CANADIAN COOK BOOK

NELLIE LYLE PATTINSON'S

CANADIAN COOK BOOK

REVISED BY HELEN WATTIE AND ELINOR DONALDSON

THE RYERSON PRESS/TORONTO/WINNIPEG/VANCOUVER

ACKNOWLEDGMENTS

Grateful acknowledgment is made to the following for the use of illustrations: Bick's of Canada Limited: p. 678; Bitner's Foods: p. 184; The Borden Company Limited: opp. p. 152 (top), pp. 101 (left), 110, 580 (bottom right), 621; Brigdens Limited: p. 265; Canada Packers Limited: opp. p. 153 (bottom); Canadian Dairy Foods Service Bureau: opp. p. 120, 280, 281 (bottom), 632 (top), pp. 196, 270, 276, 281, 416, 442, 452, 454, 514, 536, 586, 596, 602, 611; Carnation Company Limited: opp. p. 664 (bottom); Department of Agriculture, Ottawa: p. 127 (adapted from Beef Chart), 156; Department of Fisheries and Forestry, Ottawa: opp. p. 505 (top), pp. 64, 87, 219, 223, 337, 352; Dominion Stores: opp. p. 153 (top), 537, 377 (bottom), 312 (top), p. 331; Domtar Fine Papers Limited: opp. p. 504, pp. 59, 208; Fisheries Association of B.C. and the B.C. Salmon and Halibut Producers: opp. pp. 152 (bottom), 377 (top), 281 (top), pp. 221, 307, 346; General Foods: opp. p. 536, 633 (top), 664 (top), pp. 65, 75, 285, 295, 309, 364, 369, 479, 481, 485, 547, 568, 570, 580 (top right), 634, 654; Lawry's: opp. pp. 121, 505 (bottom), pp. 57, 84, 101 (right), 148, 167, 203, 258, 305, 325, 379, 384, 385, 388, 661; Lipton Soup: p. 247; Maple Leaf Mills: opp. pp. 663 (bottom), 665, pp. 272, 299, 426, 433, 438, 444, 458, 468, 471, 483, 488, 489, 501, 504, 509, 512, 540, 546, 551, 574, 576, 580 (left top and bottom), 584, 599, 665; National Duckling Council: p. 201; Nestlé (Canada) Limited: pp. 97, 418, 627, 640; Robin Hood Flour Mills: opp. pp. 312 (bottom), 632 (bottom), pp. 543, 558; Salada Tea: p. 13; Josiah Wedgwood and Sons (Canada) Limited: pp. 16, 17—photographed by Harold Brillinger.
Every effort has been made to credit picture sources. The publisher would appreciate information which would correct any errors or omissions.

PRINTED AND BOUND IN CANADA BY THE RYERSON PRESS, TORONTO

FOREWORD

Some of us are content when three meals a day emerge from our kitchens smoothly and efficiently. This is no small achievement when you include an occasional dinner party, outdoor barbecue and holiday festivities. But for others, meal production is a very personal thing, challenging the creative and discriminating instincts of those dedicated to the pursuit of perfection: the gourmets.

Philosophies of cooking vary. Cooking has been considered drudgery, fun, a challenge, a business, a science and an art; for most of us, it is probably a combination of several of these. We have our spurts of creativity and our moments of disenchantment (the fallen soufflé!) which leaven the routine of three meals a day, day in, day out. To establish oneself as a creator of superb fondues, to win acclaim for appetizers or yeast breads, to be a specialist in the preparation and serving of Chinese dinners—these are challenges and goals attainable by most cooks.

A knowledge of *basic* cooking is the underlying requirement of all cooking; it is the foundation common to the simple dish and the gourmet's delight.

Many changes appear in this edition of the *Canadian Cook Book*, caused by changing food habits, new food products, new methods and equipment. But the book continues to be a basic cook book, a role established by the late Miss Nellie Lyle Pattinson in her first edition in 1923. We have been privileged to continue her work since 1953.

New recipes have been added throughout the book, including specially-marked Basic Recipes with variations and short cuts.

The section on canning and preserving has been greatly reduced, because we find that today much less food is preserved by the home-maker. For those who wish additional information, excellent bulletins are available from the provincial departments of agriculture.

The freezing of foods is dealt with, not as a separate chapter, but within the various chapters throughout the book.

The sections on menu planning and entertaining have been greatly enlarged. The "Regional Dishes" of the previous edition now appear in suggested menu form in Chapter 1, and recipes have been transferred to the general chapters according to their category.

Recipes from former chapters "Food for the Sick" and "Outdoor Meals", among others, now appear in the chapters on vegetables, beverages, etc. and the descriptive material with recipe references appears as a section of Chapter 1.

We hope that this new edition of the *Canadian Cook Book*, completely redesigned, with new illustrations and descriptive diagrams, will meet with the approval of our followers of editions past. We hope also that it will serve as a reliable and inspiring source of information for new friends, experienced and inexperienced cooks, students, brides and homemakers—all those for whom cooking holds a challenge!

We express our sincere gratitude to the many people who have assisted in this totally revised edition of the *Canadian Cook Book*.

Helen Wattie

Elinor Donaldson

CONTENTS

1 Planning and Serving Meals

For convenience, this chapter is-divided into the following sections:

Meal Planning

Table Setting

Table Service

Entertaining

Menus for All Occasions

Meals From the Freezer

Outdoor Meals

Special Diets

Our Heritage of Food

MEAL PLANNING

MEAL TIME may be one of the few occasions today when the family is together. By making this time enjoyable, the unity of the family is strengthened. One of the most certain ways to please the family is to serve favourite dishes; another is to provide surprises with dishes that are entirely new.

1

MAKING A WEEKLY MENU

1. Rule a piece of paper so that it has seven columns across and three down.

2. Fill in the horizontal columns across the top for the days of the week, beginning with whichever day is most suitable. Some people like to start with Sunday when they have a roast or fowl to provide leftovers; others shop on Thursday and so begin then.

3. The three columns down the side are for Breakfast, Lunch and Dinner or for Breakfast, Dinner and Supper, according to the meal pattern adopted by the family.

4. Since the planning of the other two meals does not depend on breakfast to a great extent, breakfast may be filled in first.

5. Plan next the main meal of the day; a new magazine, cook book or television programmes provide new ideas. Keep in mind the factors to be considered which are outlined below.

6. Plan next the third meal of the day with an eye to leftovers and quick combinations. When a busy day can be foreseen, a simple menu should be planned for that day.

7. Check now the week's meals to be sure that the meals within each day provide combinations of food, in adequate amounts, evenly distributed throughout the day. Do the meals meet the requirements of Canada's Food Guide (page 4)? The meals for the week should show variety in the foods served and in the forms of serving them.

8. Prepare a market order based on the menus with alternate suggestions in case some food is not available. A planned menu does not prevent the substitution of another food; rather, it makes possible planned marketing. With proper storage facilities, it should be possible to buy the foods required for one week at one time. This eliminates extra trips to the store.

9. Fasten the menu to a cupboard door in the kitchen so that the family can see what has been planned and begin preparations when mother has been delayed.

SOME FACTORS TO CONSIDER
WHEN PLANNING A MENU

THE OCCASION: It is evident that special occasion menus will be more elaborate than those for every day. Often, just to vary a basic recipe and to serve simple food with style are the only requirements if the colour scheme and motifs of the occasion are observed.

THE SEASON: Advantage should be taken of the fact that foods in season are more economical and have a better flavour than those which are imported. To be ahead of the season always is extravagant; to weary people by a surfeit of food because it is in season shows lack of imagination.

THE HABITS AND CUSTOMS: People have strong food habits which when they are common to a group are known as a custom. These habits can be changed by a process of tact, education and time. Not more than one new food or method of cooking a food should be introduced at one time and it should be presented with a favourite. This is also true of food patterns which are based to a great extent on our daily activities. The breakfast which includes potatoes and pie is not unreasonable for a farmer who has done several hours of chores before breakfast.

VARIETY: Colour in a menu is as important as in a wardrobe. Avoid monotony; only a little imagination is required to picture a meal of mashed potato, cauliflower and creamed chicken served on a white plate—and to see the change when the potato is baked, the cauliflower changed to broccoli. Colours should not clash; there can be colourful but unpleasant combinations, too. Colours which are similar should be separated by a contrasting food.

Flavour, like colour, must be varied. Never serve the same food twice during a meal in such combinations as tomato soup then, later, tomato in a salad; avoid the routine of roast beef on Sunday, cold roast beef Monday, beef stew Tuesday. If another meat is served on Monday the cold beef will be more acceptable on Tuesday.

Texture is as important as colour or flavour in providing variety and interest. Crisp, raw vegetables and fruit are a pleasant contrast to the soft foods. Two mashed vegetables, two leafy vegetables or two creamed foods on the same plate are the result of poor menu planning.

The form in which the food is presented offers many opportunities for variety. Vegetables can be diced, sliced, julienned, cut in finger strips or fancy shapes or left whole.

NUTRITIVE VALUE: It is sometimes said that colourful meals are nutritious meals. Although this may be true in many cases, a more accurate index of nutritional adequacy is Canada's Food Guide (page 4). Avoid a sweet first course or appetizer which dulls the appetite or too many starches or sweets which provide calories without other essentials.

TIME, ENERGY AND EQUIPMENT available to prepare the meal must also be considered.

CANADA'S FOOD GUIDE

These foods are good to eat—Eat them every day for health—Have three meals each day.

MILK—Children (up to about 11 years) 2½ cups (20 ounces); Adolescents, 4 cups (32 ounces); Adults, 1½ cups (12 ounces); Expectant and nursing mothers, 4 cups (32 ounces).

FRUIT—Two servings of fruit or juice. Include oranges, grapefruit or tomatoes three times a week.

VEGETABLES—One serving of potatoes. Two servings of other vegetables, preferably yellow or green and often raw.

BREAD AND CEREALS—Bread (with butter or fortified margarine). One serving of whole grain cereal.

MEAT, FISH AND POULTRY—One serving of meat, fish or poultry. Eat liver occasionally. Eggs, cheese, dried beans or peas may be used in place of meat.

In addition, eggs and cheese each three times a week.

Vitamin D: 400 International Units for all growing persons and expectant and nursing mothers.

Approved by the Canadian Council on Nutrition
NUTRITION DIVISION,
DEPARTMENT OF NATIONAL HEALTH AND WELFARE, OTTAWA

CANADA'S FOOD GUIDE AND WHY WE SHOULD FOLLOW IT:

MILK is an excellent source of calcium. Unless we include milk or cheese daily in our diets, we do not obtain sufficient calcium.

FRUIT is our best source of vitamin C. Tomatoes and peaches are the best buy in August and September, frozen orange juice in October and November, fresh oranges and cabbage as a source of Vitamin C between January and May.

VEGETABLES provide vitamins A and C and iron.

WHOLE GRAIN CEREALS and enriched bread contribute the B vitamins and a little protein and iron. Refined cereals provide carbohydrate only. Butter contains vitamin A and fat.

MEAT, FISH AND POULTRY provide protein. B vitamins and iron are found in meat—iodine in fish. Eggs contain protein, vitamins A, B_2 and D. Cheese provides protein and calcium.

VITAMIN D is necessary for the utilization of calcium to form strong bones.

FUNCTIONS OF FOOD FACTORS IN NUTRITION

VITAMINS AND MINERALS are the food factors which aid the regulating processes of the body. The welfare of the eyes, gums, teeth and nervous system are but a few of the processes directly affected by the vitamins in our diets. Calcium is a mineral needed for strong bones and teeth; iron for rich blood and vitality. Vitamins and minerals do not produce calories. They are merely the "spark in the engine," not the "fuel."

PROTEINS build and repair body tissues; they are needed in larger amounts during periods of growth   adolescence, pregnancy and lactation. After wasting illnesses and injuries, an increased intake of protein in a readily assimilated form (milk, eggs, cheese and meats) hastens recovery. Proteins produce calories but are not considered to be energy foods and the need for them is affected very little by our activity.

CARBOHYDRATE is the family name for starches and sugars; breads, flour, sugar, candy, cereals, macaroni and other Italian pastes. Soft drinks are high in carbohydrate except, of course, those which contain artificial sweeteners. Root vegetables contain more carbohydrate than do leafy vegetables; meats and dairy products contain almost none. Carbohydrates act as fuel which is converted into energy. The amount of fuel-producing foods we require depends almost entirely upon our activity; if we take too little, we are listless and easily tired. Excess carbohydrate is stored fat. Particularly for people who are overweight, it is unwise to eat foods containing only carbohydrate—no vitamins and minerals. Actually, we derive sufficient carbohydrate for energy from vegetables and fruits without eating it in concentrated forms such as sugar. Sugar contributes to tooth decay.

FATS, which include butter, margarine, oils and shortening, are found in large quantities in fat meats, mayonnaise and nuts. Fats are able to produce more than twice the number of calories than are produced by an equal amount of carbohydrate. Certain vitamins are found dissolved in fats and some fat is necessary in the diet. However, fats should be used in moderation, particularly those of animal origin, as they contain substantial amounts of cholesterol—a substance considered to be one of the many factors which contribute to heart disease.

CONVENTIONAL MEAL PATTERNS

BREAKFAST

FRUIT OR FRUIT JUICE

WHOLE GRAIN CEREAL
(hot or cold)

EGG AND/OR BACON
OR PANCAKES

TOAST OR MUFFINS
(JAM)

BEVERAGE

The size of the breakfast eaten depends on our activity—and often the amount of time we allow ourselves for eating. Breakfast consisting of fruit, cereal and toast, or fruit, egg and toast are recommended for the average person. A very active person might want fruit, cereal, egg and toast, whereas the combination of fruit and toast might be sufficient for the late-riser who expects an early lunch.

When the main meal is in the middle of the day:

DINNER

APPETIZER OR CLEAR SOUP

MEAT, FISH OR FOWL
POTATOES

YELLOW, GREEN OR
RAW VEGETABLE

ANOTHER
VEGETABLE

PUDDING, PIE, CAKE OR FRUIT

BEVERAGE

SUPPER

APPETIZER

SUPPER DISH
OR OMELET $+$ SALAD GREENS

OR SALAD PLATE

BREAD, ENRICHED OR WHOLE GRAIN

PUDDING OR FRUIT

COOKIES

MILK

When the main meal is in the evening:

LUNCH

SOUP

SALAD PLATE, CASSEROLE, SANDWICHES
OR EGGS

VEGETABLE STICKS

BREAD, ENRICHED OR WHOLE GRAIN

PUDDING OR FRUIT

MILK

DINNER

APPETIZER OR CLEAR SOUP

MEAT, FISH OR FOWL

POTATOES

YELLOW, GREEN OR   ANOTHER
RAW VEGETABLE   VEGETABLE

PUDDING, PIE, CAKE OR FRUIT

BEVERAGE

The practice of eating 4 or 5 small meals a day is sometimes advocated in the treatment of disease or during convalescence.

TABLE SETTING

An attractive table sets the stage for good eating. Food tastes better because it looks better, thus providing greater enjoyment and satisfaction. An attractive table encourages children to consider table manners. Rules for table setting are based on convenience and should be used as a guide—not followed slavishly at the expense of one's comfort and means.

TABLE APPOINTMENTS

Table appointments should be chosen to harmonize with the room and the furniture.

LINEN: Large damask cloths are now usually reserved for formal dining. They require padding underneath. Mixtures of linen and rayon and of cotton and rayon are often used in place of pure linen. Pastel colours are popular. Lace dinner cloths are frequently used with linen napkins and are usually used without a pad. They are more easily cared for than damask cloths. All large cloths ideally should have a drop of at least 12 inches to help prevent slipping.

Place mats of cork, raffia, bamboo, plastic, novelty cotton, fine linen or lace are very popular because of their gaiety and their ease of laundering. They should be at least 12 by 8 inches; rectangular mats are better than round. It is not essential to have a runner or mat in the centre of the table, but if used, it should match the other mats. Napkins 18 inches square, to match or contrast, are used with place mats.

Luncheon cloths of novelty cotton are gay but usually small; 50 by 60 inches is the largest. Drapery material or dress goods may provide the texture and colour needed, especially for buffet tables.

Table linen should be immaculate. The fold of the cloth must be in the centre. Large cloths should have as few folds as possible. Place mats should be ironed without folds and kept flat. Napkins should have the fold pressed in by hand to prevent wear on the fold. Simple folds are most suitable.

DINNERWARE, SILVERWARE AND GLASSWARE: Dinnerware may be of bone china, semi-porcelain, porcelain or earthenware. Bone china is fine and dainty; porcelain and earthenware are porous in texture, and heavier in weight and line. Semi-porcelain ware may possess the features of either; usually it is more neutral in design and construction.

Silverplate, sterling silver or stainless steel should be chosen to be used with the dinnerware. Fine bone china requires dainty patterns in silverplate or sterling, whereas the stainless steel with its modern lines may be suitable only with modernistic styles of earthenware or porcelain.

Glassware should be in keeping with the personality of the dinnerware and silverware. Fine crystal and cut glass should be used with dishes and silverware of fine lines; heavy glassware is designed to be used with dishes similar to it in weight and line. Again, all appointments should be in keeping with each other to give overall appearance of unity and interest. Sometimes, to take the centre course—neutrality in choosing table appointments is easiest and most practical.

DECORATIONS: There should always be a centre of interest on the table—not necessarily in the centre. Flowers are beautiful and always suitable but sometimes too expensive. They are always used on a formal table. A small flowering plant in an attractive bowl, a figurine, a piece of driftwood with green leaves, a bowl or tray of fruit shows imagination and individuality.

Flowers should be arranged in a container which is in harmony with the other appointments. Use silver or crystal with fine damask and lace, and pottery with heavier fabrics. The flowers should be kept low so that the guests may see over them. Today there are attractive artificial flowers which can be used in areas where real flowers are not available. They should not be left on display at all times; otherwise they are soon absorbed into the background and their purpose is defeated.

A potted plant such as a chrysanthemum can grace both dining room and living room. Pick off a few inside flowers and float them or arrange them in a low bowl with a few leaves. Or, spare the flowers and use artificial chrysanthemum flowers of similar colour, with the leaves from the real plant. The leaves of artificial plants are usually less realistic than their flowers and in candlelight this arrangement works well. For other winter bouquets, small branches, painted or left bare, can be decorated with little birds, pink popcorn blossoms or such motifs as little shamrocks for St. Patrick's Day. Special days provide inspiration for a theme which can be carried out with coloured linens, paper table napkins as well as an appropriate centrepiece.

Candles are used only if they are to be lighted. Their colour should be in keeping with the general colour scheme.

BASIC RULES OF TABLE SETTING

All basic rules of etiquette are merely guides, to be understood and interpreted for the comfort of the family and guests. These are some general rules to remember:

1. Allow 24 inches for each cover.
2. Choose all appointments in harmony.
3. Set the table with only those pieces that will be needed; be sure that all the pieces needed are there.

4. Silver for serving is placed beside the food and not in it.
5. Place mats are placed in line with the edge of the table and directly opposite one another, unless an odd number of people is being served.
6. The cutlery and the plates are placed an inch from the edge of the table and in a straight line. Each piece should be set on the table carefully, with the pattern, if there is one, arranged in the same way.
7. Bread, butter, relishes and other foods should be placed on the table so that it appears balanced and not crowded in the centre.
8. Water and bread should not be placed on the table until just before the guests come to the table.
9. Soup should be served after the guests are seated; cold appetizers may be on the table.

The rules for the cover or arrangement of each place are:

Place:
1. Silver in order of use from the outside in toward the plate.
2. Forks on the left unless a knife is not being used.
3. Spoons outside the knife, on the right.
4. Butter spreader on the butter plate either parallel to the fork or at right angles.
5. Butter plate to the left and at the top of the fork.
6. Napkin folded in square or oblong placed to the left of the fork; fold to right or left as seems balanced.
7. Water glass at the tip of the knife.
8. One set of salt and pepper should be allowed for each two people.

TABLE SERVICE

INFORMAL SERVICE

Formality, or the lack of it, is a matter of degree. What is considered informal to one family might seem very formal to another. The following are the three conventional forms of table service:

RUSSIAN-STYLE: This is a formal type of service; the food is brought to the table on platters and served to each guest by the waitress. A modified form of Russian service would be to bring in the plates from the kitchen, already served.

ENGLISH-STYLE: With this style of service, the meat is carved and served at the table by the host—the vegetables by the hostess. The plates are passed to the left or carried by the waitress.

FAMILY-STYLE: The meat and vegetables are placed in front of the hostess who passes them, beginning with the meat, then potatoes and vegetable. Each person helps himself. This style lacks dignity and is best suited for picnic meals.

The Compromise-style of service is a flexible form of table service which combines some of the features of all the forms. It can be moulded to the needs of the individual family, and thus seems to be the most suitable.

The cold appetizer is on the table when the meal begins; a hot appetizer or soup is brought from the kitchen when the guests have been seated. The waitress, hostess or one of the younger members of the family does the serving. The warm plates are brought in and placed in front of the host by the server, from the left side. If the meat is covered, the cover is removed, inverted and set to one side. The meat is carved, served onto the plates and carried by the waitress or passed by the persons at the table to the lady guests. The vegetables are either passed to each guest by the waitress or served by the hostess after the meat has been served. When there is no waitress, the plates are passed to the left when served.

At the end of the first course the meat platter, then the vegetable dishes, are removed. Beginning with the person who was served first, the dinner plate, then the side plate, are next removed with the right hand from the right side. Each cover should be completely cleared before beginning another. Salts and peppers and any silverware not needed for the dessert course are removed. If necessary, the table is crumbed with a napkin and the water glasses refilled.

The dessert may be served and brought in from the kitchen or served at the table by the hostess. Coffee is served at the table by the hostess and passed to the guests, to the left. If the coffee is passed by the waitress, it is placed from the right with right hand. Coffee may be served from a coffee table in the living room or on the garden terrace.

All members of the group should leave the table together on the suggestion of the hostess. If it is necessary for a person to leave the table before that time, he should ask the host or hostess for permission.

BUFFET-STYLE MEALS

Buffet suppers are gaining greater popularity in this age of diminishing dining rooms and kitchen help —whether we feed four people or forty! This informal style of meal service can be focused about the dining room table, a buffet, tea wagon or television cart—each having its own possibilities and limitations. Each person serves himself, then finds a chair in another part of the room or in an adjoining room. A nest of tables cuts down on the need for knee-juggling—and on mishaps, too. Card tables covered with similar, attractive table cloths can be set up to accommodate guests. Often the tables are set for four, with silverware, napkins and salt and pepper being provided here instead of at the buffet table. If space permits, one large table which allows all to sit down together is ideal for maintaining the unity of the group.

TABLE LINEN: A solid-coloured cloth provides the most attractive background to set off the food to the best advantage. It should be suitable in size to the table, and the texture should be in keeping with the dishes and all other appointments. Solid-coloured mats or runners, used instead of cloths, create dramatic effects when grouped to set off particular dishes or foods. Dinner napkins (22 to 24 inches square) in matching or contrasting colour should be used.

DINNERWARE: Because a buffet supper is usually informal, pottery and gay ovenware are favourites. Any type of dinnerware is suitable as long as the cloth, silver ware, dinnerware and the table used are in harmony with each other. Chafing dishes are particularly suited to buffet suppers.

TABLE DECORATION: The decorations or centrepiece should be in proportion to the size of the table or buffet and in keeping with the nature of the appointments. Arrangements of fruit, flowers, potted plants, statuary, interesting ornaments and candles used separately or in combination are suitable. Special occasions (Christmas, Hallowe'en, St. Patrick's Day, etc.) and special events (bon voyage party, Grey Cup game, etc.) provide themes for decoration.

SERVICE: Because guests help themselves to the food, everything should be laid out in a logical sequence for smooth-running service. Fruit juice or other forms of appetizers may be passed by the host before the guests proceed to the table, or the juice may be picked up last at the end of the table. The usual and most convenient sequence is: dinner plates, the main dish (meat and vegetables, or a casserole mixture) and salad. Relishes, sauces and dressings are placed together or near the foods with which they are usually served. Breads, napkins and silverware follow in the sequence. The dessert and beverage may be placed on the table or side table with the main course. More often, they are arranged at the table after everyone has had the opportunity for "refills" and the main course has been cleared. Dessert may also be passed if there is no variety.

Some provision should be made for keeping hot foods hot, especially if many people are being served; the hot dish can be prepared in several medium-size oven dishes which are brought to the table one at a time just before the need arises. A chafing dish eliminates this problem because it has its own source of heat.

For a crowd, it is often advisable to serve a variety of foods. This is known as a smorgasbord. Experience has proven that it is wise to be extra generous with the quantities of foods prepared. Some say "we eat with our eyes" and when the food looks attractive and we're helping ourselves, by the end of our tour of the table most plates are carrying a peak load!

MENU FOR A BUFFET SUPPER

TOMATO JUICE
TUNA NOODLE CASSEROLE
TOSSED SALAD
CORNMEAL MUFFINS AND GARLIC BREAD
PICKLED ONIONS   RADISHES
STRAWBERRY REFRIGERATOR CAKE

TABLE SETTING AND SERVICE FOR THE
FORMAL DINNER

A formal dinner, because it is served Russian-style, requires competent help. Today the buffet type of entertaining has largely replaced the formal dinner in the home.

FORMAL DINNER MENU

VEGETABLE COCKTAIL

CONSOMMÉ AU PARMESAN   ROYAL CUSTARD

FILLET OF SOLE   LEMON BUTTER

ROAST DUCK   ORANGE SAUCE

NEW POTATOES IN PARSLEY BUTTER

ASPARAGUS

CAESAR SALAD

STRAWBERRY CREAM JELLYROLL

COFFEE

TABLE LINEN: Since the formal dinner is served at a long table, a long cloth has a unifying effect. This cloth, traditionally white, may now be a pastel colour. The napkins match in colour and are dinner size (22 to 24 inches square).

TABLE DECORATION: A somewhat higher floral arrangement is used to balance the length of the table. Candles are customary and must be either tall themselves or in tall candelabra; they are white or pastel in colour.

TABLE SETTING: The table setting for a formal dinner is illustrated on pages 16 and 17.

Place cards are usual if more than eight people are to be seated. These should be simple and placed above the napkin.

Salt and pepper shakers are placed one for each guest at the top of the plate, or to the left at the top if to be shared by one other guest.

The service plate, which is 9 or 10 inches, is often not the same china as the rest of the service, but it must be similar in feeling and is usually ornate.

The napkin is placed on the service plate. There is no butter plate since bread is not served at a formal dinner; a square of bread is sometimes placed on the tablecloth beside each place but this custom is disappearing.

THE TABLE SETTING
FOR A FORMAL DINNER

One cover as it would appear when the guests entered the dining room to be directed to their places by the hostess.

The Appetizer Course.
The round glass bowl holds ice to chill the cocktail. The oyster fork, with which any fish cocktail is eaten, is placed to the right side of the knife.

The Soup is served.
The cocktail service has been removed and the soup is in place. This is the cream soup, china and spoon. Such a heavy soup would never be served, but the pieces are attractive and more frequently found today than the bouillon service. Cream soup cups come with saucers.

The Fish Course.
The fish course, following the soup, is the first hot plate. The service plate is removed and the fish plate is placed so that there is never an empty space ahead of the guest. The small knife and fork may be used or there is a special fish service.

The Main Course.
The dinner plate is in place.
The fish service is removed.

The Salad Course.
The salad course is the last course
before the dessert. Notice how the
table is being cleared as the meal
progresses.

The Dessert Service.
The fingerbowl, dessert silver and
plate are placed before the guest.

THE TABLE SETTING
FOR AN INFORMAL DINNER

The same china, silver, linen and
flowers have been used.

The water glass is placed at the top of the dinner knife with other glasses to the right on a slight angle.

TABLE SERVICE: The water glass is filled just before the dinner is announced.

Water is served from the right; ices if served are placed above the plate from the right.

Used plates are removed one at a time from the right side with the right hand, the next plate being placed immediately with the left hand so that the guest is never left, until the dessert course, without a plate before him.

Food is held in a serving dish on a folded napkin on the left hand, and is offered from the left side.

At the end of the salad course all the dishes except the water glasses are removed; a small tray in the right hand is used to hold the salt and pepper shakers and any unused silver. The table is crumbed with a folded napkin, onto a small plate.

The dessert service is placed before the guest, who sets the silver onto the table, then, picking the doilie up in her left hand and the fingerbowl in the right, sets them onto the table at the upper left of the plate.

The dessert is served onto the plate by the waitress.

After the dessert is eaten, the fingerbowl is used. It should be not more than two-thirds full of water. The fingers of one hand, then the other, are dipped into the water and wiped on the napkin.

Coffee may be placed on the table in front of the guest after the table is cleared of the dessert. It may be served to the right of the guest after the dessert is served, or more often it is served in the living room.

INFORMAL DINNER MENU

VEGETABLE COCKTAIL

ROAST DUCK   ORANGE SAUCE

NEW POTATOES IN PARSLEY BUTTER

ASPARAGUS

CAESAR SALAD

HOT ROLLS

STRAWBERRY CREAM JELLYROLL

The menu and setting for a formal dinner have been modified to make it possible for the hostess who has no maid to entertain graciously. The water, butter and the appetizers are on the table when the guests come to the dining room. The soup and fish courses have been eliminated; the salad and hot rolls are passed during the main course. The main course and the dessert may be served by the English or Compromise method. Coffee is served at the table or in the living room.

TRAY SERVICE

THE BREAKFAST TRAY: This and trays for the sick are discussed in the section, Food for the Sick, page 52.

AFTERNOON TEA AND AFTER-DINNER COFFEE: Afternoon tea or after-dinner coffee may be served from a tray in the living room. The tray should be attractive and in keeping with the surrounding furnishings and the appointments used. If a tray cloth is used, usually linen or lace, it should be spotless. A coffee table, covered card table, tea wagon or trestle table should be cleared or set up to accommodate the tray; the hostess sits at the table to pour.

A tea pot or coffee pot of silver or china and the matching cream jug and sugar bowl are filled and placed on the tray along with the required number of cups and saucers of different or matching patterns. A fork and a plate of lemon slices are placed on the tea tray as well. Cubed sugar is most suitable and this may be accompanied by sugar tongs. The size of the spoons used should be in keeping with the size of the cups and saucers. For after-dinner coffee cups, coffee spoons are used; demi-tasse spoons are required for demi-tasse cups.

With a small group, the hostess may serve the tea or coffee according to the guests' preferences. With a larger group, it may be more convenient to pass cream, sugar and lemon slices on a small tray. When there is no waitress, the host passes the cups and saucers to each guest.

For a tea party where no gentlemen are present, the ladies may take their tea from the hostess as it is poured; with a large group, certain guests are usually designated to assist.

DINING ETIQUETTE

In order to avoid confusion, it is best for the hostess when giving verbal invitations to state what time she would like the guests to arrive, rather than merely stating the hour at which the meal will be served.

Guests are invited to formal dinners by written invitation only and arrive 5 to 10 minutes before the appointed hour.

RESPONSIBILITIES OF THE HOSTESS: The hostess greets each guest on arrival and sees that the meal is served at the appointed hour.

She directs the seating of her guests; lady guests are seated at the right of the host, gentlemen guests at the right of the hostess. Where there are more than 2 guests, alternate men and women at the table.

The hostess serves the vegetables at an informal meal. At a formal dinner, she merely supervises the serving of the meal by the waitress.

Since the hostess is responsible for the meal, she should plan to be at the table throughout the meal except for short intervals between courses if she has no help. Children should be taught to help with the serving. A tea wagon or small side table facilities serving.

If coffee is served in the living room, it is poured by the hostess and passed by the host or waitress.

RESPONSIBILITIES OF THE HOST: The host sees that the conversation is running smoothly and steers it into more neutral grounds should it become heated by controversial subjects. He seats the lady guests as directed by the hostess. At a formal dinner, the host offers his arm to the lady guest of honour and leads the guests into the dining room. At an informal dinner, the meat is carved by the host.

RESPONSIBILITIES OF THE GUEST: It is the responsibility of the guest to arrive on time dressed according to the occasion. The guest uses the accepted forms of etiquette, converses with the other guests and enters into the spirit of the occasion.

Guests remain about two hours after dinner is finished unless bridge, music or the theatre has been suggested in the invitation.

The guest of honour should be the first to depart, but where there are only intimate friends some may leave while others remain.

On departing, the guest thanks the hostess, and may under certain circumstances follow up the verbal thanks with a note or phone call within a few days.

ENTERTAINING

To share the hospitality of our homes with our friends is to give them a little of ourselves. For every home and every budget there is a gracious form of entertaining, whether it be a casual coffee party, a dinner party for a group of intimate friends or a barbecue for the neighbours out on the patio.

Friendly entertaining allows a hostess to enjoy her guests and to spend maximum time with them. If this is to be achieved, pre-planning and organization are essential. A harassed hostess does not enjoy her own parties and may even cause her guests to feel ill-at-ease. Consideration should be given to the choice of guests: the smaller the party, the more important it is that they should be congenial, with personalities and interests that complement each other.

One of the most popular forms of entertaining is the dinner party, partly because it comes at the end of the day when all have finished their work and are ready to enjoy themselves, and partly because it is so versatile. The hostess sets the tone, always within the scope of her own capability, time and budget. Some of the suggestions which follow can be adapted to other occasions as well.

PLANNING A DINNER PARTY
(preferably a week or more before the party)

MENU: The hostess should prepare a menu with which she is familiar and which she does well; completely new dishes should have a "dry run." The amount of time available for preparation should be considered, and, when possible, items which can be prepared in advance should be included. Casserole dishes are very popular for that reason, as are cold meats. Desserts are usually prepared in advance. For advance preparation, a freezer is a friend indeed. (Some people plan parties on 2 consecutive nights, using the same menu and confining their advance preparations to one big effort.)

SHOPPING LIST: A list should be prepared based on the menu, purchasing in advance things that can be stored, and determining at what time perishables such as salad greens, cream, etc., should be purchased.

APPOINTMENTS: Decide in advance on the choice of table cloth, napkins, dishes and silver to be used. Be sure all is presentable—silver polished, dishes free of dust. Are the salts and peppers filled? Will the table need boards to extend it? Candles, if needed, should be purchased and consideration should be given to a centrepiece. (See page 9 for Table Appointments).

TIME MANAGEMENT: Plan remaining time to include all preparations, keeping to the absolute minimum those which must be done at the last minute. Avoid too tight schedules which cannot accommodate probable disturbances and interruptions, especially if there are children in the family. Their need to be fed is unfortunately just as great on busy days as on other days, so be ready with a supply of easily-served food for the day of the party.

Allow time for cleaning the house on the day before the party or earlier. If the evening includes card playing, games, etc., arrangements should be made in advance.

ADVANCE PREPARATION: If a freezer is available, prepare and freeze foods suitable for freezing. If not, the same foods can often be prepared about 2 days before needed, then covered and chilled in the refrigerator. French dressing, croutons, herb bread can all be prepared in advance; the latter should be wrapped tightly in foil and tied, then frozen or chilled until needed. Potatoes can be baked and stuffed, then refrigerated for 2 days until reheated in the oven. Sweet potatoes or beets can be cooked in advance and stored as Fruity Sweet Potatoes or Harvard Beets, until needed. Potato salad improves in flavour when prepared the day before serving, rather than on the same day. Cooked spaghetti can be rinsed in cold water and chilled for 2 days until needed, then restored to use by heating in boiling water. Gelatine mixtures covered and stored in the refrigerator up to 3 days before serving suffer no loss of flavour.

Fortified with ideas and recipes which utilize the storage facilities of her particular household, the hostess can develop a few stock menus which are perfected through repetition and which are more easily prepared with each presentation.

PREPARATION ON THE DAY OF THE PARTY: Early in the day, fasten menu to kitchen wall or cupboard near the working area. For items which are to be served hot, mark beside each at what time cooking should begin. Frozen casseroles or other dense foods which must be thawed should be removed from the freezer early. To eliminate confusion at serving time, don't let dirty dishes accumulate beforehand; keep counters clear. Reserve certain counters or areas for specific things: the coffee pot, coffee, and the tray of cups and saucers, cream jug and sugar should be placed in one area, dessert plates and utensils required for serving dessert in another. Set table as soon as it becomes available. Check facilities for storing guests' coats; are extra coat hangers needed? Are there guest towels in the bathroom?

As the day progresses, foods should be put into the oven at the required times. Green salads should be assembled and kept in a cool place without dressing until serving time. Check regularly to see that all items have been taken care of. Try to leave time, about half an hour, to get rested and ready before guests arrive. Greet them with confidence, knowing that all is under control!

THAT EXTRA INGREDIENT: Just as seasonings add zest to a dish, so does a pinch of drama add to its presentation. Often a menu will be planned around a particularly attractive serving dish. Cold appetizers, served in iced dishes surrounded by ice or snow, introduce the meal with a flourish as do hot fish appetizers in little scallop shells. Soup bowls with lids are perfect for onion soup, and a large tureen creates a focal point for a chowder party. Individual bowls for such things as salads and rice add interest—so do baskets big and little. A handsome chafing dish might call for Meat Balls Romanoff for the main course or Cherries

Jubilee for dessert. The family meat loaf becomes more festive when cooked in a ring mould and served on a platter surrounded by colourful vegetables.

The use of long-stemmed comportes adds a touch of elegance to the lowliest of puddings, while desserts such as charlottes, ices or instant puddings gain prestige when served in graceful parfait glasses. Melons cut in zig-zag fashion and topped with a scoop of sherbet are natural scene-stealers—as are platters of fruits and cheeses. Orange halves, scooped out, serrated, filled with orange charlotte and topped with mint, add much to eye appeal and little to the budget. Flaming foods are spectacular. The list is as endless as the imagination, but the wise hostess will choose only a few novelty appointments or creations for each occasion!

Candlelight, background music, maybe even incense for a Chinese meal may contribute to the scene. Costly things are *not* necessary to make a meal memorable—rather, good food, good friends and a setting which reflects the subtle efforts of a caring and imaginative hostess.

MENUS FOR ALL OCCASIONS

ECONOMY MEALS
to be enjoyed by family and friends:

TOMATO BOUILLON

SWEET & SOUR CHICKEN WINGS

BOILED RICE   GREEN BEANS

CARROT STICKS

FRUIT TAPIOCA PUDDING

PINEAPPLE JUICE

HAMBURGER PIE

or

CHOP SUEY

COLE SLAW

GINGERBREAD

CHICKEN BROTH

FRENCH-FRIED CODFISH BALLS

WITH TARTAR SAUCE

SPINACH

SLICED TOMATOES IN SEASON

or CANNED TOMATOES

COFFEE SPANISH CREAM

CONSOMMÉ

MACARONI AND CHEESE

GREEN SALAD

TOMATO ASPIC

DEEP APPLE PIE

TOMATO JUICE

BRAISED BEEF TONGUE

CREAMED ONIONS

GREEN BEANS

LEMON SNOW WITH CUSTARD SAUCE

VEGETABLE COCKTAIL

BAKED SALMON LOAF

HOT POTATO SALAD

SPINACH OR BROCCOLI

LEMON SPONGE PIE

OVEN-COOKED MEALS
When most of the items of the menu are cooked together in the oven, there is a saving of fuel; if the oven has an automatic timer, the cook can enjoy extra time off!

½ GRAPEFRUIT	APRICOT NECTAR
PRAIRIE CASSEROLE	SAUSAGES
GREEN SALAD	SCALLOPED POTATOES
GINGERBREAD	GREEN PEAS
	CHEESE APPLE CRISP

CREAM OF POTATO SOUP	TOMATO JUICE
SUNSET CASSEROLE	SAVOURY BAKED BEANS
GREEN PEPPERS STUFFED	CARROT STICKS AND CELERY
WITH KERNEL CORN	FOAMY LEMON PUDDING
FUDGE PUDDING	

PINEAPPLE JUICE	APRICOT ORANGE COCKTAIL
HAM CUPS	NOODLE RING WITH
BROCCOLI IN CHEESE SAUCE	CREAMED TUNA
DUTCH APPLE CAKE	BAKED CARROTS
	SLICED TOMATOES
	JAM CUPS WITH LEMON SAUCE

CLEAR SOUP	RHUBARB COCKTAIL
BAKED HADDOCK OR COD	BEEF ROLL
BAKED POTATOES	BAKED POTATOES
BUTTERED OR HARVARD BEETS	WAX BEANS
BAKED APPLES	GREEN ONIONS AND RADISHES
	APPLE BETTY

OUTDOOR MEALS

Some of these menus require a barbecue; others need only be prepared indoors and kept warm outdoors.

<table>
<tr>
<td>

BARBECUED HAM
ON A SPIT

POTATO SALAD

SLICED TOMATOES
AND CUCUMBERS

FRESH PEACH OR BERRY
SHORTCAKE

</td>
<td>

HOT CHOWDER
IN MUGS

HEARTY CHEF'S SALAD

POTATO CHIPS

CARROT STICKS AND CELERY

CHERRY PIE

</td>
</tr>
<tr>
<td>

RAW VEGETABLE RELISHES

FOIL-COOKED LIMA BEANS

FRENCH FRIED POTATOES
(FROZEN)

SLICED TOMATOES

ASSORTED MELONS

</td>
<td>

HAMBURGERS OR
PATIO PUPS

KETCHUP   MUSTARD

COLE SLAW   PICKLES

SLICED TOMATOES

WATERMELON

</td>
</tr>
<tr>
<td>

CONSOMMÉ IN MUGS

SHISH KABOBS

FOIL-BAKED POTATOES

CAESAR SALAD

LEMON SHERBET AND
ANGEL CAKE

</td>
<td>

CLEAR TOMATO SOUP

ASSORTED COLD MEATS

BAKED STUFFED POTATOES

JELLIED LIME LAYERS

GARLIC BREAD

BLUEBERRY PIE

</td>
</tr>
</table>

MEALS FOR TWO

HALF GRAPEFRUIT

BROILED, MARINATED
FLANK STEAK
(1 MEAL HOT, 1 MEAL COLD)

FRENCH FRIED POTATOES
(FROZEN)

PARTY ONIONS

TOSSED GREENS

ICE CREAM WITH LIQUEUR TOPPING

SEAFOOD COCKTAIL

MEAT-STUFFED PEPPERS
or
STUFFED PORK CHOPS

SCALLOPED POTATOES

CARROTS

BAKED APPLE

JELLIED CONSOMMÉ

CHICKEN LIVERS IN WINE
or
SALMON STEAK

HOT POTATO SALAD

ZUCCHINI OR PEPPER SQUASH

SLICED TOMATOES

HALF GRAPEFRUIT WITH
MAPLE SYRUP

VEGETABLE JUICE

BAKED HAM SLICE

SPEEDY SWEET POTATOES

SPINACH

CABBAGE AND APPLE SALAD

FOAMY LEMON PUDDING

PINEAPPLE JUICE

BREAST OF CHICKEN IN
CURRY SAUCE

RICED POTATOES

GREEN BEANS OR BRUSSEL
SPROUTS

RAW VEGETABLE RELISHES

ASSORTED CHEESES
AND FRUITS

TOMATO JUICE

CHICKEN LEGS IN SWEET
AND SOUR SAUCE
or
FOIL-BAKED TURKEY LEGS

GREEN BEANS RISI

CAESAR SALAD

SHERBET IN MERINGUES

THE SCHOOL LUNCH BOX

From the humble lunch box can emerge a meal that is exciting, nutritious and enjoyable, one that provides ⅓ of the food needed for energy and good looks.

If soup or milk is available at school, a paper bag will contain all the lunch that is carried. If not, such extra items will have to be transported in a thermos in a heavier container. Small plastic or glass jars can hold puddings or salad. A wide assortment of wrappings—waxed paper, plastic wraps and foil—enables each food to be properly wrapped; dried out or oozing foods are inexcusable!

An area in the refrigerator should be reserved for leftovers which are suitable for lunches. With a freezer, a week's supply of sandwiches can be prepared at one time.

MONDAY	TUESDAY
HAM SANDWICH WITH MUSTARD OR PICKLES	FROZEN TOMATO JUICE (will be thawed by noon but keeps the pudding cold)
TOMATO WEDGES	
BAKED CUSTARD COOKIE	BAKED BEANS OR SANDWICH
HOT CHOCOLATE	A DRUMSTICK
	CARROT AND CELERY STICKS
	ORANGE INSTANT PUDDING
	GINGER COOKIE AND MILK

WEDNESDAY	THURSDAY
DEVILLED EGG	VEGETABLE SOUP
POTATO SALAD IN PLASTIC JAR	CHEESE-STUFFED CELERY
BUTTERED RYE BREAD	SAUSAGE ROLLS
BUTTER TARTS	APPLE SAUCE
BANANA	CUP CAKE
MILK SHAKE	

FRIDAY

CORN CHOWDER

TUNA ROLL

FRUIT SALAD

DATE SQUARES

LET'S ENTERTAIN

AFTER THE THEATRE

TOASTED SANDWICHES

PICKLES

FROSTED CAKE

COFFEE

SUNDAY SUPPER

CHICKEN TETRAZZINI

SALAD BOWL

ONION BISCUITS

ICE CREAM CAKE

TEA   COFFEE

LUNCH BEFORE THE GAME

BAKED HAM AND EGG SANDWICH

HOT EGG OR TUNA AND EGG BUNS

or

SANDWICH BUFFET

ICE CREAM SUNDAES   COOKIES

COFFEE

BEFORE-THE-DANCE BUFFET

FRUIT JUICE   ONION DIP

BISCUITS   POTATO CHIPS

SHRIMP JAMBALAYA

FRENCH BREAD   ROLLS

GREEN SALAD

CHOCOLATE ÉCLAIRS   COFFEE

DINNER FOR THE BOSS

APRICOT ORANGE COCKTAIL

STUFFED TENDERLOIN
WITH APPLE RINGS

GREEN BEANS WITH PICKLED ONIONS

or

GREEN PEAS WITH MUSHROOMS

LETTUCE WEDGES   FRENCH DRESSING

INDIVIDUAL BAKED ALASKAS
Made the night before and frozen

COFFEE

AT HOME AT CHRISTMAS

CHICKEN BOUCHÉES

CELERY AND PICKLES

CHRISTMAS CHEESE BALL

BISCUITS

FRUIT CAKE   SHORTBREAD

CHRISTMAS EGGNOG

A "LITTLE" DINNER

(FOR 6)

ICED SEAFOOD

BEEF FONDUE

BAKED POTATOES   GREEN SALAD

FRENCH BREAD

ICE CREAM MERINGUES
WITH FROZEN OR FRESH RASPBERRIES

COFFEE   MINTS

DINNER FOR ALL OCCASIONS

FRUIT JUICE

LIVER SAUSAGE SPREAD ON
MELBA TOAST

BAKED HAM

SWEET POTATOES   BROCCOLI

HERB-BAKED TOMATOES

GREEN SALAD

ROLLS   BUTTER

DUTCH FRUIT SQUARES

TEA   COFFEE

FAMILY BARBECUE

VEGETABLE JUICE

SHISH KABOBS
(self-assembled)

CABBAGE SALAD

BUTTERED BREAD

WATERMELON

SOFT DRINKS   COFFEE

A DESSERT AFTER BRIDGE

STRAWBERRY SHORTCAKE

RHUBARB CHARLOTTE

LIME PIE   RASPBERRY PIE

BLACK BOTTOM PIE

COFFEE

A POT LUCK SUPPER FOR A FRIEND WHO IS LEAVING TOWN

COLD MEATS   SCALLOPED POTATOES

JELLIED VEGETABLE SALADS

MUFFINS   HOT ROLLS   BISCUITS

GLAMOURIZED ICE CREAM

FRUIT SAUCE

COFFEE

A FONDUE FOURSOME

CHEESE FONDUE

FRENCH BREAD

TOSSED GREENS

COFFEE   WHITE WINE

STRICTLY FOR THE GIRLS

A SHOWER FOR THE BRIDE

FRUIT SALAD PLATE

HOT ROLLS

MERINGUE TORTE

TEA   COFFEE

A COFFEE PARTY FOR NEIGHBOUR'S MOTHER

COFFEE CAKES

BUTTERSCOTCH MUFFINS

APPLESAUCE MUFFINS

FRUIT BREAD   COFFEE

A TEA FOR THE OFFICE STAFF

FANCY SANDWICHES

BOUCHÉES WITH CHICKEN SALAD

VEGETABLE RELISHES

SMALL CUP CAKES   MERINGUES

FANCY COOKIES

TEA   COFFEE

BREAKFAST MEETING OF THE PROGRAMME COMMITTEE

FRESH FRUIT

BERRIES   MELON

BROILED GRAPEFRUIT

DANISH PASTRIES   COFFEE CAKE

MELBA TOAST

BLACK CURRANT   CINNAMON APPLE
JAM   JELLY

COFFEE

LUNCH ON THE PATIO

VICHYSSOISE

RIBBON SANDWICH LOAF

PLATTER OF ASSORTED

FRUITS

TEA   COFFEE

LUNCHEON FOR THE VISITING SPEAKER

FRUIT SALAD   CHEESE MUFFINS

CRÈME BRÛLÉE

COFFEE

WHEN FATHER ENTERTAINS

Usually there is an unwritten law with the Men's Club as to how elaborate the menu should be, and usually the focus falls in the first course.

Varieties of breads—rye, French, homemade and foreign—all make wonderful sandwiches; so do rolls which have been heated for about 15 minutes. For those do-it-yourself sandwich fans, put the breads on a tray, serve rows of assorted cold meats, cheese slices and slices of Spanish onions and tomatoes, along with a variety of substantial pickles such as garlic dills, mustard pickles or homemade relishes.

Coffee should be hot and strong. Here are a few favourite combinations:

SANDWICHES OR BUNS
FILLED WITH
HAM WITH HOT MUSTARD
SLICED CHICKEN
RELISHES
COFFEE

SAUSAGE ROLLS
HOT CHILI SAUCE
PICKLES   OLIVES
COFFEE

LASAGNA
GREEN SALAD   GARLIC BREAD
SYRUP TARTS
COFFEE

ASSORTED CHEESE
FRENCH BREAD
BISCUITS   PICKLES
FRUIT
COFFEE

CABBAGE ROLLS
POTATO CHIPS   RELISHES
COFFEE

ASSORTED COLD MEATS
(TONGUE, HAM, SALAMI)
SPANISH ONIONS   DEVILLED EGGS
RYE, HOMEMADE, FRENCH BREADS
APPLE PIE   CHEESE
COFFEE

TEENS ENTERTAIN

PYJAMA PARTY

SANDWICH BUFFET

or TOAST VARIATIONS

ICE CREAM SUNDAE

COCOA

AFTER THE DANCE

PIZZA

or HAM 'N' EGG BUNS

or BREAKFAST BUNS

PEPPERMINT STICK CAKE

TUTTI FRUTTI PUNCH

RECORD PARTY

COCKTAIL TIDBITS

PLATTER PARTY COOKIES

BROWN COW

or COLA EGG NOG

KITCHEN PARTY

FILLED WIENERS

or HAMBURGER SPOON-ONS

BUTTER TARTS *or* CINNAMON ROLLS

HOT SPICED CIDER, GRAPE JUICE

or PINEAPPLE JUICE

WINTER PICNIC

DEVILLED STEAK BUNS

or HAMBURGERS PLUS

or TUNA AND EGG BUNS

or BACON BUNS *or* FISHBURGERS

DOUGHNUTS *or* BROWNIES

THERMOS OF HOT CHOCOLATE

or COFFEE

AFTER THE GAME SUPPER

CHEESE FONDUE

or

FRENCHBURGERS

CUP CAKES

or

WAFFLES

LEMON ICE CREAM, MAPLE SYRUP

COFFEE

SMALL FRY FROLICS

A BIRTHDAY PARTY FOR A FIVE-YEAR-OLD DAUGHTER

SANDWICHES:

RAISIN BREAD AND JAM

PEANUT BUTTER AND BANANA

ICE CREAM

BIRTHDAY CAKE

STRAWBERRY MILK

A BIRTHDAY PARTY FOR AN EIGHT-YEAR-OLD SON

WIENERS OR HAMBURGERS

BUFFET STYLE

KETCHUP   RELISHES   MUSTARD

ICE CREAM

BIRTHDAY CAKE

ASSORTED SOFT DRINKS

HALLOWE'EN PARTY FOR BROWNIES AND CUBS

ASSORTED SANDWICHES

HOT CHOCOLATE WITH MARSHMALLOW

TAFFY APPLES

MEALS IN A HURRY

These foods can be invaluable when time is short and stocks of fresh foods are low: canned frozen or dehydrated soups to use as bases for quick casseroles (tomato, cream of celery, chicken, mushroom and shrimp); canned ham, salmon, tuna, chicken, used alone or in mixtures; cheese, eggs, instant potatoes, tea biscuit mix and instant puddings. Consult Supper Dishes, Chapter 11, for quick recipes.

TOMATO JUICE	CHEESE-STUFFED CELERY
HAM SLICE (CANNED OR FRESH)	SPEEDY BEEF STROGANOFF
WITH ORANGE MARMALADE *or*	NOODLES *or*
CRANBERRY SAUCE GLAZE	INSTANT MASHED POTATOES
CANNED SWEET POTATO SLICES	FROZEN GREEN VEGETABLES
FROZEN GREEN VEGETABLE	SLICED TOMATOES
FRESH FRUIT CHEESE COFFEE	7-MINUTE FRUIT WHIP
	TEA OR COFFEE

(DEHYDRATED) FRENCH ONION	HALF GRAPEFRUIT
SOUP WITH GRATED CHEDDAR	CURRIED BEEF, LAMB OR EGGS
SWEET AND SOUR PORK	*or*
FROZEN GREEN VEGETABLES	SCALLOPED TUNA OR SALMON
INSTANT RICE	SLICED TOMATOES AND CUCUMBERS
SIDE SALAD OF GREENS OR FRUIT	POTATO CHIPS
QUICK CHERRY TORTONI	QUICK PINEAPPLE CHARLOTTE
COFFEE	COFFEE

VEGETABLE JUICE	CLEAR SOUP
FISH PATTIES	SCRAMBLED EGGS AND
WITH SANDWICH SPREAD	BACK BACON
TARTAR SAUCE	BROILED TOMATO HALVES
PRESSURE-COOKED SCALLOPED	WITH GRATED CHEDDAR
POTATOES	APPLE WHIP *or*
GREEN VEGETABLES	ASSORTED FRUITS
CELERY	TEA OR COFFEE
SHERBET	
TEA OR COFFEE	

MEALS WITHOUT OVENS

Establish a tradition: "Come to lunch after church" or "Come to dinner before the Saturday movie or television special."

COME TO LUNCH AFTER CHURCH

MENU I

HEARTY SOUP   CRACKERS

SMORREBROD

LEMON ANGEL MOULD

TEA OR COFFEE

Try any of these soups: Lentil Soup, Fish Chowder, Supper Corn Chowder, French Onion Soup, Borscht, Oyster Stew, Canned Soup Combinations.

MENU II

SCRAMBLED EGGS OR OMELET

CANNED CHERRIES

DANISH PASTRIES

TEA OR COFFEE

Add any of these: Sausage or Bacon and Toast; thick tomato slices sprinkled with finely sliced green onions or chives and French Dressing; Tossed Salad.

DINNER BEFORE THE SHOW

CRANBERRY JUICE—ASSORTED BISCUITS

BEEF STEW WITH DUMPLINGS *or* INSTANT MASHED POTATO

FROZEN BROCCOLI

CUCUMBERS IN SOUR CREAM

BAKERY PIE WITH A GLAMOUR TOPPING

TEA   COFFEE

Another night try one of these for the meat dish: Swiss Steak, Veal Birds, Steamed Salmon, Chicken Livers Supreme.

MEALS FROM THE FREEZER

When food is prepared or purchased for the freezer, it helps to have a menu in mind. If this menu is posted on the freezer the planning has been done and the food is ready. Unexpected visitors, friends invited after an occasion, house guests with whom we wish to spend time will be more easily fed. Even day-to-day meals are simple when children or the automatic oven-timer can start the dinner.

One must remember that food will not keep forever. By planning menus as the food goes into the freezer, there is less likelihood that certain items will be kept too long. In the frozen-food storage compartments in refrigerators, temperatures can often rise to 20° or higher, so that food should be used within 2-4 weeks; fish within a day or two. Ice creams at this temperature do not keep well, especially in waxed cartons; plastic containers are more successful.

Included here are menu suggestions which make use of both commercially frozen foods and those for which recipes are to be found in the pages which follow.

BAMBINOS	TOMATO FRAPPÉ
CHICKEN RICE	FISH STICKS WITH SHRIMP SAUCE
HARVARD BEETS	BROCCOLI POTATO SALAD
ICE CREAM SPICE CAKE	CHEESE BISCUITS
	LEMON SHERBET OATMEAL CRISPS

BAKED VEAL WITH	HAMBURGER PATTIES
MUSHROOM SAUCE	BUNS
BROILED TOMATO SLICE	BARBECUE SAUCE
POTATO PANCAKES	MUSHROOMS
ESCAROLE SALAD	VEGETABLE STICK DIP
STRAWBERRIES AND	FRESH FRUIT
WHIPPED CREAM ROSETTES	AND
LEMON SAUCE	COFFEE CAKE
	or
	CHEESE CAKE

GRAPEFRUIT

MINT SHERBET

SWEET AND SOUR SPARE RIBS

BOILED RICE   GREEN PEAS

CRÊPES SUZETTES

APPLE JUICE

SUNSET CASSEROLE

SALAD BOWL

STUFFED BAKED POTATO

HERB BREAD

BAKED ALASKA

GAZPACHO

PARTY MEAT BALLS AND GRAVY

MASHED POTATOES OR NOODLES

GREEN BEANS OR ZUCHINI

FROZEN FRUIT SALAD

CREAM PUFFS WITH CHOCOLATE

MINT SAUCE

TOMATO SOUP

CHEESE STRAWS

CURRIED LAMB

BOILED RICE

MIXED VEGETABLES

BAKED APPLE CRISP *or*

DUTCH APPLE CAKE

BORSCHT

ASSORTED SANDWICHES

or

PIZZA

TOSSED GREEN SALAD

FRUIT PIE

CHILI CON CARNE

LETTUCE WEDGES

BLUE CHEESE DRESSING

PINEAPPLE SHERBET

RASPBERRY SAUCE

OUTDOOR MEALS

Good food tastes even better when eaten outdoors—whether it is cooked indoors and transported to the patio, or barbecued in the garden with everybody helping. Outdoor meals can provide enjoyment and good eating for family and friends alike and can be the solution to entertaining when space indoors is limited.

As with most meals, pre-planning of menu and equipment can do much to ensure success. Until one becomes experienced in the art of serving outdoors, it is very wise to keep the menu simple. Even then, it should be in keeping with the atmosphere of informality. Fresh air is the best appetizer and the wise hostess will order her supplies with a generous hand.

HELPFUL EQUIPMENT FOR GARDEN MEALS

Serving table to hold plates, cold foods, condiments, etc., for self service; a card table, or two or more card tables grouped together, will serve the purpose. The table should be located on level ground, out of the wind.

Chairs and benches should be grouped informally in twos and threes; upright ones make for easier eating.

Little tables to be shared by 2 or 3 guests for holding beverages and extras are very useful.

Barbecue and/or electrical appliances and extensions to enable food to be prepared on the spot or kept hot will save trips to the kitchen. Electric percolators, frying pans, hot plates and warmers are all useful.

Candle warmers, sterno (canned heat) keeps hot foods hot.

Trays and baskets for serving foods.

Plenty of large paper serviettes. Individual vacuum-sealed paper towels which have been impregnated with skin freshener are very helpful for cleaning greasy hands at the end of a barbecue meal; these are sold at most drug stores.

BARBECUE COOKING

There are two matters of prime importance for successful barbecueing. The first concerns the fire; food must be cooked over a deep bed of coals with *no flame*. The second requisite is that meats and fish require marinating and/or basting to prevent their drying out during cooking. For this, an unlimited variety of barbecue sauces, high in fat content and pungent in flavour, can be prepared or purchased.

PREPARATION OF THE FIRE: The fire must be started *at least* 45 minutes before cooking is started. Sufficient wood or charcoal should be used to produce a good, deep bed of coals after the fire has burned down, which will retain high heat for the entire cooking period. The fire should not be disturbed during the cooking period by poking or by the addition of more wood, as this results in a loss of heat and in uneven cooking. As each barbecue is a little different from another, experience will be the guide in determining just how much time and how much wood will be required to arrive at the right stage for cooking. It is helpful to record such information in a notebook. Briquettes of charcoal make a beautiful fire but they are more difficult to ignite. The fire should be started with kindling wood, then a few briquettes added. When these are hot, more briquettes should be added until there is a glowing bed of coals. A charcoal fire must be started at least an hour before the food is to be cooked, in order to prevent the meats being overdone from too slow cooking. Charcoal should be glowing and coated with a white ash before cooking is commenced. A very little bit of dampened hickory wood added to the fuel gives a characteristic flavour to beef which may or may not be popular with your crowd; never use it for chicken.

EQUIPMENT FOR BARBECUING

A barbecue ranges from the very simple to the most elaborate; a portable iron grill, an outdoor stone fireplace or an electric rotisserie will do the job effectively. A revolving spit is a worthwhile addition.

One or more 2-sided broilers or wire racks for grilling flat meats and vegetables such as steaks, hamburgers; stainless steel skewers or a wiener wheel for shish kabobs.

Long handled fork; long-handled tongs.

Saucepan and wide brush for basting; drip pan, preferably made of aluminum foil, to catch basting sauce from the spit.

A table beside the barbecue to hold supplies.

A rack for spices and sauces, a carving board and knife.

Mitts; asbestos mitts are best.

Aluminum foil is extremely useful as a cooking utensil and for keeping wrapped foods warm at the back of the fire box; often foods can be served right in the foil after cooking; it can be disposed of after use and thus eliminate dishwashing.

A bucket of sand beside the barbecue for putting out the fire.

A notebook to record such facts as the time required to get the fire to the right stage for cooking, how much fuel was required, how much meat to buy, how long it had to be cooked, and recommendations for another time. This will be a valuable reference for future occasions.

A WORD TO THE WISE

Nothing dampens the party faster than accidents; do all cooking in the open, away from anything that might catch fire. Place the grill on solid footing, preferably near a hedge or other windbreak. Do not put it in the line of traffic. Start the fire with wood shavings, kindling wood or sticks—never with kerosene, gasoline or lighter fluid. Special liquid fire starters are available but their use should be reserved for adults; keep only one pint on the premises at one time. Keep a bucket of sand near the grill. Use it to douse any fire caused by the flaring up of grease (the chief cause of burns at cook outs).

Dress for the job; wear a large, heavy, non-frilly apron and thick oven mitts. Keep toddlers and young children away from the grill until they are old enough to realize the danger. Sharp-pronged tools should be kept out of the way where they will not cause injury to anyone or where they could be used in horseplay. Use caution when using an electric grill that is hooked up with extension cords from inside the house. When the grass is wet or when the hands are wet, grabbing a makeshift connection could cause severe shock or electrocution. Be prepared to treat minor burns; serious ones should always receive doctor's attention. If clothing catches on fire, roll on the lawn, don't run.

PLANNING THE MENU

There is no limit to the variety of foods which can be barbecued. Any food which can be broiled or roasted can be barbecued; those which are usually braised can be wrapped in aluminum foil and cooked over the coals. It is difficult to be specific in recipes as to cooking times as this will vary from one barbecue to another, and with the size and intensity of the fire. Record in a notebook all details as to cooking.

Usually when a complete meal is being served outdoors, it is the meat course that is barbecued, perhaps with one or more vegetables. When serving a crowd, unless the barbecue is equipped with a spit, it is often impossible to accommodate more than the meat over the fire box; then hot scalloped potatoes, broiled frozen French fries or herb-flavoured rice might be brought from the kitchen and kept in a warm place. If the barbecue has a hood and the top is flat, it is usually hot and makes a good warming place; candle warmers, sterno and electric frying pans are very useful for these additional hot dishes. Rolls and breads can be kept warm in the same way.

In the menu include salads for self service, prepared in advance and refrigerated until needed; jellied salads are not very practical for outdoors, especially in hot weather. For desserts, fresh fruits such as peaches, a variety of melons or berries are always popular. If there are facilities for storage, ice cream or sherbet are favourites with or without fruit. Serve tea or coffee made on the barbecue, in electric tea or coffee makers, or indoors and kept warm on the candle warmer or barbecue.

SPECIAL DIETS

Although dieting without medical advice is a foolish and risky thing to do, there are occasions when a knowledge of special diets may be needed to vary a convalescent diet or prepare for a dieting visitor.

The best special diet is one which resembles as closely as possible what the person has been accustomed to eating. Not only is such a diet more likely to be followed but it will be easier to prepare.

All special diets are normal diets modified in one of three ways. There may be a change in the number of calories, in the texture of the food or in one particular element.

TO LOSE WEIGHT

Today overweight is a major North American health problem. But to lose weight it is not necessary to follow some strange dietary regime; rather it is necessary to know the foods and recipes which provide many or few calories so that a wise choice may be made.

A calorie is a unit of measurement. Inches measure length, pounds measure weight and calories measure the amount of energy that food supplies to the body. If we wish to lose weight we must use up more energy than our daily food is providing; if we wish to gain weight we must provide more energy from our food than we are using up in our daily work and play.

There are 2 kinds of work which the body performs. There is the work done by our heart in beating, by our lungs in breathing, by our cells in growing, which we cannot control and must always provide for. This is why starvation diets and queer reducing diets may do much lasting harm. This internal work of the body which is known as our Basal Metabolism requires for women 1200-1500 calories a day; for men 1500-1800.

The second kind of work that the body does is the kind we can see. If we are still growing, active, energetic, in a job that requires running up and down stairs, fond of dancing, golf and tennis, we will be able to eat large quantities of high calories foods, enough to provide another 1000-2000 calories, without gaining any weight. But if we ride to work, take the elevator, sit down at our job, do not exercise and have stopped growing, then those last 1000-2000 calories are going to add weight. For every 3500 calories our food provides which we do not use up, we will gain 1 pound, so 500 calories a day in excess of our energy needs will mean a gain of 1 pound a week.

One pound a week does not sound like very much but it is 50 pounds gained or lost in a year. Add 500 calories as supplied by any of these foods:

1 doughnut	200	1 piece of pie	300
1 hot dog in a bun	300	1 piece of cake	300
	500		600
1 handful of peanuts	500	1 malted milk shake	600

The Table of Calorie Values in the Appendix lists some of the common foods in each group, with their caloric value.

To lose weight it is necessary to decide how many pounds you wish to weigh, and how many you must lose.

Suppose you weigh 145 pounds but would like to weigh 125. This weight multiplied by 15 gives you the number of calories you need—in this case 125 x 15 or 1875. But to take off the extra 20 pounds you will have to eat 500 calories a day less than this to lose 1 pound a week. This means you can have 1875—500 or 1375 calories a day until you reach your desired weight, and then you can have an extra 500 a day, or 1875 calories.

Put down the food pattern you have been following and count the number of calories. Now alter each meal to obtain the calories you need and no more.

The weight loss will not be immediate or constant. You reach levels where your body seems to adjust itself to the new programme and then all at once you have lost 5 pounds.

This day's food supplies 4745 calories

BREAKFAST

ORANGE JUICE (65)

SUGARED CEREAL (150) RICH MILK (200)

BUTTERED TOAST (2) (200)

BACON (2) (200)   MARMALADE (50)

COFFEE (100)

CREAM   SUGAR

This day's food will provide 1510 calories

BREAKFAST

ORANGE JUICE (65)

POACHED EGG (75)

TOAST: TWO SLICES BUT CUT VERY THIN AND WITH ONLY A VERY LITTLE BUTTER ADDED AFTER THE TOAST WAS COOL (100)

CAFÉ AU LAIT MADE WITH SKIMMED MILK HEATED AND POURED INTO STRONG COFFEE HALF AND HALF (50)

LUNCH

HAMBURGERS (300)   CHIPS (500)

CATSUP (50)

PIE (300)   ICE CREAM (100)

SOFT DRINK (100)

LUNCH

CONSOMME (50)   MELBA TOAST (50)

LARGE BOWL OF SALAD WITH FRENCH
DRESSING (100)

CHICKEN SANDWICH,
NO MAYONNAISE (300)

FRESH FRUIT OR CANNED
DIETETIC FRUIT (100)

COFFEE WITHOUT CREAM AND SUGAR

OR

SKIMMED MILK (85)

DINNER

PORK CHOPS (450)   GRAVY (200)

MASHED POTATOES (120)   CORN (85)

ROLL (100)   BUTTER (50)

SALAD (25)   MAYONNAISE (50)

CANNED FRUIT (100)   CAKE (300)

TEA (100)

CREAM   SUGAR

DINNER

A SLICE OF ROAST BEEF (VEAL,
LAMB, TURKEY OR FISH) (250)

CABBAGE (35)   YELLOW BEANS (35)

SALAD WITH FRENCH DRESSING (50)

CANTELOUPE (40)

CLEAR TEA WITH LEMON

EVENING SNACK

A HANDFUL OF PEANUTS (500)

A COUPLE OF HARD CANDIES (50)

A CUP OF COCOA (200)

AND 3 COOKIES (100)

EVENING SNACK

1 FRUIT GLASS OF ORANGE JUICE (25)

CELERY STICKS

CARROT STICKS

BUTTERMILK (85)   RYE CRISP (15)

OR SKIMMED MILK

A FEW TRICKS TO HELP

Reward yourself with one food you want very badly each time you lose another 10 pounds. You may find to your surprise that you don't enjoy it as much as you thought you would. We soon get used to less rich foods, less sugar, no sweetening in tea and coffee.

Buy a new dress one size too small so that you will have to continue to lose weight to wear the dress.

Buy a pair of really nice shoes of the kind that your feet couldn't stand when you were overweight.

In a sauce replace 4 tablespoons fat with 1 tablespoon oil and 1 tablespoon butter. Replace flour with cornstarch, which requires only half the amount. Use a Teflon-coated pan which needs less fat to keep the food from sticking.

Sour cream contains approximately the same amount of butterfat as light cream, and only half as much as heavy cream. Sour cream may be used instead of heavy cream; it can be substituted for whipped cream as a topping for gelatine or fruit (sweeten with a little sugar or non-calorie sweetener); sour cream can replace mayonnaise (it contains only ⅓ of the calories) or be blended half and half with mayonnaise.

Yoghurt, which is even lower in calories and fat than sour cream, may be used in making salad dressing, or in place of sour cream for dips.

Replace milk in a cream sauce with chicken stock; thicken by beating 1 egg yolk with 2 tablespoons milk; add hot liquid, return to the heat, stir until thick.

TO GAIN WEIGHT

Although it is just as difficult for the person who is underweight to gain as it is for the overweight person to lose, the problem is not as common. Exactly the same principles apply; to gain 1 pound a week it is necessary to eat foods that provide 3500 calories more than we have been eating or to eat an extra 500 calories a day. If each night a malted milk shake with a scoop of ice cream and an egg was added and no other change was made in the diet at the end of a month there should be a gain of 5 pounds.

See Beverages, Chapter 15, for suggestions; fortified beverages to use for liquid diets may also be used by the person who wishes to gain weight.

FORTIFIED BEVERAGES

A liquid diet can provide as many calories as a normal diet if the liquids used are fortified with nourishing substances which will dissolve in them. Below are listed some valuable additions to liquids.

SKIM MILK POWDER: The addition of 2 tablespoons of skim milk powder to 1 cup of fresh milk makes the milk twice as nourishing in protein and calcium. It contains approximately 37% protein, which aids the convalescent in gaining back normal strength and vigour.

EGGS: The addition of eggs to milk makes a delicious drink when the mixture is flavoured and chilled; eggs contribute protein also.

ICE CREAM: Added flavour and richness are provided by the sugar and fat; these contribute calories— and therefore energy.

SUGAR: Various sugars can be added to liquids to increase their caloric value; lactose, which is milk sugar, is the least sweet of all sugars and can be added in greater amounts without making the beverage taste too sweet.

CREAM: Cream can replace part of the milk and thus add more calories to the mixture.

HIGH RESIDUE DIETS

One of the materials which our food provides for the body is cellulose. This is the part of cereals, fruits or vegetables which forms the framework in the same way that our bones and skin provide the structure that supports us. Since this cellulose is not digested, it remains as a soft bulk to exercise the digestive tract and so keep it functioning smoothly. To increase the cellulose content of the diet, serve the following:

SALADS: Either fruit or vegetable.

FRUITS: Best eaten raw. Substitute fresh fruit and cheese for cake, ice cream and custard-type desserts; baked apple instead of applesauce rhubarb sauce instead of canned peaches or pears; sliced oranges with coconut instead of orange jelly; half a grapefruit instead of orange juice, raisin or prune and apricot pie instead of apple pie.

VEGETABLES: Serve baked potato instead of mashed; cabbage instead of cauliflower; corn instead of squash; spinach instead of turnips, canned tomatoes instead of tomato juice.

CEREALS: Serve rolled oats instead of cream of wheat; brown bread instead of white; oatmeal crisps, date squares and hermits to replace the shortbread-type cookie.

SERVE jams, conserves and honey instead of jellies.

LOW RESIDUE DIETS

When it is necessary to rest the digestive tract a *low residue* diet is required; this would be the opposite of the one preceding. It is usual at the same time to avoid anything which would irritate the lining of the digestive tract. If one thinks of the foods that would hurt a sore in the mouth one would avoid not only rough, coarse foods but salt, pepper and acids. Such a diet is known as a *bland* diet. Since the diet list provided by the doctor will list the forbidden food, the problem is rather one of making attractive those that are permitted.

Use canned baby vegetables for soups; try combinations of them. Heat a slice of onion, a few onion flakes or a little scraped onion juice in the milk to add flavour.

Add sieved fruit to egg white to make fruit whips.

Sieved or mashed vegetables may be used in soufflés, in cream soups or may be baked in small muffin tins to make timbales.

Serve scalloped potatoes, sweet potatoes, baked potato (do not serve the skin).

Cottage or cream cheese may be seasoned with fruit juice.

For desserts there are all the custards, snow puddings, charlottes, cornstarch and cereal puddings as long as nuts, dates and spices are omitted; angel cake and ice cream, sponge cakes and chiffons do not need icing.

The lack of cellulose in this diet may make it necessary to provide bulk by a commercial preparation recommended by the doctor.

LOW SALT OR LOW SODIUM DIET

The connection between sodium in the diet and disorders of heart, kidney and blood pressure is clearly indicated.

Salt is the most widely-used source of sodium, and by removing it from the diet our sodium intake is quickly reduced. However, when cooking for someone on a salt-free or low sodium diet these foods should also be considered.

Avoid these seasonings: salt, garlic salt, onion salt, celery salt, celery seed, dried celery flakes, parsley flakes, mixed seasoning salts, monosodium glutamate.

Use instead: fresh onion juice, chives, green onion tops, tarragon, rosemary, oregano, thyme, mint.

Avoid baking soda and baking powder and therefore bakery goods. Cakes, especially angel cakes, muffins, tea biscuits and quickbread may be replaced by home-made cookies made without baking powder on soda and by pastry and yeast bread.

Avoid smoked or salted meats or fish, including sausage, bacon, salami, cooked ham, corned beef, chipped beef, wieners. Serve instead hamburgers, chili con carne, spaghetti and meat sauce, cold home-roasted meats, all prepared without added salt.

Replace bouillon cubes and canned soups with homemade soups, remembering that onion and celery salt must be left out of the soup.

Replace the egg white with the yolk in custards, cookies and puddings.

Avoid pickles and condiments, because of the salt and also because they may contain sodium benzoate as a preservative. Instead of ketchup, chili sauce, meat sauce, soy sauce and prepared mustard, use lemon, chives, peppergrass or water cress, thyme, basil, pepper, cranberry-orange relish, ketchup, watermelon rind pickle (if the rind is soaked overnight in limewater instead of salt). Use poppy seed, cardamon seed, cumin seed, caraway seed, lemon and orange rind, candied ginger and coconut.

Avoid cheese, salted nuts, cocktail mixtures, salted crackers, pretzels and potato chips.

Avoid dried fruits which may have been treated in the drying; all fresh fruits may be used.

Small pots of chives, mint, thyme and rosemary may be bought in the fall at the market. If they are sprayed with a fine mist of water each day they will last until Christmas and add much to the flavour of meats and vegetables. An unsalted, poached egg on toast buttered with salt free butter may not have much appeal, but made into scrambled egg with chives and a little fresh thyme it will be enjoyed even by those who are not on a diet.

LOW FAT AND LOW CHOLESTEROL DIET

Fats in our diet are of two types, the animal and the vegetable. The animal fats are in butter, whole milk, cream, cheese, fat meat, egg yolk and lard. The vegetable fats are in nuts, salad oils, shortening and avocados. Baked goods, especially pastries, and foods cooked in fat (such as potato chips, fish and chips, doughnuts) contain a high content of fats.

The difference is that the animal fats are saturated with hydrogen and are solid. The vegetable oils are unsaturated. Vegetable oils which have been persuaded to take up more hydrogen become solid fats; they are then saturated fats.

Is any fat responsible for high blood cholesterol, or, is it just the saturated fats or just animal fats which are the culprits? This is a medical controversy which results in two diets, Low Fat and Low Cholesterol. A Low Fat diet would avoid both animal and vegetable fats. A Low Cholesterol diet does not restrict the use of vegetable oils or unsaturated fats. Also restricted is the use of eggs, cheese, cream, whole milk and meat.

Where the gall bladder or liver is involved, both animal and vegetable fats must be omitted; also a High Residue diet is to be avoided. The following foods are generally permitted:

Rice cereals, including macaroni, spaghetti, most bread and crackers, fruits cooked without seeds or skins.

Vegetables, except those such as cabbages, turnips, or onions which seem to be troublesome.

White meats of both poultry and fish, veal, lamb; roast meats with fat removed.

Cottage cheese, skimmed milk, skimmed milk cheese, egg whites.

Jams, jellies, syrups.

This is a diet in which emphasis may be placed on desserts. Any of the charlottes made with skim milk topping instead of whipped cream; any of the gelatine mixtures using egg whites, white cake or angel cakes; fruit sauces thickened with cornstarch but without the butter; fruit whips; applesauce; tapioca—these are all desserts which are high in carbohydrate but low in fat and cellulose.

A LOW FAT MENU

BREAKFAST

ORANGE JUICE

SUGAR FLAKE CEREAL   SKIM MILK

UNBUTTERED TOAST   JELLY

CLEAR COFFEE

LUNCH

CREAM OF VEGETABLE SOUP (LOW FAT)

CHICKEN SANDWICH

APPLE SAUCE

ANGEL CAKE

SNOWY LEMON FROSTING

CLEAR TEA

DINNER

ROAST BEEF   MASHED POTATO

(NO FAT)   (CREAMED WITH SKIMMED MILK)

SHREDDED BEETS   ORANGE SAUCE

LETTUCE WITH BUTTERMILK SALAD DRESSING

LEMON SHERBET

CLEAR COFFEE

DIABETIC DIET

Diabetes is a condition of the body in which more sugar is released into the blood by the liver than can be controlled by the insulin manufactured in the pancreas. The kidneys work hard to get rid of it, but without help the sugar accumulates in the blood. Insulin can be given to the person to make up the amount that is lacking. In this case the amount of food prescribed must be eaten at the proper time and in the proper amounts. Since all the food we eat—meat, eggs, fruits, vegetables, cereals and fats—will finally by chemical action in the body produce some sugar, it is necessary to control all the food that is eaten, not just the sugar.

Anyone who knows he is diabetic will have a diet carefully planned for him, so the purpose of this section is to offer some ideas to the person who has to prepare food for a diabetic visitor and to assure the cook that no upheaval of the kitchen is necessary.

The American and Canadian Dietetic Associations have worked out groups of foods that can be substituted one for another. These groups are known as exchange groups. On the diet worked out for our visitor, if she is allowed two milk exchanges it means she may eat any two items of milk or milk products on the milk exchange list and must eat two and no more than two.

Now suppose we wish to have a tea for our friend when she is visiting. If we tell her our plans she will be able to adjust her meals to save some bread and meat so she may eat a sandwich. Coffee or tea served clear does not have to be considered.

In the same way if we wish to have a picnic, sliced cold meats, a chicken leg, cheese or hard cooked egg would replace some of the meat allowed, while potato salad would replace a slice of bread. If a hamburger has no bread crumbs or rolled oats in the meat, it will be the same as 3 ounces of meat. A wiener (9 to the pound) is equal to 1 ounce. So our visitor could have a hamburger or she could have a wiener and 2 slices of cold meat. The hamburger or wiener roll is equal to 2 slices bread.

Barbecues and cook-outs can be managed equally well. Cook meat without sauces, have plenty of green salad, vegetable relishes, fresh fruit and cheese and the diabetic will be able to have a meal that will have people exclaiming, "But I thought you were on a diet."

Desserts present a greater problem because they usually have a fairly high proportion of sugar. For this reason raw fruit is a better choice. There are today dietetic counters in the large stores where fruits canned in water instead of syrup, gelatines sweetened with non-caloric sweeteners and dietetic pudding mixes are available. However, un-restricted use of these "dietetic" foods is not recommended for "diabetic" people.

ALLERGY DIETS

If someone in the family has an unusual reaction to shrimp or chocolate it is easy to avoid these foods, but the allergen may be one which poses more problems.

Egg is not difficult to avoid except in baked goods such as muffins, cakes and cookies. Rolls and fancy yeast doughs may contain egg while bread is unlikely to.

Instead of milk, fruit or vegetable juices or bouillon will be easy substitutes in some recipes, but other sources of protein will have to be provided especially for children. Care must be taken that packaged food does not contain dried milk powder.

When the gluten of wheat is the allergen it is necessary to avoid any bread except that sold as gluten-free. Rye flour or corn meal may be used.

Rice or barley makes a good substitute for macaroni and spaghetti; corn or cornmeal may be used for breakfast cereals.

Shortbread and other cookies may be made with cornstarch or rice starch.

FOOD FOR THE SICK

Every effort should be made to make meal time a pleasant time for a patient. Rapid recovery depends upon adequate nourishment and we need a generous supply of vitamins and minerals—and of proteins to repair broken-down tissues! As much as possible, the meals served to a patient should be similar to those normally eaten.

The patient who is convalescing from surgery, or who has had a high fever or a stomach upset is often fed light foods before being given a full meal. In some cases, it may be necessary to sieve vegetables and mince meat. Use infant foods to save time.

Clear Fluids, No Milk	Add Milk	Proceed to Soft Diet	Continue With Light Diet
BREAKFAST:			Soft Diet plus any foods that are not highly seasoned, very rich or sweet, or those with coarse seeds or fibre.
Strained Orange Juice	Fruit Juice	Fruit Juice	
Clear Tea or Coffee	Cream of Wheat Milk	Refined Cereal—Milk	
	Tea or Coffee	Poached Egg Beverage Toast made from white bread	
10 A.M.:			
Strained Lemonade	Tomato Juice or Milk	Milk	
DINNER:			
Fruit Juice	Strained Soup	Chicken or Fish (without skin or bones)	
Clear Gelatine Dessert	Junket Ice Cream Milk	Mashed Potatoes Green Beans and Carrots Applesauce	
3 P.M.:			
Canned Fruit Juice	Milk Shake or Egg Nog	Milk and Vanilla Wafers	
SUPPER:			
Hot Consommé	Cream Soup	Cream Soup	
Clear Gelatine Dessert	Gelatine Dessert (without fruit)	Foamy Omelet Asparagus Tips	
Clear Tea	Custard Tea	Orange Charlotte Beverage	
9 P.M.:			
Broth	Cocoa	Cocoa Enriched Bread—Butter	

Whether a tray is used for a patient or a guest, the setting should be similar to that used for table service.

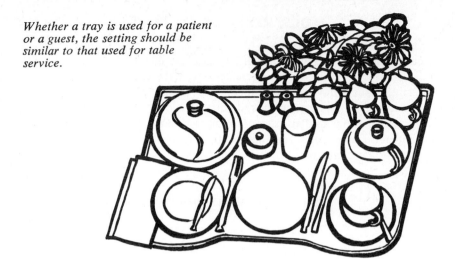

FACTS TO CONSIDER IN SETTING UP A TRAY

1. The tray should be clean and attractive; it should be made of a washable material. The size should be large enough to hold at least one course of the patient's meal.
2. The tray cover should add to the appearance of the tray; it should be spotless. Often, one from a set of place mats can be used. Where an invalid adds to a busy family schedule, a paper tray cover which can be changed after each meal is better than soiled linen.
3. Dishes should be attractive and of a suitable size for a tray. Alternating the sets of dishes and tray cloths used will aid in breaking the monotony of eating in bed. The occasional appearance of a little bouquet or gay figurine on the tray adds interest.
4. The plates and silverware should be arranged in their usual order.
5. Hot foods should be hot and cold foods cold. Use heated plates and covers for a hot main course and other hot foods. It is easier to control the temperatures of foods if one course only is served on the tray at one time. However, this may be impossible or impractical from the standpoint of distance. A chair or bedside table should be convenient for holding the tray after use.
6. Water is not put on a tray because it should always be available to the patient.
7. Plates under cereal bowls, soup bowls, and dessert dishes are not used; the tray makes them unnecessary and they add to the weight.
8. There should be a convenient arrangement for holding the tray securely at the bed.

OUR HERITAGE OF FOOD

In Canada there are people of many nationalities: those whose forebears came years ago to begin a new life and to become Canadians, those who have come recently for the same reason. With each group have come recipes which have been changed and adapted until they, too, are Canadian. As each group moved across the country they made use of the native foods and so regional recipes became part of the Canadian heritage. The recipes for the menus which follow can be found in appropriate chapters.

THE ATLANTIC PROVINCES

The newest province, Newfoundland, became the tenth by vote of its people on March 31, 1949. Though many of its children have gone from this rugged maritime island to the industrialized parts of Canada and the United States, their own food is still dear to them.

Nova Scotia, New Brunswick and Prince Edward Island are known for their seafood. Potatoes from Prince Edward Island and New Brunswick, and fruit from the Annapolis Valley of Nova Scotia, are important additions to the food supply of our country. Salmon from the Gaspé, the Restigouche and St. John rivers; lobster from the Atlantic, the Malpeque oysters, scallops, and even the delicious Digby Chicks (smoked herring) come to mind when we think of food and the Atlantic Provinces.

The Atlantic Provinces have many native foods other than fish. Visitors to Nova Scotia are always amazed to find Pork and Beans on the menu for Sunday breakfast; Beans and Brown Bread are a tradition for Saturday night supper. Fiddleheads, the frond of the ostrich fern, may now be obtained frozen.

STEAMED RESTIGOUCHE SALMON

FIDDLEHEADS

BAKED ISLAND POTATOES — WITH DIKE

MUSHROOMS

BROWN BREAD

APPLE GINGERBREAD

COFFEE

QUEBEC

In 1608, Champlain founded Canada's third settlement, a trading post at Quebec. Here five years later came the first true settlers on the Grand Allée—Abraham Martin, his wife and daughter; Nicholas Pivert, his wife and niece; Pierre Desportes, his wife and daughter, and Guillaume Collard, bachelor.

From Quebec come dishes French and "Canadien."

FRENCH	CANADIEN
VICHYSSOISE	ONION SOUP
RAGOUT	HORS D'OEUVRES
GREEN SALAD	TOURTIÈRE COQ AU VIN
CRÊPES SUZETTE	BÛCHE DE NOËL
	FERLOUCHE

ONTARIO

Ontario was first settled by the United Empire Loyalists who came up the Mohawk and Champlain Trails to find homes under the British flag. They brought to Canada not only their British food habits but also those they had developed in the Thirteen Colonies; the Thanksgiving turkey dinner is an example. More completely English were the settlers along Lake Erie, brought out by Colonel Talbot, and those of the Huron district established by the Canada Company, chartered to John Galt.

The Scottish settlement in the Ottawa Valley; the Irish one at Peterborough; the German group at Kitchener (formerly called Berlin); the Italians who came in the railway building era; the Dutch who, settling in the marshes of the Holland River, turned this great wasteland into a fertile vegetable garden; the Central Europeans who came to the mines of Northern Ontario, the Jewish people who even in the small towns kept their own food habits; all these people built Ontario and established her food customs. More recently the arrival of Hungarians, Czechoslovaks, West Indians and those from the East Indies have stimulated interest in new foods and flavours.

BRITISH

ROAST BEEF

YORKSHIRE PUDDING

HORSERADISH CREAM

MASHED POTATO   BRUSSEL SPROUTS

LEMON CHEESE TARTS

GERMAN

BARBECUED PIG TAILS

HOT POTATO SALAD

GREEN BEANS VINAIGRETTE

SOUR CREAM PIE

CENTRAL EUROPEAN

BORSCHT

BOHEMIAN PORK ROAST

RED CABBAGE—PARSLEY POTATOES

DOBOSCH TORTE

JEWISH

SMOKED SALMON

CANAPÉ

ROAST DUCKLING

NEW CABBAGE

POTATO PANCAKES

GLAZED STRAWBERRY TARTS

ITALIAN

ANTIPASTO

CHICKEN CACCIATORE

RICE   ZUCCHINI

ESCAROLE SALAD

PEACH WITH BURGUNDY

WEST INDIAN

SWEET AND SOUR PORK

LUAU SALAD

BANANA FLAMBÉ

MACADAMIA CHEESE BISCUIT

THE PRAIRIE PROVINCES

Between the years of 1896 and 1911 more than a million settlers poured through the bottleneck at Winnipeg or across the United States-Canadian border into Manitoba and the Territories. Ten thousand Icelanders settled around Winnipeg; Northern Europeans from Scandinavia, Scotland and Germany; Eastern Europeans from Russia, Poland and the Ukraine; Doukhobors, Mormons and Mennonites from the United States settled from Winnipeg to the Rockies—each group contributing to Canadian food habits.

The smorgasbord is an old custom in Sweden which is now very popular in Canada. The origin is the country party to which everyone brought food, which was spread out on a long table. (Our Potluck Supper is similar.) It is eaten in stages: first fish dishes, next meat or poultry and last cheeses, with clean plates for each course. Salads go with each course and cheese may be the dessert course with fruit, or may be eaten after dessert. The Cold Board or Koldt Bord of Denmark replaces the smorgasbord of Sweden. If a foundation of bread is used the cold foods become hearty open-faced sandwiches or Smorrebrod.

Smorrebrod from Denmark.

FISH DISHES	MEAT AND POULTRY DISHES
PICKLED HERRING	SWEDISH MEAT BALLS
LOBSTER SALAD	SPICED BEEF-WESTERN STYLE
WINNIPEG GOLD EYE	CABBAGE ROLLS OR DOLMA
	CHICKEN PAPRIKASH

CHEESE DISHES	SALADS AND RELISHES
ONION CHEESE PIE	CUCUMBER IN SOUR CREAM
CHEESE BALL	POTATO SALAD
	RED CABBAGE

DESSERTS

STOLLEN   APRICOT PIE   HVORST

PLATTAR WITH BLUEBERRY SAUCE   (PANCAKES)

BRITISH COLUMBIA

British Columbia brings us to the last of the provinces and, in the words of our national motto, "A Mari Usque ad Mare."

The Okanagan Valley, like the Annapolis Valley of Nova Scotia and the Niagara Peninsula of Ontario, is renowned for its fruit. The coast of British Columbia is a rich fishing ground. Indeed, the first international treaty which Canada signed without Great Britain also signing was the Halibut Fisheries Convention of 1923, in which the United States and Canada took steps to preserve and restore the halibut in the waters off the west coast.

From across the Pacific, China, Japan and India have also contributed colour and variation to traditional British Columbian menus.

Curried Shrimp are complemented by Sambals of contrasting flavours.

CHINA

CANTONESE   SWEET AND
CHICKEN   SOUR SHRIMPS
BOILED RICE
GINGER FRUIT COMPÔTE
SESAME COOKIES   CHINA TEA

JAPAN

SUKIYAKI
or
TEMPURA
NOODLES
CANNED LYCHÉE FRUIT

INDIA

CURRY
(LAMB, BEEF, CHICKEN)
CAULIFLOWER AND PEAS
KHEER

WEST COAST DINNER

CRAB CURRY CANAPÉ
HALIBUT TURBANS
BROCCOLI
SCALLOPED TOMATOES
PEACH BERRY PIE

YUKON AND NORTHWEST TERRITORIES

The Yukon, "Sourdoughs" and Robert Service are synonymous. A sourdough is a prospector who of necessity learned the art of bread-making with "sourings" instead of yeast. In the intense cold, bread is useless after a few hours and yeast soon freezes; yet starchy foods are needed to sustain energy on the long trails. Some sourings are kept to make sponge for the next day, and so it goes on. The older the sourings the better they work, and it is with pride that the age of the sourings is disclosed.

The Canadian Northland is famous for more than its sourdough bread; recipes for game and fish will be found in appropriate chapters.

SHERRIED CONSOMMÉ

ARCTIC CHAR

FRENCH	GREEN
BREAD	SALAD

HOT SCONES WITH
STRAWBERRY JAM

2 Appetizers

APPETIZERS include Cocktails, Canapés and Hors d'Oeuvres, and are of unlimited variety. Those which follow are merely suggestions to stimulate the imagination. Appetizers such as fruit cocktail, shrimp cocktail and tomato juice are served at an elaborate dinner as a course before the soup; at a simpler dinner in place of the soup course. Since appetizers may be on the table before the guests arrive, they are more easily served than soup for the hostess without help. Increasingly popular is the idea of serving this first course in the living room.

COCKTAILS (LIQUID)

TOMATO JUICE

3 cups tomato juice	2 teaspoons lemon juice
2 teaspoons horseradish	⅛ teaspoon pepper
¼ teaspoon onion juice	8 drops Worcestershire Sauce
¾ teaspoon salt	parsley, mint or celery leaves

1. Combine the juice and seasonings. Add a sprig of parsley, a stalk of mint, or a few celery leaves.
2. Refrigerate several hours.
3. Remove the leaves. Serves 6.

TOMATO FRAPPÉ

This is a low-calorie, economical recipe; additional calories can be added in the form of a dollop of sour cream or mayonnaise.

1 cup tomato juice	few drops Worcestershire
1 teaspoon lemon juice	Sauce
	salt to taste

Freeze to a mush; beat smooth. Serves 2-3. Garnish with parsley and serve with vegetable-flavoured biscuits.

CRANBERRY JUICE COCKTAIL

2 cups cranberries	½ cup sugar
3 cups water	2 cups any combination of fruit

1. Wash cranberries, add water, cover and simmer until the skins pop.
2. Strain through a sieve without mashing the berries.
3. To the juice add the sugar and stir until it dissolves.
4. Combine this juice (there will be about 2 cups) with 2 cups of other fruit juice, using lemon or orange juice with leftover fruit juices.
5. Dilute with ice and ginger ale. Serves 12.

   If the pulp in the sieve is boiled again with ½ cup sugar for five minutes it will make a jelly glass of cranberry sauce.

RHUBARB MINT COCKTAIL

4 cups rhubarb	2 lemons
2 cups water	1 orange
1½ cups sugar	1 sprig fresh mint
1 cup hot water	

1. Chop the washed rhubarb; add the water.
2. Add the grated rind of the orange and lemons; cover; simmer.
3. When the rhubarb is soft, strain through a sieve.
4. Dissolve the sugar in the hot water; add to the rhubarb juice.
5. Add the juice of lemons and orange.
6. If a clear juice is desired, strain through cheesecloth.
7. Refrigerate with the mint until a faint flavour of the mint is obtained. Serves 6.

CIDER PUNCH

1 quart sweet cider	1 cup water
1 lemon	1 cup sugar
3 sprigs mint	1 quart ginger ale

1. Combine the cider, strained lemon juice, and crushed mint and let stand in the refrigerator 3 to 4 hours.
2. Make a syrup by boiling sugar and water 3 minutes. Chill.
3. Remove the mint, add the syrup to the cider and just before serving add the ginger ale.
4. Pour over ice cubes. Serves 20.

HOT SPICED GRAPE JUICE

1 quart grape juice
1 quart boiling water
½ cup sugar
2 tablespoons grated orange rind

2 tablespoons lemon juice
4 cloves
3 sticks cinnamon

Simmer the ingredients 5 minutes. Remove the spices. Serves 8.

TOMATO BOUILLON

Combine equal amounts of tomato juice and consommé. Heat. Serve in cups.

See also recipes for hot and chilled soups in Chapter 4.

SEAFOOD COCKTAILS

HOT SEAFOOD APPETIZERS

1 7-ounce tin cohoe or sockeye
    salmon, or tuna
1 7-ounce tin lobster or crab
½ cup finely chopped celery
4 tablespoons butter
1½ cups medium White Sauce

½ teaspoon Worcestershire Sauce or
1 tablespoon sherry
    salt and pepper
1 cup fine, soft bread crumbs
2 tablespoons melted butter
    pimento, parsley

1. Remove bones and skin from salmon; save liquid. Rinse oil from tuna. Remove any body material from lobster. Break into small pieces.
2. Sauté celery in 4 tablespoons butter until just tender.
3. Lift out celery, and prepare White Sauce (see Chapter 3) in the pan, using liquid from salmon for part of the milk. Season.
4. Add celery and fish and stir only until combined. Transfer mixture to 6 shells or ramekins.
5. Toss crumbs lightly with melted butter, and spoon a thin layer onto each serving of fish. Garnish with strips of pimento.
6. Bake at 375° for 20-25 minutes until mixture bubbles and crumbs are golden. Garnish with parsley. Serve with lemon wedge.

   Any combination of fish or seafood can be used. Grated cheese can be added to the topping or to the White Sauce. Crushed potato chips can be substituted for buttered crumbs, or the topping omitted entirely.

Shellfish are used in this simple but impressive Seafood Cocktail.

SEAFOOD COCKTAIL

1. Allow ¼ cup per serving of cooked cleaned shrimp, flaked canned lobster, flaked crabmeat, flaked sockeye salmon, or a combination of these.
2. Add 1 tablespoon cocktail sauce before serving. Serve chilled with lemon wedge. Garnish with a sprig of parsley.

COCKTAIL SAUCE

3 tablespoons chili sauce	⅔ teaspoon Worcestershire sauce
¾ cup catsup	2 tablespoons lemon juice
2 tablespoons horseradish	1 teaspoon salt

Mix all the ingredients and chill. Serve over chilled seafood.

OYSTER COCKTAIL

See Fish and Shellfish, Chapter 6.

OYSTERS OR CLAMS ON HALF SHELL

See Fish and Shellfish, Chapter 6.

VEGETABLE COCKTAILS

TOMATO COCKTAIL

6 medium sized fresh tomatoes or
1 28-ounce can of tomatoes
¼ cup finely diced green pepper
½ cup finely chopped celery

¼ cup chopped green onions
1 teaspoon prepared horseradish
pepper and salt

1. Scald and peel fresh tomatoes. Dice. Empty canned tomatoes into a sieve and leave to drain. (Save liquid for other purposes.)
2. Combine tomatoes or pulp with other ingredients; chill, preferably for several hours.
3. Serve over small pieces of lettuce in sherbet or cocktail dishes.

These appealing Fruit Cocktails will make a lasting impression on guests, and they are easily prepared ahead of time.

FRUIT COCKTAILS

When served at the beginning of a meal, mixtures of fruits should not be too sweet. Combine grapefruit sections, or a little lemon or lime juice with canned fruits or canned fruit cocktail. When possible serve some raw fruit in the mixture.

MELON BALL COCKTAIL

Using a melon-ball cutter or the ½ teaspoon of a measuring-spoon set, scoop out balls from cantaloupe, honeydew or watermelon. Chill. Arrange in sherbet glasses. Top with a sprig of mint; grapefruit juice; lemon ice; or coconut.

APRICOT ORANGE COCKTAIL

1 pint orange ice   1 can apricot nectar

In each sherbet or parfait glass place a scoop of orange ice. Pour over it the apricot nectar. Serve at once. Garnish with a sprig of mint. Serves 6.

CANAPÉS

Canapés in their original form consisted of fancy-shaped pieces of thinly sliced bread, toasted or fried on one side, spread on the untoasted side with a savoury mixture and decorated with a garnish. Today, one can buy many varieties of cocktail biscuits, potato chips and tiny pastry shells which can also be used for canapé bases. They must be spread just before serving time to prevent softening. A variety of canapés is usually served on a large tray. To freeze canapés with bread bases, follow directions for freezing sandwiches (open-face), Chapter 12. If they are to be served hot, broil thawed canapés just before serving.

CANAPÉ SPREADS

Butter may be creamed with highly seasoned ingredients. To ¼ cup butter add any one of the following:

   1 tablespoon anchovy paste, 1 teaspoon lemon juice
   2 tablespoons chili sauce
   2 tablespoons finely minced chives
   2 tablespoons horseradish
   2 tablespoons finely chopped stuffed olives
   2 tablespoons finely minced parsley
   1 tablespoon Roquefort, Danish blue or other soft cheese
   smoked turkey minced finely, 1 tablespoon cream, seasoning

CANAPÉ GARNISHES

Cut ¼ pound thinly sliced smoked salmon into thin strips. Spread with a paste of hard-cooked egg, mayonnaise and prepared mustard. Decorate with strips of pimento.

Cut 6-ounce fillet herring into strips 1 by 1½ inches. Place on buttered bread. Trim with tiny pickled onion and water cress.

Sliced cucumber on squares of bread decorated with shrimp.

Cream cheese tinted, forced through a pasty tube.

Sardine on bread sprinkled with sieved egg yolk.

Slices of radish, stuffed olives or hard-cooked egg.

SELF-SERVE DIPS AND SPREADS

Dunking bowls are popular with hostess and guest alike. They require much less preparation than canapés and contribute informality to the occasion. Leftover mixtures can be refrigerated and used again. For easy blending, basic ingredients such as cream cheese should be at room temperature; an electric blender is particularly helpful.

Thick mixtures can be shaped into large balls about 3 inches in diameter and served on a tray with potato chips or biscuits. A spreader is placed on the tray and guests help themselves. For dunking, mixtures must be thinner to prevent breaking biscuits or chips. Most dip and spread mixtures can be prepared several days before needed, if desired, or frozen up to 4 months.

TROPICAL CHEESE BALL

½ pound old Cheddar cheese	½ teaspoon Worcestershire Sauce
1 3-ounce package soft white cream cheese	dash of celery and onion salts
	¾ cup angel flake coconut
3 tablespoons sherry or orange juice	2 tablespoons concentrated frozen orange juice
¼ cup coarsely chopped pitted ripe olives	

1. Grate Cheddar cheese into large bowl; combine with cream cheese, sherry or juice, olives, Worcestershire Sauce and seasonings. Blend until smooth.
2. Shape mixture into a ball, about 3 inches in diameter; refrigerate until needed.
3. About 30 minutes before serving, combine frozen orange concentrate and coconut, mixing thoroughly. Roll cheese ball in mixture until evenly coated.

To freeze after step 2, wrap thoroughly; freeze up to 4 months. Thaw slowly; if mixture crumbles, knead slightly to restore texture.

COCKTAIL CHEESE

Have all ingredients at room temperature and put into a blender (if a blender is not available, grate cheeses): ½ pound aged Cheddar cheese, ¼ pound Roquefort or Danish blue cheese, ¼ pound cream cheese, ¼ cup butter, 2 teaspoons Worcestershire Sauce and ½ teaspoon Tabasco. Blend until smooth. Pack at once into a lightly oiled mould and chill until firm enough to hold its shape. Unmould cheese onto a platter and serve with plain crackers or melba toast.

BLUE CHEESE BALL

½ pound wedge Danish blue or Roquefort cheese	1 tablespoon minced celery
1 8-ounce package soft white cream cheese	2 or 3 green onions, finely chopped
½ cup commercial sour cream	1 cup coarsely chopped parsley or ⅔ cup chopped walnuts

1. Grate blue cheese into a large bowl; combine with cream cheese, sour cream, celery and chopped onions. Mix until fluffy.
2. Shape into a ball about 4 inches in diameter; refrigerate until needed.
3. About 30 minutes before serving, roll ball in chopped parsley or walnuts.

   To freeze, see preceding recipe.

CREAM CHEESE DIP

To an 8-ounce package of softened white cream cheese add any of the following combinations of ingredients:

2 small tins devilled ham, tongue, liver spread or pâté, ¼ cup mayonnaise, 1 teaspoon minced onion, 2 tablespoons chopped stuffed olives, 2 tablespoons prepared mustard and ¼ teaspoon Tabasco sauce.

1 cup mashed avocado pulp, 3 tablespoons lemon juice, 1 teaspoon finely chopped onion, 1 teaspoon salt and ½ teaspoon Worcestershire Sauce.

¾ cup cooked or canned shrimp, drained and chopped, 2 tablespoons cream, 2 teaspoons lemon juice, 1 teaspoon chopped chives, and ½ teaspoon Worcestershire Sauce. Add shrimps last to avoid mashing.

PARTY GOUDA

A blender is needed for this novelty dip for vegetables.

1 baby Gouda cheese (10 ounces)	½ cup chili sauce
½ cup sour cream	½ pound butter, cubed
	2 tablespoons chopped chives

1. Cut circle from the top of the cheese; scoop out cheese from the inside, leaving a ¼-inch shell.
2. Combine loose cheese, sour cream, chili sauce and cubed butter and blend until smooth. Stir in chives.
3. Refill cheese shell with filling. Chill.
4. Serve on a tray surrounded with raw chilled strips of celery and green pepper, radishes, carrot sticks, cauliflower flowerets.

HOT CHEESE DIP

½ pound sharp Cheddar cheese, coarsely grated
¼ cup Sauterne wine
½ teaspoon Worcestershire Sauce

¼ cup sweet pepper jelly or relish
approx. 12 bread sticks

1. In chafing dish or double boiler, melt cheese slowly; add remaining ingredients except bread sticks.
2. Break bread sticks into pieces, about 1 inch in length; spear each with a toothpick.
3. Serve sauce in chafing dish or casserole and place bowl of prepared bread sticks beside the sauce for guests to serve themselves.

Leftover dip can be frozen and reused.

GOLDEN DIP FOR VEGETABLES

1 cup mayonnaise
1½ tablespoons curry powder
1 teaspoon lemon juice

1 teaspoon Worcestershire Sauce
½ teaspoon celery salt
few grains cayenne

Stir all ingredients together. Serve on a tray, surrounded by raw vegetables or shrimps for dipping.

HOT SEAFOOD DIP OR FILLING

1 small jar or tin shrimps or oysters
1 tin frozen shrimp or frozen oyster soup

½ teaspoon onion juice
1 teaspoon chopped parsley

1. When using shrimps, remove the black line from each; discard the liquid.
2. When using oysters, retain the liquid and add to oyster soup.
3. Cut oysters or large shrimps with scissors into ½-inch pieces.
4. Allow soup to thaw in the top section of a double boiler.
5. Make the thawed soup mixture into *sauce*, according to directions on the soup tin—i.e., using the reduced quantity of liquid.
6. Add onion juice and prepared seafood: heat mixture in a chafing dish or casserole over a candle-warmer. Sprinkle with parsley.
7. Serve as a dip with bread sticks, broken into 1-inch pieces and speared with a toothpick. As a filling, spoon mixture into tiny, baked tart shells. Serve on a heated platter. Makes 2 cups of filling.

GUACAMOLE (AVOCADO SPREAD)

Blend the pulp of 1 avocado with 2 teaspoons lemon juice, ½ teaspoon salt and either onion juice or Worcestershire Sauce to taste. Serve as a dip or spread.

CHICKEN LIVER PÂTÉ

Prepare one or two days before a party.

2 pounds chicken livers	2 green onions finely chopped
1 medium onion, quartered	1 tablespoon prepared mustard
1 cup chopped celery	1 cup broken stuffed olives,
1 teaspoon salt	chopped
¼ teaspoon pepper	½ cup sweet wine or chicken
2 bay leaves	stock
½ teaspoon thyme	1 tablespoon gelatine
2 sprigs parsley	¼ cup mayonnaise
3 cups water	gherkins or stuffed olives
½ cup butter	

1. In a saucepan, bring to a boil the first 9 ingredients; cover and simmer 20 minutes more. Cool, strain and reserve stock.
2. Put livers through food grinder or electric blender; blend in butter, green onions, mustard, olives and wine. Chill.
3. Shape pâté into a pyramid or any other desired shape and chill thoroughly.
4. Soften gelatine in ½ cup reserved stock; heat over hot water until dissolved. Stir into mayonnaise and chill until partially thickened.
5. Spread mayonnaise mixture over the shaped pâté; chill 5 minutes.
6. Slice gherkins or olives and arrange on the surface of the pâté to make an attractive garnish. Chill until serving time. Makes about 1 quart.

MOCK PÂTÉ DE FOIE GRAS

True pâté de foie gras is a paste of goose liver, specially fattened.

⅛ pound liver sausage	1 teaspoon grated onion
1 tablespoon chili sauce	2 tablespoons minced parsley
1 tablespoon mayonnaise	

1. Buy the sausage in one piece; slit the casing with a sharp knife and discard it.
2. Mash the meat; add the other ingredients, creaming well.
3. Spread on canapés or serve as a dip.

PIGS IN BLANKETS

1. Cook cocktail sausage or small pork sausage. If the larger ones are used, cut them in 3 pieces; cool.
2. Cut pastry into 1½-inch squares and wrap around the sausage.
3. Bake in a hot oven 450° 10 minutes. Serve hot.
   Three cups of flour make pastry to cover 40 cocktail sausages, which weigh 1 pound.

CHEESE DAINTIES

Recipe on page 520.

CHEESE PUFFS

1 cup grated sharp Cheddar cheese (¼ pound)	¼ teaspoon salt
¼ cup soft butter	½ teaspoon paprika
½ cup sifted all purpose flour	24 stuffed olives

1. Blend cheese and butter; stir in flour, salt and paprika. Mix well to form a dough. Drain and dry the olives.
2. Pat 1 teaspoonful of the pastry around each olive, covering it completely. Arrange on an ungreased baking sheet and refrigerate.
3. About 20 minutes before serving, bake puffs for 10-12 minutes at 400°. Serve hot. Makes 24.

These may be frozen on a cookie sheet, transferred to plastic bags and baked when needed; bake frozen balls at 400° for 20 minutes.

MUSHROOM TARTS

Make tiny tarts, using pastry to which ½ cup grated cheese has been added. (3 cups flour should make 48 small tarts.)
Fill with 1 teaspoon of the following mixture:

¼ cup butter	1 tablespoon chili sauce
2 tablespoons minced onion	½ teaspoon salt
1 pound mushrooms, chopped	⅛ teaspoon pepper

1. Melt the butter; sauté the onion; add the mushrooms; fry over low heat, stirring occasionally, for 10 minutes.
2. Add the chili sauce and let stand 5 minutes to absorb the juice.
3. Season. Bake in pastry shell at 450° 10 minutes. Serve hot.

Filled tarts can be frozen before or after baking.

BAMBINOS

Using recipe for Tea Biscuit Pizza (page 324) make tiny individual pizzas. Bake and serve hot.

CHEESE TARTS

Use Tart Variations of Cheese Pie (page 280).

TINY TURNOVERS

Prepare Pastry, using 4 cups flour (page 472). Cut into 2-inch rounds. Place 1 teaspoon filling on ½, dampen edge, fold over other half. Seal edges with the tines of a fork. Make 3 short slits to allow steam to escape. Bake. Makes 60 turnovers.

Chicken Liver Turnover Filling:

Sauté 1 pound chicken livers and ¼ cup chopped onions in ¼ cup butter. Add 1 teaspoon steak sauce. Mash or blend mixture. Prepare turnovers, and before baking brush each with melted butter, sprinkle with grated cheese and paprika. Bake at 400° for about 15 minutes.

Ham and Pickle Turnover Filling:

Combine 1 pound devilled ham and 12 ounces of finely chopped mixed sweet pickles. Prepare turnovers. Bake at 450° for about 12 minutes.

BOUCHÉES

Make according to recipe for Cream Puff (Basic Recipe) on page 502. When cold, fill with lobster, chicken or tuna salad.

HORS d'OEUVRES

This term, pronounced "or derv," means literally "outside the work," and the making of these appetizing little morsels was so considered by the French chef. The Italians call them antipasto.

Today we use hors d'œuvres as an accompaniment to cocktails; or arranged on a plate they may constitute the first course.

STUFFED EGGS

1. Hard cook eggs, chill in cold water. Peel off the shell.
2. Cut in halves lengthwise; remove the yolk with a teaspoon.
3. Set the whites aside in pairs.
4. Mash the yolks with a fork until fine and crumbly.

5. Add mayonnaise, prepared mustard, salt and pepper to season.
6. Chopped chives, parsley, minced ham, fried mushrooms or anchovies may be added.
7. Pile the yolk mixture back into the whites. (To force yolk through a pastry tube omit No. 6.)

STUFFED CUCUMBER OR DILL PICKLE

1. With an apple corer remove the centre from a small cucumber or a large dill pickle. Sprinkle with salt. Drain. Dry.
2. Stuff with a white or yellow cream cheese seasoned with Worcestershire Sauce.
3. Chill. Cut in ¼-inch slices.

STUFFED CELERY

1. Separate a bunch of celery by cutting off the root end with a sharp knife. Save the coarse outside stalks and the leaves.
2. Crispen the white inside pieces in ice water. Cut into 1½-2-inch lengths; dry on a tea towel.
3. Cream grated yellow, white or Danish blue cheese with a little mayonnaise and stuff the celery, using a small flexible knife or pastry tube.
4. After the cheese is stuffed, wipe off surplus cheese with a damp cloth or paper towel.

CELERY PINWHEELS

1. Choose a small celery heart, and remove each stalk. As each stalk is separated place in order in a shallow pan of ice water to chill.
2. Beginning with the inside piece stuff with creamed yellow or tinted white cheese. As each piece is stuffed press it firmly onto the one before and so build up the heart again.
3. Fasten it if necessary with elastic bands. Chill.
4. Cut in ¼-inch slices.

ROLL-UPS

1. Use thin slices of ham, chipped beef, tongue, salami, or lettuce.
2. Spread with cream cheese, seasoned with horseradish, catsup, prepared mustard or Worcestershire Sauce.
3. Roll tightly. Chill in the refrigerator.

CHEESE SLICES

1 pound Cheddar cheese, grated	2 tablespoons mayonnaise
1 3-ounce package pimento	½ cup walnuts chopped
cheese	2 tablespoons parsley chopped
5 tablespoons sherry	¼ teaspoon garlic minced

1. Cream the cheeses together.
2. Add the other ingredients; mix well.
3. Shape into two rolls about 1½ inches in diameter; roll in waxed paper and refrigerate over night.
4. Slice thinly and serve on round crackers.

COCKTAIL TIDBITS

1 pound butter or margarine	1 box Cheerios
1 teaspoon celery salt	1 box pretzel sticks
1 teaspoon cayenne	1 box Chex cereal
3 tablespoons Worcestershire	1 pound peanuts
Sauce	2 pounds mixed nuts
½ bottle garlic salt	

1. Melt the fat, add cayenne, salts and sauce.
2. Pour over the other ingredients in a large pan.
3. Bake at 300° for 1 hour, stirring every 10 minutes.

TOOTHPICK HORS d'OEUVRES OR PIERCED SAVOURIES

Pierce tasty morsels with coloured toothpicks:

From the centre piece of a cocktail tray, or apple, grapefruit or cabbage, serve tiny pearl onions, gherkins, cubes of dill pickle, watermelon pickle, olives; cubes of snappy cheese, smoked meat; tiny balls of cream cheese, rolled in minced parsley, chives or nuts (recipes for cheese balls on pages 67 and 68 can be made using half the quantities).

From a heated platter, serve broiled, buttered mushroom caps sprinkled with seasoned salt; broiled breakfast bacon pieces wrapped around ripe olives, mushrooms or a ball of poultry dressing.

From a chafing dish serve tiny cocktail sausages, or cooked chicken livers in Barbecue Sauce (page 86) or cocktail wieners in Mustard Sauce (page 89); tiny meat balls or shrimp in Sweet and Sour Sauce (page 90); or cubes of tender steak prepared by marinating 2-inch tender steak in 1 cup red wine and ½ cup cooking oil, broiling medium-rare, and cutting into half-inch squares. Serve steak in Hot Wine Butter (page 149).

From a deep platter of crushed ice, serve pineapple chunks; balls of watermelon, cantaloupe, honeydew melon sprinkled with lime or lemon juice; fresh strawberries, avocado pieces, cherries, mandarin orange sections; spear fruits separately or combine 2 different fruits on one toothpick.

Tangy dips will make these colourful dippers even tastier.

RAW VEGETABLE RELISHES

These are served as hors d'œuvres, as garnishes or accompaniments to sandwiches or salad plates, or as appetizers to be dunked in savoury dips.

CARROT STRAWS

Cut tender, cleaned carrots into ⅛-inch lengthwise slices; cut each slice again into narrow strips; sprinkle with minced parsley, cover with a damp towel and chill. Sprinkle with salt just before serving. (Turnip, cucumber, kohlrabi or the midrib of Chinese lettuce may be used in the same way.)

CARROT CURLS

Using a vegetable peeler, remove broad slices of peeled carrot. Shape into tight curls around forefinger and fasten with toothpicks or tuck tightly together in a bowl of ice; chill; remove toothpick before serving.

CAULIFLOWER BUDS

Separate raw cauliflower into small flowerets; chill.

CELERY—CLUB STYLE

Do not remove the root end from the celery but pare it to a point; with large knife cut through the celery lengthwise, dividing it into four or six; use a brush to remove sand between the stalks; chill.

CELERY CURLS

Cut cleaned celery into 3-inch lengths. Slit each end in narrow strips almost to the centre. Chill in ice water.

RADISH ROSES

Select small round radishes; leave one or two small leaves. With a sharp, pointed paring knife held firmly near the point, cut the red skin part way through into petal-like pieces, working from the stem end to the top. There will be a small bit at the bottom of each slice holding it on. As the radish chills in ice water the strips will curl back.

RADISH FANS

Select small long radishes; wash well. With a sharp paring knife cut thin slices crosswise almost through the radish. Chill in ice water.

APPLE WEDGES

Choose red apple; cut into quarters; remove the core. Cut into thin slices. Drop each slice into lemon, orange or grapefruit juice to keep it from discolouring; drain.

STUFFED RAW MUSHROOMS

Choose small white mushrooms; wash and dry; remove stems. Fill the cap with a mixture of $1\frac{1}{2}$ ounces cream cheese, 1 teaspoon Worcestershire Sauce, 2 tablespoons chives, $\frac{1}{4}$ pound of mushrooms. Yields 12.

PLANNING A PARTY

For a reception, cocktail party or sherry party, plan accompaniments according to the occasion, the number of people being served, and the amount of time available for preparation and serving. The choice should include a variety of textures, flavours and temperatures. The outline which follows is intended merely as a guide, and is based on the assumption that, on such occasions, the longer the guest list, the more elaborate is the menu.

Begin with Group A, adding one or more from subsequent groups as the situation demands. Within each group, the first mentioned item is the most easily prepared.

For impromptu occasions:

A 1. Celery, olives, pickles, gherkins
   2. Raw vegetable relishes

B 1. Assorted nuts, cocktail tidbits, purchased cocktail biscuits and mixtures, Cheese Dainties. Omit this group if more than 3 groups are to be used

With the addition of any of these a party begins to shape up:

C 1. Cheese Ball or Dip
   2. Pâté
   3. Hot Dips, Cocktail Wieners

These require someone in the kitchen on "oven duty":

D 1. Broiled mushroom caps or mushroom tarts
   2. Pigs in Blankets, Bambinos, Cheese Tarts, etc.

Now we pass from casual entertaining to more serious efforts:

E 1. Pierced Shrimps with Curried Mayonnaise

Bouchées and Canapés are the more formal additions to the party:

F 1. Seafood or Chicken Bouchées
   2. Canapés

3 Sauces

A good sauce is rich in flavour, smooth in texture and seasoned with care. It can convert the simplest food into a gourmet's delight.

Most sauces, whether for meat, vegetables, desserts or prepared dishes are variations of one simple recipe. Skill in the use of herbs and seasonings pays rich dividends in sauce making. See chart (page 734).

SAUCES FOR MEAT, FISH AND VEGETABLES

Sauces are used to enhance—never to disguise. One sauce is sufficient during a course; if sauce is served on the meat, leave the vegetables unadorned.

Some sauces, such as Hollandaise, must be served immediately on cooking—a fact which should be considered when dinners are destined to be held over. Many sauces with White Sauce bases can be converted to soups by thinning.

BASIC INGREDIENTS

Fat: Butter is the fat considered most desirable from a flavour standpoint; fats from roasts or fowl will give a distinct flavour; shortening may be used if other highly flavoured ingredients are present, but since the chief purpose of a sauce is to contribute flavour, shortening is not recommended. Butter contributes a richness of flavour to sauces that cannot be duplicated by margarine.

Liquid: Milk, meat or vegetable stock are the liquids most commonly used.

Thickening material: Flour is usually used because it is inexpensive and readily available. It has a definite flavour which changes as the flour cooks, so that recipes often say "cook until there is no taste of raw starch." Either pastry or all purpose flour may be used. Cornstarch is another common thickener. To substitute cornstarch or other ingredients for 1 tablespoon flour, consult Table of Replacement Values on the front end papers.

WHITE (CREAM) SAUCE (Basic Recipe)

PROPORTIONS FOR 1 CUP OF SAUCE

Sauce	Description	Liquid	Flour	Fat	Use
		CUPS	TABLESPOONS	TABLESPOONS	
Thin	Pours like milk	1	1	1	Soup
Medium	Like rich or whipping cream	1	2	2	Gravy Pudding Sauce Vegetable Sauce Scallops Casseroles
Thick	Still pours; makes a well when a little is dropped from a spoon back into the sauce; does not pile up	1	3	3	Croquettes Soufflés
Very thick	Makes a pattern when stirred; will mould, or hold its shape	1	4	(Usually for flavour only)	Puddings as Cornstarch Pudding

METHODS

1. Measure ingredients, using quantities required for thin, medium, thick or very thick sauce.
2. Combine ingredients by one of the following methods, being careful never to allow mixture to scorch. Use a double boiler or heavy saucepan.

Melted Fat Method—particularly suitable when fat is hard:

HEAT: as fat melts, stir in dry ingredients. Let mixture bubble.

Stir in cold liquid until smooth.

Cook until thick and there is no taste of raw starch.

If a large quantity of sauce is being prepared, use only 1 cup cold milk to blend into fat-flour mixture; heat remaining milk and stir into blended mixture.

Creamed Fat Method—a simple method to use when fat is soft. It is particularly convenient when a large quantity of sauce is required:

Heat liquid.

In a small bowl, cream fat and dry ingredients.

Stir blended mixture into hot liquid; cook until thick and there is no taste of raw starch.

Cold Liquid Method—When thickening pan gravy, pot roast gravy or stew, there may not be enough fat to separate the starch granules of the flour. This method is then used. A small jar with a tight-fitting top is required:

Estimate the amount of liquid to be thickened. For each tablespoon of flour required, measure twice the quantity of water or milk into jar.

Cover jar and shake vigorously.

Stir mixture into hot liquid until thick and smooth. Cook until there is no taste of raw starch.

WHITE SAUCE MIX OR ROUX

A roux is a mixture of a large amount of fat and flour cooked together and added to the liquid as needed.

1 cup fat (butter, margarine, part   1 cup flour
    butter and part margarine)

1. Melt or cream the fat; blend in the flour; cook gently over boiling water with constant stirring.
2. Store in a covered jar in the refrigerator.
3. Label with the following information.

Sauce Desired	Liquid Used	Roux Required
Thin	1 cup	1½ tablespoons
Medium	1 cup	3 tablespoons
Thick	1 cup	4½ tablespoons

4. Combine the required amount of roux with hot liquid. Stir until sauce thickens. Taste and season.

When Adding Egg to Hot Sauce: Beat egg or egg yolk; add to it a little (2-3 tablespoons) hot sauce while stirring egg constantly. After the egg mixture is thoroughly blended, stir it into remaining hot sauce.

To Heat Leftover Sauce: Often more sauce than is required for one dish may be made up, and used later. For example, when making sauce for Macaroni and Cheese, it would be easy to make enough for one of the scalloped dishes at the same time; especially for the small family this is a wise practice. When the cold sauce is taken from the covered container, it should be placed in the top of a double boiler and, without stirring, be allowed to heat over hot water. When hot, a little more liquid may be added if necessary and the sauce made smooth by beating.

To Freeze Sauces: Cream sauce, Bearnaise, Hollandaise and brown sauces and gravies freeze well. Always thaw the sauce first, then reheat in the top section of a double boiler, over boiling water. With Bearnaise or Hollandaise sauce, begin by reheating 2 tablespoons of sauce, then stirring in 2 more, and so on until all is hot. Sauces frozen in cubes (use icecube tray and transfer cubes to plastic bags) are convenient when only one or two servings of vegetables or meat are being served. Do not freeze sauces that have mayonnaise bases as they will separate.

MEDIUM WHITE (CREAM) SAUCE (Basic Recipe)

Unless thickness is specifically designated, use proportions given below in recipes calling for White (Cream) Sauce.

2 tablespoons flour	1 cup milk
2 tablespoons butter	seasonings
½ teaspoon salt	

Prepare by any of the methods outlined above. Makes ¾-1 cup sauce.

Sauce	Serve with	Additions to basic recipe
Cheese Sauce	Vegetables, macaroni, rice, toast	2 tablespoons to ⅓ cup grated cheese
Egg Sauce	Fish, toast	2 hard-cooked eggs, chopped
Parsley Sauce	Fish rice and fish casserole	1 tablespoon parsley, chopped
Caper Sauce	Fish, lamb	¾ cup capers
Oyster Sauce	Chicken, turkey, fish	½ cup oysters dash of nutmeg
Shrimp Sauce	Fish, fish timbales	¼ cup shrimps, cooked

SHORT-CUT WHITE SAUCES

1. To one 10-ounce can of condensed celery or mushroom soup, add ¼ can of cream. For additional flavour, add any of ¼ cup of chopped parsley, canned pimento or toasted slivered almonds. Heat in double boiler. Makes about 1⅔ cups sauce—enough for 4-6 servings of vegetables.

2. To one 1½ ounce package dehydrated cream soup add gradually 2 cups cold liquid (part milk). Stir over low heat until thickened. Add any of the additions suggested.

VELOUTÉ SAUCE (Basic Recipe)

2 tablespoons flour	1 cup white stock made from
2 tablespoons butter	veal, chicken or chicken bouillon cube

Prepare by any of the methods outlined above. Makes ¾-1 cup sauce.

Sauce	Serve with	Additions to basic recipe
Allemande Sauce	Fowl, lamb	Blend in 1 beaten egg yolk, 1 teaspoon lemon juice
Horseradish	Veal, beef	2 tablespoons prepared horse-radish
Currant Sauce (use brown stock)	Roast lamb	Reduce stock to ¾ cup and add ¼ cup stiff currant jelly, cut in cubes. Blend until smooth
Mushroom Sauce (use brown stock)	Beefsteak	½ cup mushrooms, simmered in sauce

SHORT-CUT VELOUTÉ SAUCE

To 1 10-ounce can condensed cream of chicken soup add ¼ can water or white stock and 1 tablespoon minced onion. Heat in double boiler. Makes 1⅔ cups.

TOMATO SAUCE (Basic Recipe)

2 tablespoons flour	1 cup tomato juice or strained
2 tablespoons butter	tomatoes or
	tomato paste mixed with an
	equal quantity of water

Prepare by any of the 3 methods outlined under White (Cream) Sauce (Basic Recipe).

Serve on fish, veal cutlets, macaroni, spaghetti or use as a binding ingredient in casserole mixtures.

Tomato Sauce complements Fish Fillets.

SHORT-CUT TOMATO SAUCE

To 1 10-ounce can condensed tomato soup add ¼ can water.

SPANISH SAUCE

Chop ½ green pepper, 1 medium onion and celery to make ½ cup. Sauté in 3 tablespoons butter, and use butter remaining in the pan to prepare sauce.

CREOLE SAUCE

Chop and sauté vegetables as for Spanish Sauce; ¼ cup sliced mushrooms could be added. Add 2 cups canned tomatoes but do not add flour. Season. Simmer uncovered until mixture thickens.

TOMATO GARLIC SAUCE

Sauté 1 clove garlic, crushed in 2 tablespoons butter. Drain liquid from raw, peeled tomatoes; add tomatoes to garlic. Chop with a pastry blender. Heat to boiling. Season.

MEAT SAUCE (Basic Recipe)

This highly-seasoned meat mixture is the basis of many casserole mixtures such as Spaghetti and Meat Sauce, Lasagna, and Prairie Casserole. It can be prepared in a large quantity and frozen, or made up into a variety of casseroles which can be frozen until needed. The proportions and varieties of tomato ingredients can be varied according to what is on hand, giving a thicker or thinner mixture which may or may not require additional seasoning.

2 cloves garlic, crushed	12 cups tomato mixture made up
2 green peppers, chopped	approximately as follows:
1½-2 cups chopped onion	2 cups tomato juice or beef
¼ cup salad oil	stock
3 pounds beef chuck, minced	8 cups canned tomatoes or
	tomato sauce
	1 cup condensed tomato soup,
	tomato paste or ketchup

1. Sauté raw vegetables slightly in oil; remove from pan and set aside.
2. Brown the beef. When preparing a large quantity, brown the beef a little at a time, setting it aside and adding more as it browns.

3. Combine all the ingredients in a large pot and cook slowly for about 2 hours. Taste and season.

4. Serve over hot spaghetti or in casseroles. Serves 12 when used in this way.

SAUCES WHICH ARE SERVED HOT

BARBECUE SAUCE

There are many different recipes for Barbecue Sauce; this one can be used on all meats.

½ cup ketchup	2 teaspoons sugar
½ cup water	½ teaspoon salt
¼ cup vinegar	½ teaspoon celery seed
2-8 tablespoons butter or cooking oil*	1 tablespoon Worcestershire Sauce
2 tablespoons chopped onion	1 garlic clove, minced
1 tablespoon green peppers, chopped	few drops Tabasco sauce
	2 teaspoons paprika

1. Combine all the ingredients; heat to boiling; simmer 15 minutes.

2. Use to baste spare ribs, or serve with beef patties. Can be used to marinate chicken pieces before cooking and for basting on the barbecue; pour over sausages for baking. Makes approximately 1¼ cups.

* Use smaller quantity of fat if sauce is to baste fat meat such as pork; use larger quantity for chicken and lean meats.

Basting Sauces and Marinades are in Chapter 5 with the meats with which they are served.

HOLLANDAISE SAUCE

3 tablespoons butter	dash of cayenne
2 yolks of eggs	⅛ cup boiling water
¼ teaspoon salt	1 tablespoon lemon juice

1. Cream the butter; add beaten yolks of eggs.

2. Add seasonings and water.

3. Cook over gently boiling water until thick; stir constantly.

4. Remove from heat; add lemon juice.

5. Serve at once with fish steaks, baked fish or cutlets, asparagus or broccoli.

The flavour of Halibut Steaks and Asparagus is enhanced by Hollandaise Sauce.

MOCK HOLLANDAISE SAUCE

1 cup rich White Sauce or
1 tin cream of chicken soup,
    heated

2 tablespoons butter
¼ cup mayonnaise
1 tablespoon lemon juice

1. Add butter, 1 tablespoon at a time, to hot sauce; blend well.
2. Stir in mayonnaise; heat but do not boil.
3. Add lemon juice. Serve over hot vegetables or fish.

BÉARNAISE SAUCE

1 teaspoon dried tarragon
2 teaspoons chopped parsley
2 teaspoons chopped green
    onion

3 tablespoons wine vinegar
1 tablespoon water
    salt, pepper
    Hollandaise Sauce

1. Cook together all the ingredients except the Hollandaise Sauce until little liquid remains.
2. Prepare Hollandaise Sauce according to the recipe above, beating in this mixture after the addition of the egg yolks.
3. Continue to beat over hot water until the sauce is thick. Serve on broiled meat or fish.

MAYONNAISE SAUCE

1. Blend ½ cup mayonnaise with any of:
   a) ½ cup milk; salt and pepper to taste.
   b) ¼ cup milk, ½ cup ketchup, 1 teaspoon lemon juice and 1 tea-spoon salt.
   c) 2 tablespoons lemon juice, 2 tablespoons water or fish stock.
2. Cook over low heat for 3 minutes, stirring constantly.
3. Serve a) as a substitute for White Sauce,
   b) on rice, macaroni and egg dishes,
   c) on fish, meats or vegetables.

MINT SAUCE

¼ cup mint leaves, finely chopped	¼ cup vinegar
¼ cup hot water	2 tablespoons sugar

1. Mix water, vinegar, sugar; stir until sugar is dissolved.
2. Pour over mint; let stand in a warm place 30 minutes. Serve with roast lamb.

ORANGE MINT SAUCE

Add ⅓ cup orange juice and ½ teaspoon grated orange rind to Mint Sauce ingredients.

CURRANT MINT SAUCE

1 glass currant jelly	2 tablespoons grated orange rind
2 tablespoons mint, finely chopped	

1. Break the jelly with a fork.
2. Add mint and orange rind.
3. Serve with roast lamb or lamb chops.

ROYAL MUSHROOM SAUCE

This enhances the most elegant filet and the lowliest meat patty.

½ cup fresh mushroom stems, chopped	steak drippings or butter
¼ cup finely chopped green onions	1½ tablespoons cornstarch
	½ cup water or stock
	1 cup red wine

1. Sauté vegetables until just tender in drippings left in pan after cooking steak.

2. Blend cornstarch with water and add with wine to vegetables in the pan.
3. Cook with constant stirring until thick. Serve 2 tablespoonfuls over each filet when serving, and pass additional hot sauce during the meal.

HOT MUSTARD SAUCE

1 egg	3 tablespoons mustard (dry)
1 tablespoon sugar	½ cup vinegar
¼ teaspoon salt	2 tablespoons butter and salad oil

1. Beat the egg in the top of a double boiler; add remaining ingredients except the fat.
2. Place over hot water and stir until mixture thickens. Add fat. This sauce can be served hot or cold; when serving the sauce cold, add salad oil after cooling. Serve with ham, roast beef or wieners.

ORANGE SAUCE

This is good with duck.

3 tablespoons flour	½ cup orange juice
2 tablespoons fat	1 tablespoon grated orange rind
1 cup stock or boiling water	1 tablespoon sherry

1. Stir the flour into the fat in the roasting pan.
2. Add the stock or boiling water; stir until thick.
3. Add the orange juice, rind and sherry. Serve at once.

RAISIN SAUCE

½ cup brown sugar	⅓ teaspoon salt
¼ cup water or ham stock or apple juice	dash of pepper
½ cup stiff, red jelly*	1 teaspoon mustard
1½ tablespoons vinegar	½ cup raisins, cut in pieces
	1 tablespoon butter

1. Make a syrup of sugar and water; boil 3 minutes.
2. Add jelly, broken in pieces, vinegar and seasonings; cook 5 minutes.
3. Add raisins; cook until plump. Add butter.
4. Serve hot with ham, pork chops or sausage.
* Jelly may be omitted and juice and grated rind of 1 orange added.

SWEET AND SOUR SAUCE

½ green pepper, coarsely chopped
2 tablespoons cooking oil
½ cup vinegar*
6 tablespoons brown sugar
1 tablespoon soy sauce

¾ cup ketchup
1 19-ounce tin pineapple cubes
1 tablespoon cornstarch
1 tablespoon chopped preserved ginger (optional)

1. Sauté green pepper in oil over medium heat until almost tender but still bright green.
2. Add vinegar, sugar, soy sauce, ketchup and juice from the pineapple (there should be about 1 cup) and bring to boil.
3. Combine cornstarch with 2 tablespoons cold water and stir into hot mixture; cook and stir until mixture is thick and transparent. Add pineapple cubes.
4. Makes about 2 cups. Serve hot over cooked pork, chicken wings, spare ribs, meatballs, shrimps and fish.

* Leftover juice from pickles can be substituted for the vinegar.

WINE SAUCE

See also recipe for Hot Wine Butter (page 149).

¼ cup butter
¼ cup dry white wine
1 tablespoon lemon juice

dash of cayenne
2 tablespoons chopped parsley

Heat butter, wine and juice in saucepan until just hot. Stir in remaining ingredients. Serve hot with fish.

SAUCES WHICH ARE SERVED COLD

CUCUMBER SAUCE

1 cup sour cream
¼ cup unpared chopped cucumber
4 radishes, thinly sliced or
1 teaspoon chopped pimento

2 teaspoons prepared horseradish
1 teaspoon lemon juice
¼ teaspoon salt
dash of cayenne
dash of tarragon vinegar

1. Combine and chill for 1 to 2 hours.
2. Serve with broiled or steamed fish or with fish moulds.

CREAM HORSERADISH SAUCE

2 tablespoons drained prepared
   horseradish

1 cup sour cream or whipped
   cream
¼ teaspoon salt

Combine all ingredients. Serve on cold meats or salads.
2 tablespoons chopped fresh dill may be substituted for horseradish
in the sour cream.

MÂITRE D'HÔTEL SAUCE (PARSLEY BUTTER)

¼ cup butter
½ teaspoon salt
   dash cayenne

½ tablespoon parsley, finely
   chopped
¾ tablespoon lemon juice

1. Cream the butter; add seasonings and parsley.
2. Add lemon juice slowly; chill.
3. Shape into balls. Serve on beefsteak.

MUSTARD SAUCE

Mix ½ cup dry mustard with 3 tablespoons cold water or stale beer.

TARTAR SAUCE

1 cup mayonnaise
½ tablespoon chopped olives
½ tablespoon chopped pickles
½ tablespoon capers

½ tablespoon parsley, finely
   chopped
   few drops onion juice

1. To mayonnaise, add remaining ingredients.
2. Serve with fish or fish cutlets, scallops, oysters.
   Chopped pickle relish can be substituted for the pickles, etc. To
   serve hot, substitute cooked salad dressing for mayonnaise; heat over
   boiling water. Serve with fish or seafood.

QUICK TARTAR SAUCE

Serve commercial sandwich spread either hot or cold.

CHAUD FROID SAUCE

The chef's touch for cold meats and fish at a formal buffet; use with Aspic glaze (below).

2 tablespoons butter	1 egg yolk, beaten
3 tablespoons flour	⅓ cup cream
1 cup stock—chicken, veal or fish	1 teaspoon lemon juice
	1 teaspoon gelatine
¼ teaspoon salt	1 tablespoon cold water
dash of cayenne	

1. Cook the first 5 ingredients as a White Sauce, in a double boiler.
2. Beat egg yolk thoroughly, stir in the cream.
3. Add a little of the hot mixture to egg mixture, blend thoroughly and stir into remaining hot mixture. Cook 5 minutes, stirring until thick.
4. Add gelatine to cold water; let stand 5 minutes.
5. Add lemon juice and softened gelatine to the sauce.
6. Chill, stirring often, until mixture begins to thicken. Coat chilled, cooked chicken or fish.
7. Decorate before the sauce sets. When firm, coat with Aspic Glaze (next recipe).

ASPIC GLAZE

1 cup seasoned white stock	2 tablespoons cold water
¾ tablespoon gelatine	

1. Heat stock to boiling.
2. Soften gelatine in cold water, dissolve in boiling stock.
3. Chill; when beginning to set, use for coating Chaud Froid Chicken or Fish.

CHINESE SAUCE

Make a smooth paste of 2 tablespoons cornstarch and 1 cup water. Add ¼ teaspoon M.S.G. (monosodium glutamate) and 1 tablespoon soy sauce. Cook, stirring constantly, until thick and clear.

CHINESE PLUM SAUCE

Drain juice off a 28-ounce can (3½ cups) of green gage plums. Work fruit through a sieve, food mill or electric blender until puréed. Put plum purée in a saucepan, add 1 clove crushed garlic, 1 cup sugar and 2 tablespoons vinegar. Cook slowly for about 30 minutes, then cool.

CRANBERRY RELISH

2 cups cranberries   ¾ cup sugar
1 large orange

1. Pick over and wash cranberries; put through mincer, using medium knife.
2. Squeeze juice from orange; remove seeds and coarse membrane; put through mincer.
3. Mix cranberries and rind with juice and sugar.
4. Refrigerate in a covered container.
5. Serve with meat or chicken.

CRANBERRY RELISH MOULD

½ orange, cut in pieces and   2 tablespoons gelatine
    seeded   ½ cup cold water
3 cups cranberries   ½ cup boiling water
1¼ cups sugar

1. Prepare fruits as in the preceding recipe. Add sugar.
2. Soften gelatine in cold water for 5 minutes; add boiling water and stir until dissolved.
3. Combine gelatine and prepared fruit thoroughly; turn into a 4-cup mould or into individual moulds, which have been rinsed in cold water or very lightly greased with cooking oil.
4. Chill until firm for several hours. Unmould on a bed of chicory or other greens.

Blender Method:
1. Soften gelatine in cold water in the container of an electric blender for 5 minutes.
2. Add boiling water, cover and blend until gelatine dissolves.
3. Add sugar and orange; blend until orange is finely chopped.
4. Stop blender, add cranberries, cover and blend until cranberries are finely chopped. Mould and serve as in preceding directions.

WHOLE CRANBERRY SAUCE

1 pound (4 cups) cranberries   ½ cup boiling water
2 cups sugar

1. Pick over and wash cranberries.
2. Make syrup of sugar and water; boil 2 minutes.
3. Add prepared cranberries, cook gently until berries are clear.

CRANBERRY JELLY

4 cups cranberries   2 cups sugar
1 cup water

1. Pick over and wash cranberries.
2. Add water; cook until very soft.
3. Press through a sieve; add sugar, stir till dissolved.
4. Cook without stirring until it will jell—about 5 minutes.
5. Pour into moistened moulds; refrigerate. Serve with hot or cold fowl.

SAUCES FOR PUDDINGS AND ICE CREAM

These can be made up and stored in a covered jar in the refrigerator, ready for an easy dessert or sundae. Sauces containing flour or cornstarch should not be kept longer than a week in the refrigerator; they can be kept frozen up to 1 month.

VANILLA SAUCE (Basic Recipe)

½ cup sugar   1 tablespoon butter
1 tablespoon cornstarch   1 teaspoon vanilla
¼ cup cold water   dash of salt
½ cup boiling water

1. Mix sugar and cornstarch thoroughly; add cold water and stir to a thin paste; add to hot liquid.
2. Cook with constant stirring until there is no taste of raw starch; add butter; cool; add vanilla and salt. Makes about 1 cup sauce.

SHORT-CUT VANILLA SAUCE

To vanilla pudding mix, add 1½ times the quantity of liquid required for pudding.

VARIATIONS OF VANILLA SAUCE

Sauce	Basic Ingredients	Additional Ingredients
Lemon Sauce	½ cup sugar 1 tablespoon cornstarch ¾ cup water	2 tablespoons butter ½ teaspoon grated lemon rind 2 tablespoons lemon juice
Brown Sugar Sauce	½ cup brown sugar 1 tablespoon cornstarch ¾ cup water	2 tablespoons butter ½ teaspoon vanilla or 1 tablespoon brandy

VARIATIONS OF VANILLA SAUCE—*Continued*

Sauce	Basic Ingredients	Additional Ingredients
Butter Sauce	2 tablespoons sugar 2 tablespoons flour ¾ cup water	3 tablespoons butter 2 tablespoons lemon juice, vanilla, rum or sherry
Chocolate Sauce	½ cup cocoa ⅔-¾ cup sugar 1 cup water	1 tablespoon butter 1 teaspoon vanilla
Fruit Sauce	sugar (may not be necessary) 1 tablespoon cornstarch ¾ cup fruit juice or left- over syrup from canned fruit	lemon juice as needed to add flavour 2 tablespoons butter drained fruit may be added
Maraschino Sauce	¾ cup sugar 1 tablespoon cornstarch ¾ cup water	¼ cup cherries, chopped 1 tablespoon butter ⅓ cup syrup from maraschino cherries

BLUEBERRY SAUCE

Perfect accompaniment for pancakes.

1 pint fresh blueberries or	⅔ cup sugar
1 box frozen blueberries or	2 tablespoons cornstarch
2 15-ounce tins blueberries	¼ cup water
1 cup orange juice	½ teaspoon almond extract
1 cup water	⅛ teaspoon cinnamon

1. Place fresh or thawed berries in a saucepan with orange juice, 1 cup water and sugar. If canned berries are used, omit water and add only ½ cup orange juice.
2. Heat mixture to boiling point.
3. Blend cornstarch with ¼ cup water and stir into blueberry mixture.
4. Simmer gently until there is no taste of starch.
5. Add almond extract and cinnamon. Serve over waffles, pancakes or ice cream.

CARAMEL SAUCE

⅔ cup brown sugar
1 cup boiling water
⅔ tablespoon cornstarch
   dash of salt

1 tablespoon cold water
1 tablespoon butter
½ teaspoon vanilla

1. Melt sugar, brown slightly, add boiling water; simmer until smooth
2. Mix cornstarch and salt with cold water.
3. Add to syrup; cook until there is no taste of raw starch.
4. Remove from heat; add butter and vanilla. Makes about 1¼ cups.

BUTTERSCOTCH SAUCE

¾ cup brown sugar
2 tablespoons butter
½ cup corn syrup

⅓ cup light cream or
   evaporated milk
   dash of salt

1. Heat sugar, butter and corn syrup over very low heat and cook without stirring to 234° or until a soft ball forms when a little of the mixture is dropped into cold water.
2. Cool slightly; stir in cream and salt.
3. Serve sauce warm or cold; dilute with a little cream if sauce thickens excessively on storing. Makes 1¼ cups.

MARSHMALLOW SAUCE

½ cup granulated sugar
¼ cup boiling water
16 large marshmallows
1 egg white

½ teaspoon vanilla or
   few drops of peppermint or
   almond flavouring

1. Boil sugar and water 2 minutes.
2. Press marshmallows into syrup until melted; do not stir mixture.
3. Beat white of egg until stiff, add marshmallow mixture, slowly beating until smooth.
4. Add flavouring. Makes 2 cups.

MOCK MAPLE SYRUP

1 cup brown sugar
1 cup boiling water
½ cup sugar

1 teaspoon butter
½ teaspoon vanilla or
   maple flavouring

1. Combine brown sugar and water and bring to a boil.
2. Caramelize white sugar by heating it in a frying pan until sugar melts and turns brown.

3. Add brown sugar syrup from step 1; simmer until smooth and thick.
4. Pour into a pitcher containing butter and vanilla or other flavouring.
   Makes 1½ cups.

RUM RAISIN SAUCE

½ cup rum
½ cup seedless raisins
½ cup sugar
¼ cup water

½ teaspoon cinnamon
1 tablespoon grated orange rind
1 tablespoon grated lemon rind
¼ cup chopped nuts

1. Soak raisins in rum until plump.
2. Combine sugar, water and cinnamon in a saucepan and boil 2 minutes.
3. Add raisins and rum and cook 5 minutes more. Add rind and nuts. Serve warm over ice cream. Makes about 1¼ cups.

An elegant and different touch to an evening's entertainment is this Chocolate Fondue. Speared marshmallows, fruits and cakes are dipped in the hot Chocolate Sauce. Strong, black coffee may be served with it.

QUICK CHOCOLATE SAUCE

See also recipe for Chocolate Sauce on page 95.

2 1¾-ounce Milk Chocolate bars	14 caramels
¼ cup milk	2 teaspoons vanilla

Melt chocolate in milk over hot water; add caramels and melt. Stir until smooth. Add vanilla. Serve with ice cream, or as a base for chocolate fondue.

CUSTARD SAUCE

3 eggs or 5 egg yolks	2 cups hot milk
5 tablespoons sugar	¾ teaspoon vanilla
⅛ teaspoon salt	

1. Beat eggs just enough to blend the whites and yolks, or if yolks are being used alone, beat slightly; add sugar, salt and milk.
2. Cook mixture in the top section of double boiler over water which is kept just below the boiling point.
3. Stir until mixture coats a metal spoon; test frequently to avoid over-cooking.
4. Cool by straining into a bowl; chill, and add vanilla.
   If the custard begins to curdle, immerse top section of the double boiler in cold water and beat custard with an egg beater.

MOCK CUSTARD SAUCE

1 teaspoon cornstarch	1½ tablespoons sugar
1 tablespoon cold water	dash of salt
¾ cup milk, heated	½ teaspoon vanilla
1 egg yolk	

1. Mix cornstarch and cold water; add to hot milk; cook till it thickens.
2. Beat egg yolk; add sugar and salt.
3. Add hot milk mixture slowly to the egg mixture.
4. Cook over hot water, stirring constantly until mixture will coat a silver spoon.
5. Remove from heat, strain; flavour with vanilla. Makes about ⅔ cup.

WHIPPED CREAM SAUCE

Serve on wedges of angel cake or Christmas plum pudding.

2 egg yolks	¼ cup sherry, rum or orange
½ cup sugar	juice
	½ cup cream, whipped

1. Combine egg yolks, sugar and flavouring.
2. Fold in whipped cream. Makes about 1½ cups.

For convenience, sauce can be shaped into dollops with a spoon or into rosettes with a pastry tube and frozen until needed. Shape sauce directly onto sheets of waxed paper and store in a covered container or plastic bag, excluding as much air as possible.

FOAMY SAUCE

1 egg, separated
⅓ cup fruit sugar

flavouring

1. Beat egg white until just stiff; gradually beat in half of sugar.
2. Beat yolk of egg until very thick.
3. Add rest of sugar and flavouring (sherry, rum or fruit juice) gradually.
4. Fold mixtures together. Serve at once. Makes ¾ cup.

FOAMY ORANGE SAUCE

3 egg whites
¾ cup fruit sugar
grated rind of 1 orange

½ cup orange juice
3 tablespoons lemon juice

1. Beat egg whites until stiff.
2. Add sugar gradually, beating constantly.
3. Add rind and fruit juice. Makes 1½ cups.

FOAMY LEMON SAUCE

¼ cup butter
⅔ cup sugar
2 egg yolks

2 tablespoons milk
1 tablespoon lemon juice
2 egg whites

1. Cream the butter; blend in sugar and egg yolks. Add milk.
2. Cook over hot water until thick; stir constantly.
3. Add lemon juice. Pour slowly over stiffly beaten whites; beat thoroughly; serve at once. Makes about 1¼ cups.

HARD SAUCE

Serve on hot plum pudding, mince meat pie.

⅓ cup butter
½ teaspoon vanilla

1 cup sugar
(fruit, brown or icing sugar)

Cream butter and flavouring; fruit juices such as cherry or pineapple, or brandy or rum can be substituted for the vanilla. Add sugar slowly, creaming until light and fluffy. Shape into rosettes with a pastry tube, or pat flat and cut into squares. Chill. Makes about 1 cup, enough for 12 servings. Beaten white of 1 egg may be folded into mixture before chilling.

4 Soups

Even with the many excellent canned, dehydrated and frozen soups available today, there are some we prefer to make at home. Varying and fortifying purchased varieties are other ways of giving a personal touch to this versatile dish. Always serve hot soups piping hot in heated bowls or tureen. Likewise, chilled soups should be iced or served in chilled dishes.

Among the basic ingredients of soups are:

Vegetable stock—the liquid remaining after vegetables have been boiled or steamed. An efficient cook has a covered jar for saving such liquids. When the refrigerator is being defrosted, small ends of vegetables, outside leaves of lettuce, tops of celery etc. can be simmered in a little water, then strained into the stock jar. Too much cabbage, onion or turnip makes the stock strong in flavour.

Meat stock— the liquid derived from simmering meat, bones or skin in water. Bouillon cubes and water can be used as a substitute for meat stock.

Although some soups have characteristics of more than one category, most can be classified in this way:

I. Cream Soups— these have a White Sauce base with vegetable or meat stock and pulp added.

II. Soups Made Without Meat Stock—these include vegetable soups, thickened vegetable soups and chowders.

III. Soups Made With Meat Stock—these include thick soups and cleared soups such as consommé.

Soup tureens may be used in formal or informal settings. Here Mushroom Bisque is served in cream soup bowls, while Vegetable Soup with Meat is served in mugs.

CREAM SOUPS

Cream Soup is a filling soup which is better served at lunch or supper than at dinner.

The ingredients include:

VEGETABLE OR MEAT STOCK

Vegetable Pulp: Canned baby foods; leftover mashed potato; cream style corn; finely diced celery, cooked; grated carrot, cooked; chopped mushrooms; canned tomatoes—all make delicious soups in a very few minutes. Leftover vegetables can be frozen until needed.

Cream Sauce: The recipe and method for a cream or white sauce is one which every cook should know perfectly since it is the basis of so many recipes. Soups thicken quickly when served and lose liquid by evaporation during cooking. Hence, the thin sauce is best for all soups. Do not hestitate to thin a soup if necessary; it should be the consistency of rich cream, not of porridge. Butter used in the sauce adds to the flavour of the soup; chicken fat is also good.

Seasoning: This is the mark of the artist in cooking. Salt and pepper are essential. Monosodium glutamate and seasoning salt are also valuable additions to soup. Consult chart in the appendix for use of herbs. A little onion juice or a piece of onion floated in the milk will add flavour, if there was not onion in the vegetable stock. Celery leaves or celery salt may be added in the same way.

CREAM OF VEGETABLE SOUP (Basic Recipe)

Corn, Potato, Carrot, Celery are popular cream soups.

3 cups thin White Sauce made from	stock made from
3 cups milk	1½ cups cooked vegetable
3 tablespoons fat	1½ cups vegetable stock
3 tablespoons flour	seasoning: 1 teaspoon salt
	minced onion or
	celery salt
	monosodium
	glutamate

1. Prepare White Sauce (page 79).
2. Add the vegetable stock and pulp; preheat if desired.
3. Reheat, taste and season. Serve in heated bowls. Garnish. Serves 6.
   Good source of calcium and riboflavin.
   Cream Soup can be frozen up to 4 months.
   Refrigerating a large quantity of Roux (see page 81) for soups and sauces is the most practical method of preparing cream soups quickly.

POTATO CHEESE SOUP

Prepare Cream of Potato Soup from basic recipe. Just before serving, stir in 1½ cups grated Cheddar cheese. Allow it to melt on low heat and beat until smooth. Garnish with paprika.

CREAM OF TOMATO SOUP

2 cups canned tomatoes, heated

2 cups thin White Sauce well seasoned and hot

1. Combine the two only when ready to serve; try to have them at the same temperature.
2. *Always* add the tomato *slowly* to the sauce.
3. Reheat quickly if necessary, but do not allow the mixture to boil; taste; add more seasoning if necessary.
4. Serve as soon as the soup is hot.
5. A few crushed soda crackers may be added just before serving. Serves 4-6.

For additional flavour, cook until tender ¼ cup chopped celery and 2 tablespoons chopped onion in the tomatoes, before adding to White Sauce.

CREAM OF CHICKEN SOUP

4 cups rich seasoned chicken broth

2 cups table cream or top milk

6 tablespoons chicken fat and butter

6 tablespoons flour

¼ cup toasted almonds slivered

1. Combine the broth and cream; thicken with White Sauce (page 79).
2. Taste; season.
3. Serve hot, garnished with almonds. Serves 6.

CREAM OF CHEESE SOUP

4 cups milk

1 blade mace

1 tablespoon flour

¾ teaspoon salt

dash of pepper

1 tablespoon butter

2 egg yolks

½ cup grated cheese

1. Heat milk with mace over low heat; remove mace.
2. Make sauce of flour, seasonings, butter and milk (White Sauce page 79).
3. Beat egg yolks; add a little of the hot sauce and blend thoroughly. Return to the sauce, stirring constantly.
4. Add cheese, stir until cheese melts and sauce thickens. Serve at once.

CHEESE AND ONION SOUP

A meal in itself.

2 medium-sized onions, thinly sliced	2 cups grated strong Cheddar cheese
2 tablespoons butter, melted	salt, pepper
1 tablespoon flour	4 slices French bread
1 teaspoon dry mustard	½ cup grated Cheddar cheese (extra)
2 cups milk	

1. Stir onions into melted butter in a saucepan; cover and cook over low heat until tender, about 20 minutes.
2. Mix together flour and mustard; add enough milk to make a thin paste; add remaining milk to onions; heat; stir in thickening.
3. Cook mixture over medium heat for about 5 minutes with constant stirring.
4. Add cheese; remove mixture from direct heat and allow cheese to melt; stir; season.
5. Place bread in soup bowls; pour in the hot soup.
6. Sprinkle remaining cheese over bread; broil to brown cheese on bread. Serve at once.

TOMATO NEPTUNE BISQUE

1 cup cooked clams (10 oz. tin)	1 slice onion
lobster (7 oz. tin)	1 teaspoon Worcestershire Sauce
or shrimp (7 oz. tin)	2 or 3 drops Tabasco sauce
1½ cups tomato juice	2½ cups rich milk
2 tablespoons flour	

1. Grind seafood in meat grinder, shake flour in a covered jar with tomato juice and combine all ingredients except milk. *OR* put these ingredients in electric blender and blend until smooth.
2. Heat milk; gradually stir tomato mixture into it. Heat thoroughly, stirring frequently. Taste and season. Serve with croutons or Mayonnaise Garnish (page 115). Serves 6.

TOMATO BISQUE

4 cups milk	2 cups tomatoes
½ small onion, chopped	2 teaspoons sugar
6 cloves; piece of bay leaf spray of parsley	1½ teaspoons salt
¾ cup dry bread crumbs	⅛ teaspoon pepper
	3 tablespoons butter

1. Scald milk with onion, spices, parsley and bread crumbs; press through a sieve or mix in a blender.
2. Cook tomatoes with sugar 15 minutes; press through a sieve. Add seasonings and butter.
3. Combine the mixtures by adding the tomato slowly to the milk.
4. Serve at once with croutons or crisp crackers. Serves 6.

VEGETABLE CHOWDER

This soup is filling, nutritious, inexpensive, and best of all it tastes good.

4 potatoes, diced	2 tablespoons rolled oats
3 carrots, grated coarsely	1 cup vegetable stock or water
1 onion, diced	(approximately)
1 stalk celery, diced	2 cups milk (approximately)
2 tablespoons bacon fat, butter	2 cups tomatoes (canned) or
or chicken fat	juice
	2 teaspoons salt

1. Lightly brown raw vegetables in the fat in a large saucepan.
2. Add the rolled oats and enough water or vegetable stock to cover.
3. Cover and simmer until the vegetables are tender (20 minutes).
4. Measure liquid and add milk to make 3 cups.
5. Slowly add the tomatoes; season, reheat and serve immediately. Serves 6.

SUPPER CORN CHOWDER

5 slices bacon	1 10-ounce can cream
3 tablespoons bacon fat	mushroom soup
1 medium onion	2½ cups milk
1 can cream style corn	salt, pepper, butter, 6 soda
1 cup diced cooked potatoes	biscuits

1. In large saucepan or top of double boiler cook bacon slowly until crisp; remove and drain on paper towel or brown paper; crumble.
2. Pour off the fat; measure 3 tablespoons and return to the pan.
3. Slice the onion thinly; separate into rings; fry slowly in the fat until yellow and clear.
4. Add corn, potatoes, soup, milk and seasonings; bring just to a boil stirring constantly, or heat in a double boiler.
5. Add crumbled bacon, a soda biscuit crumbled and a teaspoon of butter to each serving. Serves 6.

ATLANTIC CHOWDER

¼ pound salt pork	1 cup boiling water
3 onions, sliced	¾ pound cod or haddock fillets
4 small potatoes, pared and sliced 1 inch thick	3 cups milk
	1 tablespoon butter
1 teaspoon salt	2 tablespoons chopped parsley

1. Dice the pork; fry it slowly to a crisp golden brown in a 3-quart heavy pan; lift out the bits of pork and set them aside.
2. Add the onions to the fat and fry slowly until yellow and clear.
3. Add the potatoes, the seasoning, and the water; heat.
4. Cut the fish into 2-inch squares; drop onto the potatoes; cover and simmer until the potatoes are tender and the fish flakes (20 minutes).
5. Add the milk and heat; add more salt if necessary.
6. Just before serving, drop the butter and bits of fried pork and parsley into the chowder; do not stir. Serve with soda biscuits.

Bacon or Bacon Square may be used in place of the fat pork.

CLAM CHOWDER

Substitute 1 cup of clams and 1 cup of clam liquid for the fish in the preceding recipe.

BOUILLABAISSE

There are many versions of this hearty fish soup.

2 pounds mixed fish and shellfish	1 cup canned tomatoes
¾ cup sliced onions	¼ teaspoon saffron or turmeric
1 clove garlic, crushed	1 bay leaf
1 leek, sliced (optional)	½ teaspoon thyme
4 tablespoons cooking oil	½ cup white wine
4½ cups water	

1. Cook shellfish (except oysters) in a pot of water until tender; oysters need only to be shucked. Discard water and shells.
2. Sauté onions, garlic and leek in oil until soft.
3. Combine the fish, seafood, 4½ cups water, onions and remaining ingredients; cover and simmer for 20 minutes. Serves 6.

CLEAR TOMATO SOUP

2½ cups cooked tomatoes	1 tablespoon chopped onion
2 cups water	2 teaspoons sugar
12 pepper berries	3 tablespoons flour
4 cloves	1 teaspoon salt
1 bay leaf	2 tablespoons butter

Simmer first six ingredients 20 minutes; sieve. Add salt and sugar; thicken with flour and butter (White Sauce, page 79).

IBERIAN BEAN SOUP

Serve with French bread as a meal in itself.

2 cups dried kidney beans (2 cans cooked)	1 teaspoon monosodium glutamate
2 small onions, sliced	2 cups canned tomatoes
1 garlic clove, minced	4 cups water
3 medium potatoes, diced	2 tablespoons lemon juice
1 tablespoon salad oil or fat	1 teaspoon sugar
1 teaspoon salt	2 cups shredded cabbage
few drops tabasco	1 cup elbow macaroni, uncooked
½ teaspoon oregano	

1. Wash beans; cover with cold water and let stand overnight.
2. In the morning, pour beans and any remaining water into a kettle, add fresh water to cover beans. Cover kettle.
3. Simmer about 2 hours or until skins burst when tested with a fork.
4. Add remaining ingredients except cabbage and macaroni. Cook 15 minutes.
5. Add cabbage and macaroni; cook 15 minutes longer or until macaroni is tender. Makes 8 servings.

MEATLESS VEGETABLE SOUP (Basic Recipe)

3 tablespoons beef drippings or butter	1½ cups potatoes, diced
⅓ cup carrot, diced	4 cups boiling water
⅓ cup turnip, diced	½ tablespoon chopped parsley
⅓ cup celery, diced	1 teaspoon salt
1 tablespoon onion, chopped	⅛ teaspoon pepper

1. Cook carrot, turnip, celery and onion in drippings until lightly browned.
2. Add potatoes, cook 2 minutes longer, add water.
3. Cover and simmer 1 hour; add water to keep amount of liquid 1 quart.
4. Add parsley and seasonings. Serves 6.

   Fresh peas and beans can be added at the end of step 2; cooked vegetables should be added 15 minutes before serving.
   For Maigre Soup, press vegetables through a sieve before adding parsley.

MEAT STOCK SOUPS

Veal or chicken provides the basis for white soup stock while fresh beef or cooked meats (beef, lamb or pork) are used to make brown stock.

FLAVOURED SOUP STOCK

2 pounds meat and bone	1 bay leaf
6 cups cold water	1 teaspoon mixed herbs, thyme,
1 small onion	marjoram, savoury
½ cup carrot	1 sprig parsley
4 cloves	2 stalks celery
6 pepperberries	1 teaspoon salt

1. Cover the meat with cold water; bring to a boil; simmer 2 hours.
2. Add vegetables and seasonings; cook 1 hour longer.
3. Take out the meat; discard the skin and bones. (The meat may be served separately or may be cubed and added to the soup.)
4. Strain; let the stock cool; remove the fat. The stock should form jelly when it is cold. If it does not, soup cubes may be added to reinforce the flavour. Use as a base for the following recipes. Makes about 4 cups.

Soup stocks freeze perfectly. It is sometimes convenient to have a supply of frozen stock cubes, made by freezing stock in ice-cube trays. When small quantities of stock are needed for sauces or soups, the cubes are easily thawed.

Canned consommé, bouillon cubes or dehydrated soups may be substituted.

TO CLEAR SOUP STOCK

1 quart soup stock	¼ cup cold water
1 white of egg and 1 shell	

1. Let stock become cold; remove fat.
2. Beat white of egg slightly; add shell, crushed; add to stock; mix thoroughly.
3. Heat slowly to boiling point, stirring continuously; boil 5 minutes; add seasonings, as desired.
4. Set back; let stand 5 minutes; add cold water.
5. Let it stand to settle; strain through a thick piece of cotton placed over a strainer; remove the fat completely by blotting it up with brown paper or pieces of paper towel.

CONSOMMÉ

3 pounds lean beef	1 tablespoon salt
3 pounds veal knuckle	1 teaspoon pepperberries
bones from a 4-5 pound	4 cloves
chicken	¼ bay leaf
1 quart water	2 sprigs parsley
½ cup each chopped celery,	
onion, carrot	

1. Prepare as Flavoured Soup Stock. Clear and remove all fat.
2. Use in any of the following ways:

CONSOMMÉ MADRILENE: Heat equal amounts of tomato juice and consommé.

CONSOMMÉ À LA ROYAL: Garnish with royal custard.

CONSOMMÉ AU PARMESAN: Garnish with Parmesan cheese.

CONSOMMÉ JULIENNE: Add cooked carrots, turnip and string beans cut in matchlike strips.

SHERRIED CONSOMMÉ: Add 2 tablespoons sherry to 1 cup consommé; heat.

JELLIED CONSOMMÉ

Serve jellied soups in warm weather. Use a cleared meat stock, well seasoned, or canned consommé. If the meat stock does not form a stiff jelly when chilled, gelatine should be added. Soften 1 tablespoon gelatine to each 2 cups of stock in cold water; dissolve in hot soup. Pour into a pan to a depth of ½-inch, allow to set, then cut into cubes. To serve jellied consommé, pour 1 tablespoon sherry or sour cream on top. Garnish with minced chives or parsley. Serve with lemon wedge.

JELLIED WINE CONSOMMÉ

2 tablespoons gelatine	1 teaspoon sugar
½ cup water	½ teaspoon lemon or lime juice
2 10-ounce cans consommé	salt
4 cups water	pepper
½ cup red wine	lemon wedges

1. Soften gelatine in ½ cup water for 5 minutes.
2. Heat 1 cup consommé, 4 cups water, wine and sugar to boiling; add gelatine and stir until gelatine is dissolved; add lemon juice.
3. Season and pour into a bowl; chill until set.
4. Dice with a fork and serve in chilled glass dishes with lemon wedges. Serves 6.

Jellied Beet Soup is a good start for a hot meal.

FRENCH ONION SOUP

6 medium onions	dash of pepper
2 tablespoons butter or drippings	1 teaspoon Worcestershire Sauce
4 cups cleared soup stock or consommé	1 French roll grated cheese
½ teaspoon salt	
⅛ teaspoon celery salt	

1. Peel onions; cut into thin slices.
2. Brown onion lightly in fat.
3. Add stock; simmer until onions are tender; add seasonings.
4. Slice a French roll into ½-inch slices; toast in a slow oven.
5. Sprinkle thickly with grated hard cheese (Parmesan is the cheese commonly used); brown under the broiler.
6. Serve one slice in each dish of hot soup. Serves 4-6.

BORSCHT (BEET SOUP)

This is a recipe common to all the Eastern European countries, and one with many variations. It may be made without stock; sometimes vinegar or cream of tartar is added to give acidity.

2 cups water	2 tablespoons butter
2 cups finely grated beets	1 cup tomato juice
½ cup finely shredded carrots	½ cup finely shredded cabbage
1 cup finely chopped onion	½ cup finely shredded beet tops
2 potatoes (new potatoes are best) cut in chunks	pinch of green dill
	1 cup thick sour cream, at
2 cups soup stock or consommé	room temperature

1. Boil the beets, carrots, onions in the water until tender.
2. Boil the potatoes separately so they do not become coloured.
3. Combine the stock, cooked vegetables except the potatoes, and the other ingredients except the cream; simmer 15 minutes; taste and season.
4. Add the potatoes and cream; or add sweet cream and pass the sour cream at the table. Serves 10.

   If canned shredded beets are being used, substitute spinach leaves for the beet tops.

INSTANT BORSCHT

Add beet juice from canned beets (not pickled) to 1 cup soup stock or consommé; add 1 cup tomato juice. Heat; season; serve with sour cream.

VEGETABLE SOUP (WITH MEAT)

1 quart flavoured soup stock	2 cups vegetables, diced or
1 cup diced meat, hamburger or diced cooked meat	shredded
	1 tablespoon rice or barley

1. Combine the ingredients; simmer until the vegetables are tender.
2. Taste; season.
3. Serve in heated dishes.

   Any combination of vegetables may be used; cabbage and turnip should be used sparingly, as the flavour is strong. Potatoes should be cut in somewhat larger pieces since they cook more quickly than other vegetables and become mushy.

TURKISH SOUP

3 tablespoons rice	piece of bay leaf
5 cups brown soup stock	1 teaspoon salt
1½ cups cooked tomatoes, strained	¼ teaspoon celery salt
1 small onion	2 tablespoons butter
10 pepperberries	1½ tablespoons flour

1. Cook rice in stock until soft.
2. Add seasonings to tomatoes; simmer 20 minutes.
3. Combine stock and tomatoes; rub through a sieve.
4. Blend together butter and flour. Stir into hot liquid.

TURKEY BROTH

turkey bones, scraped clean of dressing	celery leaves
1 carrot	1 teaspoon salt
1 onion	1 quart water
	few black peppers

1. Simmer all the ingredients until the meat comes off the bones.
2. Strain; add meat shredded from the bones.
3. Taste; season. Serves 5-6.

CHICKEN BROTH

4 cups chicken broth	2 tablespoons rice
1 cup celery, diced	1 teaspoon salt
1 onion, diced	

1. Add the vegetables to broth; simmer until tender.
2. Taste; season. Serves 4-5.
   Chicken carcass can be used to make stock; see Turkey Broth.

FRENCH CANADIAN PEA SOUP

1 cup split peas	1 onion, thinly sliced
3 cups cold water	celery leaves, bay leaf
2 pounds smoked ham shank or ham bone	1 teaspoon salt
3 quarts boiling water	⅛ teaspoon pepper
	2 carrots, shredded

1. Soak the peas in cold water overnight; drain.
2. Combine the peas, ham and bone, onion, celery leaves and bay leaf, and boiling water.

3. Cover, bring to a boil; simmer 2 to 3 hours, stirring often to prevent sticking.
4. During the last hour of cooking add the seasonings and carrots.

GOOD COMBINATION OF CANNED SOUPS

USING CONDENSED TOMATO SOUP

1. 1 can condensed Pea Soup, 1 can condensed Tomato Soup, 2 cans milk or vegetable stock. This is called Purée Mongole.
2. 1 can condensed Celery Soup, 2 cans condensed Tomato Soup, 2 cans milk or vegetable stock.
3. 1 can Clam Chowder, 1 can condensed Tomato Soup, 2 cans vegetable stock.
4. 1 can Chicken Gumbo, 1 can condensed Tomato Soup, 2 cans vegetable stock.
5. 1 can consommé, 1 can condensed Tomato Soup, 2 cans vegetable stock.

USING CONDENSED CREAM OF CHICKEN SOUP

1. 1 cup mashed potato, 1 can Cream of Chicken soup, 2 cans milk. Combine, heat in double boiler; beat until smooth. Leftover baked potato is especially good; scrape out and press through a sieve.
2. 1 can Cream of Asparagus, 1 can Cream of Chicken, 2 cans milk.
3. 1 can Cream of Mushroom, 1 can Cream of Chicken, 2 cans milk.

MISCELLANEOUS

1. 1 can Cream of Mushroom soup, 1 can Chicken Noodle, 2 cans water or vegetable stock.
2. 1 can condensed Green Pea Soup, 1 can Chicken Noodle Soup, 2 cans water or vegetable stock.
3. 1 can Clam Chowder, 1 can Cream of Celery Soup, 2 cans water or vegetable stock.
4. 1 can Green Pea Soup, 1 can Vegetable Soup, 1 can water, ½ pound cooked sliced sausage, 1 onion sliced thinly. Cook the sausage; add the onions and cook slowly until soft but not brown. Drain off the fat; slice the sausage in ½-inch pieces. Add the soup; reheat.

CHILLED SOUPS

CUCUMBER SOUP

This chilled soup is easy on calories.

4 cups buttermilk	1 tablespoon fresh dill
1 cup sour cream	1 teaspoon salt
1 cup diced cucumber	¼ teaspoon pepper
1 tablespoon finely chopped green onion	

1. Beat the buttermilk and sour cream until smooth; add the vegetables and seasonings; chill thoroughly. Serves 6-8.

GAZPACHO

This is a chilled Spanish soup. As an appetizer, soup can be strained and additional chopped onions and green pepper passed when soup is served. As a soup, it is served as is—with bread and butter, cheese and maybe wine. With added gelatine it is served as a salad.

1 cup finely chopped peeled tomato	1 teaspoon chopped chives
½ cup finely chopped green pepper	1 small clove garlic, minced
½ cup finely chopped celery	2 tablespoons wine vinegar or lemon juice
½ cup finely chopped peeled cucumber	2 tablespoons salad oil
¼ cup finely chopped onion	1 teaspoon salt
2 teaspoons chopped parsley	¼ teaspoon pepper
	½ teaspoon Worcestershire Sauce
	2 cups tomato juice

1. Combine all ingredients in a glass or china bowl; refrigerate at least 4 hours.
2. Serve in chilled bowls, preferably iced. Serves 6.

VICHYSSOISE

A chilled soup of French origin.

3 leeks	2 teaspoons salt
1 small-medium onion	3 cups rich milk
2 teaspoons butter	¾ cup whipping cream
4 medium-sized potatoes	chives
3 cups chicken broth	

1. Slice the white part of leeks, and the onion, and sauté in butter until tender but not brown.
2. Slice potatoes thinly (there should be about 3 cups); cook in a saucepan with broth, salt, leeks and onions until soft (35-40 minutes).
3. Rub through a fine sieve or blend in an electric blender, return to heat, add milk, stir while heating just to the boiling point.

4. Cool. If necessary, sieve or blend again.
5. Add cream and chill 2-3 hours. Serve in chilled cups, preferably iced. Garnish with chopped chives. Serves 6.

INSTANT VICHYSSOISE

Using frozen potato soup, follow directions on the can. Season to taste.

GARNISHES

CUSTARD

2 egg yolks	2 tablespoons milk
dash of salt	

1. Beat egg yolks slightly; add salt and milk.
2. Pour into small, buttered mould; oven-poach or steam until firm; chill.
3. Turn out; cut in fancy shapes; serve in clear soup.

ROYAL CUSTARD

1 egg	⅛ teaspoon salt
3 egg yolks	dash of cayenne
½ cup cleared stock	dash of nutmeg

Combine and cook as Custard (above).

FORCEMEAT BALLS

¾ cup cooked meat, minced	1 teaspoon chopped parsley
¼ cup soft bread crumbs	⅛ teaspoon grated onion
¼ teaspoon salt	1 egg yolk
dash of cayenne	flour
¼ teaspoon thyme	fat
1 teaspoon lemon juice	

1. Mix all together; form into balls the size of a small marble.
2. Roll in flour; brown in hot fat.
3. Place 3 or 4 in each serving of clear soup.

MAYONNAISE GARNISH

⅓ cup mayonnaise	¼ teaspoon lemon juice
½ teaspoon minced parsley	

Blend thoroughly and add any of

½ teaspoon Worcestershire Sauce, prepared horseradish, or curry powder	¼ teaspoon grated lemon peel, seasoned salt or garlic salt
	¾ drops Tabasco sauce

Serve one spoonful on hot or cold soup.

ADDITIONAL GARNISHES

For Clear Soups: lemon slices, chopped parsley or chives, pepper cress or watercress, thin slices of avocado, thin slices of lemon or orange.

For Meat Soups: slices of cooked sausage or wieners on pea or bean soups, grated cheese, croutons, crisp crumbled bacon or other bits of cooked meat, parsley, corn chips.

For Cream Soups: Sour cream or salted whipped cream, both at room temperature, shredded toasted almonds, chopped parsley, chives or watercress, croutons, grated cheese, cheese popcorn.

For Chilled Soups: Chilled sour cream, thin slices of cucumber or radishes, lemon wedges, watercress.

5 Meats

Meat is one of the most expensive items in our diet, worthy of maximum care in purchase, storage and cooking. The most popular cuts bring high prices while less expensive cuts can be equally enjoyed when the right cooking methods are used.

The use of dressings and stuffings in chops and roasts, and of fillers with minced meats, helps to extend the meat, giving more servings per pound.

There is good nutrition in all meat. Protein, iron and some of the B vitamins are to be found in the cheaper as well as the more expensive cuts. Meat is a highly satisfying food and is usually the focal point about which a menu is planned.

GRADING OF MEAT

The round purple stamp indicates federal inspection for health and sanitation. Only meat which is to move in interprovincial trade must be so inspected except where there are local by-laws. The ribbon stamp is a grade stamp, found as yet only on beef. Red is the indication of choice or top quality; blue indicates good. Grades below this which are Commercial and Utility are not usually labelled, although sometimes high grade Commercial will be given a brown ribbon stamp. Only meat which has had the federal inspection may be grade labelled.

In order to provide meat inspection in areas where federal inspection is not available, some provinces provide their own inspection services with standards similar to those provided by federal agencies.

AMOUNT TO PURCHASE

Allow $\frac{1}{3}$ to $\frac{1}{2}$ pound per person if there is some bone; $\frac{1}{4}$ pound boneless meat, $\frac{1}{8}$ pound sliced cold meat.

STORAGE OF MEAT IN THE HOME

Meat should be unwrapped as soon as it is brought from the store because the wrapping paper draws the juices out of the meat.

If the meat has bits of ground bone on the surface it may be wiped with a damp cloth; it should not be washed.

Place the meat on a clean plate and cover loosely with wax paper.

Keep the meat as cold as possible.

Ground meat spoils easily because of the extra handling and because it is exposed to the air. It should be used within 2 days unless it is frozen.

Jellied meats also provide a good base for the growth of bacteria, and so should be refrigerated and used promptly.

Cooked meat should be allowed to cool, then be covered and kept cold.

Stews and meat soups which have been thickened with flour will spoil easily and so should not be kept more than a few days.

TO FREEZE MEATS

Fresh meats must be thoroughly wrapped in air-tight wrappings or containers to prevent loss of moisture during freezing. Such a loss results in "freezer burn," a condition characterized by dry, stringy meat of poor flavour. For large cuts, an over-wrapping of cotton stocking or other cloth protects the air-tight wrapping from tears and punctures. Charts giving the length of storage time should be consulted (Appendix) so that flavour change will not result from over-storage. This is particularly important in the freezing of pork.

METHODS OF COOKING MEAT

Meat cuts are divided into those which are *tender* and those which are *less tender*. A cut which is tough if the meat is of poor quality may very well be a tender cut when a better grade of meat is bought; for example, rump roast and round steak in beef may be more or less tender depending upon the quality of the beef and the method of cooking.

The less tender cuts contain as much food value and even more flavour than tender cuts since the extractives which give the flavour are developed by exercise.

The problem with these less tender cuts, then, is to cook them so that the fine flavour can be enjoyed. Since the less tender cuts comprise a much larger part of the carcass and are less in demand, they are less expensive.

METHODS OF COOKING THE LESS TENDER CUTS

POT ROASTING and BRAISING: These terms mean cooking slowly, below the boiling point, in moist heat; the former term applies to large cuts (roasts), while the latter applies to small cuts. Although they are tender, small cuts of veal and pork are usually braised; moist heat dissolves the large amount of connective tissue found in veal; it allows pork to be well-cooked, as is necessary, without being dried out.

STEWING: Meat is cooked slowly in liquid.

COOKING IN A LARGE AMOUNT OF LIQUID: This method, which is usually called "boiling," is misnamed since meat should always be cooked below the boiling point. It differs from braising in the amount of liquid used. Also the meat is usually not browned.

The kettle should be large enough that the meat can be completely covered with water. Simmer 2-4 hours.

After cooking, the meat is allowed to cool in the stock; this prevents shrinkage, makes the meat more juicy and improves the flavour.

The stock may be boiled to reduce the volume, flavoured and served with the meat, or it may be used for soup.

PRESSURE COOKING: All the moist-heat methods for tenderizing meats are involved.

GRINDING: All ground meat is tender because the coarse fibres have been cut through; it may be treated as a tender cut.

POUNDING AND WAFFLING: These methods also break down the connective tissue.

USE OF ACID: Meat may be soaked in a flavoured oil and acid mixture called a marinade, or the acid may be added in the cooking. Tomatoes or tomato juice are commonly used for this purpose. Acid breaks down connective tissue.

USE OF TENDERIZERS: These contain enzymes which predigest the meat and so change its character. They are more successful with thin pieces of meat than with roasts. Meat may be purchased already tenderized by the packer, and bears a brand name which indicates this treatment. Usually, a shorter period of cooking is required for such meat, and cuts which are ordinarily considered to be marginally tender can be cooked by the methods recommended for tender meat.

METHODS OF COOKING THE TENDER CUTS

Tender cuts of meat are usually cooked by dry heat methods as in roasting. However, some tender cuts, especially pork and veal, which need to be well cooked, are better braised, to prevent them from drying out.

ROASTING: Cooking uncovered by dry heat in an oven. If a roast has water added or is covered during cooking, it is being braised, not roasted. It is not wise to pay the high prices demanded for tender meat and then to cook it as a less-tender cut.

Research has proven conclusively that roasting meat at a low temperature, without preliminary searing:

saves fuel.

reduces shrinkage. All meat loses weight on cooking. Roasts cooked at 450° will have double the weight loss of roasts cooked at 300°.

leaves the juices in the meat, making it moist and flavoursome.

prevents fat from burning on the racks and oven.

makes carving easier because the meat fibres hold together better.

Temperatures recommended are: 350° for fresh pork, 300 to 325° for all other meat. For details of Method, see method for cooking Roast Beef, page 141.

A *Meat Thermometer*, an inexpensive piece of equipment which may be purchased at any hardware store, will insure that the meat is cooked to the desired degree. It will not however, indicate the approximate amount of time required; use the timetable below as a guide. The thermometer should be placed in the thickest part of the roast, not touching the bone, or resting in fat. Never attempt to insert a thermometer into frozen meat. It will break!

TIMETABLE FOR ROASTING MEATS

Meat	Description	Weight in Pounds	Temperature	Minutes per Pound	Time in Hours
BEEF	Compact roast, without bone to be well done	3	325°	40	2
	Large, with bone, to be rare	6	325°	20	2
LAMB	Rolled shoulder	4	325°	30	2
	Leg	7	325°	25	3
VEAL	Rolled roast	3	325°	50	2½
	Leg	5	325°	35	3
PORK, Fresh	Boneless Butt	4	350°	45	3
	Leg (fresh ham)	6	350°	40	4
Cured, Bone in	Whole ham, small	8-10	300°	20	3¼
	large	15-18	300°	15	3¾
	Half ham	5-8	300°	—	—
Bone out	Whole ham	8-10	300°	25	4
	Half ham	3	300°	30	1½
Picnic Shoulder		4	300°	30	2

Note: Frozen roasts require ¾ to ½ as long again as unfrozen roasts.

Quality Beef, barbecued on the patio or roasted indoors, is without rival.

Two meal-in-one dishes are Beef Stew and Spaghetti with Meatballs.

BROILING: Another dry-heat method for cooking tender meat—usually small to medium-size cuts. Meat is placed 2 to 4 inches below the heating element, depending upon the thickness of the meat. It is cooked on one side, then turned and cooked on the other. For details, see basic recipe for Broiled Steak, page 146. The oven door of an electric oven should always be kept ajar during broiling.

TIMETABLE FOR BROILING

Meat	Cook Each Side
A large sirloin, 1 inch thick..........................	10-14 minutes
Individual pieces, 1 inch thick.......................	5-7 minutes
Meat patties, 1 inch thick............................	8-10 minutes

PAN-BROILING: Tender meat is cooked quickly in a frying pan which has been lightly greased, usually with pieces of fat cut from the meat. It is browned on one side and then on the other and the heat reduced.

PAN-FRYING: Small tender cuts of meat which are breaded, or cuts low in fat, such as liver, are used. Meat is cooked in fat to a depth of $\frac{1}{8}$ inch over moderate heat, on one side and then on the other. Fat is poured off as it accumulates, or more is added as required.

DEEP-FAT FRYING: See Chapter 21.

TIPS TO CARVERS

Of first importance is the quality of the steel in the carving knife. A blade that will take and hold a keen edge is more important than a fancy handle.

To get the full co-operation of a carving set it must be given good care. Keep it separated from other cutlery so the knife will not be dulled or nicked. A good blade needs only occasional sharpening but it should always be steeled before using.

Electric carving knives are effective and require little maintenance.

If it is easier, stand up to carve.

Avoid changing the angle of the blade while making a slice; neat uniform slices look better and go farther.

A large roast or fowl can be carved more easily after it stands in a warm place for 15 to 30 minutes in the roasting pan to absorb the juices.

Give the carver plenty of platter room and plenty of elbow room. Place glasses and dishes where they will not interfere with the carver.

When garnishing, don't be over-generous; leave space for the work to be done.

Servings cool quickly so plates and platter *must* be heated.

An inexperienced carver will appreciate a hostess who keeps the guests' attention diverted from his carving.

Roast Leg of Lamb

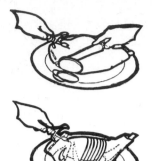

The leg of lamb should be placed before the carver so that the shank bone is to his right and the thick meaty section, or cushion, is on the far side of the platter.

Insert the fork firmly in the large end of the leg and carve two or three lengthwise slices from the near thin side.

Turn the roast so that it rests on the surface just cut.

Insert the fork in the left of the roast. Starting at the shank end, slice down to the leg bone. Parallel slices may be made until the aitch bone is reached.

With the fork still in place, run the knife along the leg bone, releasing all the slices.

Standing Rib Roast

The roast is placed on the platter with the small cut surface up and the rib side to your left.

With the guard up, insert the fork firmly between the two top ribs. From the far outside edge slice across the grain toward the ribs. Make the slices ⅛ to ⅜-inch thick.

Release each slice by cutting close along the rib with the knife tip.

Rolled Rib Roast

The roast is placed on the platter with the larger cut surface down.

With the guard up, push the fork firmly into the roast on the left side an inch or two from the top.

Slice across the grain toward the fork from the far right side. Uniform slices of ⅛ to ⅜-inch thick make desirable servings.

Remove each cord only as it is approached in making slices. Sever it with the tip of the blade, loosen it with the fork and allow it to drop to the platter.

Other Rolled Roasts

Since many of them make a long roll, you will find carving easier with the roast lying horizontally on the platter. Slice across the face in the same way as the rolled rib.

Porterhouse Steak

Holding the steak with the fork inserted at the left, cut close around the bone. Then lift the bone to the side of the platter where it will not interfere with carving.

With the fork in position, cut across the full width of the steak. Make wedge-shaped portions, widest at the far side. Each serving will be a piece of the tenderloin and a piece of the large muscle.

Serve the flank end last if additional servings are needed.

A board cut to fit the centre section of the steak platter protects the cutting edge of the knife.

Blade Pot Roast

Hold the pot roast firmly with the fork inserted at the left and separate a section by running the knife between two muscles, then close to the bone.

Turn the section just separated so that the grain of the meat is parallel with the platter. Holding the piece with the fork, cut slices of ¼ to ⅜-inch thick.

Separate the remaining sections of the roast; note the directions of the meat fibres and carve across the grain.

Baked Whole Ham

The ham is placed on the platter with the fat or decorated side up and the shank end to the carver's right.

Insert the fork and cut several slices parallel to the length of the ham on the thin side.

Turn the ham so that it rests on the surface just cut. Hold the ham firmly with the fork and cut a small wedge from the shank end.

Keep the fork in place to steady the ham and cut thin slices down to the leg bone. Release slices by cutting along bone at right angles to slices.

For more servings turn the ham back to its original position and slice at right angles to the bone.

Picnic Shoulder

Procedure is the same as for Baked Ham.

Pork Loin Roast

It is much easier to carve a pork loin roast if the backbone is separated from the ribs at the market. The backbone then becomes loosened during roasting.

Before the roast is brought to the table remove the backbone by cutting between it and the rib ends.

The roast is placed on the platter so that the rib side faces you.

Insert the fork firmly in the top of the roast. Cut close against both sides of each rib. If the loin is large it is possible to cut two boneless slices between the ribs.

Roast Suckling Pig

Split pig in half by cutting through tender backbone. Separate head from body.

Separate legs from body on one side.

Cut between ribs, allowing 2 per serving, along with some meat from ham and shoulder and some skin. Repeat for other side of pig.

Chicken or Turkey

Remove all trussing equipment, such as skewers and string, in the kitchen.

Hold the drumstick firmly with fingers, pulling gently away from the body. At the same time cut through skin between leg and body.

Press leg away from body with flat side of knife. Then cut through joint joining leg to backbone and skin on the back. Separate drumstick and thigh by cutting down through the joint to the plate.

Slice drumstick and thigh meat. Chicken drumsticks and thighs are usually served without slicing.

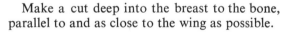

Make a cut deep into the breast to the bone, parallel to and as close to the wing as possible.

Begin at front, starting halfway up the breast, cut thin slices of white meat down to the cut made parallel to the wing.

Remove individual servings of stuffing from an opening cut into side where leg has been removed.

For half turkey, remove wing tip and first joint, then the drumstick. Continue as above.

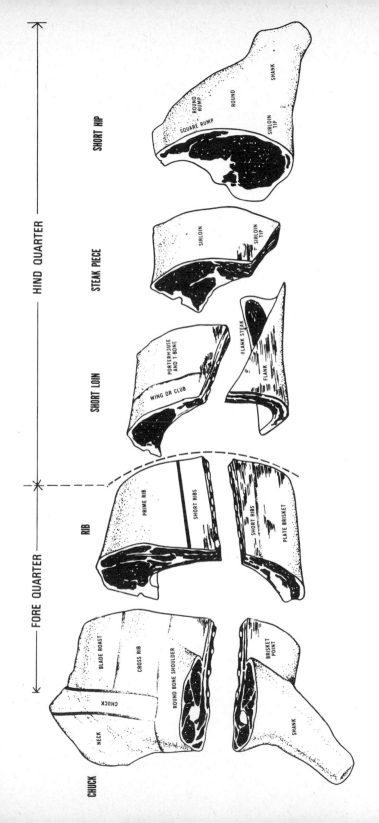

CUTS OF BEEF

The dividing line between the front and hind quarter is taken as the price line; the farther from it the cheaper the cut.

Study the cuts in relation to an animal in the field. The parts which receive the most exercise will be stronger and therefore less tender. At the same time they are developing the extractives which give good flavour.

Today when so much meat is cut and packaged for sale, it is more important to recognize the appearance of the cut than its location on the carcass.

Beef should have a creamy white fat which is brittle and crumbly. Dark yellow soft fat indicates poor beef, usually cow grade. Beef cannot be of high quality without a reasonable amount of fat within the muscles as well as that which forms the exterior covering. This intermingling of fat and lean is called marbling. Fat increases the flavour and helps to retain the moisture of the muscles. The flesh should be a bright, rich red with velvety appearance. The bone should be soft and porous with a pinkish colour. A flinty white bone indicates age.

COOKING THE LESS TENDER CUTS OF BEEF

The recipes which follow make use of some of the less expensive cuts of beef in ways which give attractive, flavourful dishes. A Dutch oven or deep casserole dish with cover would be suitable; an electric frying pan especially convenient. A pressure cooker could be used successfully in most recipes by reducing the liquid and the cooking time.

BRAISING

Name	Weight	Description
CHUCK STEAK	2 pounds	The first cut taken from the rib end.
ARM STEAK	2 pounds	From the shoulder; this steak has a round bone like the round steak, but a different muscle formation. It is less tender than the round and should be less expensive.
FLANK STEAK	¾ pound to 1 pound	This small lean steak is stripped from the flank. It has good flavour but has coarse muscle fibres, running lengthwise. It is not a good buy unless considerably less expensive than round steak.
SHORT RIBS		The rib ends, cut in 2-inch pieces, may be braised with vegetables. They have a high proportion of bone and fat and are not economical for families who wish lean meat.
ROUND STEAK	2 pounds	If this piece is cut from red or blue brand beef it may be tender enough to pan-fry; from commercial or utility beef should be braised. The top round steak, which is one large muscle, is the most tender portion of round steak.

BRAISED BEEF (Basic Recipe)

meat suitable for braising
flour
seasonings

hot liquid (water, stock or
tomato juice)

1. Trim the bone and superfluous fat from the meat.
2. Dredge meat in seasoned flour; if a small piece, pound it with a meat hammer or with the edge of a heavy plate.
3. In a heavy pan which has a tight-fitting lid, or in an electric frying pan, brown the meat on all sides in a small amount of hot fat.
4. Add a small amount of liquid; cover tightly and simmer until meat is tender, adding more liquid, if necessary, to prevent scorching. If desired, browned meat may be cooked in a covered pan in a moderate oven.
5. Use the liquid for gravy, thickening it if necessary with flour shaken with cold water in a covered jar.

SWISS STEAK

2 pounds steak, 1 inch thick
¼ to ⅓ cup flour
1 teaspoon salt
⅛ teaspoon pepper

fat
1 small onion
2 cups boiling water, or
2 cups tomatoes

Prepare according to recipe for Braised Beef, adding chopped onion to liquid ingredients. Cook 2 hours. Serves 4-5.

Potatoes and carrots can be cooked with the meat to make a casserole; add during last hour.

MOCK DUCK

2 pounds steak
flour
1 teaspoon salt
¼ teaspoon pepper

2 cups bread dressing
fat
liquid

1. Prepare meat according to steps 1 and 2 in recipe for Braised Beef.
2. Roll and tie securely with strings.
3. Finish as Braised Beef, baking at 350° for 1½-2 hours. Uncover during last ½ hour of cooking.
4. Remove strings before serving. Serve with gravy. Serves 4-6.

BEEF BIRDS

Using 1 pound of mushrooms, chop stems and add to Mock Duck dressing. Simmer browned meat, cut in individual servings, with the mushroom caps.

BRAISED SHORT RIBS WITH VEGETABLES

2 pounds short ribs	½ cup water
3 tablespoons flour	2 small onions, sliced
2 teaspoons salt	2 carrots, sliced
⅛ teaspoon pepper	2 potatoes, cubed
fat	½ cup celery

1. Cut the short ribs into 8 pieces; brown; drain off fat. Follow recipe for Braised Beef beginning at step 4.
2. Simmer 2 hours; add the vegetables; cook 30 minutes.
3. Thicken the liquid for gravy.

COOKING IN FOIL (Basic Recipe)

Aluminum foil is particularly useful in the cooking of many of these less tender cuts, as meat can be cooked in its own steam with little or no additional liquid—thus retaining all its flavour.

Tear off a length of aluminum foil, preferably heavy-duty foil, 2½ times the length of the meat. Centre the meat on the foil, bring up the cut edges over the meat and triple fold top and sides to make a tight, leak-proof package. Be careful not to tear or puncture the foil. If desired, a double thickness of foil can be used for added strength.

Bake on cookie sheet. See 2 recipes with follow.

STEAK IN FOIL WITH MUSHROOMS

2 pounds 1-inch round steak	⅛ teaspoon pepper
½ package dehydrated onion soup mix	1 cup mushrooms
	2 tablespoons water

1. Centre steak on foil; slice mushrooms and sprinkle over meat with remaining ingredients.
2. Seal carefully. Bake at 375° about 1½ hours or until tender. Serves 4-5.

SWISS STEAK IN FOIL

2 pounds 1-inch round steak	⅛ teaspoon pepper
1 cup ketchup	1 large onion, sliced
¼ cup flour	2 tablespoons lemon juice or
¼ teaspoon salt	1 lemon, thinly sliced

1. Combine ketchup and flour, spoon half of the mixture into the centre of the foil, put steak on top and season.
2. Cover steak with onion slices and remaining ketchup mixture.
3. Sprinkle with lemon juice or top with slices of lemon.
4. Seal carefully. Bake at 375° for 1½ hours or until tender. Serves 4-5.

STEWED BEEF

Meat for stewing should be ordered by the cut. If trimmings are purchased as "Stew Meat" there will be some tender and some less tender meat; it will be impossible to cook the meat until tender without making some of it stringy.

Allow 1 pound of boneless meat for stew for 4; this amount may be reduced if more vegetables are added. Some cuts for stewing:

SHIN OR SHANK BEEF	Coarse, has no bone or gristle and has a good flavour
NECK BEEF	Dark in colour; has a good flavour; needs long cooking
FLANK BEEF	Stringy and has more fat
PLATE BEEF	Has layers of fat and lean
CHUCK BEEF	Is more expensive; requires less cooking

BEEF STEW (Basic Recipe)

1½ pounds beef	6 carrots, halved
⅓ cups seasoned flour	6 potatoes, quartered
fat	1½ teaspoons salt
1 small onion sliced	⅙ teaspoon pepper
vegetable stock or water	flour
⅓ cup celery sliced	

1. Trim the fat and coarse tissue from the meat; cut in 1-inch cubes.
2. Dredge at least half the meat with flour; brown slowly in a little hot fat in a heavy kettle which has a tight-fitting lid.
3. Add the rest of the meat and the onion; add just enough stock or water to cover the meat (about 1 quart). Cover the kettle.
4. Simmer 1 hour; add the vegetables, and more water if necessary, and simmer another hour. Add ⅓ cup white wine if desired.
5. Thicken with flour mixture (page 79).
6. Taste and season. Stew may be served with or without any of the toppings which follow.

Speedy Stew (Pressure-cooked)—Brown prepared meat in fat in an uncovered pressure saucepan. Transfer meat to rack of saucepan, add liquid. Add vegetables which have been halved or left whole so that they will not be overcooked. Pressure-cook all for 12 minutes at 15 pounds pressure. Allow pot to cool slowly; thicken.

To Freeze: If freezer space is limited, it is often preferable to freeze the stewed meat only; when needed, cook vegetables with the thawed meat. If vegetables are frozen together, omit potatoes. Can be kept frozen up to 4 months.

HUNGARIAN GOULASH

2 pounds stewing beef	1 teaspoon salt
fat	½ teaspoon marjoram
1 cup chopped onion	⅛ teaspoon caraway seed
1 clove garlic, crushed	vegetable stock, tomato juice
1 teaspoon paprika	or water, or a combination

1. Cut the meat into 2-inch cubes; brown slowly in a little fat.
2. Add onion and garlic and cook until the juice is absorbed; add paprika and seasoning.
3. Finish according to Beef Stew (Basic Recipe).

HUNGARIAN GOULASH WITH SAUERKRAUT

Heat 2 cups cooked sauerkraut and 1 cup of sour cream; add to the stew mixture just before serving.

TOPPINGS FOR STEW

Turn the hot stew into a 2 quart casserole or into individual serving dishes; cover with any of the following toppings.

PASTRY

1 cup pastry flour or	⅓ cup fat
⅞ cup all-purpose flour	water, about 3 tablespoons
½ teaspoon salt	

1. Make plain Pastry (method page 472); roll ¼ inch thick to fit the casserole.
2. Crimp the edges; brush with milk. Score in a few places to allow steam to escape.
3. Bake the uncooked pastry on a baking sheet at 450° for 15 minutes. Serve it on top of the hot stew. Or, place the uncooked pastry on top of the casserole of hot stew (use an inverted cup or funnel or pastry bird in the centre to support the pastry if a large amount is being made). Bake at 410° for 25 minutes.

POTATO

Leftover mashed potato can be used as topping.

4 large potatoes	1 teaspoon salt
2 tablespoons butter	⅓ cup milk

1. Boil the potatoes; drain; mash with the butter, seasonings and milk.
2. Spread the potatoes on top of the casserole. A pastry bag with a large tip may be used to make a professional-looking dish, or swirl potatoes with a fork.
3. Bake at 400° until the potato begins to brown.
   A beaten egg or egg yolk may be beaten into the potatoes (step 1) to give them a creamy appearance.

DUMPLINGS

2 cups sifted pastry flour or	4 teaspoons baking powder
1¾ cups all purpose flour	¼-⅓ cup fat
1 teaspoon salt	⅔ cup milk

1. Mix and sift the flour, salt and baking powder.
2. Cut in the fat until it is the texture of meal.
3. Stir in the milk to make a sticky dough.
4. Cut out dumplings with a tablespoon and place on a plate which has been sprinkled with flour.
5. Have the unthickened stew boiling gently in a 9-inch saucepan with a tight-fitting lid. There should not be so much liquid that the dumplings cannot rest on the meat and vegetables; allow a space of at least 3 inches for the dumplings to rise.
6. Drop dumplings quickly into the stew, spacing them evenly; cover the pan.
7. Keep the stew simmering and do *not* lift the lid for 15 minutes.
8. Lift the dumplings onto a plate; thicken the stew; pour the stew into a serving dish; arrange the dumplings on top. Makes 12.
   2 tablespoons chopped parsley, chives or finely shredded spinach may be added to the flour to give the dumplings an attractive appearance.

CHEESE DUMPLINGS

Add ½ cup grated Cheddar cheese to dry ingredients for Dumplings and use ¼ cup fat. Prepare as Dumplings.

BISCUIT TOPPING

1. Make tea biscuit dough from the ingredients for Dumplings.
2. Roll dough and shape by any of the following methods:
   (a) Shape into a circle or square to fit the casserole; score with a sharp knife almost through the dough.
   (b) Cut individual biscuits with a round cutter.
   (c) Roll out dough into a rectangle, about ¼ inch in thickness; sprinkle with poultry spice, roll up like a small jellyroll and cut into ½ inch slices.
3. Arrange dough on stew. Bake at 425° for 20-30 minutes.

BOILED BEEF

CUTS FOR "BOILING"

Name	Weight	Description
BRISKET		
Point	8 pounds	This part of the brisket has a larger percentage of fat than the plate end.
Plate End		A well-flavoured, inexpensive piece of meat.
Rolled Brisket		May have too much fat for some families.
PLATE	Up to 10 pounds	Layers of fat and lean. The meat is not as fine as the brisket.
SOUP BONES		
Shank Bones	5 to 6 pounds	Where the stock is wanted more than
Neck	Any weight	the meat, parts which contain much
Tail	1 to 1½ pounds	cartilage and connective tissue are used. The long, slow cooking extracts the gelatine and makes a rich stock.
CORNED BEEF		This is a piece of meat which varies a great deal in quality with the grade of the meat, the cut and the method of curing. The saltpetre in the curing liquid gives the meat a red colour.

"BOILED" BRISKET WITH HORSERADISH SAUCE

3 to 4 pound piece of brisket
fat
boiling water
½ teaspoon salt

⅛ teaspoon pepper
1 cup chopped celery and leaves
1 onion sliced

1. Brown the meat slowly in a little hot fat.
2. Cover with boiling water; add seasonings and vegetables; simmer until tender, about 3 hours. Drain.
3. Serve with Horseradish Sauce (page 91).

OLD FASHIONED "BOILED DINNER"

3 to 4 pounds beef for boiling	6 small onions, whole
6 potatoes, quartered	1 small turnip, cut in large cubes
6 small carrots, whole	1 small head cabbage

1. Cover meat with boiling water and simmer until tender; about 3 hours.
2. One hour before serving add the potatoes, carrots, onions and turnips; half an hour later add the cabbage, cut in wedge-shaped pieces.
3. Serve meat on a platter surrounded with the vegetables.
4. Pour the stock into a pitcher; pass with the dinner.

CORNED BEEF

This is a pickled meat, usually rolled rib or brisket.
1. Wipe meat, place in kettle, cover with cold water.
2. Heat to boiling point, boil 5 minutes, remove scum.
3. Reduce heat; cook below boiling until tender, 3 to 4 hours.
4. Serve hot or cold.

If meat is to be pressed, cool slightly in the water in which it was cooked. Place in a meat press or in a bowl or crock. Cover and weight down, leave until cold.

Vegetables may be cooked with the corned beef as in "Boiled Dinner" recipe.

CUTS FOR POT ROASTING

Name	Weight	Description
ROUND STEAK		
ROASTS	3 pounds	These four roasts are of good quality,
Sirloin Tip		fine texture and have little waste; the
Top of the Round		first two will be more tender but there
Silverside		is a difference in price. The last two
Eye		make excellent pot roasts.

Name	Weight	Description
RUMP ROASTS Square End Aitch Bone or Round End	4 to 5 pounds	This is the better of the two. The meat from any rump roast is excellent in flavour; the large amount of bone makes it fairly expensive and difficult to carve.
CHUCK ROASTS Blade Short Rib Arm Bone	3 to 6 pounds	These roasts are listed in order of quality. All have good texture and little waste. Since they are from the front quarter they are cheaper than the round and rump roasts. The arm bone roast may be cut into three pieces. Use the round end for stew, the centre portion for a pot roast and the square end, sliced into thin steaks, for Swiss Steak. This is an economical way for the small family to avoid leftovers.
SHANK PIECE	4 to 5 pounds	The heavy end of the shank may be boned and tied; it will be much less expensive than the other roasts but the meat is coarse. It is better for "boiled" beef.
PLATE MEAT	Up to 10 pounds	May be boned and rolled; has a large percentage of fat.

POT ROAST (Basic Recipe)

3 to 5 pound pot roast	¼ teaspoon pepper
⅓ cup flour	fat
1 teaspoon salt	½ cup vegetable stock

1. Wipe meat with a paper towel or clean cloth; combine the flour and seasonings and rub them into the meat.
2. Heat fat in a heavy pan (a cast-iron Dutch oven is ideal for this) and brown meat on all sides. Because much of the colour and flavour of the meat depends on the browning, this step should be done carefully.

3. Transfer meat to a rack and place in a pot along with water, vegetable stock or tomato juice. Cover and cook over low heat. If necessary, hot liquid may be added during cooking. Avoid excess liquid for the best flavour and colour of the roast.

4. About an hour before the meat is cooked, add vegetables: small potatoes or large ones quartered, small whole onions or large onions quartered, small whole carrots or diced carrots, green beans or peas. As the flavour of turnip is strong, it is usually cooked separately, if used, and added at serving time.

5. Continue cooking until meat and vegetables are tender. Season. Total cooking time will be 2½-3 hours for a 3-pound pot roast.

6. Remove meat and vegetables to a platter. If necessary thicken the gravy with flour.

Some variations for added flavour:

Wedge several cloves into an onion and cook it with the roast.

Insert a garlic clove, cut into slivers, into gashes cut in the surface of the roast.

After browning, cover meat with ½ cup prepared horseradish; add the liquid and continue at step 3, Basic Recipe.

Add to the liquid before thickening any good meat sauce.

FLEMISH POT ROAST

5 pound pot roast	1 egg
2 teaspoons salt	2 cups bread dressing
2 teaspoons allspice	fat
1 blade of mace	1 onion
1 cup vinegar	cloves
1 5½ ounce can tomato paste	flour

1. Heat salt, allspice and mace in vinegar for 5 minutes; pour it over the roast, cover and let stand several hours.

2. Combine tomato paste, egg and bread dressing.

3. Remove the meat from the vinegar; brown slowly in a little hot fat in a deep pot.

4. Gash the meat deeply in several places; fill with dressing mixture.

5. Pour the seasoned vinegar around the meat and add an onion stuck with 4 cloves.

6. Cover and simmer 2 to 3 hours; thicken liquid.

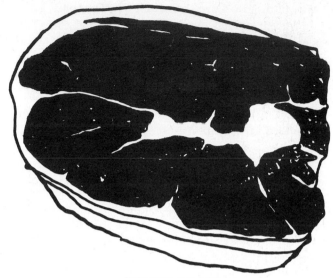

ROUND ROAST

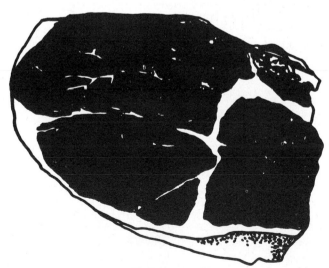

RUMP ROAST

SOUR BEEF (SAUERBRATEN)

4 to 5 pound beef pot roast
2 cups cider vinegar
2 onions, sliced
1 small piece bay leaf
1 teaspoon cinnamon
1 teaspoon allspice

1 teaspoon cloves
1 teaspoon salt
½ teaspoon pepper
2 cups vinegar
2 cups water

1. Over the roast in a large bowl pour the combined vinegar, onions and spices; leave in a cool place for 2 days, turning the meat every 12 hours.
2. Remove the meat; drain; place in a heavy, covered pan.
3. Add vinegar and water
4. Simmer on top of the stove or bake covered at 300° 3 hours.
5. Thicken the liquid with flour. Sour cream may be combined with flour and stirred into the hot liquid. Allow ½ cup sour cream and 2 tablespoons flour for each cup of liquid.

SPICED BEEF

Ideal on the Christmas buffet.

9 pound rump roast of beef
½ pound brown sugar
12 ounces salt
1 ounce saltpetre

½ ounce cloves
½ ounce mace
1½ ounces allspice
½ ounce black pepper

1. Mix together sugar, salt and saltpetre and rub well into meat; let stand 24 hours in a cool place.
2. Combine spices and rub into meat; let stand in a crock in a cold place and turn the meat every day for 2 weeks in the liquid which forms in the crock.
3. Place meat in a large kettle and cover with water; add liquid from crock.
4. Bring to a boil. Simmer the meat for 1 hour.
5. Replace meat in crock; add boiling liquid. Cover the crock with blankets to hold in the heat. Cool slowly 2-3 days. Serve cold, thinly sliced.

COOKING THE TENDER CUTS OF BEEF
Cuts for Roasting

A roast less than 3 pounds is not a good buy.

From Red and Blue Brand beef all the cuts listed below may be roasted; from Commercial brand those marked (*) will be better pot-roasted.

Cuts for Roasting	Weight	Description
TENDER ROASTS		
TENDERLOIN (or fillet or undercut)	2½ to 4½ pounds	Tender, juicy but not highly flavoured; very expensive; seldom removed in the piece.
RIB ROASTS		
Standing	3½-10 pounds (1 rib weighs 3½ pounds)	A delicious flavour; this roast has a high percentage of bone but is not difficult to carve. The first 5 or 6 ribs on the forequarter are the Prime ribs.
Hotel Style		The back bone or chine and the short ribs may be trimmed off to make a more compact roast.
Rolled		A high-priced roast, it has a good flavour and little waste.
*Short rib		Is less tender but has a larger amount of lean; it is more economical.
WING ROAST	3 to 8 pounds	An expensive roast. Has a large proportion of bone, but a good flavour, and tender meat.
PINBONE ROAST	5 pounds	Have 'The tenderloin removed to be served as filet mignon. The remaining is boned and rolled for roasting. Expensive.
PORTERHOUSE ROAST	3 to 8 pounds	This roast contains the tenderloin but at the same time considerable bone and the tough flank end. It is carved much like the standing rib roast.
BONELESS PORTERHOUSE	3 to 6 pounds	The most expensive roast but very tender and easy to carve.

Cuts for Roasting	Weight	Description
*SIRLOIN		
Tip	4 to 10 pounds	This roast has the appearance of the rolled rib roast; it is cut from the round.
Top Cut	4 to 10 pounds	May have the end of the tender loin in it. Is an expensive roast the better of the two.
LESS TENDER ROASTS		
*ROUND STEAK		
Top Round		This roast is a good buy.
*RUMP		
Boned Rump	3 to 5 pounds	This is fairly expensive meat but has good flavour and is a good size for a small family.
Square End Rump	4 to 5 pounds	These roasts have a high percent-
Aitch-bone Rump	5 to 6 pounds	age of bone. The meat is somewhat dry but has a good flavour.
*CHUCK		
Blade	3 to 6 pounds	A continuation of the prime ribs. From graded beef this is an excellent buy, tender, not too much waste. Look for one with a pliable blade bone.

ROAST BEEF

1. Note weight of meat; wipe with a damp cloth or paper towel and place fat side up on a rack in a shallow, uncovered roasting pan. If the meat is very lean, a piece of suet should be ordered with it and placed on top, or the top of the meat should be spread with a paste of 1 tablespoon dry mustard, 2 teaspoons flour and 2 tablespoons dripping or fat.
2. Insert meat thermometer, cook meat at 325° at approximately 30 minutes per pound. See table following.
3. When roast is cooked, remove the thermometer and transfer the meat to a hot platter, leaving it in a warm place or warming oven for 10 minutes. This will allow time for some of the juices of the meat to be reabsorbed, facilitating carving, and providing time for making the gravy.

   Roasts which are frozen need not be thawed before cooking; allow 15 minutes more cooking time per pound. Do not use thermometer with frozen roasts.

PRIME RIB ROAST

ROLLED PRIME RIB ROAST

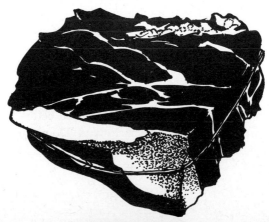

SHORT RIB ROAST

AVERAGE COOKING TIMES FOR ROAST BEEF

Type of Roast	Minutes per Pound	
Standing Rib (with bone)	Rare	23
	Medium	27
	Well Done	34
Rolled Rib or Loin (without bone)	Rare	32
	Medium	35
	Well Done	40

GRAVY

1. Remove the roast from the pan; keep it hot in a warming oven.
2. Pour off the fat; for each cup of gravy return 2 tablespoons fat to the pan.
3. Stir in 2 tablespoons flour for each cup of gravy; stir until smooth.
4. Remove the pan from the stove; stir in a little cold water to make a smooth paste; thin with measured hot water or vegetable stock.
5. Return the pan to the heat; stir until the sauce thickens; add liquid if necessary. The gravy should be a creamy consistency.
6. Season well; if necessary add a little gravy colouring. 1 cup of gravy serves 3. A 3-4 pound roast makes 1-2 cups.

YORKSHIRE PUDDING

1 cup sifted pastry flour or   1 cup milk
⅞ cup all-purpose flour   3 eggs
½ teaspoon salt   beef dripping (about ½ cup)

1. Sift flour with salt. Add milk, gradually, to prevent lumping.
2. Add eggs and beat 2 minutes with an egg beater. Chill 20 minutes in the refrigerator. Preheat oven to 425°.
3. Cover the bottom of an 8-inch square pan with drippings from the roast or pour a tablespoon of drippings into each of 8 large muffin tins; place in the oven until sizzling hot.
4. Quickly pour in the batter to a depth of ¾ inch.
5. Place pans in oven and immediately reset temperature control to 375°. Bake; large pan 50 minutes, muffin tins 30 minutes.

Yorkshire pudding should puff up and become crisp; serve around the roast. When transferred to individual plates, pour gravy over it.

BARBECUED RUMP ROAST

Order from the butcher a boned rump roast and have it larded generously with salt pork. Place the meat on a spit and cook 15 minutes to the pound, basting frequently with Barbecue Sauce (page 86). If the spit is not rotated electrically, turn it often to insure even cooking. Place a drip pan under the meat each time it is basted; remove after each use. Remove meat from the heat; let stand 5 minutes before slicing.

Cuts for Broiling, Pan-Broiling

From Red or Blue Brand Beef the following cuts will be tender enough to broil or pan-broil.

Cut	Weight	Description
TENDERLOIN STEAK (Filet Mignon)	2 to 3 steaks to the pound	This muscle is stripped out of the side of beef, thereby removing it from the porterhouse steaks. For this reason it is very expensive and must be specially ordered. It is juicy, tender, but not as flavoursome as other steaks. It is cut into 1-inch steaks; order by number rather than weight.
PORTERHOUSE STEAK	1 to 2 pounds	This steak contains the tenderloin. The tail, which is tough, should be cut off before cooking and used for stew or marinated for shish kabobs (page 168). Usually one steak is served to each person but sometimes it is cut 3 inches thick and carved. Expensive.
T-BONE STEAK	¾ to 1 pound	A smaller steak than the porterhouse, it has less tenderloin and less tail. Buy one for each serving.
WING OR CLUB STEAK	½ pound	This is still smaller with little or no tenderloin. Buy one for each serving.
SIRLOIN STEAK	¾ to 3 pounds	This steak has a wide variation in the amount of bone and in the tenderness. Serves 2-4.
PIN-BONE SIRLOIN STEAK		This, the least desirable of the sirloin steaks, has a large amount of bone and fat and tail end.

Cut	Weight	Description
DOUBLE-BONE SIRLOIN STEAK		The most desirable.
ROUND-BONE SIRLOIN STEAK		Has less bone than the other bone sirloins but is cut from the loin end next to the round and will be less tender.
WEDGE-BONE SIRLOIN STEAK	2 pounds	The last steaks from the round end of the sirloin are economical but less tender.
ROUND STEAK		Contains only the small round bone. If Commercial Grade, this should be braised.

ADDITIONAL CUTS FOR BROILING AND PAN-BROILING

Marinating meats for 18-24 hours renders many meats of marginal tenderness sufficiently tender for broiling and pan-broiling. This is also true of meats which have been treated with meat tenderizer, commercially or at home.

These include flank steak, chuck steak or round steak.

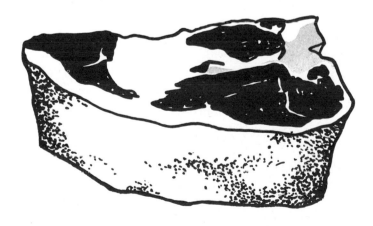

PORTERHOUSE ROAST

BROILED STEAK

1. Place oven rack about 3 inches below element and preheat broiler. If steak is thick, use a meat thermometer.
2. While broiler is heating, wipe steak, trim off superfluous fat, slash rounded edges to prevent curling.
3. If steak is very lean, coat each side lightly with melted butter or drippings.
4. Broil on one side, turn and broil on the other. With an electric stove leave oven door ajar. For a 1-inch steak allow 15-20 minutes; for $1\frac{1}{2}$ inch steak 20-25 minutes; for a 2-inch steak allow 30-35 minutes.
5. Season. Serve sizzling hot on heated plate with onions, mushrooms or parsley butter.

Rare Steak: interior of steak is rose in colour.
Medium Steak: interior pinkish, outer brown layer deeper than for rare.
Well-done Steak: brownish gray throughout.

PAN-BROILED STEAK

1. Wipe meat with a damp cloth; trim off superfluous fat. Slash rounded edges to prevent curling.
2. Melt about 2 tablespoons fat in a heavy frying pan (extra fat cut off meat can be rendered down). Heat frying pan.
3. When the pan is very hot, put in the meat and sear on one side. Reduce heat and continue cooking about 3 to 6 minutes, according to the degree of cooking desired.
4. Increase heat again, turn meat and sear. Continue cooking on reduced heat until done. Season with salt and pepper. Serve sizzling hot on heated plates or platter with pan gravy, mushrooms or butter mixed with lemon juice and/or chives.

   The type of pan, and the size and thickness of steak influence the length of time required to pan-broil (pan-fry) steak. To determine if steak is cooked, cut a small gash close to the bone near the end of the cooking period and note the colour of the meat.

Usually a 1-inch, individual portion of steak will be cooked—rare in approximately 5-7 minutes—medium in 6 to 8 minutes—well-done in 8 to 10 minutes. Steaks 1½ inches in thickness will require approximately 10 minutes longer to cook, while those 2 inches thick will require approximately 20 minutes longer.

MARINATED STEAK

Flank steak lends itself to this treatment beautifully. Prepare a marinade (page 168) or combine cooking oil, lemon juice and spices to generously coat both sides of steak. Place in a porcelain or glass dish of suitable size to hold steak. Marinate steak 18-24 hours, turning it over occasionally. Drain. Broil 7-10 minutes on each side.

BARBECUED STEAK

Choose a tender steak—porterhouse, sirloin, etc.—cut 1½ to 2 inches thick; for a crowd, sirloin is the most satisfactory cut. Allow approximately ¾ to 1 pound per person. Let steak remain at room temperature for at least an hour before cooking. Trim off excess fat, then score edges every 2 inches. Rub with a clove of garlic and sprinkle generously with salt and pepper. Coat with Barbecue Sauce (page 86), using a wide brush. Place steak in a 2-sided wire broiler on the grill, or on the grill directly, and cook over a very hot fire, burned down to coals. Sear quickly on one side, about a minute, turn and sear on the other side. Continue cooking about 6 to 8 minutes longer, turn and finish cooking the other side for about the same length of time. A 2-inch steak will require a total of about 15 minutes to be cooked rare. As red juices will ooze from a well-cooked steak as well as from one which is cooked rare, care must be taken to avoid overcooking. Season with salt and pepper.

BUDGET BARBECUED STEAK

Choose a 1½ to 2 inch thick chuck, blade or round steak. Trim fat and score edges every 2 inches. Sprinkle meat tenderizer lightly and evenly on both sides, about ½ teaspoon per pound of meat. Pierce meat with a fork on both sides at 1-inch intervals and let stand at least 30 to 40 minutes at room temperature for steaks up to 1-inch thick, 1 hour for thicker ones; or cover meat loosely and refrigerate over night. Let refrigerated steak stand at room temperature for an hour before cooking, and cook as in preceding recipe, allowing a total cooking time of about 20 minutes.

*Beef Bourguignonne is an
increasingly popular fondue.
Guests will enjoy cooking and
eating the delicious cubes of steak.*

BEEF FONDUE (BEEF BOURGUIGNONNE)

This is fun for a small dinner party when meat is cooked in a fondue pot or chafing dish at the table. Beef fondue can also be served as a hot appetizer.

For each person, cut into ¾ inch cubes about 6-8 ounces of beef tenderloin. Fill fondue pot about ⅓ full of cooking oil and bring to boiling point. Adjust heat to keep oil boiling very gently. Each person spears meat with a fondue fork and cooks the meat in the oil until it is cooked to his liking.

A variety of sauces, hot and cold, are served with the meat. Sour cream can be mixed with any of horseradish, blue cheese, or cream cheese seasoned with garlic. Flavoured mayonnaise—mayonnaise mixed with curry powder, or with a little ketchup and a dash of Worcestershire Sauce—makes a zesty accompaniment to the beef. Hot Barbecue Sauce (page 86) or Hot Wine Butter (below) might also be served.

When Beef Fondue is served as a main course at dinner, serve with it baked potatoes and a green salad.

TO SERVE WITH STEAK

Although good steak requires little embellishment, these butters and sauces do contribute to an occasion.

SAVORY STEAK SPREADS: Blend 4 tablespoons butter with any of: 1 tablespoon lemon juice, 1 tablespoon chopped chives, 1 teaspoon prepared mustard; or with 3 tablespoons blue cheese blended with 2 tablespoons mayonnaise. Spread on hot, cooked steak.

MAÎTRE D'HÔTEL SAUCE: page 91.

HOT WINE BUTTER: Combine the following ingredients and heat (do not boil): ½ cup butter, 1 tablespoon dry mustard, ½ teaspoon garlic salt, 1 teaspoon Worcestershire Sauce, 2 tablespoons red wine and a dash of pepper. Serve with steak or Beef Fondue.

ROYAL MUSHROOM SAUCE: page 88.

GROUND BEEF

There are three grades of ground beef which may be purchased.

HAMBURGER: This is made from the trimmings and may contain too high a percentage of fat to be economical or appetizing. Hamburger, purchased from a reliable meat store, is excellent; bought at special sales it may shrink greatly when cooked.

GROUND BEEF: Ask to have neck, chuck or shin beef put through the grinder.

ROUND STEAK, MINCED: This is much more expensive and has no better flavour than the ground beef.

HAMBURGER PATTIES (Basic Recipe)

1½ pounds ground beef	1 teaspoon parsley, finely
1 teaspoon salt	chopped
⅛ teaspoon pepper	2 tablespoons chopped green
2 tablespoons grated onion	pepper (optional)

1. Add the seasonings to the meat; mix in; overmixing toughens.
2. Shape into patties ½ inch thick, rounding them with the palm of the hand. Makes 6. For use in buns pat flat to ¼ inch thickness. Makes 12.
3. Sauté in a little hot fat, or broil 5-7 minutes on each side.

   Any one of the following seasonings may be added: ½ teaspoon dry ginger, 1 teaspoon prepared horseradish, 1 teaspoon prepared mustard, 3 tablespoons ketchup, 1 clove minced garlic, ½ cup mushrooms, 1 cup medium-grated potato, 1 teaspoon finely-grated lemon rind.

To extend the meat and to make a patty of lighter texture add: ½ cup soft bread crumbs or ½ cup quick-cooking rolled oats and ¼ cup milk. This will make 8 patties or 16 for use in buns.

To Freeze: Place the number of patties required for one meal on a sheet of waxed paper on a firm backing of cardboard (if many, use two sheets). Cover with waxed paper, another layer of patties and another sheet of waxed paper. Add more layers as needed; overwrap with foil or freezer wrap. Remove frozen patties by layers, returning remaining to freezer.

PARTY HAMBURGERS

1. Shape a favourite hamburg recipe into a long roll about 3 inches in diameter.
2. On a sheet of waxed paper lay out rindless side-bacon strips, allowing one strip for each inch of roll.
3. Place the roll on the strips of bacon; bring each strip up around the roll and fasten with a toothpick.
4. Wrap in the paper and chill.
5. When ready to use, cut with a sharp knife between each strip.
6. Broil; turn and broil until beginning to brown.
7. Place a large mushroom, containing a little butter, cap side up on the hamburger; continue to cook until the mushroom looks done.
8. Turn the cap, brush with a little melted butter and finish cooking.

MEAT BALLS (Basic Recipe)

1 pound ground beef	1 teaspoon salt
1 tablespoon finely chopped onion	½ - 1 egg flour
1 tablespoon finely chopped green pepper (optional)	1 tablespoon fat
¼ cup fine, soft bread crumbs	2½ cups liquid*

1. Combine the meat, onion, green pepper, bread crumbs, salt and egg. Shape into 1½-inch balls and roll each in flour.
2. Heat fat in a deep frying pan or electric skillet; brown balls on all sides. Pour off fat.

3. Prepare liquid ingredients and pour over meat balls. Cover and simmer 15-20 minutes. Makes about 18 meat balls. Serves 4-5.

 *Use any of the following liquids:

    1 10-ounce can cream of mushroom, celery or tomato soup diluted with 1 cup water or stock, or dehydrated cream soup reconstituted with 2½ cups cold water, or leftover beef gravy diluted with an equal quantity of water.

    2½ cups tomato juice, vegetable stock, meat stock or bouillon made from cubes, or constituted onion soup mix.

 Thicken liquid with flour (page 79). Serve meat balls and their gravy with noodles, spaghetti, rice or potatoes.

 For economy: Increase bread crumbs to ¾ cup.

To Freeze: Follow preparation directions to the end of step 2. Freeze quickly in a single layer on a cookie sheet; transfer to a plastic bag and tie. If a large quantity is being prepared, use several bags, indicating the quantity on each. Remove the required number of meat balls as needed, heat any of the liquids suggested in a saucepan or chafing dish, simmer meat balls, thawed or frozen depending on the amount of available time.

To prepare a large quantity: For a party or church supper, or for many little spontaneous supper parties during the Christmas season, prepare several pounds of meat into balls and freeze as indicated in preceding instructions. When cooking a large quantity of meat balls, cook with preheated liquid in a covered roasting pan in a 350° oven until done; transfer to serving dishes. See Party Meat Balls (below) for party touches.

VEAL AND PORK MEAT BALLS

Substitute a mixture of veal and pork for half of the beef in Meat Balls (Basic Recipe).

PORCUPINE MEAT BALLS

To the ingredients for Meat Balls (Basic Recipe) add ½ cup uncooked rice; form into balls. Do not brown. Dilute 1 10-ounce can tomato soup with 1 cup water. Simmer balls in liquid in a covered pan or bake in a covered casserole at 350° for 50 minutes.

PARTY MEAT BALLS

Prepare meat balls using double the quantity of Meat Balls (Basic Recipe). Cook browned meat balls in liquid made from a combination of dehydrated onion soup and cream of mushroom soup, plus water. Stir in 1 cup of sautéed, sliced mushrooms if desired, and serve from a casserole or chafing dish. Garnish with strips of pimento and coarsely chopped parsley.

MEAT BALLS ROMANOFF

Prepare Party Meat Balls. Shortly before serving, stir in 1 cup sour cream.

SWEDISH MEAT BALLS

2 tablespoons chopped onion	¼ teaspoon pepper
2 tablespoons bacon fat	⅛ teaspoon mace
¼ cup brown bread crumbs	⅛ teaspoon allspice
½ cup milk	⅛ teaspoon mustard
1 pound ground beef	⅛ teaspoon sage
¼ pound ground lean pork	1 tablespoon chopped parsley
1 egg yolk	2 tablespoons butter
½ cup cold mashed potatoes	1 cup water
1½ teaspoons salt	

1. Sauté the onion in fat until golden brown.
2. Soak the crumbs in milk until soft; add the meat, onion, egg yolk, potatoes and seasoning; knead together until smooth.
3. Shape into small balls, using 2 spoons dipped in cold water.
4. Cook the meat balls in the butter, shaking continually to make the balls round, until an even brown.
5. Add the water; cover and simmer 30 minutes. Thicken the gravy. Serve hot or cold. The water may be omitted and the meat balls served dry; in this case meat balls should be cooked for a few minutes more, after browning.

BEEF ROLL

1 pound ground beef	½ teaspoon salt
½ cup chopped onion	⅛ teaspoon pepper
¼ cup celery thinly sliced	½ teaspoon Worcestershire Sauce
¼ cup chopped green pepper	1 recipe of Tea Biscuit dough
fat	

1. Brown the meat and vegetables in a little fat; add seasonings; cool.
2. Make the Biscuit Dough according to recipe on page 440. Roll to a sheet ¼ inch thick, and about 10 inches in width.

Ham Rolls (page 333) are a delicious and attractive Supper Dish.
Seafood-stuffed avocadoes, tomatoes or melons are hot-weather favourites.

Roast Turkey is a fine traditional meal. Ham appears regally in its many roles—as a roast with bone, as a boneless rolled roast, or as canned pressed ham.

3. Brush with a little melted fat; spread with the meat mixture; roll as a jellyroll; chill in the refrigerator.
4. Cut into 1½-inch slices; place cut side up in a greased 10 by 6½-inch pan; brush with melted butter.
5. Bake at 400° for 30 minutes.
6. Serve with Spanish Sauce or hot home-made Chili Sauce (page 684). Serves 6.

BEEF LOAF

1½ pounds ground beef	½ teaspoon grated lemon rind
1 cup bread crumbs	1 tablespoon chopped parsley
1 teaspoon salt	1 tablespoon melted fat
¼ teaspoon pepper	1 egg
1 small onion finely chopped	

1. Combine all the ingredients, mixing lightly and as little as possible.
2. Press into a greased 9 by 5-inch loaf tin and cover lightly with foil.
3. Bake at 350° 1 to 1½ hours. Serves 8.
   If dry crumbs are used add 1 cup liquid. Vegetable stock, tomato juice or milk may be used.

VARIATIONS

1. Substitute veal, or pork, for ½ pound of beef.
2. Add any of 1 cup grated carrot, 1 green pepper, 1 clove garlic, minced or 1 cup grated raw potato.
3. Line the bottom of the pan with half the meat mixture; cover this with 1 cup bread dressing; add the remaining meat; finish as above.
4. Shape the mixture into 8 individual loaves; place in a shallow pan or muffin pans; bake 45 minutes at 350°, basting once or twice.
5. Baste individual or large meat loaves as they cook with Barbecue Sauce (page 86).
6. Substitute 1 cup quick-cooking rolled oats for the bread crumbs.
7. Serve with Tomato Sauce or Mushroom Sauce (pages 84, 88).

Other recipes containing ground beef may be found in Chapter 11, Supper Dishes.

VEAL

Meat from young beef animals 3 to 10 months of age is known as veal.

Since veal has little fat but considerable connective tissue it requires long, slow cooking. Roasting, pan-frying or braising are the most suitable methods; broiling is not recommended. The flesh of veal should be a light grayish pink in colour with a velvety texture. There will be less fat than on beef but this fat should also be firm and white. The bone should be porous and red.

VEAL FOR ROASTING

Roast	Weight	Description
LEG		
Whole Leg	18 pounds	Too large for most families.
Leg with Rump off		The large rump bone is off, making easier carving.
Shank Half		Can be a good buy. Have the shank sawed through and use for stew.
Rump Half		Too large a bone makes it expensive and difficult.
Round	4 pounds	A good roast with only the round bone.
LOIN		
Loin	3 to 12 pounds	This roast when cooked has tender, white meat, mild in flavour. It is expensive.
Sirloin		As in beef the round end is less tender; the pin-bone has more waste.
RIB		This is a better buy as chops.
SHOULDER		
Square Cut	6 to 8 pounds	This roast has a large amount of bone. It is often boned out and resembles the rolled rib. It has a good flavour and will be more economical.
Blade	3 to 4 pounds	An economical small roast; it is usually boned and dressed.
Arm	3 to 4 pounds	Has only the small round bone but is less tender.

When any cut of veal is being roasted a piece of fat should be placed on top to baste the meat as it cooks.

Slivers of garlic may be inserted in 2 or 3 cuts made on the surface of the roast.

Roast uncovered on a rack in a roasting pan at 325° for approximately 35 minutes per pound for a leg roast (with bone) and approximately 50 minutes per pound for a rolled roast (boneless).

Veal should always be cooked well done.

For more detail of cooking, see method for cooking Roast Beef, page 141.

VEAL FOR POT-ROASTING

Roast	Weight	Description
HEEL OF THE ROUND	3 to 4 pounds	An excellent piece.
BREAST	4 pounds	Is thin and stringy; it is inexpensive and makes a more attractive roast if dressed.

For method of Pot-roasting, see page 136.

VEAL FOR BRAISING OR PAN-FRYING

Cuts	Weight	Description
CHOPS		
Loin	3 to 1 pound	Least amount of bone.
Rib	3 to 1 pound	
Shoulder	2 to 1 pound	More bone than the loin but much less expensive.
CUTLETS	1 slice is 1-1¼ pounds	This is the same as round steak in beef.
ARM STEAK	½-¾ pound	These pieces are less expensive and may be served in the same way as the chops and cutlets.
BLADE STEAKS		
SCALLOPS		Very thin slices of the leg, pounded flat.
RIBLETS		Little meat; see short ribs of beef.

Breaded Veal Cutlets with Mushroom Sauce.

BREADED VEAL CUTLETS

1. For cutlets, use ¾-inch slice from leg or shoulder of veal.
2. Wipe meat, remove bone and skin; cut meat into pieces for serving; skewer small pieces together with toothpicks.
3. Cover bones and skin with cold water, heat slowly, cook below boiling; use this stock for gravy.
4. Season pieces of veal with salt and pepper, crumb.
5. Brown in hot fat.
6. Reduce heat and continue cooking until tender, adding more fat if necessary, or add stock and a dash of Worcestershire Sauce. Cook below boiling point 1 hour, or until tender. Garnish with parsley.

VARIATIONS

SPANISH VEAL: Substitute, for gravy, 1 cup Creole Sauce (page 85).

SMOTHERED VEAL: Substitute for stock and Worcestershire Sauce 1 can mushroom soup (10-ounce) mixed with ½ can water.

DEVILLED VEAL CUTLETS: Add 1 teaspoon prepared mustard and 3 teaspoons prepared horseradish to the stock in Breaded Veal Cutlets. Omit Worcestershire Sauce.

VEAL PAPRIKAS

3 medium onions
2 tablespoons paprika
2 tablespoons fat
1½ pounds arm steak
2 cups stock or cold water

3 tablespoons flour
⅛ teaspoon pepper
2 teaspoons salt
½ cup sour cream

1. Sauté the sliced onions and the paprika slowly in the fat for 10 minutes
2. Add the steak; sauté slowly until golden brown.
3. Add the stock; cover; simmer until tender (1-1½ hours).
4. Blend the flour, seasonings and sour cream. About 5 minutes before the meat is done, stir mixture into the stock slowly; heat to just below the boiling point.
5. Serve with dumplings or noodles.
   A 4 pound fowl, disjointed, may be substituted for the veal.

VEAL BIRDS

See recipe for Beef Birds, page 130.

SCALLOPINE OF VEAL

This dish of Italian origin can be prepared in advance up to the end of step 5, then easily finished at serving time.

1½ pounds veal steak,
    ½-inch thick
½ cup salad oil
¼ cup lemon juice
1 clove garlic, crushed
¼ teaspoon mustard
1 teaspoon paprika
1 teaspoon salt
¼ teaspoon nutmeg

½ teaspoon sugar
¼ cup flour
¼ cup fat
1 medium onion
1 green pepper
1½ cups chicken stock
¼ pound mushrooms
1 tablespoon butter
6 stuffed olives

1. Cut meat into serving pieces. Pound thin.
2. Prepare a marinade from the next 8 ingredients by shaking them together in a covered bottle.
3. Spread pieces of meat in the bottom of a flat pan; pour marinade over meat and soak for 15 minutes, turning meat occasionally.
4. Lift veal from marinade. Dip meat in flour, brown on both sides in hot fat in frying pan.
5. Add thinly sliced onion, strips of green pepper, chicken stock and the remaining marinade.

6. Cover and cook over low heat or in a 350° oven until the veal is very tender, about 40 minutes.
7. Slice mushrooms and brown them lightly in butter. Slice olives and add with mushrooms to veal.
8. Spoon sauce over veal while cooking for 5 minutes more.

SCALLOPINE A MARSALA

Omit onions and pepper; to the fat left after the meat is cooked (step 4) add ¼ cup Marsala. Cook 1 minute to loosen the browned bits in the pan; pour over the veal. Serve with mushrooms and tomatoes.

VEAL RIBLETS WITH PARSLEY DUMPLINGS

2 pounds veal riblets
¼ cup fat
1 teaspoon salt
½ teaspoon pepper

½ cup chopped celery
½ cup chopped onion
2 cups vegetable stock or water

1. Have the veal cut in 2-inch pieces; brown in hot fat; season.
2. Simmer with the vegetables and stock until tender, about 1 hour.
3. 15 minutes before serving add the dumplings (page 133). Cook without lifting lid for 15 minutes. Transfer to a platter.

VEAL FOR STEWING

Name	Weight	Description
KNUCKLE	4 pounds	This large bone has little meat but makes excellent jelly.
BREAST	4 pounds	Has layers of meat and skin; the rib end may be cut off and braised.
SHANK	2 pounds	Fine-textured meat and at the upper end a good piece. It will make jelly if only a small amount is needed.
NECK	3 pounds	Contains a heavy bone.

VEAL STEW

1½ to 2 pounds veal
⅓ cup seasoned flour
4 tablespoons fat
3 cups vegetable stock or water

2 teaspoons salt
¼ teaspoon pepper
1 large onion, chopped
1 cup diced celery

1. Cut the veal into 1-inch pieces; roll in seasoned flour.
2. Brown in the hot fat; cover with water or stock; add seasoning; cover and simmer 1½ to 2 hours.
3. Add the vegetables and simmer until tender, about 15 minutes.
4. Thicken the gravy if necessary (page 143).

JELLIED VEAL

This makes an attractive mould for a buffet supper.

1 veal shank or neck	1 large onion
2 quarts water	leaves from 1 bunch celery
½ teaspoon black pepper	1 small bunch parsley
2 teaspoons salt	1 bay leaf
1 slice lemon	

1. Cover the meat, including the skin and bone, with cold water; add remaining ingredients.
2. Simmer about 2 hours until the liquid is reduced to ⅓ the amount; drain off and save the stock. Refrigerate all overnight.
3. Skim off the fat; observe if the jelly is firm enough to cut.
4. Skin the meat; remove the bones; shred or chop the meat finely.
5. Heat the stock; if the jelly was not firm add 1 teaspoon gelatine to 2 cups of liquid; heat but do not boil until the gelatine is dissolved; season well; clear if desired.
6. Chill stock until it begins to thicken; combine with the meat and pour into a loaf tin or individual moulds.

   To decorate the mould pour in a thin layer of jelly and allow it to set fairly stiff; arrange on this layer the decoration (see paragraph following), remembering that it will be reversed. When the decoration is in place, spoon over it a thin layer of jelly and leave a few minutes to set; spoon the meat and jelly mixed together into the mould.

   An attractive decoration is a border of sliced radish or green peas, well drained, around a flower of sliced, hard-cooked egg with the stem and leaves of water cress. Sliced gherkins arranged symmetrically with stuffed olives make another decoration.

   Chicken may be jellied in the same way, or chicken and veal may be combined.

   The meat may be left in larger pieces and packed into a bowl. Add just enough stock to hold the meat together. Place a plate and a weight on top to press it firmly. Chill. Unmould.

LAMB

Lamb is the flesh of young sheep. The Dorset sheep which breeds three times a year now makes it possible to have young lamb if not "spring" lamb throughout most of the year. Young lamb will have red, porous bones. The "break joint" where the forefeet are taken off in young lamb will have a sawtooth effect and will be moist and red. The flesh in young lamb will be pink; it darkens with age to a dark red. The fat is slightly pink in very young animals, becoming creamy, then finally white and brittle.

Since lamb is a young animal, all the cuts are tender and only the shank, neck and breast need long cooking.

It is important to serve lamb either very hot or very cold since the fat hardens quickly and, on lukewarm plates, it will become unappetizing.

There is a thin papery covering over the lamb carcass called the fell; it is removed from steaks and chops but may be left on the leg.

CUTS FOR ROASTING

Cut	Weight	Description
LEG		
Full Leg	5 to 7 pounds	The meat is tender and juicy; should be thick and heavy for its size.
Boned Leg		Easy to carve; more expensive.
Half Leg		A good buy if not the rump end, which has a high proportion of bone.
Short Leg		Shank end; more bone but will be less expensive; is difficult to carve; other less expensive cuts are a better buy.
LOIN	7 to 8 pounds (12 chops)	A well-flavoured tender roast containing the tenderloin; the backbone must be cut so carving is simplified.
SHOULDER Ribs and Shoulder	8 pounds	This is a good buy if used wisely. Remove ribs to broil; shank for stew; neck for devilled neck slices; dress and roast the rest.
Square cut	4 to 6 pounds	The shank and neck are trimmed off. Shoulder bone removed.
Cushion	4 to 6 pounds	The shoulder is boned and stuffed to form a square, cushion-like roast.
Rolled	4 pounds	This roast is more expensive but has no waste.

Cut	Weight	Description
RIB Crown Roast		It is not usually sold as a roast. An even number of ribs from the rack are turned back and tied to make a crown. It is expensive because of the time required to shape it, and is a large roast.
BREAST	2 to 2½ pounds	This is a thin piece of meat with a stringy texture and considerable fat. It is inexpensive.

ROAST LAMB TIMETABLE

	Weight in Pounds	Oven Temperature	Minutes per Pound	Time Hours
Rolled Shoulder	4	325°	35	2⅓
Leg	7	325°	30	3½

When a meat thermometer is used, the meat will be medium cooked when the thermometer registers 175°, well cooked at 182°.

ROAST LEG OF LAMB

1. Remove thick skin. Note weight, and wipe meat.
2. Place on rack in roasting pan, season with garlic or herbs, salt and pepper.
3. Roast according to Timetable.
4. Serve with Brown Gravy (page 143) and Mint Sauce (page 88) or Currant Jelly.
5. Leg of lamb may be boned and stuffed if desired.

GRILLED LEG OF LAMB IN FOIL

Ideal for a barbecue dinner.

Trim off all fat from a whole or half leg of lamb which has had the shank bone removed. Rub meat all over with a cut clove of garlic, then with lightly seasoned flour. Place meat in the centre of a large sheet of heavy aluminum foil and brush generously with soy sauce or with a mixture of ½ cup bottled thick meat sauce, ¼ cup ketchup and 2 to 3 tablespoons chopped fresh mint. Wrap and seal meat carefully, using triple folds on all edges. Roast on the grill about 6 inches above glowing coals, allowing about 30 minutes per pound. Slit foil and pour off the juice into a pitcher, remove meat; let stand in a warm place for 5 minutes before carving. Serve with the hot juices which collected in the foil during cooking.

LAMB CUTS

1. LEG—Roast.

2. LOIN—Roasts and Chops.

3. RIBS (or hotel rack)—Roasts and Chops.

4. BREAST—Roasts and Stews.

5. CHUCK (Shoulder)—Roasts and Stews.

6. SHANK—Broth, Soups and Stews.

7. NECK—Broth, Soups and Stews.

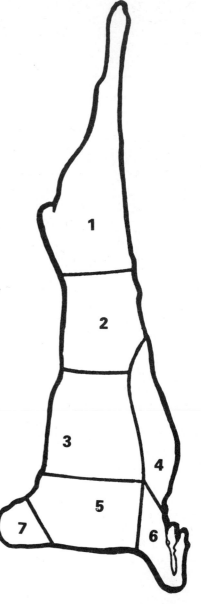

CROWN ROAST OF LAMB

1. Have the crown set up, using ten ribs or more; keep the number even.
2. Pack trimmings in centre of crown; cover with weighted bowl to keep crown in shape; bread dressing may be used.
3. Wrap ends of chops with greased paper to prevent burning, or stick a piece of fat pork on each.
4. Place on rack in roasting pan, season, roast at 325° for 30 minutes per pound.
5. Remove paper from ends of bones; garnish with paper frills.
6. Fill centre with potato balls or green peas and carrots.
7. Serve with Brown Gravy and Currant Jelly, Mint Sauce or Orange Mint Sauce. (page 88). Allow 2 ribs per serving.

ROAST BREAST OF LAMB

4 to 5 pounds breast of lamb   salt
2 cups bread dressing   pepper
   flour

1. Remove bones from roast.
2. Wipe meat; season; cover with dressing; roll up and tie firmly.
3. Dredge with flour; sprinkle with salt and pepper.
4. Place in roasting pan; add ½ cup water or vegetable stock, cover and cook 2 hours at 350°. Remove cover during last half hour to brown meat.

3 cups diced vegetables may be added during the last hour of the cooking.

CUTS FOR BROILING OR PAN-BROILING

Chop	Weight	Description
LOIN	4 to the pound	Contains the tenderloin.
ENGLISH		A double loin chop, boned and rolled with the kidney rolled in.
RIBS	4 to the pound	Contains little meat in proportion to the bone; good flavour.
FRENCH		The rib bone is cleaned back about an inch; after cooking it is decorated with a paper frill.
SHOULDER	3 to the pound	The most economical chop.

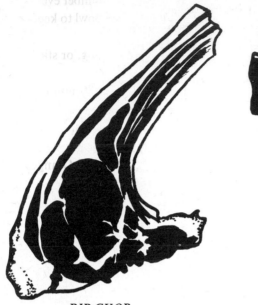

RIB CHOP   *LOIN CHOP*

PAN-BROILED LAMB CHOPS

Thin chops are best cooked in this way.
1. Pull the fell or thin papery covering from the edge of the chop.
2. Trim off a little fat; use it to grease a hot skillet; add the chops; season.
3. Reduce the heat and cook slowly for 5 minutes on each side, turning once only. Serve with mint jelly.

BROILED LAMB CHOPS

Ideal method for cooking chops 1-1½ inches thick.
1. Prepare chops as in preceding recipe; slash edges to prevent curling.
2. Broil 3 inches below source of heat; when using an electric stove, leave door ajar.
3. Broil on one side, 6-7 minutes for chops 1-inch thick, 9-11 minutes for chops 1½ inches thick. Turn and broil for the same length of time on the other side.

   For added flavour, brush chops before broiling with French dressing or rub surface with a cut clove of garlic.

STUFFED LAMB CHOPS

6 lamb chops, 1¼ inches thick   salt
1 cup bread dressing   pepper

1. Trim chops; wipe with a damp cloth or paper towel.
2. Split lean meat to the bone to make a pocket.
3. Place dressing between the meat; press sides together; fasten with toothpicks; season.
4. Pan-broil or bake. To bake—place in greased baking pan; bake 1 hour at 350° turning once during the cooking. Serves 4-6.
   Chops may be dipped in crumbs, beaten egg and crumbs, before baking.

CUTS FOR STEWING OR BRAISING

Cut	Weight	Description
SHANK	1 pound	Makes a good meat for stew; it may also be braised; served with a barbecue sauce.
NECK		Neck slices may also be braised or cut for stewing meat.
BREAST	2 to 3 pounds	The breast meat is inexpensive but stringy.
RIBLETS		These may be cut in small pieces and used for stew.
SHOULDER CHOPS		From heavier lamb will be more tender if braised.

BRAISED LAMB SHOULDER CHOPS

6 shoulder chops   ⅛ teaspoon pepper
  fat   1 tablespoon Worcestershire
2 tablespoons flour   Sauce
1 teaspoon salt   1 cup milk

1. Brown the chops slowly in hot fat.
2. Lift them from the pan; add the flour and seasoning; stir until the flour is brown.
3. Add the Worcestershire Sauce and milk; stir until thick.
4. Place the chops in the gravy; cover; simmer over very low heat or bake at 350° for 30 minutes. Serves 4-6.

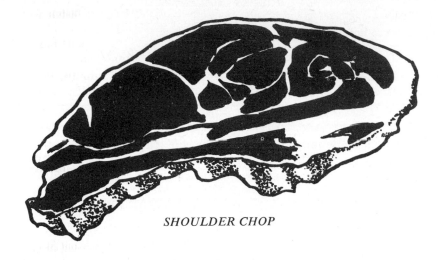

SHOULDER CHOP

BARBECUED LAMB SLICES

Cut ½-inch slices from a boned leg of lamb which has had the thin out-side skin left on. Marinate the meat for 24 hours in Barbecue Sauce (page 86) or in Marinade for Lamb (below) with one sliced onion. Drain the marinade from the meat, allowing some of the onions to cling to the slices. Arrange slices on 2-sided wire broilers and cook over a medium-hot fire for 15 minutes on each side, turning several times. Serve with heated Barbecue Sauce.

IRISH STEW

1 to 1½ pounds lean lamb	6 small new carrots, scraped
1 teaspooon salt	½ cup new green peas
⅛ teaspoon pepper	1 sprig mint
12 small new potatoes, scraped	1 tablespoon chopped parsley
12 small new onions	

1. Cut the meat into cubes; add seasoning and water to cover.
2. Cover the pan and simmer until the meat is almost tender, about 1 hour.
3. Skim off any fat; add the vegetables except parsley and more liquid if necessary; simmer again until the potatoes are tender, about 30 minutes; remove the mint.
4. Thicken the stock. This stew should be rather thin.
5. Sprinkle with parsley.

DEVILLED NECK SLICES

2 pounds neck slices
   fat
2 large onions, chopped
1 teaspoon salt

½ teaspoon dry mustard
2 cups water or stock
1 tablespoon vinegar

1. Brown the meat in a little hot fat; add the onions and cook until they are clear.
2. Add the seasonings, water or vegetable stock and vinegar; simmer until tender, about 1 hour; remove the meat.
3. Thicken the stock. Serves 4-6.

Brochettes (Shish Kabobs) charcoal broiled on an hibachi.

BROCHETTES (SHISH KABOBS)

This is the term applied to meat cooked on a skewer. Shashlik is the Persian name.

The meat is cut into 1-inch cubes; it is frequently marinated; beef tenderloin, lamb or veal leg slices, sweetbreads par-boiled, oysters, scallops or shrimps may be used; if pork is used it must be well cooked. 1½ to 2 pounds meat serves 6.

Skewers should be firm and 6 to 10 inches long.

Other ingredients are mushroom caps, bacon or salt pork squares, strips of bacon, tiny onions, tomatoes, chicken livers, cubed pineapple, olives or squares of green pepper. Alternate these ingredients in any desired combination with the meat; it is best to combine foods which require approximately the same cooking time.

Brush with melted butter or Barbecue Sauce (page 86) if not previously marinated. Broil approximately 10 minutes, turning often.

Serve on a bed of fluffy rice.

The skewer should be removed carefully so that the pieces stay in the same order; for outdoor serving, the skewer may be left in.

MARINADE FOR LAMB

A marinade is a combination of oil, vinegar and seasonings; when meat is marinated or soaked for several hours in this mixture, it becomes more tender and gains additional flavour.

½ cup of oil	1 tablespoon chopped parsley
¼ cup wine vinegar or lemon juice	2 cloves garlic
1 teaspoon salt	sprinkling of marjoram, or oregano and thyme

Combine ingredients. Let stand several hours in a non-metal container.

MIXED GRILL

A mixed grill is made up of a broiled lamb chop with a mushroom cap on it, 2 or 3 small pork sausages, 1 or 2 strips of bacon and a broiled tomato slice.

PORK

Pork is the meat from the pig, marketed usually between 7 to 12 months. It may be fresh or cured. Fresh pork is tender enough that all the suitable cuts may be roasted; chops and steaks are better pan-fried or braised rather than broiled. *Pork should never be served unless it is well-cooked.*

FRESH PORK ·

Fresh pork should be a grayish white with firm hard fat.

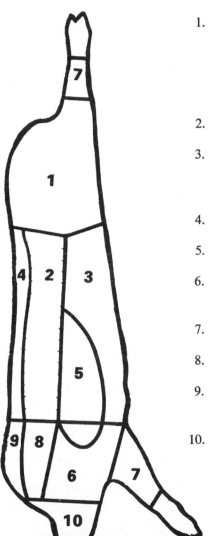

CUTS OF FRESH PORK

1. HAM—It is more economical to buy a whole ham. The butt may be baked, the centre sliced, fried or broiled, the shank boiled, and the rind used for seasoning.

2. LOIN—Roasts and chops.

3. BELLY—Used for bacon. The best grade of bacon, "Certified" brand, is the heart of this cut.

4. FAT BACK—Smoked or pickled.

5. SPARE RIBS.

6. PICNIC BUTT (Shoulder)—Roasts, steaks, chops, hams.

7. HOCK—Pickled and stewed.

8. BOSTON BUTT—Steaks and roasts.

9. CLEAR PLATE—Pickled and smoked.

10. JOWL—Used for cheap bacon, and generally cooked with baked beans.

CUTS FOR ROASTING

Cut	Weight	Description
TENDERLOIN	½ to 1 pound in each	Tender, has no waste, no fat, is expensive.
LOIN		
Loin Roast	4 to 5 pounds	Very sweet, white meat; the centre cut is the best. It must be properly cut to make carving easy. Have the backbone loosened by sawing at right angles to the ribs.
Trimmed Loin	4 to 5 pounds	The loin is trimmed and the tenderloin cut out so that it may be stuffed before the tenderloin is replaced. An expensive but superior roast.
Sirloin Blade Loin		Cut from either end of the loin, these cuts are less in demand but good buys.
FRESH LEG	14 to 17 pounds	Not usually purchased.
Butt End Middle Cut Shank End	4 to 5 pounds	These may vary in price; the middle cut is the best because it has much less bone.
SHOULDER		
Picnic Shoulder	3 to 5 pounds	The lower half of the shoulder, this cut is less desirable than the butt.
Butt Roast or Boston Butt		An excellent roast; it may be boned and tied loosely so that it may be dressed.
Arm Roast		A good roast but less tender.
SPARE RIBS		Back ribs, 2 to 3 inches long, much higher priced; side ribs, 6 inches long. Not economical but good eating.

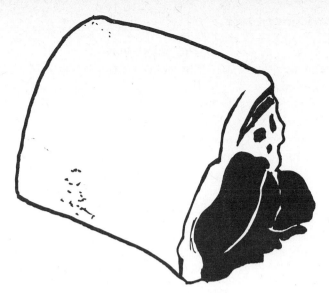

LOIN OF PORK

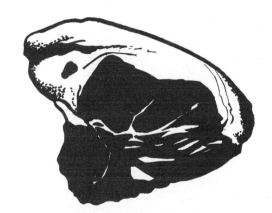

PORK CHOP

PORK SHOULDER

BAKED SPARE RIBS

1. Use a long piece of spare ribs of 8 ribs or more; allow 1 pound of ribs per person.
2. Wipe, place skin side down on a board.
3. Season with salt and pepper; spread ½ with dressing (see end of this chapter); turn remaining ribs over to form a "sandwich" roll.
4. Skewer or tie in shape; place in baking pan with a little dripping, bake 1½ to 1¾ hours at 325°.

BARBECUED SPARE RIBS

1 teaspoon salt	1 tablespoon Worcestershire
¼ teaspoon pepper	Sauce
4 pounds spare ribs	1 teapsoon dry mustard
3 tablespoons fat	1 cup juice from peaches or
1 medium onion chopped	sweet pickles
4 tablespoons lemon juice	½ cup diced celery
2 tablespoons brown sugar	⅛ teaspoon cayenne
1 cup ketchup	

1. Sprinkle meat with salt and pepper.
2. Bake meat side up at 400° for 30 minutes.
3. Heat the fat. Fry the onion to a light yellow.
4. Add the other ingredients; heat to boiling.
5. Pour over the ribs.
6. Cover and bake at 350° about 1 hour, basting every 15 minutes.

   For another Barbecue Sauce recipe, see page 86.

ROAST FRESH HAM OR LEG OF PORK

4 pound leg roast	¼ cup flour
1 teaspoon salt	¼ cup brown sugar
¼ teaspoon pepper	whole cloves

1. Leave the rind on the roast; sprinkle with salt and pepper; rub with flour.
2. Place on a rack in an open pan, fat side up, with a meat thermometer in position.
3. Bake at 350° until the thermometer registers 185°, approximately 40 minutes per pound.
4. Remove from the oven; with a sharp knife remove the rind.
5. Score the fat in straight lines or in diamonds; rub with brown sugar and place a clove in the centre of each diamond.

6. Put the roast back in the oven until it browns. Serve with applesauce or currant jelly.

The scored skin cooks crisp and is called Crackling.

ROAST SUCKLING PIG

Order a suckling pig (10 to 12 pounds; the butcher will eviscerate it and remove eyes). Wash pig thoroughly with salted water; rinse. Sprinkle inside with more salt and rub with half a lemon. Stuff with bread dressing flavoured with rosemary. Tie the legs in a forward bend position so that the roast will sit well. Prop mouth open with a ball of tightly rolled foil. Place pig on racks or foil in a roasting pan; bake at 325° for 3-4 hours, brushing frequently with a basting sauce (use Marinade for Lamb, page 168). Prick any blisters which form on the surface of the skin.

Remove pig to a larger platter; remove strings and ball or foil. Put a red apple in mouth and encircle neck with cranberries, strung into a decorative necklace; place cranberry in each eye. Tuck parsley around the base of the pig and garnish with red pickled crabapples. Serves 8.

BAKED STUFFED TENDERLOIN

2 large tenderloins	flour
1 cup bread dressing	1 tablespoon butter, melted or
¼ teaspoon salt	3 strips bacon
pepper	

1. Trim and wipe tenderloins. Split lengthwise, and flatten to ¾ inch.
2. Prepare dressing (end of this chapter).
3. Sprinkle meat with salt and pepper; spread one piece with dressing.
4. Place other tenderloin over this; tie securely or skewer the edges.
5. Season with salt and pepper. Dredge with flour.
6. Place on rack in baking pan; cover with strips of bacon, a piece of fat pork, or baste with 1 tablespoon butter in 1 cup hot water.
7. Bake 1 hour at 350°.
8. Serve with red currant jelly or apple rings.

BAKED STUFFED PORK CHOPS

1. Use rib chops cut ¾ to 1 inch thick.
2. Have each chop slit so it may be filled with dressing; sew or skewer the chop.
3. Finish as stuffed tenderloin in preceding recipe.

Diced apple, kernel corn, chopped celery are good additions to the bread dressing.

CUTS FOR BRAISING OR PAN-FRYING

Cut	Size	Description
TENDERLOIN		
Frenched	10 to 12 in the pound	The tenderloin is cut in 1-inch pieces and flattened with a cleaver.
CHOPS		
Loin	3 to the pound	The choice chops; ask for the centre chops.
Rib	3 to the pound	More bone, but good flavour.
Shoulder	2 to the pound	More economical but not as tender.
STEAKS		
Pork	1 steak weighs about ¾ pound	Similar in appearance to the shoulder chop, it is cut from the leg. It is more expensive than the chop but has less waste.
Arm		These are from the shoulder, and should
Blade		not be as expensive.
PORK HOCKS	about 1 pound	Allow 1 to a serving.
GREEN BACON		Uncured bacon may be fried.

PORK TENDERLOIN

1. Trim and wipe "Frenched" tenderloin; cut into 1-inch crosswise slices; roll in seasoned flour.
2. Sear on both sides in a greased frying pan, reduce heat and cook thoroughly.

TENDERLOIN WITH APPLE RINGS

1. Follow directions for Pork Tenderloin; to each seared slice add a small piece of bay leaf; cover with a slice of apple, cored; sprinkle with paprika.
2. Reduce heat, cover, cook slowly 15 to 20 minutes.
3. Garnish with parsley.

BRAISED PORK STEAK OR CHOPS

1. Trim off a little fat from the meat; rub over a hot frying pan.
2. Mushroom soup diluted with ½ the quality of water.
3. Reduce the heat and cook the meat slowly, if necessary pouring off excess fat.
4. Enough liquid, to cover the pan to a depth of ½ inch, may be added and the pan covered; simmer on top of the stove or in the oven. Thicken liquid, if necessary, before serving.

Suitable Liquids for Braising Chops

1. Water or vegetable stock.
2. Mushroom soup diluted with ½ the quantity of water.
3. Canned tomatoes, diluted tomato soup or ketchup.
4. Barbecue Sauce (recipe page 86).
5. Consommé and onions; add during last 10 minutes of cooking 1 cup sour cream blended with 2-3 tablespoons flour.
6. Frozen orange juice, undiluted (about 2 tablespoons per chop). Sprinkle with cinnamon; place a clove in each chop.
7. Combine 3 tablespoons canned tomato paste with 3 tablespoons white wine, 1 green pepper chopped, ½ pound sliced mushrooms, ½ clove garlic crushed. When poured over browned chops and baked, this makes Neopolitan Pork Chops.

CURED PORK

Pork may be cured, then smoked, or it may be cured (or pickled) and not smoked. Smoked pork today usually requires no soaking, less cooking time, and more careful refrigeration than earlier varieties.

CUTS OF CURED PORK

Cut	Size	Description
SMOKED PORK		
HAM		
Whole Ham, bone in		
Uncooked	10 to 20 pounds	A 10-pound ham will yield 20 servings; a 15-pound ham 35. While this ham presents more carving problems it is economical and has a fine flavour.
Cooked	10 to 18 pounds	Expensive but convenient.
Whole Ham, boneless		
Uncooked	8 to 12 pounds	Easy to carve; no waste; not as much flavour.
Cooked	10 pounds	Ready to eat.
Part Ham, uncooked		
Shank End	5 pounds	Cheaper; more bone but economical if the bone is used for pea soup, etc.
Centre Piece	3 to 5 pounds	This is more expensive, but has no waste.
Butt End	3 to 6 pounds	Less expensive than the centre cut and has less waste than the shank end. It is a good buy.
Ham Steaks		
Centre Slice		Have the ham sliced 1 to 2 inches thick for baking; ½ inch for frying.
SHOULDER		
Picnic Shoulder	4 to 7 pounds	This cut has more fat but is much less expensive than the ham; it should not appear fat.
Boned Picnic		
Smoked Butt or		
Cottage Roll	4 to 6 pounds	A boneless roll, rather fat. Ends may be purchased cheaply.

CUTS OF CURED PORK—*Continued*

Cut	Size	Description
BACON Canadian Style or Back Bacon	12 to 15 slices per pound	This cut from the loin is similar to the tenderloin; it is cured, then smoked. A 2-pound piece makes an economical and delicious substitute for a baked ham for a small family.
Breakfast or Side Bacon	18 to 22 slices per pound	May be purchased sliced or in the piece; rindless or with the rind. It is cut from the side, leaving the spareribs, and is streaked with lean and fat.
Bacon Square	1 to 1½ pounds	Jowl meat, this small square has much fat, but a flavour of bacon makes it useful in pork and beans, etc.
WET CURED OR PICKLED PORK		
COTTAGE ROLL	2 to 4 pounds	Boneless, sweet pickled butt. It is usually rolled in peameal. It may be too fat. This may be baked like the back bacon, but will not be as tender.
COOKED HAM	1 pound thinly sliced, 20 slices	As purchased in the store, this is sliced. It is pickled but not smoked, it is boiled, trimmed and pressed into a square shape.
CANNED HAM	5 to 8 pounds	Is the same as above but cooked in a tin in its own juices.
DRY CURED PORK		
FAT SALT PORK FAT BACK		These pieces cured in salt are used for chowder, pork and beans. They may be sliced, soaked in milk, and fried; this was a popular dish in lumber camps and on farms, but with better methods of refrigeration and transportation it is less used.

CURED SIDE OF PORK

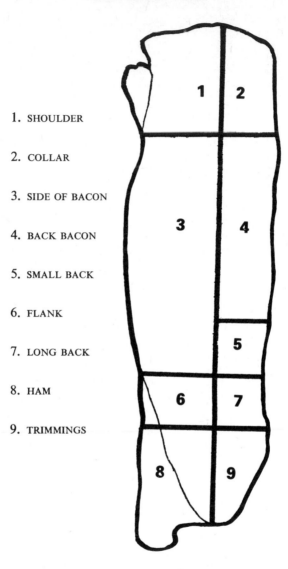

1. SHOULDER

2. COLLAR

3. SIDE OF BACON

4. BACK BACON

5. SMALL BACK

6. FLANK

7. LONG BACK

8. HAM

9. TRIMMINGS

GLAZED BAKED HAM

This method is for mild, high-grade, commercially cured hams.
1. Scrub the skin of the ham well with cold water.
2. Place the ham, fat side up, on a rack in a pan. Add a little water.
3. Bake covered at 250° to 300° according to the directions if the ham is partly cooked, or use the timetable following. If a thermometer is used it should register 165° when the ham is cooked.
4. Remove the ham from the oven; remove the rind by loosening with a sharp knife as the rind is pulled gently up from the ham.
5. Score the fat in diamonds (cutting not too deeply because they open up); or cut a series of pinwheels on the surface.
6. A clove may be stuck into the centre of each diamond or pinwheel or ground cloves may be added to the glaze. Each has an advantage; the ground cloves give more flavour and make carving easy; the whole cloves look attractive.
7. Glaze ham by spreading mixture evenly over the fat, upper surface of the ham; use any of the glazes which follow.
8. Bake the ham at 400° to brown and glaze.
9. To garnish the ham use whole pineapple slices centred with a cherry, pineapple wedges around red maraschino cherries, peach or orange sections arranged, daisy fashion, around green cherries. If the pineapple is to stand any length of time it should be simmered in a thick syrup for 20 minutes to keep it from drying out.

HAM GLAZES

SUGAR GLAZE: Blend 1½ cups brown sugar, 1½ teaspoons dry mustard, ¾ teaspoon ground cloves.

ORANGE GLAZE: Blend ¼ cup orange marmalade, ½ teaspoon dry mustard, ½ cup brown sugar, 1 tablespoon flour and sufficient pineapple juice to make a thick paste.

JELLY GLAZE: Before scoring ham, sprinkle hot fat with a little dry mustard, score, and spread over it 1 cup red currant jelly which has been beaten with a fork until runny. Or, similarly apply 1 cup cranberry jelly which has been beaten with 1 tablespoon lemon juice.

PINEAPPLE GLAZE: Blend 1½ teaspoons dry mustard, 1½ cups brown sugar, ¾ cup well-drained crushed pineapple.

GINGER GLAZE: Blend 1 teaspoon ground ginger, 1 teaspoon dry mustard, 1½ cups brown sugar with enough canned pear or peach syrup to make a thick paste; add 1 teaspoon lemon juice.

CHILI SAUCE GLAZE: Blend ½ cup thick chili sauce, commercial variety, with ¼ cup corn syrup.

TIMETABLE FOR BAKING HAM AT 325°

Type	Weight in Pounds	Minutes to the Pound
BONE IN		
Whole Ham	8 to 10	18-20
	10 to 15	18
	15 to 18	15
Half Ham	5 to 8	25
Picnic Shoulder	4 to 6	30
BONE OUT		
Whole Ham	8 to 10	25
Half Ham		30

Tenderized hams have had the pickling solution pumped through them before smoking. Since they may at the same time have been steamed, the directions on the package for cooking times should be followed.

PARTY HAM

When purchasing a large canned ham or a fully-cooked boned ham, take to the store a shallow baking pan or heavy-duty aluminum foil. Ask the butcher to slice ham on his slicing machine, then tie it firmly into its original shape; place in baking pan or wrap in foil.

Bake uncovered, at 325°, 20 minutes per pound for a small canned ham (about 6 pounds) or 10 to 15 minutes per pound for larger hams (8-10 pounds). For the last 30 minutes, cover ham with orange marmalade to form a glaze. Remove strings and serve.

BOILED HAM

Use this method for home-cured salty hams.
1. Cover ham with cold water; let stand overnight.
2. Drain, put in kettle, cover with fresh cold water.
3. Heat to boiling, boil 5 minutes, remove scum.
4. Cook below boiling point.
5. Time—for ham weighing 7 pounds allow 3½ hours; for ham weighing 10 pounds allow 5 hours.
6. If to be served cold, cool ham in water in which it was cooked; lift out; remove skin.

BAKED PICNIC SHOULDER

1. Scrub the surface of the ham; cover with hot water; simmer 1 hour; save the stock.
2. Bake in the oven at 300° for the remaining time according to preceding timetable. Add a little stock.
3. Half an hour before the ham will be finished, remove it; remove the skin and finish as Glazed Baked Ham above.
4. A 4-pound picnic shoulder serves 8, with leftovers for Cauliflower and Ham Scallop, Ham and Pickle Sandwiches, and bits of ham to add to 1 can of French Canadian style pea soup.

BREAKFAST BACON

1. Remove rind from bacon with scissors if rind has not been removed; allow very cold bacon to warm before separating strips, to avoid tearing, or separate after cooking has begun.
2. Place in a cold frying pan over a slow heat.
3. Cook slowly; pour off the fat as it collects; turn often.
4. Drain on paper towelling; keep hot.

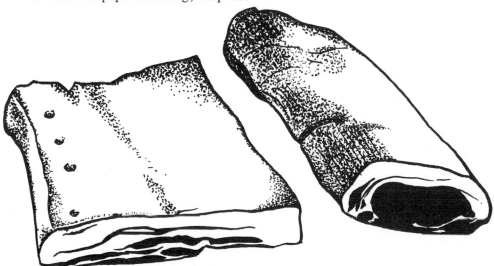

SMOKED SIDE BACON OR BREAKFAST BACON (left)

SMOKED BACK BACON OR CANADIAN STYLE BACON (right)

OVEN-COOKED BREAKFAST BACON

This is a useful method for cooking a large amount.
1. Arrange slices of bacon on a rack (a cake rack works well) in a pan; or arrange in a shallow pan and pour the fat off several times as it accumulates.
2. Bake at 375° or broil 4 inches from the heat.
3. Use a spatula to slip under the slices to turn them.
4. Drain on paper towelling, or brown paper.

BACK BACON ROAST

1. Use a piece, 1 pound or more, smoked or pickled back bacon.
2. Place on a rack in a roasting pan; add 1 cup stock or fruit juice.
3. Cover and bake at 350° for ¾ to 1 hour. Finish as Glazed Baked Ham.

FRIED CANADIAN STYLE BACON

1. If the bacon is very lean, put a little fat in the pan so bacon will cook without hardening.
2. Cook slowly until lightly browned.

BOILED PEAMEAL BACON

This loin bacon has been pickled but not smoked.
Place a piece of peameal bacon, 1 pound or more, in boiling water to cover. Simmer until tender, about 1 hour or more. Serve hot or cold.

HAM WITH CRANBERRIES

2 1-inch slices ham (centre cut)   1 cup brown sugar
2 cups cranberries

1. Wash cranberries; chop.
2. Slash fat edges of ham, and place 1 slice of ham in a casserole.
3. Cover with ½ berries and ½ sugar.
4. Place the other slice on top.
5. Cover with the remaining berries and sugar.
6. Stud the fat around the edge with cloves.
7. Bake at 300° to 350° for 1 hour, basting with the liquid in the pan. Raisin or Cherry Pie Filling (page 491) may replace cranberries and sugar between the slices. Leave the top slice uncovered; add a little water and cover the casserole.

HAM SLICE WITH PINEAPPLE

1. Place 1-inch slice of ham in baking pan. Slash fat edges.
2. Mix a little mustard, sugar and vinegar; spread over the ham.
3. Pour in ½ cup milk or fruit juice; bake at 350° until ham is tender, about 1 hour.
4. Place pineapple on ham; brush with fat; continue baking until pineapple is lightly browned.
5. Sliced oranges, apples, canned peaches or apricots may be used instead of pineapple.

BAKED HAM WITH POTATOES AND ONIONS

2-pound slice of smoked ham	2 onions
6 potatoes	milk
flour	

1. Place the ham in a covered casserole.
2. Cover with a layer of potato slices.
3. Sprinkle lightly with flour.
4. Add a layer of onion, sliced or chopped.
5. Repeat, having potato on top.
6. Pour in milk until it is halfway up in the dish.
7. Cover. Bake at 350° for 1 hour.
8. Uncover during the last few minutes to brown.

FRIED HAM

1. Have the ham sliced about ¼ inch thick; slash edges to prevent curling.
2. Cut off bits of the fat around the edge and rub over a hot pan.
3. Fry the ham slowly to brown lightly and cook thoroughly.
4. Serve with eggs cooked in the ham fat or in butter or with pineapple slices cooked in the same pan.

BROILED HAM WITH PINEAPPLE

1. Have smoked ham cut ¼ inch thick; cut in pieces for serving and slash edges.
2. Broil; turn; on each piece place a slice of pineapple.
3. Brush with melted butter, sprinkle with a little brown sugar.
4. Broil until the pineapple browns slightly and the ham is cooked, about 10 minutes.

VARIETY MEATS

This term is used to include those portions of the animal used for food which are classed as organs, not muscle, and also those meats such as sausage which are a combination of meats.

Since the organ meats are generally much superior to the muscle meats in minerals and vitamins, they should be used often. Unless frozen, they should be used within 24 hours of purchase.

Variety Meats are combinations of meats, such as these, as well as the organ meats. There is a wide selection available of this convenient form of meat.

LIVER

1 pound of liver serves 4 to 6; it is best thinly sliced.

Calves' liver is tender and delicate in flavour; while it is more expensive than the other liver, it is still cheaper than most muscle meats suitable for broiling. Baby beef liver is mild, tender and less expensive.

Pork liver, which is the most reasonable in price, is also the highest in the vitamins; lamb liver is delicate in flavour; beef liver is sometimes coarse and not suitable for broiling.

The tough membrane on the outer edges of liver should be removed. All liver should be thoroughly rinsed.

BROILED LIVER

1 pound liver, thinly sliced	salt
¼ cup melted butter	pepper

1. Brush liver with melted butter; place on the rack 3 inches from the heat.
2. Broil until brown, turn and season; broil until done. Approximately 3 minutes on each side should be sufficient time, but it is well to cut into 1 piece to be sure. There should be no pink colour. Avoid overcooking which gives a leathery result.
3. Bacon and thin slices of onion brushed with butter may be broiled at the same time.
   Chicken livers are especially delicious when broiled on shish kabobs.

PAN-FRIED LIVER

1 pound liver thinly sliced	¼ cup seasoned flour

1. Shake liver in a paper bag with the seasoned flour.
2. Sauté until brown; turn and brown; reduce the heat and finish cooking; serve at once.

LIVER AND ONIONS

Slice 3 medium onions thinly; fry in butter until yellow; remove and keep hot. Fry the liver; serve with onions on top of each slice.

LIVER AND BACON

Fry bacon; dry; keep warm. Fry liver in bacon fat; serve with strips of bacon.

LIVER WITH VEGETABLES

2 cups celery and leaves	2 tablespoons fat
1 teaspoon salt	2 onions
1 pound liver, thinly sliced	6 carrots
2 tablespoons flour	1 cup tomatoes

1. Chop the celery and spread in a greased casserole; sprinkle with a little salt.
2. Dredge prepared liver in flour; brown in hot fat; place on top of the celery; sprinkle with salt.
3. Add the other vegetables (cut in small pieces) and the rest of the salt.
4. Cover and bake at 350° for about 1 hour.

STUFFED LIVER

Even "non-fans" of liver enjoy this dish.

1 pound liver, thinly sliced	pepper
1 cup bread dressing	1 10-ounce can condensed
2 tablespoons fat	tomato soup
salt	½ can water or vegetable stock

1. Spread the prepared liver with a dressing from the end of this chapter; roll from the short end; fasten with a toothpick or small skewer.
2. Brown in the hot fat; lift into a casserole; sprinkle with salt and pepper.
3. Pour on the soup diluted with water.
4. Cover; bake at 350°. The cooking time will depend upon the kind of liver and the thinness; calves' liver sliced thin may cook in 30 minutes; beef liver will usually require 60 minutes.

CHICKEN LIVERS SUPREME

1 pound chicken livers	⅔ cup milk
½ pound mushrooms, sliced	1½ cups cooked rice*
butter	2 tablespoons chopped parsley
1 10-ounce can condensed	2 tablespoons shredded almonds
mushroom soup	

1. Flour livers and brown in hot fat.
2. Sauté mushrooms in butter.
3. Empty soup into a casserole dish, stir in milk; add liver, mushrooms. rice and parsley.
4. Bake at 350° for 10 to 15 minutes. Serve topped with shredded almonds. Serves 4-5.
   *About ½ cup regular rice before cooking.

KIDNEY

Beef, veal, lamb and pork kidneys may be used. Half a beef kidney, 1 veal or pork kidney, or 2 lamb kidneys would provide 1 serving.

KIDNEY STEW

2 to 3 beef kidneys	2 cups chopped onions
½ cup flour	2 tablespoons fat
1 teaspoon salt	2 cups boiling water

1. Wash the kidneys; cut in half; pour on boiling water; leave 10 minutes.
2. Drain; cut out all the white tubes; cut the kidney into ½-inch cubes; dry well and roll in seasoned flour.
3. Sauté the onions in hot fat; lift out; put in the meat and stir until brown.
4. Add the hot water and stir continuously until the liquid thickens.
5. Add the cooked onion and continue to simmer for 10 minutes.

BEEFSTEAK AND KIDNEY PIE

1 small beef kidney	2 tablespoons fat
1 pound stewing beef	4 cups water and vegetable stock
2 teaspoons salt	flour for thickening
⅛ teaspoon pepper	pie crust
1 large onion, chopped	

1. Prepare kidneys as for Kidney Stew.
2. Cut the stewing beef into 1-inch cubes; season.
3. Sauté the onions in hot fat until golden brown; remove from the fat.
4. Brown the meat in the same fat; replace the onions; add the water or stock; cover and simmer until tender, about 1½ hours.
5. Thicken the stew.
6. Pour into a casserole; add the crust.
7. Bake at 425° for 20 minutes, or until golden.

BROILED KIDNEY

6 veal or 12 lamb kidneys	6 large mushroom caps
2 tablespoons butter, melted	6 strips bacon
3 tomatoes	2 tablespoons lemon juice

1. Wash the kidneys in cold water; skin; cut crosswise into slices.
2. Arrange on the broiler pan; brush with butter.
3. Place each tomato, halved, and each mushroom cap, round side up, and the bacon on the pan; brush the tomato and mushroom with butter.
4. Place the pan so the surface of each tomato is 3 inches below the heat.
5. Broil until brown; turn; brush the kidneys with butter and lemon juice; fill each mushroom cap with butter; season and cook about 15 minutes longer.

HEART

A baby beef heart weighs about 1½ pounds and serves 6; a veal heart weighs about 1 pound and serves 4; pork hearts weigh about ½ pound each and serve 2.

STUFFED HEART

1 baby beef heart	2 tablespoons fat
1 cup bread dressing	1 cup water or vegetable stock
¼ cup seasoned flour	

1. Wash the heart in cold water. At one side at the top is a little sac which should be slit open; remove the veins and sinews; dry.
2. Prepare dressing (end of this chapter) and stuff the heart. Sew or close with skewers.
3. Dredge with seasoned flour and brown slowly in hot fat; add liquid; cover.
4. Bake at 350° or simmer on a very low heat for about 2 hours or until tender, or pressure cook for 45 minutes at 15 pounds pressure.
5. Thicken the gravy; serve in a separate dish.

   To serve the heart, slice from the pointed end, discarding the coarse top piece. Serves 6.
   Serve hot heart sliced, with gravy.
   Cold sliced heart is an excellent addition to a cold meat plate.

BRAISED HEART

1 baby beef or 2 veal hearts	¼ cup flour
1 onion	½ cup celery
¼ teaspoon pepper	1 cup tomatoes
½ teaspoon salt	2 tablespoons fat

1. Wash the heart as in preceding recipe; steam or simmer ½ hour; cool.
2. Dice, removing any fibres or fat; dredge with seasoned flour.
3. Brown in the hot fat; add the vegetables.
4. Cover and simmer or bake until tender, about 2 hours. Serves 6.

   Heart may also be cooked whole in a pressure cooker, for 45 minutes at 15 pounds pressure.

SWEETBREADS

Sweetbread is the thymus gland of young beef; veal sweetbread is the most desirable. As the animal grows the gland disappears so that "beef sweetbread" is not truly a sweetbread but is the pancreas gland, a much larger and softer organ. One pound of sweetbreads makes approximately 4 servings. They should be used while very fresh and before being prepared in any other way should be parboiled by the following method:

1. Soak in cold salted water ½ hour; drain.
2. Put into boiling water to which has been added ½ tablespoon vinegar or lemon juice and ½ teaspoon salt.
3. Simmer 20 to 30 minutes, according to size.
4. Drain and plunge into cold water.
5. Peel off the thin membrane

CREAMED SWEETBREADS

1 pound sweetbreads	dash of cayenne pepper
2 tablespoons flour	2 tablespoons butter
¼ teaspoon salt	1 cup rich milk
dash of pepper	

1. Prepare sweetbreads; cut into ½-inch slices.
2. Make White Sauce from remaining ingredients (page 79); add sweetbreads, and any of the suggested additions below.
3. Reheat; serve in Swedish timbales, patty shells or bread cases.

Additions:
Sautéed mushrooms, cooked green peas, diced cooked chicken or chopped cooked ham may be added.
One tin condensed mushroom or chicken soup plus ½ cup milk may be substituted for the White Sauce.

BROILED SWEETBREADS

Serve from the barbecue on fresh French bread.
1. Prepare sweetbreads; split in half.
2. Brush with melted butter; sprinkle with salt, pepper and celery salt.
3. Broil about 3 inches from the heat, until brown; turn and broil.

BREADED SWEETBREADS

1. Prepare sweetbreads; dry; season.
2. Roll in fine, dry bread crumbs, in egg and in crumbs.
3. Sauté in butter; serve on toast.

BRAINS

Brains when cooked resemble sweetbreads, being somewhat softer, and much less expensive. They should be prepared and parboiled in the same way as sweetbreads and may be creamed, or combined with scalloped tomatoes. One pound makes approximately 4 servings.

CHIPPED OR DRIED BEEF

This smoked, thinly sliced beef is usually bought in 4-ounce jars. It may be cut with scissors and mixed with an unsalted cream sauce and served on toast or over split, baked potato. To lessen saltiness, pour boiling water over chipped beef in a sieve; dry.

Dissolve 1 teaspoon gelatine in a can of hot consommé; chill. When beginning to set, add shredded chipped beef. This makes a quickly prepared, delicious addition to a salad plate.

TRIPE

The lining of the second stomach of beef is cleaned and partly cooked, and may be pickled. This is the honeycomb type of tripe which is superior to the plain tripe from the first stomach. One pound makes approximately 4-5 servings.

STEWED TRIPE

A thin stew—serve with biscuits.

1 pound honeycomb tripe	1 teaspoon salt
2 cups water	pepper
2 cups chopped onion	1 cup milk
1 cup chopped celery	

1. Wash the tripe well; cut into 1-inch strips and then into diamond-shaped pieces.
2. Add the water, vegetables and seasoning; simmer until tender, about 2 hours, or pressure cook 15 minutes.
3. Add the milk; reheat; thicken. Serves 4-5.

TONGUE

Beef, veal, lamb or pork tongue may be used. Tongue may be fresh, pickled or smoked. After cooking, pickled and smoked tongues are red, fresh tongue is grey. One pound of tongue makes 4-5 servings.

"BOILED" TONGUE

1 beef tongue (3 to 4 pounds)	1 onion
1 teaspoon salt	2 stalks celery and leaves
1 teaspoon peppercorns	water

1. Add only enough boiling water to cover the tongue; add the seasonings and vegetables; simmer until tender, about 1 hour per pound.
2. Strain off the stock and save it for soup stock.
3. Remove the roots of the tongue and skin it. To skin the tongue, cut off the bone and gristle from the root end; slit the skin on the underside from root to tip; loosen the skin around the root end with a

sharp knife; turn the tongue right side up, grasp the loosened skin and pull off.

4. Slice the tongue on a slant to get larger pieces.
5. Serve hot with mustard or horseradish, or serve cold.

Pickled or smoked tongue: cover in cold water and soak for several hours, or bring to a boil. Discard this water. Continue as for fresh tongue.

JELLIED TONGUE

2 small veal tongues	2 tablespoons mixed pickling
1 veal knuckle or shank, split	spice
cold water, about 1 quart	1 small onion
1 teaspoon salt	

1. Wash the tongue and soak in cold water; drain; add the knuckle.
2. Cover with fresh cold water; add the seasonings and onion; simmer until tender, about 2 hours; the skin should come off easily; cool.
3. Skin the tongues; curl them into a bowl so that it holds them tightly.
4. Boil down the liquid if necessary until there are approximately 2 cups; season; pour over and around the tongues in the bowl.
5. Set a plate on top of the tongues and weight down so they will hold their shape; cool until set.
6. Unmould; serve with Horseradish Sauce (page 91).

BRAISED OXTAILS WITH VEGETABLES

Long slow cooking makes the flavour.

2 pounds disjointed oxtails	2 cups water (or 1 cup water and
3 tablespoons fat	1 cup tomato juice)
1 large onion, chopped	2 cups diced carrots
2 teaspoons salt	1 cup diced celery
¼ teaspoon pepper	1 green pepper, chopped
1 tablespoon vinegar	4 medium potatoes, cut in half

1. Rinse the oxtails; pat dry.
2. Melt fat in a heavy, deep pan and add the oxtails.
3. Brown in hot fat; add the onion.
4. Add salt, pepper, vinegar and water; cover tightly and simmer 3 hours, adding more water if necessary to prevent burning.
5. Add vegetables and increase heat until mixture returns to boiling point. Reduce heat and simmer 45 minutes.
6. Place vegetables and meat on a hot platter; thicken stock for gravy (method page 143).

SAUSAGES

Sausages are on the market in great variety, both ready-to-eat and uncooked.

Ready-to-eat Sausages

DRY OR "SUMMER" SAUSAGES: These may be made of pork and beef. They are dried and some varieties are smoked before drying. They include salami, cervelat, pepperoni and mortedella.

SMOKED SAUSAGES: These, like the dry sausage, may be of beef or pork. They are seasoned and smoked. Common examples are the frankfurter or wiener, bologna and thuringer.

COOKED SPECIALTIES: These are made from a wider range of meats, and are not usually smoked. Included are liver sausage and braun-schweiger.

WIENERS: These can be cooked by several different methods. Dropped into a kettle of boiling water, they can be simmered 5-8 minutes. They can be baked or broiled in the oven on a lightly greased pan or on top of a casserole mixture. Slashing the surface of the wiener helps it to keep its shape during cooking, by dry heat. Recipes will be found in Supper Dishes, Chapter 11.

Fresh Sausage

Fresh sausage is marketed in three forms:

LINK SAUSAGE: The meat should be rosy pink if fresh. The links may be twisted to make long or short sausages. They may be all pork, considered the best, or a mixture of pork and beef.

1 pound small pork sausages contains 14 to 16 sausages.

SAUSAGE MEAT: This is the same meat but has not been put into a casing. It is sold in bulk form.

FARMER'S SAUSAGE: The meat is packed into larger casing, not linked, and sold in a coil. It may be seen more commonly at a farmers' market; it should be purchased only if it has a good colour and odour.

To avoid the danger of trichinosis, all fresh pork products must be well cooked.

PAN-FRIED SAUSAGE

1. Place sausage links in frying pan; add a little water to a depth of ¼ inch; cover and simmer for 5 minutes. (Do not boil, and do not prick the links with a fork to let juice escape.)
2. Drain off water and pan fry slowly. Continue to cook until the sausage is brown, and cooked throughout. Serve the sausage with fried apple rings or with hot chili sauce.

BAKED SAUSAGE

1. Spread a single layer of sausages in a shallow pan.
2. Bake at 400° for approximately 30 minutes. Turn to brown evenly. For added flavour, pour ½-1 cup Barbecue Sauce (page 86) over the sausages just before baking or pan-frying.

TO USE LEFTOVER COOKED MEATS

1. Slice and serve cold with vegetables or salad.
2. Grind; season and add enough mayonnaise to make a spread for crackers and sandwiches; prepare in electric blender to make a paste for appetizers; grind and stuff green peppers; make croquettes.
3. Dice; add mayonnaise, chopped celery, pickle and serve on salad plate; add to soup, consommé; use in casserole mixtures and meat pies.
4. Simmer bones for soup.
   Many recipes using leftover cooked meats will be found in Supper Dishes, Chapter 11.

POULTRY

Poultry may be sold *Market Dressed*. This means the insides have not been removed (drawn) nor the head and feet cut off.

Ready-to-Cook fowl has had the head and feet cut off, the entrails removed and the giblets cleaned. Pin feathers will need to be removed and the inside thoroughly washed. An 18-pound ready-to-cook fowl equals a 22-pound market-dressed fowl.

Poultry may be cooked immediately after being killed. If not, it should be kept chilled for 72 hours.

Preparation of Poultry

Poultry is usually sold already eviscreated; if not, it should be done as follows (Steps 1, 2, 9 and 11 apply to all forms of poultry):
1. Remove the pin feathers by using a pair of tweezers or pressing the feathers between the thumb and a paring knife, then pulling.
2. Singe over a flame to remove the hair. A candle or cigarette lighter is useful.
3. If the feet have not been cut off it is easier to remove the tendons. Make a lengthwise cut along the skin over the leg joint; pick up the tendons with a wire skewer or a nail; hold the leg firmly and twist the skewer until the tendons pull out; cut off.
4. Twist the wing toward the breast to dislocate the shoulder joint.

5. Cut off the head; slit the skin along the back of the neck; cut off the neck close to the body.

6. Remove the windpipe and the crop.

7. Cut out the oil sac on the back near the tail.

8. Cut a slit above the vent, toward the right leg, just long enough to insert the hand. Insert a finger through the cut around the intestine; cut around the vent; loosen the skin around the organs until the gizzard is able to be pulled down. This will bring the liver, gizzard and intestines out. The gall bladder, which is a green ball attached to the liver, must not be broken. It contains a bitter fluid which gives a bitter taste to any meat it touches. Remove the heart, kidneys.

9. The lungs are a soft, spongy mass against the ribs and even from drawn fowl the lungs must be removed. Wash the fowl inside and out with lukewarm salted water; let cold water run through; dry inside before stuffing; sprinkle with salt.

10. Prepare the giblets.
    (a) Heart—cut away arteries and veins; press to extract blood; wash in cold, salted water.
    (b) Liver—cut away gall bladder carefully; wash liver in salted water.
    (c) Gizzard—remove fat; cut carefully with a sharp knife in through the thick part to the sac; remove outer part from sac. Cut away the thick, white lining; wash gizzard in salted water.

11. To cook giblets, cut gizzard in small pieces; cover gizzard and heart with cold water; heat to boiling, then cook below boiling point until tender. When these have cooked 20 minutes add liver and simmer 10-15 minutes longer. The neck may be cooked with the giblets.

To Dress or Stuff a Bird

1. Place the fowl in a bowl, neck up.

2. Fill the neck and plump out the breast; pull the neck skin down and back to hold the dressing in. Reverse the bird in the bowl.

3. Fill in at the vent; do not pack the dressing too tightly since it will swell in cooking and if too full will be soggy.

4. Skewer the slit closed with poultry pins; lace with string (illustrations *a, b*); or sew the slit, using a darning needle and coarse white thread; or if the slit is slanting, and not too long, the leg will hold it shut when the fowl is trussed.

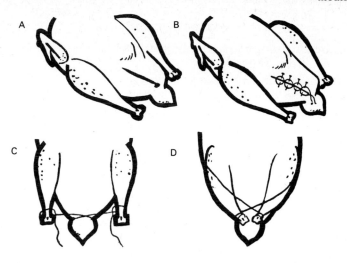

CHICKENS

Broilers, Fryers, Barbecue Chickens or Spring Chickens are young, tender birds weighing about 2-3½ pounds. Allow ¾ pound per person.

Roasting Chickens weigh 3 to 6 pounds; 5 pounds is an economical size. Allow ½ to ¾ pound per person. A chicken should have a smooth skin, smooth, soft feet, and a flexible tip to the breastbone. There may be pin feathers, but long hairs are a sign of age. Milk-fed chickens are a white colour and in general are superior.

Capon, an unsexed male, is a larger bird. It weighs 6 pounds and up. One serves 8.

Fowl or Hens or Stewing Chickens are mature female birds. They weigh 3 to 8 pounds. The breastbone is rigid, the feet dry, hard and scaly. A 5-pound fowl yields 12 servings of creamed chicken.

They require a cooking method which will tenderize them.

Cut-up Chicken is chicken which has been cut into pieces. Any part desired may be purchased. Legs and breasts are favourites; wings are a good buy if plump.

TIMETABLE FOR ROASTING CHICKEN

Kind	Ready to Cook Weight	Market Dressed or Stuffed Weight	Temperature	Minutes per Pound Dressed Weight	Time in Hours
CHICKEN	2½ to 3½	3 to 4	350°	35	1½ to 2½
	3½ to 5	5 to 6	325°	35	3 to 3½
CAPON	5½	7	325°	35	4

ROAST CHICKEN

1. Prepare a roasting chicken; stuff it (recipes for bread dressing are at the end of this chapter).
2. Truss for roasting by turning the tips of the wings under the back; press the legs close back against the body.
3. Tie a piece of string about 3 feet long around the tail, leaving long ends; bring these ends up over the ends of the legs, pulling them down against the body; carry each string along the side to the wing, up over the wing joint and tie over the neck skin at the back (illustrations *c, d*). Or, use skewers to hold legs and wings close to the body and to close the vent.
4. Brush the skin with melted fat; sprinkle with salt and pepper.
5. Place breast down in a roasting pan; add no water; do not cover. There are many ways suggested for cooking fowl. Some are: cover with a cloth, soaked in butter; bake in a brown paper bag; cover with aluminum foil; baste every 10 minutes; coat with a paste of flour and butter. If a low temperature is used none of these is necessary.
6. Roast at 325°; see the timetable above; when done the leg will break away at the body; the thick part of the thigh is tender when pierced with the point of a small knife.

Oven-Baked Chicken with Potato Puffs.

7. Allow it to stand in a warm place 20 minutes after it comes out of the oven. This gives time for the juices to be absorbed; the meat sets and is easier to carve.
8. Remove the strings and skewers before it is taken to the table. Garnish with parsley.

TO CUT CHICKEN FOR STEWING OR FRYING

1. Thoroughly rinse chicken from which viscera, head and feet have been removed. Remove all pin feathers.
2. Cut off legs, separate into drumstick and thigh.
3. Cut off wings; remove tips.
4. Cut behind the wishbone and separate it from breast.
5. Separate breast from back by cutting through ribs.
6. Cut the back into two pieces crosswise. Each piece should have its own skin.

TO BROWN CHICKEN

1. For each pound of chicken, combine in a paper bag:

¼ cup flour	½ teaspoon salt
1 teaspoon paprika	⅛ teaspoon pepper

2. Cut the chicken into pieces.
3. Shake the chicken, two or three pieces at a time, in the paper bag to coat evenly with flour.
4. Have hot fat ½ inch deep in a heavy pan; sauté over medium high heat until chicken is golden. Turn chicken often and avoid crowding pieces during cooking. If dark sediment collects in the pan, as it will when a large amount of chicken is being browned, discard oil, clean pan and continue with fresh oil. Otherwise it will be impossible to develop the desired colour.

   Steps 1 and 3 may be omitted and chicken browned without flour to give a somewhat transparent appearance to the skin. Chicken must be thoroughly dried before browning.

FRENCH FRIED CHICKEN

Recipe for this will be found in French Frying, Chapter 21.

PAN-FRIED CHICKEN

1. Brown chicken, reduce heat, cover tightly and cook slowly until tender, about 30 minutes. If the pan cannot be covered tightly, it may be necessary to add a small amount of water.
2. Uncover during the last 10 minutes to crispen the skin.
3. The chicken is done when the meat on the thickest part of the drumstick is tender when tested with the point of a knife.
4. Serve chicken piping hot in a napkin-lined basket with corn fritters, or on a platter with gravy made from the pan juices.

   For variety rub chicken with lemon and let dry for a few minutes before browning, or marinate it (Basting Marinades, page 199).
   If several chickens are being fried, finish the cooking in a moderate oven in a shallow pan, basting occasionally with a mixture of melted butter and water to prevent drying.

OVEN-FRIED CHICKEN

Both browning and cooking take place in the oven.

1. Coat chicken with flour and arrange pieces in greased shallow pan, dotting them generously with fat or cooking oil.
2. Bake at 475° for about 15 minutes, turning pieces and cooking to a golden colour.
3. Open oven door for a few minutes to reduce heat to 325° (reset thermostat), cover pan closely and cook chicken 35 to 50 minutes longer, according to the size of the pieces, until tender.
4. Uncover pan for final 10 minutes to restore crispness to the coating.

   See preceding recipe for serving and variation suggestions.

GLAZED CHICKEN

1. Brown 1¾ pounds of chicken pieces with oil only, omitting flour; this can be done on top of the stove or in the oven.
2. Arrange chicken in a large, shallow baking dish, season, and pour over it either of the following mixtures:

   4 tablespoons concentrated frozen orange juice mixed with 4 tablespoons mint jelly and 2 tablespoons lemon juice.
   ¾ cup ginger or orange marmalade or apricot jam mixed with ¼ cup water.
3. Bake at 375°, uncovered, for about 45 minutes. Baste often during cooking.

MARYLAND CHICKEN

12 chicken legs or breasts or	egg
2 young chickens	dry bread crumbs
seasonings	½ cup melted butter
flour	2 cups rich White Sauce

1. Cut chickens in pieces for serving; season; dip in flour, beaten egg, then in crumbs.
2. Place in well-greased pan; bake at 350°, 45 to 60 minutes, or until tender, basting with the butter.
3. Serve with White Sauce (page 79) or a variation of it. Serves 6-8.

BROILED CHICKEN

1. Use young chicken, allowing ½ for each serving.
2. Have them split in half, lengthwise.
3. Break the joints and skewer the wing and leg to the body to keep them flat and compact; season with salt and pepper.
4. Place in a broiling pan, skin side down, but not on the rack; brush with melted butter or any of the marinades which follow.
5. Broil slowly, about 7 inches below the heat; turn and brush more fat on each piece as it browns. Cook 30 to 50 minutes.

BASTING MARINADES FOR CHICKEN

These add extra flavour to chicken when used as a marinade and/or basting sauce.

Mix ⅓ cup melted butter, or salad oil, and 3 tablespoons lemon juice.

Mix equal parts of sherry, soy sauce and cooking oil.

Mix ½ cup melted butter, ⅓ cup white wine and 1 tablespoon dried tarragon.

CHARCOAL BROILED CHICKEN

Prepare chicken as for Broiled Chicken, cutting broilers into quarters or halves or using only legs and breasts. Baste frequently with Barbecue Sauce (page 86), or with any of the Basting Sauces. When chicken is cooked, no blood should run when the thickest part of the second leg joint is pierced with the point of a knife. Allow 30 to 45 minutes for broilers.

COQ AU VIN

See Perdrix au Vin (page 215).

BROILED CHICKEN BREASTS

Remove meat from the bones of raw chicken breasts, keeping it intact as much as possible. Pound the meat thin with a mallet or rolling pin; avoid tearing it. Crush 1 small clove of garlic with ½ cup of butter and spread over chicken. Roll tightly in a jellyroll fashion, wrap in foil and chill thoroughly. Slice rolls into ½-inch pinwheels and thread onto skewers. Brush with any of the Basting Sauces for chicken. Broil.

BARBECUED CHICKEN ON A SPIT

Secure a roasting chicken or broiler on a spit and cook over glowing coals, allowing 45 to 60 minutes for a 2½ to 3 pound chicken, about 1 to 1¼ hours for a 3½ to 4 pound chicken and about 1½ hours for a 4 to 5½ pound chicken. A bunch of sweet herbs, tarragon, celery, green onion, etc. can be tied together and placed in the body cavity during cooking, or the chicken can be stuffed with bread dressing. Legs and wings of large chickens should be tied or skewered in place, close to the body. Baste frequently with Barbecue Sauce (page 86), or with any of the Basting Sauces.
Rock Cornish hens may be cooked in the same manner; allow 1 per person.

SMOTHERED CHICKEN (Basic Recipe)

Variations of this recipe are unlimited.

6-8	chicken legs or breasts, or	2 cups cream, or
3-4	pound young chicken	1 can cream of mushroom or
¾	cup flour	celery soup diluted with
2	teaspoons salt	½ can water
¼	teaspoon pepper	¼ pound mushrooms, sliced
¼	teaspoon ginger (optional)	
½	cup fat or oil	

1. Brown chicken in a heavy pan, using first 6 ingredients (Method page 197). Pour off any excess fat remaining in pan.
2. Heat the cream and pour it with the mushrooms over the chicken.
3. Cover and bake at 350° for about 1 hour, or cook on top of the stove in a covered container until tender, about 45 minutes. Serves 4-6.

SWEET AND SOUR CHICKEN

Substitute Sweet and Sour Sauce (page 90) for liquid of Smothered Chicken, or use Barbecue Sauce (page 86). Plump chicken wings make an economical and delicious dish when served in this way; omit flour when browning.

Any of pineapple cubes, green pepper and fresh tomato wedges can be added.

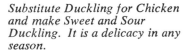

Substitute Duckling for Chicken and make Sweet and Sour Duckling. It is a delicacy in any season.

QUICK CHICKEN ITALIANO

For the liquid ingredients, mix the contents of 1 envelope of spaghetti sauce mix and 2 cups tomato or vegetable juice; pour over browned chicken and finish cooking as Smothered Chicken. Serve with buttered noodles.

CHICKEN VALENCIA

½ cup orange juice	1 cup pitted black olives
1 cup white wine or chicken stock	1 sweet red pepper, cut in strips
1 teaspoon salt	2 tablespoons cornstarch
⅛ teaspoon garlic salt	3 tablespoons water
1 teaspoon ginger	1 orange, peeled and sliced

Combine first 7 ingredients and pour over browned chicken. Cook according to Smothered Chicken or cook uncovered in oven at 375°, basting frequently to produce a glazed crisper skin. Just before serving mix cornstarch and water; add to the liquids; stir until the liquid thickens. Heat orange slices quickly in mixture. Serve chicken over a platter of rice with orange slices on top. Garnish with parsley.

TARRAGON CHICKEN

Cook browned chicken in 1 cup chicken stock (part of liquid may be white wine), until tender. Mix in 1 teaspoon tarragon. Before serving, shake 1 cup cream and 2 tablespoons flour in a covered jar, and stir into pan juices to make gravy. Stock may be prepared from chicken bouillon cubes.

JAVANESE CHICKEN

1 clove garlic, crushed	½ teaspoon salt
2 chopped onions	½ teaspoon or more curry powder
½ pound mushrooms	¼ teaspoon thyme
2 cups tomato juice	¼ teaspoon cayenne pepper
2 green peppers, chopped	½ cup raisins or currants

1. In the pan in which chicken was browned, sauté the first 3 ingredients until just soft.
2. Combine remaining ingredients and simmer 5 minutes; pour over chicken, cover and finish cooking as Smothered Chicken.
3. Serve over rice; garnish with toasted almond slivers and parsley.

CHICKEN VÉRONIQUE

Before browning chicken, rub pieces with halves of a lemon; sprinkle with salt and let dry for a few minutes; brown chicken without coating with flour. Cook chicken in ⅔ cup white wine or chicken stock until tender. Just before serving stir in 2 cups seedless green grapes and heat through. Sprinkle with paprika; serve sauce separately.

CHICKEN CACCIATORE

In the pan in which the chicken was browned, cook 1 thinly sliced onion and 1 clove garlic, crushed until golden brown. Blend in 1 cup water, 1 8-ounce tin tomato paste, 2 teaspoons salt and ½ teaspoon pepper; cover and simmer until the chicken is tender, about 1 hour. Add ½ cup sliced mushrooms and ½ cup dry red wine (optional) and cook uncovered for 5 minutes more.

CHICKEN PAPRIKAS

Use recipe for Veal Paprikas, page 157.

Chicken Cacciatore can be served with noodles.

STEWED CHICKEN (Basic Recipe)

1 4-5 pound chicken or fowl	2 slices lemon
1 medium onion	2 teaspoons salt
½ cup celery stalks and leaves	cold water

1. Disjoint and cut chicken into large pieces.
2. Place in large kettle with vegetables, seasonings and enough water to cover.
3. Cover and heat to boiling, then simmer until tender. Chicken will be tender in about 2 hours, fowl in about 3 hours.
4. Lift out chicken, remove skin and bones, cut chicken unto cubes or thin, flat slices. Save stock for soup, for a base in jellied chicken, or thicken for gravy.

STEWED CHICKEN AND VEGETABLES

Cook cubed potatoes or potato balls, diced carrots, green peas in chicken stock. Thicken stock with flour. Add chicken; heat; season.

JELLIED CHICKEN

1 tablespoon gelatine	2 cups hot chicken stock
¼ cup cold water or	1 cup chicken and vegetables
chicken stock	

1. Soften gelatine in cold water or stock for 5 minutes; dissolve in hot seasoned chicken stock.
2. Chill until mixture begins to set.
3. Moisten a mould, put in layers of jelly and chicken and any of diced celery, green pepper or sliced olives.
4. Chill until firmly set. Makes 6 4-ounce moulds.

CHICKEN FRICASSEE

1. Cut chicken into pieces and cook as for Stewed Chicken.
2. When tender, drain from stock; season each piece with salt and pepper; roll in flour; brown in frying pan in butter or bacon drippings.
3. Keep hot; add stock to the drippings in the pan; thicken if necessary with flour which has been shaken with a little cold water in a covered jar.
4. Arrange the chicken on a platter; pour the gravy over.

STIR-FRIED CHICKEN

Chicken is cut into strips or cubes and cooked quickly in a little oil over high heat, and stirred frequently with a fork until it turns white. Shredded or diced vegetables plus a little chicken stock and seasonings are added, and the pan covered to finish cooking. The juices are thickened, usually with cornstarch. This rapid method of cooking retains the crispness and flavour of the foods, and is used skilfully by the Chinese. The next recipe is an example.

CHICKEN AND ALMONDS

1½ cups raw chicken meat	½ cup fresh or frozen green peas,
2 tablespoons fat	cooked
½ cup bamboo shoots	½ teaspoon salt
½ cup mushrooms, sliced	1 tablespoon soy sauce
1 cup celery, finely diced	1 cup water
½ cup water chestnuts	½ cup browned almonds

1. Blanch the almonds; cook slowly in 1 tablespoon butter until just beginning to brown.
2. Cut the chicken in 2-inch strips; brown in hot fat; cook until tender.
3. Add all ingredients except the almonds; simmer 5 minutes.
4. If much liquid remains, thicken it by stirring into it a paste made by combining 1 tablespoon or more of cornstarch with 2 or more tablespoons cold water.
5. Add the almonds to the chicken mixture; serve at once.
   Diced lean pork may be substituted for half the chicken.

BRAISED FOWL

1. Prepare as for roasting but do not stuff or truss.
2. Brown on all sides by cooking in hot fat in a heavy pan, turning until all is brown.
3. Place breast up in a deep pan; add 2 cups of water.
4. Cover and cook slowly until tender, 2 to 3 hours.
5. Leave the lid off for the last ½ hour to crispen the skin.
   ½ cup uncooked rice, washed and drained, and 2 onions, sliced, may be cooked in the pan around the fowl and served with it.

CREAMED CHICKEN (Basic Recipe)

2 cups White Sauce	salt
1½ cups cooked diced chicken	pepper
¼ teaspoon celery salt	chopped parsley

1. Prepare White Sauce from recipe on page 79, substituting equal quantities of light cream and chicken stock for the milk.
2. Heat chicken in sauce, stirring frequently.
3. Season to taste.
4. Serve in patty shells, ramekins or on toast. Sprinkle with chopped parsley. Serves 3-4.

CHICKEN À LA KING

Prepare twice the quantity of sauce for Creamed Chicken (Basic Recipe). Beat yolks of 2 eggs, stir in a little hot sauce, then stir egg mixture into remaining sauce. Strain in ½ teaspoon lemon juice and 3 cups cooked, diced chicken. Add any of ½ cup sautéed mushrooms, 1 cup cooked green peas and 2 tablespoons chopped pimento. Heat and serve as Creamed Chicken. Serves 6-8.

ORIENTAL CHICKEN

To Creamed Chicken add:

¼ cup almonds, blanched and cut in strips	½ cup cooked, diced celery or sliced water chestnuts
½ cup cooked peas or sautéed mushrooms	¼ cup sherry

Serve with crisp Chow Mein Noodles. Serves 4-5.

INDIVIDUAL CHICKEN PIE

½ cup cooked diced carrots	¾ cup chicken gravy or
5 small cooked onions	½ can cream chicken soup
¼ package frozen peas	¾ cup cooked or canned chicken
½ cup milk	tea biscuits

1. Combine ingredients, except tea biscuits, pour into a casserole and bake at 400° for 10 minutes.
2. Prepare Tea Biscuits from recipe (page 437) using ½ quantity of ingredients.
3. Place biscuits on top of hot mixture. Bake at 400° for 25 minutes. Serves 6-12.

SPANISH TIMBALES

1 tablespoon butter	½ teaspoon celery salt
½ cup diced green pepper	½ teaspoon salt
3 tablespoons minced onion	⅛ teaspoon pepper
1¼ cups toasted bread crumbs	⅛ teaspoon oregano
2 eggs	1 cup hot chicken stock
1½ cups cooked shredded chicken	6 stuffed olives sliced

1. Melt the butter; sauté the pepper and onion until tender; add crumbs.
2. Beat the eggs lightly.
3. Combine all the ingredients except the olives.
4. Place the sliced olives in the bottom of 6 greased individual custard cups.
5. Pack the chicken mixture into the custard cups.
6. Bake in a pan of hot water at 350° until firm, about 45 minutes. (Serves 4-6.)

DEVILLED BONES

cooked chicken—drumsticks, second joints and wings	½ tablespoon Worcestershire Sauce
salt, pepper	½ teaspoon mustard
flour	dash of cayenne
2 tablespoons butter	1 cup chicken stock
1 tablespoon tomato ketchup or chili sauce	½ tablespoon finely chopped parsley

1. Cut several small gashes in each piece of chicken.
2. Season with salt and pepper; roll in flour.
3. Melt butter, add sauces, mustard and cayenne.
4. Cook chicken in the seasoned butter until well browned.
5. Add stock; simmer 5 minutes.
6. Arrange chicken on serving dish; pour sauce over; sprinkle with parsley.

CHICKEN CROQUETTES

Recipe is in French Frying, Chapter 21.

CHICKEN CASSEROLES

The recipes for many casserole dishes made with chicken will be found in Supper Dishes, Chapter 11.

ROAST DUCK

Allow 1 to 1¼ pounds per person. The breastbone is soft and flexible if the duck is young. The under bill will break easily.

1. Dress, stuff and truss as for Roast Chicken (page 196).
2. Place on a rack in a roasting pan; season; brush with melted butter.
3. Roast according to the timetable following; after 30 minutes pour off the fat in the pan and baste with orange juice.
4. Serve with Orange Sauce (page 89); garnish with glazed apple rings and parsley.

Roast Stuffed Duckling with Orange Sauce spells old-fashioned dining elegance.

TIMETABLE FOR ROASTING DUCK

Ready-to-Cook Weight	Time Required to Cook at 325°
2 to 3	1½-2 hours
3 to 5	2-2½ hours

ROAST GOOSE

Allow 1 to 1¼ pounds per person. Feet should be soft, fat and yellow; legs covered with soft down. A red bill is a sign of age.

1. Using a brush, scrub the skin with water to which is added 1 teaspoon baking soda to 1 quart water; rinse well.
2. Singe, dress and truss goose; prick the skin in several places.
3. Instead of using dressing, place a couple of apples, cut in half, in the cavity.
4. Place on a rack in a roasting pan; season with salt.
5. Roast according to the table below; drain away the fat as it collects in the roaster. Serve with Pickled Crabapples (page 686).

TIMETABLE FOR ROASTING GOOSE

Ready-to-Cook Weight	Oven Temperature	Minutes per Pound	Time in Hours
7 to 8	325°	30	3½ to 4
9 to 11	325°	25	4 to 4½

If the goose is old, simmer 1½ hours, then roast the remaining time.

TURKEYS

Choose broad-chested, roundish turkeys rather than long sinewy ones. If the feet are still on the bird, they should be black, not grey. Hens weigh 6 to 16 pounds and are more tender than tom turkeys. Toms weigh 12 to 20 pounds.

Allow 1 pound per person; 1½ pounds will allow second-day snacks.

Large turkeys provide more meat at a lower price than small turkeys and are a good buy for the family which can use one. In order to have 2 meals of hot roast turkey, the bird can be cut in half lengthwise and cooked on 2 different occasions.

Frozen turkey should be thawed completely before stuffing. Do not refreeze turkeys once thawed.

Thaw in the original moistureproof wrapping in the refrigerator. Or thaw the wrapped bird in a pan set under *cold running water*. Turkey may be left in the refrigerator 1 day, then completely thawed under cold running water.

Ready-to-cook Weight (lbs.)	*Approximate Thawing Time Required* In Refrigerator	Under Cold Water
4 to 12	1 to 2 days	4 to 6 hours
12 to 20	2 to 3 days	6 to 8 hours
20 to 24	3 to 4 days	8 to 12 hours

Free legs and tail from tucked position carefully as soon as possible. Remove turkey from bag. Remove neck and giblets from the neck and main cavities. Refrigerate turkey if not to be used immediately. Use the turkey within 24 hours after thawing.

ROAST TURKEY

1. Dress, stuff and truss a turkey in the same manner as for a chicken.
2. Place, breast down or on its side, on a rack in a roasting pan.
3. Brush with melted fat; cover lightly with foil or several thicknesses of cheesecloth.
4. Roast choice birds *uncovered*, basting occasionally. If time is limited, if one cannot be on hand to baste bird if needed, or if bird is of marginal tenderness, cover with a lid for part of the cooking time; the bird should be uncovered during the last hour of cooking.
5. Roast at 325° according to the timetable which follows:

TIMETABLE FOR ROASTING TURKEY

Weight (lbs.) (Ready To Cook)	*Approximate Roasting Time in Hours (Uncovered)*	*Approximate Roasting Time in Hours (Covered)*
6 to 8	4 to 4½	3 to 3½
8 to 10	4½ to 5½	3½ to 4
10 to 13	5½ to 6¼	4¼ to 5
13 to 16	6¼ to 6¾	5 to 5¾
16 to 20	6¾ to 7¼	6 to 6¼
20 to 24	7¼ to 8	7 to 7¼

TO STORE COOKED TURKEY

Before refrigerating the remains of a cooked turkey, take it apart so it will not dry out.

1. Pull off large pieces suitable for slicing. Wrap in waxed paper or metal foil.
2. Cut off small pieces suitable for dicing. Cover in a refrigerator dish.
3. Remove the dressing into a casserole in which it can be heated, or wrap and serve cold.
4. Break up the bones for soup.

TO SERVE LEFTOVER TURKEY

Leftover turkey can be served cold, alone or in combination with other cold meats such as ham or roast beef.

It makes delicious sandwiches and salads. It can be served hot in croquettes or as a substitute for chicken in many of the casserole mixtures calling for cooked chicken.

Freezing leftover turkey for use at a later date reduces the tendency toward over-repetition.

CORNISH HENS WITH RICE

Allow 1 bird per person for this company fare.

2 frozen Rock Cornish hens each about 1¼ pounds	½ tin cream of mushroom soup
salt and pepper	½ cup heavy cream
butter	⅛ teaspoon marjoram
½ cup rice	dash of basil
1 tablespoon butter	dash of tarragon
2 tablespoons minced onion	¼ teaspoon curry powder
1 tablespoon minced green pepper	¼ teaspoon salt
6 mushrooms, sliced	⅛ teaspoon pepper
	fresh dill

1. Thaw hens, preferably overnight in the refrigerator, and wash inside thoroughly. Giblets will not be needed.
2. Sprinkle hens with salt and pepper and arrange in an open shallow pan without a rack; melt butter and brush over birds. Roast, uncovered, with frequent basting until done, 45-60 minutes.
3. Cook rice.
4. Melt 1 tablespoon butter in saucepan, sauté onion, green pepper and sliced mushrooms for 5 minutes; stir in undiluted soup, cream, and seasonings, except dill. Heat 10 minutes longer.
5. Stir in cooked rice and heat through; arrange on a small platter.
6. Arrange cooked hens on top; garnish with fresh dill. Serves 2.
   Birds are more easily eaten if cut in half lengthwise before placing on platter. Wild Rice with Mushrooms may be used as dressing, allowing ½ cup cooked rice for each bird.

GAME

All game is protected in Canada and may be shot only in season. The amount which may be taken is regulated, as is the length of time it may be kept in freezer lockers. These regulations may be obtained from The Department of Game and Fisheries of the Province.

Venison

Canadian deer or venison is probably the game with which most wives are confronted. We trust that the man of the house knows how to have the animal hung for at least two weeks where it will not freeze, and that he is an expert who can prepare it for cooking! After that, venison is cooked by the same methods as veal.

If the deer was young and not run too long by the hunters, the meat will be tender but rather dry. The fat is hard, so that if venison is to be served hot it must be very hot.

Cuts of venison are similar to those of lamb. The best cuts for roasting are the leg, or haunch, and the saddle. Steaks and cutlets are slices from the leg and loin. Other pieces, as the flank, breast and neck, should be used in stews. The flank is sometimes included with the saddle, in which case a few pieces of celery, or celery and carrot, may be rolled in each flank, which is then skewered underneath, close to the backbone. Venison, when roasted or broiled, may be served rare.

BROILED VENISON STEAK

1. Rub steak with a cut clove of garlic and softened butter.
2. Broil quickly, unless steaks are very thick, turning them only once.
3. Season. Drippings may be flavoured with a little sherry; pour over steaks and serve at once with Maître d'Hôtel Sauce (page 91).

ROAST VENISON

1. Weigh and wipe meat; place on rack in roasting pan. The meat may be larded or pieces of beef or pork fat may be laid on top of saddle.
2. Dredge meat with flour.
3. Baste every 15 minutes with fat from pan.
4. Season when half cooked; roast 15 minutes per pound at 325°.

TO PRESERVE VENISON

1. Cut the less tender parts of the meat into 2-inch cubes; cut off all gristle and fat.
2. Simmer, in water to cover, adding 1 teaspoon salt to each quart; cook until the meat is tender.
3. Pour the meat into sterilized jars.
4. Strain and season the stock; bring to a boil; pour over the meat. Process in a pressure cooker according to directions. If this is not possible, process in boiling water 2 hours. Unless the pressure method is used, be certain that when a jar is opened for use it is emptied into a saucepan, and the contents boiled 10 to 15 minutes before it is tasted. Thicken by shaking a little flour and water together in a covered jar and adding this to the liquid. Use in meat pie or serve with vegetables as stew.

VENISON PIE

1. Cut the less tender meat into small cubes; brown in hot fat.
2. Add water just to cover, salt, pepper, onion; simmer until tender; thicken (method page 79). Cool.
3. Pour into a casserole, lined with rich pastry; put on the top crust; brush with milk.
4. Bake at 425° for 30 minutes.

Other Game

Other game less commonly eaten are moose, bear and buffalo. Buffalo is available only when the government reduces the size of the herds in the national park at Wainwright, Alberta. Like venison, the quality of these meats depends upon the age and condition of the animal. Bear meat, which is fat, should be treated like pork, the others like beef.

SPANISH MOOSE STEAK

2 pounds moose or caribou steak	1 green pepper, chopped
¼ cup flour	1 clove garlic, chopped
½ teaspoon salt	6 small onions, sliced
pepper	1 cup tomatoes
2 tablespoons fat	1 cup peas

1. Dredge the meat with the seasoned flour; brown on both sides in hot fat; remove from the pan.
2. Sauté the pepper and garlic in the same fat until tender.

3. Place the pepper and garlic on the meat; replace it in the pan; add the onions and tomatoes; simmer until tender, about 2 hours.
4. Shortly before the meat is cooked add the peas and more seasoning if necessary.
5. Arrange on a platter with the vegetables on top; surround with a border of potato puffs.

MOOSE OR CARIBOU YUKON

2 pounds moose or caribou	⅓ cup flour
2 tablespoons lemon juice	2 tablespoons fat
1 teaspoon salt	½ cup chopped olives
1 teaspoon chili powder	

1. Cube the meat as for stew; sprinkle with lemon juice; stir well.
2. Season with salt and chili powder; roll in flour.
3. Brown well on all sides in the fat; add hot water to cover.
4. Simmer covered about 2 hours; 20 minutes before serving, remove the lid and allow the liquid to cook down to a rich gravy.
5. Add the olives. (Pimento may be substituted if desired.) Serve with noodles or rice.

Wild Fowl

DUCK: All varieties of wild duck are not edible. Edible varieties—the mallard, red-head, canvas back, black duck and teal—are roasted, usually without dressing but with sliced apple in the cavity. Lay strips of bacon over the breast and bake at 300° for 30 to 60 minutes. Baste with red currant jelly dissolved in hot water. Serve with wild rice.

GOOSE: The age of the goose may be determined by the size. Also, a red bill is a sign of age.

If the goose is young, cook it as wild duck, but cook it at least 2 hours. Since the fat is strong, do not stuff the bird but fill the cavity with sliced apple or onion which is discarded before serving. Keep the fat drained off as it collects and baste the fowl with currant jelly in hot water.

PARTRIDGE: This little bird, which is almost all breast, may be cooked by broiling as chicken (page 199), or it may be roasted.

To roast, clean; do not stuff. Cover with strips of bacon and bake in a slow oven at 300° for 40 to 60 minutes, or in an electric frying pan.

PHEASANT: Stuff as chicken. Roast 1½ to 2 hours at 300°.

PRAIRIE CHICKEN: Cook as partridge.

PERDRIX AU VIN (PARTRIDGE IN WINE)

Duck and pheasant can also be cooked in this manner; substitute chicken for partridge and voilà—Coq au Vin!

3 partridges	1 whole clove
1½ tablespoons cooking oil	⅔ cup sherry
1 tablespoon butter	1¾ cups canned tomatoes
1 medium onion, thinly sliced	¼ teaspoon salt
few celery leaves	⅛ teaspoon pepper
1 bay leaf	½ teaspoon monosodium
dash of thyme	glutamate
dash of marjoram	

1. Brown partridge in a deep kettle, containing oil, butter, onion, celery leaves and spices, until the birds are golden coloured on all sides.
2. Add sherry, and let simmer 15 minutes, covered.
3. Add tomatoes, salt, pepper and monosodium glutamate. Simmer, covered, for 2 hours longer. Serve with rice or wild rice.

BRAISED CANADA GOOSE

1. Remove meat from the bones of the goose to produce fillets.
2. Soak fillets in salt water (about 1 teaspoon salt to 1 quart water) for 1 hour. Dry.
3. Lightly rub the inside of a roasting pan with oil; add fillets.
4. Add chopped pulp of 1 orange, ½ cup chopped onion, ½ cup chopped celery, ½ teaspoon thyme, a little salt and pepper and 2 cups chicken stock.
5. Cover pan and cook goose in the oven at 350° for 2½-3 hours, or until tender.
6. Thicken pan juices with flour and stir in ¼ cup wine.

DRESSING

Allow 1 cup of dressing to each pound of fowl; 1 to 2 cups for fish or a roast.

A 1-pound loaf makes 8 cups of dressing; or allow 2 slices of bread for each serving.

Day-old bread is best; if dry bread is used a little warm milk will need to be added; when the dressing is pressed together into a ball lightly, it should break apart when released.

Do not stuff a fowl to be frozen; either completely thaw the bird, then stuff it, or bake the dressing separately in a pan during the last hour to reduce the danger of bacterial poisoning.

Always cool dressing before stuffing a bird which is not to be cooked immediately.

To stuff a half turkey partially roast it, skin side up; when about half done shape up the dressing on a sheet of aluminum foil and set the turkey over it.

BREAD DRESSING (Basic Recipe)

4 cups soft crumbs or cubes	1 teaspoon salt
¼ cup butter	⅛ teaspoon pepper
½ cup celery, chopped	1 teaspoon sage, poultry dressing
¼ cup onion, chopped	or savoury

1. Melt the fat; add the celery, onion; cook slowly to prevent browning.
2. Combine the crumbs and seasoning; mix all together.
3. Pack lightly into the fowl; the dressing swells as it cooks.

Use the basic recipe to make any of the following variations:

PARSLEY DRESSING: Add 4 tablespoons minced parsley; omit sage.

CELERY AND ALMOND DRESSING: Add ½ cup almonds, blanched and chopped; omit sage.

MUSHROOM DRESSING: Sauté 1 cup mushroom with the celery and onion.

OYSTER DRESSING: Chop ½ pint oysters; add to the cooked celery and onion.

APPLE DRESSING: Chop 2 cups apples finely; mix with the bread.

APRICOT DRESSING: Chop 1 cup tenderized dried apricots and ⅔ cup washed, seedless raisins. Omit the onion and sage.

APRICOT RICE DRESSING: Substitute 4 cups cooked rice for bread; omit onion and sage; add 1 cup tenderized chopped apricots.

ORANGE DRESSING: Add 1 cup orange sections. Omit the onion and sage.

ROLLED OATS DRESSING: Substitute rolled oats for part of the bread.

SAUSAGE DRESSING: Crumble ⅓ pound sausage meat and brown it in a frying pan; use the fat to cook the onion and celery.

CHESTNUT DRESSING: Add 1 cup boiled chopped chestnuts.

GIBLET DRESSING: Add finely chopped, cooked giblets and ½ cup giblet stock.

CRANBERRY DRESSING: Add to the basic dressing: 1 cup chopped cranberries, ½ cup washed raisins, ¼ teaspoon cinnamon, 2 teaspoons grated lemon rind, 4 tablespoons sugar. Omit the onion and sage.

CAPER DRESSING: Add 2 tablespoons chopped pickle or capers. Omit the sage.

WALNUT DRESSING: Add ⅓-½ cup chopped walnuts.

6 Fish and Shellfish

Fish in its many varieties is a delicious, nutritious food, abundant in Canadian waters. It is rich in protein and is an excellent source of minerals. It is relatively lean. Fish requires a short cooking period and so can be prepared quickly. The addition of a sauce to the more bland varieties of fish adds extra flavour and richness. Fish may be fresh, frozen, smoked, pickled or dried.

Among the fish in our stores:

Cod—an all purpose fish, one of the least expensive, but delicious when cooked by any of the conventional methods, especially when served with a sauce. Its pronounced flavour becomes milder when it is served in mixtures, such as fish balls.

Haddock—an all purpose fish like cod, slightly milder in flavour and a little more expensive.

Sole—a delicately-flavoured fish, usually purchased as fillets which are broiled or fried.

Halibut—a rich fish with a higher fat content than preceding varities. It has a pronounced fish flavour and is usually broiled or baked.

Salmon—also rich in fat, its flesh varied in colour from creamy Pink to bright orange Sockeye. Slightly paler than Sockeye, Cohoe salmon is very desirable and less expensive. Salmon is usually steamed, baked or broiled and is widely canned.

Trout—lake and brook trout are treats often "hard-to-come-by." These fish, too, have flesh of pinky-peach tones. Brook trout are usually pan-fried or broiled; lake trout baked or broiled.

Arctic Char—a delectable fish found only in specialty fish markets in large centres, harvested by Canadian Eskimos. It is a rich creamy-fleshed fish; broil or bake to bring out its superior flavour.

Some of the fish available are: (clockwise from left) Halibut Steak, Salmon Steak, Fresh Sole, Canned Cohoe Salmon, Canned Canadian Sardines, Fresh Whole Lobster, Fresh Smelts, Hard Shelled Clam, (centre, bottom) Whole Yellow Pickerel, (centre, top) Whole Mackerel.

Fish is marketed in the following forms:

Whole—This is the form in which the fish come from the water; they must be scaled or skinned, beheaded and have the entrails removed before use.

Drawn—These fish have had only the entrails removed.

Dressed—The entrails, head, tails and fins have been removed.

Steaks—These are cross sections of large, dressed fish, each providing one serving.

Fillets—These are the meaty sides of the fish cut lengthwise away from the backbone; they should be free of bones. Fillets are usually sold packaged and frozen.

Grading and government inspection are not compulsory; however, packaged fish bearing a maple leaf government seal have been processed under government approved conditions.

Quantities to Buy: When buying whole fish, allow 2 servings per pound; drawn fish, 2½ servings per pound; and filletted fish, 4 servings per pound.

To Prepare Whole Fish for Cooking

1. Remove scales. Hold fish by tail; loosen scales with knife, keeping knife close against the fish, to prevent scales from flying. Fish may be scaled under water in a large pan, so that scales will not fly about. Remove fins.
2. Remove head and tail. These are sometimes left on if fish is to be baked, also in case of small fish, such as smelts. If head is left on, remove eyes, using sharp knife or pair of scissors to loosen membrane.
3. Cut underside of fish lengthwise with a sharp knife. Remove entrails and any clotted blood which clings to backbone.
4. Wash inside and out; sprinkle inside of fish with salt, then wash thoroughly with cold water; rinse and dry.

To Bone Fish

1. Clean fish; remove head, tail and fins.
2. Remove large bones near the head, then slip a sharp knife under flesh close to backbone.
3. Work the flesh from bones on one side, from head to tail, then from the other side.
4. Remove all small bones remaining.
   Fish is frequently boned for broiling and when preparing it for children or invalids. It is necessary to bone whole fish when cooking on a plank.

To Skin Fish

1. Lay fish flat side down on the cutting board.
2. Holding the tail end with one hand, cut with a sharp knife through the skin to the flesh about ½ inch above the tail.
3. Flatten the knife along the skin and cut the flesh away from the skin by pushing the knife forward while holding the free end of the skin firmly with other hand.

BROILED FISH

Fish fillets, steaks or split whole fish are suitable for broiling.

1. Prepare fish for cooking; sprinkle with salt and a few drops of lemon juice or vinegar and place on a wire rack or greased broiling pan.
2. If fish is very dry, as is whitefish, brush over with melted butter. Preheat broiler.

3. Broil on one side, cooking the split or cut side first. Turn and broil other side. Time required, 6-10 minutes, depending upon thickness of fish.
4. Serve, garnished with parsley and lemon.

Lemon juice brings out the flavour of Broiled Fish Steaks.

BARBECUED FISH

Any fish can be broiled over an outdoor fire; the fire should be less hot than those for cooking steak or fowl. Spread split whole fish, small fish or fish steaks with Barbecue Sauce (page 86) or Basting Sauce (below) and put into the 2-sided broiler or directly onto the grill. Broil on one side, turn and broil on the other side. Cook 5 to 10 minutes on each side according to the thickness of the fish.

BASTING SAUCES FOR FISH

Mix a few teaspoonfuls of white wine or lemon juice with 3 or 4 tablespoons of softened butter.

Mix mayonnaise with half the quantity of lemon juice.

FRIED FISH IN BATTER

Recipe on page 633.

SAUTÉED WHOLE FISH

Cooking fish in a pan helps to keep them moist; broiled fish has a tendency to become dry. Fish may or may not be sprinkled with seasoned flour before being sautéed lightly in a little melted butter in a frying pan. Turn once and cook until the fish is golden in colour. Barbecue Sauce may then be poured over the cooked fish and heated through; or the sauce may be omitted altogether. Fish is improved with a pinch of dill.

To avoid cooking odours, cook fish outdoors!

SAUTÉED FISH STEAKS

1. Clean fish; cut into 1-inch slices.
2. The bones may be removed; skewer fish into circle; fasten with toothpicks or small skewers.
3. Season; dip in (a) flour, or (b) flour and cornmeal, equal parts, or (c) sifted crumbs, eggs and crumbs.
4. Have frying-pan hot; put in fat—vegetable oil or butter.
5. When fat is hot, put in fish; cook 5 or 6 minutes on each side until evenly browned.
6. Serve with drawn butter or other fish sauce; garnish with parsley and slices or sections of lemon.

STEAMED FISH

1. To serve 6-8, buy a piece 2 to 3 pounds in weight, cut from the tail end; have it scaled and drawn.
2. Place the fish on a piece of porous cloth in the top of a steamer; cover loosely with a piece of foil; cover the steamer.
3. Steam 10 minutes to the pound and 10 minutes extra.
4. When the fish flakes when tested with a fork, lift it out of the steamer onto a pan.

5. Peel off the dark skin; arrange the fish on a heated platter. Remove upper half of fish, lift out bone; reassemble. Serve HOT with a fish sauce, or chill and serve with mayonnaise. (See also Fish Baked in Foil.)

To improvise a steamer, use a large sieve, colander or meat rack over a pan of boiling water.

BAKED FISH

1. Prepare fish for cooking; sprinkle inside with salt. Preheat oven to 400°.
2. Fill with Parsley Dressing (page 216); sew or skewer edges together.
3. Wrap tail in greased paper.
4. Place in greased baking-pan or on foil in pan.
5. Lay strips of fat salt pork over top of fish; hold in place with toothpicks.
6. Bake about 10 minutes per pound and 10 minutes extra; or about 10 minutes per inch thickness of fish.
7. Lift out carefully; remove skewers and paper.
8. Garnish with parsley and lemon; serve with Tartar or Hollandaise Sauce (page 86). 2-3 pounds serves 6.

Fish in Foil (on the coals) and Grilled Whole Fish are a treat for everyone.

FISH BAKED IN FOIL

This method is a combination of steaming and baking. It is convenient and effective for cooking fish outdoors on a barbecue or buried in hot coals of campfire; equally good indoors in the oven.

Tear off a length of aluminum foil, preferably heavy-duty foil or a double thickness of regular foil, 2½ times the width of the fish. Centre the fish, rub lightly with butter or add a slice of bacon. Bring up the cut edges over the fish, triple fold top and sides to make a tight, leak-proof package. Be careful not to tear or puncture the foil. Bake at 450° about 10-15 minutes, according to the thickness of the fish; on hot coals, allow 5-10 minutes.

BAKED FISH STEAKS

1. Prepare fish steaks in pieces for serving.
2. Dip in salted milk (2 teaspoons salt to 1 cup milk), then in sifted crumbs.
3. Place in well-greased baking pan; dot with small pieces of butter.
4. Bake, uncovered, in hot oven, 500°, 10 to 20 minutes; or bake, uncovered, in oven 350°, 30 to 35 minutes.
5. Serve with Creole Sauce (page 85); garnish with parsley and lemon sections.

PLANKED FISH

Best results are obtained if fish is fairly thick, or if steaks of large fish, such as salmon or halibut, are used.
1. Prepare fish for cooking, removing bones.
2. Place, skin side down, on fish plank.
3. Brush over with melted butter; season.
4. Place on upper rack in oven and bake 20 to 25 minutes at 350°; remove from oven.
5. Prepare hot mashed potatoes; press through large pastry tube to form border around fish.
6. Brown at 400°.
7. Garnish with watercress or parsley and lemon.

ROLLED FISH FILLETS (FISH TURBANS)

Use fillets of fresh or frozen (thawed) fish or large fish steaks, boned.
1. Sprinkle fish with salt and pepper; spread each piece with filling following.
2. Roll up and fasten with toothpicks or skewers, or wrap in partly cooked bacon.
3. Place rolls in a shallow greased casserole, brush with melted butter.

4. Bake at 400° 20-25 minutes, or remove from oven after 15 minutes and pour 1 cup White Sauce or any of the cream soup variations over the fillets. Sprinkle with grated cheese, if desired, and return casserole to oven to finish baking.

ROLLED FISH FILLINGS

Bread Dressing (page 216): about 1 cup per pound of fish. Add 4 tablespoons chopped celery or grated, peeled cucumber for additional flavour. Moisten dressing with 1-2 tablespoons dill pickle juice or water.

Cracker Crumb Dressing: crush vegetable-flavoured crackers to make 1 cup (enough for 1 pound of fish). Moisten with 1 tablespoon piquant French dressing and about 3 tablespoons water.

Asparagus: enclose 3 or 4 spears of cooked asparagus in each fillet. Pour White Sauce or cream soup sauce over fillets before baking.

Shrimps: chop about 8 large cooked shrimps and add to ½ cup Bread Dressing (page 216). Sauté 1 small clove garlic, crushed, 3 tablespoons finely chopped onion and 3 tablespoons finely-chopped green pepper, and add to filling. Serve fish with Hollandaise or Maître d'Hôtel Sauce (pages 86, 91) and garnish with additional cooked shrimps, lemon wedges and parsley.

FISH LOAF (SALMON LOAF)

15-ounce can of salmon makes 1 loaf; use Cohoe or pink varieties.

2 cups cooked fish, flaked	1 teaspoon lemon juice
1 cup soft bread crumbs	2 eggs
½ teaspoon salt	½ cup milk
¼ teaspoon paprika	1 tablespoon finely chopped
½ teaspoon grated onion	parsley

1. Mix all ingredients together; more milk may be needed if fish is dry.
2. Turn into buttered baking dish, cover.
3. Oven-poach or steam until firm in centre—about ½ hour.
4. Serve hot with Hollandaise Sauce, Cheese Sauce (page 86) or serve cold with salad. Serves 4-6.

FISH BALLS OR CAKES

1½ cups flaked cooked fish	¼ teaspoon pepper
2 cups mashed potatoes	1 teaspoon finely minced onion
1 egg, beaten	1 cup fine dry bread crumbs or
1 tablespoon melted butter	crushed corn flakes
1 teaspoon salt	2-3 tablespoons fat

1. Combine all ingredients except crumbs or corn flakes and fat.
2. Form into balls or cakes and roll in crumbs. Chill.
3. Cook fish balls in fat over medium heat until golden brown and heated through, about 3-5 minutes. Serves 6.

FISH PATTIES

Quickly prepared for hurry-up meals.

1 15-ounce tin salmon or	½ teaspoon salt
2 cups any cooked fish	⅛ teaspoon paprika
2 eggs, beaten	2-3 tablespoons fat
½ cup cracker or dry bread crumbs	

1. Flake fish and combine with all other ingredients except the fat.
2. Form into flat cakes and sauté in fat until golden brown on each side. Serve with Tartar Sauce (page 91).

FISH CROQUETTES

Recipe in French Frying, Chapter 21.

KEDGEREE

⅓ cup rice	1 teaspoon parsley, finely chopped
1 cup cooked fish, flaked	salt and pepper
2 tablespoons butter, melted	
1 egg yolk	

1. Boil the rice and drain.
2. Add fish; mix lightly with a fork; reheat.
3. Add melted butter, yolk of egg, beaten, parsley and salt and pepper.
4. Cook 2 minutes; pile on serving dish; serve with Parsley or Egg Sauce (page 83). Serves 3-4.

CODFISH BALLS

Recipe in French Frying, Chapter 21.

FINNAN HADDIE OR SMOKED FILLETS IN MILK

2 pounds finnan haddie or smoked fillets	2 tablespoons butter
	1 cup milk

1. Cover fish with boiling water and simmer 10 minutes. Drain.
2. Add butter and milk to fish and bake at 350° for 15 minutes or simmer until the fish flakes apart. Serves 6.
   For frozen fillets simmer in water for 20 minutes.

CISCOES AND GOLDEYES

1. Place fish in a greased pan; bake at 400°, 12-15 minutes.
2. Remove skin; take out backbone, being careful to leave flesh unbroken.
3. Place fish on hot platter or on toast.
4. Serve, garnished with lemon and parsley.

WINNIPEG GOLDEYE IN FOIL

Allow 1 goldeye per person. Sprinkle with fresh black pepper. Leaving head and tail on, wrap each fish tightly in well greased aluminum foil. Double-fold the seam and pinch ends closely so package is moisture-tight. Place on baking sheet in 450° (hot) oven and allow 10 minutes per inch of thickness of the fish.

The goldeye may be skinned and head removed for serving—a matter of preference. Serve with wedges of lemon.

FRIED SMELTS

1. Clean smelts. Make a cut under the gills, remove intestines; sprinkle with salt; wash and dry.
2. Season; dip in flour, beaten egg and crumbs.
3. Fry in fat which browns a cube of bread in 60 seconds. After putting in fish, reduce heat, so that fish may be sufficiently cooked without becoming too brown. Cook 3 to 4 minutes.
4. Drain; garnish with lemon and parsley or watercress; serve with Hollandaise or Tartar Sauce (pages 86, 91).

PICKLED HERRING

A Scandinavian treat! It may be served as an appetizer, or be offered as one of many delicacies of a smorgasbord.

1 large salt herring	2 tablespoons chopped onion
½ cup white vinegar	2 tablespoons mixed pickling
2 tablespoons water	spice
¼ cup sugar	

1. Clean the fish; remove the head; soak in cold water overnight.
2. Bone; slice in pieces 1 inch wide; place pieces in a long dish to resemble a whole fish again.
3. Mix the ingredients for the dressing; pour it over the fish. Refrigerate several hours.

Oysters

This delicate-flavoured sea food is available all year round, not just in the R-containing months as was formerly believed. Because oysters come from different localities there are prime quality oysters available in every season. They are usually marketed less frequently in the summer months because of their high perishability.

Oysters are sold in the shell or shucked. Shucked oysters have been removed from the shell and are sold frozen, canned and fresh. Shells should be scrubbed with a brush, pried open with a sharp knife and the cord (membrane attaching the oyster to the shell) severed. To clean oysters, strain oyster juice through a cheese cloth, or fine strainer, and save. Pick over oysters to remove pieces of shell, place in a colander and pour cold water through—about ½ cup of water to 1 quart of oysters.

OYSTERS OR CLAMS ON HALF SHELL

Allowing 6 clams or oysters per person, arrange open shells on a bed of ice.

Serve with containers of lemon juice and horseradish, and freshly ground black pepper, or a dish of Cocktail Sauce (page 64). Sink dish in bed of ice.

SCALLOPED OYSTERS

2 cups buttered crumbs*	dash of cayenne
1 pint oysters, cleaned	⅓ cup oyster juice
½ teaspoon salt	

1. Butter a baking dish or scallop shells.
2. Place ¼ of crumbs over bottom of dish; add ½ the oysters, cutting them in half if large; sprinkle with seasonings.
3. Repeat crumbs, oysters, seasonings; add oyster juice.
4. Cover with remaining crumbs.
5. Bake at 350°, 30 to 40 minutes, for casserole dish, 15 minutes for shells. Serves 4-5.

    *If shells are used, 4 cups crumbs will be required.

OYSTER STEW

2½ cups top milk	¾ teaspoon salt
2 tablespoons fine cracker crumbs	dash of pepper
⅓ cup oyster juice	1 pint oysters
2 tablespoons butter	chives or green onions and parsley

1. Heat the milk and crumbs over low heat.
2. Add the juice from the oysters, the seasoning and the butter.
3. When the milk is hot and the butter melted, add the oysters.
4. Cook until the oysters are plump and the edges begin to curl.
5. Serve at once. Sprinkle chopped chives or green onions and parsley on top. Serves 4-5.

FRICASSEED OYSTERS

2 tablespoons butter	Sauce for Oysters
1 teaspoon salt	1 cup milk and oyster juice
⅛ teaspoon pepper	2 tablespoons butter
dash of cayenne	2 tablespoons flour
1 pint oysters, cleaned	2 yolks of eggs
	1 teaspoon lemon juice

1. Place butter and seasonings in a chafing dish or saucepan. Heat slowly.
2. When hot, add oysters, cover; shake the pan occasionally.
3. When oysters are plump, remove and keep hot.
4. Add milk to liquid in pan, to make 1 cup.
5. Make White Sauce from butter, flour and liquid (page 79).
6. Beat eggs until thick; add sauce and lemon juice.
7. Reheat oysters in sauce; serve on toast or wafers, in canapés or timbales. Serves 4.
   ½ cup white wine may be added to replace milk.

FRIED OYSTERS
Recipe in French Frying, Chapter 21.

BROILED OYSTERS
1. Clean oysters; dry.
2. Dip in melted butter, then in very fine, seasoned crumbs.
3. Broil until plump.
4. Serve garnished with parsley and lemon sections, or serve with bacon or on toast with White Sauce in which oyster juice is part of the liquid.

BROILED OYSTERS DE LUXE
1. Clean oysters, drain and marinate for 1 hour in French dressing or white wine to which has been added a little grated garlic and pepper.
2. Drain oysters and wrap each in ½ thin slice of bacon.
3. Broil until bacon is crisp. Serve as an appetizer or with cocktails.

Lobsters

Lobster is the aristocrat of sea foods because of its distinctive flavour and because of its high price. Lobster can be served hot or cold, plain or in flavoursome mixtures.

Live lobsters should be heavy for their size; the meat of smaller lobsters is more tender than that of large.

Cooked lobsters should be used within 18 hours after cooking. Test by straightening tail; if it springs back quickly, lobster was alive when put on to cook.

Lobsters are usually killed by plunging them head first into boiling water. It is considered more humane to bring them to the boiling point in fresh cold water as the fresh water anaesthetizes this salt-water inhabitant. They may also be killed by cutting the spinal cord (see Broiled Lobster recipe).

BOILED LOBSTERS

Using a large kettle with a large quantity of water, kill lobster by either of the methods outlined. Simmer 20 to 25 minutes, according to size. Drain; place on back to chill.

1. When cool enough to handle, split down the front from head to tail; remove the intestinal vein, and the stomach.
2. The liver, green in colour, may be left as is or mixed with bread crumbs, salt and pepper and replaced.
3. A heavy knife is needed for cracking claw and arm shells.
4. Serve hot with melted butter to which a few drops of lemon juice have been added; or
   Serve cold on a bed of lettuce, garnished with hard-cooked eggs, tomato slices, mayonnaise and capers.

BROILED LOBSTER

1. Place live lobster on its back, cross the large claws and hold firmly.
2. With a sharp-pointed knife, make a deep incision near the mouth to cut through the spinal cord; cut down through the body from the mouth to the end of the tail.
3. Remove the intestinal vein, liver and stomach and crack the claw shells.
4. Sprinkle with melted butter; broil 8 to 10 minutes on the flesh side and 6 to 8 minutes on the shell side.
5. Season and serve with melted butter.

LOBSTER THERMIDOR

This mixture can also be served in ramekins, timbales or small tart shells.

3 tablespoons butter	1 cup cream
2 tablespoons flour	2 cups cooked lobster
½ teaspoon mustard	¼ cup chopped, sautéed
½ teaspoon minced onion	mushrooms
dash of pepper	small finger rolls
½ teaspoon salt	2 tablespoons grated cheese

1. Make a White Sauce of butter, flour, seasonings and cream (page 79).
2. Add lobster and mushrooms; serve in scallop shells, patty shells, or cut tops from rolls, scoop out centres and heat. Fill heated rolls with lobster mixture. Sprinkle with grated cheese.
3. Brown in hot oven; serve at once.

LOBSTER NEWBURG

1. Sauté 2 cups of cooked lobster in ¼ cup of butter. Add 1 tablespoon of sherry, 1 tablespoon of brandy.
2. Combine with 2 cups of Allemande Sauce (page 83), made with light cream for stock.
3. Serve as Lobster Thermidor.

Crab

Alaska King Crab, available fresh on the west coast of Canada, can be purchased frozen or canned in other parts of the country. Similar to lobster in flavour, it can be substituted for it in any of the lobster recipes.

Shrimp

Shrimp are particularly popular when served as hors d'oeuvres or tangy seafood cocktails. Large, jumbo shrimp may be dipped in batter and fried, while all sizes lend themselves to the Latin American treatment of cooking in a mixture of rice, tomatoes and spices.

Shrimp may be purchased fresh, cooked, dried or canned. Fresh or cooked shrimp should be kept refrigerated or frozen to insure freshness. Fresh shrimp are greenish in colour and are cooked in rapidly boiling salted water for 5 minutes; the shells are then peeled off. Cooked shrimp are light orange in colour.

The intestinal vein should be removed by making a shallow cut along the outside curvature of the shrimp and lifting out the black line with the point of the knife. After fresh shrimp have been cooked the head is also removed.

SHRIMP CREOLE WITH RICE

1½ pounds shrimp, cooked	¼ garlic clove, chopped fine
4 tablespoons butter	dash of basil
3 tablespoons green pepper strips	½ teaspoon black pepper
3 tablespoons chopped onion	⅛ teaspoon salt
3 tablespoons celery strips	½ cup vegetable stock or wine
1 medium-sized tomato, cut into pieces	½ cup tomato sauce

1. Brown the shrimp in butter for 5 minutes; add remaining ingredients except stock or wine and sauce; sauté all for 10 minutes longer.
2. Add stock and cook uncovered for 2 minutes longer.
3. Add tomato sauce and cook 10 minutes more. Serve with rice.

FRIED SHRIMP

Recipe in French Frying, Chapter 21.

SHRIMP COCKTAIL

See recipe for Seafood Cocktail, page 64.

SHRIMP CURRY

See page 320.

Scallops

Scallops, another form of seafood, consist of one large muscle and a tiny one. Drain off the liquid; remove and discard the tiny muscle. There are 25 large scallops to a pound, and up to 50 if they are small.

SAUTÉED SCALLOPS

1 pound scallops	¾-1 teaspoon salt
flour, about 1-1½ cups	6 tablespoons fat

1. Mix flour and salt and thoroughly coat each scallop.
2. Melt fat in a frying pan and cook scallops in the fat over low heat until delicately browned.
3. Serve with Tartar Sauce (page 91).

COQUILLES ST. JACQUES

Particularly attractive when served in scallop shells, this light luncheon dish can be prepared ahead, and refrigerated or frozen until needed.

1 pound scallops
½ pound mushrooms
¾ cup white wine
¼ cup water
½ bay leaf
2 sprigs parsley
½ small onion
few grains pepper
¼ teaspoon salt

3 tablespoons butter
4 tablespoons flour
1 cup stock
¾ cup milk
2 egg yolks
½ cup heavy cream
lemon juice
fine, buttered crumbs
Parmesan cheese

1. Rinse scallops, slice mushrooms and combine with the next 7 ingredients; simmer 4-5 minutes.

2. Strain off stock and keep it warm; set aside scallops and mushrooms.

3. In top of a double boiler or in a heavy saucepan, melt butter, blend in flour and heat gently until mixture bubbles.

4. Remove from heat, blend in heated stock from scallops, then the milk; heat 1 minute more.

5. Combine beaten egg yolks and cream. Add a little hot sauce to the egg mixture, stirring constantly; stir egg mixture back into the remaining hot sauce.

6. Cook 1 minute more—over hot water, if a double boiler is used, or over direct heat, watching carefully to prevent burning.

7. Taste; add a few drops of lemon juice, and salt and pepper if needed.

8. Cut scallops into quarters and combine with about ⅔ of the sauce; spoon into 6 buttered scallop shells or ramekins and cover with remaining sauce.

9. Top with very fine, buttered crumbs and sprinkle with Parmesan cheese; arrange shells on a shallow pan and refrigerate. If shells are to be frozen, add topping after thawing; frozen shells must be thoroughly thawed.

10. About 15 minutes before needed, place shells 8 to 9 inches below a heated broiler and heat through until bubbly with the top lightly browned. Serve at once, garnished with a sprig of parsley. Serves 6.

In the sauce, step 3, reduce flour to 1 tablespoon, stock to ½ cup; substitute 1 10-ounce tin frozen shrimp soup for the milk, add only 1 egg yolk.

To Use Leftover Cooked Fish

1. Add mayonnaise, seasonings, serve in salads or as a spread for appetizers and sandwiches.
2. Make croquettes, fish loaf, soufflé, chowder, fish balls and patties.
3. Use in jellied salads, aspic or mousse.
4. Add White Sauce, vegetables and serve on toast, in ramekins or sea shells.
5. Blend with other fish for seafood cocktail.

7 Vegetables

CANADIAN VEGETABLES have no rivals! Cooking techniques can maintain or destroy their natural beauty of colour, texture and flavour and determine the fate of their vitamins and minerals. Serving vegetables raw occasionally is good practice since Vitamin C levels are higher in raw than cooked vegetables; their crisp texture stimulates the appetite.

Facts to Consider When Buying and Storing Vegetables

Buy vegetables in season; they are fresher, less expensive and have more flavour and nutritional value. Shop in person for vegetables and choose those with the brightest colours; buy root vegetables which are firm and heavy for size in quantities in keeping with available storage space. Leafy vegetables should be crisp and bought in small quantities. All should be free of blemishes and soft spots. Storing vegetables in a cool, moist atmosphere away from sunlight helps to preserve their quality.

To Freeze Vegetables

Raw vegetables do *not* freeze well. Exceptions are green pepper, cabbage and celery; the latter two wilt on thawing but are quite acceptable for use in cooked dishes. Other fresh vegetables to be frozen must first be blanched or par-boiled for a short, timed period, then quickly plunged into cold water. Detailed information for freezing the many varieties of fresh vegetables is available in bulletins from the provincial departments of agriculture.

Most cooked vegetables freeze well. Exceptions are boiled (white) potatoes which become mealy and corn on the cob which suffers a loss of flavour and texture.

Vegetable casseroles freeze well. Leftover baked potatoes can be converted to baked stuffed potatoes, foil-wrapped and frozen for future use—or they can be prepared in advance with a special occasion in mind. Many of the recipes in this chapter are marked "can be frozen."

Preparation of Vegetables

Vegetables should be thoroughly clean; if the skins are left on the vegetable they should be scrubbed with a brush. When peeling, remove only a thin layer of peeling as most of the iron in root vegetables is found in the area just under the skin. It may be necessary to soak cauliflower and broccoli in cold, salted water for about 15 minutes before cooking in order to draw out any organisms which may be lodged between the flowerets. Leave vegetables in as large pieces as possible; the more exposed surfaces there are, the greater will be the loss of vitamins and minerals.

General Directions for Cooking Vegetables

Do not Overcook Vegetables. Cook vegetables until they are just tender when tested with the point of a paring knife. Season with salt, pepper and butter or use some of the herbs listed in the chart in the appendix.

BOILING: The general rule is to cook vegetables in a small quantity of boiling water covered with a tight-fitting lid. Bring vegetable to the boil as quickly as possible, then reduce heat and boil gently until the vegetable is tender. This method of boiling ensures the maximum retention of vitamins and minerals. Leafy vegetables like spinach require only the water which clings to the leaves when washing. If vegetables have become strong in flavour through storage, such as winter cabbage, increasing the amount of water used or leaving the lid off the pot for part of the cooking period will reduce the strong flavour. When cooking green vegetables, leaving the lid off the pot during the last few minutes of cooking results in a brighter green. Always start with boiling water;

unless the vegetable is particularly strong in flavour, save the cooking water (vegetable stock) to dilute canned soups, to reconstitute dehydrated soups, for soup stocks or gravies.

STEAMING: Because the water is not in direct contact with the vegetable, steaming retains more of the water-soluble vitamins than does boiling. Boiling water is placed in a large pot and the vegetable is placed over it on a rack or in a separate compartment which has holes in the bottom to allow the steam to penetrate. The pot is tightly covered. This method of cooking is suitable for most vegetables.

PRESSURE COOKING: Follow directions given with the pressure cooker. In this method, little water is used and the cooking time is short. Therefore retention of vitamins and minerals is good. This method of cooking is suitable for all but the leafy vegetables.

BAKING: Scrub vegetables with a brush. In the case of potatoes, leave skins on and prick in several places with a fork to enable steam to escape. Vegetables may be peeled and baked in large or small pieces in a covered casserole dish. Baking retains vitamins and minerals to a high degree and is most suited to root vegetables, squash and onions.

COOKING IN FOIL: Vegetables are cooked in an oven or over coals of a barbecue or campfire, by a combination of steaming and baking.

Prepare foil packets by tearing a length of heavy aluminum foil, about 20 inches long; fold in half to make a 10-inch sheet. Triple-fold edges at the top and on side, making all folds flat and firm. With open end up, put in about 1 pound of fresh or frozen vegetables with 2 tablespoons of water. Triple fold remaining end and check all sides of packages to be sure it is thoroughly sealed. Cook 45 to 60 minutes according to the type of vegetable and the size of the pieces. Carrots and squash are particularly good when cooked in foil.

PAN-SAUTÉING: Vegetables are shredded, diced or thinly sliced and cooked in a frying pan containing about 3 to 4 tablespoons melted butter, with a tight-fitting lid. The butter prevents the vegetables from sticking while the vegetable juices are turning into steam. The steam finishes the cooking. This method of cooking can be used effectively with most young vegetables, especially those with a high moisture content—cabbage, kale and spinach. Occasionally, it is necessary to add a few tablespoons of water if vegetable lacks moisture.

ROASTING: This is a variation of baking, in which vegetables are cooked in the oven around roasting meat. Sometimes vegetables are precooked in water for 10 to 15 minutes. When uncooked vegetables are to be roasted, soaking in ice water for a few minutes, then drying thoroughly, reduces the absorption of fat. Vegetables are brushed with dripping and roasted in the pan with the meat. The oven temperature should be increased to 350°.

FRENCH FRYING: The cooking of vegetables by this method is described in French Frying, Chapter 21.

VEGETABLES ON SKEWERS (ON A BARBECUE): Scrub potatoes, yams, white turnips, onions and tomatoes; leave whole and unpeeled. Thread each kind of vegetable onto its own skewer. Rotate frequently over hot coals which are lined up in rows between the skewers. Start cooking the potatoes and yams first, approximately 60 minutes, then onions and turnips for about 40 minutes. Tomatoes will cook in 5 to 10 minutes and so should be cooked at the very last. Vegetables can be kept warm without further cooking if wrapped in foil and placed at the back of the fire box.

COOKING FROZEN VEGETABLES: Frozen vegetables require less cooking since the processes of blanching, freezing and thawing tend to soften the cellulose. Follow directions given on the packages of commercially frozen vegetables. Others should be allowed to thaw slightly and then be cooked with no or very little added water in a tightly covered sauce pan. To ensure uniform cooking, break the melting mass apart with a fork.

COOKING CANNED VEGETABLES: Place the stock from canned vegetables in a saucepan and heat until liquid has been reduced to ⅓ to ½ the original volume. Add vegetables and heat just to boiling. Save the cooking water to dilute canned soups, for gravy or soup stock. All *home-canned* vegetables except tomatoes must be boiled in an open saucepan 10 to 15 minutes before tasting or using.

Various Forms in Which Vegetables May Be Served

When several vegetables are served together on one plate, there should be variation of the size and shape, as well as colour and texture. Here are some variations of shape:

JULIENNE (vegetables cut into thin strips, sometimes referred to as shoe-string): Potatoes, carrots, beets.

FINGERS (vegetables cut into strips, longer and wider than Julienne): Carrots, parsnips.

WHOLE: Peas, potatoes, asparagus, tiny beets, corn on the cob. Cauliflower is sometimes cooked whole and served with other vegetables from a platter.

ROUNDS OR SLICES: Beets, potatoes, tomatoes, onions.

DICED OR CUBED: Turnip, potatoes, beets.

MASHED OR WHIPPED: Potatoes, turnip.

RICED (vegetables forced through tiny holes of a ricer or food press): Potatoes.

CHOPPED: Hashed brown potatoes, onions.

FLOWERETS: Cauliflower, broccoli.

SHREDDED: Cabbage.

WEDGES: Cooked cabbage, lettuce (raw).

For variety, or to enhance the flavours of vegetables which have had a long storage period during winter months, try any of these:

Use herbs such as chopped mint, chives, chervil or marjoram on root vegetables.

Add orange or lemon juices to buttered carrots, a teaspoon of sugar to mashed turnips.

Serve sour cream on potatoes, curried sauce or cauliflower on mixed vegetables.

Mix garlic croutons with green beans, and a mixture of fine, buttered crumbs and grated cheese with brussels sprouts or cauli- flower.

Use seasoned salt on any vegetable, garlic butter on mushrooms or broccoli.

Serve with sauces, Hollandaise, Cheese, French Dressing (Vinaigrette). (See Chapter 3.)

Combine with other vegetables which complement them in flavour and colour.

VEGETABLE COOKERY TIMETABLE

Cooking Time in Minutes*

Kind	Preparation	Boil	Steam	Pressure Cook	Pan-Sauté (shred)	Bake 350°	Amount for 6 in Pounds	Serving Suggestions
MILD ARTICHOKES Jerusalem	Clean and scrape. To boil add ½ teaspoon vinegar to cooking water.	20-30	30-40	10			2½	Serve with butter, salt and pepper or Vegetable or Cheese Sauce.
ASPARAGUS	Wash, cut off tough ends; to boil, tie in bunches and stand up in deep pot with water half way up stalks. (An old coffee pot works well.)	15-20	30-40	9			1	Serve with Maître d'Hôtel or Cream Sauce; or on toast with Cheese Sauce.
BEANS Wax or Green	Wash, remove stems and tips; cut into 1-inch lengths or slice into long, thin strips.	15-25	30-35	2-2½	5-8		1½	Serve with butter, salt and pepper; cook with herbs or mushrooms.
BEETS Whole Sliced	Cut tops 2 inches from root; wash and do not break the skin; if using the pressure cooker, peel before cooking.	25-45 15-25		15-18 8-10	10	90	2½	Serve with butter, salt and pepper; or with vinegar or lemon juice.
CARROTS	Wash; scrape or peel. Leave whole if small; slice or dice.	15-20	20-30	2-3	5-8	35-45 young covered	1½	Season with butter, salt and pepper; pour over a little orange juice and melted butter; garnish with mint. Add tarragon to boiled carrots.
CELERY	Clean with brush; remove leaves and cut into ¾-inch pieces. Time is for 1½ bunches.	30-40		10-12				Serve with Vegetable Sauce.
CORN	Remove leaves and silk; cook in boiling water to cover when boiling. 8-10 cobs.	6-10		5	10-12			Serve with butter, salt and pepper.

Cooking Time in Minutes

Kind	Preparation	Boil	Steam	Pressure Cook	Pan-Sauté (shred)	Bake 350°	Amount for 6 in Pounds	Serving Suggestions
EGGPLANT	Peel just before using to avoid discolouration; dice or slice.	10-20				30	1½-2	Garnish with onions or tomatoes. Serve with cheese or celery.
MUSHROOMS	Tender, fresh mushrooms need no peeling; leave whole, slice or dice.			1	4-5			Season with butter, salt and pepper. Serve with green pepper, onion or tomato.
PARSNIPS	Peel or scrape; cut lengthwise or crosswise; remove cores if tough.	20-30	30-45	10			1½	Serve with butter, salt and pepper and chopped parsley.
PEAS	Remove from pods; rinse.	15-25	15-25	1			3	May be cooked with mint; drain, serve with salt, pepper and butter or Vegetable Sauce.
POTATOES Irish	Wash and peel, or cook in skins.	35-40	40-50	8-10		425° 50-60	2	Serve with melted butter, finely chopped parsley, and salt and pepper; may be sprinkled with paprika. Sweet potatoes may be served with a sweet sauce or candied.
Sweet/ Yams	Scrub and cook in skins.	30-40	34-45	8		425° 50	2	
SALISFY	Scrub, peel and cut into slices or cubes.	20-25						Serve with Vegetable Sauce or butter, salt and pepper.
SQUASH Hubbard	Cut into chunks, remove seeds and bake; for mashing peel, dice and steam.	35-45	45-50	12-15		60-90	2-3	Season with butter, salt and pepper.
Pepper and Acorn	Cut in half; remove seeds and bake or steam cut side down.		45			50		Fill hollow with butter, salt and pepper and a little brown sugar or honey.
ZUCCHINI	Wash, do not peel. Slice thinly and boil or sauté. Can be parboiled and baked under a topping of buttered crumbs (leave whole or cut in lengthwise halves).	5-10	5		7		3	Serve with butter, salt, pepper. Grated Cheddar cheese, chopped fresh tomato are good additions. Often served in a macedoine of vegetables.

Cooking Time in Minutes*

Kind	Preparation	Boil	Steam	Pressure Cook	Pan-Sauté (shred)	Bake 350°	Amount for 6 in Pounds	Serving Suggestions
STRONG								
Broccoli	Soak in salted water 10 minutes, trim and cut off flowerets from main stalk; split ends of stalks.	15-20	20-30	1½-2			2	Serve with melted butter, salt and pepper or Cheese Sauce, Hollandaise Sauce or lemon mayonnaise.
Brussel Sprouts	Remove wilted leaves; leave whole.	12-20	20-25	2			1½	Serve with butter, salt and pepper or Vegetable Sauce.
Cabbage	Remove wilted outside leaves; cut into quarters or shred. 1 pound = ½ head.	5-15	10-20	1-1½	5-8		1	Serve with butter and seasonings or Cheese Sauce.
Cauliflower	Remove leaves and stem; soak 10 minutes in salted water; leave whole or divide into flowerets.	10-20 / 25-30 whole	15-30	2-3			2½	Serve with butter and seasonings or Cheese Sauce.
Onions	Peel onions under water; quarter or leave whole.	30-40	25-30	5-8	10-15	45-60	1½	Serve with butter and seasonings or either Cheese or Vegetable Sauce.
Turnips Yellow or White	Wash, cut in ½-inch slices and peel; dice.	20-30	25-35	10	5-8		1½	May be cooked with a little chopped onion; season, serve in cubes or mash.
LEAFY								
Spinach, Beet Tops	Remove roots, coarse stems; wash in warm water and rinse twice. Cook in water which clings to leaves—no more!	8-10	15-20		5-6		3	Serve with butter, salt and pepper or a little chopped crisp bacon; nutmeg gives extra flavour.
Swiss Chard	Remove roots, coarse stems; wash in warm water and rinse twice. Cook in water which clings to leaves—no more!	10-15	20-35	5	8-10		3	Serve with butter, salt and pepper or a little chopped crisp bacon; nutmeg gives extra flavour.
Kale	Remove roots, coarse stems; wash in warm water and rinse twice. Cook in water which clings to leaves—no more!	15-25		3½-5	5-8		3	Serve with butter, salt and pepper or a little chopped crisp bacon; nutmeg gives extra flavour.

*Cooking times for vegetables which have been frozen will be somewhat less. If vegetables are commercially frozen, follow cooking directions on package. Sauces mentioned may be found in Chapter 3.

BAKED POTATOES

Choose thick, regular-shaped potatoes for baking. If time is scarce, potatoes may be parboiled for 10 minutes while waiting for oven temperature to be reached.

1. Scrub and rinse potatoes; prick with a fork in several places and grease lightly.
2. Place on rack in oven 400-425°; bake 45-60 minutes. New potatoes will require longer cooking than old.
3. Crack or cut skins to allow steam to escape immediately on taking from oven.
4. Serve uncovered; add 1 pat butter to each.
5. Garnish with parsley and/or paprika; or add 1-2 tablespoons of any of the following toppings:

   divide ½ cup sour cream evenly on top of 6 baked potatoes and sprinkle chopped chives or finely chopped green onions and/or crumbled crisp bacon on each

   mix sour cream with ½ cup grated Cheddar cheese (or use part blue cheese) and 1 tablespoon chopped chives or finely chopped green onions

   mix sour cream with 1 tablespoon chopped fresh dill or 1 teaspoon dried dill, or 2 teaspoons prepared horseradish

   mix sour cream with 3 tablespoons chopped peeled cucumber, 3 tablespoons chopped radishes and 1 tablespoon minced onion. Or, use 1 8-ounce package cream cheese mixed with ⅓ cup light cream and beaten until light and fluffy. Add 1 teaspoon lemon juice, ½ teaspoon garlic salt and 1 tablespoon chopped chives.

BAKED STUFFED POTATOES

Can be baked and stuffed one day and, if desired, reheated the next.

6 baked potatoes	2 tablespoons butter
¾ teaspoon salt	¼ to ⅓ cup hot milk
⅛ teaspoon pepper	

1. Cut a slice from the top of the potatoes; scoop out the insides.
2. Mash; add seasonings, butter and milk; beat until light. Stir in any of the additions desired.
3. Refill shells, heat in hot oven until mixture is heated through and lightly browned, about 20 minutes.
4. Garnish with parsley and/or paprika.

For extra flavour, use toppings suggested in preceding recipe or any of the additions below.

1 tablespoon very finely chopped parsley or chives	¼ cup minced raw onion
1 cup grated Cheddar cheese	½ cup sour cream
½ to 1 cup chopped, cooked meat—ham, veal, chicken or hash	

SCALLOPED POTATOES

1. Wash potatoes; cut in 1/8-inch slices.
2. Butter a baking dish; put in a layer of potatoes; sprinkle with salt and pepper, flour and dot over with small pieces of butter. Minced onion may be added.
3. Repeat until dish is full.
4. Pour in milk until it may be seen through top layer.
5. Bake at 325° 1 hour, or until soft. Cover dish during first half of cooking. Too hot an oven will curdle the milk.

SCALLOPED POTATOES WITH BACON

Omit butter from Scalloped Potatoes; place strips of cooked bacon in layers with potatoes, having potatoes on top, or cut bacon or ham in small pieces and put between layers of potatoes.

SCARLET SCALLOPED POTATOES

1. Mix together ¼ cup flour, ½ cup skim milk powder, ½ teaspoon salt, ¼ teaspoon pepper, dash of seasoning salt.
2. Butter a casserole dish, and in it place alternating layers of thinly sliced potatoes (about 6), 1 cup minced onion and the mixed dry ingredients; dot generously with butter.
3. Pour over it a mixture of 1 20-ounce can of mixed vegetable juices and 1 cup of water.
4. Cover, and bake at 350° for 2 hours. Remove cover at the beginning of the last half hour. Serves 8.

POTATOES AND CREAM IN FOIL

4 medium potatoes	chopped parsley
3 tablespoons butter	½ cup grated Cheddar cheese
salt and pepper	½ cup cream
seasoning salt	

1. Peel potatoes and cut lengthwise in strips.
2. Tear off a length of aluminum foil, preferably heavy-duty or a double thickness of regular foil, about 2½ times the length of the mass of potatoes when centred on it.
3. Dot the potatoes with butter, seasonings, parsley and cheese.
4. Triple-fold cut edges at the top and one of the sides; holding the package with the open side up, pour in the cream; seal remaining side to form a tightly closed package, but do not press!
5. Place on cookie sheet or shallow pan and bake at 425° for about 45 minutes.
6. Serve in opened foil package in a basket or on a platter. Sprinkle with extra chopped parsley.

FRANCONIA POTATOES

Potatoes are baked and served around a roast.

1. Wash and peel potatoes; soak in ice water 30 minutes; dry.
2. Place in roasting pan, around meat; sprinkle with salt and pepper.
3. Bake at 350° until tender, 1-1½ hours, turning them occasionally in the melted fat.

FRENCH FRIED POTATOES

Recipe in French Frying, Chapter 21.

BROILER-FRIED POTATOES

1. Wash and peel 6 medium potatoes; cut lengthwise into strips ½ inch thick.
2. Soak in a bowl of cold water for 30 minutes.
3. Preheat the broiler for 5 minutes.
4. Meanwhile drain potatoes and dry thoroughly with a clean tea towel.
5. Place potatoes in a broiler pan; pour over ½ cup cooking oil and stir well.
6. Broil 15 to 18 minutes, stirring frequently until brown.
7. Season with salt; serve immediately.

MASHED POTATOES

6 medium-sized peeled potatoes, boiled	½ teaspoon salt
	pepper
¼ to ⅓ cup hot milk	parsley or chives
1½ tablespoons butter	

1. Mash potatoes or put through ricer.
2. Add milk, butter and seasonings.
3. Beat until very light; pile lightly in hot dish.
4. Sprinkle with very finely chopped parsley or chives.
5. Serve at once.

DUCHESS POTATOES

Use fresh or leftover mashed potatoes or instant mashed potatoes.

1. Prepare mashed potatoes; 1 egg or 2 yolks, well beaten, may be added.
2. Butter a shallow baking dish; put in potatoes, mound in centre, smooth the surface and brush over with melted butter. Brown in a 400° oven.

POTATO NESTS: Add 1 slightly beaten egg yolk to 2 cups stiff, mashed potatoes and form mixture into 4 nests on a greased cookie sheet. Brush with egg white. Fill nests with cooked mixed vegetables; sprinkle with grated Cheddar cheese and bake 25 to 30 minutes at 350° until lightly browned and cheese melts.

POTATO ROSES: Add 2 egg yolks, 3 tablespoons butter and seasonings to 2 cups hot mashed potatoes and beat until very light. Put mixture into pastry bag with large rose tube and force out mixture onto a buttered cookie sheet. Brown at 400°. Use as a garnish for fish or meat.

POTATO PUFFS

3 cups warm mashed potatoes	salt and pepper to taste
3 eggs, separated	½ to 1 teaspoon minced onion
2 tablespoons chopped parsley	

1. Beat egg yolks; add mashed potatoes, parsley, seasonings and onions.
2. Beat egg whites until stiff; fold into potato mixture.
3. Bake in greased muffin pans at 350° until browned.

POTATO BOATS (MOCK BAKED STUFFED POTATOES)

1. Shape squares of aluminum foil into boat-like containers.
2. Prepare mashed potatoes using fresh or instant mashed potatoes, season and add butter. For extra flavour, stir in any of the additions given at the end of the recipe for Baked Stuffed Potatoes, page 243.
3. Pile potato mixture into boats and heat in oven at 375° until mixture is heated through, about 20 minutes.
4. Serve potatoes in boats garnished with parsley, sliced stuffed olives or chopped chives or with a dollop of sour cream, sprinkled with chopped chives.

Hash Brown Potatoes, a household favourite.

HASH BROWN POTATOES

1. Dice boiled potatoes; thinly sliced onions, chopped pimento or finely chopped green pepper may be added for additional flavour.
2. Melt butter or fat in a heavy frying pan and brown potatoes until crisp.
3. Turn and brown on the other side. Season.

SOUR CREAM POTATO CASSEROLE

Ideal for the party buffet.

½ cup finely chopped onion	½ cup grated Cheddar cheese
2 tablespoons butter	2 eggs
5 large potatoes, boiled or	1 cup sour cream
5 cups cooked potatoes	salt, pepper
¼ cup dry bread crumbs	

1. Sauté onions in butter until soft.
2. Slice the cooked potatoes into a buttered 1-quart casserole dish. and sprinkle over them the onions, crumbs and ¼ cup grated cheese.
3. Beat together eggs, sour cream and seasonings and pour over the potatoes.
4. Sprinkle on the remaining ¼ cup cheese and bake at 350° until tender. Garnish with chopped parsley. Serves 6.

FRUITY SWEET POTATOES

6 medium sweet potatoes	dash of salt
1 tablespoon cornstarch	1 cup orange juice or
⅓ cup brown sugar	1 cup crushed pineapple and
¼ cup sugar	juice
3 tablespoons melted butter	1 tablespoon orange rind, grated

1. Boil potatoes in skins until tender, about 30 minutes; or use canned sweet potatoes. Drain.
2. Combine cornstarch, sugars and melted butter in a saucepan and mix until smooth; add remaining ingredients and cook, with frequent stirring until thick.
3. Peel potatoes, cut in halves, ½-inch slices or leave whole if not too large.
4. Arrange potatoes in a shallow, greased baking dish and pour the fruit sauce over them.
5. Cover dish and bake at 350° for about 20 minutes; remove cover and bake 15 minutes longer. Serves 6-8.

As a speedy variation, combine ½ cup liquid from canned sweet potatoes, the juice and grated rind of 1 orange, 3 tablespoons butter and 2 tablespoons sugar; heat to boiling. Add potatoes and heat through, turning only once.

HERBED GREEN BEANS

1 pound green beans	½ clove garlic, crushed
⅓ cup butter	¼ teaspoon basil
⅓ cup chopped onion	¼ teaspoon rosemary
⅓ cup chopped celery	salt and pepper

1. Cut green beans into lengthwise strips.
2. Sauté onion, celery and garlic in butter until just tender.
3. Add beans and seasoning; cover and cook over low heat until tender, about 15 minutes.

GREEN BEANS VINAIGRETTE

½ cup tart French dressing	6 strips crisp-cooked bacon
1 tablespoon finely chopped onion	⅓ cup sliced ripe olives
	⅓ cup commercial sour cream
2 pounds cooked green beans, drained	1 tablespoon vinegar
	½ teaspoon prepared mustard
6 hard-cooked eggs, chopped	salt to taste

1. Shake together the French dressing and minced onion and pour over the green beans arranged in a shallow dish; turn beans to coat thoroughly and let chill several hours.
2. Toss together the chopped hard-cooked eggs, crumbled bacon and ripe olives with a mixture of sour cream, vinegar and mustard; add salt to taste.
3. At serving time, arrange marinated green beans on a platter and spoon egg and bacon mixture over top. Makes 8 servings.

GREEN BEANS RISI

An easy and very festive dish.
Combine equal parts of cooked julienne green beans and cooked rice. Add butter and salt and pepper. Stir in chopped pimento and toasted slivered almonds.

QUICK SHREDDED BEETS (PAN-SAUTÉED BEETS)

Peel and coarsely shred 6-8 medium-sized beets. Add ¼ cup water, 2 tablespoons vinegar and 1 teaspoon sugar. Cover and cook 10 minutes or until tender—stirring twice during cooking. Add butter and season with salt and pepper.

HARVARD BEETS

8 to 10 cooked beets	¼ cup wine vinegar
½ cup sugar	¾ cup water
1 tablespoon cornstarch	2 tablespoons butter
¼ teaspoon salt	
dash of pepper	

1. Cut beets in slices or cubes or use canned rosebud beets.
2. Mix sugar, cornstarch, seasonings; add vinegar and water. Stir until smooth.
3. Cook until thick; add beets and let stand 30 minutes where they will keep hot.
4. Add butter just before serving.

ORANGE BEETS

Follow recipe for Harvard Beets, substituting orange juice for the vinegar and reducing sugar to ¼ cup.

BEETS AND PINEAPPLE

Follow recipe for Harvard Beets, substituting 1 cup pineapple tidbits (include some juice) and 1 tablespoon lemon juice for vinegar and water. Reduce sugar to 2 tablespoons and use brown sugar.

QUICK SHREDDED CABBAGE (PAN-SAUTÉED CABBAGE)

1. Split a medium-size head of fresh green cabbage; then shred coarsely with a sharp knife and cut shreds crosswise into about ½-inch lengths.
2. Place cabbage in a heavy saucepan. Sprinkle generously with salt and pepper; add ½ teaspoon monosodium glutamate. Dribble over it 2-3 tablespoons of melted butter or cooking oil. Add a very small amount of water (scarcely more than enough to cover bottom of pan).
3. Cover and cook quickly over high heat. Remove cover to stir through a couple of times. Total cooking time will be 5 to 7 minutes or when cabbage has wilted (no longer "crunchy"), is still green and has body.
4. Remove from heat and serve immediately. Serves 6.

   Beet tops, escarole, spinach and chard can be cooked in the same way.

RED CABBAGE AND RAISINS

4 cups shredded red cabbage	⅓ cup water
3 tablespoons raisins	1½ tablespoons brown sugar
2½ tablespoons lemon juice	dash of ground cloves

1. Thoroughly combine all ingredients in a saucepan.
2. Cover and cook slowly with occasional stirring until cabbage is tender, about 10 minutes.
3. Add more water if needed.

GLAZED CARROTS OR PARSNIPS

6 medium-sized carrots	½ teaspoon salt
1½ tablespoons butter	dash of pepper
½ cup sugar	⅓ cup stock

1. Wash and peel carrots; cut in half lengthwise.
2. Cook in boiling, salted water 15 minutes; drain; reserve ⅓ cup stock.
3. Add butter, sugar, stock and seasonings; cook carefully until tender and glazed, turning in the syrup.
   1 tablespoon fresh chopped mint may be added while glazing.

CHEESE-GLAZED CARROTS

1. Prepare and boil carrots as in preceding recipe.
2. Dip each half in honey (¼ cup) and sprinkle each with grated Cheddar cheese (1 cup). Broil or bake in a hot oven until cheese melts.

MAPLE-GLAZED CARROTS AND ONIONS

6 medium-sized carrots	4 tablespoons butter
6 small white onions	½ cup maple-flavoured syrup

1. Peel carrots; halve crosswise, then quarter lengthwise. Peel onions.
2. Cook carrots and onions together, covered, in boiling salted water in a medium-size frying pan 30 minutes, or until tender; drain. Return to frying pan.
3. Add butter and syrup. Cook slowly, stirring several times, 10 minutes, or until vegetables are glazed. Serves 6.

QUICK SHREDDED CARROTS (PAN-SAUTÉED CARROTS)

Peel and shred coarsely 8 carrots. Add 3 tablespoons butter and 3 tablespoons water. Cover and cook about 10 minutes or until tender, stirring twice. If necessary, add more water during cooking. Season.

BAKED CARROTS

1. Peel carrots, cut in half lengthwise, if large, and place in a shallow casserole with a little water—about ¼-½ inch depth.
2. Dot with a little butter and sprinkle with salt and pepper.
3. Cover tightly and bake until tender—about 35-45 minutes at 350°. Old carrots can be grated or sliced for baking.

CAULIFLOWER AU GRATIN

1. Boil a whole cauliflower; place on serving dish.
2. Cover with buttered crumbs; brown in hot oven.
3. Pour 1 cup Cheese Sauce (page 83) around cauliflower and serve.

CAULIFLOWER WITH CURRY SAUCE

1. Boil a whole cauliflower.
2. In 2 tablespoons butter, sauté until soft 1 small peeled apple, chopped, and 1 medium onion, sliced.
3. Blend in 2 tablespoons flour and 1 teaspoon curry powder and add 1 cup water (use cooking water from cauliflower) to make a smooth sauce.
4. Simmer 5 minutes and pour over cauliflower.
5. Sprinkle with paprika and chopped parsley.

CORN ON THE COB

There are two "musts" for corn on the cob. It must be freshly picked and it must not be overcooked!

1. Have a large open kettle about ⅔ filled with rapidly boiling water.
2. Husk corn, removing all the silk.
3. Drop cobs, one by one, into the water so as not to cool the water too quickly. Cover.
4. When water returns to boiling point, time the cooking from 4 to 8 minutes. (Test the kernel for tenderness with the point of a knife at the end of 4 minutes.)
5. Drain, serve at once with butter, salt and pepper.

ROASTED CORN

Dampen the husks of the corn with salted water (use sea water if you're a Maritimer). Lay the ears on hot but well-burned-down coals. There must be no flames. Turn frequently to prevent the husks from becoming burned through. Cook 8 to 10 minutes. Serve with butter, salt and pepper.

CORN IN FOIL

This method is recommended for the barbecue. Husk corn and sprinkle with water. Brush with soft butter and season with salt and pepper. Wrap snugly in foil. Cook 10 minutes on the grill, turning frequently.

CORN PUDDING

2 cups cooked kernel corn	3 eggs
2 tablespoons sugar	2 tablespoons melted butter
1 teaspoon salt	2 cups hot milk
⅛ teaspoon pepper	

1. Chop the corn; add seasonings.
2. Add eggs, slightly beaten, then butter and milk.
3. Pour into greased baking dish or ramekins.
4. Oven poach until firm at 350° for 30-45 minutes. Serve with broiled tomatoes and bacon. Serves 4-6.

CUCUMBERS IN CREAM DILL SAUCE

These are known as "Soused Cucumbers" in the Lunenburg area of Nova Scotia.

Slice 3 medium-sized cucumbers *thinly*; sprinkle with salt and leave for about 20 minutes. Combine 2 cups sugar, 2 cups white vinegar and ¼ teaspoon white pepper. Press as much juice as possible from the cucumber slices and marinate in the vinegar. Again press as much liquid as possible from the cucumbers and combine them with a sauce made by mixing 1 cup mayonnaise with ½ cup whipped cream, ½ cup sour cream and 2 tablespoons finely chopped fresh dill. Add salt and white pepper to taste. Serve with cold meats and dishes of Russian or Scandinavian origin; serve in place of tossed salad.

BROILED EGGPLANT

This vegetable is also known as Eggfruit and Aubergine.

Cut a large eggplant into ½-inch slices, leaving the skin on. Blend ½ cup of softened butter with ½ teaspoon basil, ½ teaspoon oregano, a dash of salt and paprika. Spread each side of the eggplant slices with the seasoned butter. Broil until tender, turning once. If desired, grated Parmesan cheese may be sprinkled on each slice just after turning.

EGGPLANT PARMIGIANA

Slice eggplant into ½-inch slices. Bread each slice by dipping first into a pan containing beaten egg, then into another containing fine, soft bread crumbs. Pan fry lightly in cooking oil until golden. In a large shallow casserole, alternate slices of eggplant and Mozzarella cheese and pour over them the contents of an 8-ounce tin of tomato sauce. Sprinkle with ½ teaspoon basil, ½ teaspoon oregano and ½ cup grated Parmesan or Cheddar cheese. Bake at 325° until the cheese melts.

SCALLOPED EGGPLANT

1 medium-sized eggplant	1 teaspoon salt
3 tablespoons butter	1 tablespoon brown sugar
3 tablespoons flour	1 cup grated old Cheddar
1 medium-sized onion, chopped	cheese
3 large ripe tomatoes	½ cup fine dry bread crumbs

1. Peel and dice eggplant; cook in boiling salted water for 10 minutes, drain thoroughly and transfer to an 8-cup buttered casserole.
2. Melt butter, blend in flour and stir over low heat until a smooth paste is formed.
3. Peel and cut up tomatoes, add onions and stir into butter mixture.
4. Sprinkle with salt and brown sugar; continue cooking over low direct heat, stirring constantly, until mixture is thick and smooth. Pour over eggplant.
5. Combine cheese and bread crumbs; sprinkle over casserole. Bake at 350° until bubbly and brown, about 30 minutes. Serves 6.

Artichoke

FRENCH ARTICHOKES

Artichokes are usually about 4 inches high and are a great delicacy.

1. Trim stems, leaving on about ½ an inch, remove outside bottom leaves and cut off any discoloured tips; do this just before cooking to prevent discolouration.
2. Wash thoroughly to remove all sand; stand upright in a deep saucepan and do not allow the vegetable to tip over.
3. Sprinkle each with salt and about 2 teaspoons salad oil.
4. Pour in boiling water to a depth of 1 inch; garlic cloves or onion can be added for extra flavour.
5. Cook with a cover on the saucepan for 45 to 60 minutes, adding a little more water if necessary.
6. Vegetable is cooked when a leaf can be pulled out easily and the base is soft.
7. Lift out with tongs or 2 spoons, invert to drain and cut off the base of the stem.
8. Serve with Drawn Butter Sauce, Cheese Sauce or Hollandaise Sauce (Chapter 3).

STEWED MUSHROOMS

1 pound mushrooms	1 cup rich milk or stock
4 tablespoons butter	½ teaspoon salt
2 tablespoons flour	dash of pepper

1. Wash mushrooms; peel caps only if discoloured.
2. Slice whole mushrooms lengthwise or chop stems separately.
3. Melt butter in saucepan; add mushrooms, sauté 2 minutes.
4. Sprinkle with flour; when flour is blended, add milk or stock.
5. Cook slowly 5 to 15 minutes or until tender; season, serve on fingers of toast; garnish with parsley. Serves 3.

Mushrooms may be sprinkled with 1 teaspoon lemon juice before serving.

GOURMET MUSHROOMS

Using 1 pound mushrooms, ¼ cup finely chopped onion and ⅓ cup of butter, prepare as Stewed Mushrooms, substituting the following for the liquid:

½ cup white wine	1 teaspoon brown sugar
1 teaspoon soy sauce	

MUSHROOMS À LA RUSSE

To 1 pound sautéed mushrooms add 1 teaspoon lemon juice, 1-1½ cups sour cream and 1 teaspoon paprika. Heat through; serve on grilled steak.

STUFFED MUSHROOMS

6 large mushrooms	1 teaspoon parsley, finely chopped
3 tablespoons chopped cooked meat—veal, chicken, ham or lobster	⅓ teaspoon salt
	dash of pepper
3 tablespoons bread crumbs	3 tablespoons butter
1 tablespoon finely chopped walnuts (optional)	⅔ cup tomato sauce or diluted tomato paste
1 teaspoon minced onion	½ cup buttered crumbs

1. Wash mushrooms, set aside the caps. Chop stems finely.
2. Mix meat, crumbs, walnuts, onions, parsley, stems and seasonings; cook in butter 3 minutes.
3. Add about 3 tablespoons tomato sauce to mixture to moisten and fill mushroom caps with the mixture; cover with buttered crumbs.
4. Place in baking pan; pour remaining tomato sauce around mushrooms. Bake at 400° for 15 minutes. Serves 3.

FRIED ONIONS

6 medium onions	salt
3 tablespoons butter	

1. Peel onions; slice thinly.
2. Melt butter in frying pan; add onions; sauté until browned, turning frequently; season.

FRIED ONION RINGS

3 medium-large onions	½ teaspoon salt
¾ cup milk	fat
½ cup flour	

1. Slice onions across into rings.
2. Dip in milk; drain and dredge lightly in seasoned flour.
3. Sauté in fat or fry in deep fat (French Frying, Chapter 21).

GLAZED ONIONS

3 cups small onions	4 tablespoons butter
4 tablespoons sugar (or honey)	

1. Peel onions; parboil 15 minutes; drain and dry.
2. Melt butter, add sugar, mix well; add onions; cook carefully until lightly browned, about 20 minutes.

PARTY ONIONS

6 large white onions
⅓ cup dry white table wine
½ teaspoon salt
3 tablespoons corn syrup

1 or two whole cloves
1 tablespoon butter
1 tablespoon flour

1. Cut peeled onions into ½-inch slices and place in a heavy pan with wine, salt, syrup and cloves.
2. Cover and simmer until onions are tender, about 20 minutes.
3. Thicken with blended butter and flour.
4. Garnish with chopped parsley. Serves 4-6.

PAN-FRIED PARSNIPS

A good way to use up leftover cooked parsnips.
Cut boiled parsnips in 1-inch pieces. (If the parsnip has a hard central core, remove it.) Pan fry in a little beef dripping or butter until brown.

STUFFED PEPPERS

6 sweet green peppers
1 cup cooked rice
½ teaspoon salt
1 tablespoon butter, melted

1½ cups ground meat
¼ teaspoon grated onion
tomato juice, about ½ cup
½ cup buttered crumbs

1. Select peppers of suitable size and shape for stuffing; cut slice from end; remove tongue and seeds. Parboil for 5 minutes.
2. Combine next 5 ingredients; add enough tomato juice to moisten mixture.
3. Fill peppers with the mixture; cover with buttered crumbs.
4. Place in baking pan, add a little hot water to the pan to a depth of about ¼ inch.
5. Bake at 375° for 30 minutes.
6. Serve as an entrée or luncheon dish.

STUFFED ONIONS

Onions may be parboiled 10 minutes, centres removed and finished as Stuffed Peppers.

STUFFED TOMATOES

Remove centres of raw tomatoes; do not peel. Stuff and bake without added water.

STUFFING FOR PEPPERS, ONIONS OR TOMATOES

For each pepper allow ¾ to 1 cup of stuffing
For each onion allow ½ cup of stuffing
For each tomato allow ½ cup of stuffing

Cooked and minced ham, veal or chicken.

Ground beef which has been browned in a little fat with green pepper, onion or tomato (do not use the same ingredient in the stuffing as the original vegetable).

Pimento or cream style corn.

Cooked spaghetti in tomato sauce, sprinkled with grated cheese.

Baked Stuffed Tomatoes.

BAKED SQUASH

1. Cut squash in halves; remove seeds and stringy fibres.
2. Place downward in baking pan, having a little water in the pan; cover; bake in a moderate oven until soft, 1 to 1½ hours.
3. Scrape from shell; mash; season with butter, pepper and salt. If squash is small, serve in halves, thirds or quarters, without mashing; add butter and, if desired, any of 1 teaspoon brown sugar, 1 teaspoon honey or 1 tablespoon drained crushed pineapple to each half.

STEAMED SQUASH

Cut squash in pieces; remove seeds and fibres; place downward in steamer. Steam until soft, about 30 to 40 minutes; remove skin, mash and season.

PUMPKIN

Cook as Steamed Squash. For pies, do not season; scrape from shell and press through a sieve.

STEAMED VEGETABLE MARROW

Sometimes called Summer Squash.
1. Cut marrow in slices 1-inch thick; remove skin.
2. Place on plate in steamer.
3. Steam until tender, about 20 to 30 minutes.
4. Life out carefully; serve with butter, pepper and salt.

Marrow may be mashed and seasoned with butter, pepper and salt.

SAUTÉED ZUCCHINI SQUASH

Wash, and slice into thin crosswise slices; sauté in a little butter until tender, turning them frequently. Season with salt and pepper, basil or marjoram. For additional flavour, add chopped onion or ½ clove garlic, crushed in the butter while sautéing. Sprinkle with grated cheese, chopped parsley or chives. Sour cream or tomato sauce may be served with the zucchini.

ZUCCHINI MEDLEY

Sauté zucchini slices with chopped green pepper and ½ garlic clove, crushed, in butter, until tender. Stir in 1 or 2 chopped fresh tomatoes, heat through. Season and serve.

BROILED RED OR GREEN TOMATOES

1. Wipe tomatoes; cut across in thick slices or halves.
2. Season with salt and pepper; brush over with butter and sprinkle with seasoned salt and fine cracker crumbs.
3. Broil until tender, about 5 minutes.
   For added flavour, crush ½ clove of garlic in the butter, blend and brush over tomatoes. Serve with sour cream.

TOMATOES WITH DILL SAUCE

1. Cut tomatoes in half crosswise. Season cut side with salt and pepper. Dot with butter.
2. Broil, until heated through.
3. Spoon over each a mixture made by combining ½ cup sour cream, ¼ cup mayonnaise, 2 tablespoons finely chopped onion and 1 teaspoon chopped fresh dill (or 1 teaspoon dried dill). Serves 6-8.

CASSEROLE OF TOMATOES

1 28-ounce tin of tomatoes	3 tablespoons butter
½ cup chopped celery	3 tablespoons flour
1 medium onion, chopped or	½ teaspoon salt
thinly sliced	⅛ teaspoon pepper
¼ green pepper, cut in strips	

1. Empty tomatoes into a saucepan, reserving ½ cup of juice. Heat to nearly boiling.
2. Prepare celery, onion and green pepper and cook in butter in a frying pan until nearly tender; add to tomatoes, leaving butter in the frying pan.
3. Combine melted butter, flour and tomato juice to form a smooth paste; stir into tomato mixture. Season.
4. Pour mixture into baking dish; crushed cornflakes and grated cheese may be sprinkled over top. Bake at 350° for 35 minutes. Serves 4-6.

Variation: Omit step 3; add 1 cup Garlic Croutons (page 359).

VEGETABLES ORIENTALE

Crisp but tender vegetables in sweet and sour sauce. Kinds and quantities of vegetables used are flexible.

6-8 large outside celery stalks	1½ cups chicken stock
2 large sweet red peppers	¼ cup brown sugar
1 package fresh spinach	¼ cup cider vinegar
1 head chinese cabbage	2 tablespoons soy sauce
3 tablespoons cooking oil	3 tablespoons cornstarch
1 package frozen snow peas, or	1 5-ounce can water chestnuts,
green beans	drained and sliced

1. Cut celery into diagonal slices, cut red peppers into 1-inch squares, remove any coarse stems from spinach. Shred chinese cabbage.

2. Heat oil in a large frying pan. Stir in celery; push to one side. Stir in red peppers and push to one side. Add peas or beans in the same way.
3. Add 1¼ cups chicken stock and heat to boiling. Cover and steam 5 minutes.
4. Place spinach and cabbage in separate mounds in pan. Cover and steam 5 minutes more or until vegetables are tender but still crisp.
5. Carefully lift vegetables from pan, placing each variety in its own separate mound on a heated deep platter. Keep warm while preparing sauce.
6. Combine sugar, vinegar and soy sauce with vegetable juices in pan, heat to boiling.
7. Blend cornstarch with remaining chicken stock to form a smooth paste. Stir into hot liquid and continue stirring while cooking mixture until thick. Cook and stir for 3 minutes more. Stir in the prepared water chestnuts.
8. Spoon sauce over vegetables on platter. Garnish with toasted almond halves, and serve with additional soy sauce. This is especially delicious served with barbecued chicken or pork tenderloin. Serves 4-6.

RATATOUILLE

This dish from southern France is a casserole of highly flavoured vegetables. It can be completely cooked the day before needed, then reheated or served cold as an accompaniment to hot or cold meats. It may be served cold as an appetizer.

2 medium onions, thinly sliced	1 clove garlic, crushed
3 tablespoons olive or cooking oil	3 tomatoes, peeled
	½ teaspoon basil
1 large green pepper, chopped	½ teaspoon marjoram
1 small eggplant	1½ teaspoons salt
2 zucchini, cut in ½-inch slices	pepper

1. In a large saucepan, sauté onion slices in oil until clear.
2. Add chopped green peppers and sauté 2 minutes more. Remove to a side dish.
3. Add eggplant which has been peeled and cut into finger-length strips about ½ inch wide and ⅓ inch thick. Sauté 1 layer at a time for about 1 minute on each side. Remove to side dish.

4. Sauté zucchini slices in the same way. Stir in 1 clove garlic, crushed, and sauté with the zucchinis.
5. Cut tomatoes in half, crosswise, and squeeze gently to remove seeds. Discard seeds. Chop tomatoes coarsely.
6. Combine all vegetables with remaining oil in saucepan or casserole. Cover and cook over low heat for about 45 minutes, with occasional stirring.
7. Add seasonings and cook 5 minutes longer. Serve hot or cold. Serves 6.

SCALLOPED VEGETABLES

2 cups cooked vegetables	1½ cups buttered crumbs
1 cup medium White Sauce	
grated Cheddar cheese	
(optional)	

1. Use cooked potatoes, cabbage, cauliflower, onions, etc.; place in buttered casserole.
2. Prepare White Sauce (page 79); stir in grated cheese and blend until smooth.
3. Pour sauce over vegetables; cover with buttered crumbs.
4. Bake until crumbs are brown in a moderate oven.

For variety or convenience, ½ can condensed cream of celery or mushroom soup plus ¼ cup of milk may be substituted for White Sauce.

TO USE LEFTOVER COOKED VEGETABLES

1. Reheat in hot Vegetable Sauce, Cheese Sauce or White Sauce (Chapter 3) and serve with meat, or serve on toast or in ramekins; reheat in a frying pan with butter (Hash Brown Potatoes).
2. Marinate in French dressing or serve with mayonnaise in salads.
3. Chop and add to stew, soufflé, scrambled eggs, meat pies, casseroles and soups.
4. Purée or mash for cream soup, croquettes, toppings (Duchess Potatoes).

8 Eggs

EGGS ARE a nutritious food served alone or combined with other foods. They hold ingredients of a batter together by emulsifying them and cause soufflés and meringues to rise by holding in air which expands on heating. Eggs thicken custards and sauces and are used for coating chops and croquettes for breading. High quality protein, iron and vitamins A, B$_2$ and D, all present in eggs, make them a valuable food for young and old. They can be served as an alternative to meat.

GRADES: Eggs are graded according to quality, A1, A, B, C and cracks. Of these, Grade A is the most common in our stores and Grade B eggs are usually reserved for commercial purposes such as bakeries. Within the A grade, there are 5 sizes: extra large, large, medium, small and peewee; of these, large and medium are generally available. Medium-sized eggs are a better buy than large if their price is at least ⅛ less than that of large eggs and are quite acceptable in most recipes.

FRESHNESS: Eggs have a better flavour and are more efficient in baking when they are fresh. A fresh egg has a dull finish on the shell called the "bloom." As the egg ages, this bloom wears off. When an egg is opened out onto a saucer, the thick white (the area of white immediately surrounding the yolk) should be much greater in quantity than the thin, runny white, and should be very thick. The yoke should have a glossy surface, not wrinkled or blotchy, and the cords should be prominent.

CARE: Eggs should be stored in a cold atmosphere above freezing temperature, away from strong-flavoured foods. Wash off eggs just before using them, and when baking remove eggs from the refrigerator earlier so that they may reach room temperature. When storing extra egg yolks, cover with a thin layer of cold water to prevent drying and cover tightly. Whites should be stored in a covered jar. Both may be frozen until needed.

PRESERVATION: Buying eggs when they are cheap and plentiful and storing for several months may be an economical practice if there is a considerable range of prices between the seasons. Sodium silicate, a preservative also called water glass, is obtainable in cans at the drug store. This is diluted with boiling water in a crock, and allowed to cool. The eggs are immersed in it with pointed ends down. They may be kept 8 to 9 months.

TO FREEZE: Pack eggs in the quantity needed for a single use, in small bags, heat seal and pack in a carton.

Whole Eggs: Break into a clean bowl; beat slightly with a fork.

Egg Yolks: Beat slightly. If to be used in making cake or puddings add 1 teaspoon sugar or corn syrup to 6 yolks; for other purposes add ½ teaspoon salt to 6 yolks.

Egg Whites: Separate and pack without beating. They may be beaten like fresh egg white when thawed.

To defrost leave in a warm room 2 hours, or place an envelope of egg in a bowl of warm water 30 minutes.

Equivalents: 1 cup thawed whole egg equals 5 eggs
1½ tablespoons thawed egg white equals 1 egg white
1 tablespoon thawed egg yolk equals 1 egg yolk

COOKING: Eggs should be cooked below the boiling point of water, never boiled. Custards, soufflés and other oven dishes rich in eggs should be baked in an ovenware dish placed in a pan of hot water. This process is called *oven-poaching*. High temperatures cause the egg protein to become rubbery and indigestible.

SEPARATING EGG WHITES AND YOLKS: Collect two bowls, one for yolks and another larger bowl for whites. If more than one egg is being broken, have a saucer convenient. Hit the centre area of a washed egg with a dull knife, just sufficiently to cut the shell sharply, but not to go through into the egg. Using both thumbs, pry the shell apart at this cut and allow the white of the egg to drop into the bowl for egg whites. Transfer the yolk from one section of the shell to the other until all the white has been removed. Drop the yolk into its respective bowl. When separating more than one egg, collect each subsequent white separately in the saucer, check to be sure that it is fresh and that there is no yolk present, then add to the other white in the bowl. If egg yolk does become mixed in with the white, it can sometimes be removed with a spoon.

BEATING EGG WHITES: Egg white is beaten because it will hold a great deal of air. In a batter, this will expand and leaven the product. Egg yolk contains fat and fat in any form will break down this egg white foam or even prevent it from forming. Therefore, it is very important that when separating eggs for beating, no yolk is allowed to become mixed in with the white. Have egg whites at room temperature for beating, choose a deep bowl with a small bottom, and a fine beater. The addition of a little salt or cream of tartar to the egg white stabilizes the foam. Beat only until the egg white is stiff and still shiny. Overbeating knocks out the air and the foam will collapse.

Foamy Omelet with pieces of turkey enclosed.

SOFT AND HARD-COOKED EGGS

Method I—When eggs are at refrigerator temperature.
1. Place eggs in a saucepan of warm water (about 2 cups for 1 or 2 eggs and ½ cup extra for each additional egg).
2. Heat slowly to boiling point; set back where water will keep hot; for soft-cooked eggs 3 to 5 minutes; hard-cooked 20 to 30 minutes.
3. If hard-cooked eggs are to be served cold, immediately after cooking they should be plunged into cold water.

Method II—When eggs are at room temperature.
1. Boil water (about a pint for 1 or 2 eggs and ½ cup extra for each additional egg).
2. Set back where water will keep hot; put in eggs, cover.
3. Let stand. For soft-cooked eggs leave 4 to 6 minutes; hard-cooked eggs 25 to 30 minutes.
4. Cool eggs in cold water if they are to be served cold.
   When many eggs are being cooked together, they may require a longer cooking time. Test 1 egg.

POACHED EGGS

1. Have water, at least 1½ inches deep, boiling gently in a shallow pan; add salt.
2. Break egg into saucer, stir the water briskly and slip the egg into the water.
3. Cover; set back off the burner, where water will keep hot.
4. Cook until white is firm and a film has formed over yolk.
5. Lift up with a skimmer; drain; serve on buttered toast, garnish with parsley.

   To poach many eggs, break into metal sealer rings in a large frying pan of boiling water.

SHIRRED EGGS

1. Butter a ramekin; put in a layer of fine buttered crumbs.
2. Break an egg into a saucer; slip into ramekin.
3. Sprinkle lightly with salt; cover with seasoned, buttered crumbs.
4. Place in shallow pan of hot water; cook in moderate oven until white is firm.

SHIRRED EGGS WITH VEGETABLES

1. Substitute mashed potatoes or finely chopped cooked spinach for the crumb base. Season with butter, pepper and salt.
2. Place in a buttered casserole; smooth the top, then make a depression for each egg. Finish as in preceding recipe.

SCRAMBLED EGGS

1 to 2 eggs per person	salt and pepper
1 tablespoon milk per egg	butter

1. In a bowl, beat eggs, milk and seasonings together.
2. Melt butter in a frying pan, allowing about ½ teaspoon per egg.
3. Pour in egg mixture; cook over low heat until mixture coagulates, stirring only enough to prevent mixture from sticking. Serve on toast.

   Scrambled eggs can be made from a combination of egg yolks and whole eggs; substitute 2 yolks per egg.

CREAMY EGG

Useful when serving a large number.

Use 3 tablespoons of milk to each egg and cook in the same manner as scrambled eggs in the top section of a double boiler over hot (not boiling) water.

Egg yolks can be substituted for whole eggs.

MAKING AN OMELET

1. *Pour Omelet mixture into hot pan.*
2. *Loosen edges with spatula.*
3. *Crease Omelet and fold over.*
4. *Slide Omelet off pan onto a heated plate.*

FRENCH OMELET (Basic Recipe)

1. Using 1-2 eggs per person and 1 tablespoon milk or water per egg, combine eggs, liquid, salt and pepper in a bowl using a fork or rotary beater.
2. Choose a frying pan or omelet pan of suitable size for the number of eggs being used; melt butter in it, allowing about ½ to ¾ teaspoon per egg. Tip the pan to coat bottom and sides.
3. Pour in the mixture and cook over low heat.
4. As the omelet cooks, lift it up with a broad knife or spatula to allow liquid to run underneath, until the whole mixture is lightly cooked.
5. Increase the heat to brown the omelet.
6. Fold into a hot platter; garnish and serve.

FOAMY OMELET (Basic Recipe)

1. Preheat oven to 350°; place serving plate in warming oven to heat.
2. Allow 1 to 2 eggs per person. Separate eggs and beat egg whites until stiff, but not dry.
3. Beat egg yolks with milk or water, allowing 1 tablespoon to each egg; add seasonings.
4. Heat an omelet pan or a frying pan of suitable size for the number of eggs being used; melt butter, allowing about ½ to ¾ teaspoon per egg; have sides and bottom of pan well buttered.
5. Cut and fold beaten egg whites into yolk mixture.
6. Have pan hot, pour in the omelet mixture, spread evenly.
7. Cook over low heat until the omelet has set or congealed in the pan; place in oven until omelet puffs and becomes dry on top.
8. Using a spatula or egg lifter, fold in half and turn out onto a heated plate.
9. Serve with any of: parsley, Spanish sauce, braised chicken livers or sautéed mushrooms. Serve at once.

PARSLEY OMELET

To the ingredients for French or Foamy Omelet stir in finely chopped parsley (about 1 teaspoon per egg); in the case of Foamy Omelet, add the parsley to the yolk mixture.

MEAT OR VEGETABLE OMELET

Prepare ingredients for French or Foamy Omelet. Add to the egg-milk mixture any of minced cooked chicken, veal, bacon, fish or vegetables and finish according to the basic recipe. Or, prepare and cook omelet and when folding it over, enclose hot minced cooked meat or vegetables. Asparagus tips can be left whole. Allow about 1-2 tablespoons meat or vegetable for each egg used.

JELLY OMELET

Omit pepper; add 1 teaspoon sugar per egg to egg whites.
When cooked, spread with jelly, jam or marmalade.
Fold, turn out, sprinkle with fruit sugar.

ORANGE OMELET

Substitute orange juice for milk and add 1 teaspoon of sugar per egg to the beaten egg whites; omit pepper.

CHEESE OMELET

Sprinkle cooked Foamy Omelet with grated cheese. Fold, turn out, garnish and serve.

BREAD OMELET

½ cup bread crumbs	¾ teaspoon salt
½ cup milk	⅛ teaspoon pepper
4 eggs, separated	2 teaspoons butter

1. Add milk to bread crumbs; soak 10 minutes.
2. Add beaten yolk and seasonings.
3. Finish as Foamy Omelet. Serves 4 to 6.

FRENCH TOAST

See page 361.

The basic steps in making a Soufflé.

SOUFFLÉ (Basic Recipe)

4 tablespoons butter	4 egg yolks
½ cup flour	1 cup cooked finely chopped or
1 teaspoon salt	minced vegetables, meat,
dash of pepper	fish—or cheese, grated
1¼ cups milk	4-5 egg whites

1. Melt butter in top of double boiler; blend in flour and seasonings until smooth and gradually add milk. Set oven at 400°.
2. Cook with constant stirring until mixture thickens.
3. In separate bowl beat egg yolks and to them add the hot mixture slowly, with constant stirring; stir in prepared vegetable, meat, fish or cheese.
4. When cool, fold in stiffly beaten egg whites.
5. Pour into a 6-cup or individual greased casserole dishes. Reset oven at 375° and bake 30-35 minutes for a large casserole and about 20 minutes for individual casseroles. The soufflé is cooked when a silver knife can be inserted into the soufflé and be removed without mixture adhering to it. Small soufflés can be unmoulded, if desired. Serve at once. Serves 4-6.

Minced chicken, ham or chopped bacon mixed with chopped green pepper, celery or Cheddar cheese may be added.

MUSHROOM SOUFFLÉ

Sauté ½ pound sliced mushrooms in 3 tablespoons butter. Stir in 2 teaspoons lemon juice. Add at end of step 3 in basic recipe for Soufflé.

CREAMED EGGS

1 cup White Sauce	toast
3 hard-cooked eggs	parsley

1. Prepare White Sauce (page 79). Season.
2. Cut eggs into quarters; place on serving dish or on toast.
3. Pour sauce over eggs; garnish with toast points and parsley. Serves 2-3.

CURRIED EGGS

Add ½ teaspoon curry powder to Creamed Eggs.

TO CHOOSE A SOUFFLÉ MOULD

For a capacity of 6 cups (using 4 eggs) choose a metal or ovenware pan about 5½ inches in diameter and about 3½ inches high. To use a shallower pan or a quantity of mixture greater than 6 cups, a double strip of buttered foil or brown paper can be tied around the dish to increase its capacity. Or choose a dish with a diameter greater than 5½ inches.

Shallow, ovenware soufflé dish is given a buttered paper collar to increase its capacity.

CHEESE AND CRUMB SOUFFLÉ

1 cup milk	1 cup grated cheese
1 cup soft bread crumbs	1 tablespoon butter
3 eggs, separated	½ teaspoon salt

1. Add milk to crumbs. In a separate bowl beat egg yolks.
2. When bread is soft, add cheese, butter, salt and beaten yolks.
3. Beat whites until stiff; fold into yolk mixture.
4. Finish as Soufflé in basic recipe. Serves 4-6.

STUFFED EGGS (DEVILLED EGGS)

1. Hard cook eggs, chill in cold water. Peel off the shell.
2. Cut in halves lengthwise; remove the yolk with a teaspoon.
3. Set the whites aside in pairs.
4. Mash the yolks with a fork until fine and crumbly.
5. Add mayonnaise, prepared mustard, salt and pepper to season.
6. Chopped chives, parsley, minced ham, fried mushrooms or anchovies may be added.
7. Pile the yolk mixture back into the whites. (To force yolk through a pastry tube, omit step 6.)

STUFFED EGGS À LA MODE

Serve as a main dish at lunch with asparagus or broccoli. Lengthwise halves are stuffed and put back together, evenly and neatly. The broad bases are trimmed so that the eggs will stand upright in a serving dish or ramekin. Then the eggs are chilled and dressed with any of these colourful mayonnaise sauces.

WITH HERB SAUCE

STUFFING: 6 mashed yolks, ¼ cup finely chopped water cress, garden cress or parsley, 1 teaspoon prepared mustard, salt and pepper to taste, mixed together throughly.

SAUCE: combine ½ cup mixed finely chopped water cress or garden cress, and parsley. Add a pinch of tarragon and basil, ½ clove garlic, crushed, ½ cup sour cream, ½ cup mayonnaise, 1 teaspoon lemon juice and salt and pepper as needed.

WITH CURRY SAUCE

STUFFING: 6 mashed yolks, ¼ cup chutney, sieved, salt as needed. Blend together until smooth.

SAUCE: 1 cup mayonnaise, 1 tablespoon or more curry powder, 2 teaspoons soy sauce, ⅓ cup cream. Mix until smooth.

WITH TOMATO MAYONNAISE

STUFFING: 6 mashed egg yolks, 2 slices pimento, drained and finely chopped, 1 tablespoon chopped chives, 1 tablespoon ketchup, salt and pepper as needed.

SAUCE: 1 cup mayonnaise, ¼ cup tomato paste or ketchup, ½ teaspoon grated lemon rind, 1 teaspoon lemon juice. Add salt and pepper if tomato paste was used. Stir until smooth.

To Use Leftover Cooked Eggs

Add mayonnaise to make devilled eggs (see preceding recipe), chopped egg filling for sandwiches or salads. Slice to garnish salads, canapés; add to potato salad and aspic. Combine with White Sauce to make scallops, casserole dishes. Sieve to make topping or garnish for creamed mixtures and appetizers.

If eggs are not quite hard-cooked, place in boiling water and continue cooking until whites and yolks are firm.

To Use Leftover Raw Eggs

LEFTOVER EGG YOLKS: Yolks may be used up in any of: scrambled eggs, egg-nogs, French toast, baked custard, custard sauce, butter icing, mashed potatoes, meat patties and for breading chops and croquettes.

LEFTOVER EGG WHITES: Whites may be used up in any of: meringues, seven-minute or boiled frosting, divinity fudge, macaroons, sponge desserts, sherbets, fruit whips, angle cake and white cake.

9 Cheese

CHEESE is a versatile food. Because of its content of high quality protein, it can take the place of meat when served along with other nutritious foods. It adds the finishing touch to a meal when it appears in its many forms on a cheese tray. As a between-meal snack, it is both satisfying and nourishing. Being a milk product, cheese is an excellent source of calcium; cheese or milk must be taken daily if the calcium requirement is to be met. Cheese should be kept in a cool, dry place and wrapped in metal foil.

As in the case of eggs and meat, temperature is the important consideration in cooking. Cheese should be cooked only to the point of melting; beyond that, the proteins become tough and indigestible. Cheese should be combined with foods already cooked, or those requiring very short cooking, and should be cooked at a low temperature.

Varieties of Cheese

Most of the many types of cheese produced are European in origin. Although some are still imported into this country, Canadian cheesemakers are now able to produce nearly all of the famous names in cheese.

There are cheeses with unique flavours and those which provide the characteristic cheese flavour required for soufflés and casseroles. Blue cheeses have a sharp flavour which makes them suitable for appetizers. Aged Cheddar cheese and Swiss cheese (Ementhal) are excellent choices for cooked cheese mixtures and grated toppings, just as they are suitable choices for almost any role requiring cheese.

Cheeses that melt well are Mozzarella, Swiss, Gruyère and Cheddar. Cheeses that grate well are dry and aged Parmesan, Swiss and Cheddar. (To grate one's own cheese is less expensive than to buy it already grated in small containers. Compare the price per pound.) Rich creamy cheeses such as Camembert, Brie and Pont-l'Evêque are runny cheeses with a hard outer crust; they make ideal desserts when served with rounds of French bread, biscuits and fruit.

If one is limited to a few varieties of cheese, always include aged Canadian Cheddar for its all-purpose excellence—and economy.

A Cheese Tray: (centre) Gouda, (under Gouda) Camembert, (clockwise) Swiss, Blue, Brie, Cheddar, Liptauer, Brick, Colby.

YOGURT

Yogurt is really not cheese, but rather a cultured milk product. Because of its similarity to Cottage Cheese, in flavour and use, it is included in this chapter. It is slightly sour in flavour, low in calories and is easily digested. Serve as a snack, a low-calorie meal or a dessert.

To make yogurt, begin with yogurt culture; buy 1 small container of plain yogurt at the store, and use as directed in the recipe following. Save 1 tablespoon yogurt from each batch to serve as a culture for the next.

Heat 4 cups milk in a 2-quart pan carefully only until milk rises to the top of the pan. Remove from heat and cool milk to *lukewarm*. To 1 cup of the lukewarm milk, add 1 tablespoon yogurt and ½ cup skim milk powder; mix thoroughly to dissolve. Stir into remaining milk and mix well. Pour the mixture into 1 large or 5-6 individual non-metallic bowls. Cover with a plate, and cover all with a bath towel and leave in a warm place 4-5 hours, or until thick. Chill well before serving.

For additional flavour, add to the mixture before the long setting period 1 tablespoon drained crushed pineapple or 2 juicy maraschino cherries for each serving. Serves 5-6.

CHEESE AND FRUIT TRAY

The choice of cheeses and fruits used will, of course, be influenced by personal preference and availability. The following provide a pleasant combination of flavours and textures; serve about 4 of them: Gouda, Aged Cheddar, Blue, Camembert, Boursault and Port du Salut with any of luscious apples, pears, grapes and avocados. Home-make jam or jelly and a variety of biscuits can be included.

WINE AND CHEESE PARTY

When the party is held before dinner, allow about 4 ounces of cheese per person when ordering, and about half that amount if the party takes place after dinner. Serve 4-8 different kinds of cheese, according to the number of guests, and use the following as a nuclcus, adding on and subtracting as required: Brie, Boursault, Roquefort or Blue, and Port du Salut. Aged Cheddar and Gouda make good additions. See chart of varieties of cheeses.

Choose a light wine to serve with mild cheese and a heavier wine for the stronger varieties, a combined total of approximately 12 ounces per person.

SOME VARIETIES OF NATIVE AND IMPORTED CHEESE

Name	Origin	Characteristics	Mode of Serving
BLUE	Denmark, France	Semi-hard, white with blue streaks; made from whole, cow's milk	On cheese tray, crushed in mayonnaise and sauces. Mixed with butter and spread on hot steaks
BOURSAULT	France	Soft creamy cheese, high in butterfat. A new-comer to the cheese world	Spread on biscuits for dessert or serve on cheese tray
BRICK	Early Mennonites in America	Semi-hard, white coloured with tiny gas holes; flavour strong, between Limburger and Cheddar; made from whole cows' milk	On cheese tray, with salads
BRIE	Paris, France	Soft, mild cheese similar to Camembert; made from whole cows' milk	On cheese tray; for desserts
CAMEMBERT	Camembert, France	Soft, cream-coloured, full-flavoured cheese; made from whole cows' milk	On cheese tray; for desserts
CHEDDAR (Canadian Cheese)	Cheddar, England	Hard, yellow to orange in colour; mild to nippy in flavour according to age; made from cows' milk, whole or partly skimmed	On cheese tray. Grated in sauces, casseroles
COTTAGE	Universal	Soft, white, curdy with mild, sour flavour; made from whole or skimmed cows' milk	In a dish on cheese tray; in salads; cheese cake
CREAM	Not known	Soft, smooth; mild and slightly sour flavour; made from cows' milk and cream; often pimento, fruits or nuts added	As a spread for sandwiches, crackers; in balls, or slices on salads
EDAM	Holland	Hard, red-coated orange-coloured, rubbery cheese; shape of a flattened ball, flavour of Cheddar; from cows' milk, partly skimmed	On cheese tray
GORGONZOLA	Gorgonzola, Italy	Semi-hard, cream coloured, marbled with blue mould; nippy flavour	On cheese tray; with salads; as an appetizer
GOUDA	Holland	Semi-hard, flavour similar to Edam; made from partly skimmed cows' milk	On cheese tray; spread on crackers
GRUYÈRE	Gruyère, Switzerland	Hard with gas holes; salty flavour; made from partly skimmed cows' milk. In this country it is usually sold in the processed form, in individual foil-wrapped portions	On cheese tray

SOME VARIETIES OF NATIVE AND IMPORTED CHEESE—*Continued*

Name	Origin	Characteristics	Mode of Serving
LIMBURGER	Germany, Belgium	Soft, very full flavoured with a strong aroma; made from cows' milk, partly skimmed	Spread on sandwiches and crackers
MOZZARELLA	Italy	Firm, cream coloured unripened; usually sold in slices	On cheese tray; in casserole mixtures
MUENSTER	Muenster, Germany	Semi-hard, strong flavour not quite as strong as Limburger; usually a mixture of cows' and goats' milk	Spread on sandwiches and crackers
OKA	Trappist Monasteries— France, Canada	Semi-hard rubbery with a flavour between Cheddar and Limburger; made from whole cows' milk	On cheese tray
PARMESAN	Parma, Italy	Hard cheese with a granular texture, sharp flavour	On spaghetti; for seasoning and toppings
PONT-L'ÉVÊQUE	France	Runny, rich texture	On cheese tray; as a dessert
PORT DU SALUT	France	Semi-soft, buttery, mild to mellow flavour; creamy yellow with tiny holes	Dessert, with fruit; on cheese tray
PROCESSED	United States	Semi-hard mild flavoured, a blend of Cheddar cheeses which have been emulsified to form a smooth mass	On cheese tray; spread on bread and crackers
PROVOLONE	Italy	Hard, cream-coloured, sharp-flavoured; usually pear-shaped; made from whole cows' milk	On cheese tray and in Italian cookery
ROQUEFORT	Roquefort, France	Semi-hard, white cheese marbled with blue mould; sharp flavoured	On cheese tray; with salads; as an appetizer
STILTON	Stilton, England	Semi-hard, white with blue mould, rich spicy flavour; made from whole cows' milk with added cream	On cheese tray; with salads and in cooked foods; as an appetizer
SWISS	Switzerland	Hard, cream-coloured with large gas holes; mild flavoured; made from partly skimmed cows' milk	On cheese tray with salads; cheese fondue

CHEESE PIE (Basic Recipe)

1 9-inch unbaked pie shell
1 cup grated Swiss or Cheddar
   cheese
3 eggs
1½ cups rich milk

½ teaspoon salt
   pinch nutmeg
   pinch cayenne
1 teaspoon sugar

1. Chill unbaked pie shell for 1 hour.
2. Sprinkle grated cheese into the bottom of the pie shell.
3. Beat eggs, add milk, seasonings and sugar and pour over the cheese in the pie shell.
4. Bake at 400° for 10 minutes, then reduce heat to 350° and continue to cook until the custard is cooked. (Insert a silver knife into the custard and it should come out free of custard.) Do not overcook as the custard will continue to thicken out of the oven.

CHEESE ONION PIE

Lightly sauté 1 cup thinly sliced onions. Spread over grated cheese in pie shell. Pour egg-milk mixture over and continue with Basic Recipe.

QUICHE LORRAINE

Follow basic recipe for Cheese Pie, reducing the cheese to ½ cup. Crumble 6 slices of cooked bacon and add to the grated cheese. When the pie is baked, garnish with 2 additional strips of crumbled cooked bacon, and with parsley.

CHEESE TARTS

Cut pastry into 18 2½-3-inch rounds and line 2-inch muffin or tart pans, dividing the filling for Cheese Pie among each. Bake at 375° until tarts are cooked.

LOBSTER CHEESE TARTS

Prepare Cheese Tarts from preceding recipe. Before baking, add a small chunk of cooked lobster to each. One 7-ounce tin of lobster is enough for 12-18 tarts.

Welcome at any hour or occasion is the attractive Cheese Tray. Cottage Cheese is at home with fresh fruit or vegetables and in cooked mixtures.

Cheese Pie (Quiche) and Beef Stroganoff are popular Supper Dishes.

WELSH RAREBIT

½ pound cheese, grated	2 teaspoons butter
½ teaspoon mustard	¼ cup top milk
½ teaspoon salt	1 egg
cayenne	dry toast or wafers

1. Place cheese in chafing dish or double boiler.
2. Mix seasonings; sprinkle over cheese.
3. Add butter, in pieces, and milk.
4. When cheese begins to melt, stir until smooth.
5. Beat the egg; stir in a little hot mixture, blend well and return to pan; cook 1 minute.
6. Serve at once on toast slices or cubes.

Cheese Fondue is a delightful Swiss dish.

CHEESE FONDUE

This Swiss dish brings together a group of friends (no more than 10) to a common pot. Serve as a supper dish with a green salad or in the evening to climax a visit. Serve with a hot drink or white wine.

1 pound Swiss cheese, diced or
    coarsely grated
3 tablespoons flour
1 clove garlic
2 cups dry white wine
1 tablespoon lemon juice

3 tablespoons kirsch or brandy
    nutmeg, pepper or paprika
    to taste
2 loaves crusty French bread,
    cubed so that each has a
    piece of crust

1. Dredge cheese lightly with flour.
2. Rub fondue pot or utensil with garlic; pour in wine and heat gently until air bubbles rise to the surface.
3. Add lemon juice; add cheese by handfuls, stirring constantly with a wooden spoon until cheese melts. Add kirsch and spices, and stir until blended.
4. Serve bubbling hot. Spear bread cubes through crust with a long-handled fork, dunk and swirl in fondue.

10   Cereals

Cereals comprise any grasses cultivated for their seed and the products resulting from their processing and refinement. Every country of the world has some native grain. Northern peoples use wheat, oats and barley; in the south, more corn products are used. The Orient lives on rice; Central Europe lives on rye.

Cereals are cheap, relatively abundant and good sources of energy. Supplemented with milk, or with small amounts of meat or cheese, they are an important part of a low-cost diet.

Cereals may be divided into groups based upon the part of the kernel that is used. *Refined* or starchy cereals have had the bran layers and germ removed; *whole grain* cereals contain the inner, starchy portion of the grain plus bran layers and at least part of the germ. The latter supply not only carbohydrate for energy, but also incomplete proteins, iron, B vitamins and cellulose.

Today, many of the refined cereals have had restored the minerals and vitamins which were removed by the milling process. These are known as *enriched cereals* and are especially important if cereal is a major constituent of the diet.

Another classification of cereals is based upon the amount of cooking they receive during the manufacturing process. *Precooked* cereals are ready to eat, *partially cooked* cereals are those which have been steamed to soften them during processing and which require only a short cooking time. *Uncooked* cereals require a long, slow period of cooking.

GENERAL PROPORTIONS FOR COOKING CEREALS

Type	Example	Cereal	Water	Salt	Time
Fine Cereals	Cornmeal				30 minutes.
	Cream of Wheat	¼ cup	1 cup	¼ teaspoon	If pre-cooked needs 5 minutes
Rolled or Flaked Cereals	Rolled Oats Flaked Wheat	½ cup	1 cup	¼ teaspoon	5-15 minutes
Coarse Cereals	Cracked Wheat	⅓ cup	1 cup	¼ teaspoon	1 hour

The amount of cereal when cooked will be about the same as the amount of liquid used.

METHOD FOR COOKING CEREALS (PREPARING PORRIDGE)

1. Have the water boiling in the top of a double boiler; add salt.
2. Add cereal slowly, stirring with a fork until the water boils again and the cereal thickens.
3. Place over the boiling water in the bottom of the double boiler; cover tightly; leave without stirring until cooked. For cereals requiring a long cooking period, this much may be done at night and the porridge heated in the morning while the rest of the breakfast is being prepared. If the cereal is to be cooked the previous night, or if added food value is desired, pour a little milk over the top and stir it into the porridge as it is being served.

   Rich milk, brown sugar, salt or butter, maple sugar or maple syrup, a handful of raisins—all are popular additions to a bowl of satisfying porridge.

   To reheat leftover cereals, place cereal with a small amount of milk in the top of a double boiler; do not stir. Cover and heat over hot water. When hot stir with a fork.

Rice is the central dish of an oriental dinner.

Rice

Rice may be purchased as whole-grain or brown, refined or polished rice of many varieties. Polished rice is available raw, pre-cooked and partly prepared. Wild rice is not a true rice but a product of a water grass from Northern Manitoba. The kernel is long, greenish black in colour and much prized as an accompaniment to game.

Raw and converted (partially cooked) rice expands 3 to 4 times when cooked. Quick-cooking rice expands to twice its volume when cooked.

TO COOK RICE

Follow package directions for cooking quick-cooking and converted rice. When cooking mixtures calling for raw regular rice, adjustments must be made to quantities of rice used, and to cooking times, if quick-cooking rice is substituted. In most cases, it is neither practical or economical to cook quick-cooking rice for long periods.

The following methods are recommended for cooking regular raw rice.

BOILED RICE

1 cup rice   1 teaspoon salt
4 cups water

1. Wash the rice well by rubbing in a sieve as cold water runs through; this removes excess starch.
2. Have water boiling rapidly in a large kettle; add salt.
3. Add rice, slowly stirring with a fork until the water boils again.
4. Keep the water boiling until the rice is tender. Test by tasting or by rubbing a kernel between thumb and forefinger. There should be no "bone" in the centre.
5. Drain in a sieve; rinse with boiling water; set the sieve over hot water to steam for a few minutes. Serves 4-6.
   The addition of 1-2 tablespoons lemon juice or ¼ teaspoon cream of tartar to cooking water helps to keep rice white.

STEAMED RICE

Combine 1 cup rice with 1⅔ cup boiling water or chicken stock in a saucepan. Cover and bring to boiling. Reduce heat and continue cooking until "pock" marks appear on the surface of the rice and all the liquid has been absorbed, about 15-20 minutes. Let rice "rest" in a warm place for 20-30 minutes to prevent kernels from sticking together. Toss lightly with a fork. Serves 4-6.

RISOTTO

3 tablespoons butter   1 cup rice
1 cup onions   3 cups chicken stock
1 cup celery   ½ teaspoon salt

1. Sauté the onions and celery in the fat until the onions are golden.
2. Add the well washed rice; stir constantly until brown.

3. Add the chicken stock; pour into a buttered baking dish; taste and season. Cover and bake at 350° for 45 minutes or cover and simmer on top of the stove until liquid is absorbed, about 25 minutes.

Variations: Chicken stock can be flavoured with garlic; mushroom slices may be added. Serve risotto with generous sprinkling of grated Parmesan cheese. Cook 1 fresh seeded chopped tomato in the mixture; stir in cooked fresh or frozen green peas when rice is cooked.

Use the following recipes with regular, quick-cooking or converted rice, using the specific cooking method for each:

BROWNED RICE

Brown 1–1⅓ cups raw rice in 2 tablespoons butter with 2 tablespoons chopped onion. If quick-cooking rice is used add the same quantity of water or consommé; if converted or regular rice is used add 3 cups liquid. Bring to boiling point and finish according to package directions in the case of quick-cooking rice, or to recipe for Steamed Rice (page 286) for regular or converted rice.

CHEESE RICE

Into 2 cups cooked rice, stir ⅔ cup grated Cheddar or Parmesan cheese. Serve with bacon, sausages, minced beef patties, fried liver etc.

COCONUT RICE

Into 2 cups cooked rice, lightly stir ½ cup moist, flaked coconut. Serve with chicken, curried mixtures or with foods which would be enhanced by the sweet flavour of coconut.

LEMON RICE

Into 2 cups cooked rice, stir lightly 1 teaspoon grated lemon rind, ⅓ cup chopped almonds and 1 tablespoon butter. Serve with seafood.

ORANGE RICE

Substitute grated orange rind for lemon rind of Lemon Rice. Serve with seafood.

PARSLEY OR CHIVE RICE

Finely chop 2 tablespoons parsley or chives (or green onions) or a mixture of the 2, and toss into 2 cups cooked rice. Serve Parsley Rice where the colour adds to the attractiveness; serve Chive Rice where both colour and chive flavour are desired.

PINEAPPLE RICE

Into 2 cups cooked rice, stir ½ cup thoroughly drained crushed pineapple. Serve with ham, veal or chicken.

SAFFRON RICE

Add a pinch of saffron to 2 cups cooked rice and stir lightly. Turmeric is less costly than saffron and can be substituted for it; the colour is not quite as bright. Serve with seafood, curries or chicken.

WILD RICE

This rice is the gourmet's accompaniment to game; it is too expensive for frequent serving.

1 cup wild rice	1½ teaspoon salt
5 cups cold water (or chicken stock)	

1. Wash the rice very well in several waters; place it in a saucepan with the cold water and salt; cover; place over medium heat and bring slowly to a boil, stirring with a fork to be sure it does not stick.
2. Boil without stirring until the rice is tender and well opened (about 30-40 minutes).
3. Drain; shake gently over the heat to dry, or place in a warm oven 10-15 minutes. Add seasonings and butter or use in the following way. Serves 4-6.

WILD RICE WITH MUSHROOMS

¼ cup butter	salt and pepper
1 tablespoon finely chopped onion	1 cup wild rice, cooked
½ pound mushrooms	1 tablespoon chopped parsley

1. Melt the butter; fry the onion until wilted; add the mushrooms washed, dried and thinly sliced; cook about 5 minutes; season; stir in 1 cup cooked wild rice and parsley; heat and serve. Serves 3-4.

CASSEROLES containing Rice Recipes in Supper Dishes, Chapter 11.

KASHA

Kasha is buckwheat groats, a popular dish in eastern Mediterranean countries. It is served with meat and vegetables.

1 cup buckweat groats	2 cups chicken stock
1 egg	4 tablespoons butter
salt	

1. Heat a heavy frying pan which has a tight-fitting lid; add the groats.
2. Beat the egg and stir quickly into the groats and continue cooking and stirring until mixture is thoroughly blended and cooked dry.
3. Add stock and salt to taste; cook, covered, over low heat until groats are cooked and liquid absorbed, about 30 minutes.
4. Mix with butter and serve.

MACARONI, SPAGHETTI AND NOODLES

These are only three of the dozens of varieties of "Pasta" or Italian Pastes. Rigatoni, Lasagna, Shells and Bow ties are all made from a paste of flour and water, shaped and dried. *They expand to about twice their original size when cooked.*

1. Measure the quantity of macaroni desired. About 1 ounce per serving (¼ cup uncooked) is sufficient when sauce is to be added.
2. Have a large amount of water boiling rapidly; add salt, 1 teaspoon per quart.
3. Add macaroni slowly, boil uncovered until tender—15-20 minutes. (Dip the ends of spaghetti or noodles in to soften; push down. Lasagna and manicotti noodles should be handled very carefully to prevent tearing.)
4. Drain small pasta in a sieve; rinse with cold water if not to be used immediately. Using a slotted spoon, transfer lasagna and manicotti noodles carefully to a container of cold water until needed, and then remove one at a time, as needed, with a slotted spoon, in order to prevent tearing.

For extra flavour a slice of onion or a few celery leaves may be boiled while the macaroni is cooking; chicken broth may be used instead of water.

The addition of 1 tablespoon salad oil to the cooking water reduces the tendency for the pasta to stick together.

Recipes for casseroles containing pasta will be found in Supper Dishes, Chapter 11.

BARLEY CASSEROLE

Not only does barley add nourishment to soups, it stands alone nobly in this casserole. Serve with meat and salad.

1 large onion, chopped	1 cup pearl barley
½ pound mushrooms, sliced	2 cups chicken or meat stock
4 tablespoons butter	

1. Sauté onion and mushroom slices in butter until soft; lift out; add barley and brown it lightly.
2. Taste stock and add salt and pepper if necessary; pour 1 cup broth over barley, cover and bake at 350° for 30 minutes. Add remaining broth and vegetables. Continue cooking until the liquid is absorbed and the barley is tender.

LEFTOVER CEREALS

Use cooked rice in Chicken Fried Rice; Spanish Rice, with Chicken Livers, with Sweet and Sour Chicken Wings, or for dessert as Rice Custard or Bavarian Rice.

Macaroni may be mixed with vegetables to make a salad, with a thick meat soup to make a substantial supper dish, or with any stew.

Noodles seasoned with butter and poppy seeds make a pleasant change from potatoes; serve with Scallopine (page 157). Consult Supper Dishes, Chapter 11.

---

11 Supper Dishes

Supper dishes have been divided into the following categories and appear in this order:

Scallops
Casseroles made with Pasta
Casseroles made with Rice
Casseroles made with Beans
Chafing-Dish Specialties
Curries
Supper dishes made with Tea Biscuit, Yeast Dough or Pastry
Miscellaneous Casseroles
Supper Dishes made with Bread
Supper on a Bun
Ways with Wieners
Ways with Hamburgers

Recipes labelled "Speedy" plus regular recipes which include short-cut versions and suggestions have been included throughout this chapter.

All the recipes may be considered speedy in these sections: Scallops, Supper on a Bun, Ways with Wieners, Ways with Hamburgers.

A basic pattern for quick supper dishes is to heat the protein part of the main course in a sauce, and to serve it on or with a starchy food. The meal is rounded out with another vegetable and/or a salad. The chart which follows illustrates this pattern.

FOOD ON HAND	HEAT OR COOK FOODS IN	SERVE ON OR WITH
wieners sausages chicken liver leftover roast cut in strips *corned beef, luncheon meat *frozen meat balls	*Barbecue Sauce prepared (page 86) or purchased	toasted buns *noodles and grated cheese *rice (quick-cooking) rice toasted buns noodles, grated cheese
leftover roast pork *cooked or canned chicken browned (uncooked) chicken wings canned *seafood, *tuna frozen meat balls	*Sweet and Sour Sauce prepared (page 90) or purchased	rice or noodles
cheese, grated canned or cooked tuna, chicken or seafood hard-cooked eggs frozen meat balls	White Sauce (page 79) made from *roux or *cream celery, *mushroom, *chicken or vegetable soups, canned or dehydrated. See Scallops (page 232) Curry Sauce made by adding 2 teaspoons curry to any of the White Sauces above	toast, tea biscuits (hot), noodles, rice noodles or rice
*fish fillets fish patties hamburger patties fresh or frozen meat balls fresh or frozen	Tomato Sauce made from *tomato soup, *sauce or *paste Spaghetti Sauce made from *spaghetti sauce mix plus tomato sauce or juice leftover gravy	rice *instant scalloped potatoes noodles or spaghetti noodles, rice or spaghetti, *instant mashed potatoes

Items marked with * should be kept on hand.

SCALLOP (Basic Recipe)

A scalloped dish is a combination of cooked meat, fish or vegetables arranged in layers with White (Cream) Sauce and topping. It is baked in the oven long enough so that the mixture bubbles and the topping browns. Cream soup variations of White Sauce add interest to these dishes.

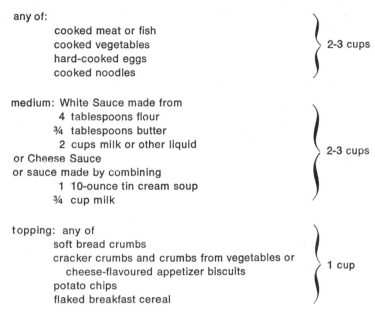

any of:
cooked meat or fish
cooked vegetables   2-3 cups
hard-cooked eggs
cooked noodles

medium: White Sauce made from
4 tablespoons flour
¾ tablespoons butter
2 cups milk or other liquid   2-3 cups
or Cheese Sauce
or sauce made by combining
1 10-ounce tin cream soup
¾ cup milk

topping: any of
soft bread crumbs
cracker crumbs and crumbs from vegetables or
   cheese-flavoured appetizer biscuits   1 cup
potato chips
flaked breakfast cereal

1. Prepare meat and vegetable ingredients as required.
2. Prepare White Sauce (method page 79) or cream soup variation.
3. Grease a 2 quart casserole. Add a layer of meat or vegetable, and a layer of White Sauce; repeat.
4. Top with one of the topping mixtures. If crumbs are used, additional flavour can be added by mixing them with butter or cheese.
5. Bake at 350° until mixture bubbles and the crumbs are brown, about 30 minutes. Serves 4-6.

To Extend Scallop: add any of cooked rice, noodles or macaroni.
For Added Zest: add to the White Sauce 2 tablespoons salad dressing or mayonnaise, or 3-4 tablespoons sherry.
To Freeze: cool quickly, cover. Can be frozen 4 months.

To Prepare Cheese Crumbs: Stir lightly with a fork 2-3 tablespoons grated Cheddar or Parmesan cheese into 1 cup soft bread crumbs.

To Prepare Buttered Crumbs; Stir lightly with a fork 1-2 tablespoons melted butter into 1 cup soft bread or cracker crumbs.

SPEEDY SCALLOP

Prepare 1 package of dehydrated scalloped potatoes according to package directions, adding 1 cup cooked seafood, fish or cooked vegetable. If foods being added are very dry, increase liquid slightly.

HAM AND NOODLE SCALLOP

Add to the White Sauce 2 teaspoons prepared mustard and 1½ cups sautéed mushrooms and alternate mixture with layers of cooked noodles (about ⅓ of a package) and chopped cooked ham. Top with cheese crumbs.

SALMON AND CELERY SCALLOP

Use 1 16-ounce tin salmon and 2 cups chopped, cooked celery. Use liquid from salmon and cooking liquid (stock) from celery for half the liquid required in the White Sauce. Green peas and their stock can be substituted for the celery and celery stock. Alternate layers of salmon and vegetable with White Sauce and top with buttered crumbs.

OLD FAVOURITE SALMON SCALLOP

Alternate layers of cooked salmon (1 16-ounce tin) plus 1 tablespoon lemon juice (save salmon stock for use in the White Sauce as part of the liquid) with layers of coarsely crushed soda biscuits (1 cup) and White Sauce. Top with buttered soda biscuit crumbs.

CAULIFLOWER AND HAM SCALLOP

Arrange flowerets or 1 whole cooked cauliflower in bottom of casserole dish. Combine White Sauce, 2 cups diced ham and ¼ cup blanched almonds, and pour over cauliflower. Top with buttered cracker crumbs.

TUNA FISH AND MUSHROOM SCALLOP

Rinse, drain and flake a 7-ounce tin of tuna and add 2 tablespoons lemon juice. Sauté 1 cup mushrooms and add White Sauce. (Mushroom or celery soup varieties of sauce are particularly good here.) Alternate with layers of tuna and sauce. Top with potato chips.

ASPARAGUS AND EGG SCALLOP

Cook 1 10-ounce package frozen asparagus spears or use fresh asparagus. Alternate layers of asparagus, 4 sliced hard-cooked eggs and White Sauce (or cream of chicken or celery soup sauce). Top with cheese crumbs.

CURRIED HADDIE AND EGGS SCALLOP

Stir-fry or lightly cook diced celery, green pepper and peeled cucumber to make a total of 1½ cups. Alternate layers of vegetables, 1 can chicken haddie flaked and 4 sliced hard-cooked eggs with White Sauce (or sauce made from cream or celery soup). Top with buttered crumbs.

BEAN AND CORNED BEEF SCALLOP

Cook a variety of frozen beans, (yellow, green and lima) or use packaged mixed vegetables, saving cooking water for part of the liquid in the White Sauce. Add ½ teaspoon Worcestershire Sauce to White Sauce or Cheese Sauce and alternate with layers of beans and diced corned beef. Top with buttered crumbs.

Several appetizing Supper Dishes are: Hungarian Goulash (top), Cabbage Rolls and Curried Shrimp.

CASSEROLE COOKERY

Family meals and party meals benefit from the use of casseroles. Ingredients range from the simplest to the most expensive; leftovers are incorporated into casseroles with unprecedented dignity.

These versatile dishes can be prepared hours or days before needed, reducing last-minute pressures. When serving a crowd, food will always be hot if many casserole dishes are used, some keeping hot in the oven while others are in use.

By tripling a favourite recipe and freezing several casseroles at one time for extra-busy days, we are never caught unprepared—and what an incentive it is to plan a party, knowing that the main dish is ready and waiting in the freezer. Economy is added to convenience when we build up a file of recipes for favourite casserole dishes, and then take advantage of special sales of featured ingredients. They can be made up at one time into many casseroles.

Some casserole ingredients are used in such small quantities that it may be more advantageous to freeze them separately. These are some:

mushrooms—slice, sauté in butter until just tender; sprinkle with lemon juice and freeze.

green pepper—remove seeds and stem. Chop; do not blanch; freeze.

broccoli slices—when broccoli is being prepared for a meal, set aside 2 or 3 flowerets. Slice lengthwise into paper-thin slices and drop into boiling water. After about 7 seconds, remove and rinse in cold water. Freeze. When preparing Chinese dishes, add a few broccoli slices for colour and texture contrast.

egg plant— peel, cut into ⅓ inch slices or dice. Blanch 4 minutes. Dip into a solution containing 1 quart cold water and ½ cup lemon juice; freeze.

parsley— chop parsley finely; do not blanch; freeze.

Partially used cans and jars of water chestnuts, bamboo shoots, pimento and cream soups can be frozen and kept on hand for casserole making.

HOW TO FREEZE CASSEROLES

Most casserole mixtures of cooked or partially-cooked ingredients freeze well. Those containing potatoes or hard-cooked eggs do not. Onions lose strength on freezing; herbs and sour cream are best when added when food is being reheated. Mixtures containing uncooked, beaten egg should be completely thawed before cooking to permit even cooking. It is best to undercook mixtures slightly so that the processes of freezing, thawing and reheating will not result in dry or over-processed food.

To freeze casseroles, line casserole dishes with foil, using a large piece which will extend up and beyond the sides of the dish. Fill with mixture and freeze. Remove the frozen mass and fold over the extended foil to enclose the mixture, making it airtight. Label and return package to freezer; the dish is available for other uses until the casserole is to be used. Then the foil is peeled off the frozen food and the mixture returned to the dish for thawing and reheating.

Combination dishes containing meat can be kept frozen at 0° for a period up to 4 months; those containing poultry can be kept frozen up to 6 months. When possible, thaw casseroles overnight in the refrigerator before heating. Thawing at room temperature will take place in about ⅓ to ½ that time. If time does not permit complete thawing, place casserole dish in a pan of water and bake, allowing up to 1½ times the normal time required for reheating.

CASSEROLES MADE WITH PASTA
(Macaroni, Spaghetti and Noodles)

Italian pasta or pastes include dozens of varieties—Rigatoni, Cannelloni, Lasagna, Bows, Shells—all of which can be used in these casseroles.

During Cooking

1 cup uncooked pasta equals 2 cups cooked pasta

Detailed instructions for cooking pasta are on page 289.

MACARONI RING

1 cup cut raw macaroni	2 tablespoons chopped parsley
2 slices bread, cubed	1 tablespoon grated onion
½ cup grated cheese	1 tablespoon mayonnaise
2 cups milk	

1. Cook macaroni. Drain.
2. Combine all the ingredients.
3. Bake in a greased ring mould or 2-quart casserole in a pan of hot water at 350° for 40 minutes.
4. Allow to stand 10 minutes; unmould. Fill the centre with creamed chipped beef, chicken or fish.

NOODLE RING

½ package broad noodles	1 tablespoon butter
1⅓ cups milk	Seasoning (onion or celery salt,
3 eggs	Worcestershire Sauce)

1. Cook the noodles; drain and rinse with cold water.
2. Combine the milk, beaten eggs and melted butter; add the noodles; season and pour into greased ring mould; set in a pan of hot water.
3. Bake at 350° for 1 hour or until set; unmould.
4. Serve with hot homemade chili sauce in the centre and cooked farmers' sausage (1-1½ pounds) around the outside.

NOODLES ALFREDO

1 pound broad noodles	2 cups grated Parmesan or
¾ cup butter	Cheddar cheese
	½ cup rich cream

1. Thoroughly drain cooked noodles; place in hot casserole with butter and toss gently with fork until noodles are buttered.
2. Add cheese and toss again; pour in cream and toss.
3. Season with pepper or seasoned salt. Serve with meat balls, Beef Stroganoff, Smothered Chicken or other foods which have their own gravies or sauce.

MACARONI WITH CHEESE SAUCE (Basic Recipe)

Cook in the oven or on top of the stove.

2 cups White Sauce	1 8-ounce package macaroni,
1¾ cups grated Cheddar cheese	cooked
(½ pound)	⅔ cup soft, buttered crumbs

1. Prepare White Sauce in the top section of a double boiler (page 79).
2. Add grated cheese and stir over hot water until melted; combine with cooked macaroni.
3. Mixture may be heated on top of the stove or baked at 350° in a greased 2 quart casserole, topped with buttered crumbs. Bake until crumbs are browned, about 35 minutes. Serves 4-6.

Any of chopped green pepper, 1 teaspoon minced onion, Worcestershire Sauce or partly cooked bacon may be added.
A bouillon cube may be dissolved in the milk; Cheese Sauce may be prepared from cream of mushroom, celery or cheese soups. Grate only half of the cheese and add to the sauce; leave remaining cheese in very thin flat pieces and carefully stir into the combined mixture.

BLENDER MACARONI

In an electric blender, place flour, butter, salt, pepper and ungrated cheese, ½ cup skim milk powder and 1½ cups milk; blend until smooth. Cook macaroni; drain. Combine macaroni and cheese mixture; omit crumb topping. Bake.

MACARONI SUPREME

Combine 2 cups cottage cheese, 1 cup sour cream and 1 beaten egg; substitute (White Sauce) in basic recipe. Finish according to recipe.

This casserole has been attractively garnished for Valentine's Day.

BUFFET CHICKEN CASSEROLE

This attractive and delicious casserole can be prepared the day before a party, or earlier if frozen. Begin by stewing a 4-5 pound fowl. Save chicken stock and meat for casserole.

½ cup chopped onion	1 cup pitted ripe olives
½ green pepper, chopped	4 tablespoons pimento cut in
1 cup mushrooms	strips
2 tablespoons butter or fat	1 10–12 ounce package frozen
12 ounces thin, flat noodles	peas
3-4 cups cooked chicken, diced	celery salt, salt and pepper
1 10-ounce tin cream of	1½ cups grated Cheddar cheese
mushroom soup	

1. Sauté onion, green pepper and mushrooms in butter.
2. Combine chicken stock, liquid from canned olives and water to make 6 cups; heat to boiling and add noodles. Cook until tender. Do not drain.
3. Stir in chicken, soup, pimento and olives, sautéed vegetables and thawed peas. Season to taste.
4. Pour half of the mixture into a large (3 quart) casserole dish. Sprinkle over it half of the grated cheese.
5. Pour in remaining mixture and top with remaining cheese.
6. Cover and bake at 325° for about 45 minutes; uncover and bake for 15 minutes more until top is browned. Garnish with parsley. Serves 8-10.

CHICKEN TETRAZZINI

2 tablespoons fat	½ pound spaghetti, macaroni or
½ pound mushrooms	broad noodles, cooked
2 tablespoons flour	½ cup grated Cheddar cheese
2 cups chicken stock and cream	½ cup table cream
3 cups diced cooked chicken	paprika
¼ cup toasted almonds	

1. Sauté the mushrooms in fat about 5 minutes; add flour; stir until well blended.
2. Add the chicken stock and cream mixture; stir until it bubbles; add the chicken and almonds.
3. Combine the cooked spaghetti, half the cheese and the ½ cup of cream; heat.
4. Arrange the spaghetti around the outside of a platter.

5. Pour the creamed mixture into the centre of the spaghetti; sprinkle with the rest of the cheese and with paprika. Serves 6.

¼ cup sherry may be added to the mixture a few minutes before serving.

TUNA TETRAZZINI

2-3 tins solid-pack, white meat tuna can be substituted for chicken.

TUNA NOODLE CASSEROLE

⅓ package noodles
2 cups crushed potato chips
1 7-ounce tin tuna fish
1 cup cooked green peas
   (optional)

1 10-ounce can cream of
   mushroom soup
½ cup milk
1 tablespoon grated cheese

1. Cook noodles in boiling water until tender; drain.
2. Butter a 2-quart casserole dish and line bottom and sides with ½ cup crushed potato chips.
3. Rinse oil from tuna fish with cold water, drain, and flake lightly.
4. Place a layer of tuna fish in the bottom of the casserole, cover with a layer of noodles; add peas if desired; add another layer of fish and another of noodles.
5. Add a layer of the remaining potato chips.
6. Using a knife or skewer, make holes in the mixture and pour the soup and milk over all. Sprinkle with grated cheese.
7. Bake at 350° about 1 hour. Serves 4-6.

MACARONI AND SAUSAGE LOAF

1 cup seasoned medium White
   Sauce
1 cup grated cheese
2 eggs

seasoning
2½ cups cooked macaroni
   (1 cup uncooked)
1 pound sausage

1. Make the White Sauce (page 79), add the cheese; beat eggs and stir into them a little of the hot sauce. Stir egg mixture into remaining hot sauce. Taste and season.
2. Add macaroni to mixture.
3. Brown the sausage in a frying pan; stand them up along the sides and end of a loaf pan.
4. Pour the macaroni mixture into the centre.
5. Bake at 350° until the loaf is set, about 40 minutes.

MACARONI AND TOMATO CASSEROLE

Substitute 2½ cups tomatoes for the milk in Macaroni and Cheese Sauce (Basic Recipe) page 83.

MACARONI WITH TOMATO SAUCE (Basic Recipe)

¼ cup fat	2 teaspoons salt
¼ cup chopped onion	¼ teaspoon pepper
½ cup green pepper, chopped	2 teaspoons brown sugar
½ cup chopped celery	1 cup grated cheese
2 cups canned tomatoes	
4 cups cooked macaroni	
(2 cups uncooked)	

1. Sauté the onion, pepper and celery in the fat until clear.
2. Combine the ingredients in a greased casserole, saving the cheese to sprinkle on top.
3. Bake at 350°, uncovered, 30 minutes. Serves 6.

Any of the following may be added:

1-2 cups cooked kernel corn, green beans or lima beans.

½ pound minced beef, browned, or 8-10 sausages which have first been simmered in water for 5 minutes.

1 cup sautéed eggplant cubes, or 4 or 5 slices; or 1 cup chopped, peeled cucumber or slices of zucchini squash.

MEXICAN SKILLET

1 pound pork sausage	1 teaspoon chili powder
2 cups uncooked macaroni	2 teaspoons salt
1 cup chopped green pepper	2 tablespoons sugar
1 cup chopped onion	2 cups sour cream
1 28-ounce tin tomatoes	

1. Brown sausages thoroughly on all sides; they should be almost cooked. Drain off fat.
2. Add rest of ingredients except sour cream; bring to a boil; reduce heat and cook, covered, until done, about 30 minutes. Stir occasionally.
3. Stir in sour cream and serve.

If more liquid is needed before mixture is cooked, add a little tomato juice, or diluted ketchup, tomato paste or tomato sauce. Serves 4-6.

MANICOTTI CASSEROLE

Manicotti noodles, large pasta tubes, are filled with savoury meat and cheese mixtures, and baked in tomato sauce. (Squares of pasta dough, rolled into tubes after filling, are called cannelloni.)

This casserole requires considerable time for preparation. However it can be prepared in advance and refrigerated or frozen until needed.

1 package manicotti noodles (about 12 ounces)	12 ounces cottage cheese
1 pound finely ground beef or	1 package (3–4 ounces) cream cheese
1 cup finely chopped leftover beef	3½ cups tomato sauce
1 9–10 ounce package frozen spinach or	½ teaspoon oregano
12 ounces fresh spinach	1 4–6 ounce package Mozzarella cheese slices
2 eggs, beaten	
salt, pepper	

1. Cook noodles according to directions on page 289, and when tender, lift out with a slotted spoon into a container of cold water. Handle carefully to avoid breaking.

2. Brown raw beef in a little fat in a frying pan; remove from pan and cool. Drain excess fat from frying pan.

3. If spinach is frozen, thaw it and drain it thoroughly. Chop spinach finely and sauté in frying pan for 3-4 minutes, stirring constantly. Cool.

4. Combine meat, half of the spinach, 1 beaten egg and 1 teaspoon salt. Blend well.

5. In another container, combine cottage cheese, cream cheese, ½ teaspoon salt, 1 beaten egg and remaining spinach. Mix until smooth.

6. Lift noodles, one at a time, from the water. Drain and fill with either the meat mixture or cheese mixture, so that there will be equal quantities of meat-filled noodles and cheese-filled noodles.

7. Cover the bottom of a 13 by 9 by 2-inch pan with 2 cups of tomato sauce, using canned sauce or sauce prepared from the recipe on page 84. Carefully arrange noodles in rows in the sauce; cover with remaining sauce. Sprinkle with oregano.

8. Cover and bake at 350° for about 30 minutes. Uncover and top with overlapping triangles of Mozzarella cheese. Bake 10 minutes or until cheese melts. Garnish with chopped parsley. Serves 8-10.

The casserole can be varied as follows:

Combine meat and cheese fillings to make one combination filling, or make only meat or only cheese filling.

top the filled noodles with White Sauce (½ of recipe on page 79) instead of tomato sauce; retain 2 cups tomato sauce for the bottom layer.

sprinkle grated Parmesan or Cheddar cheese over filled noodles before topping them with sauce.

SPAGHETTI AND MEAT BALLS

1. Prepare Meat Balls from recipe on page 150; brown.
2. Prepare Creole Sauce (page 85) and season with a little garlic salt and ¼ teaspoon oregano, *or* substitute spaghetti sauce mix and tomato juice for the Creole Sauce.
3. Cover and cook browned meat balls in sauce for about 15 minutes.
4. Pour over hot, cooked spaghetti (about 8 ounces). Garnish with parsley. Serves 6.

PASTA CASSEROLES MADE FROM MEAT SAUCE

Using the recipe for Meat Sauce on page 85, many different casseroles can be prepared and frozen until needed. Here are some:

SPAGHETTI AND MEAT SAUCE

Using ½ the Meat Sauce recipe, serve sauce hot over 8 ounces of spaghetti, cooked. Garnish with parsley and serve with grated Parmesan or Cheddar cheese. Serves 6.

PRAIRIE CASSEROLE

½-1 package broad noodles	2 teaspoons Worcestershire
½ Meat Sauce recipe	Sauce
1 cup canned kernel corn	salt, pepper
½ pound processed cheese, grated	

1. Cook noodles according to directions on page 289. Drain.
2. Combine all ingredients in a 3-quart casserole and bake at 350° for 30 minutes or until the mixture bubbles. Serves 6-8.

LASAGNA

This Italian specialty is best baked in a square or rectangular 3-quart casserole.

6 lasagna noodles (⅓ package)	¼ pound grated Parmesan or
½ Meat Sauce recipe	Cheddar cheese
½ pound Mozzarella cheese	½ package spinach, cooked
slices	(optional)
½ pound cottage cheese	

1. Cook lasagna noodles according to directions page 289, until tender; test with the point of a sharp knife. Handle carefully to avoid tearing.
2. Cover the bottom of the casserole with a layer of Meat Sauce, about ½ inch deep. Cover with a single layer of noodles, a layer of Mozzarella cheese slices and a layer of cottage cheese. Sprinkle with grated Parmesan or Cheddar Cheese.
3. A layer of drained, chopped, cooked spinach may be added.
4. Repeat Step 2 and finish with a layer of meat sauce.
5. Bake at 325° for about 30 minutes or until mixture bubbles. Remove from oven and keep casserole in a warm place for about 5 minutes before serving. Garnish with parsley. Serves 6-8.

Lasagna, served with Garlic Bread and a tossed salad.

CASSEROLES MADE WITH RICE

	Uncooked	Cooked
Regular Rice	1 cup equals 3 cups (approx.)	
Quick-cooking Rice	1 cup equals 2 cups (approx.)	

Detailed instructions for cooking rice will be found on page 286.

RICE RING

1¼ cups uncooked rice	½ cup toasted almonds
¼ cup butter	¼ cup golden raisins
2½ cups chicken stock	½ teaspoon salt

1. Brown rice in butter, add stock, cover and cook until tender.
2. Add remaining ingredients and press into a 4-cup buttered ring mould.
3. Keep in warm place for 10 minutes. Unmould. Serve filled with Smothered Chicken, creamed mixtures or curries.

SPANISH RICE

2 tablespoons butter	1 can tomatoes (28 ounces)
1 cup onion	1 teaspoon sugar
1 clove garlic	1 teaspoon salt
½ cup celery	2 whole cloves
½ cup green pepper	3 cups cooked rice

1. Sauté the fresh vegetables in the fat; remove the garlic.
2. Add the tomatoes, sugar and seasonings; bring to a boil; simmer 10 minutes; remove the cloves.
3. Stir in the rice; pour into a greased casserole.
4. Bake at 350° for 30 minutes.

   Cold roast beef may be cubed and added to the casserole.

SPEEDY SPANISH RICE

Prepare ingredients to end of Step 2. Stir in 1⅓ cups instant rice. Simmer for 5-10 minutes. Serve.

Jambalaya can be made with fish, ham or chicken.

JAMBALAYA

Prepare Spanish Rice by any of the preceding methods. When the rice is tender and much of the liquid has been absorbed, stir in 2 cups cooked shrimp, ham or chicken. Serves 4-6.

CASSEROLE OF RICE AND BEEF

4 cups cooked rice	1 16-ounce can green beans,
1½ pounds ground beef	drained
¼ teaspoon salt	garlic salt
⅛ teaspoon pepper	1 cup condensed mushroom or
¼ cup ketchup or tomato paste	celery soup
2 tablespoons minced onion	2 cups canned tomatoes

1. Spread rice in greased, shallow 1½ quart casserole.
2. Cook meat until lightly browned; drain off fat, spread meat on rice.
3. Sprinkle with salt and pepper and spread with ketchup or tomato paste.
4. Sprinkle onions and beans over this; sprinkle lightly with garlic salt.
5. Top with soup and tomatoes and spread evenly. Bake at 350° for about 40 minutes. Serves 6.

DJUVECE

A dinner-in-a-dish from Poland.

3 large onions (chopped)	1 large green pepper
2 tablespoons fat	(seeded and chopped)
3 large potatoes (sliced)	½ cup rice
2½ cups tomato juice and	6-8 lamb or pork chops
3 large tomatoes (sliced)	¾ teaspoon salt
	⅛ teaspoon pepper

1. Sauté onions in fat until straw-coloured; place half in a 9 by 14-inch baking dish (2 quart). Add half the potatoes, the green pepper, the tomato slices and half the juice.
2. Wash the rice well; sprinkle over the vegetables; add the remaining onion, potato and juice. Add part of the seasoning.
3. Trim the chops and brown in the pan in which the onions were cooked; arrange them on top of the vegetables; add the remaining seasoning.
4. Bake covered at 325° for 30 minutes. Uncover, baste and bake until the chops are brown (about 15 minutes).

SEVEN-LAYER CASSEROLE

1 cup uncooked rice	½ cup finely chopped onion
1 cup canned kernel corn, drained	½ cup finely chopped green pepper
salt, pepper	¾ pound ground beef
2 8-ounce tins tomato sauce	4 strips bacon
¾ cup water	

1. In a large greased casserole, arrange ingredients in layers thus: rice, corn (sprinkle with salt and pepper), one tin of tomato sauce and a half tin (half cup) of water, chopped onion and green pepper, beef, (sprinkle again with salt and pepper) and the second tin of tomato sauce and ¼ tin of water. Top with bacon strips which have been cut in half.
2. Cover and bake at 350° for 1 hour. Uncover and bake about 30 minutes more. Serves 6-8.

   1⅓ cups ketchup and ⅔ cup water may be substituted for the tomato sauce; less salt and pepper will be required.

   To reduce cooking time to about 40 minutes, use quick-cooking rice, and sauté onion, green pepper and beef (separately) in a little fat, before assembling casserole. Heating tomato sauce and water together beforehand reduces cooking time further.

CASSEROLE OF RICE AND FISH

2 cups cooked fish, flaked	2 tablespoons melted butter
¼ cup soft bread crumbs	2 tablespoons milk
1 teaspoon salt	1 tablespoon lemon juice
¼ teaspoon pepper	1 egg
¼ teaspoon grated onion	2½ cups cooked rice

1. Mix the fish, crumbs and seasonings.
2. Add butter, milk, lemon juice and egg, well beaten.
3. Grease a 1-quart mould; line with rice, using about ⅔ of it.
4. Pack the centre with the fish mixture; cover with rice.
5. Cover tightly; steam 45 minutes.
6. Unmould; serve with Parsley or Egg Sauce (page 83).

CASSEROLE OF RICE AND MEAT

Substitute 2 cups minced cooked meat for the fish in Casserole of Rice and Fish. Omit lemon juice and milk; add ¼ cup gravy.

Rice can be used in preparing many Supper Dishes. Here the rice is prepared separately and served with sautéed strips of sirloin topped with marinated mushrooms.

CHINESE FRIED RICE

½ cup finely diced ham, cooked chicken or cooked pork
2 tablespoons salad oil
1 3-ounce can sliced broiled mushrooms

1½ tablespoons finely chopped green onions
2 cups cold cooked rice
3 eggs
2 to 3 tablespoons soy sauce

1. Brown meat in oil; add mushrooms, onions and rice and continue to cook over low heat for 10 minutes or until the rice is slightly brown.
2. Make a well in the centre; stir in the eggs lightly beaten; as the eggs begin to set stir into the rice; add soy sauce. Serves 6-8.

SPEEDY HAWAIIAN SUPPER

Cooking time has been reduced in this recipe by the use of quick-cooking rice. It can be reduced further by substituting previously-prepared Sweet and Sour Sauce (page 90) for the sauce in this recipe.

2½ cups cooked ham, cut in strips
2 tablespoons butter
1 green pepper, cut in strips
1⅓ cups pineapple juice and water
4 teaspoons vinegar
2 tablespoons brown sugar
2 teaspoons prepared mustard
½ teaspoon ginger
½ teaspoon salt

2 tablespoons cornstarch
1 14-ounce tin pineapple chunks, drained
1⅓ cups hot water
½ teaspoon salt
few grains pepper
2 tablespoons chopped green onions
1⅓ cups quick-cooking rice

1. Sauté ham in butter until browned, add green pepper strips and sauté 2 minutes more.
2. Combine pineapple juice and water, vinegar, brown sugar, mustard, ginger, salt and cornstarch. Mix well and stir into ham mixture, cooking and stirring until sauce is transparent and thick.
3. Cover and simmer 10 minutes. Add pineapple.
4. Combine hot water, salt, pepper, green onions and quick-cooking rice. Make a well in the centre of the sauce; pour in rice mixture.
5. Bring to a boil, cover and simmer for 5 minutes.
Luncheon meat may be substituted for ham.

TUNA RICE CASSEROLE

Substitute cooked rice for noodles in recipe for Tuna Noodle Casserole (page 301).

SPEEDY TUNA RICE CASSEROLE

Quick-cooking rice shortens the cooking time.

1 10-ounce tin cream mushroom
  soup
⅓ cup finely chopped onion
1⅓ cups water
1 teaspoon lemon juice
¼ teaspoon salt
  few grains pepper

1⅓ cups quick-cooking rice
1 10-ounce package frozen peas,
  partially thawed, or
1½ cups cooked or canned peas
1 7-ounce tin tuna
½ cup grated Cheddar cheese
  paprika

1. Combine first 6 ingredients in a saucepan, bring to a boil, stirring occasionally; pour half of the mixture into a greased 1½ quart casserole.
2. Add, in layers, rice, peas and tuna fish, which has been drained and flaked.
3. Add remaining soup, sprinkle with cheese and paprika.
4. Cover and bake at 375° for 15 to 20 minutes. After 10 minutes of baking, cut through mixture with a knife to help distribute soup mixture.

SHRIMP FRICASSEE

2 cups milk
1 can condensed cream of
  chicken soup
2 5-ounce cans shrimp
1 tablespoon lemon juice
4 tablespoons fat
¼ cup chopped onion

½ cup chopped celery
4 tablespoons flour
¼ teaspoon salt
  dash of pepper
2 cups cooked rice
¼ cup slivered toasted almonds
2 cups potato chips

1. Heat the milk and soup in the top of a double boiler.
2. Clean the shrimp; sprinkle with lemon juice.
3. Melt the fat; sauté the onion and celery until clear.
4. Add the flour; blend it into the fat; stir quickly into the hot liquid; stir until thick; taste and season.
5. Fold in the rice, shrimps and almonds; pour into a greased casserole; cover with potato chips.
6. Bake at 350° until brown and bubbling. Serves 4-6.

Cream of mushroom, frozen shrimp or oyster soup may be substituted for the chicken soup; 2 cups of White Sauce (page 79) can replace both milk and soup.

PAELLA

This Spanish dish combines chicken and seafood. Clams in the shell garnish the top.

3-4 chicken breasts	1 cup frozen peas
½ cup cooking oil	1 cup canned tomatoes, drained
2 cloves garlic, crushed	4 cups chicken stock
½ cup onion, chopped	¼ teaspoon saffron or turmeric
1 green pepper, cut in strips	1 pound raw shrimp, shelled
¼ cup pimento, cut in strips	and cleaned
½ teaspoon oregano	12 clams in the shell
½ teaspoon pepper	lemon wedges
2 cups uncooked rice	

1. Cut chicken breasts into halves, and each half into 3 or 4 pieces, to include bones. Brown each piece in oil in a large Dutch oven.
2. Add garlic, onion and green pepper and sauté until just soft.
3. Add pimento, seasonings, rice, peas and coarsely chopped tomatoes.
4. Add saffron (or turmeric) to chicken stock and heat to boiling; add to chicken mixture and bring mixture to boiling again. Cook gently, uncovered, for about 10 minutes, with minimum stirring.
5. Add shrimp, pushing them down into the liquid. Cover and cook gently for about 15 minutes, until all foods are cooked.
6. Stir through mixture gently to distribute the liquid. Transfer pot to oven (350°) and continue cooking, uncovered, until mixture is almost dry, about 15 minutes.
7. While mixture is in the oven, scrub clam shells with a brush. Steam in a covered container over boiling water. (A metal sieve in a covered saucepan can be used for this). Shells should open after about 10 minutes of steaming. Arrange opened shells on top of paella with wedges of lemon. Serves 8.

CABBAGE ROLLS (Koldomar, Holupchi, Holubsti)

Each of the Central European countries has a different version of this recipe. The names mean "little pigeons."

1 green cabbage	a few small rib bones of lamb
½ cup rice	2 teaspoons salt
1 pound of shoulder lamb	1 teaspoon pepper
3 tablespoons bacon fat	1 to 1½ cups tomato juice
1 onion, chopped	

1. Leave the cabbage whole; pull off any discoloured leaves; remove all the core; pour boiling water into the core to cover the cabbage; let it stand over low heat until the leaves are pliable and will not break when folded.

Eggs are an essential part of our diet and there are many ways they can be prepared. Home-made fresh cherry pie is a favourite dessert.

French Canadian Pea Soup and a hearty salmon sandwich are a lunchtime favourite. Fancy sandwiches and a sandwich loaf and cookies are the makings of a party.

2. Wash the rice well in cold water; add to ½ cup boiling water; boil 1 minute; cover tightly; turn off the heat and leave until the water is absorbed.
3. Cut the meat into small cubes.
4. Fry the onion in bacon fat until golden brown.
5. Combine the rice, which will still be firm, the meat, onions and seasoning.
6. Remove the cabbage; cool under cold water; separate the leaves carefully.
7. On the long side of each leaf place a tablespoon of the mixture; roll up, tucking in the ends to make a tight roll; fasten with a toothpick if necessary; brown in hot fat.
8. If the cabbage rolls are to be cooked on top of the stove, place the rib bones in the kettle, and arrange the rolls in layers removing any toothpicks; sprinkle with salt and pepper; pour the tomato juice on to barely show; cover tightly and simmer about 1 hour. (The bones will help to prevent scorching but the rolls will have to be watched, especially if the kettle is thin). The rolls may be placed in a casserole with a tightly fitting cover and baked an hour or longer. In this case the bones are not necessary although they do add some flavour. Also, the cabbage rolls may be pressure-cooked at 15 pounds for 10 minutes.
9. Uncover when cooked, brush with a little butter and leave to brown either in the oven or under the broiler. Serve with crisp crumbled bacon and sour cream. Serves 8.

Add 2 cloves garlic, crushed; a little cayenne pepper will give a hot flavour.

Use ground beef instead of lamb for variety.

QUICK CABBAGE ROLLS

⅓ large green cabbage	½ teaspoon pepper
1½ cups rice	⅔ 10-ounce can tomato soup
⅓ pound ground beef	2 slices bacon
½ onion, chopped	sour cream
1 teaspoon salt	

Using the directions from the preceding recipe, prepare cabbage leaves and fill with a mixture of the next 5 ingredients. Pour soup over the rolls and cook 30-40 minutes. Serve with crisp crumbled bacon and sour cream.

DOLMAS

Prepare the mixture for Cabbage Rolls, omitting rice. Substitute for cabbage leaves 40-50 grape leaves. Place a tablespoon of filling near the stem end of the underside (veined side) of a cooked grape leaf. Fold the sides over the filling and roll up from the stem end. Heat a little fat (butter or cooking oil) in a heavy saucepan. Cover bottom of pan with a few grape leaves and place rolls tightly together on them; pour tomato juice over rolls. Cook as cabbage rolls.

Grape Leaves packed in brine may be obtained in specialty shops. To use, rinse in warm water, drain thoroughly on a rack and remove stem.

Fresh, young, tender leaves (Thompson seedless are considered best) may be frozen for later use. To cook, drop leaves into boiling water to which 1 teaspoon lemon juice per 2 cups of water has been added. Remove leaves after 3-5 minutes when soft. Drain. To freeze, dry with a cloth first. Pile cooked leaves in bundles of 10; separate each bundle from the next with foil. Package and freeze.

CASSEROLES MADE WITH BEANS
SAVOURY BAKED BEANS

4 strips bacon	2 tablespoons brown sugar
¼ cup chopped onions	⅛ teaspoon dry mustard
1 28-ounce can pork and beans in tomato sauce	¼ cup chili sauce

1. Dice the bacon; fry crisp; crumble.
2. Add the onions and cook until clear.
3. Combine all the ingredients in a baking dish; cover.
4. Bake at 350° for 30 minutes.

BAKED BEANS

1 pound white beans	pepper
1 onion	1 tablespoon mustard
¼ pound salt pork	4 tablespoons molasses
1 teaspoon salt	

1. Pick over the beans; rinse; soak overnight in water to cover.
2. Drain; cover with cold water; boil gently 1 hour; drain.
3. Place the onion and pork in the bean pot or in an oven dish.
4. Pour in the beans.
5. Sprinkle with salt, pepper and mustard; add the molasses and hot water to cover.
6. Bake, covered, for 6 hours at 300°, adding water as necessary.
7. Remove the pork and onion.

HAWAIIAN BEAN POT

1 28-ounce can pork and beans
1 8-ounce can pineapple
  tidbits, drained
1 tablespoon soy sauce
2 tablespoons instant minced
  onions

½ teaspoon hickory smoked salt
  or
¼ teaspoon celery salt
4-5 slices lean bacon

Combine all ingredients, except bacon, in a 1½-2 quart casserole. Top with bacon slices, and bake at 350° for 30 minutes. Serves 4-5.

CHILI CON CARNE

½ cup onions, thinly sliced
2 tablespoons fat
½ pound ground beef
1 teaspoon Worcestershire
  Sauce

1 teaspoon chili powder
1 28-ounce can tomatoes
1 20-ounce can kidney beans

1. Cook the onion in the fat until clear and yellow. Lift out.
2. Brown the meat; add the seasonings and the onions.
3. Add the tomatoes and simmer slowly, covered, for 1 hour.
4. Uncover; add the beans and simmer until thick and tender.
5. Taste and season with salt, pepper and more chili if desired.

SPEEDY CHILI CON CARNE

To 3 cups of Meat Sauce (page 85) add 1 can of Kidney beans and chili powder to taste.

LIMA BEAN AND SAUSAGE CASSEROLE

This casserole is as good on reheating as it is on the first time around Serve with a crisp salad.

2 cups dried lima beans
½-1 pound pork sausage
1 clove garlic, crushed
1 medium onion, chopped
1 green pepper, chopped
1 teaspoon chili powder
½ teaspoon dry mustard
½ teaspoon thyme

2 teaspoons Worcestershire
  Sauce
½ teaspoon salt
1 10-ounce can condensed
  tomato soup
Parmesan or Cheddar cheese,
  grated

1. Soak limas overnight in about 6 cups water; next day add additional liquid to make 6 cups.
2. Cook covered in a large pot until tender, about 1 hour.
3. Drain and reserve stock.

4. Brown sausage in a frying pan, being sure that all sides are well browned. Remove from pan, and slice half of the sausages into ¼ inch slices; set aside remaining sausages.
5. Discard all but 3 tablespoons fat from sausages, and sauté garlic, onion and green pepper in it until tender.
6. Add remaining ingredients, except cheese, to the limas. Add 1 cup stock and mix all thoroughly.
7. Bake uncovered in a greased 2-3 quart casserole for about 35 minutes. Remove from oven and cut remaining sausages lengthwise and place cut-side-down on the top of the casserole.
8. Bake for 10-15 minutes more. Serve with grated cheese. Serves 6-8.

SPEEDY BEAN, BACON AND ONION CASSEROLE

1 20-ounce can lima or navy beans	2 teaspoons Worcestershire Sauce
1 small can whole boiled onions	few grains Cayenne
1 8-ounce can tomato sauce	8 slices bacon squares
1 teaspoon prepared mustard	2 tablespoons brown sugar

1. Drain beans and onions. Combine all ingredients in a 1 or 2 quart casserole.
2. Bake at 400° for 20 minutes.

DESPERATE BEANS

It's the cook who is desperate, not the beans, and in need of something good in a hurry.

Combine 1 20-ounce can lima beans, drained, 1 10-ounce can tomato soup, 2 teaspoons Worcestershire Sauce and ½ cup liquid from the beans. Bake at 400° until bubbly. The addition of any or all of chopped onion, grated cheese, sour cream (up to ¾ cup) or leftover cooked meat improves this dish.

CHAFING DISH SPECIALTIES

There are almost as many different varieties of chafing dishes as there are mixtures to go in them. They vary from the basic skillet-type pan to the double boiler (bain marie) which has a removable water-bath compartment, for use in keeping foods hot after cooking.

A source of heat which can be regulated, such as alcohol, canned heat or electricity, is most satisfactory. While the elegant chafing dish can be the focal point of a supper party, the electric frying pan can often do the same job quietly in the kitchen.

WELSH RAREBIT

See Cheese, Chapter 9.

CHEESE FONDUE

See Cheese, Chapter 9.

BEEF FONDUE

See Meats, Chapter 5.

BEEF STROGANOFF

1 pound beef sirloin or tenderized round steak	1 tablespoon ketchup or tomato paste
1 tablespoon flour	1 10-ounce can consommé or
2 tablespoons butter	1¼ cups beef stock
1 cup thinly sliced mushrooms	½ teaspoon salt
½ cup chopped onion	⅛ teaspoon pepper
1 clove garlic, crushed	½ teaspoon basil
2 tablespoons butter	1 cup sour cream
3 tablespoons flour	2 tablespoons sherry

1. Dredge ¼-inch wide strips of beef in flour; melt butter in chafing dish or frying pan and brown strips of meat on all sides, quickly.
2. Add mushroom slices, onion and garlic and cook until golden. Remove from pan.
3. In the frying pan or chafing dish, prepare sauce from the 2 tablespoons of additional butter, the flour, ketchup and consommé, using the method preferred from those on page 79 for making White Sauce.
4. Return the meat, mushrooms and onions to the pan and stir in seasonings, sour cream and sherry. Heat through.
5. Serve on buttered noodles.

SPEEDY BEEF STROGANOFF

Cook ½ cup chopped onions in 4 tablespoons butter or cooking oil until almost tender; push to 1 side of the pan. Cut 6 minute steaks into strips ½-inch wide; brown quickly in frying pan, adding a little more cooking oil if necessary. Dilute 1 10-ounce can cream of mushroom soup with 1 cup water and add to steak with 1 cup sour cream. Heat through, season with 1 teaspoon Worcestershire Sauce and garlic salt to taste. Serve at once over cooked noodles or instant rice. Serves 4-6.

LOBSTER THERMIDOR

See Fish and Shell fish, Chapter 6.

SEAFOOD SUPPER

This elegant fare takes little preparation time.

2 cans cream of mushroom soup	1 7-ounce can crab meat
1 10-ounce can mushrooms	1 tablespoon sherry
1 7-ounce can shrimp	1 tablespoon heavy cream
2 7-ounce cans lobster	

1. Combine soup, mushrooms and their juice in the top of a large double boiler.
2. Drain juices from seafood; clean and rinse shrimps in cold water.
3. Add seafood, sherry and cream to mushroom mixture and mix lightly.
4. Heat about 10 minutes or until very hot. Serve in pastry shells, on toast or on rice. Serve with a tossed salad.

SUKIYAKI

Pronounced skiyaki, this Japanese word means "cook in a pan." Foods to be cooked are set out in a colourful arrangement on a tray, then cooked in a skillet over an hibachi or stove, or in a chafing dish or electric frying pan. The cooking may take place in the presence of the partakers!

¼ cup salad oil	1 can bamboo shoots, drained
1 pound tender beef sliced thin (½-inch by 2-inch strips)	2 tablespoons shirataki or 1 can transparent yam noodles,
½ cup consommé	bean threads
½ cup soy sauce	2 squares bean curd or 1 can
2 cups green onions—halved and cut in 2-inch strips	bean sprouts
1 cup celery sliced on an angle	2 cups fresh spinach (small leaves, shredded) or
¼ pound mushrooms, sliced	1 can water chestnuts
2 tablespoons sugar	2 bunches water cress
1 teaspoon monosodium glutamate	rice, cooked

1. On a board or tray arrange all the food in attractive rows.
2. Heat the salad oil to 360° in fry pan.
3. Brown the meat; push to one side. Add half the consommé and soy sauce, add small amounts of onion, celery and mushrooms in separate groups. Cover and cook 5 minutes; push to one side.
4. Add the rest of the liquid, sugar, monosodium glutamate, bamboo shoots, noodles, bean curd and chestnuts; cook 3 minutes. Stir carefully so the vegetables remain separate.
5. Add water cress; cook 3 minutes or until wilted.

6. To serve, spoon a serving of hot fluffy rice onto each plate; top with a serving of sukiyaki; cook remaining food in the sauce as needed. Serves 6.

If bean threads are used, soak 2 hours in cold water.

CURRIES

Meats, vegetables, fruits and spices combine to produce these exotic dishes. Orientals serve them "red" hot; for Western tastes, a lighter hand with the spices, plus frequent tasting while seasoning, is advised.

Curries are served with rice and any number of accompaniments (sambals)—small dishes of foods, crisp, sweet, hot and tart. Each person adds a spoonful or more of any of these according to his own preferences. Suggestions for sambals are given following the curry recipes.

CURRIED LAMB

10 small white onions	2 cups celery cut diagonally
3 tablespoons butter or cooking	into 1-inch chunks
oil	2 teaspoons curry powder
1 or 2 garlic cloves, crushed	(or more to taste)
1 teaspoon salt	½ teaspoon ginger
¼ teaspoon pepper	1 teaspoon Worcestershire
½ teaspoon marjoram	Sauce
¼ cup flour	2 green peppers
3 pounds well-trimmed lamb cut	2 tablespoons lemon juice
in 1-inch cubes	2 teaspoons lemon rind
1 20-ounce tin tomato juice	½ cup raisins
(2½ cups)	

1. Sauté onions in butter or oil in a heavy stew pot or skillet until lightly browned; set aside. Sauté garlic until golden.
2. Combine salt, pepper, marjoram and flour and dredge lamb cubes in the mixture.
3. Brown lamb cubes, a few at a time; add a little cooking oil to pan if needed to prevent sticking.
4. Add tomato juice, celery, curry powder, ginger and Worcestershire sauce; cover and cook slowly until lamb is tender, about 1-1½ hours.
5. Cut green pepper into ¼-inch strips and add with browned onions to lamb. Add lemon juice, rind and raisins, cover and cook until all is tender, about 25 minutes.
6. Adjust seasoning, if necessary, and serve with hot rice. Serves 6-8.

CHICKEN CURRY

Javanese Chicken (page 202) is another recipe for Curried Chicken.

3 pounds cut-up chicken
½ cup flour
¼ cup butter or cooking oil
1 clove garlic, crushed
1 large onion, chopped
½ teaspoon chili powder or
  turmeric
2 teaspoons curry powder
1 teaspoon salt
½ teaspoon ground ginger

3 tablespoons flour
2 cups coconut milk
1 cup chicken stock
1 cup peeled diced cucumber or
  sliced mushrooms
½ cup sultana raisins
1 teaspoon lemon juice
  ground cinnamon, cloves and
  cardamom

1. Cut chicken breasts into 4, and legs into thighs and drumsticks.
2. Measure flour into a small paper bag, add chicken pieces and shake.
3. Sauté chicken pieces in butter or oil until golden on all sides.
4. Remove from pan and sauté garlic and onion until just soft; remove from heat and stir in next 5 ingredients.
5. Stir in gradually the coconut milk and stock; cook until thickened.
6. Add vegetable, raisins and chicken; cover and cook slowly for about 30 minutes or until chicken is tender. Add more chicken stock if necessary.
7. Add lemon juice. Taste and adjust seasoning if necessary.
8. Sprinkle surface very lightly with each of the 3 spices. Serves 6.

*For Coconut Milk: Pour 2 cups boiling water over contents of 1 8-ounce package of shredded coconut; let stand 5 minutes, then drain thoroughly. Use this liquid. (Remaining coconut can be mixed with fruit or nuts and served as a sambal. If coconut milk is not available, substitute additional chicken stock or milk.)

SHRIMP CURRY

¼ cup butter
2 tablespoons flour
1 teaspoon finely minced onion
1 cup milk
1 cup sour cream
1-2 tablespoons curry powder
3 cups cleaned shrimp
  (2 pounds in shell)

1 tablespoon finely chopped
  ginger
1 tablespoon lemon juice
  dash of Worcestershire Sauce
  salt, pepper

1. Prepare a White Sauce using the first 4 ingredients (method page 79), blending in the minced onion with the butter and flour.

2. Blend in sour cream and curry powder; add remaining ingredients and heat through. Adjust seasoning if necessary.
3. Serve with hot rice and sambals.

To obtain more than 4 servings, sautéed chopped peeled apple, and/or sautéed chopped green pepper may be added.

HURRY CURRY I

Use with seafood, fish or chicken.

½ cup chopped onion
1 garlic clove, crushed
3 tablespoons butter
2 tablespoons curry powder

1 10-ounce can cream celery soup
1 cup tomato juice

1. Sauté onion and garlic in butter until soft; blend in curry powder and remaining ingredients. Heat with frequent stirring until smooth.
2. Pour over any of the following cooked or canned foods: 2 cups shrimps, tuna or other fish, or chicken. Heat through.
   OR
2. Combine all the above ingredients without sautéeing onion or cooking sauce. Add to these ingredients 8 uncooked large chicken wings or 4 disjointed legs (brown first), or uncooked fish or seafood. Cover and cook slowly until foods are tender. Serve with rice.

HURRY CURRY II

Use with lamb or beef.

2 cups diced, cooked roast lamb
   or roast beef
1 large onion, chopped
1 green pepper, chopped
¼ cup celery, chopped
1 clove garlic crushed (optional)

3 tablespoons butter
1 tablespoon curry powder
2 cups lamb or beef gravy or stock
salt, pepper

1. Meat should be trimmed to remove all fat or gristle. Dice, or slice into strips.
2. Sauté chopped onion, green pepper, celery and garlic until soft.
3. Stir in curry powder and gravy, using beef gravy with roast beef and lamb gravy if roast lamb is used. If meat stock is used instead of gravy, thicken it with flour.
4. Add meat and continue cooking until meat is heated through.
5. Season with salt and pepper. Serve with hot rice. Serves 4-6.

SAMBALS

The choice of sambals is usually influenced by the tone of the curry. Very hot curries are complemented by sambals which are mild in flavour, While a more pungent array of sambals often accompanies a milder curry. Choose 3 or more from the following, considering contrasts of flavours, colours and textures.

Mild or Sweet

banana slices sprinkled with
   lemon juice
avacado slices sprinkled with
   lemon juice
hard-cooked egg, chopped
shredded coconut—plain or toasted
crisp bacon, crumbled
peeled cucumber, chopped
tomato, chopped

green pepper, chopped
peanuts, almonds or cashews,
   chopped
raisins, plumped in water or fruit
   juice
Mandarin orange sections, drained
pineapple cubes, drained
sweet pepper jelly or relish

Hot or Sharp

chutney
preserved kumquats
hot pepper relish

preserved ginger, chopped
green onions, sliced
chili pepper seeds (very hot)

SUPPER DISHES MADE WITH TEA BISCUIT, YEAST DOUGH OR PASTRY

MEAT OR FISH ROLL

1. Using recipe for Tea Biscuits (page 437), prepare dough and roll it into a rectangle ¼-inch thick.
2. Spread lightly with soft butter.
3. Prepare 1 of the following 3 filling mixtures:
   a. 2 cups finely chopped or ground leftover roast beef or lamb or meat loaf, crumbled, ½ cup chopped onion, 3 tablespoons chopped green pepper and/or celery and gravy to moisten.
   b. ½ can luncheon meat, 2 tablespoons chopped sweet pickles, 1 tablespoon mayonnaise and 1 teaspoon prepared mustard.
   c. 1 7-ounce can salmon or tuna, 1 tablespoon lemon juice, 1 teaspoon finely chopped onion and 1 tablespoon mayonnaise.
4. Dough and filling can be made into a roll by any one of the following methods:

a. Place filling in a roll down the centre of the dough. Bring up edges of dough to enclose filling; pinch edges together. Bake on greased pan at 400° for 30 minutes.

b. Spread filling on the entire surface of the dough; roll up dough from long side. Place on greased pan with cut edge of roll down. Close ends and bake at 400° for 30 minutes.

c. Slice roll from (b.) into pinwheel slices. Place on a greased pan and bake at 425° for 20 minutes.

5. Serve with gravy, tomato sauce or White Sauce, or a cream soup variety of White Sauce (page 79).

SHRIMP PIE WITH FIESTA BISCUITS

¼ cup chopped onion	2 tablespoons chopped pimento
3 tablespoons chopped green pepper	1 teaspoon Worcestershire Sauce
2 tablespoons butter	¼ teaspoon salt
2 10-ounce tins condensed cream of mushroom soup	⅛ teaspoon pepper
3 tablespoons milk	1 recipe of tea biscuit dough
1½ pounds fresh shrimp, cooked, diced (¾ pound cleaned)	⅓ cup chopped pimento
	½ cup grated Cheddar cheese

1. Sauté onion and pepper in butter until tender.
2. Add the canned soup and the next 6 ingredients; heat, and pour into a 3-quart casserole.
3. Prepare Tea Biscuit dough (page 437) and roll into a rectangle ¼ inch thick; sprinkle with chopped pimento and grated cheese.
4. Roll lengthwise, jellyroll fashion, and cut into ½-inch slices. Place on top of shrimp mixture. Bake 25 minutes or until biscuits are thoroughly baked. Serves 6.

DUMPLINGS WITH TOMATO SAUCE

2 tablespoons fat	dash of pepper
1 small onion, chopped	1 cup flour
1 tablespoon green pepper, diced	2 teaspoons baking powder
2 tablespoons celery, diced	½ teaspoon salt
1 28-ounce can of tomatoes	2 tablespoons fat
1 teaspoon sugar	½ cup grated cheese
½ teaspoon salt	⅓ cup milk

1. Choose a 10-inch skillet with a tight-fitting lid.
2. Melt the fat; simmer the fresh vegetables until they are transparent.
3. Add the tomatoes and seasonings; simmer, covered, until the vegetables are tender.

4. Combine remaining ingredients into Dumplings.
5. Cut out the batter by tablespoonfuls and drop into a plate of flour. This recipe makes 12 dumplings.
6. Drop all the dumplings into the tomato sauce, spacing them evenly.
7. Quickly cover the saucepan and simmer 10 minutes without lifting the cover. Be careful that the heat is kept low so the tomatoes do not scorch.
8. Allow two dumplings with sauce for each serving. Bacon or sausage goes well with these. Serves 6.

TEA BISCUIT PIZZA

Delicious for supper, or after an evening of bridge.

1 recipe tea biscuit dough	¾ cup grated Danish blue
1 6-ounce tin tomato paste	or Cheddar cheese
½ cup chopped onion	salt and pepper
½ cup chopped green pepper	oregano
	2 tins sardines, drained

1. Prepare Tea Biscuit dough (page 437).
2. Knead dough into a large ball and press flat on a greased cookie sheet to form a large circle, about ⅓-inch thick, or two small circles of the same thickness.
3. Spread dough with tomato paste; sprinkle with onion, green pepper, cheese and seasonings.
4. Arrange sardines in a radiating fashion around the circle.
5. Bake at 400° until the edges of the pizza are a golden brown.
6. With the aid of an egg lifter, slide the pizza onto a warm platter. Serve at once. Serves 6-8.

Any of the following may be substituted for sardines: anchovy fillets, crumbled corned beef, wiener slices, bulk sausage meat well cooked and drained. Bacon which has been cooked separately can be arranged on the pizza just before serving.

Mozzarella cheese may be substituted for the Danish blue cheese.

BAMBINOS

Make tiny pizzas, about 1½-2 inches in diameter, and serve hot as appetizers or cocktail accompaniments (Bambinos).

A variety of toppings can be used for Italian Pizza.

ITALIAN PIZZA

1 package dry granular yeast	½ pound sausage meat
½ cup lukewarm water	1 4-ounce can mushrooms
1 teaspoon sugar	1 28-ounce can tomatoes,
½ cup scalded milk	drained, or 1 cup tomato
¼ cup fat	sauce
1 teaspoon salt	½ pound Mozzarella cheese
1 egg	⅓ cup Parmesan cheese
4 to 6 cups all-purpose flour	oregano
1 2-ounce can anchovy fillets	salt, pepper
1 clove garlic, minced	

1. Prepare dough from the first eight ingredients (page 449); let rise until double in bulk.
2. Divide the dough into two pieces; round up; let rest 10 minutes.
3. Soak the garlic in the oil drained from the anchovies.
4. Stretch each ball to cover a greased baking sheet, let rise until double in bulk; crimp the edge as for pie.
5. Brown the sausage meat; drain the tomatoes.
6. Brush the risen dough with oil from the anchovies or with salad oil, cover with the sausage meat; season; add the mushrooms and tomatoes.

7. Arrange the cheese and anchovies on top; sprinkle with oregano; bake at 400° for 15 to 20 minutes. Makes two large pizzas.
To Freeze: Do not add anchovies or sausage. Bake at 450° for 10 minutes and cool. Wrap in a double layer of freezer paper; seal. To serve add meat; bake at 425° for 15-20 minutes.

TOURTIÈRE (PORK PIE)

These pies are traditional French-Canadian Christmas-Eve fare, often served when the family returns from midnight mass.

2 pounds lean shoulder pork and veal	¼ teaspoon pepper
1 cup water	½ teaspoon nutmeg
1 onion	dash of mace, cayenne
1 clove garlic	¼ teaspoon celery salt
1 teaspoon salt	pastry (using 3 cups flour)

1. Chop the meat finely but do not grind; place in a saucepan with water, seasonings and any bone that was left in the meat; cover and simmer until the meat is tender, about 1 hour, adding water if necessary as the meat cooks. The mixture when cooked should be thick. Sometimes bacon is added and the meat, onions and bacon are browned before the water is added.
2. Remove the bone; season if necessary; cool.
3. Prepare the pastry; line 2 8-inch or 8 individual pie tins.
4. Fill with the meat mixture; add a top crust, cut to let the steam escape.
5. Bake at 425° for 40 minutes. Serves 6-8.

These cooked pies can be wrapped and frozen. Heat at 350° for about 30 minutes; serve hot with Chili Sauce.

MISCELLANEOUS CASSEROLES

For convenience only, these casseroles appear in the following order: those made with uncooked meat or fish, and those made with cooked or leftover meat or fish. Many other recipes containing cooked and uncooked meat or fish appear throughout the chapter, but in special categories.

MISCELLANEOUS CASSEROLES MADE FROM UNCOOKED MEAT OR FISH

HAMBURGER PIE

1 medium onion, chopped
2 tablespoons fat
1 pound ground beef
   salt and pepper
2½ cups cooked or canned green
   beans (20 ounce can),
   drained
1 10-ounce tin condensed
   tomato soup

5 medium potatoes, cooked
½ cup warm milk
1 egg, beaten
½ teaspoon salt
½ teaspoon pepper
¼ teaspoon monosodium
   glutamate

1. Brown onion in the hot fat, brown meat in the same fat; add salt and pepper.
2. Stir in the beans and the soup; pour into a large greased casserole.
3. Mash the potatoes; add milk, beaten egg and seasonings. Arrange over meat mixture in a ring or form into 6 mounds.
4. Bake at 350° until potato peaks are lightly browned. Serves 6.

   *4 cups leftover mashed or instant mashed potatoes can be substituted for the potatoes and milk.

SUNSET CASSEROLE

Tasty and economical.

½ cup sliced onion
2 tablespoons fat
1½ to 2 pounds fillet of fish

1 10-ounce can condensed
   tomato soup
½ cup water

1. Cook the onion in the hot fat until a pale yellow; place in a greased casserole.
2. Cut the fish in serving-size pieces; place on top of the onions.
3. Pour the soup diluted with water over the fish.
4. Bake at 350° for 30 minutes. If the fillets are frozen increase the time to 50 minutes.

MUSSAKA

This Greek casserole consists of layers of eggplant and meat; it can be made up ahead and baked when needed.

2 medium eggplants	1 clove garlic, crushed
salt	¼ teaspoon pepper
flour	¼ cup oatmeal or fine bread
4 eggs	crumbs
½ cup salad oil	4 tablespoons flour
1 cup chopped onions	1½ cups milk
6 tablespoons butter	½ teaspoon nutmeg
½ pound ground lean pork	2 egg yolks
and/or beef	sour cream
1 pound ground lean lamb	

1. Cut peeled eggplants in ¼-inch slices; sprinkle with salt and let stand for 15 minutes. Drain. Dust slices with flour.
2. Beat eggs; dip slices in eggs and brown quickly in hot oil in a frying pan. Remove slices to a platter. Save left over egg.
3. Melt 3 tablespoons butter in frying pan, add onions and cook until golden.
4. Combine meats, leftover egg, garlic, pepper, ¼ teaspoon salt, oatmeal or crumbs. Add to onion and cook and stir until meat is browned and crumbled.
5. Prepare a White Sauce of remaining 3 tablespoons butter, 4 tablespoons flour and the milk (page 79). Add nutmeg and ½ teaspoon salt.
6. Beat egg yolks, and stir while adding a little of the hot sauce to them. Stir egg mixture into remaining sauce so that it is completely blended.
7. Line a shallow 3-4 quart casserole with a layer of eggplant. Cover with a layer of meat. Repeat until all eggplant and meat are used, ending with eggplant.
8. Pour sauce evenly over the casserole; bake at 375° for about 50 minutes.
9. Cut in squares; serve with sour cream. Serves 6-8.

MEAT AND SAUERKRAUT CASSEROLE

1½ pounds cubed lean pork	1 19-ounce can tomatoes
1½ pounds cubed veal	2 tablespoons caraway seed
4 tablespoons vegetable oil	1 pint sour cream
2 pounds bulk or canned	¼ teaspoon salt
sauerkraut	⅛ teaspoon pepper

1. Brown meats in oil; rinse sauerkraut in cold water and drain thoroughly.
2. Place sauerkraut in the bottom of a 3-quart casserole and add meats.
3. Mix remaining ingredients together and pour over meat and sauerkraut.
4. Cover and bake 1½ hours at 350°. Serves 6-8.

SWEET AND SOUR PORK

1½ pounds boneless lean pork cut in 1-inch cubes	1 cup pineapple chunks
2 eggs	4 tablespoons cornstarch
3 tablespoons flour	6 tablespoons sugar
½ teaspoon salt	4 tablespoons soy sauce
⅛ teaspoon pepper	6 tablespoons vinegar
4 tablespoons cooking oil	¾ cup pineapple juice
3 green peppers	Chinese noodles or
1 cup diagonally-sliced celery	cooked rice

1. Coat cubes of pork in a mixture of beaten egg, flour and seasonings.
2. Brown meat on all sides in hot oil in frying pan; cover and cook slowly for about 30 minutes.
3. Cut green peppers into 1-inch squares; cook with celery slices in about 2 cups of water for about 12 minutes. Drain.
4. Add vegetables and pineapple to meat. Cover and simmer 10 minutes.
5. Combine cornstarch, sugar, soy sauce, vinegar and juice, cook and stir until clear, about 3 minutes.
6. Pour over meat mixture and simmer 5 minutes. Serve hot over noodles or cooked rice. Serves 6.

Speedy Sweet and Sour Pork: see page 334.

CHOP SUEY

1½ tablespoons butter	½ cup chicken stock
½ cup chopped onion	2 tablespoons flour
½ cup cooked chicken, pork or veal, shredded	½ cup mushrooms
	½ cup toasted almonds, slivered
1 cup diagonally-sliced celery	2 tablespoons soy sauce
1 cup cooked bean sprouts	

1. Sauté onions in butter until soft, about 3 minutes.
2. Add meat, celery, bean sprouts and half fo the chicken stock.

3. Make a paste of remaining stock and flour, and stir into the meat-vegetable mixture. Cook and stir until tender.

4. In another pan, sauté mushrooms in 1 tablespoon butter. Add to mixture. Stir in almonds and soy sauce. Serve with hot rice.

For additional flavour, marinate meat for about 15 minutes before cooking, in the following marinade:

1½ tablespoons soy sauce 2 teaspoons brown sugar
2 tablespoons salad oil

Omit additional soy sauce in the recipe.

EGG FOO YONG

1 cup cooked ham, pork, chicken, shrimp or lobster
1 No. 2 can (2½ cups) bean sprouts
2 tablespoons flour
3 green onions
6 water chestnuts (optional)

1 3-ounce can sliced mushrooms
½ teaspoon salt
dash of pepper
5 eggs
salad oil for frying

1. Chop the meat finely; drain bean sprouts and toss them around in the flour; slice the green onions and water chestnuts; drain mushrooms; mix vegetables with meat.

2. Add salt and pepper to eggs and beat slightly; stir into meat mixture. Heat salad oil in a skillet and fry one large spoonful of the mixture at a time over a medium heat. Fry each side 3 to 4 minutes or until golden. Keep warm in a low oven until all are fried. Serve with Chinese sauce (page 92).

EGG ROLLS

Filling

½ pound cooked lean pork
1 large onion
½ pound fresh or 1 6-ounce can mushrooms
1 cup (½ pound) cooked shrimp

1 19-ounce can (2½ cups) bean sprouts
2 teaspoons salad oil
2 teaspoons sesame seeds
1 teaspoon monosodium glutamate

1. Grind or chop finely pork, onion and mushrooms; chop shrimp into little chunks; drain and chop bean sprouts.

2. Heat oil in a saucepan, pour in sesame seeds and cook until brown and toasted; mix all filling ingredients together.

Egg Rolls, a necessary part of a Chinese dinner.

Wrappers

6 eggs	½ teaspoon salad oil
1½ cups sifted all-purpose flour	shortening or salad oil for
1½ teaspoons salt	deep frying
2¼ cups water	

1. Beat eggs until light; add flour and salt and beat until smooth; stir in the water.
2. Heat oil in a 6-inch skillet; spoon about 2 tablespoons of batter into skillet and tilt pan so batter covers entire bottom. Fry over low heat until the edges begin to curl away from skillet. Fry one side only, then lift from pan and store on a tray until all batter, with the exception of ¼ cup, is used.
3. On the fried side of the wrapper put a heaping tablespoon of filling; fold in 2 ends of wrapper. Brush edges with remaining batter to seal, then roll up other 2 edges to shape a little roll.
4. Heat oil until a cube of bread turns brown in 1 minute (360°) and fry egg rolls until pale gold. Makes about 30. Reheat in oven before serving. Serve with Mustard Sauce (page 91).

MEXICORN CASSEROLE

2½ cups cooked or canned kernel corn	¼ teaspoon salt
1 cup White Sauce	⅛ teaspoon pepper
1 green pepper, chopped	1¼ cups crumbled crisp cooked bacon/or minced cooked
1 pimento, chopped	ham
2 egg yolks	2 egg whites

1. Drain liquid from canned corn; use this liquid plus light cream to make the White Sauce (page 79).
2. Add corn, chopped green pepper and pimento and cook until mixture bubbles. Watch carefully to prevent burning.
3. Remove mixture from the heat; beat egg yolks and add a little hot sauce to them, beating constantly.
4. Stir egg mixture into remaining hot mixture and cook 2 minutes more; season with salt and pepper.
5. Cover the bottom of an ungreased 2 quart casserole with prepared bacon or ham.
6. Beat egg whites until stiff; fold into corn mixture.
7. Bake at 325° for 10 minutes; increase heat to 350° and bake until firm, about 20 minutes. Serves 6.

If recipe is doubled, casserole must be baked about 3 times as long as for a single recipe.

VEAL AND HAM PIE

2 cups diced cooked veal	1½ cups leftover gravy or
1 cup diced cooked ham	1 can cream of celery soup
½ cup diced cooked potato	heated with ¼ cup milk
1 cup cooked green peas, carrots or celery	topping for stew

1. Combine the meats, vegetables and sauce; taste and season.
2. Add a topping of Pastry or Biscuit Dough (page 472).
3. Bake as required for the topping. Serves 4-6.

HAM AND SWEET POTATO CASSEROLE

1 cup diced cooked ham	2 eggs, beaten
2 teaspoons steak sauce	2 cups mashed, cooked sweet
⅛ teaspoon pepper	potato
¼ cup orange juice	2 tablespoons brown sugar
½ cup rich cream	

Mix all ingredients, except brown sugar, and put in shallow 1-quart baking dish. Sprinkle with brown sugar. Bake in moderate oven (350°) 30 to 40 minutes.

HAM ITALIENNE

1½ cups cooked macaroni (about ⅔ cup before cooking)	1 cup grated Cheddar cheese cooked ham shredded or finely chopped
2 cups seasoned tomato sauce	

Combine all the ingredients; reheat, taste and season. Serves 3-4.

DEVILLED HAM CASSEROLE

½ cup ground cooked ham	4 slices bread
2 tablespoons chili sauce	¼ cup grated cheese
1 teaspoon prepared mustard	2 teaspoons butter
1 teaspoon minced onion	3 eggs, beaten
1 teaspoon Worcestershire Sauce	½ teaspoon salt
1 teaspoon prepared horseradish	2 cups milk

1. Combine the first 6 ingredients.
2. Spread bread with ham mixture; cut into ½-inch cubes.
3. Alternate layers of cubes and cheese in a greased casserole, with bread as top layer; dot with pieces of butter.
4. Combine beaten eggs, salt and milk; pour over bread mixture.
5. Set casserole in a pan of warm water and bake at 350° for 1¼ hours.

A can of devilled ham may be used in the same way; omit the ham and seasonings.

HAM ROLLS (Basic Recipe)

Rice is only one of the many delicious fillings suited to this dish.

1½ cups cooked rice	8 thin slices cooked ham
2 tablespoons parsley	1 can cream of chicken soup
¼ cup toasted almonds	½ can water
2 tablespoons butter	

1. Mix the rice, parsley, nuts and melted butter.
2. Roll a rounded tablespoon of the mixture in each slice of ham.
3. Place in a casserole; cover with the soup and water.
4. Bake at 350° for 20 minutes. Serves 4-6

HAM AND BANANA ROLLS

Spread ham slices lightly with prepared mustard and substitute bananas (halved lengthwise if large) for the Ham Roll filling. Sprinkle sauce with grated cheese before baking.

ASPARAGUS HAM ROLLS

Substitute cooked asparagus spears for Ham Roll filling, using 2 or 3 in each roll if thin. Cover with sauce, grated cheese and bake.

HAM NOODLE ROLLS

Combine equal quantities of highly-seasoned cheese sauce and cooked spaghetti or noodles. Roll in slices of cooked ham. Omit soup and water; bake as Ham Rolls. Serve hot; garnish with parsley.

SPEEDY SWEET AND SOUR PORK

Arrange four ½-inch slices of cold roast pork and 4 sliced cooked sweet potatoes (1 20-ounce tin) in a shallow open pan. Pour over Sweet and Sour Sauce (use half the recipe page 329). Broil about 5 inches from heat 5-10 minutes.

SPEEDY PATTIES DIVINE

1 or 1½ cups corned beef or canned fish or minced beef	¼ cup fat
½ cup finely chopped onion	3 slices sharp-flavoured processed cheese
½ cup finely chopped green pepper	1 10-ounce tin cream of vegetable soup
½ cup mayonnaise	⅓ cup milk or meat stock
¾ cup fine bread crumbs	3 hamburger buns

1. Prepare flat patties from first 4 ingredients; roll in crumbs and press patties between hands to make crumbs adhere.
2. Brown patties on both sides in fat. Patties made from raw beef should be cooked, covered, for about 4 minutes longer.
3. Place patties in a single layer in the bottom of a 12 by 9-inch pan. Cut cheese slices into triangles, 4 per slice, and overlap 2 on each patty. Combine soup and milk or stock and pour around patties.
4. Bake at 350° for about 12 to 15 minutes until heated through.
5. Serve on hot or toasted bun halves. Serves 6.

FISH PIE

1 7-ounce can salmon	seasoning
1 tablespoon chili sauce or ketchup	1 tablespoon grated or finely chopped onion
1 cup milk	¼ cup grated cheese
2 tablespoons fat	2 to 3 medium potatoes, mashed
2 tablespoons flour	

1. Flake the fish into the bottom of a greased baking dish; sprinkle with chili sauce.
2. Make a White Sauce from the next 4 ingredients (page 79), add the onion and ½ the cheese; pour over the fish.

3. Cover with a 1-inch layer of mashed, seasoned potatoes; sprinkle with the rest of the cheese.
4. Bake at 350° until brown and bubbly.

    4 cups mashed potatoes, leftover or instant, can be substituted; cream of celery soup can be used to make the sauce.

SHEPHERD'S PIE

2 cups minced cooked meat	½ cup gravy or stock
salt and pepper	3 cups mashed potatoes
1 teaspoon grated onion	1 egg, beaten

1. Mix meat, seasonings and gravy; heat. Stir to prevent sticking. Worcestershire Sauce, tomato ketchup or parsley may be added.
2. Warm the leftover potatoes, beat well, add egg and seasonings; add milk if necessary.
3. Butter a baking dish; put in a layer of potato, then a layer of meat; repeat, having potato on top.
4. Bake in hot oven until potatoes are browned and mixture heated through. Serves 4-6.

BROWNED HASH

1 cup minced cooked meat	stock, gravy or strained tomato
2 cups mashed potatoes	½ tablespoon fat
1 teaspoon grated onion	1 teaspoon finely chopped
salt and pepper	parsley
1 egg	

1. Mix meat, vegetables, seasonings and beaten egg; add enough stock to hold mixture together.
2. Melt fat in heavy pan.
3. Spread mixture evenly in pan; reduce heat.
4. Cook slowly so that mixture browns evenly.
5. Fold as an omelet.
6. Garnish with parsley; serve with tomato ketchup or hot tomato sauce. Serves 2-3.

    The mixture may be shaped into round flat cakes and browned.

SUPPER DISHES MADE WITH BREAD

BAKED CHEESE CUBES

2 cups bread, cut in ⅔-inch cubes	2 cups milk
1 cup grated cheese	2 tablespoons butter, melted
2 eggs	1 teaspoon salt
	dash of cayenne

1. Butter a baking dish; arrange cubes of bread and cheese in layers, having bread on top.
2. Beat eggs; add milk, butter and seasonings.
3. Pour on the bread; let stand 20 minutes.
4. Oven-poach at 350° until firm—large amount, 35 to 40 minutes; individual, 20 minutes.

   Sliced stuffed olives baked in the casserole add flavour.

CHEESE STRATAS

12 half-inch slices dry bread	1 tablespoon chopped parsley
12 slices processed cheese (½ pound)	dash of each of pepper, paprika and seasoned salt
4 eggs	1 teaspoon minced onion (optional)
2⅔ cups milk	
¾ teaspoon salt	

1. Arrange alternate layers of bread and cheese in 6 individual 1½-cup baking dishes or 1 large dish, having the top layer of cheese.
2. Beat eggs and milk with an egg beater; add seasonings; pour part of the liquid into each of the baking dishes; chill.
3. Oven-poach at 350° about 30 minutes for small dishes, 45 minutes for large, or until custard is just set and bread has puffed up. Serves 6.

SALMON STRATAS

Remove skin and bones from contents of 1-pound can of salmon; add liquid to milk. Omit cheese, and instead cover bottom layer of bread with flaked salmon. Finish as Cheese Stratas. Serves 6.

SUPPER ON A BUN

Hot dog buns, salad buns, hamburger buns or English muffins lend themselves to this informal presentation of lunch, supper or late-evening snacks. When hot foods are to be served on buns, the buns should always be heated—in a bun warmer (improvise this by using a rack in a pot) on top of the stove, or in a paper bag or in foil in the oven. When heating many buns, use a covered roasting pan. Buns can also be toasted or heated with the filling under the broiler.

Fishburgers are something a little different for casual entertaining.

BARBECUED BEEF BUNS

1 small onion	4 slices cold roast beef or
3 tablespoons butter	1 12-ounce tin corned beef
1 cup ketchup	

1. Chop onion finely and sauté in butter until tender.
2. Cut beef into 2-inch strips; add with ketchup to the onion.
3. Simmer about 20 minutes and spoon onto toasted buns. Serves 6.
   Barbecue Sauce can be substituted for the first three ingredients.

DEVILLED STEAK BUNS

1. Rub very thin minute steaks with a little dry mustard and a dash of Worcestershire Sauce; broil; turn; broil. Do not overcook.
2. Sprinkle with salt and spread with grated cheese (try blue cheese crumbled); broil again to melt the cheese.
3. Serve in toasted buttered buns. Serves 6.

HAM 'N' EGG BUNS

1 cup cooked ham	1 tablespoon cream
3 eggs	1 green pepper, chopped
¼ teaspoon salt	

1. Chop the ham finely; sauté until golden brown; remove from the heat.

2. Beat eggs well; add all the other ingredients.
3. Spoon into a little hot fat in a frying pan to make a small pancake. Cook slowly, turning once until golden brown. Serve in toasted buttered buns. Serves 6.

BREAKFAST BUNS

2 eggs	3 hamburger buns
2 tablespoons milk	⅓ cup devilled ham
salt, pepper	3 tablespoons grated cheese
1 tablespoon melted butter	

1. Beat eggs, milk, salt and pepper; pour into frying pan containing butter; scramble eggs until just firm. Do not overcook.
2. Split the buns; toast both sides under the broiler 3 inches from the heat for 1 minute.
3. Spread with devilled ham, then with egg and grated cheese.
4. Broil until the cheese melts. Serves 6.

HOT EGG SALAD BUNS

1½ cups grated cheese	3 tablespoons sliced stuffed
3 tablespoons green pepper	olives
⅓ cup chopped onion	½ teaspoon Worcestershire Sauce
2 cups hard-cooked egg (6)	3 tablespoons ketchup

Combine all the ingredients; spread the mixture on ½ of bun and broil 6 inches from heat for about 5 minutes. Toast remaining halves of buns; butter and put halves together. Or, fill buns with mixture, wrap in foil and bake at 400° for 15 minutes. Serves 6.

TUNA AND EGG BUNS

1 cup grated cheese	¼ cup hot dog relish
2 hard-cooked eggs, chopped	¼ cup mayonnaise
1 cup tuna, flaked	6 hamburger buns

Combine all ingredients and bake as in preceding recipe.

BUNS DE LUXE

6 wiener buns	½ cup finely sliced celery
1 can tuna*	⅛ teaspoon salt
¼ teaspoon grated onion	4 tablespoons mayonnaise

1. Partly hollow out the top and bottom part of a bun; save the crumbs to dry for bread crumbs for other purposes; brush the top and bottom half of bun with soft butter.

2. Drain the tuna; rinse with boiling water; flake into a bowl; combine with other ingredients.
3. Press gently into the hollow in the bottom half of the bun; close the two halves.

   *Chicken, salmon, shrimp, crabmeat or lobster may be served in the same way.

FISH BURGER BUNS

Prepare fish patties (page 226). Place in toasted, buttered bun; garnish with pickle, chips or thin slices of lemon.

WAYS WITH WIENERS

Wieners or frankfurters (the names are used interchangeably) can be dressed up to provide tasty, speedy snacks and supper dishes.

FILLED WIENERS

1 pound wieners (10-12)	canned baked beans mixed
strips of cheese	with hot dog relish
sweet pickle relish	cole slaw
crushed pineapple or	dill pickles cut in long wedges
pineapple spears	10 to 12 strips bacon

1. Slit the wiener lengthwise not quite all the way through; add any one of the materials suggested above except bacon.
2. Fry the bacon until partly cooked; drain on paper towel; wrap, spiral fashion, around the wiener.
3. Bake at 425° for 15 to 20 minutes or heat 5 inches from the broiler until the bacon is cooked and the wiener hot; or fry over medium heat.
4. Serve in a hot buttered wiener bun, in a buttered toasted bun, or on a slice of buttered bread spread with mustard. Place the wiener diagonally on the bread; bring up the opposite corners and fasten with toothpicks; broil 7 inches from the heat until brown.

BARBECUED WIENERS

Here are 3 different versions:
(a) Simmer 1 pound of wieners in a pan with ½ cup chopped onion and 1 cup Barbecue Sauce (page 86) for about 10 minutes or until the onions are cooked.
(b) Place wieners on grill of barbecue or on a shish kabob wheel. Baste with Barbecue Sauce. Cook and turn, basting frequently.
(c) Slit frankfurters lengthwise to a depth of about ½ inch (almost but not quite through). Open flat; brush with Barbecue Sauce and broil.

FRANKABOBS

These are really shish kabobs with weiners predominating. Cut wieners into 1-inch chunks and thread onto skewers. See recipe for Shish Kabobs (page 168) for suggestions for additions. Baste with Barbecue Sauce or any basting mixture. Broil, turning frequently

BARBER POLE FRANKS

1 pound wieners	1 recipe tea biscuit dough

1. Prepare Tea Biscuit Dough (page 437); roll to form a 9 by 12-inch rectangle; spread with mustard.
2. Cut into ¾-inch strips lengthwise; wrap each strip spiral fashion around the wieners, pinching the dough at each end to seal it.
3. Bake at 425° for 12 to 15 minutes. Serve with catsup, chili sauce or mustard sauce.

WAYS WITH HAMBURGERS

HAMBURGERS

Use the recipe for Hamburger Patties (page 149) to prepare the following variations:

SURPRISES

1. Roll hamburger patties thin between sheets of waxed paper; on 1 patty spread 1 of the fillings below not quite to the edge.
2. Place the other patty on top and press the edges together until none of the filling shows. Cook as usual. Serves 8.
   ¼ cup chili sauce thickened with 1 cup grated cheese.
   ¼ cup green onions sliced.
   ½ cup grated blue cheese mixed with 2 tablespoons mayonnaise, 2 teaspoons prepared mustard and 2 tablespoons Worcestershire Sauce.

TOPPINGS

Before broiling, spread with any ketchup, mustard sauce, relish, chili sauce, sharp cheese, grated or sliced; after broiling add onion rings, chopped chives, green onions or sliced Spanish onion.

Spoon one of these on top of 8 cooked hamburgers:

ONION SAUCE: 1 package onion soup mix, 2 cups water, 2 tablespoons flour, 4 tablespoons soft butter. Mix the soup with water; bring to a boil. Combine butter and flour to a smooth paste; stir into the hot liquid; stir until smooth and thick.

CHILI BEAN SAUCE: 1 can chili con carne, 1 sliced Spanish onion. Place the hamburger and onion on ½ of toasted bun; spoon heated chili over top.

MUSHROOM SAUCE: Sauté ¼ pound mushrooms, washed and chopped, in 2 tablespoons chicken fat or butter until they brown; add 1 chicken bouillon cube, ½ cup water, 1 tablespoon ketchup; simmer 5 minutes; add 1 tablespoon flour mixed with a little water and stir to thicken.

12 Sandwich and Toast Variations

SANDWICHES

Sandwiches come in all styles and sizes, from hearty to formal, with many intermediary varieties. The same principles are involved in their making.

FACTS TO CONSIDER

1. Bread should be a day old and of a fine, even texture. Very fresh bread should be chilled in the refrigerator before slicing.
2. Use white and brown breads alone or in combination.
3. Sandwiches may be made with or without the crust; for formal occasions remove the crusts before applying butter and filling.
4. Leave the butter, margarine or mixture of the 2 out of the refrigerator several hours before using, and soften by creaming.
5. Fillings should be moist; excess moisture causes sogginess, while dry sandwiches are unpalatable. Tomato sandwiches should be made as near to serving time as possible. Fillings should be well seasoned and of spreading consistency.
6. Butter and sandwich filling should extend right out to the edges of each slice.
7. Sandwiches may be kept fresh by wrapping in waxed paper so that no air can enter, then placing them in a crisping pan covered with a damp tea towel and storing in a refrigerator. Not cutting the sandwiches until just before serving time also ensures freshness.

TO FREEZE SANDWICHES

Prepare sandwiches without lettuce, tomatoes or cucumber. Do not use mayonnaise in quantities constituting more than ⅓ of the volume of the filling. Jelly does not freeze well, and if hard-cooked eggs are to be frozen, they should be thoroughly mashed to prevent them from becoming rubbery in texture.

Sliced or ground meat, poultry, meat loaf and corned beef freeze well. Creamed cheese fillings tend to crumble; if frozen separately (without bread) the texture of the filling can be restored by kneading, after thawing.

Cover bread generously with butter or margarine, before spreading filling; this prevents filling from making bread soggy.

Freeze open-faced sandwiches on trays, covered with a sheet of heavy-duty wax paper or foil; freeze quickly. Then transfer to rigid, air-tight containers. Other sandwiches should be wrapped before freezing, in individual sandwich bags if sandwiches are to be used at different times in lunch boxes, or in lots to be served at one time, packaged for ease of wrapping and freezing.

Thaw open-face sandwiches on serving trays, covered with a clean tea towel. Thaw other sandwiches in original wrappings, opened, to allow the escape of excess moisture. Allow 30-60 minutes at room temperature for thawing to take place.

Sandwiches may be kept frozen up to 6 weeks.

FACTS ABOUT SANDWICH INGREDIENTS

BREAD: 24-ounce loaf (average size) cuts into approximately 28 slices ⅜ inches thick or about 22 slices ½ inch thick. Bread cuts to best advantage when a day old.

BUTTER OR MARGARINE: When softened, 1 pound of butter or margarine will spread approximately 96 slices of bread if 1 teaspoonful is used for each slice.

CHEESE: 1 pound of processed cheese cuts into approximately 16 to 18 slices when cut thinner than ¼ inch; when grated, 1 pound of cheese makes 4 cups; 1 pound of cottage cheese is equivalent to 2 cups.

CHICKEN: 1 5-pound fowl averages 7 cups cooked, diced meat, enough for approximately 40 sandwiches if 2 tablespoons of chicken are used in each.

EGGS: 1 dozen hard-cooked eggs, chopped, averages 3½ cups, which is sufficient for 25 sandwiches if 2 tablespoons are allowed for each sandwich.

LETTUCE: 1 medium head averages 15 leaves; wash and dry thoroughly before using.

MAYONNAISE: 1 cup (8 ounces) will spread approximately 25 slices of bread if 1 tablespoon is used per slice.

MEAT: 1 pound of cold (cooked) meat averages 8 slices; bologna averages 15 slices per pound; minced cooked meat averages 3 cups to a pound, enough for approximately 2 dozen sandwiches, if about 2 table-spoonfuls are allowed for each sandwich.

CANNED SALMON AND TUNA: I pound averages 1 pint of flaked fish, which makes approximately 15 sandwiches if about 2 tablespoonfuls are used for each sandwich.

SANDWICH FILLINGS AND SPREADS

CUCUMBER

1. Cut peeled cucumber in thin slices; remove large seeds.
2. Cover with diluted vinegar to which a little salt has been added, or with sour cream; let stand ½ hour; drain.
3. Place on buttered bread; spread with salad dressing; cover with buttered bread.

ADDITIONS: Lettuce; thin tomato slices; sliced Bermuda or Spanish onions.

TOMATO

1. Peel and cut tomato into thin slices; sprinkle with salt; allow to drain.
2. Spread salad dressing on buttered bread, cut a little thicker than for other sandwiches. Place tomato slices on lettuce on one slice of bread. Cover with buttered bread.

ADDITIONS: Olives, chives.

SPINACH

1½ cups shredded fresh spinach	salt and pepper
1 hard-cooked egg, chopped	1 tablespoon mayonnaise or
1 teaspoon chopped celery	salad dressing
1 teaspoon onion juice	

Combine ingredients; mix lightly. Spread on buttered bread. Makes 1¼ cups, 8 or 9 sandwiches.

LETTUCE

Leaf lettuce needs to be well washed. Dry on clean towel.

Use very thin fresh bread; butter; spread each piece with salad dressing. Shred lettuce or pile several leaves together.

WATER CRESS, PEPPERGRASS OR PEPPER CRESS

Remove coarse stems of water cress and chop. Spread greens on thin slices of buttered bread. If desired, chopped cucumber can be added to the greens; it should first be put through meat grinder, then drained for several hours.

OLIVES

Chop stuffed or plain ripe or green olives.
  Mix with salad dressing.

  ADDITIONS: Cheese, nuts, chicken, veal.

NUTS

Chop walnuts, almonds, pecans or peanuts very finely.
  Combine with salad dressing.

  ADDITIONS: Cheese, pimento, olives, green pepper, raisins.

PEANUT BUTTER

Mix peanut butter with any one of honey, orange marmalade, crisp crumbled bacon, mashed or sliced banana; or spread one slice of bread with peanut butter, one with jam; put together with sliced banana, raisins or slivered dates.

DATES

Chop dates finely; moisten with cream, mild salad dressing and/or cream cheese.

  ADDITIONS: Nuts, preserved ginger, orange juice and rind or orange marmalade.

RAISINS

Use seeded raisins or soak seedless raisins 15 minutes in hot water.
  Chop finely; mix with salad dressing or cream cheese.

  ADDITIONS: Nuts, preserved ginger, chopped pineapple, shredded carrot.

CHOPPED MEAT

Chop cooked chicken or veal, stuffed roast pork, roast beef, ham.
  Season, add salad dressing to moisten.
  Spread on thin slices of buttered bread.

  ADDITIONS: Finely chopped celery, crisp lettuce leaves, chopped olives, green pepper, horseradish, mustard or sweet pickles.

MEAT SPREAD

2 chicken bouillon cubes	¼ cup chopped sweet pickle
2 tablespoons boiling water	¼ cup chopped peanuts
¾ cup cooked pork, chopped	⅛ teaspoon pepper
¼ cup chopped celery	4 tablespoons mayonnaise

Dissolve the bouillon cubes in water; add other ingredients.
Taste and season. Spreads 10-12 sandwiches.

BAKED BEAN FILLING

1 cup baked beans	½ teaspoon salt
½ cup crumbled crisp bacon	⅛ teaspoon dry mustard
(8 slices)	4 tablespoons mayonnaise
2 tablespoons sweet pickle	

Drain the beans well; mash with a fork.
Add the remaining ingredients; taste and season. Spreads 6-8
sandwiches.

Salmon on a bun topped with Swiss cheese, grilled and garnished.

FISH

SALMON (COHOE OR SOCKEYE): Drain well, remove skin and bones; flake apart with fork. To each 7-ounce tin of salmon add 1 teaspoon lemon juice, ¼ teaspoon grated onion, ¼ cup finely chopped celery, salt and small amount of salad dressing. A 7-ounce tin spreads 6-8 sandwiches.

TUNA: Drain off the oil; rinse with boiling water; finish as salmon.

SARDINES: Prepare as tuna; mix a little ketchup with sardines. 1 tin spreads 4 sandwiches.

SHRIMP: Rinse canned shrimp; remove the black line; mash slightly with a fork. Add a little lemon juice and mayonnaise. Add thinly sliced celery if desired.

LOBSTER OR LOBSTER PASTE: Add a little lemon juice; celery and salad dressing may be added to make it go farther.

SLICED CHICKEN

Cold boiled fowl is best if many sandwiches are to be made; slice it thinly. Spread the bread with butter, then mayonnaise. Cover with slices of chicken; season with salt and pepper. Canned chicken can be used in the same way; jellied juices should be removed. The addition of a leaf of dry, crisp lettuce to each sandwich provides a contrast of texture.

CHICKEN SALAD FILLING

Mix together 1 cup diced, cooked chicken, ½ cup finely chopped celery, ¼ cup mayonnaise, 1½ teaspoons lemon juice, salt and pepper to taste. 1 or 2 hard-cooked eggs, chopped, can also be added. Spread on buttered bread.

EGG

2 hard-cooked eggs	pepper
speck of dry mustard	mayonnaise
salt	chives or minced onion

Mash the egg with a fork or chop finely. When using several eggs, use a pastry blender or potato masher to chop eggs. Season. Add enough mayonnaise to give a spreading consistency. Spreads 3-4 double sandwiches. Chopped green or ripe olives give extra flavour and colour.

CHEESE

Grate cheese or mix processed cheese until soft. Combine with chopped sweet pickle; chopped salted peanuts; prepared mustard. *Or*, blend cream cheese with equal quantities of pickle relish and liver sausage.

MINCED HAM

Mix minced ham with chopped mustard pickles; add salad dressing to moisten to spreading consistency.

MINCED COLD ROAST BEEF

Add horseradish and sufficient mayonnaise to make it of spreading consistency.

SLICED COLD ROAST BEEF

Flavour ½ cup sour cream with 2 teaspoons onion soup mix and 1 teaspoon prepared horseradish, drained. Spread thin slices of beef on 4 slices of buttered bread. Cover each slice with a leaf of lettuce and a spoonful of sour-cream mixture. Cover with a second slice of buttered bread. Makes 4 sandwiches; serve with slices of dill pickle.

EVERYDAY SANDWICHES

Closed sandwiches are popular for their ease of preparation and their versatility. Served toasted or plain, or with lettuce as salad sandwiches, they can be cut into generous halves for lunch boxes or into smaller and more intricate shapes for afternoon tea. It is important that slices of bread be matched before butter is applied. The following are suggested ways for cutting made-up sandwiches into smaller ones:

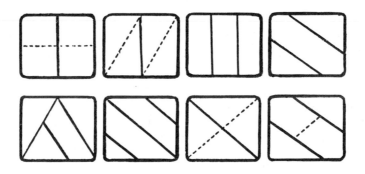

Cut 4 or 5 at one time with a very sharp knife, allowing no ragged edges of filling or lettuce to remain.

BROILED AND TOASTED SANDWICHES
CHICKEN, HAM AND TOMATO

1. Toast 3 slices bread; butter.
2. Spread one slice with salad dressing, cover with chicken slices, cover with second buttered toast slice.
3. Butter top side of this slice, spread with salad dressing; place tomato and ham slices.
4. Cover with third slice of toast.
5. Cut across from corner to corner; garnish with parsley, sweet pickles or olives; serve at once.

CHEESE, BACON AND FRIED EGG

1. Toast bread; butter. Fry bacon; drain. Fry egg.
2. Cover first slice with bacon strips and cheese. Cover with toast buttered on both sides.
3. Cover second slice with fried egg. Cover with third slice of buttered toast.

MIDNIGHT SPECIAL

1. Toast bread slices on one side. Spread untoasted side with butter, then peanut butter.
2. Mash 1 cup canned baked beans; add 2 tablespoons each chopped onion, ketchup, and chopped pickle or relish.
3. Spread over peanut butter. Top with partly-cooked bacon slices.
4. Broil about 5 minutes. Top with thin, peeled tomato slice. Broil 3 or 4 minutes.

CHEESE DREAMS

1. For each sandwich, toast 1 slice bread (crusts trimmed) on one side. Spread untoasted side with mayonnaise.
2. Top with tomato slice. Sprinkle with salt. Add a generous slice of cheese, then a strip of partially broiled bacon.
3. Place sandwich about 6 inches below broiler and broil until cheese is melted and bacon crisp. Serve while hot.

BROILED CHEESE

Toast bread and cut off crusts. Spread with thin slices of processed cheese and sliced sweet pickle. Broil until cheese melts, then top with second slice of hot buttered toast.

TOASTED ROLLS

1. Make rolled sandwiches, using thinly sliced bread cut crosswise from the loaf.
2. Spread with creamed yellow cheese, or with sandwich spread, or with mushroom soup undiluted, to which finely chopped fried mushrooms have been added.
3. Roll; brush with melted butter. Toast under broiler.
   These rolls may be made up in advance and left covered, to be toasted when required.

BACON

12 bacon strips, fried crisp	butter or margarine
8 slices white or whole-wheat bread	maple syrup

1. Place 3 strips of bacon between 2 slices of bread.
2. Spread outsides of sandwich with butter or margarine.
3. Cook in skillet or on a grill till brown on both sides.
4. Serve with hot maple syrup.

GRILLED CHEESE

Butter a slice of bread on one side; put buttered-side down on a frying pan or grill. Cover with a thin slice of processed cheese and another slice of bread, buttered on the top side only. Cook over low-medium heat until golden brown, turn and cook on the other side.

PIZZA-STYLE

Layer salami, pizza sauce, and cheese between slices of bread, sprinkled with garlic salt and brushed with soft butter. Cook on a frying pan or grill until golden brown.

SAUTÉED CLUB SANDWICH (FRENCH TOAST SANDWICH)

Butter a slice of bread, cover it with sliced, lean, baked ham and sliced, cooked chicken. Butter a second slice of bread on both sides and place it on the meat. Cover this with thinly-sliced Swiss cheese. Butter a third slice of bread and place it, buttered-side down, over cheese. Trim off crusts and cut sandwich in half; secure each half with toothpicks. Beat 1 egg in a flat dish with 2 tablespoons of milk. Dip sandwiches in the egg, on both sides. Melt 2 tablespoons butter in a frying pan and sauté sandwiches until golden brown. Remove picks and serve sandwich with currant jelly, sweet pickle relish or cranberry sauce. Serves 1.
See also recipes in the section "Supper on a Bun," pages 336.

SMORREBROD

The Cold Board or Koldt Bord of Denmark, the smorgasbord of Sweden, usually features hearty open-faced sandwiches or Smorrebrod.

Use a variety of shapes and flavours of the bread on which the sandwiches are made and slice it thinly. Butter the bread and arrange the food attractively. Some suggestions are:

Smoked Salmon with a diagonal ribbon of scrambled egg; garnish with chives.

Canned Salmon with a twist of lemon garnished with water cress or sliced cucumber.

Sliced hard-cooked egg with anchovies and sliced tomato garnished with cress.

Sliced chicken or turkey with a ribbon of cranberry sauce or slices of cranberry jelly.

Lobster and mayonnaise on lettuce decorated with asparagus tips.

Many small shrimps in even rows with a teaspoon of mayonnaise and a cucumber twist.

A thin slice of Danish blue cheese with radish rings and cress to decorate.

Cold roast pork or spiced meat roll, with chopped pickle, sliced tomato.

Salami with thin onion rings.

Liver paste with tomato slices and crisp bacon.

Cold ham with hot mustard and onion rings or with cottage cheese and green pepper.

Sardines, a whole row, well drained, with a twist of lemon and chopped chive.

Cooked chicken livers chopped; sliced hard-cooked eggs.

Baked beans, fresh onion rings, crisp bacon.

Swiss cheese triangles with triangles of tongue, chicken loaf or cold cuts.

Date paste, thin round slice crisp apple cored and dipped in orange juice; fill centre with chopped nuts.

Peanut butter, sliced bananas, orange or apricot marmalade glaze.

As a final finish to these attractive pictures a glaze is sometimes poured over the sandwiches and allowed to set.

SMORREBROD GLAZE

1⅔ cup water	1 package lemon jelly powder
⅛ teaspoon pepperberries	3 tablespoons vinegar
½ bay leaf	½ teaspoon salt
½ teaspoon dill seed	pepper

1. Combine water, seasonings; cover and simmer 10 minutes, strain.
2. Dissolve the jelly powder in the hot water; add vinegar and seasoning; chill; when the jelly begins to set spoon a thin layer over the decorated sandwiches on a rack.

This Seafood Sandwich Torte is different and attractive. One loaf of bread is cut horizontally into 6 slices. They are then cut in half and fitted together with different fillings in each layer, and garnished.

PARTY SANDWICHES

ROLLED SANDWICHES

1. Cut fresh bread into as thin slices as possible; remove crusts. Roll each slice once with a rolling pin to keep bread from cracking.
2. Spread with butter; place a small bunch of cress at each end of the bread, extending a little beyond the edge.
3. Roll closely on a damp towel covered with waxed paper.

SUGGESTED FILLINGS: Cheese; chopped olives; chopped nuts; pimento and nuts; crushed pineapple and cream cheese. Gherkins, tiny sausages (cooked), celery sticks, asparagus can be used for centres.

PINWHEEL SANDWICHES

1. Cut the crust from the top of a fresh loaf of bread; turn loaf on its side and cut ⅓-inch lengthwise slices.
2. Remove crusts and roll each slice with a rolling pin to keep bread from cracking.
3. Spread each slice with butter and filling.
4. Place a row of olives or pickles along the nearest edge . When rolled this will make a distinct centre in the pinwheel. Strips of pimento can be placed across the filling at regular intervals to form a pattern when rolled.
5. Roll sandwiches, starting at the edge which has the edge of olives or pickles; wrap and chill.
6. Cut in ⅓-inch slices.

SUGGESTED FILLINGS: Pimento cheese mixed to a paste with mayonnaise; chopped egg filling; mushroom filling; egg and olive filling. For an attractive Christmas sandwich-spread with white cream cheese or cottage cheese; arrange olives along one end; at 2-inch intervals place alternate strips of green pepper and pimento.

BANANA PINWHEELS

1. Cut bread as for pinwheel sandwiches.
2. Spread with peanut butter, softened with dressing or orange juice.
3. Place a banana along edge of bread and roll firmly. Wrap and chill.
4. Cut in slices.

RIBBON SANDWICHES

1. Cut 1 slice of white bread and 2 slices of brown bread ½-inch thick; butter 1 slice of brown.
2. Spread brown bread with filling; cover with white bread buttered on both sides; spread with filling.
3. Cover with 1 slice buttered brown bread; press.
4. At serving time cut in ¼-inch slices or in ½-inch slices, cut in thirds.

SUGGESTED FILLINGS: For 1 layer, use cheese, pimento, green pepper, nuts, olives, gherkins or radish, finely chopped, and moistened with salad dressing.

For the second layer, use ham and relish; egg and parsley; salmon, shrimp, lobster or chicken with celery, salad dressing.

Another popular combination is, first layer, cream cheese with chopped preserved ginger; second layer, slivered dates and chopped walnuts with enough cheese to hold them together.

CHECKERBOARD SANDWICHES

1. Cut 6 ½-inch slices of bread, 3 brown, 3 white. Remove crusts.
2. Butter and spread with tinted cheese to which flavour has been added (chives, Worcestershire Sauce, orange rind, horseradish, capers).
3. Pile 3 slices together with first group having 2 white slices and 1 brown between, and group 2 having 2 brown slices with 1 white between.
4. Slice in ½-inch slices.
5. From group 1 take 2 ½-inch slices and take 1 slice from group 2; spread with butter and coloured cheese and pile alternately.
6. Cut a thin slice of bread in a contrasting colour to the checker-boards (if checkerboard is predominately white bread, use brown). Spread slice with butter and cheese and wrap it around a checker-board group. Chill and slice.

Ribbon   *Checkerboard*

CORNUCOPIA SANDWICHES

1. Cut bread into thin slices; trim crusts; butter.
2. Spread with any seasoned filling.
3. Cut each slice into 4 squares; roll each into tiny cornucopia, fasten with a toothpick.
4. Wrap or cover with damp towel, chill 2 hours. Remove toothpick, garnish with parsley.

RIBBON SANDWICH LOAF

1. Remove crusts from a loaf of day-old bread.
2. Cut four ½-inch lengthwise slices.
3. Spread each slice with different fillings which go well together, e.g. pimento cheese, tomato, lettuce and mayonnaise with chicken, ham or lobster.
4. Ice the loaf with 3 packages of softened cream cheese to which has been added a little mayonnaise to make it of spreading consistency.
5. Chill for approximately an hour and serve on a platter garnished with water cress or parsley. Slice about 1 inch thick.
   Individual loaves may be made, using bread cut in small rounds.

OPEN-FACED SANDWICHES

1. Prepare fillings and decorations; keep covered.
2. Cut crusts from top and sides of a sandwich loaf; leave one crust to help support the loaf while slicing.
3. With a sharp knife slice the loaf lengthwise; keep each slice on damp tea towel covered with waxed paper; cover with waxed paper and a damp towel.
4. Cut a slice into squares, fingers, triangles, or with cookie cutters into fancy shapes.
5. Spread with softened butter, then with filling; if cheese is being used the butter is not necessary. Mix cheese with a little sour cream or mayonnaise; flavour with onion juice.
6. Decorate each sandwich.

SUGGESTED DECORATIONS: Sliced radish or stuffed olives; pickle fans or slices; tiny sardines with criss-crossed pimento strips; two or three small cleaned shrimps; thin, neat slice of hard-cooked egg; slice of tomato or cherry tomatoes, smaller slice of cucumber topped with a bit of mayonnaise and a tiny sprig of parsley, mint or cress; a slice of cooked sausage or salami.

Hard-cooked eggs, sieved and sprinkled in the centre of any open-faced sandwich, is decorative.

Cream cheese softened and mixed with a little mayonnaise may be piped around the edge with a pastry tube.

For large open-faced sandwiches, see Smorrebrod, the Danish Sandwich, page 351.

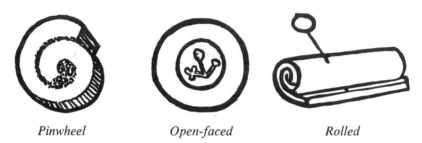

Pinwheel *Open-faced* *Rolled*

OPEN-FACED FRUIT SANDWICHES

Serve with tea or punch at summer-time parties. Cut a variety of thinly-sliced breads (including fruit and nut breads) into fingers, about 1½ inches wide and 2½ inches long. Spread with softened cream cheese; give some fingers an additional thin layer of jam or jelly. Arrange different sliced fresh or preserved fruits on each—for example, 6 grape halves, seeded and placed cut side down, about 6 slices of fresh strawberries, banana slices or Mandarin orange slices. Arrange in attractive rows according to the size of the fruit. Chopped nuts may be added for garnish. Chill until serving time but serve soon after preparation.

TOAST VARIATIONS

For quick preparation of many pieces of toast use the broiler. Preheat; spread the bread on the rack; place about 2 inches below the heat; toast to the desired shade of brown; turn and toast.

Many spreads may be used on toast for quick accompaniments to salads, or for afternoon tea or evening refreshments. Cut toast in fingers or triangles.

CINNAMON TOAST I

Toast bread; spread with paste of 2 tablespoons butter, ¼ cup brown sugar, 1½ teaspoons cinnamon. Place in hot oven or under the broiler until sugar melts. Serve hot, cut into triangles or fingers.

CINNAMON TOAST II

Toast bread; butter; sprinkle with cinnamon-sugar mix. Broil 4 inches from heat until the mixture bubbles. Cut into triangles or fingers.

CINNAMON-SUGAR MIX: Combine 1 cup granulated sugar, 3-4 teaspoons cinnamon. Keep in a tightly covered screw-top jar.

CINNAMON TOASTIES

Cut loaf of unsliced white bread lengthwise into 1-inch slices. Slash each slice into squares or diamonds, not all the way through. Mix ½ cup soft butter or margarine with 1 cup granulated sugar and 2 teaspoons cinnamon; spread over bread. Refrigerate. Start heating oven to 375°. Bake bread 15 to 20 minutes, or until bubbling. Serve warm. Makes about 12 toasties.

ORANGE TOAST

½ cup sugar   2 tablespoons orange juice
grated rind of orange

1. Toast thin slices of bread; butter them.
2. Blend ingredients and spread on hot toast.

TOASTED HAM FINGERS

1. Mix 1 cup ground boiled ham, 1 cup grated cheese, ½ cup condensed tomato soup, ½ teaspoon mustard and ½ teaspoon horseradish.
2. Toast bread, trim off crusts and cut each slice into three or four strips.
3. Spread with mixture, then toast under broiler. Serve with hot chocolate.

SAUSAGE TOAST

Cook sausage meat. Spread on buttered toast. Place small square of cheese on sausage meat on each slice and broil lightly to melt cheese.

CREAM CHEESE TOAST

Here are 2 varieties. Blend 3-ounce package cream cheese with 2 tablespoons peach or raspberry jam or orange or ginger marmalade; or with 2 tablespoons soft butter, 2 tablespoons milk, ⅛ teaspoon onion juice and 2-3 tablespoons of each of chopped nuts and chopped stuffed olives. Spread on toast.

CHEESE TOAST

Sprinkle grated cheese on buttered toast; place under the broiler until the cheese melts.

CHEESE FINGERS

1. Cut wiener buns in half lengthwise then in half lengthwise again.
2. Spread on 3 sides with soft butter; roll in grated cheese; sprinkle with poppy or sesame seeds; or in minced parsley, chives or nuts.
3. Toast in a hot oven (450°) about 8 minutes. (Hamburger buns may be sliced into thin circles.)

CHEESE PUFF-UPS

1. Cream ½ cup butter or margarine. Mix in 1 cup shredded sharp Cheddar cheese. Blend in 1 stiffly beaten egg white.
2. Spread 4 slices of bread generously with mixture.
3. Bake in hot oven (400°) for 15 minutes or until puffy.

FOLD-UPS

1. Remove crusts from bread; butter the slices. Sprinkle lightly with grated cheese.
2. Fasten opposite corners together with a toothpick.
3. Bake in very hot oven (450°) for 10 minutes. Serve with soup or salad.

COCONUT STICKS

3 thick slices of bread	¾ cup coconut
½ cup condensed milk	

1. Trim the crusts from the bread; cut each piece into 3 strips.
2. Spread 3 sides with the condensed milk; roll 3 sides in coconut.
3. Place on a greased baking sheet; broil 4 inches from the heat until light brown, turning once.

HONEY SQUARES

Mix equal amounts of honey and brown sugar; spread on buttered squares or slices of bread. Sprinkle with chopped nuts; bake at 375° for 15 minutes.

PARSLEY TEA STRIPS

4 tablespoons butter	1 tablespoon minced parsley
2 tablespoons grated cheese	1 teaspoon prepared mustard
1 tablespoon cream	6 slices bread

Cream butter and blend in other ingredients. Spread on bread; cut bread into strips, 3 per slice. Broil.

SPICY MARMALADE BREAD

1 loaf French bread
(about 12 inches long)
⅓ to ½ cup soft butter or
margarine

½ cup orange marmalade
cinnamon

1. Cut bread in 1- to 1½-inch diagonal slices.
2. Spread with butter, then generously with marmalade.
3. Sprinkle cinnamon generously over top.
4. Place slices, marmalade side up, on ungreased cookie sheet. Heat in hot oven (400°) about 8 minutes, or till hot. Makes 8 to 10 slices. Apricot jam can be substituted for marmalade.

GARLIC BREAD

1 loaf French bread
¼ pound butter

½ teaspoon powdered garlic or
1 sliced garlic clove

1. Soften butter, add garlic. Blend thoroughly. Let butter stand for half an hour if garlic cloves are used. Remove garlic.
2. Cut French bread into ½-inch slices; spread flavoured butter on both sides and reassemble loaf.
3. Wrap loaf in metal foil. Heat in a moderate oven 30 minutes. Serve hot, turning foil down to make a basket.

Celery seed may be substituted for garlic in garlic bread or used with it.

Rolls can be buttered with garlic butter; several rolls can be wrapped together or they can be individually wrapped, in foil.

CROUTONS

Cut slices of dry bread ⅓-inch thick; cut into cubes. Place in baking pan and brown in a hot oven.

GARLIC CROUTONS (GARLIC BREAD CUBES)

Cut unsliced loaf of day-old bread into cubes about ½ to ¾ inches in size, to make 2 cups. Combine ¼ cup butter, margarine or salad oil in a frying pan with a half clove of garlic, crushed, or with ¼ teaspoon garlic powder. Heat bread cubes in this mixture until golden brown, over medium heat; stir frequently. Cubes will become crisp. Serve them in Scalloped Tomatoes, as a topping on casseroles or in Caesar Salad Cooled croutons can be kept fresh in a covered jar, for several days; reheat before using.

QUICK-STICKY BUNS

1. Start heating oven to 375°.
2. From loaf of day-old unsliced white bread, trim crusts. Cut loaf in half lengthwise. Cut each half crosswise into 1½-inch slices, almost through to bottom; then cut each half lengthwise, almost through to bottom, to form squares.
3. Spread cut surfaces with soft butter or margarine. Then cover both halves with one of mixtures below.
4. Bake on cookie sheet 10 to 15 minutes.
5. To serve, break "rolls" apart. Makes 16 to 20 servings.

   NUT: Mix ¼ cup brown sugar, 2 tablespoons chopped nuts.

   COCONUT: First top with ¼ cup sweetened condensed milk, then with ½ cup shredded or flaked coconut.

   HONEY: Mix 3 tablespoons honey with ¾ cup brown sugar; top with 2 tablespoons chopped walnuts or ¼ cup flaked coconut.

SOUP STICKS

1. Cut dry bread into ⅓-inch slices; remove crusts.
2. Spread thinly with butter.
3. Cut into strips ⅓ inch wide and 2½ to 3 inches long.
4. Brown in a hot oven.
   Leftover toast may be used in making croutons or soup sticks.

BREAD CASES OR CROUSTADES

1. Cut dry bread into slices 2 inches thick.
2. Remove crusts; cut into rounds or squares.
3. Remove part of bread from centre, leaving case about ⅓ inch thick.
4. Brush over lightly with butter and brown in oven.
5. Fill with hot creamed fish, meat or vegetables.

BREAD CUPS

1. Cut crusts from fresh bread slices; flatten with rolling pin.
2. Brush both sides with melted butter to which minced parsley has been added.
3. Press into muffin pans; toast in hot oven (400°) about 10 minutes.
4. Fill with any creamed mixture or chicken salad topped with cheese sauce.

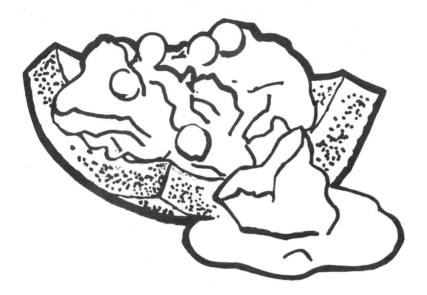

Bread Cup

MELBA TOAST

Cut bread into very thin slices, ¼ inch or less; cut into pieces as desired.
Dry slowly in oven (250°) until crisp and golden brown, about 1 hour.

FRENCH TOAST

2 eggs or 3 yolks	1 teaspoon sugar
⅛ teaspoon salt	6 slices bread
⅓ cup milk	fat for frying

1. In a casserole or deep pie plate, beat eggs; add salt, sugar and milk.
2. Dip bread in egg mixture; lift carefully onto hot griddle on which a small amount of fat has been melted.
3. Brown slowly on both sides; sprinkle with sugar or serve with syrup, sour cream, ketchup or strawberry jam.

BANANA FRENCH TOAST

2 eggs slightly beaten	8 slices enriched white bread
⅔ cup milk	shortening
1 teaspoon nutmeg	3 medium size bananas, sliced

1. Combine eggs, milk and nutmeg.
2. Dip bread slices into egg mixture, turning them to coat both sides.
3. Brown bread, on both sides, in small amount of hot shortening in a skillet.
4. Place a layer of sliced bananas on each of 4 slices of French toast.
5. Cover with a second slice of French toast. Serve with maple syrup. Makes 4 servings, 2 slices toast per serving.

BREAD CRUMBS

Soft bread crumbs are those prepared by crumbling day-old bread or older bread, but not dry bread. This may be done by scraping the bread with a fork or by rubbing two thick slices together, or grinding in the electric blender.

Dry bread crumbs are made by rolling fine or grinding dry, unbuttered bread. They keep well.

LEFTOVER BREAD

Use as desserts: Fruit Betty, Bread Pudding, Orange Marmalade Pudding, Carrot Pudding, Hunter's Delight.

Use as topping for casseroles; stuffing for fowl, fish and roasts; extender in hamburg patties.

Prepare croutons, garlic croutons, Melba Toast.

13 Fruits

NUTRITIONISTS ADVISE that ⅕ of our food money should be spent for fruits and vegetables. Not only do fruits add important minerals and vitamins to our diet, but they also add colour and flavour to our menus.

All fresh fruits should be well washed to remove harmful sprays and the dust and germs which may have collected.

When paring or slicing fruit a stainless steel or silver knife will prevent darkening of the surface.

Since many fruits darken as soon as they are cut, and lose flavour and vitamins on exposure to air, they should not be prepared in advance. Orange, lemon, grapefruit or pineapple juice may be sprinkled on fruit such as banana or apples to prevent this darkening.

Those fruits which we wish to soften, such as unpeeled fruit, fruit to be made into sauce, or dried fruit, we cook first in water, then add sugar to sweeten. When we wish the fruit to hold its shape, as we do rhubarb and peeled fruits, we first make a syrup and simmer the fruit in it.

FRESH FRUITS

APPLES

Apples are plentiful, versatile and delicious. They are not as rich in vitamins and minerals as some fruits but since they are more plentiful, they can be used frequently enough to make a substantial contribution of these elements to our diet.

Good varieties to use for both cooking and eating raw are: Baldwin, Spy, McIntosh, Gravenstein, Wealthy and Cortland; Astrachans are an early apple. For eating raw there are the Delicious, Talman Sweet and Russet. For cooking only, use the Duchess, which is an early apple.

There are 2 basic ways to make applesauce. The results differ in both flavour and appearance. Applesauce freezes well up to 8 months, leave a space in the container to allow for expansion.

APPLESAUCE

This retains more of the shape of the apple. It is a creamy colour.

1. Wash, quarter, core and pare the apples into a saucepan.
2. Add water to come up in the saucepan to the depth of 1 inch.
3. Cover the pan and simmer until the apples are soft; if necessary evaporate the liquid by cooking without the lid.
4. Add sugar, allowing 1 to 2 tablespoons to each apple, depending on their natural sweetness. Stir until the sugar is dissolved.

Fruits can be used in many ways. Here are Glazed Pears, Baked Apples and a moulded Fruit Salad.

SIEVED APPLESAUCE

This method makes a smooth, pink applesauce, quickly and easily.

1. Wash red apples; remove the stems; do not pare.
2. Cut the apple into small pieces into a saucepan.
3. Add water to fill the pan to a depth of 1 inch.
4. Cover tightly and simmer until the apples are soft; if necessary remove the lid and allow the excess liquid to evaporate.
5. Press through a sieve or fruit mill.
6. Add sugar (white or brown), allowing 1 to 2 tablespoons to each apple, depending on their natural sweetness; stir to dissolve the sugar. Spice should be added only when apples have lost flavour, at the end of the season.

APPLE COMPÔTE (Basic Recipe)

1 cup sugar	8 apples
1½ cups water	1 tablespoon lemon juice
shavings of ¼ lemon rind	

Make a syrup of sugar, water and lemon rind; bring to a boil. Remove lemon rind.

Using Whole Apples: Wash, peel and core apples of medium size. Cook slowly in syrup which comes up halfway on the apples. When the bottom of the apple is soft, invert apples and cook until all is tender. Lift out carefully into a serving dish. Add lemon juice to syrup and if necessary strain before pouring it over the apples. Centres of apples can be filled with Apple Jelly if desired (page 671).

Using Cut-up Apples: Wash, peel and core apples; cut into eighths. Add half of the prepared apples to syrup and cover and cook slowly until clear. Using a slotted spoon, carefully transfer to serving dish. Cook remaining apples, and transfer to serving dish. Add lemon juice to syrup and strain over apples.

BLUSHING APPLES

Cook whole apples without peeling first; carefully remove skin after cooking. When cool, fill the centres with Apple Jelly (page 671).

CINNAMON APPLES

Add 2-3 tablespoons cinnamon candies to the syrup before cooking apples.

APPLE PORCUPINES

Chill cooked, whole apples and fill centres with jelly. Blanch and split almonds in halves lengthwise and stick into apples. If desired, place apples under broiler for a few minutes to brown nuts. Pour syrup around apples and serve with cream.

BAKED APPLES

1. Wash the apple; core; cut a strip of skin from around the centre, or pare down an inch from the top, to keep the skin from splitting.
2. Place the apples in a baking dish; a tin dish will discolour the syrup.
3. Fill each centre with one of the following: brown sugar and cinnamon (1 teaspoon to 1 cup sugar), raisins, dates, mincemeat, walnuts, rum and butter caramel candy.
4. Sprinkle brown sugar in the dish around the apples, allowing 2 tablespoons sugar to each apple.
5. Pour water in the dish until it is an inch deep around the apples.
6. Bake at 350° until tender, about 40 minutes; baste two or three times. A syringe-type baster is convenient to use.
7. Serve the apples hot, with cream, or a marshmallow, placed on each apple just before they are removed from the oven; or serve the apple cold with a whipped cream topping.

PARTY BAKED APPLE

1. When the apples are almost cooked remove from the oven.
2. Top with a generous spoonful of meringue (page 482). Sprinkle with coconut, nuts and sliced maraschino cherries.
3. Return to the oven for 15 minutes or until lightly brown.

GLAZED APPLES

8 red-skinned apples   boiling water
⅔ cup white sugar

1. Choose red baking apples; wash; pare the top quarter, and core.
2. Place upside down in a baking dish.
3. Pour in boiling water to a depth of 1 inch; add the sugar.
4. Cook at 325°, turning the apples 3 or 4 times so they will cook evenly.
5. When partly cooked turn right side up in the pan and finish under the broiler, basting frequently. Serve cold with whipped cream.

For other apple recipes see Desserts, Chapter 19.
Recipe for Taffy Apples is on page 646.

GLAZED APPLE RINGS

Serve these with roast pork, pork tenderloin or sausages.

2 large apples	1 tablespoon vinegar
½ cup sugar	3 sticks cinnamon
½ cup water	2 cloves

Arrange thick slices of cored apples in a baking dish or frying pan. Combine remaining ingredients and pour over apples. Bake uncovered at 375° or cook slowly over direct heat for 30-40 minutes until the apples are transparent and tender.

Omit cinnamon and add a few drops of red colouring to make a rosy-coloured syrup in which to cook the apples.

AVOCADOS

The avocado is a tropical fruit with a dark, greenish-black skin which resembles coarse leather—the origin of its alternative name, Alligator Pear. The flesh of the fruit is pale yellowish-green in colour; it has a smooth, buttery texture. The flavour of this fruit can be appreciated only when it is fully ripe. At that stage, the skin shows some black markings on a green background. Also when the fruit is held in the palm of the hand and lightly pressed, it yields.

Unlike other fruits, the avocado has a high fat content and a substantial amount of thiamin. It is delicious served in fruit or vegetable salads; cut lengthwise, halves can be stuffed with cream cheese, seafood or chicken salads. As an appetizer, serve in wedges or mash to make a dip or spread for crackers. The flavour is accentuated by the addition of a little salt. To freeze, mash and add 2 teaspoons lemon juice per cup of avocado.

BANANAS

Bananas are fully ripe and best for eating when the peel is yellow flecked with brown.

If bananas have green tips they contain starch which has not yet turned to sugar. They should not be placed in the refrigerator, where they will darken without ripening. Do not attempt to freeze bananas.

BAKED BANANA

1. Peel the banana; place in a greased baking dish.
2. Brush with melted butter and sprinkle with salt.
3. Bake at 350° for 15 minutes; to brown, broil 1 to 2 minutes.

Brown sugar can be used in place of the salt.

BANANA AMBROSIA

2 oranges
2 ripe bananas

2 tablespoons sugar (optional)
1 cup shredded coconut

1. Peel the oranges and slice. Arrange a layer in a fruit dish. Sprinkle with sugar, if desired.
2. Cover with a layer of sliced bananas.
3. Continue to add fruit and sugar in layers until the dish is almost full. Sprinkle with coconut. Chill well before serving.

BANANAS WITH FRUIT JUICE

Slice bananas into a sauce dish. Pour any of the following juices over them: pineapple, orange or bottled cranberry juice.

FRENCH TOAST WITH BANANAS

See recipe on page 362.

BERRIES

Blueberries keep well if cold and dry. They may be poured into dry sealers, covered and kept in the refrigerator until needed. To wash, sprinkle them into cold water; lift out, removing leaves and stems.

Serve with cream and sugar; in melons; with cereal. 1-quart box serves 6.

Boysenberries are a large berry of the thimbleberry variety. The berries have a bright red colour and make delicious juice, but are seedy and sour when canned as fruit.

Loganberries are similar to the Boysenberry but brighter in colour and smaller.

Saskatoons resemble the blueberry crossed with black currant. Use as blueberries.

Strawberries should be bought in small quantities, as these berries spoil easily. Do not buy sandy berries. Wash by sprinkling the berries gently into a pan of cold water; lift out. Remove the hulls; sprinkle with sugar. Serve with sweet or sour cream. 1 quart serves 6. Strawberries may have the hulls left on; arrange the berries around a small dish of powdered sugar.

Raspberries are even more fragile than strawberries; handle in the same way. 1 quart serves 6.

To freeze berries: Wash and dry thoroughly; spread 1 layer deep on a flat pan. Freeze quickly; transfer to plastic bags or covered containers.

Most berries can be used in muffins or as pie filling.

Well chosen desserts can add health as well as pleasure to a meal. Chilled, sliced fresh fruits, Citrus and local, will add vitamins to any diet.

CITRUS FRUIT

All citrus fruits are imported into Canada, but are widely used because of their high vitamin C content. It is not practical to freeze citrus fruits.

GRAPEFRUIT

Choose grapefruit which are heavy for their size, with smooth, thin skins; the colour of the skin is not an indication of quality. Rinse the grapefruit under cold water before it is stored.

BROILED GRAPEFRUIT

1. Cut grapefruit in half; remove seeds and cut around sections.
2. Sprinkle each half with 1 teaspoon white and 1 teaspoon brown sugar; dot with 1 teaspoon butter; let stand 20 minutes.
3. Broil about 10 minutes, or until lightly browned.

GRAPEFRUIT HALVES

1. Cut in halves crosswise.
2. With a sharp paring knife or a serrated grapefruit knife cut the pulp from the membrane, in each section.
3. Run the knife around the outside edge of the pulp; do not cut into the bitter white membrane.
4. With scissors cut around the core, lift it out.
5. Sweeten if desired with sugar, syrup or honey. Garnish; chill.

GRAPEFRUIT SECTIONS

1. Using a sharp knife, cut the rind from a grapefruit, removing all the white skin. This skin contains bitter oil and should be completely removed.

2. Cut out one section, by cutting along the inside of the membranes on each side of the section. Subsequent sections can be easily removed by cutting down the opposite side of the membrane already exposed, and with an upward turn of the knife along the next membrane, flicking out the next section. Use sections in fruit cup or fruit salad.

ORANGES

California oranges are of two varieties: Navel oranges which are in season from November to May, and Valencia oranges, in season from May to November.

Florida oranges are of many varieties. They are lighter in colour, have many seeds and a large amount of juice.

Valencia oranges are best for sectioning. The large number of seeds in Florida oranges makes them less suitable for sectioning, as does the navel of Navel oranges.

Temple oranges, from Florida, are large, juicy and easily peeled and a favourite for eating out of the hand.

Tangerines or *Mandarin* Oranges, like Temple Oranges, are easily peeled and eaten, but are smaller.

New varieties of citrus fruit are always being developed—often crosses of different species—like the Tangelo, a cross between a tangerine and a grapefruit.

To remove the white skin, a quick method is to drop the unpeeled fruit into boiling water to cover. Leave about 2 minutes, remove, hold under cold water. The white membrane comes off with the skin.

For Orange Sections, follow method for sectioning grapefruit.

GRAPES

Canadian grapes are on the market in September and October. Grapes should not fall off the bunch, and bunches should have no mouldy fruit. Pour cold water over them. Drain. Serve in small bunches, clipped from the main stem, on fruit or cheese platters.

FROSTED GRAPES

1. Brush small bunches of grapes with egg white beaten with a little water.
2. While still damp, sprinkle with coarse sugar; allow to dry. Serve on fruit salad plate as a garnish.

MELONS

Canteloupe should be chosen by their fragrance. Canadian melons appear on the market in August. Melons do not freeze satisfactorily.

1. Wash and chill the melon.
2. Cut in half crosswise if small; lengthwise in quarters if large.
3. Remove the seeds and stringy fibres with a spoon.
4. Serve with salt, sugar, lemon wedge.

Small canteloupe are sometimes filled with blueberries, raspberries, fruit cocktail, ice cream or sherbet.

Halves of canteloupe or honeydew melon can be substituted for cake in Alaska Mary Anns (page 626); put filled melon halves in crushed ice before browning meringue.

A fluted edge may be easily obtained by tracing a zigzag line lightly around the centre of the melon. Cut deeply on this line and the melon pulls apart, each half having the same pattern. See diagram.

Cutting a Canteloupe with a fluted edge

Honeydew Melon is the pale green, smooth-skinned variety. It is prepared and served in the same way as canteloupe. As with most fruits, it is most important that this melon be eaten when "just ripe" if the true flavour is to be appreciated. The green of the skin should have a *slight* creamy colour.

Watermelon should sound hollow when thumped with the knuckle. If ripe, the thin green skin will peel easily.

Serve in wedges or thick slices with a fork for an appetizer or dessert.

Prosciutto con Melone is a popular Italian appetizer consisting of wedges of melon draped with thin slices of Italian ham (Prosciutto).

Melon Ball Cocktail recipe is on page 65.

PEACHES

The Niagara Peninsula of Ontario, the Okanagan Valley of British Columbia and the Annapolis Valley of Nova Scotia provide peaches in great abundance from August to October.

Golden Jubilee, Valiant, Vedettes and Elbertas, all freestone varieties, are the most popular. They should be firm, but ripe enough that the skin will peel off readily.

Peaches can be frozen but special care must be taken to minimize darkening of their colour. For the method, consult the bulletins on freezing available from the provincial Department of Agriculture.

SLICED PEACHES

If skin cannot be removed easily, dip the peaches into boiling water, then into cold; do only a few at a time. Since they darken on standing, they should not be peeled until needed. Sprinkle peaches with sugar immediately after slicing; sugar will combine with juice to form syrup.

FRIED PEACHES

1. Peel and halve each peach; remove pit. Pan-fry slowly with cut surface down.
2. Turn and cook slowly on the round side; allow about 5 minutes for each side.
3. Serve hot with meat.

BROILED PEACHES

1. Peel and halve the peach, remove pit; brush with lemon juice.
2. Place rounded side up on the broiler rack; broil 3 minutes; turn.
3. Fill the hollow with mayonnaise or grape jelly.
4. Broil until tender and beginning to brown. Serve with hot or cold meat.

GLAZED PEACHES

3 tablespoons butter	¼ cup lemon juice
½ cup currant jelly	6 peach halves

1. Combine butter, jelly and juice in a saucepan.
2. Simmer ripe peach halves, turning often until they are glazed and tender. Serve with meat.

PEARS

Bartlett pears, old favourites, are in season early. The Anjou, Bosc, Kieffer and Seckel are other popular varieties. Pears ripen well in storage so may be bought green.

A pear is usually served whole, with a knife, so that it may be cut into quarters, and the core removed.

BAKED FRESH PEARS

4 fresh pears	2 tablespoons maple syrup
6 tablespoons orange juice	

1. Cut pears in half lengthwise, remove core and place cut side up in a casserole.
2. Fill centres with juice; dribble maple syrup over all.
3. Bake at 350° for 20 minutes or until pears are tender when tested with the point of a knife.

Omit orange juice; bake or simmer pears in sufficient maple syrup to cover. Add a dash of ginger.

Cook pears in a syrup made from ½ cup sugar, 1 cup water and shavings from the peel of ½ lemon. Cool and drain; serve with Custard Sauce, Sour Cream or Whipped Cream Sauce (page 98).

PINEAPPLE

Choose short square fruit, heavy in relation to size, with a distinct pineapple odour. The leaves should pull out easily. The best pineapple is on the market in May. A 2-pound pineapple yields about 5 cups diced fruit and requires ½ to 1 cup sugar. Although it is not economical to freeze fresh pineapple in Canada, it can be frozen diced or in slices without additional processing.

With a sharp knife, slice the skin off the pineapple; cut out the eyes with a sharp knife or vegetable peeler; if the pineapple is to be sliced, it is easier to remove the skin after it is sliced. Do not leave bits of skin on the fruit.

Spears: Cut the pineapples lengthwise into 8 pieces; remove the core from each piece.

Slices: Cut the pineapple crosswise in ½-inch slices; remove the core.

Cubes: Dice slices.

The waste from the pineapple, if covered with water and simmered, makes an excellent base for fruit drinks or fruit jelly.

PLUMS

Damsons, the little sour purple plums; Lombards, the large blue; Prune plums, dark purple blue, Green Gages, the large green plums, are some of the many varieties of plums available. They should be ripe and unblemished.

To freeze, plums are packed in a cold syrup to which ascorbic acid had been added. Department of Agriculture bulletins provide details of this method.

RHUBARB

Rhubarb is best early in the spring when it is young. It is always cooked before freezing.

To freeze, trim and cut into desired lengths. To retain flavour, drop into boiling water and after 1 minute, drain thoroughly and cool quickly. Pack dry in a container; granulated sugar mixed in with the rhubarb in proportions required for pie, stewed rhubarb etc., helps to eliminate some of the air from the container.

RHUBARB SAUCE

4 cups rhubarb   1 to 1½ cups sugar

1. Choose young, tender rhubarb of red colour.
2. Discard the root and leaves; wash the stalks.
3. Cut into 1-inch pieces.
4. Place in a saucepan or in a covered casserole; sprinkle the sugar over the fruit and mix well; let stand 20 to 30 minutes.
5. Cook slowly over low heat or in a 350° oven.

   Oven-cooking develops a rich colour in the rhubarb, eliminates the need for constant watching and is an economical cooking method if the rhubarb is part of an oven-cooked meal.

FRUIT MIXTURES

These mixtures in which fresh fruits predominate make delicious desserts. For appetizers, choose a combination of fruits which is less sweet.

FRUIT CUP

1 grapefruit, sectioned	1 apple, cut-up
2 oranges, sectioned	½ cup white grapes
2 bananas, sliced	½ cup maraschino cherries
½ cup diced pineapple	½ cup sugar

1. Arrange fruit in a bowl; bananas should be added just before serving.
2. Cover fruits with their own juices or with grape juice for added colour.
3. Add sugar; let stand to dissolve. Serves 4-6.

   Add fresh berries in season.

   Add canned peaches or pears, or fresh fruit in season.

   Add 1 tablespoon preserved ginger and pour ginger ale over the cut fruit.

   Add 6 after-dinner mints, which will dissolve in the juice.

FRUIT AMBROSIA

3 oranges, sectioned	1 banana, sliced
6 green cherries, quartered	1 cup diced pineapple
1 grapefruit, sectioned	¾ cup shredded coconut
½ cup miniature marshmallows	

Arrange the fruit and marshmallows in a bowl; cover with one variety of fruit juice or a combination.

Add sugar if necessary. Sprinkle with coconut.

A few mint wafers or after-dinner mints may be crumbled into the bowl if this is a popular flavour.

ORIENTAL FRUIT CUP

1 19-ounce can sliced peaches	2 teaspoons finely chopped
1 cup orange juice	candied ginger
	2 bananas, sliced

Drain peaches and combine with orange juice and ginger. Chill for several hours. Add sliced bananas and serve. Serves 6-8.

DRIED FRUITS

Apples, apricots, peaches and certain plums are commercially dried when fully ripe to give food of high nutritive value and versatility.

Approximate Yield

1 pound prunes when cooked yields 4 cups or about 12 servings.

1	"	apricots	"	"	"	4½	"	"	"	10	"
1	"	peaches	"	"	"	4	"	"	"	11	"
1	"	figs	"	"	"	4½	"	"	"	12	"
1	"	raisins	"	"	"	4	"	"	"	9	"

Prunes are graded as follows: small contain 60 to 80 to the pound; medium, 50 to 60, large, 40 to 50; extra large, 20 to 40.

COOKING DRIED FRUIT

To soften dried fruit it must be cooked in water before the sugar is added. Allow ⅓ to ½ cup sugar to 1 pound prunes; 1 to 1½ cups to 1 pound apricots.

The dried-fruit industry recommends that fruit be cooked without soaking. This method requires 30 to 40 minutes, slow cooking: soaked first, it will cook in 10 minutes.

STEWED PRUNES

½ pound prunes
2½ cups cold water

¼ cup sugar
1 tablespoon lemon juice

1. Rinse the prunes thoroughly in warm water.
2. Cover with cold water; soak several hours.
3. Simmer prunes in the water in which they were soaked, until tender, about 10 minutes.
4. Add the sugar; stir until dissolved; add lemon juice.
5. Serve very cold.

¼ cup orange juice may be added instead of the lemon. Orange slices or sections served with the stewed prunes are colourful and make a delicious variation.

For easy preparation, combine prunes and water in a jar. Cover, leave overnight and serve.

14 Salads and Dressings

SALADS AND DRESSINGS

Colour, crispness and flavour are a salad's contributions to mealtime. Vitamins and minerals are a bonus!

The ideal salad is a thing of beauty and a delight to the palate.

FACTS TO CONSIDER

Ingredients should be thoroughly chilled, also the plates on which the salads are to be served.

Salad greens and other vegetables should be clean, crisp and dry.

Ingredients should be cut into attractive and varying shapes and if used for mixtures should be of sufficient size to retain their identity. Strive for a variety of flavours, colours and textures.

When using several vegetables, marinate each one separately and allow to stand; for salad mixtures, dressing should not be applied until serving time with the exception of heavy mixtures like potato salad.

Add a dressing suitable to the mixture, a little at a time, so that the foods are just moist; excess dressing makes foods soggy.

Salads being served as a main course should contain some form of protein food (meat, fish, cheese or egg) as well as vegetables or fruits.

Salads being served as an accompaniment to a main course are usually served as a side salad, or in a large bowl to be passed. These salads should contain little or no protein as that is provided elsewhere in the main course. Salads being served as a dessert should also be low in protein.

Appetizer salads should be small in size and sharp in flavour in order to tempt the appetite and not satisfy it.

Choose a plate or bowl of glass, wood or solid shade of china which is sufficiently neutral to form a background for the salad. The outer edge of a salad plate should be left uncovered so that it "frames" the picture.

SALAD GREENS

This term usually refers to the leafy green vegetables which include head and leaf lettuce, romaine, water cress, garden cress, endive, chicory, spinach, parsley and cabbage.

To freshen, place in ice water about half an hour before using. Remove discoloured and very coarse leaves.

Wash carefully in plenty of cold water, being careful that no sand or insects are left on the leaves.

Cut out the heart end of head lettuce and hold the head under running water with the end upward so that the leaves are separated by the force of the water. Keep hearts and loose leaves for use in tossed salads and reserve cup-shaped leaves for salad plates.

Dry greens thoroughly by patting gently with a clean tea towel, or leaving to drain in a wire basket or dish drainer for a few minutes.

Keep greens fresh by placing in crisping pan of a refrigerator or by keeping in an air-tight dish in a cold place.

GARNISHES

Keep garnishes simple.

Whenever possible, use 1 of the ingredients of the salad in garnishing; garnishes should always be edible.

The appearance of almost all salads is improved by a careful arrangement of a bed of head lettuce or shredded leaves. Water cress and endive can also be used.

To make "curled celery," cut the celery stalk into small 2½-inch strips. Slash from each end of the strip to within ½ inch of the centre. place in cold salted water to curl.

To make "radish roses," cut radish into six or eight sections to within ¼ inch of the bottom; leave stem and leaf on, place in cold water to open. Do not crispen radishes before cutting.

Sprigs of parsley, water cress, mint or young celery leaves make simple but effective garnishes.

Do not have more than one centre of interest when garnishing.

UNCOOKED VEGETABLE SALADS

Serve as salad course at luncheon or dinner; with main course at luncheon or supper.

A variety of uncooked vegetables can be used in salads.

PREPARATION OF VEGETABLES

Cabbage

1. Soak ½ hour in cold salted water to freshen.
2. Remove outer leaves if discoloured.
3. Cut in quarters, remove the heart and shred as finely as possible.
4. Add mayonnaise diluted with a little pickle juice or fruit juice, or add French Dressing (page 398). Mix and chill for several hours.

Celery

1. Separate stalks; freshen in cold water.
2. Wash thoroughly, using vegetable brush.
3. If celery is to be diced, cut upper and outside stalks in small lengthwise sections; lay 2 or 3 stalks together on a board and cut crosswise.

   Keep heart and lower stalks for club celery, served separately as appetizer.
   Small leaves and stalks may be used for garnishing; large leaves may be added to soup stocks.

Radishes

1. Cut off stem end, leaving a ¼-inch "handle." Cut off root end.
2. Brush to remove all sand; crispen in cold water for 15 minutes.

Tomatoes

1. Wash. If tomato is to be peeled, cover with boiling water for 15 seconds to loosen skins, plunge into cold water.
2. Cut out stem end and remove skin.
3. If tomato cup is to be used, do not scald or peel. Wash and cut slice from stem end, scoop out pulp; sprinkle inside with salt, invert to drain.

TOSSED SALAD

One medium-large head of lettuce will provide lettuce cups for 5-6 salad plates, or tossed greens for 8 servings.

1. Rub inside of salad bowl with a slice of onion or cut clove of garlic.
2. Have salad ingredients dried and chilled.
3. Cut or break as desired; put in layers in bowl.
4. Just before serving time add French Dressing (page 398). Toss lightly with two forks until ingredients are blended. Season.

INGREDIENTS FOR TOSSED SALADS:

Lettuce, leaf or head.
Spinach, tender leaves and stems.
Endive, leaf or root.
Dandelion and nasturtium leaves.
Water cress, parsley, garden cress.
Green beans, slivered.
Cabbage, Chinese cabbage, shredded.
Celery, green pepper, cucumber, green onions, tomatoes, carrots, turnip, raw cauliflower, radishes.
Herbs such as chives, mint, basil and tarragon as flavour boosters when used in small quantities.
Cheese, grated or finely diced Cheddar, Parmesan or blue.
Crumbled crisp bacon, sliced olives or pickles for variety.

CABBAGE SALAD (COLE SLAW)

1. Cut cabbage into sections; slice very finely with a sharp French knife or slicer, discarding heart section.
2. Additions—green pepper; pimento; carrot, grated or slivered; sliced radishes; sliced olives; chopped apple and raisins; diced pine-

apple, cut in pieces; slivers of browned almonds; peanuts, toasted sesame seeds.

3. Add French or boiled dressing or mayonnaise. Season. Chill, preferably for several hours.

CAESAR SALAD

⅔ cup salad oil
1 clove garlic, crushed or
    ¼ teaspoon garlic powder
8 cups torn leaf lettuce or
    romaine
1½ cups ½-inch dry bread cubes

½ teaspoon salt
    pepper
2 eggs, boiled 1 minute
¼ cup lemon juice
½ cup grated Parmesan cheese

1. Add garlic to oil and leave at room temperature for at least 15 minutes (the longer the better).
2. Prepare greens, drain, and chill in a covered bowl lined with paper towels.
3. Brown bread cubes in 3 tablespoons of the prepared garlic oil.
4. Remove towels from bowl, add salt and a little pepper, preferably freshly-grated from a pepper mill. Pour on remaining oil and toss salad lightly.
5. Add eggs and lemon juice; toss well. Sprinkle with cheese and toss again.
6. Add bread cubes and toss just until mixed. Serves 6-8.

ENDIVE AND BACON SALAD

This delicious salad is low in calories.

½ head endive
2 slices bacon
1½ tablespoons vinegar

1 teaspoon sugar
¾ teaspoon salt
    pepper

1. Wash the endive well; dry on tea towel; shred into a salad bowl.
2. Fry the bacon until crisp; remove from the pan; drain and crumble; sprinkle over the endive.
3. Pour off all the bacon fat but ½ tablespoon; add the vinegar, sugar, salt and pepper; mix; pour over the endive, mixing with two forks. Serve this as a salad or as a vegetable.
Cook a slice of onion with the bacon to give flavour.
Substitute lettuce broken into small chunks for the endive.

CARROT AND RAISIN SALAD

½ cup raisins	1 tablespoon lemon juice
⅓ cup orange sections (optional)	1 teaspoon sugar
1½ cups grated raw carrots	¼ teaspoon salt
¼ cup mayonnaise or salad dressing	

1. Pour boiling water over raisins to cover. Let stand 5 minutes, drain.
2. Chop orange sections, and add with carrots to raisins.
3. Combine mayonnaise, lemon juice, sugar and salt and toss into carrot mixture.

TOMATO SALAD

1. Peel and chill tomatoes; cut in thick slices or wedges.
2. Serve on lettuce with cucumber, green pepper, celery, chives, olives, cheese.
3. Use French Dressing, mayonnaise, sour cream or Sour Cream Dressing (page 402).
4. Garnish with parsley, mint, celery tips, cress.

STUFFED TOMATO SALAD

1. Make tomato cup as given in Preparation of Tomatoes (page 380), or slice in 3, crosswise.
2. Fill hollowed tomato or cover slices with diced celery; cucumber; cubes of chicken, veal or ham; fish; cottage cheese and olives; mix separately or in combinations with salad dressing.

COOKED VEGETABLE SALADS

Serve with meat course at luncheon or supper, or as a salad course at dinner. Exceptions are such salads as potato and lima bean, which are very filling; they might be served instead of potatoes.

Use freshly-cooked, left over or canned vegetables. Marinate vegetables in French Dressing; when different varieties are marinated separately, maximum flavour is preserved. Serve with additional French Dressing or mayonnaise.

WHEN SERVED FROM SALAD BOWL:

Prepare green salad ingredients; add pieces of cooked vegetables and toss with French Dressing just before serving.

WHEN ARRANGED ON PLATES:

1. Prepare cooked vegetables and marinate separately.
2. Arrange 3 or 4 nests of lettuce on plates; fill these with the separate vegetables.
3. Serve dressing in a separate lettuce cup or in a mayonnaise bowl.

VEGETABLES TO USE:

Asparagus—Pile 3 or 4 stalks on lettuce or on a thick tomato slice; garnish with pimento, green pepper, celery, cress.

Beets—Beets may be cubed, sliced or chopped. Marinate with French Dressing; garnish with finely chopped mint, cress, parsley.

Broccoli—Use tips or stalks. Serve on lettuce with French Dressing or mayonnaise.

Cauliflower—Cut into fairly large sections; serve with French Dressing; garnish with pimento, green pepper, peas, radish roses, cress.

Lima Beans, Kidney Beans—Use alone or mixed with celery, tomatoes, pimento; garnish with cress. Cooked bean sprouts need not be marinated; combine with cooked or raw vegetables and toss with French Dressing.

LIMA BEAN SALAD

Prepare in advance and chill until needed. A nutritious addition to a meal.

1 10-ounce package frozen lima beans	1 clove garlic, crushed
½ cup sour cream	1 teaspoon sugar
1 tablespoon vinegar	¼ teaspoon salt
1 tablespoon salad oil	paprika

1. Cook limas according to package directions. Drain and chill.
2. Combine remaining ingredients with enough paprika to colour lightly; mix thoroughly.
3. Combine with chilled limas, tossing them lightly to coat with dressing.
4. Chill for at least 1 hour, preferably longer. Serve in lettuce cups.

FOUR-BEAN SALAD

1 can kidney beans	1 cup diced celery
1 can lima beans	¼ cup sugar
1 can yellow wax beans	¼ teaspoon ginger or
1 can green beans	1 clove garlic, crushed
2 onions, sliced	French Dressing

1. Drain liquids from beans. Combine beans and remaining ingredients with enough French Dressing to coat all (about 1-1½ cups). Toss vegetable in dressing and chill overnight.

2. Toss vegetables again, drain and season with salt and pepper as needed. Serve in lettuce cups. Serves 6-8.

CHICK PEA SALAD (CECI)

Drain a can of chick peas; marinate in French Dressing; drain and toss with thinly-sliced Spanish onion.

Four-Bean Salad is especially delicious in the summer.

POTATO SALAD

3 cups cooked potatoes, in ⅓
   inch cubes
½ cup chopped onion, green
   onion or part chives

One of:
   1 cup mayonnaise or salad
     dressing
   ⅔ cup sour cream plus ⅓ cup
     mayonnaise
   ⅓ cup French Dressing

Any of:
   chopped celery, green pepper
     or pimento
   innermost leaves of head
     lettuce, chopped
   thinly sliced radishes, olives
   cooked green peas, carrots
     (chopped), corn
   hard-cooked egg, chopped or
     sliced
   crisp bacon

Combine diced potatoes and chopped onions with any of the suggested additions and mix with one of the dressings. Chill for at least 1 hour, preferably several. If French Dressing is used, potatoes can be diced and marinated while hot, in the dressing, then cooled and mixed with other ingredients.

Top with any of hard-cooked egg slices, radish slices, crisp bacon, onion rings, chopped green onions, chives or chopped fresh dill. Serves 5-6.

Potato Salad is a staple on hot days.

HOT POTATO SALAD

Slice cooked potatoes to make 3 cups. Cook 6 slices bacon until crisp; remove from pan and add ½ cup chopped onion. Cook until soft. Add potatoes and bacon (crumbled).

In a large saucepan, combine ½ cup mayonnaise, 3 tablespoons water and 1 tablespoon pickle juice (or 1 teaspoon vinegar, plus 1 teaspoon sugar). Heat with constant stirring. Add potato mixture and toss lightly with a fork. Season with salt and pepper to taste. Serve immediately, garnished with chopped parsley and radish slices. Serves 4-6.

EGG SALADS

Serve as a main course at luncheon or supper, or at picnics.

Eggs should be cooked according to directions for "hard-cooked eggs" (page 265); drop into cold water to prevent darkening. Serve sliced, stuffed or chopped with mayonnaise and chives. (Recipe for Devilled Eggs is on page 273).

For variation, gherkins, olives, nuts, celery, minced ham, chicken or veal may be added to the yolk mixture for stuffed eggs.

Serve on lettuce or endive, garnish with any of parsley, cress, pimento, tomatoes, radishes.

CHEESE SALADS

Serve as a main course at luncheon or supper.

CHEESE BALLS

1. Use hard cheese, grated, or soft cream cheese, mashed; moisten with salad dressing.
2. Add chopped nuts, olives, parsley, pimento or green pepper.
3. Shape into balls and serve on lettuce or cress or with a fruit or vegetable salad.

CHEESE SHAMROCK SLICES

1. Wash green pepper; cut slice from stem end; remove seeds and tongue.
2. Pack centre with cheese mixture prepared as for Cheese Balls.
3. Chill; slice across with sharp knife.
4. Serve on lettuce, cress or endive.

Other uses for cheese in salads are given with Moulded Salads and Fruit Salads.

MEAT AND FISH SALADS

Serve as a main course at luncheon or supper.

These salads are improved if the meat or fish is marinated with French Dressing and allowed to stand some time before combining in the salad. Dressings used are French, Mayonnaise, Boiled and Cream. (Salad Dressing, end of this Chapter).

VEAL, CHICKEN, TURKEY OR PORK TENDERLOIN SALAD

1. Remove skin and bone; cut meat into ⅓-inch to ½-inch cubes; season and marinate with French Dressing.
2. Add up to an equal quantity of diced celery; blend with dressing.
3. Chopped olives, green pepper, gherkins, pimento strips, toasted almonds may be added. Chill.
4. Serve in salad bowl on a bed of lettuce or endive, or arrange on individual plates.

HEARTY CHEF'S SALAD

¼ pound sliced Swiss cheese or crumbled Blue cheese	½ bunch green onions
	1 bunch radishes
½ pound sliced boiled smoked tongue or sliced boiled ham or mixture	½ cucumber
	2-3 tomatoes
	salad greens
4 hard-cooked eggs	French Dressing

1. Cut cheese and meat into thin strips; slice eggs, onions and radishes.
2. Peel and chop cucumber finely; cut tomatoes into wedges.
3. Line salad bowl with crisp greens; arrange prepared foods in groups on the greens. Chill.
4. Toss lightly with garlic-flavoured French Dressing just before serving.

AVOCADO CHICKEN SALAD

Substitute 1 cup cooked diced chicken and 1 diced avocado for the meat in Hearty Chef's Salad. Omit green onions and instead use 1 tablespoon chopped chives.

Niçoise Salad is a French classic.

NIÇOISE SALAD

This famous French salad always features tomatoes, anchovy filets or paste, and black olives. Frequently tuna fish, onions, cooked green vegetables and hard-cooked eggs are added.

½ pound fresh or frozen green beans	½ cup ripe pitted olives
1 large green pepper	1 7-ounce tin tuna
4 tomatoes	1 tin anchovy filets
½ Spanish or Bermuda onion	1 head lettuce or other greens
	3 hard-cooked eggs

1. Cut fresh beans into 2-inch lengths or choose frozen beans which are not frenched. Cook, drain and chill.
2. Slice green peppers into thin rings; peel and cut tomatoes into small wedges; slice onion into thin rings; slice olives.
3. Drain tuna and break into chunks; rinse anchovies in cold water and drain.

4. Combine all these ingredients with broken lettuce or salad greens and toss lightly with French Dressing.
5. Quarter eggs into wedges. Serve salad in a bowl with tomato wedges, tuna chunks and egg wedges on top. Serves 6.

FRUIT CHICKEN SALAD

3 cups diced cooked chicken	½ cup sliced toasted almonds
1 cup diced celery	2 tablespoons salad oil
1 cup orange sections, diced	2 tablespoons orange juice
1 can pineapple tidbits, drained	2 tablespoons vinegar
1 cup seedless grapes	½ teaspoon salt
6 ripe pitted olives	½ cup mayonnaise

1. Lightly toss diced chicken, celery, fruits and almonds.
2. Shake together salad oil, orange juice, vinegar and salt and pour over chicken mixture; let stand 1 hour.
3. Drain off the liquid from the chicken; toss lightly with mayonnaise.
4. Serve in lettuce cups or as bouchées. Serves 8-10.

CURRIED CHICKEN SALAD

1 cup diced cooked chicken	6 pitted ripe olives, silvered
½ cup diced unpeeled apple	(optional)
½ cup seedless raisins	½ cup mayonnaise (approxi-
1 cup finely diced celery	mately)
¼ cup finely diced green pepper	curry powder

Combine chicken, fruits and vegetables. Add curry powder (about ½ teaspoon) to mayonnaise, and toss salad lightly. Serve in lettuce-lined salad bowls or in avocado halves, allowing ½ per person. (Sprinkle avocado halves with lemon juice after cutting, to prevent darkening.)
Substitute prepared horseradish for curry powder, if preferred.

LOBSTER SALAD

1. Cut cooked lobster meat into cubes, reserving claw meat for garnishing; marinate with French Dressing.
2. Add an equal quantity of diced celery; season with salt, cayenne; blend with mayonnaise.
3. Serve on lettuce or in lobster shell; garnish with claw meat, and any of celery tips, cress, olives, cucumber slices.

CRAB MEAT SALAD

Follow directions for Lobster Salad.

SALMON SALAD

1. Use freshly cooked or canned salmon; if canned, drain off liquid.
2. Remove skin and bones; break into pieces.
3. Add diced celery; peas.
4. Season; add dressing to blend ingredients.
5. Serve on lettuce or pack in moistened moulds and turn out on lettuce.
6. Garnish with celery, gherkins, cucumbers, olives, hard-cooked eggs, cress.

SHRIMP SALAD

1. Drain shrimps, remove intestinal vein, leave in salted water for a few minutes, rinse and dry; leave whole or break into pieces.
2. Combine with diced celery, season and blend with dressing.
3. Peas, cucumbers, olives or green pepper may be added.
4. Serve on lettuce, garnished with any of celery tips, green pepper, gherkins, olives, parsley or cress.

TUNA FISH SALAD

1. Rinse oil off canned tuna with cold water.
2. Break fish into pieces; add an equal quantity of diced celery.
3. Pimento strips, green pepper, olives, gherkins may be added.
4. Season and blend with mayonnaise.
5. Serve on lettuce, or each serving may be piled on drained, canned pineapple slices placed on lettuce or endive.
6. Garnish with any of cress, parsley, pimento, olives, hard-cooked egg.

Left over fish, as whitefish or salmon, may be used in this way.

FISH SALAD BOWL

1. Prepare salad bowl of lettuce, celery, tomatoes, cucumbers, beans, peas.
2. Add prepared fish, as whitefish, salmon, shrimps, tuna fish, lobster.
3. Add French Dressing and toss together.

FRUIT SALADS

Serve as a salad course, at luncheon, supper or dinner, as a dessert course at luncheon, supper or dinner or as a main course at luncheon when a protein food is included.

When served as dessert, combine with sweet salad dressing or fruit sugar; may be served in fruit glasses, topped with whipped cream. In other cases, combine salad with French, boiled, mayonnaise or cream dressing, and arrange on lettuce or endive.

WALDORF SALAD

1. Dice or coarsely grate apples to make 1½ cups; the skins of red apples may be left on.
2. Blend with either boiled, mayonnaise or cream dressing.
3. Add 1 cup finely diced celery.
4. Serve in lettuce cups sprinkled with chopped nuts; garnish with celery tips, parsley or cress.

   Dates, stoned and cut, may be added. Cheese balls may be served on the salad. Cabbage, finely shredded, may be used instead of celery. Fresh pears may be substituted for apples or a mixture of pears and apples used.

   Walnuts give a purple colour when mixed with apple and dressing so should be reserved for a garnish.

FRUIT SALAD PLATE

1. Arrange several lettuce cups on salad plate.
2. Prepare different fruits, or fruit mixtures: Waldorf Salad from diced apple; grapefruit or orange sections; melon balls; avocado wedges; grapes, in small clusters; pineapple, pears, peaches or apricots, fresh or canned. A scoop of fruit sherbet is an attractive and refreshing addition to a salad plate, as is jellied fruit, moulded or cut into individual servings.
3. Arrange fruit or fruit mixtures in separate lettuce cups so that flavours and colours harmonize.
4. Garnish with mint, water cress, cheese balls, ripe olives, cherries, stuffed prunes or dates.
5. Serve with whipped cream dressing, sour cream, or sweetened fruit dressing.

MOULDED SALADS

Moulded salads are both decorative and appetizing when set off by a background of lettuce or endive. Meats, vegetables and fruits all lend themselves favourably to this treatment. Fresh or canned fruits set in a colourful base of tinted fruit juice or commercially prepared jelly powder provide glamour on a salad plate. *Fresh pineapple must be cooked before adding to a gelatine mixture.* Otherwise the mixture won't jell.

Before filling mould, rinse it in cold water *or* rub it lightly with a piece of paper napkin which has been sprinkled with cooking oil. If the latter method is used, the mixture must be cooled before pouring it into the mould.

The setting of the jelly can be speeded up, if desired, by placing the mould in the freezing section of the refrigerator until set. Once the mixture is set, remove it from this area to prevent freezing. Jelly set at room temperature will not melt as readily when served in warm weather as will jelly that is set at refrigerator temperature.

To Unmould: If mould is non-fluted, loosen first by running a sharp-tipped thin-blade knife around the edge of the mould. All moulds, including fluted ones, should be dipped very quickly in and out of hot water to loosen. Place a serving dish face down over mould, and invert all quickly. Store in a cool place until needed.

TOMATO JELLY (ASPIC) (Basic Recipe)

1⅓ tablespoons gelatine	⅛ teaspoon dried celery leaves
⅓ cup cold water	4 cloves
2½ cups tomatoes (20-ounce tin)	4 pepperberries
¼ cup water	1 teaspoon sugar
1 bay leaf	1½ teaspoon salt
1 slice onion	2 teaspoons lemon juice

1. Soften gelatine in cold water.
2. Simmer all other ingredients except lemon juice for 20 minutes; add lemon juice.
3. Pour over softened gelatine, stir till gelatine is dissolved; press through a sieve (there should be 2 cups).
4. Cool, then pour into moulds; chill.
5. Unmould on lettuce. Serves 6.

   When mixture is partially set, add any of chopped parsley, hard-cooked egg, cooked peas, diced celery, sliced, stuffed olives or peeled chopped tomato. The addition of ¼-½ cup mayonnaise beaten into the partially set jelly makes a delicious variation.

   Jelly may be moulded in a shallow pan, then cut in shapes for garnishing.

QUICK TOMATO ASPIC

1 3-ounce package lemon jelly powder	1 clove
1¾ cups tomato or mixed vegetables juices	1 slice of onion
	½ bay leaf
	1 chicken bouillon cube

1. Heat tomato or mixed vegetable juices with clove, onion and bay leaf. Simmer 5 minutes; remove clove and bay leaf.
2. Stir in jelly powder and bouillon cube and continue stirring over very low heat until completely dissolved. Pour into prepared moulds. (See Additions in preceding recipe.) Serves 6.

CARDINAL TOMATO ASPIC

1 3-ounce package strawberry jelly powder	1 tablespoon minced onion
1¾ cups tomato or vegetable juice	1 cup sliced celery
1 tablespoon vinegar	2 carrots, shredded
1 teaspoon prepared horseradish	¼ green pepper, chopped

Prepare as Quick Tomato Aspic. Add vegetables when jelly is partially set.

PERFECTION SALAD (Basic Recipe)

Variations are as unlimited as the imagination.

⅓ cup dilute vinegar	juice of 1 lemon
1⅓ cups boiling water	few drops of food colouring
¾ teaspoon salt	⅔ cup cabbage, shredded finely
⅓ cup sugar	1½ cups celery, diced
1⅓ tablespoons gelatine	⅛ cup sweet red pepper, chopped
⅓ cup cold water	

1. Mix vinegar, boiling water, salt and sugar; heat to boiling point.
2. Soften gelatine in cold water; dissolve in boiling liquid.
3. Add lemon juice; strain; add food colouring; chill, stirring occasionally.
4. When slightly thickened, add vegetables.
5. Turn into moistened or oiled moulds; chill. Unmould and serve on crisp salad greens.

The jelly mixture of this salad, *Perfection Jelly*, may be used for moulding other vegetables, as asparagus and pimento, beets and celery, carrots and peas. Vegetable stock may be used as part of the liquid in the jelly.

Reduce boiling water to 1 cup; stir ½ cup mayonnaise into partially set jelly.

Cooked shredded pineapple, chopped dates and nuts may be added and the vinegar reduced to 1 tablespoon.

Cubed, processed cheese and sliced stuffed olives may be added.

Substitute other combinations of vegetables.

QUICK PERFECTION SALAD

Dissolve 1 3-ounce package lemon jelly powder in 1½ cups boiling water; add ½ teaspoon salt and ⅓ cup dilute vinegar. Finish as indicated in preceding recipe, beginning with step 4. Use vegetables indidicated, or variations. Salad jelly powders can also be substituted.

PARTY PERFECTION MOULD

Dissolve 1 3-ounce package lemon jelly powder in 1 cup boiling water; add ¾ cup ginger ale and 1 tablespoon lemon juice. Chill. When slightly thickened, add 1 cup shredded cabbage, ½ cup grated carrots and 6 sliced radishes. Pour into prepared mould and chill until set.

JELLIED SALMON, TUNA FISH

To Perfection Jelly or Quick Perfection Jelly add:

½ pound can of fish, flaked	2 tablespoons green pepper,
½ cup celery or cucumber, diced	chopped

The mayonnaise variation is particularly suitable here.

JELLIED SHRIMP AND CRAB MEAT

To Perfection Jelly or Quick Perfection Jelly add:

1 cup shrimp and crab meat, cubed	1 tablespoon green pepper, chopped
½ cup celery, diced	6 stuffed olives, sliced

GOLDEN SALAD

Substitute lemon juice for vinegar in Perfection Jelly or prepare 1 3-ounce package lemon jelly powder. Use 1 cup of pineapple juice drained from crushed pineapple for part of the liquid. For the vegetables substitute 4 grated carrots and 1 cup cooked pineapple, drained and crushed.

FRUIT MOULD (Basic Recipe)

1 tablespoon gelatine	1 cup grapefruit juice
¼ cup cold water	1 tablespoon lemon juice
¼ cup boiling water	fruit (see below)
½ cup sugar	nuts

1. Soften the gelatine in cold water.
2. Make a syrup of boiling water and sugar; boil 3 minutes.
3. Pour over softened gelatine; when dissolved add fruit juices; strain.
4. Chill; when beginning to set add fruit sections and nuts; mould. Serves 6.

1 3-ounce package of lemon or lime jelly powder and ½ cup of boiling water may be substituted for the first 4 ingredients. For fruit add any of the following: grapefruit sections; orange sections; pineapple; cherries; grapes; avocado sections. Or add celery, shrimps.

Pineapple, grapes, nuts.
Pineapple, cherries.
Grapefruit, orange.
Fruits, nuts, marshmallows.
Melon cubes or balls.
1 tablespoon of horseradish and substitute pineapple juice for lime juice.
½ cup mayonnaise and reduce boiling water to 1 cup.
Green colouring may be added.

FRUIT AND GINGER ALE SALAD

Especially attractive when served in a ring mould.

1½ tablespoons gelatine	⅓ cup malaga grapes, cut and
2 tablespoons cold water	seeded
⅓ cup boiling water	⅓ cup celery, diced
2 tablespoons sugar	⅓ cup apples, diced
¼ cup ginger syrup	¼ cup canned pineapple, diced
¼ cup lemon juice	⅛ cup preserved ginger, cut fine
1 cup ginger ale	

Prepare as Fruit Mould. Serves 6.

Pineapple juice may be used in place of ginger syrup; grapes may be omitted and pineapple increased.

One 3-ounce package jelly powder, 1 cup boiling water and ⅓ cup of ginger ale may be substituted for the first 7 ingredients.

JELLIED LIME LAYERS

1 3-ounce package lime jelly
powder
1 cup boiling water
¾ cup pineapple juice

1 tablespoon prepared
horseradish
½ cup mayonnaise
6 slices canned pineapple

1. Dissolve jelly powder in boiling water; add pineapple juice.
2. Pour ⅓ of the mixture into a moistened mould and chill until it is firm.
3. Chill remainder until it is slightly thick; beat until fluffy.
4. Add horseradish and mayonnaise and pour over first layer of firm gelatine. Chill.
5. Unmould on greens, garnish with pineapple slices. Serves 6.

JELLIED CUCUMBER CREAM

2 cucumbers
1 3-ounce package lime jelly
powder
1 cup boiling water
1 cup sour cream

¼ cup mayonnaise
2 tablespoons lemon juice
1 teaspoon finely grated onion
salt

1. Peel cucumbers, quarter lengthwise and remove seeds. Dice and drain on a paper towel.
2. Dissolve jelly powder in boiling water in a large bowl; beat in sour cream, mayonnaise, lemon juice and onion. Add a few grains of salt.
3. Chill until mixture begins to thicken.
4. Fold in diced cucumber and pour into a prepared mould (about 4 cups) or into individual moulds.
5. Chill several hours or until firm. Unmould and serve garnished with chicory or other greens. Serves 6.

CHICKEN MOUSSE

Whipped cream in a gelatine base.

1 tablespoon gelatine
¼ cup water
¾ cup stock, seasoned
1 cup whipping cream

1 cup diced cooked chicken
¼ teaspoon salt
dash of pepper

1. Soften the gelatine in cold water for 5 minutes; dissolve in hot stock.
2. Chill until partly set.
3. Beat the gelatine mixture until frothy.
4. Whip the cream and fold into the gelatine.
5. Fold in the cut chicken and seasonings; chill until firm. Pour into a moistened or oiled mould. Serves 6-8.

MOULDED CHEESE SALAD

1 tablespoon gelatine	½ tablespoon lemon juice
¼ cup water	1 teaspoon salt
⅔ cup hot milk	½ cup cream, whipped
8 ounces fresh cream cheese, plain or relish	

1. Soften gelatine with cold water; dissolve in hot milk; cool.
2. Add cheese, lemon juice and salt; beat until smooth; chill.
3. When mixture begins to set, fold in cream; mould.

Sour cream may replace whipped cream.

Celery and green pepper, chopped celery and olives, plain or pimento may be added. Or add canned pineapple, shredded or diced. Use pineapple juice instead of milk in recipe.

Tomato Jelly—fill mould half full of tomato jelly; when set, add cheese jelly, chill.

When salad forms the main course—serve hot rolls; tea biscuits; muffins; melba toast; buttered bread (white, brown, nut, orange); bread and butter sandwiches; cress rolls.

When salad is served as an appetizer in luncheon or dinner—serve crackers, plain or crispened, with cheese; cheese straws.

When salad is served as dessert—serve cheese straws; crackers and cheese; small sandwiches.

FROZEN CHEESE AND FRUIT SALAD

1 tablespoon lemon juice	½ cup chopped dates
¼ cup mayonnaise or salad dressing	½ cup quartered maraschino cherries
1 8-ounce package cream cheese	½ cup toasted almonds
½ teaspoon salt	2 bananas, sliced
¼ cup crushed pineapple	1 cup heavy cream, whipped

1. Gradually add the lemon juice and mayonnaise to the cream cheese, blending until smooth.
2. Add the salt, pineapple, dates, ½ cup of quartered cherries, almonds and bananas. Fold in the whipped cream.
3. Pour into 6 or 8 individual moulds. Freeze until firm. Serves 6 to 8.

Variation: Add ½ cup miniature marshmallows or ½ cup shredded coconut to the ingredients.

FROZEN TROPICAL SALAD

1 tablespoon gelatine	1 cup diced canned pineapple,
¼ cup cold water	drained
½ cup mayonnaise or salad	1 cup orange sections
dressing	1 cup grapefruit sections
1 cup whipping cream	1 banana, sliced (optional)

1. Soften gelatine in cold water; dissolve over hot water, and stir slowly into the mayonnaise.
2. Whip cream and fold into mayonnaise mixture; fold in the fruits. Pour into refrigerator freezing tray and freeze until firm. Slice and serve. Serves 6.

SALAD DRESSINGS

Basic salad dressings are few in number but their variations are unlimited.

Choose a dressing suited to the texture and flavour of the salad ingredients. It is convenient to have 2 or 3 different kinds on hand in the refrigerator; often these too can be blended together to form new variations.

FLAVOURED VINEGAR

The vinegar left from pickled onions, olives and other pickles gives extra tang to a dressing when substituted for regular vinegar. Cider vinegar has a characteristic flavour of its own while malt vinegar which has less flavour is used either as is or flavoured with various herbs.

To 1 cup of malt vinegar add any one of the following:

2 crushed cloves of garlic	2 teaspoons dried herbs
2 teaspoons fresh, chopped mint	(marjoram, basil, thyme)
leaves	½ cup dried tarragon leaves

Leave vinegar with herbs in a tightly closed sealer for about 1 week. Strain. Use in salad dressings.

FRENCH DRESSING (Basic Recipe)

This liquid dressing is the most easily prepared and most versatile of dressings. It can be used on all salads with the exception of jellied and frozen salads. It is always used on tossed green salads and serves as a marinade for cooked vegetable salads. It can vary in flavour from tart to sweet, and highly-seasoned to mild!

Because it separates out into 2 layers, it must be thoroughly shaken before use, and applied just before serving time.

⅓ cup vinegar	1 teaspoon onion juice
⅔ cup salad oil	½ teaspoon sugar
1 teaspoon salt	¼ teaspoon pepper
½ teaspoon dry mustard	½ teaspoon paprika

1. Measure all ingredients into a jar which has a close-fitting top. Cover and shake vigorously, *or* combine ingredients in an electric blender, to give a more stable product.
2. Serve on leafy salad mixtures. Makes 1 cup.

If it is desirable that the oil and vinegar do not separate out into layers, an egg white may be shaken up with the ingredients. This will also thicken dressing slightly.

Additions:
Few drops Tabasco sauce.
Tomato ketchup.
Crumbled blue cheese (see recipe following).
Garlic clove; remove before serving. Finely-chopped water cress.
Chopped hard-cooked eggs and ketchup (Blackstone Dressing).
1 package salad dressing mix.

FRUIT FRENCH DRESSING

Substitute lemon, orange or pineapple, or a mixture of these juices, for vinegar. Sweeten with 2-3 tablespoons honey, if desired, and add 1 teaspoon celery seeds. Serve on fruits.

TOMATO SOUP DRESSING

Add ½ 10-ounce can tomato soup to basic recipe; serve on greens.

HOT FRENCH DRESSING (VINAIGRETTE DRESSING OR SAUCE)

Heat 1 cup French Dressing to boiling and add 2 chopped hard-cooked eggs, 1 tablespoon chopped green onions or chives, 1 tablespoon chopped parsley, 1 tablespoon chopped celery leaves, ½ teaspoon dry mustard and ½ teaspoon Worcestershire Sauce. Mix well and serve hot over hot green beans, asparagus, broccoli, hot sliced potatoes and boiled beef or tongue.

SESAME SEED DRESSING

Sauté 1 teaspoon sesame seeds in ½ cup cooking oil with 1 garlic clove. Cool and remove garlic. Add 3 tablespoons vinegar, ¼ teaspoon salt and a few grains pepper. Shake and serve.

BLUE CHEESE FRENCH DRESSING

Crumble ¼ cup Danish blue or Roquefort cheese with a few drops of lemon juice and 2 tablespoons rich cream. Using a fork, stir in ¼ cup vinegar, ½ cup cooking oil, ¼ teaspoon salt and a few grains pepper.

MAYONNAISE (Basic Recipe)

This thick dressing is an emulsion of oil, vinegar, egg and spices. Care must be taken in its preparation to develop the emulsion by the slow addition of the oil while the mixture is beaten constantly. This dressing is used for heavy salad mixtures such as potato, chicken or Waldorf salad, in sandwiches or in sandwich mixtures, or as a base for Tartar Sauce. It may be served as an accompaniment to salads in a separate dish, or in a tiny lettuce cup on the salad plate.

1 teaspoon dry mustard	1 large egg or 2 yolks
1 teaspoon salt	1 cup salad oil
½ teaspoon paprika	2 tablespoons vinegar

1. In a small but deep bowl, mix spices, egg and 1 tablespoon vinegar.
2. Add oil one drop at a time, beating constantly until an emulsion forms (mixture thickens).
3. Beat in 1 tablespoon vinegar and the remaining oil in larger portions.
4. Keep in a covered jar away from the freezing section of the refrigerator. Makes 1¼ cups.

Additions:
Chopped chives, olives, gherkins.
Capers, relish, horseradish.
Crumbled blue cheese.
Onion juice or finely chopped onion.
Chili sauce and horseradish.
Whipped cream, honey and enough maraschino cherry juice to tint the dressing a delicate pink (Whipped Cream Dressing).
French Dressing.

THICKENED MAYONNAISE

This dressing forms a more stable emulsion than regular mayonnaise; it is also slightly less expensive to make.

To the dry ingredients add 2 tablespoons flour and 1 tablespoon sugar. Mix well. Add ½ cup boiling water and cook until thick, stirring constantly. Add well-beaten egg, and beat well with an egg beater. Cool; beat in oil and vinegar in small alternate amounts.

AVOCADO MAYONNAISE

Sieve or blend in a blender 1 avocado. Combine with ⅓ cup mayonnaise, 1 tablespoon lemon juice, 1 tablespoon onion juice, a dash of Worcestershire Sauce and a dash of Tabasco sauce. Add salt to taste. Serve over sliced tomatoes or seafood salad, and sprinkle with chives.

CURRY MAYONNAISE

To ½ cup mayonnaise add 1 teaspoon lemon juice, enough curry powder to give the desired flavour (about ½ teaspoon) and ½ cup sour cream (optional). Serve with seafood or chicken salads, or as a dunking sauce for shrimps or raw vegetable relishes.

GREEN GODDESS MAYONNAISE

Chop together finely 6 anchovy filets, 1 small onion or 4 green onions, ¼ cup parsley, ¼ cup chives and 1 small garlic clove, crushed. Stir into 1 cup mayonnaise. Add 2 teaspoons lemon juice and salt and pepper to taste. Chill. Serve on seafood salads.

COOKED SALAD DRESSING (Basic Recipe)

This is a flour-thickened mixture which is used for the same purposes as mayonnaise.

½ teaspoon salt	1 egg or 2 yolks
2 tablespoons prepared mustard	½ cup water
dash of cayenne	¼ cup vinegar
1 tablespoon sugar	1 tablespoon butter
1 tablespoon flour	

1. Mix dry ingredients in upper part of double boiler.
2. Add egg, well beaten, and water.
3. Add vinegar slowly; cook over boiling water, stirring constantly until thick.
4. Remove from heat; add butter. Cool. If necessary, thin with sweet or sour cream. Makes ¾ cup.

   See Mayonnaise (Basic Recipe) for additions; add when dressing is cool.

POPPY SEED DRESSING

Add 1 tablespoon poppy seed.

SOUR CREAM DRESSINGS

Sour cream can be used alone or in combination with other ingredients as a salad dressing. As in all the recipes in this book, sour cream refers to the commercial product purchased as such in stores.

SOUR CREAM DRESSINGS FOR VEGETABLES

To *1 cup sour cream* add any 1 of the following ingredients to give the desired variation:

2 tablespoons of any of lemon juice, pickle juice or French Dressing; ½ tablespoon minced onion, ¼ teaspoon salt, ¼ cup finely chopped olives or pickles (optional). If lemon juice is used, add extra sugar if necessary. Mix thoroughly and chill; serve on green salads, cucumbers and cabbage salad.

½ cup mayonnaise, 1 teaspoon celery seed, 1 teaspoon prepared mustard and 1 teaspoon minced onion. Mix thoroughly and chill; serve on cabbage and potato salads and on sliced tomatoes.

1 teaspoon chopped fresh dill, 1 teaspoon chopped parsley, 2 tablespoons tarragon vinegar, ½ teaspoon salt and a few grains white pepper and garlic powder. Chill and serve on cole slaw, cooked vegetables or cucumbers.

3 ounces blue cheese, crumbled, 3 tablespoons milk, 2 tablespoons salad oil, dash Worcestershire Sauce, 1 tablespoon grated Parmesan cheese, a few grains of each of onion and garlic salts and pepper, 3 tablespoons malt vinegar and 4 teaspoons lemon juice. Stir ingredients to mix, leaving the cheese in its crumbled state. Chill; serve on vegetables or fruits.

SOUR CREAM DRESSING FOR FRUITS

To *1 cup sour cream* add any 1 group of the following ingredients to give the desired variation:

blue cheese (see preceding variation).

⅓ cup liquid honey, 3 tablespoons lemon juice and ⅛ teaspoon salt. Mix and chill.

2 tablespoons finely chopped mint and 1 teaspoon sugar which have stood for 5 minutes before adding to sour cream, a few grains salt and 1 teaspoon lemon juice. Chill.

6 drops almond extract, ½ teaspoon vanilla and a few grains of salt. Mix and chill.

½ cup finely-chopped candied ginger, ¼ cup finely chopped walnuts and 1 teaspoon liquid honey. Chill.

½ cup orange juice and ¼ cup icing sugar; mix and sprinkle a few grains of nutmeg or cinnamon on top. Chill.

¼ cup frozen strawberries, or fresh, sweetened strawberries, ½ teaspoon salt. Chill.

2 tablespoons lime juice, ½ teaspoon grated orange rind and ¼ teaspoon each of lemon and lime rind and powdered ginger, 1 tablespoon sugar. Chill.

WHIPPED CREAM DRESSING

Combine 3 tablespoons mayonnaise with 1 tablespoon syrup, or honey, or liquid from preserved ginger, maraschino cherries or other sweetened fruits. Whip ½ cup whipping cream and fold into mayonnaise mixture. Chill and serve. Makes 1 cup.

BUTTERMILK SALAD DRESSING

This is a low-calorie dressing.

1 cup of buttermilk	1 tablespoon lemon juice
¼ teaspoon salt	1 tablespoon chili sauce or
⅛ teaspoon pepper	ketchup

Shake well together in a tightly covered container.

PICNIC DRESSING

This dressing thickens on standing.

⅔ cup undiluted evaporated milk	3 tablespoons crumbled blue
⅔ cup salad oil	cheese
2 tablespoons lemon juice	or
½ teaspoon salt	3 tablespoons prepared mustard
¼ teaspoon Worcestershire Sauce	

1. Shake all the ingredients together in a tightly covered jar.
2. The mustard variation is particularly suitable served with cold meat, poultry and cheese. The blue cheese variation complements fruit salads and tossed greens. Makes 1⅔ cups.

LIME-MINT FRUIT SALAD DRESSING

1 3-ounce package soft cream cheese	½ cup heavy cream, whipped
2 tablespoons honey	⅛ teaspoon salt
½ cup mayonnaise	3 tablespoons lime juice
	3 sprigs of mint

1. Blend cheese, honey and mayonnaise until smooth.
2. Fold in whipped cream, salt and lime juice. Cut in mint with scissors.
3. Chill and serve on chilled fruits. Makes 1½ cups.

MAGIC MAYONNAISE

A sweet Mayonnaise.

⅔ cup sweetened condensed milk	1 egg yolk
¼ cup vinegar or lemon juice	½ teaspoon salt
¼ cup salad oil or melted butter	dash of cayenne pepper
	1 teaspoon dry mustard

Place ingredients in a pint jar, cover tightly and shake vigorously. For a thicker consistency, chill mixture for 1 hour before serving. Makes 1¼ cups.

15 Beverages

The pick-me-up in the middle of the day, the bed-time relaxer or the finishing touch to a perfect meal, a beverage is most versatile.

A fortified milk shake can give us the equivalent of a whole meal's calories in just 1 glass—the same volume of clear tea or coffee provides none!

Beverages are a focal point for hospitality—morning coffee, afternoon tea or a cool drink on a hot day can provide the setting for friendly get-togethers!

COFFEE

At a meal, coffee is usually served with the dessert course or after it. Sometimes, after-dinner coffee is served in the living room when there is no limit on time; demitasses may be used. Gay mugs bring a smile to morning coffee; regular coffee cups are always suitable.

Coffee may be purchased as beans for home grinding; it may be ground when packed or ground at the time of purchase.

Instant coffee is natural coffee essence with the water removed. Freeze-dried instant coffee retains more of the characteristic coffee flavour and aroma than does ordinary instant coffee.

FACTS TO CONSIDER WHEN MAKING COFFEE

1. Use freshly ground coffee; buy it in small amounts and keep in a covered container in a refrigerator or other cool place. Choose the blend most pleasing.
2. Use the grind of coffee suited to your coffee maker: coarse for steeped coffee; medium for percolator; fine for the vacuum type and dripolator.

3. Be sure the coffee maker is washed and rinsed after each use; never use it for tea. The size should be suitable for the amount of coffee being made; do not try to make 1 cup of coffee in a 8-cup pot.

4. Use a measured amount of coffee and water; 1 to 3 tablespoons for each cup, depending upon the strength desired. Like tea, strong coffee should be obtained by increasing the amount of coffee, not by increasing the time of heating.

5. Use boiling water, because the faster the coffee is made the better it will be. However, there are some types of automatic percolators which must start out with cold water in order to complete the percolating cycle. Do not allow the coffee to boil, nor to stand for any length of time before serving.

6. A few grains of salt will bring out the flavour, but be careful to avoid a salty taste.

DRIPOLATOR COFFEE

1. Use 1 to 3 tablespoons finely ground coffee to each cup of water.
2. Place the measured coffee in the middle section.
3. Pour the boiling water in the top section.
4. As soon as a little coffee has dripped through, place the pot over a low heat.
5. When all the water has dripped through the coffee into the lower section, remove the top two sections and serve.

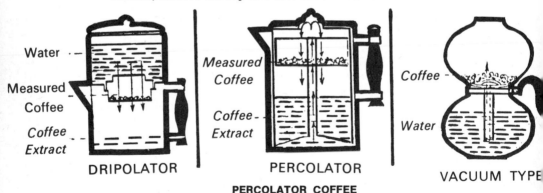

Water
Measured Coffee
Coffee Extract
DRIPOLATOR

Measured Coffee
Coffee Extract
PERCOLATOR

Coffee
Water
VACUUM TYPE

PERCOLATOR COFFEE

1. Pour the measured water into the percolator.
2. Measure 1 to 3 tablespoons (depending on the strength desired) of medium-grind coffee for each cup of water, into the basket; if there is a perforated cover put it on. Put the lid on the pot.

3. Set the percolator on high heat; as soon as the water begins to bubble up through the tube, lower the heat so the percolation continues slowly.
4. Percolate 7 minutes; remove the basket and tube; serve.

VACUUM COFFEE

1. Put measured boiling water into the lower bowl of the coffeemaker; set it on high heat. Use medium heat for a glass coffeemaker or set it on a protective grid.
2. If a cloth filter is used rinse it in cold water and hook it into position; if a glass rod is used place it in position.
3. Remove the lower bowl from the heat; place the upper bowl in the lower after dampening the rubber gasket; twist it gently to make a tight seal.
4. Measure 1 to 3 tablespoons finely ground coffee for each cup of water into the upper bowl.
5. When the water is forced by the steam into the upper bowl, leave it for 3 minutes on low heat, stirring it carefully once.
6. Remove the coffeemaker from the heat, or turn the heat off. The pressure of the air will force the coffee extract back into the lower bowl, leaving the grounds on top.
7. Remove the upper bowl.

    If the coffee will not go back down, it means that a tight seal was not formed between the upper and lower bowl, or that a grain of coffee got in under the filter. In this case place the coffeemaker back on the heat and allow the heat to send whatever coffee has dripped down back up again. This may dislodge the grain of coffee if that was the trouble; tighten the seal and proceed as before. If this happens frequently, it is possible that the rubber gasket needs replacing.

FILTERED COFFEE

There are many different methods for making filtered coffee, each with its own special pot. Some are based on principles used in standard coffeemakers; Espresso coffee is made in a special machine which uses steam pressure for extraction. A simpler version of this Italian coffeemaker is made in many different styles, but the principle is the same in each. Its description follows:

ITALIAN-TYPE COFFEEMAKER

Water is heated to boiling in the lower compartment of the coffeemaker. It passes up through a funnel-shaped compartment which contains the ground coffee, through a series of filters, and is collected in an upper chamber. Depending on the style of coffeemaker used, coffee may be poured out directly, or the whole unit inverted and the coffee-chamber disengaged for pouring.

Coffee Essence

Filters

Ground Coffee

Water

ITALIAN-TYPE COFFEE MAKER

STEEPED COFFEE

1. Allow 1 to 3 tablespoons coffee, coarsely ground, for each cup water.
2. Put the measured coffee into any covered pan of suitable size; it may be tied loosely in a cheesecloth bag.
3. Pour on the freshly boiled water.
4. Heat the water to just under the boiling point; keep it at that temperature 8 minutes; add a little cold water and allow it to stand off the heat a few minutes.

   For making coffee in large quantities, see Feeding a Crowd, Chapter 23.

CLEARED COFFEE

1 cup coffee   3 tablespoons cold water
1 egg white and crushed shell   dash of salt
8 cups boiling water

1. Combine the coffee, egg and cold water to form a paste.
2. Steep as in preceding recipe; the egg, in coagulating, encloses the tiny particles of coffee and so gives a clear appearance to the liquid. Serves 8.

CAFÉ AU LAIT

Combine equal parts of strong coffee and scalded milk.

ICED COFFEE

1. Make coffee by any method but make it double strength.
2. Pour into a tall glass full of ice cubes.
3. Serve with cream and Sugar Syrup (page 411).
   Coffee may be made in advance and poured into the ice-cube tray.
   These cubes may be used with coffee of regular strength.

COFFEE IMPERIAL

4 sticks cinnamon	¾ cup whipping cream
6 cups strong hot coffee	ice cubes
⅓ cup sugar	

1. Add cinnamon sticks to hot coffee and let stand for 1 hour.
2. Remove cinnamon sticks, add sugar to taste and ½ cup of the cream. Chill.
3. Pour liquid into 6 tall glasses and fill with ice cubes.
4. Whip remaining cream, add a little sugar and vanilla if desired; place a spoonful of cream on each serving. Serves 6.

CAFÉ BRULÔT

Hot spicy coffee to end a meal dramatically.

1 small orange	6 cubes sugar
1 lemon	½ cup cognac
6 whole cloves	4 cups freshly brewed coffee
3 cinnamon sticks	

1. Using a vegetable parer, remove peel in thin strips from orange and lemon; place in a chafing dish. Reserve pulp of fruit for other uses.
2. Combine spices, sugar and 6 tablespoons of the cognac in chafing dish and heat until just warm.
3. Warm remaining cognac in a ladle until it begins to bubble; ignite it with a match and stir into mixture in the chafing dish. Stir in coffee and heat until bubbly. Serve hot in demitasses.

TEA

Tea stars as mid-afternoon refreshment, quietly at home or at social gatherings. It is also served with meals.

HOT TEA

1 cup boiling water   1 teaspoon tea

1. Use a glass or earthenware teapot.
2. Pour hot water into teapot; let stand until thoroughly heated; empty it.
3. Measure in the tea; add freshly boiled, boiling water.
4. Let stand in a hot place to infuse for 5 to 6 minutes. Do not let it boil; to alter the strength use more or less tea, do not change the time.
5. Pour tea from leaves and serve with milk or very thin cream, or with thin slices of lemon or slices of orange with one clove in each. If tea bags are used, increase the quantity of water by ½.

ICED TEA

4 teaspoons tea   2 cups boiling water

1. Make tea; when infused, strain from leaves or remove tea bags.
2. Sweeten, if desired.
3. Pour into tall glasses ⅓ full of chipped ice.
4. Serve with a thin slice of lemon or orange.

COCOA

Serve at breakfast, at bedtime, or after winter sports.

2 to 3 tablespoons cocoa	1 cup water
2 tablespoons sugar	3 cups milk
dash of salt	½ teaspoon vanilla

1. Mix cocoa, sugar and salt in the top of a double boiler.
2. Add water; bring to a boil over the direct heat. Boil 1 minute.
3. Add the milk; set over hot water and leave until the cocoa is hot.
4. Just before serving add vanilla and beat with an egg beater until a thick froth forms. This breaks up the skin which is composed of fat and protein and so it should not be skimmed off.
5. A marshmallow may be placed in each cup or a topping of whipped cream may be added. For variety, stir in 1-2 teaspoons instant coffee. Serves 4-6.

CHOCOLATE SYRUP

If chocolate is served frequently, time is saved by making up syrup which can be stored until needed.

¾ cup cocoa	1½ cups boiling water
1½ cups sugar	3 tablespoons butter
⅛ teaspoon salt	

1. Combine cocoa, sugar and salt; mix well.
2. Add boiling water slowly; boil 5 minutes. Add butter.
3. Pour into a jar; seal; refrigerate.
4. To use, mix 1 tablespoon to 1 glass of milk, hot or cold.

   For extra nourishment and calories, stir in 2 well-beaten eggs at the end of step 2.

COCOA PASTE

A good recipe to add extra calories.

1 cup cocoa	1 cup water
dash of salt	¼ cup butter
1½ cups sugar	2 eggs (optional)

1. Mix the cocoa, salt and sugar.
2. Add the water; mix well; bring to a boil and boil 3 minutes.
3. Remove from the stove; add the butter; mix well; cool.
4. Add the well-beaten eggs; beat smooth; refrigerate.
5. Serve 2 tablespoons to 1 glass cold milk. Makes 1 pint.

FRUIT DRINKS

SUGAR SYRUP

Keep in the refrigerator to sweeten fruit drinks, iced tea and coffee.

2 cups sugar	2 cups water

Add the sugar to the water and bring to a boil. Makes about 3 cups thin syrup.

LEMONADE I

This recipe uses Sugar Syrup.

2 cups sugar syrup	1 quart ice water
⅓ cup lemon juice	

Mix well; pour over ice cubes. Makes 8 glasses (6 tall).

LEMONADE II

This recipe makes a small quantity.

1 cup water   2 tablespoons lemon juice
4 tablespoons sugar

Stir the sugar and water to dissolve; add the lemon juice; pour over ice cubes. Makes 2 glasses.

LEMONADE III

1½ cups sugar   rind of 1 lemon (thin shavings
1 cup water   without white)
                       juice of 6 lemons

1. Make syrup of water, sugar and lemon rind by simmering 5 minutes.
2. Cool; add lemon juice, strain.
3. Dilute to taste, with ice water, using about 2 tablespoons syrup to 1 glass. This makes a stronger flavoured lemonade; about 20 glasses.
4. Garnish the glass with a thin slice of lemon rind and a maraschino cherry.

LIMEADE

Follow the directions and quantities for Lemonade, reducing the sugar to taste. 6 limes make ½ cup juice.

GRAPE LEMONADE

Pink lemonade for birthday parties.

⅓ cup grape juice   ⅔ cup lemonade

Combine; pour over ice cubes. Makes 2 glasses.

DECORATIVE ICE CUBES FOR USE IN FRUIT DRINKS

1. Fill a refrigerator tray with water; the water may be coloured if desired.
2. Place in each section any one of the following: a red or green maraschino cherry; a slice of lemon or orange; a piece of pineapple or a sprig of mint.
3. Freeze and serve cubes in iced tea, lemonade or other cold drinks. Substitute lemonade, orangeade or other diluted fruit juices for water. Serve in fruit drinks.

HOT SPICED FRUIT JUICE

12 ounces fruit juice (apple, grape, etc.)	½ stick cinnamon thin shaving of orange or lemon rind
2 cloves	

Tie spices and rind in cheesecloth; add fruit juice and simmer 5 minutes. Serve hot in mugs. Serves 2.

HOT MULLED CIDER

½ cup brown sugar	1 teaspoon whole cloves
¼ teaspoon salt	3-inch stick of cinnamon
2 quarts cider	dash of nutmeg
1 teaspoon whole allspice	

1. In a large saucepan, combine sugar, salt and cider.
2. Tie spices in a piece of cheesecloth, add to cider and heat slowly to boiling point.
3. Cover and simmer 20 minutes. Remove spices.
4. Serve in mugs with an orange slice floater and cinnamon stick muddler. Serves 10.

PUNCH BOWLS

These symbols of hospitality add decoration to every garden party or Holiday Open House. For fruit punches, float slices of orange and lemon, or a fruit ice block or ring. For larger quantities, see Feeding A Crowd, Chapter 23. 1 punch cup holds about 4 ounces.

FRUIT ICE BLOCK FOR PUNCH BOWL

Use a round pan about 7 or 8 inches in diameter and about 3 inches deep. Place pineapple rings in bottom; fill centres with maraschino cherries. Mix pineapple juice with water, about half and half, and fill pan. Freeze. Remove ice block when ready to serve; place in punch bowl and add punch. The mixture may be similarly frozen in a ring jelly mould, if desired.

FRUIT PUNCH

½ cup sugar	1 cup grape juice or
¼ cup water	½ cup crushed pineapple or
1 lemon	1 cup cold tea
1 orange	1 small bottle ginger ale

Combine sugar and water; heat to boiling point to form a syrup. Cool. Add the juice of lemon and orange; add 1 cup of grape juice, pineapple or tea. Chill. Pour into punch bowl. Add ginger ale and ice cubes, a few slices of cherries and sprigs of mint. Serves 4-6.

PINK LADY PUNCH

½ cup lemon juice
1 cup pineapple juice
2 cans frozen orange juice

¼ cup maraschino cherry juice
2 quarts ginger ale
maraschino cherries

Combine fruit juices; pour over ice in punch bowl. Add ginger ale and garnish with cherries. Makes 25 punch-cup servings.

PINEAPPLE MINT PUNCH

fresh mint sprigs
2 tablespoons sugar
½ cup lemon or lime juice
1 48-ounce can pineapple juice

1 30-ounce bottle lemon-lime
carbonated drink
pineapple spears

Crush mint with sugar; add lemon juice and pineapple juice and chill for at least 1 hour. Just before serving, add carbonated drink. Pour mixture over ice in a punch bowl; serve in punch cups or glasses garnished with pineapple spears and sprigs of mint. Makes about 2 quarts, or 20 punch-cupfuls.

RHUBARB PUNCH

4 pounds rosy rhubarb (about 16
cups)
2 quarts water
3 cups sugar
3 cups boiling water

¾ cup lemon juice
1 12-ounce tin frozen orange
juice
4 quarts soda water
mint

Chop rhubarb and cook in water until tender; strain through a jelly bag without squeezing. Dissolve sugar in boiling water and add to rhubarb juice. Chill, and add remaining juices. Just before serving combine with soda water, crushed ice cubes and sprigs of fresh mint. Makes about 7 quarts or 70 punch-cupfuls.

EGGNOGS

An electric blender is most useful in making eggnogs and milk shakes; a covered glass or plastic shaker is effective also. Serve these filling drinks between meals when extra energy or calories are needed. The addition of skim milk powder to any of the milk drinks (1-2 tablespoons per serving) increases the nutritive value.

EGGNOG

3 eggs
1 tablespoon sugar
  dash of salt

1 teaspoon vanilla
2 cups milk
  dash of nutmeg

1. Beat eggs slightly; add sugar, salt and vanilla.
2. Stir in cold milk; strain and chill.
3. Pour into cold glasses and sprinkle lightly with nutmeg. Serves 2-3.

COLA EGGNOG

2 eggs, separated
2 bottles (6½ ounce) cola
  beverage

2 tablespoons icing sugar
¼ teaspoon vanilla

1. Beat egg yolks slightly and combine with the chilled cola drink.
2. Beat egg whites until stiff but not dry; gradually beat in the sugar and the vanilla.
3. Fold half of the beaten whites into the cola mixture and pour into 2 tall glasses. Top with remaining whites. Sprinkle with cinnamon, if desired. Serves 2.

CHRISTMAS EGGNOG

For a festive party.

12 egg whites
  salt
½ cup sugar
1 quart whipping cream
12 egg yolks

1 cup sugar
1 quart milk
1 large bottle ginger ale or
1 quart white rum or bourbon

1. Add a dash of salt to egg whites and beat until stiff, but not dry; gradually beat in ½ cup sugar.
2. Beat the chilled whipping cream until stiff.
3. In a large mixing bowl, beat egg yolks until thick and light; gradually beat in 1 cup sugar. Add the milk.
4. Stir chilled ginger ale or liquor into egg yolk mixture; fold in whipped cream and beaten egg whites.
5. Pour mixture into a chilled punch bowl and sprinkle with grated nutmeg. Fills about 35 punch-cups (4 ounces each).

GINGER ALE EGGNOG

1 egg	2 cups light cream or top milk
dash of salt	1 pint ginger ale
1 tablespoon corn syrup	

1. Beat egg, salt and corn syrup together; stir in chilled milk or cream.
2. Just before serving, add ginger ale. Makes 6 glasses.

Eggnog is traditional at Christmas-time.

MILK SHAKES

MOCHA FLOAT

3 cups milk	1 tablespoon sugar
2½ teaspoons instant coffee	dash of salt
6 tablespoons chocolate syrup	3 scoops vanilla ice cream

1. Combine all ingredients, except ice cream, in a blender or shaker; blend thoroughly and chill.
2. Pour into glasses and top with ice cream. Serves 3-4.

STRAWBERRY MILK SHAKE

3 cups hulled strawberries	½ teaspoon lemon juice
¼ cup sugar	3 cups milk
dash of salt	½ pint vanilla ice cream

1. Crush strawberries and press through a sieve or blend in a blender; add sugar, salt and lemon juice. Mix thoroughly and chill.
2. Add cold milk and ice cream and shake or beat until mixture is frothy and thoroughly combined. Serve at once. Serves 3-6.

   Some of the ice cream can be set aside and floated on top of each glass.

APRICOT MILK FLIP

1 13-ounce tin apricot nectar	dash of salt
1½ teaspoons lemon juice	3 cups milk
1½ tablespoons sugar	

1. Combine all ingredients except milk, thoroughly. Chill.
2. Just before serving combine with chilled milk in a pitcher.
3. Pour into glasses and garnish with a mint leaf or green cherry. Serves 4-5.

BANANA MILK DRINK

2 ripe bananas	dash of cinnamon
dash of salt	4 cups cold milk

Combine all ingredients in an electric blender or press bananas through a sieve, and beat in remaining ingredients with a rotary beater. Chill. Serves 4-5.

BROWN COW

4 large ripe bananas	1 teaspoon vanilla
½ cup chocolate-flavoured	4 cups cold milk
malted milk powder or	chocolate or vanilla ice cream
½ to ¾ cup chocolate syrup	

1. Slice peeled bananas into a bowl or blender; beat or mash to form a smooth pulp.
2. Add malt powder or chocolate sauce, vanilla and a little of the milk; blend thoroughly.
3. Add remaining milk and mix well. Top each serving with a scoop of ice cream. Serves 4-6.

GINGER FLIP

1 cup milk   1 cup ginger ale

Mix well. Serve cold. Serves 1-2.

SPICED HONEY MILK

2 teaspoons honey   ¾ cup milk
 dash of cinnamon or cloves

Mix honey and spice; add milk and beat with rotary beater. Serves 1.

Cold milk drinks add zest to a children's party.

MAPLE MILK

2 tablespoons maple syrup   1 glass cold milk

Shake or stir well to combine. Serves 1.

BUTTERMILK ORANGEADE

2 cups chilled fresh or frozen
   orange juice
2 cups chilled buttermilk

1 tablespoon lemon juice
½ to ¾ cup sugar, to taste

Combine all ingredients; blend well. Serve very cold.

PINEAPPLE BUTTERMILK

2 cups cold buttermilk
2 cups cold pineapple juice,
   preferably fresh or frozen

2 tablespoons lemon juice
½ cup sugar

Combine all ingredients; blend well. Serve very cold.

STRAWBERRY SODA

1 pint strawberries, washed and
   hulled
¼ cup sugar

2 12-ounce bottles soda water
1 pint vanilla or strawberry ice
   cream

1. Crush strawberries and press through a sieve; add sugar and mix thoroughly.
2. Set out 4-5 tall glasses and divide strawberry mixture among each.
3. Add a scoop of ice cream and a little soda water to each glass and stir well.
4. Add remaining soda water, top each glass with a scoop of ice cream and garnish with a whole strawberry. Serves 4-5.

   ¾ cup frozen strawberries can be substituted for sweetened fresh berries.

TO PASTEURIZE MILK

1. Sterilize bottles, drain, fill with milk; cork or cover.
2. Place on rack in a deep kettle; surround with cold water to the level of the milk.
3. Heat gradually to 145°, keep at that temperature 30 minutes.
4. Cool quickly; keep in a cold place.

16   Breads

A FLOUR MIXTURE obtains its structure from gluten, an elastic-like substance which is formed when the protein in flour is combined with a liquid, and from the protein of the egg which coagulates during baking. There must always be a balance between these structure-building ingredients and the tenderizing ingredients, which are shortening and sugar.

When a recipe is low in tenderizing ingredients, the method of mixing must involve little handling so that gluten formation will be kept to a minimum. This is the case with muffins and quick breads. Pancake batters contain so much liquid that the gluten develops less readily. However, extensive beating is not recommended.

In cakes, the proportion of tenderizing ingredients is so much higher that excess gluten formation is less probable. However, most of the beating must take place before the flour is added since beating after the addition of dry ingredients results in excess loss of carbon dioxide from the baking powder, producing a cake of poor volume.

INGREDIENTS USED IN PREPARING FLOUR MIXTURES

FLOURS

Canadian wheat is grown and milled for every purpose. Ontario soft wheat is ideal for cakes and pastry, while Western or hard wheat from our Prairie Provinces is the necessary ingredient for our daily bread. The difference lies in the protein content of the two flours.

Flour from hard wheat has a higher percentage of proteins than soft wheat flour and when kneaded forms more of the substance called gluten. Gluten gives the elasticity to dough. Strength is essential to contain the carbon dioxide formed when yeast is at work, but is undesirable when tenderness is required.

Bread flour from fine quality hard wheat is not available in small amounts; it might be obtained from a bake shop.

All-purpose flour, as the name implies, is designed for all types of flour mixtures. It contains a mixture of pastry and bread flour and so has some of the qualities of each.

Pastry flour or soft wheat flour contains fewer of the gluten-forming proteins and may be used for all products except yeast breads.

Cake flour is also milled from soft wheat. It is very finely milled, more velvety to touch and used when fineness of texture is of prime importance.

Enriched flour is flour to which some of the B vitamins and iron have been added to compensate for their loss during the process of refinement. Pastry, bread and all-purpose flours may be enriched.

Whole wheat flour, sometimes known as *graham flour*, is milled from soft wheat but, being less refined than pastry and cake flour, it contains more of the natural vitamins and minerals. It can be substituted for part of the flour in cookies, tea biscuits and rolls to give an equally delicious but more nutritious product. It is not sifted before measuring.

Instantized flour is a more expensive product which pours and blends more easily than ordinary flour and so is useful in sauces.

Self-rising flour has baking powder and salt added. It is used more widely in the United States than in Canada.

Presifted flour. All flour is sifted during milling, hence this term is meaningless. Use as unsifted flour.

FATS

Vegetable fats are available as *oils* which may be used when melted fat is required, or as *shortenings* which are oils which have been hardened by hydrogenation. *Emulsified fats* increase the amount of sugar which the fat can handle. These are more satisfactory in the quick-mix type of recipe. *Margarine* may be made from animal or vegetable fats or from a blend of the two; it is hydrogenated, then churned in milk to give flavour.

Animal fats make up the second group of fats. *Butter* has always been valued for the flavour it imparts. When the flavour is obscured by spices, other less-expensive fats will give equally good results. *Lard* is pork fat which has been decolourized and deflavoured. The keeping quality has been improved by the addition of anti-oxidants, and it has excellent tenderizing ability.

Shortening and lard are all fat; since butter and margarine contain some milk solids and are not all fat, their tenderizing effect is somewhat less.

BAKING POWDER
(Leavening Agent)

Two principal types of baking powder are available today: the *phosphate or quick-acting* and the *S.A.S. or double-acting*. Both give satisfactory results, but the double-acting is preferable in the quick-mix recipes where the baking powder is added at the beginning of the recipe. Unskilled cooks might find double-acting baking powder a little easier to use as all the gas does not form until the product is heated. Use either unless a recipe states that a double-acting powder is to be used. To substitute double-acting powder only ⅔ as much is required.

SUGAR

Sugar, like fat, has a tenderizing effect in flour mixtures. Granulated or white sugar is most commonly used. Today's sugar is fine in texture so that recipes which used to demand fruit or sifted sugar may be made with ordinary granulated sugar.

Brown sugar may range from dark to very light, depending upon the amount of molasses it retains. To replace an equal amount of white sugar it should be firmly packed.

Syrup—either maple, corn or honey—may be used to replace half the amount of sugar in a recipe if the liquid is reduced by ½ cup for each cup of syrup used.

LIQUID

Fresh whole milk, the liquid most commonly used, contains 3.25% fat. By law in Canada it must be pasteurized; it may also be homogenized to prevent the fat separating out as cream.

Skimmed milk, either liquid or dry, may be used to replace whole milk when it is desired to reduce the calories. (½ tablespoon butter for each cup of milk will replace the fat.) Powdered skim milk may be sifted in with the dry ingredients.

2% milk has less fat than whole milk, more than skimmed. It may be substituted without change.

Evaporated milk diluted with an equal amount of water may be substituted for an equal amount of whole milk with no change.

Condensed milk, because of the high sugar content, is not successful except in recipes especially designed for it.

Cream may be obtained by pouring off the top of a quart of milk which is not homogenized. This may be referred to as rich or top milk, and is equivalent to cereal cream, thin or light cream, with a fat content of about 10%. Coffee cream contains 16% butter fat, whipping cream contains 32-35% butter fat.

Commercial sour cream contains about 16% fat and has been soured by lactic acid bacteria. Cream soured at home may have a higher fat content and may not have a good flavour, so that it is not recommended in cheese cakes or salad dressings, but may be used in chocolate cake, scones or muffins.

Sour milk in a recipe means milk which has become sour enough to separate, at which point there is a constant acidity of 1%. *Buttermilk* may be used instead, or sweet milk may be soured by substituting 1 tablespoon of vinegar for 1 tablespoon of milk in 1 cup. To replace sweet milk in a recipe with sour milk a change must be made in the baking powder:

For each cup of sour milk, ½ teaspoon baking soda is used and the amount of baking powder is cut in half.

HOT AND QUICK BREADS

MUFFIN METHOD

Prepare pan. Add flour, sugar, salt; add egg, milk; then fat. Combine and stir to blend. Fill baking pans ⅔ full; then bake.

BISCUIT METHOD

Prepare pan. Mix and sift dry ingredients; cut in fat; measure liquid and egg; add liquid and combine until soft dough forms; knead, roll and shape; bake.

CAKE METHOD

Prepare pan. Combine soft fat, sugar and egg, beating until light and fluffy. Mix and sift dry ingredients; add alternately with milk, beating just to combine after each addition. Fill pan ½–⅔ full; then bake.

TO PREPARE PAN OR TIN FOR BAKING

Use one of these methods:

1. Coat thinly on bottom or sides with fat. Butter gives more flavour but any fat may be used.
2. Line the bottom of a cake pan with a strip of waxed paper cut to a size slightly less than the bottom of the pan; grease the sides and the bottom of the pan, including the paper.

3. Use an *ungreased tube pan* for products such as angel cake which will produce less volume if the sides of the pan are slippery.

CLASSIFICATION OF BATTERS BASED ON PROPORTION OF LIQUID TO FLOUR

Type	Amount of Liquid*	Amount of Flour	Use
	cups	cups	
Thin or Pour Batter (resembles whipping cream)	1	1	griddle cakes popovers
Thick or Drop Batter (resembles sour cream)	1	2	cakes muffins
Soft dough (can be handled)	1	3	tea biscuit bread
Stiff Dough (will crack)	1	4	pastry cookies

*The "liquid" includes those ingredients which are in liquid form during mixing, as milk, water, molasses and egg. An egg may be considered as a scant ¼ cup.

PANCAKES OR GRIDDLECAKES (Basic Recipe)

Every country makes them: plattar in Sweden, pfannkuchen in Germany, palacsinta in Hungary.

1½ cups sifted pastry flour or	2 tablespoons sugar (optional)
1¼ cups sifted all-purpose flour	1 egg
2 teaspoons baking powder	1-1½ cups milk (room temp.)
¾ teaspoon salt	3 tablespoons fat (melted)

1. Measure the flour. Mix and sift dry ingredients.
2. Beat egg, add milk and fat.
3. Add liquid to dry ingredients, slowly, to prevent lumps forming; stir and do not beat.
4. Heat a griddle or heavy frying pan; to test temperature sprinkle with a few drops of water; if they dance the pan is ready. With sufficient fat in the recipe and a good pan, no extra fat will be necessary; if the first griddle cake sticks, a small amount of fat may be added before each lot of cakes are cooked.
5. Pour the batter from a pitcher or measuring cup with a spout to get an even shape; form cakes about 3 inches in diameter. Use about ¼ cup batter to each pancake.
6. When bubbles begin to break on the surface and a rim forms around the edge, flip the cake over with a pancake turner or spatula.
7. Stacking pancakes makes a good picture but a soggy product. Spread them out on a hot plate and cover with a hot colander, or place on a heated platter in a warm oven. Makes 14-16 pancakes 4-5 inches in diameter.

Serve with maple, blueberry, strawberry or butter syrup following. If the batter is mixed in a 4-cup measuring cup it will be easy to pour and fewer dishes will be required.

Pancakes poured from a measuring cup.

BUTTERMILK PANCAKES

To substitute buttermilk for sweet milk use only half the amount of baking powder and add ½ teaspoon baking soda for each cup of milk (¾ teaspoon for the preceding recipe).

WHOLE WHEAT PANCAKES

Replace an equal amount of white flour with whole wheat flour up to ½ the quantity; add to sifted dry ingredients. Add 2 tablespoons molasses to liquid ingredients.

CORNMEAL PANCAKES

Replace an equal amount of white flour with cornmeal up to ½ the quantity; add to sifted dry ingredients.

SYRUPS TO SERVE WITH
PANCAKES AND WAFFLES

BUTTER SYRUP: Heat together 1 cup corn syrup and ¼ cup butter.

STRAWBERRY SYRUP: Add ⅓ cup strawberry preserves to butter syrup.

MAPLE SYRUP: Heat 1 pint maple syrup with 2 tablespoons butter. Serve warm.

MOCK MAPLE SYRUP: page 96.

BLUEBERRY SAUCE: page 95.

WAFFLES (Basic Recipe)

1½ cups sifted all-purpose flour or
1¾ cups sifted pastry flour
  3 tablespoons baking powder
  ½ teaspoon salt
  2 tablespoons sugar

2 large or 3 medium eggs,
  separated
1¾ cups milk
⅓ cup butter, melted

1. Sift dry ingredients.
2. Beat egg yolks; add milk and butter.
3. Combine liquid and dry ingredients; fold in stiffly beaten whites.
4. Heat waffle iron.
5. Pour 1 tablespoon of mixture in each section, near centre.
6. Bake without opening until no steam escapes and the batter ceases to "sing."
7. Makes 4-5 7-inch waffles.

When many waffles are needed, place singly on a baking sheet as they are made and keep warm in the oven.

CHEESE WAFFLES

Reduce the butter to ¼ cup; fold in 1 cup grated cheese with the egg white. Serve with bacon and tomatoes.

BACON WAFFLES

Cook 4-6 slices bacon until crisp; drain and crumble. Sprinkle 1 tablespoon over the top of each waffle before closing the iron. Serve with orange marmalade, sour cream or tomatoes.

APRICOT AND NUT WAFFLES

To the batter add ⅔ cup of drained cooked apricots before folding in the egg whites; sprinkle 2 teaspoons of finely chopped nuts on each unbaked waffle.

BLUEBERRY WAFFLES

Reduce milk in recipe to 1 cup; before folding in the egg whites, add 1 cup of fresh, frozen or drained canned blueberries.

COCONUT WAFFLES

To Waffles (Basic Recipe) add 1 teaspoon vanilla and sprinkle 1 heaping tablespoon of coconut over each waffle before baking.

ORANGE WAFFLES

Substitute 2 tablespoons (only) of orange juice for 2 tablespoons of milk in the recipe; add the finely grated rind of 1 orange.

PECAN WAFFLES

Fold ½ to 1 cup coarsely chopped pecans into the batter before baking.

PEANUT BUTTER WAFFLES

Reduce fat to ¼ cup; combine ½ cup crunch-style peanut butter with the fat.

GINGERBREAD WAFFLES

A spicy dessert waffle! Serve hot with applesauce.

1¾ cups sifted pastry flour or	1 teaspoon ginger
1½ cups sifted all-purpose flour	3 eggs, separated
1 teaspoon soda	½ cup molasses
1 teaspoon baking powder	⅓ cup melted shortening
½ teaspoon salt	1 cup sour milk or buttermilk
½ teaspoon cinnamon	

1. Mix and sift dry ingredients. Beat egg yolks.
2. Combine molasses, shortening, sour milk and egg yolks.
3. Finish as Waffles. Makes 4-5 waffles.

CHOCOLATE WAFFLES

Serve hot or cold with ice cream.

1¾ cups sifted pastry flour or	6 tablespoons cocoa
1½ cups sifted all-purpose flour	2 eggs, separated
3 teaspoons baking powder	2 tablespoons melted butter
½ teaspoon salt	1 cup milk
6 tablespoons sugar	

1. Mix and sift dry ingredients.
2. Beat egg yolks; add melted butter and milk and beat thoroughly.
3. Mix liquid ingredients with dry ingredients, and mix only until smooth.
4. Beat egg whites and fold into mixture; finish as Waffles. Makes 4-5 waffles.

HAM CRÊPES

1 recipe Crêpes	½ cup sour cream
¼ pound mushrooms	8 thin slices cooked ham
butter	1 cup seasoned medium White
salt	Sauce (page 79) or
pepper	1 cup Tomato Garlic Sauce
1 tablespoon flour	(page 85)

1. Prepare the Crêpes (Basic Recipe).
2. Wash, chop, and fry mushrooms in the butter; add seasoning; sprinkle flour over mushrooms, add sour cream, stir until mixture thickens slightly.
3. Cover each crêpe with a slice of cooked ham; spread with a layer of mushroom mixture; fold over; arrange open side down in a greased shallow baking dish.
4. Cover with sauce; sprinkle with cheese. Bake until browned and bubbling at 350° for 20 minutes.

   Quick recipe: Use frozen crêpes defrosted; combine ½ cup condensed mushroom soup (undiluted) and ½ cup sour cream; finish as Ham Crêpes.

CHICKEN CRÊPES

Substitute thinly sliced chicken for the ham in Ham Crêpes.

MUSHROOM CRÊPES

Chop cooked chicken finely and combine with the mushrooms as a filling.

SWEETBREAD CRÊPES

Add 1 cup Diced Cooked Sweetbreads (page 188) to the mushroom mixture of Ham Crêpes.

ASPARAGUS CRÊPES

Fill crêpes with cooked asparagus tips and julienned strips of ham; roll; heat in White Sauce.

CRAB MEAT CRÊPES

Combine 1 can crab meat, 2 tablespoons capers, 2 tablespoons finely minced green pepper and enough mayonnaise to moisten. Fill crêpes; brush with melted butter and heat in the oven.

NEWBURG CRÊPES

1 can crab meat, 1½ cups seasoned White Sauce, 1 can devilled shrimps. Flake seafood; add ½-cup sauce; fill crêpes. Arrange in chafing dish; cover with remaining sauce. Reheat.

CRÊPES SUZETTE

1 recipe Dessert Crêpe mixture	juice and finely grated rind of
½ cup butter, softened	1 orange
½ cup icing sugar	¼ cup Curaçao, Cointreau or
	Grand Marnier (optional)

1. Prepare the Dessert Crêpes.
2. Cream other ingredients together until smooth; melt in chafing dish.
3. Fry pancakes, roll or fold in four; place in sauce; heat.

   To flame, heat ½ cup brandy or Grand Marnier in a brandy warmer or a small pyrex teapot. Pour it around the edge of the dish; light it and spoon the flaming liquid over the crêpes.

PINEAPPLE CRÊPES

Roll drained canned pineapple spears in marmalade, then in coconut. Roll in crêpes; heat in the oven; serve with ice cream or fruit sauce.

BANANA CRÊPES

Roll banana in crêpe; heat in rum sauce; serve flambé with rum.

STRAWBERRY CRÊPES

1 recipe Dessert Crêpe mixture	½ cup almonds, blanched,
icing sugar	slivered
1 pint creamed cottage cheese	sour cream
1 pint strawberries	

1. As each crêpe is cooked slide it onto a board sprinkled with icing sugar.
2. Along one edge of each crêpe place 1 tablespoon creamed cottage cheese and 1 tablespoon sliced strawberries; fold over; arrange in baking dish.
3. Sprinkle with slivered almonds; broil 6 inches from the element until the tops begin to blister and brown slightly. Serve with sour cream. Makes 16 crêpes.

MUFFINS (Basic Recipe)

These thrive on minimum mixing.

2 cups sifted pastry flour or	3 tablespoons sugar
1¾ cups sifted all-purpose flour	1 egg
3½ teaspoons baking powder	1 cup milk
½ teaspoon salt	¼ cup melted fat or salad oil

1. Set the oven at 400°; grease muffin tins on the bottom only
2. Measure the flour; mix and sift the dry ingredients.
3. Beat the egg; add the milk.
4. Pour the liquid ingredients into the dry; add the fat; stir just enough to blend the ingredients but not to produce a smooth batter. Do not beat.
5. Fill muffin tins ⅔ full. The batter must not stand before it is in the muffin tins, but a few minutes after it is in the tins will do no harm.
6. Bake at 400° for about 20 minutes until the muffins come away from the sides of the pan and are a golden brown colour.
7. Turn out on a cake rack; serve warm. Makes 10 medium, 1½ dozen small muffins.

Muffins: Bake until golden brown.

CHEESE MUFFINS

Reduce shortening by 1 tablespoon and add ½ cup grated Cheddar cheese to the dry ingredients.

SPICE MUFFINS

Increase sugar by 2 tablespoons and sift in 1 teaspoon cinnamon, ½ teaspoon nutmeg and ½ teaspoon allspice with the dry ingredients.

BACON MUFFINS

Add ½ cup cooked chopped bacon or ham to the dry ingredients.

BLUEBERRY MUFFINS

See recipe on page 436.

ALL-BRAN MUFFINS

1 cup all-bran cereal	1 cup sifted all-purpose flour
¾ cup milk	2½ teaspoons baking powder
1 egg	1 teaspoon salt
¼ cup molasses or	½ cup chopped dates or
4 tablespoons brown sugar	seedless raisins
2 tablespoons melted fat or cooking oil	

1. Combine bran and milk in a small bowl and let soak 5 minutes.
2. Beat egg. Stir in molasses, oil and bran mixture. Sift dry ingredients together into egg mixture and stir only to blend. Fold in dates with a few strokes. Spoon into well-greased muffin tins, filling ⅔ full. Bake at 400° for 25 minutes. Makes 12 muffins.

   For dark muffins use dark molasses and increase the amount to ½ cup. The lighter the colour of molasses or brown sugar, the lighter will be the colour of the muffins. Experiment to find the flavour preferred.

BRAN-FLAKE MUFFINS

1 cup sifted all-purpose flour	1 egg
1¼ cups bran flakes	⅞ cup milk
3 teaspoons baking powder	⅓ cup shortening, melted
2 tablespoons sugar	¾ teaspoon salt

Combine as All-Bran Muffins; add flakes to sifted mixture. Makes 10-12 muffins.

BRAN MUFFINS

1 cup sifted all-purpose flour	⅓ cup molasses
1 teaspoon baking powder	⅞ cup sour or buttermilk
1½ teaspoons soda	1 egg
¼ cup brown sugar	4 tablespoons shortening
2¼ cups cooking bran	½ cup raisins or chopped dates

Combine as Muffins, adding the bran to the sifted dry ingredients. Add molasses to milk. Makes 12 muffins.

To use sweet milk omit the soda and increase the baking powder to 2 teaspoons.

GRAHAM MUFFINS

1½ cups brown sugar	1 cup dates
½ teaspoon salt	1 egg
2 teaspoons baking powder	1½ cups buttermilk
1½ teaspoons soda	2 tablespoons melted fat
1½ cups graham flour	

Combine as Muffins, adding *unsifted* flour to the other dry ingredients. Makes 10-12 muffins.

CORNMEAL MUFFINS

1 cup all-purpose flour	1 cup yellow cornmeal
1½ teaspoons baking powder	5 tablespoons shortening
¼ teaspoon baking soda	1 egg
1 teaspoon salt	½ cup sour milk
½ cup sugar	

Combine as Muffins, adding the cornmeal to the other dry ingredients after they have been sifted. Makes 10-12 muffins.

JOHNNY CAKE

The name is a corruption of journey-cake, because this corn bread was often carried by travellers! Bake Cornmeal Muffins mixture in an 8-inch square cake pan; serve hot in squares with maple syrup.

HAM AND PEANUT CORN SQUARES

1 package cornbread mix	1 cup salted peanuts,
2 4½ ounce cans devilled ham	coarsely chopped
	½ cup Cheddar cheese, grated

1. Prepare mix according to directions on package, adding devilled ham to the egg.
2. Spread on greased shallow pan.
3. Sprinkle evenly with peanuts and cheese. Bake at 375° for 20 to 25 minutes, until brown and crisp. Cut into about 48 squares.

RICH MUFFINS (Basic Recipe)

2 cups sifted pastry flour or	¼ cup sugar
1¾ cups sifted all-purpose flour	1 egg
3 teaspoons baking powder	½ cup milk
½ teaspoon salt	⅓ cup melted fat or salad oil

Combine as Muffins (page 433). Makes 8-12 medium muffins.

BLUEBERRY MUFFINS

To 1 cup fresh or unthawed frozen blueberries add half the sugar; stir gently into the batter. Do not overmix.

ORANGE MARMALADE MUFFINS

Omit the sugar; add 3 tablespoons marmalade with the milk.

JELLY CAKE MUFFINS

Prepare Streusel Topping (page 489), omitting nuts and adding 1 tablespoon orange or 1 teaspoon lemon rind. Half fill the muffin tins with batter; add 1 teaspoon jelly; cover with batter. Sprinkle Streusel Topping on the batter in each tin; bake as Rich Muffins.

GLAZED MINCEMEAT MUFFINS

Replace milk with ½ cup canned mincemeat and ½ cup apple juice. Glaze with Rum Butter Icing (page 570).

APPLESAUCE MUFFINS

Make these small to serve with tea or coffee.

1¾ cups sifted all-purpose flour or	¾ cup brown sugar
2 cups sifted pastry flour	¾ cup raisins
2 teaspoons baking powder	¼ cup unblanched almonds
2 teaspoons soda	(chopped)
¾ teaspoon salt	1 egg, beaten
1 teaspoon cinnamon	4 tablespoons melted fat
¼ teaspoon allspice	1 cup cold sieved applesauce
⅛ teaspoon cloves	

1. Mix and sift first 7 ingredients; add sugar, raisins and nuts.
2. Beat egg and fat. Add applesauce. Sift dry ingredients.
3. Bake at 400° for 15-20 minutes. Makes 10-12 medium or 24 small muffins.

TEA BISCUITS (Basic Recipe)

2¼ cups sifted pastry flour or	½ teaspoon salt
2 cups sifted all-purpose flour	½-⅔ cup firm shortening
4 teaspoons baking powder	⅔ cup milk (approximately)

1. Sift flour, baking powder and salt into a mixing bowl.
2. Cut in fat with a pastry blender, 2 knives or the fingers until no lumps of fat appear when the bowl is shaken; the mixture should have the appearance of fine crumbs.
3. Add the milk little by little with a fork or spoon until the mixture will form a ball around the spoon. (Too little milk makes a stiff dough which will crumble or crack; too much milk makes a sticky dough which will be difficult to handle.)
4. Turn the dough out onto a floured board; knead lightly until the ball of dough is smooth and beginning to spring back. (For this amount of dough it will require about 7 turns.) Turn the ball of dough so that the smooth side is up; roll ¾ inch thick for large biscuits, ½ inch for small biscuits.
5. Cut with a 1½ or 2-inch floured cookie cutter. For a shiny surface brush the top with milk or milk containing beaten egg yolk; place on an unbuttered baking sheet.
6. Bake at 400° to 425° for 10-20 minutes, depending upon the size. Makes 12-18 biscuits ¾ inch thick. Time may be saved by mixing the dough a little longer in the bowl and dropping it onto a baking sheet instead of kneading or rolling. This gives a rough looking biscuit but one with a good texture; it saves 2 steps.
   Or shape the dough into a rectangle on a baking sheet. Cut into squares with a sharp knife; separate before baking.

SKILLET BISCUITS

Preheat an electric frying pan to 380°; grease lightly; arrange the biscuits so they are not touching; cover and bake 3 minutes; turn and bake another 3 minutes.

SOUR CREAM BISCUITS

In the Tea Biscuit (Basic Recipe) replace the milk with sour cream, reduce the baking powder to 2 teaspoons and add ½ teaspoon baking soda.

Tea Biscuits: Cut with floured cookie cutter and place on ungreased pan. Have biscuits almost touching for soft-sided biscuits and 1 inch apart for crusty-sided biscuits.

Biscuits may stand for 5 to 10 minutes before baking. Bake in preheated oven until golden.

BUTTERMILK BISCUITS

In the Tea Biscuit (Basic Recipe) replace the milk with buttermilk or thick sour milk. Add ½ teaspoon baking soda and reduce the baking powder to 2 teaspoons.

CHEESE BISCUITS

To the dry ingredients in Tea Biscuit (Basic Recipe), add 1 teaspoon dry mustard, 2 cups grated, medium or old Cheddar cheese. For liquid beat 2 egg yolks in a measuring cup; add milk to make ⅔ cup. Use the smaller amount of fat. Brush the tops with milk; sprinkle with poppy seeds, celery seed, sesame seed or cumin seed.

TOMATO CHEESE BISCUITS

To the dry ingredients in Tea Biscuits (Basic Recipe) add ¾ cup Cheddar cheese, grated. Reduce baking powder to 2 teaspoons and add with ½ teaspoon soda. Replace milk with tomato juice.

FIESTA BISCUITS

To the dry ingredients in Tea Biscuits (Basic Recipe) add ½ cup grated sharp processed cheese, 2 tablespoons minced green pepper and 2 tablespoons chopped pimento. Roll into 8-inch square, cut in triangles, squares, or diamonds. Place on greased baking sheet. Bake as Tea Biscuits.

CORN BISCUITS

Beat 1 egg; add milk to make ⅔ cup and use as liquid ingredients. To the dough add 2 tablespoons chopped onion, 1 cup drained kernel corn.

WHOLE WHEAT TEA BISCUITS

Replace half the flour with whole wheat flour added to the sifted ingredients.

IRISH SODA BREAD

This biscuit cut in wedges makes a delicious substitute for bread. To the dry ingredients in Buttermilk Biscuits, add ½ cup raisins or currants, and 1 teaspoon caraway seed (optional). Shape into a round loaf about ¾-inch thick; place in a greased 9-inch pie plate. Bake 30 minutes at 375°. 6-8 wedges.

ONION BISCUIT SQUARES

(Serve hot with cold meat or salads.)

1 recipe Tea Biscuits (Basic Recipe)	dash pepper
2 cups sliced onions	1 egg
2 tablespoons butter	¼ teaspoon salt
½ teaspoon salt	½ cup commercial sour cream

1. Cook the onions in the butter, stirring until tender; sprinkle with salt and pepper.
2. Prepare biscuit dough; roll the dough into a 10 by 10-inch square; pat firmly into a greased 8 by 8 by 2-inch pan, pressing dough up the sides of the pan.
3. Top with the cooked onions; beat the egg, salt and sour cream; pour over the onions.
4. Bake at 450° until lightly browned (25 minutes); cut into squares to serve. Makes 16-20 pieces.

QUICK ONION BISCUITS

Prepare 2 cups Tea Biscuit Mix (Basic Recipe). Roll biscuits ¼-inch thick; cut with cookie cutter, press with bottom of floured custard cup to leave a rim. Fill centres with a butter-onion mixture made by stirring 2 tablespoons instant minced onion into 2 tablespoons melted butter; add the sour cream mixture. Bake on greased sheet at 425° for 20 minutes. Makes 1½-2 dozen.

FRENCH BREAD

Many interesting variations are possible, using prepared biscuits.

2 cans prepared biscuits	1 teaspoon poppy seed
1 egg white	

Place biscuits on ungreased baking sheet, pressing them together and shapping the ends to form a loaf; brush with egg white, sprinkle with poppy seed, bake at 350° for 30-40 minutes.

CHEESE FLAKES

⅔ cup cheese spread or softened sharp cheese	2 tablespoons butter
	1 package butterflake rolls

Cream the butter and cheese; separate rolls into sections; spread with the cheese mixture; arrange in muffin tins according to package directions. Bake at 375° for 15 minutes. Makes 12.

PARSLEY FLAKES

Remove the roll of biscuits from the package and coil around the edge of an 8-inch pie plate; pinch the ends of the roll together; brush well with melted butter mixed with a few drops of Tabasco and 1 tablespoon chopped parsley; sprinkle with grated cheese. Bake according to package directions.

SWEET TEA BISCUITS (Basic Recipe)

2¼ cups pastry flour or	¼ cup sugar
2 cups sifted all-purpose flour	¼ cup firm shortening
4 teaspoons baking powder	1 egg
½ teaspoon salt	milk

Sift the dry ingredients and cut in the fat. Best the egg with a fork in a measuring cup; add milk to make 1 cup. Combine as Tea Biscuits.

CURRANT SCONES

To Sweet Tea Biscuit recipe add 1 cup washed, dried and floured raisins or currants to dry ingredients. Roll dough to fit a 9-inch pie plate; score dough in triangles; sprinkle with sugar. Bake at 410° for 20 minutes.

LEMON CREAM SCONES

In Sweet Tea Biscuit recipe, substitute buttermilk or sour cream for milk, add juice and rind of 1 lemon, reduce baking powder to 2 teaspoons and add ½ teaspoon baking soda. Roll ¼ inch thick; brush with egg white, sprinkle with sugar to glaze; cut into triangles; bake well separated on a baking sheet at 425° for 15 minutes.

BUTTERSCOTCH MUFFINS

1. Prepare a pie plate by spreading liberally with soft butter; sprinkle with brown sugar; add 1 teaspoon corn syrup or a few drops of water to each pan.
2. Prepare Sweet Tea Biscuit dough (page 440); roll into a 9 by 12-inch rectangle.
3. Spread with soft butter; sprinkle with brown sugar; roll from the long side; with cut edge under, slice with a sharp knife into 1½ inch slices.
4. Place cut side down in the muffin pans; bake at 400° for 20 minutes. Makes 8 medium biscuits.

   For small biscuits cut the rectangle in half lengthwise before rolling; cut the slices ¾ inch thick; use small muffin pans. Makes 16 biscuits.

FRUIT ROLLS

1. Prepare a pie plate as in Butterscotch Muffins.
2. Roll 1 recipe Sweet Tea Biscuit dough (page 440) into a 9 by 12-inch rectangle.
3. Spread the dough with soft butter; cover with brown sugar; sprinkle with cinnamon.
4. Cover with 1 cup of any combination of dried fruit or nuts. Raisins, dates, candied pineapple, glazed or maraschino cherries, almonds or walnuts may be used, chopped finely. Well-drained, cooked apricots give a pleasant tart flavour alone or in combination with orange rind or orange marmalade.
5. Complete as Butterscotch Muffins.

COFFEE CAKE

1. Prepare 1 recipe Streusel Topping (page 489) and 1 recipe Sweet Tea Biscuits (page 440), increasing the milk to 1 cup before the egg is added.
2. Spread the batter in a buttered 9-inch square or round cake pan.
3. Sprinkle with Streusel Topping.
4. Bake at 375° for 30 minutes. Makes 16-20 pieces.

MARBLED COFFEE CAKE

1. Place ½ the batter for Coffee Cake in the cake pan.
2. Sprinkle with half the Streusel Topping.
3. Cover with the rest of the batter.
4. Draw a spatula up and down in a zigzag fashion through the batter.
5. Sprinkle the last of the Streusel Topping on the batter.

Coffee Cake with an optional sauce.

LEMON COFFEE CAKE

1. To dry ingredients of Coffee Cake add 1 tablespoon grated lemon rind.
2. Spread ½ the batter in a greased and floured large tube pan; Sprinkle with ½ the Streusel Topping; add remaining batter and sprinkle with remaining topping. Bake at 350° for about 45 minutes. Let cool 5 minutes and remove from pan.
3. Spoon a Lemon Glaze (page 578) over the ring and garnish with nuts, cherries and/or bits of lemon peel. Bake at 350° for 45 minutes. Serve while warm, accompanied with sweetened whipped cream. Serves 6-8.

BLUEBERRY COFFEE CAKE

Add 2 cups washed and dried fresh blueberries, or unthawed frozen blueberries, to the Coffee Cake batter before spreading it into the cake pan.

APPLE COFFEE CAKE

Spread Coffee Cake batter in a greased 9-inch round pan; arrange 2 apples, peeled, cored and sliced, in circles on the batter; top with Streusel mix. Bake at 400° for 25-30 minutes. Serves 6-8.

APRICOT COFFEE CAKE

1. Press ¾ of the Coffee Cake into an 8-inch cake pan.
2. Spread with apricot jam to within ½ inch of the outside edges.
3. To the remaining batter add flour to form a dough which is not sticky; divide into 8 pieces.
4. With well-floured hands roll each piece into the shape of a pencil 8 inches long.
5. Place these criss-cross fashion over the jam, having 5 pieces one way and 3 the other; brush with milk, sprinkle with sugar; bake at 350° for 25-30 minutes. Makes 16-20 pieces.

APRICOT SWIRL

Combine 1 cup jam (apricot, pineapple, strawberry) with 2 tablespoons orange juice and rind. Prepare 1 recipe Coffee Cake batter; spread ½ the batter in a greased 9-inch round pan. Alternate spoonfuls of the jam mix and the rest of the batter on top. Spiral a knife through the batter. Bake at 400° for 25 minutes. Serves 6.

APPLE PINWHEEL

1 package refrigerated crescent rolls (8 rolls)	¼ cup raisins
1 medium apple, cored, pared, and chopped (about 1 cup)	2 tablespoons sugar
	½ teaspoon grated lemon peel
	dash nutmeg
	1 tablespoon brown sugar

1. Separate crescent rolls; on greased baking sheet, arrange triangles, bases overlapping, in complete circle. (Centre of circle should be open, with points toward outside.)
2. Combine remaining ingredients; spoon over bases of triangles.
3. Fold points over filling, tucking points under bases of triangles at centre circle; brush with a little milk; sprinkle with 1 tablespoon brown sugar. Bake in a moderate oven (350°) for 25 minutes or until golden brown. Makes 8 servings.

QUICK BREADS

These loaves are leavened by baking powder instead of yeast, They may be combined by the muffin method, the cake method or the biscuit method. The muffin method, especially when salad oil is used, is the easiest method, but the cake method will give the finest, lightest product.

A search for time- and energy-saving methods is not new; these recipes were developed after the 1850's when baking powder was first sold.

Quick Breads keep well when baked and frozen. To thaw, heat muffins as biscuits 10 minutes in a bag or foil container. A loaf will thaw in 2 hours at room temperature, in 15 minutes in an oven of 350°. If sliced, the slices may be thawed in 10 minutes or toasted without thawing.

Quick Breads: Tangerine Loaf (a variation of Lemon Loaf) is in the traditional loaf pan; Corn Muffins are in a heavy cast-iron baking pan; Nut Bread is in the antique copper mould.

CHERRY LOAF (Basic Recipe)

1 6-ounce bottle maraschino cherries	¼ cup fat
2¼ cups sifted pastry flour or	¾ cup sugar
2 cups sifted all-purpose flour	2 eggs
4 teaspoons baking powder	2 teaspoons grated orange rind
½ teaspoon salt	¼ teaspoon almond extract
	⅞ cup milk

1. Line the bottom of a greased 9 by 3-inch loaf pan with a strip of waxed paper.
2. Drain the cherries; dry on paper towels and chop.
3. Measure the flour; mix and sift the dry ingredients; add the cherries.
4. Cream the fat, sugar and eggs until light and fluffy.
5. Add orange rind and almond flavouring to the milk.
6. Add dry and liquid ingredients to the fat-sugar-egg mixture, about ⅓ at a time, stirring after each addition; beat until smooth.
7. Scrape into the loaf pan; let stand 15 minutes before baking to prevent deep cracks.
8. Bake at 350° until cake tester comes out clean (60 minutes).
9. Invert on a rack; cool; wrap and store 24 hours before slicing. Makes 30 slices.

Variations:

Replace 1 cup of white flour with an equal amount of whole wheat flour added to the sifted dry ingredients.

Biscuit mix can replace the flour, baking powder, fat and salt.

Bake the loaf in a ring-jelly mould, a fancy jelly mould or a 15-ounce Coffee Tin. (To compare the capacity, pour water into the loaf pan to within ¾ inch of the top; pour this water into the pan to be checked.)

Before baking sprinkle the batter with slivered nuts, flake coconut, cinnamon-sugar mix, bits of candied fruit, crushed sweetened cereal flakes, cookie crumbs or Streusel Topping (page 489).

For shiny-topped loaves, bake first, then while still hot brush with honey, corn syrup or Icing Sugar Glaze (page 465).

LEMON LOAF

Omit cherries; replace orange rind with 2 tablespoons grated lemon rind. Combine 2 tablespoons sugar and 3 tablespoons lemon juice (1 lemon). When the cake is almost cooked, spoon this mixture over the top and return to the oven for 5 minutes.

CRANBERRY LOAF

Reduce baking powder to 2 teaspoons; add ½ teaspoon soda. Omit cherries; add 1 cup Cranberry Relish (page 93) to liquid ingredients.

ALMOND LOAF

Omit cherries; toast ½ cup slivered almonds in oven; cool; add to sifted dry ingredients.

FRUIT LOAF

Replace cherries with ½ cup glacé cherries, glacé pineapple and citron peel and ½ cup raisins; add 2 tablespoons liquid honey to the milk.

BANANA BREAD

Omit cherries. Mash 2 small bananas (¾ cup), add 1 teaspoon lemon juice or 1 tablespoon orange juice and milk to make 1 cup.

ORANGE BREAD

2¼ cups sifted pastry flour or	1 cup dates, finely chopped
2 cups sifted all-purpose flour	½ cup chopped nuts
2 teaspoons baking powder	juice and rind of 2 oranges
½ teaspoon salt	(1 cup)
½ teaspoon baking soda	2 eggs
¾ cup sugar	¼ cup fat
2 eggs	

Combine ingredients as in Cherry Loaf.

CARDAMOM LOAF

1. Toast ¾ cup sesame seeds in the oven or stir carefully over low heat; cool; add ½ cup with ½ teaspoon ground cardamom to sifted dry ingredients of Cherry Loaf.
2. Mix 2 tablespoons orange juice with 2 tablespoons sugar for glaze.
3. Combine ingredients as in Cherry Loaf; when almost cooked spoon the glaze over the top and sprinkle with remaining sesame seeds.

WHOLE WHEAT NUT BREAD

1 cup sifted all-purpose flour or
1 cup plus 2 tablespoons
   unsifted pastry flour
2 teaspoons baking powder
½ teaspoon soda
¾ teaspoon salt
2 teaspoons mixed spice
1 cup whole wheat flour
⅔ cup brown sugar, firmly
   packed

¼ cup fat
1 egg
½ cup chopped pecans or
   walnuts
1 cup chopped dates
¼ cup molasses
¾ cup milk

1. Mix and sift first five ingredients; add whole wheat flour.
2. Combine ingredients as in Cherry Loaf.

DATE LOAF (Basic Recipe)

1 cup dates
1¼ cups boiling water
⅓ cup fat
1½ cups brown sugar
1 egg

1 teaspoon vanilla
2½ cups sifted pastry flour or
2¼ cups sifted all-purpose flour
1½ teaspoons salt
1½ teaspoons baking soda

1. Chop dates into a bowl; add water, stir and cool.
2. Beat fat, sugar and egg until fluffy; add vanilla.
3. Measure flour; mix and sift dry ingredients.
4. Add dry ingredients alternately with dates to beaten mixture.
5. Bake in a lined pan 9 by 5 inches for 60 minutes at 350°.

SHERRY DATE LOAF

Substitute 1 cup sherry for the water (do not heat); add ½ cup chopped glacé cherries, pineapple. Finish as Date Loaf.

SPICED DATE LOAF

Add 1½ teaspoons mixed pastry spice to flour; add ⅓ cup of table molasses to replace an equal amount of brown sugar. Finish as Date Loaf.

DATE AND NUT LOAF

Add ½ cup coarsley chopped walnuts. Finish as Date Loaf.

TOMATO SOUP SPICE LOAF

2¼ cups sifted pastry flour or	¾ cup lightly packed brown
2 cups sifted all-purpose flour	sugar
½ teaspoon baking soda	½ cup raisins
2 teaspoons baking powder	½ cup chopped nuts
1½ teaspoons mixed spice	1 can condensed tomato soup
(cinnamon, cloves, nutmeg)	(10-ounce)
¼ cup fat	1 egg

Combine ingredients as in Cherry Loaf (page 445), using soup to replace milk.

APPLESAUCE LOAF

Substitute 1⅛ cups canned applesauce for tomato soup.

BOSTON BROWN BREAD

2 cups all-purpose flour	1 cup raisins
2 teaspoons soda	2 eggs
1 teaspoon salt	1 cup sour milk
2 cups whole-wheat flour	1 cup molasses

1. Mix and sift first three ingredients; add whole wheat flour and raisins, washed and dried.
2. Combine the eggs, sour milk and molasses; add to the dry ingredients.
3. Fill greased moulds (4 1-pound baking powder or coffee cans) ⅔ full; tie greased brown paper over the tops.
4. Place the cans on a rack in a kettle containing boiling water, which comes half way up around the cans.
5. Cover and steam 4 hours, adding boiling water if necessary.
6. Slice and serve hot or cold with Baked Beans; or spread cold bread with Cream Cheese.

YEAST BREAD AND ROLLS

INGREDIENTS USED IN PREPARING YEAST DOUGHS

Flour must provide sufficient gluten to produce an elastic dough. Bread flour is best but all-purpose flour will make an excellent bread; whole wheat flour may be used along with bread or all-purpose flour, but not alone. Pastry flour produces a loaf of poor volume.

Yeast used may be the fresh compressed (cake) variety obtainable from a bakery, or dry granular yeast. The amount of yeast used varies with the length of time available for rising. Very fast results may be obtained when the amount of yeast specified in the recipe is doubled, but a slower rising allows the development of flavour.

Liquid may be water, potato water, milk, or milk and water. The protein in potato water aids the growth of the yeast; milk sugar in milk is not fermented by the yeast so it remains to give a deep crust colour; the milk adds food value to the bread and adds flavour. Water should be boiled and cooled to lukewarm, at which temperature a drop on the wrist feels neither hot nor cold. Milk should be scalded and cooled so that undesired bacteria will be destroyed. Potato water is obtained by cooking 2 medium potatoes in 1 quart of water, mashing or ricing them, and adding them back to the liquid in which they were cooked.

Salt in yeast mixtures not only provides flavour but controls the fermentation. By retarding destruction of sugar by yeast, salt gives a deeper crust colour. Too much salt results in a very dark crust colour, also it toughens the gluten and gives a close texture.

Sugar supplies food to support the yeast activity; it furnishes material to produce carbon dioxide for leavening. Too little sugar results in a pale crust and a loaf which fails to reach its full volume.

Fat produces a soft, velvety crumb, an increased volume and a finer texture. In addition, it improves the keeping quality. Butter gives more colour and flavour; shortening a whiter loaf. Melted fat does not give as good texture.

STEPS IN THE PREPARATION OF YEAST DOUGH

Preparing the dough: it is essential that the temperatures of the ingredients added to the yeast be no hotter than lukewarm. Too high a temperature kills the yeast; too low a temperature means too slow rising with the development of other organisms and off-flavours. "Yeasty" bread is much more likely to be caused by too slow rising than by too much yeast. Thorough mixing at the beginning is necessary to distribute the yeast evenly and to develop the gluten. Kneading, the process of turning and working the dough with the heel of the hand, further develops the gluten and distributes the gas produced by the yeast throughout the dough. It is largely responsible for the texture.

Fermentation: during fermentation the yeast is growing and using the sugar. A temperature of about 80° and a slightly moist atmosphere are desirable. A closed, warm cupboard containing a large pan of boiling water may be used; an electric dishwasher, warm and steamy after use, but turned off completely, is excellent. As the dough rises it may be punched down by pushing the fist into the dough and turning in the edges to the centre. This pushes out the large gas bubbles formed before the yeast is growing actively, and gives better texture to large loaves. This step is not necessary for rolls.

Shaping: depends upon the product desired. When the dough has risen it should be cut into pieces, the cut edges turned under to make a smooth ball, covered with an inverted bowl or loosely with plastic and allowed to let rest 10 minutes before shaping.

Baking: after shaping, the dough must not be baked until it has been made light again by the gas which is developed as the yeast grows. If, however, it is allowed to stand, all the food has been used by the yeast, the gluten will be overstretched, the volume will be decreased, the texture will be close and the colour of the loaf will be pale. When the risen dough goes into the oven there will be a sudden expansion of the gas (known as the "spring"). For this reason space must be allowed in the pans. The bread is baked when it sounds hollow when rapped. It may be covered with a sheet of foil if it is becoming too brown in the oven before it is cooked.

To shorten the fermentation (rising) period the amount of yeast may be increased. One half or even one third the recipe may be made without decreasing the yeast. This adds to the expense and will not give the best flavour. It is not recommended but will allow bread-making to be taught within classroom time.

When the dough is ready for the first rising it may be put into the freezer for about 20 minutes to check the fermentation. After this, the dough will keep in a refrigerator if covered with aluminum foil or waxed paper and a damp tea towel. A deep bowl is necessary as the dough will rise slowly. If it rises to the top of the bowl before it is to be used it may be punched down once. The length of time the dough will keep will depend upon the initial temperature of the dough and the temperature of the refrigerator. If the door of the refrigerator is not being constantly opened, the dough will keep up to a week, although it may be necessary to wet the towel several times.

To freeze baked bread it should be cool and wrapped tightly with freezer wrap. Where only a few slices of bread will be needed at a time the loaf should be sliced before freezing so that it does not need to be defrosted each time.

WHITE BREAD (Basic Recipe)

1 envelope granular yeast	2 tablespoons salt
3 cups liquid	⅓ cup fat
⅓ cup sugar	12 cups all-purpose or bread flour

1. Prepare yeast as directed on the envelope.
2. Place the liquid (milk, water or potato water), in a large saucepan; heat slowly until bubbles form around the edge of the pan; cool to lukewarm.
3. Add the sugar, salt and fat; fat should soften but not melt.
4. Stir in 2 cups flour and beat to form a smooth batter.
5. Stir the yeast mixture well and stir into batter; beat vigorously until the mixture is very smooth and very elastic. Add enough flour to make a dough; turn out onto a floured board.
6. Work in remaining flour, approximately 6 cups, kneading until it is smooth and springy to touch (10 to 15 minutes); shape into a ball.
7. Turn the dough down into a large greased bowl to grease the surface lightly. Turn over, cover and let rise in warm moist place until doubled. This *first rising* will require about 3 hours.
8. Punch down; let rise again until doubled. This *second rising* will take about 1½ hours.
9. Punch down; turn out onto an unfloured board and shape into a ball; cut with a sharp knife into four; round up each piece into a ball, turning the cut edges in and under; let rest 10 to 15 minutes, covered lightly with waxed paper or an inverted bowl.
10. Shape into loaves. To do this, roll the dough on the board to a rectangle a little less than the width of the pan to be used; roll into a tight roll like a jelly roll, sealing each roll with the heel of the hand; seal the ends and turn under.
11. Have the loaf pans lightly greased with shortening or oil; excess fat on the outside of the loaf causes streaking. Place the dough in the pan; it should not quite fill the end of the pan and should be about half the height of the pan.
12. Let rise until double in bulk. The *third rising* will take about 45 minutes. The dough should appear very light, the loaf should

nicely fill the pan, the centre being slightly higher than the edges. When pressed the mark should not remain. When small bubbles are appearing under the surface this is a sign that the dough has reached the point where it must go into the oven.

13. Bake at 400° for 30 minutes, then at 375° for another 30 minutes. The bread will be firm, have a hollow sound when rapped on the bottom of the loaf with the knuckles and should come away from the sides of the pan.

14. Turn out onto a wire rack; let cool away from draughts right side up. If a soft crust is desired, brush with a little melted fat. Makes 4 9 by 5 by 3-inch loaves.

4 steps in the making of bread.

WHITE BREAD (COOL RISE METHOD)

Follow White Bread (Basic Recipe) through step 6. Then proceed as follows:

7. Cover with plastic wrap, then a towel, and let rest on board for 20 minutes. Punch down.
8. Divide dough into 2 equal portions; shape each into a loaf and place in greased loaf pans.
9. Brush surface of dough with oil. Cover pan *loosely* with oiled waxed paper, then plastic wrap.
10. Store in refrigerator for 2-24 hours.
11. Let refrigerated dough stand, uncovered, at room temperature for 10 minutes, while preheating oven to 400°. With a greased toothpick puncture any surface bubbles which may have formed.
12. Bake loaves for about 50 minutes. Remove from pans immediately; brush tops with butter and cool on rack.

WHOLE WHEAT BREAD

Substitute whole wheat flour for half the white flour. Molasses may replace the sugar for a darker loaf. If all whole-wheat flour is used, the loaf will be close or heavy in texture.

RAISIN BREAD

1 envelope granular yeast	1 tablespoon cinnamon
⅔ cup milk	1 teaspoon ginger
⅓ cup granulated sugar or	1 teaspoon each cloves, nutmeg,
⅔ cup molasses	allspice
1 teaspoon salt	5½ cups (approximately) sifted
½ cup fat	all-purpose flour
3 eggs	2 cups seedless raisins

Follow the directions for White Bread (Basic Recipe). Add slightly beaten eggs to the milk, sugar, fat mixture; sift the spices with 1 cup of the flour and add it to this mixture; wash and dry the raisins. Raisins may be combined as the flour is being added or they may be added a few at a time as the dough is being kneaded. Bake at 400° for 50 minutes. Makes 2 loaves.

CHELSEA BUNS

This recipe is included with the sweet dough variations on pages 461-463 but is frequently made from white or raisin bread dough.

HERB LOAF

¼ cup grated carrot	½ teaspoon salt
2 tablespoons grated celery	¼ teaspoon thyme
1 tablespoon grated onion	½ teaspoon sage
1 teaspoon celery salt	

Mix all ingredients; sprinkle over dough for one loaf as it is being shaped for the pan (see step 11 in White Bread, Basic Recipe); shape and finish as bread.

Herb Loaf.

DOUGHNUTS (Yeast) (Basic Recipe)

1 envelope granular yeast	2 eggs
¾ cup milk	¼ teaspoon nutmeg
¼ cup shortening	1 teaspoon lemon rind
1 teaspoon salt	3-4 cups all-purpose flour
½ cup sugar	fat for frying

1. Combine ingredients as in White Bread (Basic Recipe).
2. Cover; let rise in a warm moist place until double in bulk.
3. Roll the dough ⅓-inch thick.

4. Cut with a cookie cutter or 3-inch doughnut cutter; let rise uncovered until light (30 to 45 minutes).
5. Drop into hot fat (365°) raised side down; turn and brown.
6. Drain; shake in a bag with granulated or icing sugar. Makes 2 dozen.

FILLED DOUGHNUTS

Roll dough ⅜-inch thick; cut into rounds with floured 2¼-inch cookie cutter; brush edges of half of rounds with egg white; place 1 teaspoon strawberry jam or applesauce in centre of each. Top with rest of rounds; firmly pinch edges together. Arrange on floured cookie sheets; let rise in warm place till almost doubled and light to the touch; fry.

FORTUNES

Small bits of dough may be broken off after the first rising and dropped into the hot fat, to make interesting shapes, by which fortunes are told!

CARAMEL DUMPLINGS

Small bits of dough pulled off after the first rising may be shaped into round balls; let rise until light. Drop on top of boiling maple syrup; cover and cook 20 minutes.

FRENCH BREAD

1. Make ½ White Bread (Basic Recipe), reducing the fat to 1 tablespoon, sugar to 1 tablespoon.
2. After the second rising cut the dough into 3 pieces; roll each part with a rolling pin to an 8 by 14-inch rectangle; roll the long side of the rectangle into a tight roll 1½ inches in diameter.
3. Butter two baking sheets and sprinkle lightly with cornmeal; arrange the rolls on the baking sheet and let rise until double in bulk.
4. Brush tops with cold water and cut 3-4 diagonal slashes across each long loaf; bake at 400° for 50 to 60 minutes, brushing tops of loaves with cold water every 20 minutes.

   Keep a shallow pan of hot water in oven while the rolls are baking. The steam helps to give the crustiness.

HOT CROSS BUNS

1. Let dough for Raisin Bread rise; instead of punching it down, divide into four pieces; let rest.
2. Roll each piece ½-inch thick; cut with a cookie cutter; shape into balls on a greased baking sheet; cover and let rise until double in bulk.
3. Cut a shallow cross in top of each with kitchen scissors.
4. Brush with slightly beaten egg white; bake at 400° for 20 minutes; cuts may be filled when cool with a thin butter icing.

ROLLS (Basic Recipe)

1 envelope granular yeast	1 egg, beaten
¾ cup liquid	1 teaspoon salt
2 tablespoons shortening	3 cups bread or all-purpose flour
2 tablespoons sugar	

1. Prepare yeast as directed on the envelope.
2. Scald liquid, then cool to lukewarm; add shortening, sugar, egg and salt.
3. Beat in 1 cup flour and the yeast mixture; knead in the remaining flour.
4. Shape the dough according to any of the variations below.
5. Bake at 375°. Makes 1-2 dozen rolls.

DINNER ROLLS

1. Roll the dough about ½-inch thick. With a floured cookie cutter cut dough. Shape each piece over the thumb into a ball with the cut edges under to prevent the escape of gas.
2. Place in buttered muffin tins or side by side in a cake pan.
3. Finish according to Rolls (Basic Recipe).

PARKER HOUSE ROLLS

1. Roll the dough to ⅓-inch thickness; cut with a round cookie cutter.
2. Crease each circle of dough slightly off-centre with the back of a knife or the handle of a wooden spoon.
3. Brush the larger half with melted butter; fold the small piece over; press the edges together; arrange back to back on a buttered sheet; finish according to Rolls (Basic Recipe).

SNOWMEN

1. Roll the dough ½ inch thick; shape a 4-inch oval for the body. For the head shape a round ball. Press currants in deeply for the eyes, add a tiny bit of dough for the nose.
2. For the arms shape a 2-inch pencil-like roll; divide it. Pinch into the body.
3. Place snowmen 3 inches apart on a buttered sheet; let rise until double in bulk; brush with a little egg white slightly beaten.
4. Bake at 350° for 15 to 20 minutes.

BOW KNOTS

1. Roll the dough ½ inch thick; cut into strips ½ inch wide by 3 inches long.
2. Roll each strip between the palms of the hands and the board to make a pencil-like tube; brush with melted butter.
3. Knot each strip; tuck under the loose ends; place 1 inch apart on a buttered cookie sheet; finish according to Rolls (Basic Recipe).

EASTER BUNNIES

1. Follow the directions for Bow Knots. Pull the ends up. Pinch into points for ears.
2. When baked, ice with Icing Sugar Glaze (page 465).
3. Decorate with bits of peel, raisins or cherries for eyes and mouth.

BRAIDS

1. Proceed as for Bow Knots.
2. Join three strips by pressing firmly together onto a baking sheet; braid.
3. Sprinkle with poppy seeds, sesame seeds or coarse salt.
4. Finish according to Rolls (Basic Recipe).

BUTTERHORNS

1. Roll dough ⅓ inch thick into a 9-inch circle.
2. Cut each circle into 12 to 16 wedge-shaped pieces.
3. Roll up each wedge, starting at wide end and rolling to the point.
4. Place on greased pan with point side of rolls up.
5. Finish according to Rolls (Basic Recipe).

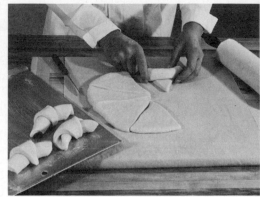

Fan Tans, Butterhorns, (below) Swedish Tea Ring, Braids.

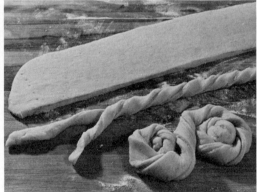

CRESCENTS

1. Prepare as Butterhorns.
2. Bend into a crescent and place point side up on greased pan.
3. Finish according to Rolls (Basic Recipe).

SESAME CRESCENTS

1. Sprinkle the wedges with sesame seeds; shape; brush with melted butter and sprinkle with more sesame seeds.
2. Finish according to Rolls (Basic Recipe).

PETAL ROLLS OR FAN TANS

1. Roll dough ⅓ inch thick; spread with softened butter.
2. Cut into strips 2 inches in width.
3. Place 4 or 5 strips on top of each other and cut into 2-inch squares.
4. Stand the squares on end in greased muffins.
5. Finish according to Rolls (Basic Recipe).

SHAMROCK OR CLOVERLEAF ROLLS

1. Roll the dough ⅓ inch thick; cut with a round cookie cutter; shape into balls.
2. Place 3 balls in each greased muffin pan.
3. Finish according to Rolls (Basic Recipe).

SHORTCUT CLOVERLEAVES

1. Pinch off pieces of dough about the size of golf balls. Pull the edges of each piece down and under to form a smooth top; place in greased muffin tins, 1 ball of dough to a cup.
2. Using a pair of kitchen shears, snip across the top of each roll, making cuts at right angles to form cloverleaves.
3. Finish according to Rolls (Basic Recipe).

SALT STICKS

1. Roll dough into rectangle about 16 by 12 inches; cut into 4-inch squares.
2. Starting at a corner, roll each square diagonally to opposite corner; round off ends by rolling lightly on board with palms of hands.
3. Place 2 inches apart on greased baking sheet.
4. Brush with 1 egg yolk, slightly beaten with 1 tablespoon water.
5. Sprinkle with coarse salt or salt crystals.
6. Finish according to Rolls (Basic Recipe). Makes 12.

LEMON SPICE PUFFS

Good with applesauce.

1 envelope granular yeast	2 tablespoons grated lemon rind
¾ cup scalded milk	1 teaspoon lemon juice
6 tablespoons sugar	3 cups bread or all-purpose flour
1 teaspoon salt	2 eggs
5 tablespoons fat	1 teaspoon cinnamon
	1 tablespoon sugar

1. Prepare yeast as directed on the envelope.
2. Cool scalded milk to lukewarm; add sugar, salt, fat, rind and lemon juice; stir until the fat is soft.
3. Add the yeast, 1 cup of flour and 1 egg; beat well; add the second egg, another cup of flour; beat well; continue adding the flour a cup at a time until all the flour is added, beating until the mixture is light after each addition. (Unless the electric mixer has a dough hook, the last additions of flour will have to be kneaded in.)
4. Cover and let rise until double in bulk; punch down.
5. Half fill buttered muffin cups with dough; sprinkle with mixture of cinnamon and sugar.
6. Cover and let rise; bake at 375° for 20 minutes. Makes about 20.

SWEET DOUGH (Basic Recipe)

1 envelope granular yeast	⅔ cup fat
1¾ cup milk	½ tablespoon salt
lemon rind	2 eggs
¾ cup sugar	8 cups bread or all-purpose flour

1. Prepare yeast as directed on the envelope.
2. Scald lemon rind with milk; strain; cool to lukewarm.
3. Add sugar, fat, salt and eggs beaten together.
4. Beat in 2 cups of flour and the yeast mixture. Stir and knead in the remaining flour.
5. Divide into three; shape into balls; let rest; shape into buns or follow the directions for the variations following. For more detailed instructions, see White Bread (page 451).

Sweet Dough can be glazed while warm with any of the glazes for Quick Bread (page 444).

CARDAMOM SEEDS

Cardamom seeds give the characteristic flavour found in Scandinavian Breads. To use with Sweet Dough, open 2 of the papery pods and remove the small black seeds. Crush them between 2 sheets of waxed paper with a rolling pin. Soak in the milk while it is heating. (Or, add powdered cardamom to the flour.)

TUTTI FRUTTI BREAD

⅓ risen Sweet Dough   1 cup chopped fruit

1. Roll dough to rectangle 12 by 16 inches. Turn over so smooth side is down.
2. Sprinkle with 1 cup of chopped fruits (glazed cherries, pineapple, citron peel, raisins, almonds). Shape and complete as White Bread, step 11 (page 451). Makes 1 loaf 9 by 5 by 3 inches.

CHELSEA BUNS

⅓ risen Sweet Dough   2 tablespoons water or corn
1 recipe Butterscotch Filling   syrup
   (page 463)

1. Coat an 8-inch cake pan with ⅓ of the Butterscotch Filling; sprinkle with water or corn syrup.
2. Roll the dough into a rectangle 12 by 16 inches; turn over so the smooth side is down; spread with the remaining filling; roll from the long side of the rectangle into a tight roll with the cut edge down.
3. Divide into 12 equal pieces; place cut side down in the prepared pans. Complete as White Bread, step 13 (page 452).
5. Bake at 375° for 30 minutes. Makes 1 dozen.

Pecan or walnut halves may be arranged round side down on the Butterscotch Filling in the pan; cinnamon may be added to the butter-sugar mixture; washed currants or raisins or glazed fruit may be sprinkled over the dough before rolling, or on the Butterscotch Filling in the pan.

BUTTERSCOTCH ROLLS

Follow directions for Chelsea Buns, using 12 medium muffin pans instead of the cake pan.

SWEDISH TEA RING

1. Follow directions for Chelsea Buns; spread filling almost to the edge; sprinkle with fruit (1 cup raisins, currants, nuts or glazed fruit).
2. Join the ends of the roll and pinch together; place the circle on a greased pie plate or baking sheet.
3. Using scissors, cut into the ring from the top and outer edge but not through it, at 2-inch intervals; pull sections apart and twist each slightly so that the spiral can be seen. Cover and let rise until double in bulk. Bake.
4. When almost cool, glaze with syrup or Icing Sugar glaze (page 465) and garnish with slices of red and green cherries. Bake at 375° for 30 minutes. Makes 1 ring.

FRUIT SCROLL

1. Prepare ingredients for Chelsea Buns.
2. Follow the directions for Swedish Tea Ring but do not turn the roll into a circle.
3. Place the roll on a buttered baking sheet; cut in 1-inch slices from the top and alternate side not quite through the roll.
4. Twist each piece to alternate sides of the centre line (see diagram following). Cover and let rise.
5. Bake; while still warm glaze. Bake at 375° for 30 minutes. Makes one scroll.

FRUIT ROLL

⅓ risen Sweet Dough Recipe   filling
   (page 460)   glaze

1. Roll the ball of dough into a rectangle 12 by 6 inches; mark the rectangle in thirds lengthwise; place on a greased baking sheet.
2. Spread the centre strip with filling (page 463).
3. Cut in 1-inch strips from the edge to the beginning of the centre strip.
4. Bring the strips alternately to the centre (see diagram following). Cover and let rise.
5. Bake at 375° for 30-40 minutes; while still warm brush with glaze (page 465).

FRUIT SWIRLS

⅓ risen Sweet Dough   glaze
1 recipe Pineapple Filling
    (page 464)

1. Grease a round or heart-shaped 8-inch cake pan.
2. Roll the dough into a 6 by 12 inch rectangle; cover ½ of the long side of the rectangle with the pineapple filling; fold the uncovered half over the filling; cut with a sharp knife into 1-inch strips.
3. Twist each strip and coil into a tight roll; place in the prepared pan; cover and let rise until double in bulk.
4. Bake at 375° for 30-40 minutes; immediately after baking brush with corn syrup; when almost cool glaze.

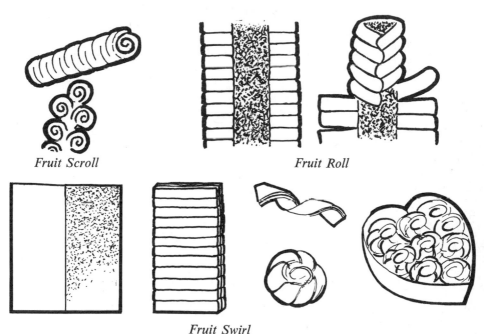

Fruit Scroll   *Fruit Roll*

Fruit Swirl

BUTTERSCOTCH FILLING

⅓ cup soft butter or margarine   ½ teaspoon cinnamon (optional)
1 cup brown sugar

Cream until smooth and soft enough to spread easily.
To the Butterscotch Filling add ¼ cup finely chopped or ground almonds or walnuts.

PRUNE FILLING

2 cups drained, pitted, cooked
    prunes (1 pound)
½ cup walnuts, coarsely chopped

¼ cup sugar
2 tablespoons lemon juice

Mix all ingredients together; spread over Butterscotch Filling.

APRICOT FILLING

2 cups drained, sieved or
    chopped cooked apricots

½ cup blanched, slivered
    almonds
½ cup sugar

Mix all ingredients together, spread over Butterscotch Filling.

PINEAPPLE FILLING

1 tablespoon cornstarch
½ cup crushed pineapple
¼ cup butter or margarine

¼ cup brown sugar
¼ cup chopped walnuts
⅛ cup cinnamon candies

1. In a small saucepan combine the cornstarch and pineapple; stir until well blended; heat, stirring constantly until thick and clear.
2. Add the remaining ingredients; cool.

   Substitute raspberry, apricot or pineapple jam for any of these fillings, or use baby-food prunes or apricots.

FRANGIPANE FILLING

1 egg white
½ cup sugar
½ cup almond paste or
    ground almonds

lemon or cream pie filling or
    pudding (about ¼ cup)
1 cup cake or cookie crumbs

1. Beat egg white until foamy; beat in sugar gradually; add ground almonds.
2. Combine cream filling and crumbs.
3. Fold the two mixtures together.

   If almond paste is used, crumble it into the cream filling; beat smooth.

ORANGE GLAZE

¼ cup orange juice

3 tablespoons sugar

1. Mix juice and sugar.
2. Spread on partially cooled baked Sweet Doughs.

ICING SUGAR GLAZE

1 cup icing sugar
2 tablespoons milk

½ teaspoon vanilla or almond
extract

1. Mix sugar, milk, vanilla and colouring if desired.
2. Spread on partially cooled, baked Sweet Doughs.

BRANDY GLAZE

2 tablespoons melted butter
2 tablespoons brandy

2-3 tablespoons heavy cream
2 cups sifted icing sugar

Mix all ingredients until smooth.

SUGARPLUM COFFEE RING

⅓ risen Sweet Dough (page 460)
¼ cup fine, dry bread crumbs
¼ cup sugar

1 teaspoon cinnamon
¼ cup butter or margarine
1 cup dried chopped fruit
and nuts

1. Roll the dough into a long rope with the hands; cut into 25 pieces and shape into balls.
2. Combine the bread crumbs, sugar and spice; melt butter.
3. Drop each ball into the fat, onto the crumb mixture, and arrange one layer in a greased 8-inch tube pan or 9-inch ring mould; sprinkle evenly with the fruit mixture; repeat; top with any remaining crumb mixture; let rise until double in bulk.
4. Bake at 375° for 25-30 minutes; invert onto a rack; cool slightly; glaze; decorate with sliced red and green cherries and nuts, while the glaze is still soft.

STOLLEN

Traditional Christmas Bread from Austria.

1 cup seedless raisins
2 tablespoons chopped candied
    orange peel
1 cup diced mixed candied fruit
¼ cup brandy
½ cup milk
½ cup granulated sugar
¾ cup soft butter
1 teaspoon salt
1 envelope granular yeast
1 cup sour cream

1 teaspoon vanilla
2 teaspoons fresh lemon juice
3 egg yolks, beaten
5 to 5½ cups all-purpose flour
¾ cup blanched almonds
2 tablespoons melted butter
½ teaspoon cinnamon
1 tablespoon granulated sugar
melted butter
icing sugar

1. Combine raisins, orange peel, candied fruit; add brandy. Let stand at least 1 hour.
2. Scald milk; cool to lukewarm, add sugar, butter, salt; stir until sugar is dissolved.
3. Prepare yeast as directed on package; add to milk mixture.
4. Add sour cream, vanilla, lemon juice, egg yolks.
5. Gradually stir in 5 cups of flour to make a light but not sticky dough; knead until smooth and elastic; let rise until double in bulk; punch down; add drained fruits and almonds; work in dough only until fruit-nut mixture is evenly distributed.
6. Cut dough in half, flatten each part into an oval about ¾-inch thick, brush with melted butter, sprinkle with sugar and cinnamon. Fold almost, but not quite in half, so that the bottom edge of dough extends beyond the top (as for an omelet). Lightly roll folded dough with a rolling pin to set fold.
7. Place stollens on well greased baking sheets. Allow to rise until puffy but not quite doubled.
8. Bake at 375° for 45 minutes until golden brown. Remove from oven, brush with melted butter while still warm. Brush again with melted butter after loaves have cooled and dust generously with icing sugar. Makes two 5 by 10-inch loaves.

JULEBROD OR JULEKAK

Traditional Christmas bread from Norway.

2 envelopes granular yeast	1 cup melted butter
2 cups top milk	2 eggs
1 tablespoon cardamom seeds	1½ cups raisins
½ cup sugar	¼ pound citron peel
1 teaspoon salt	8 cups all-purpose flour

1. Combine the yeast according to the package.
2. Scald the milk with the cardamom seeds (page 461); Cool to lukewarm.
3. Add sugar, salt and butter.
4. Beat 2 whites and 1 egg yolk together (save the other yolk for the top). Add to the milk mixture.
5. Flour the raisins and peel.

6. Mix together the milk, yeast and flour to make a batter; beat well; continue to add flour to make a soft dough.
7. Let rise in a warm place, about 2 hours.
8. Shape into 3 loaves; brush with the remaining egg yolk beaten with a little water; place in well-greased pans.
9. Let rise again; bake at 375° for 60 minutes.

PANETTONE DI NATALE

Traditional Christmas Bread from Italy.

½ cup milk	6 eggs
2 packages granular yeast	1 teaspoon vanilla
8 cups sifted all-purpose flour	1 cup black seedless raisins
¾ pound butter	1 cup white raisins
1 sup sugar	2 cups mixed candied fruit
3 egg yolks	sliced blanched almonds

1. Scald the milk; cool to lukewarm in a large bowl. Sprinkle the yeast over the milk; add ½ cup of the flour; stand in a warm place until the sponge is light and lively, about 1 hour.
2. Cream the butter and sugar until light in the large bowl of the electric mixer; Beat in the egg yolks and whole eggs, one at a time, and the vanilla.
3. Add the yeast sponge and 3 cups of the flour, and beat at low speed for 5 minutes.
4. Stir in the fruit by hand, then 3½ more cups of flour. Turn out on a board spread with the remaining cup of flour, and knead in as much of it as is necessary to make the dough leave the board clean.
5. Return to the bowl, cover loosely with plastic and allow to rise in a warm place until double, about 3 or 4 hours.
6. Butter two 9-inch ring moulds, fluted moulds, or turret moulds; Arrange slices of almonds in a pattern within the moulds. Divide the dough, and shape to fit the moulds. Allow to rise until double, about 2 hours.
7. Bake in a preheated 425° oven for 10 minutes, then reduce the heat to 350° and continue to bake for 35-50 minutes longer, depending upon the size and shape of the loaf.
8. As soon as loaves come from the oven, coat them with brandy glaze (page 465) and decorate with candied fruits and nuts if desired.

BABA

An exotic yeast-bread dessert.

1 envelope granular yeast	½ teaspoon salt
1½ cups sifted all-purpose flour	1½ teaspoons grated lemon rind
3 eggs	or
¼ cup sugar	½ inch vanilla bean
½ cup soft butter or margarine	

1. Prepare yeast according to directions on the envelope; when foamy add ½ cup flour; beat well.
2. Beat in the eggs, one at a time; add sugar, butter, salt and lemon rind or pulp from the vanilla.
3. Add the remaining flour a tablespoon at a time, beating well, until the batter resembles cake batter.
4. Butter a large ring mould or 12 custard cups; half fill; cover and let rise until double in size (about 15 minutes).
5. Bake 400° for 20 to 25 minutes or until brown.
6. Drizzle over Baba one of the hot sauces below, until no more can be absorbed. Cool; serve with whipped cream.

Rum Baba.

RUM BABA SAUCE

Simmer ½ cup boiling water and ¾ cup sugar for 10 minutes; Add ½ cup rum.

APRICOT BABA SAUCE

Simmer 1 can apricot nectar and ¾ cup sugar for 10 minutes. Add 1 tablespoon lemon juice and 1 teaspoon rum extract or 1 ounce rum.

ORANGE BABA SAUCE

Bring to a boil 1 cup sugar and 1 cup water; Add 1 tablespoon butter and 1 6-ounce can frozen orange juice concentrate.

GLAMOUR BABA

Bake the baba at 400° about 30 minutes, covering if necessary with a sheet of foil to prevent overbrowning. Turn the baba out onto a serving dish and spoon the hot syrup over; baste until all the syrup is absorbed. Garnish with almonds; pile sweetened strawberries or ice cream in the centre.

CUSTARD CUP BABA

Bake the baba in custard cups; arrange in a chafing dish; pour the syrup over and baste until no more will be absorbed; let stand several hours; reheat in a little more syrup, add 2 ounces of rum and flame.

17 Pastry, Cookies and Cakes

PASTRY

"Pastry" refers to that mixture of flour, fat, water and salt known as plain pastry or puff pastry. The difference depends upon the kind and amount of fat used and the method of mixing and rolling. Little cakes, cream puffs and meringues are sometimes referred to as pastries.

INGREDIENTS USED

Flour: In the basic recipe all-purpose or pastry flour may be used.

Fat: Lard or shortening is best for pastry. If a special method of mixing is followed, cooking oil may be used. Fat should be cold. More fat is required to tenderize all-purpose than pastry flour; more fat is required when butter is used than when the fat is lard or shortening.

Liquids: Liquid may be water, milk or fruit juice.   Flour is more moist at one time than another because of storage conditions and so the amount of liquid which is needed will vary. Since the flour soaks up moisture, if the liquid is added a little at a time less will be needed and a more tender pastry will result than if the liquid is added all at once.

TOP CRUST PATTERNS

Edging and top crust patterns are traditional in families from generation to generation. The cuts should never be so long that the pastry tears in transferring it from board to pie.

Here are some old favourites.

LATTICE TOP: Roll the smaller part of the ball of pastry to a rectangle. Cut in ½ inch strips with a sharp knife or a pastry wheel. On a sheet of waxed paper on a baking sheet mark a circle the size of the pie. Weave together crosswise and lengthwise strips of pastry as in the illustration.

Press very lightly with a rolling pin to set the cross strips; place in the freezer a few minutes; slide into position on the pie; dampen the edge and pat down the strips. Trim and edge. Variations:

Lattice Top and edging variations.

EDGINGS

PASTRY (Basic Recipe)

Makes 2 9-inch shells or 1 double crust.

2 cups flour	¼-⅓ cup very cold water
⅔ cup fat, for pastry flour, or	1 teaspoon salt
¾ cup fat, for all-purpose flour	

1. Sift flour and salt into a bowl; add cold fat; cut into the flour with a pastry blender or two knives until when the bowl is shaken, no pieces larger than a pea appear. (Cutting the fat too finely or creaming it into the flour will give a cookie-type crust known as short pastry. Flaky pastry requires small lumps of cold fat to trap layers of air.)

2. Measure the water. Sprinkle it over the flour. Mix the flour up from the bottom of the bowl with a fork. As some of the mixture appears to stick together, push it to one side and sprinkle the dry flour with water. Too much moisture makes tough pastry; too little, and the dough will be hard to roll out. Experience helps in determining the right amount.

3. When the flour appears damp, press it together into a ball; break the ball open; if it crumbles apart more water is required; shape all the dough into a ball but do not knead it.

4. Chill the dough while preparing to roll it. (If the dough is to be left, wrap it well in waxed paper. When it is removed from the refrigerator, dough must soften up a little before it can be rolled). Divide it into two pieces, the larger piece for the bottom crust, the smaller for the top.

5. Dough may be rolled on a lightly floured board, between two pieces of waxed paper or on a pastry cloth. A clean heavy linen tea towel makes a good substitute for a cloth. Let one end hang over the end of the table so that it may be kept in position. Rub a little flour into it. A child's white stocking with the foot cut off, or a knitted cotton rolling pin cover, pulled over the rolling pin, holds flour and keeps the pin from sticking. More important than any piece of equipment is the lightness of touch. If the dough becomes warm it will also be much harder to handle.

6. Roll the dough from the centre out to the edge in each direction, if a circle of dough is desired; roll it all in the same direction for a rectangle. Pinch together any cracks that form.

7. At the end of each stroke the pin should be lifted to be sure the dough is not sticking. After each 3 or 4 strokes, move the pastry on the board to pick up a little more flour, and run a floured hand over the pin. If the dough will not move freely, loosen it carefully with the side of a knife and sprinkle a little more flour on the board.

8. The dough should be rolled to about ¼ inch in thickness; there is no advantage in having paper-thin pastry. The size should be that of the bottom of the pan plus the depth. To transfer the dough to the pie pan, either fold it in 4, lift it into the centre of the pan and then unfold, or roll it loosely around the rolling pin and unroll it onto the pie pan.

For a Single Crust Pie:

9. Place the pastry in the pan, do not stretch it away from the corners but fit in slightly; trim and shape the edge.

10. For a pie shell, to be used for a cooked filling, prick the crust with the tines of a fork so that air between the dough and pan may escape to prevent bubbling. Do not prick if filling is to be baked with the dough. Bake at 425° until just beginning to colour (10-12 minutes). Because of the high amount of fat, pastry tastes burned if it darkens.

For a Double Crust Pie:

9. Place the bottom crust in position; add the filling, cooled if cooked.

10. Dampen the edge over the rim of the pan with cold water; fit on the top crust in which a vent has been cut, press the 2 pieces together along the edge with the palm of the hand. Trim and edge (page 471). Bake at 425° until beginning to colour (10-12 minutes).

Substitute orange or pineapple juice for the water in pastry to be used for fruit pie; add meat extract, Worcestershire Sauce, tomato juice to the water for pastry to be used for meat pie.

Substitute ½ cup finely ground nuts for ½ cup flour, or add ¼ cup sesame seeds or 1 tablespoon instant coffee to flour for pastry to be used for cream pies.

REFRIGERATOR PASTRY

Excellent pastry mixes are available, but for families who use pastry often this mix saves time and money.

1 egg	6⅓ cups pastry flour, or
1 tablespoon vinegar or	5½ cups all-purpose flour
lemon juice	1½ teaspoons salt
water	1 teaspoon baking powder
1 pound lard	

1. Break the egg into a measuring cup, beat with a fork; add vinegar or juice and cold water to the ¾ cup mark; beat again.
2. Finish as Pastry (Basic Recipe); pack into a container; cover tightly and refrigerate until needed. Makes three 9-inch double crust pies.

CHEDDAR CHEESE PASTRY

Add ⅓-½ cup grated Cheddar or other sharp flavoured cheese to the flour. Use for apple pie.

COTTAGE CHEESE PASTRY

Cream 1 cup cottage cheese with the fat; work into the sifted flour and salt with a fork; chill 3 hours. Good for tarts and cream pies.

CREAM CHEESE PASTRY

Substitute 2 3-ounce packages cream cheese for the cottage cheese in preceding recipe.

GALETTE PASTRY

A sweet cake-type pastry popular for the "flan" fruit pies or small tarts.

1 egg yolk	1 cup all-purpose flour
1 tablespoon water	½ teaspoon salt
2 tablespoons lemon juice	1 tablespoon sugar
	6 tablespoons fat

1. Beat together the egg yolk, cold water and lemon juice.
2. Finish as Pastry (Basic Recipe).

TO FREEZE PASTRY AND PIES

Pastry can be frozen baked or unbaked.

To prepare pastry for many pies or tarts and to save space, cut circles of pastry to fit the baking dish, freeze with circles of foil between. To use, defrost 10 minutes; press into pie plate or tart tin; prick; bake at 425°.

Although pies may be frozen either baked or unbaked, there are advantages to freezing before baking: the pastry will be flakier and the baking time will not be greatly increased. When baked and frozen the pie will require a 2-hour period for thawing at room temperature or 30 minutes in the oven at 375°. To retain moisture in the filling and prevent tearing of the top crust, do not cut a pattern in the top crust until the unbaked pie is removed from the freezer.

Do not decorate cream pies with meringue or whipped cream before freezing. Add meringue to the frozen pie and bake at 350° for 20 minutes. Defrost chiffon pies in the refrigerator for 1½ hours before decorating with whipped cream and baking.

For protection, store frozen unwrapped pies in containers.

PUFF PASTRY

2 cups sweet butter
4 cups unsifted all purpose flour
1 teaspoon salt

1 tablespoon lemon juice
1⅓ cups water

1. Work the butter into a brick shape measuring 3 by 5 by 1½ inches.
2. Spoon 3 tablespoons of flour onto waxed paper and coat butter with it. Wrap butter in waxed paper and refrigerate.
3. Place remaining flour in a large mixing bowl. With the fingers make a well in centre of flour. Add salt, lemon juice and 1 cup of water.
4. Using the fingertips in a circular motion, work flour and mixture to make a rather firm, slightly sticky dough. Gradually add remaining ¼ cup water if the dough seems to require it.
5. Knead dough 20 minutes or more. It is almost impossible to over-work it. Pound dough on the table occasionally and, while working, dip the fingers into water and dab a few drops into dough to prevent it from becoming hard and dry. It had been worked sufficiently when dough becomes smooth, satiny and elastic. Shape dough into a ball, leave for 15 minutes.
6. Place ball on a well-floured cloth. Cut a cross in the centre, then roll out four "ears" from the cross, leaving the centre a thick cushion.
7. Place the chilled butter on the cushion centre. Butter must not be too firm. Stretch the 4 rolled-out portions over the butter, over-lapping them and sealing edges and corners. There will be a cushion on the bottom and one on the top formed by the overlapping ears of dough. Wrap the whole in foil and chill 20 minutes.

8. On a well-floured cloth, gently roll dough as evenly as possible into a rectangle measuring approximately 8 by 18 inches, slightly less than ⅓ inch thick. Use a firm, even motion. Do not roll over the ends of the dough with the roller until the dough is 18 inches long. Then the rolling pin may be rolled over the ends but at a right angle to the former motion.

9. Brush off excess flour from dough and bring each end of the rectangle to centre. Press dough firmly.

10. Fold the dough in half, pocketbook fashion, to make 4 layers of dough. Wrap in·aluminum foil and chill 30 minutes.

11. Place the dough again on floured cloth with 1 of the 2 open ends facing you.

12. Roll the dough into a rectangle once more, brush off excess flour and fold as before. Repeat the rolling and folding 3 more times, chilling the dough for at least 30 minutes between each rolling and folding.

13. When the dough has been rolled, folded and chilled 5 times it is ready for use. The final chilling, however should be for 3 hours.

Purchased Puff Pastry can be made up into variations which follow.

PATTY SHELLS OR VOL-AU-VENTS

1. Roll the puff pastry to a thickness of ⅛ inch. For each patty shell, cut three 3-inch circles of dough with a biscuit cutter. Place the first circle on a baking sheet and brush it with egg yolk. Do not let egg drip on sides.

2. Using a slightly smaller cutter, cut out centre of second pastry circle to make a ring. Turn this ring over and place it on the first pastry circle. Brush with egg yolk.

3. Press the smaller biscuit cutter into the third pastry circle but do not cut through it. Place this on top of the ring and brush with egg yolk. Bake 10 minutes at 450°. Reduce heat to 350° and bake 20 minutes longer, or until golden and dry.

4. Remove the indented centre of the topmost layer of the pastry with a sharp knife. Return the shell to a 350° oven to dry. Serve the vol-au-vents with creamed mixtures such as chicken or seafood, covering with the centres. Makes 12.

PUFF PASTRY BOUCHÉES

1. Roll out the puff pastry to ⅛-inch thickness and cut into rounds or ovals with a small fluted cutter.
2. Set on a damp baking sheet, brush with beaten egg, mark a round or oval centre, then chill for 10 minutes.
3. Bake at 425° for 15 minutes.
4. Remove the centres and scoop out any soft pastry; cool; fill with cream cheese beaten with a little cream, lemon juice, pepper and smoked salmon. Or fill with hors d'oeuvres mixtures (page 72).

PALMIERS OR PALM LEAVES

1. On a cloth liberally sprinkled with granulated sugar, roll the puff pastry into a square ⅛-inch thick. Fold opposite sides into thirds toward centre so pieces overlap exactly. Fold in half again to make a compact 6-layer roll. Wrap in aluminum foil and chill 2 hours.
2. Cut down the centre of the roll about ⅔ of the way from top to bottom; cut roll into ½-inch-thick slices; dip each slice into sugar and place slices 1½ inches apart on a cookie sheet.

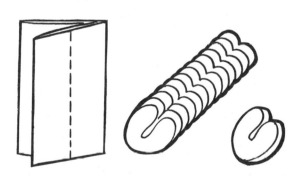

3. Bake 8 minutes at 450°. When golden at the bottom, turn with a spatula and reduce heat to 375°. Bake until cookies are crisp and no white spot shows in centres. Makes 24.

NAPOLEONS

1. Roll puff pastry or rich pastry into a 14 by 8-inch rectangle, ⅜-inch thick; with floured sharp knife, cut off all edges, prick dough thoroughly with fork to prevent uneven puffing while baking.
2. Cut in 3½ by 2-inch rectangles; place on baking sheets covered with 3 or 4 thicknesses of paper towels; chill thoroughly.
3. Brush with mixture of 1 slightly beaten egg white and 1 tablespoon ice water.
4. Bake in very hot oven (450°) for 6 minutes, then in slow oven (300°) for 25 to 30 minutes, till lightly browned and crisp. Remove from pan; cool on rack.

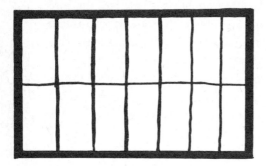 

5. Separate each pastry into 3 layers. Fill between layers with Cream Filling (page 561); spread top with Sweet Dough Glaze. Decorate with Chocolate Shadow. Makes 16.

PINEAPPLE PASTRIES

1. Roll puff pastry or rich pastry to a thickness of ¼-inch; cut with small fancy cookie cutter.
2. Place on ungreased baking sheets, prick them generously with a fork, and bake at 425° for 5-8 minutes, or until golden brown. Cool on a rack.
3. Marinate wedges of candied pineapple in Kirsch for about 30 minutes; drain, and place a wedge on each circle. Ice.
4. Decorate with bits of glacéed cherries and pistachio nuts, with sweet chocolate curls or with pastry-tube flowers.

CRUMB CRUSTS

These easy-to-make crusts add extra sweetness and flavour. They are particularly suited to cream and chiffon pies.

GRAHAM WAFER CRUST (Basic Recipe)

1½ cup graham wafer crumbs (about 18)	½ teaspoon cinnamon
3 tablespoons fine sugar	3 tablespoons melted butter or margarine

1. Grease a 9-inch pie plate.
2. Mix the crumbs, sugar and cinnamon; add melted butter. Mix well together; take out ¼ cup mixture for the topping.
3. Press mixture firmly into the pie plate to a ¼-inch thickness. For chiffon pies fill with mixture, let stand several hours before serving.

For fruit pies add fresh fruit, bake at 350° until fruit is cooked.

For lemon or cream pies fill with hot cooked mixture, cover with meringue; bake until golden brown.

Just before serving the pie, wrap a hot wet towel under the bottom and around sides of pie plate. Hold towel against plate for a few minutes. This will loosen crust so that each piece of pie slips out easily.

Chocolate wafers, ginger snaps (20 large or 30 small), vanilla wafers (30) or crushed cornflakes (4 cups) may be substituted for the graham wafer crumbs. The cookies do not require sugar.

Spicy Cream Pie in Graham Wafer Crust.

MANDARIN PIE CRUST

See page 482.

COCONUT CRUST

2 tablespoons soft butter   1½ cups shredded coconut

Spread pan with butter.
Sprinkle evenly with coconut and pat it into the butter. Bake at 350°
for 10 to 12 minutes until crisp and golden brown; cool.

CREAM PIE (Basic Recipe)

The combination of flour and cornstarch gives a good texture.

2 cups milk   ¼ teaspoon salt
2 tablespoons flour   2 large or 3 medium egg yolks
2 tablespoons cornstarch   2 tablespoons butter
½ cup sugar   ½ teaspoon vanilla
     1 9-inch baked pie shell

1. Heat 1½ cups milk in top of a double boiler.
2. Mix flour, cornstarch, sugar and salt; add ½ cup milk; stir until smooth; stir into the hot milk; cook until thick, stirring constantly; cover and let cook 10 minutes.
3. Beat egg yolks, and into them stir a small quantity of the hot mixture. Blend thoroughly and stir this mixture into remaining hot mixture; stir until thick. Cook 2 minutes.
4. Remove from heat, add butter and vanilla; cool, stirring occasionally.
5. Pour into a 9-inch baked pie shell (page 472) (or crumb crust); spread with a Meringue made from egg white (page 482); or cool and cover with whipped cream or glaze. Serves 6.

   To freeze, pour the cooked filling into a container and freeze.

GLAMOUR CREAM PIE

Beat an egg white lightly; add ½ cup crushed peanut brittle and stir. Arrange around the rim of a baked crust. Heat at 375° until the candy begins to melt. Cool and fill with Cream Pie filling.

BANANA CREAM PIE

Stir 2-3 sliced bananas into warm Cream Pie filling.

Cream Pie gets a new look with a layer of Apricot purée.

COCONUT CREAM PIE

Add 1 cup moist, shredded coconut to warm Cream Pie filling; sprinkle ½ cup coconut over meringue before browning.

PINEAPPLE CREAM PIE

Drain crushed pineapple well. Fold ½ cup into cool Cream Pie filling.

BUTTERSCOTCH CREAM PIE

Substitute ⅔ cup brown sugar for ½ cup granulated sugar; increase butter to 3 tablespoons. Add 1 teaspoon Caramel Flavouring.

LEMON MERINGUE PIE

Use yolks in filling—whites in meringue.

4 tablespoons cornstarch	3 egg yolks
5 tablespoons flour	1 tablespoon butter
1 cup sugar	⅓ cup lemon juice
1¾ cups boiling water	1½ teaspoons grated lemon rind
	1 9-inch baked pie shell

1. In the top section of a double boiler, mix cornstarch, flour and sugar; add boiling water, stir and cook over direct heat until there is no taste of raw starch.
2. Beat egg yolks; add a little cornstarch mixture to the eggs. Blend thoroughly, and stir in remaining cornstarch mixture.
3. Stir over boiling water until egg thickens.
4. Remove from heat; add butter, lemon juice and rind.
5. Cool slightly, pour into a pie shell.
6. Cover with meringue. Serves 6.

MERINGUE FOR PIES (Basic Recipe)

This makes enough for 1 9-inch pie.

2 or 3 egg whites	2 tablespoons sugar per egg white

Method I:

1. Beat whites until stiff but not dry.
2. Add sugar a teaspoon at a time and continue to beat mixture until very stiff.
3. Spread over hot pie filling and bake at 425° for 4 minutes or at 350° for 15 minutes.

Method II (for an electric beater):

1. Add sugar to unbeaten egg white; beat until the mixture stands in peaks.
2. Spread over hot pie filling and bake at 425° for 4 minutes or at 350° for 15 minutes.

MANDARIN PIE

Crust
- ½ cup butter
- 1 cup all-purpose flour
- ¼ cup brown sugar
- ⅛ teaspoon ginger
- ½ cup finely chopped walnuts

Filling
- ¾ cup milk
- 1 cup sour cream
- 1 tablespoon grated orange rind
- 1 package (3¾ ounces) instant vanilla pudding mix
- ½ cup well-drained mandarin orange segments
- ½ cup orange marmalade
- 1 to 2 tablespoons water

1. Melt butter in 9-inch pie plate; add flour, sugar, ginger, nuts; mix well.
2. Bake at 350° for 20 minutes, stirring occasionally until the crumbs are dried and beginning to brown.
3. Save out ⅓ cup of this mix; press the remainder into sides and bottom of the pie pan, shaping a firm edge.
4. Beat milk, sour cream, rind and pudding mix till thick; pour into crust, chill.
5. Arrange orange segments in the centre; rim with remaining crust mix.
6. Heat marmalade with water, stirring constantly until melted; spoon over orange segments to glaze them. Chill.

Meringue: Sugar is added gradually to make a fine-textured meringue.

Finished meringue is spooned onto cooled pie filling.

Here meringue has been swirled onto pie filling.

LEMON SPONGE PIE

1 9-inch unbaked shell	3 egg whites
½ cup butter	¼ cup sugar
¾ cup sugar	1 cup milk
1 tablespoon cornstarch	1 large lemon (juice and rind)
3 egg yolks	

1. Line a 9-inch pie pan with pastry; do not prick; bake 5 minutes at 400°.
2. Cream the butter; combine ¾ cup sugar with cornstarch and blend into butter.
3. Add the egg yolks 1 at a time, beating after each addition until light and fluffy.
4. Beat egg whites stiff but not dry with ¼ cup sugar.
5. Stir the milk, lemon juice and rind into the butter mixture; fold in stiffly beaten egg whites.
6. Pour into the partly baked shell. Bake 35 minutes at 350°. Serves 6.

CHIFFON PIES

Any of the gelatine desserts (page 608) can be transformed into a chiffon pie merely by the addition of a crust; whipped cream fillings in Cake Fillings and Frostings, Chapter 18, may be used also.

EGGNOG CHIFFON PIE

Use the Spanish Cream recipe (page 611).

BLACK BOTTOM PIE

1 9-inch pastry shell, baked	1 tablespoon gelatine
1½ cups milk	(1 envelope)
½ cup dark brown sugar	¼ cup cold water
1¼ tablespoons cornstarch	1 teaspoon vanilla
¼ teaspoon salt	1 tablespoon brandy or
4 egg yolks	1 teaspoon rum flavouring
1½ ounces unsweetened	4 egg whites
chocolate	½ cup sugar

1. Make a cream filling from the first 5 ingredients by heating 1 cup of the milk; combine sugar, cornstarch and salt; and the remaining ½ cup milk; blend well; add to the hot milk; stir until the mixture thickens and has no taste of raw starch; remove from the heat. Beat egg yolks; stir in a little of the hot mixture; return entire mixture to the heat and stir until thick and smooth; remove from the heat.

2. Melt the chocolate over hot water in a bowl; to it add approximately 1 cup of the hot cornstarch mixture; stir until smooth; add vanilla; cool slightly and pour into the pie shell.
3. Soften the gelatine in cold water; dissolve it in the remaining cream filling; add the flavourings; chill until syrupy; beat.
4. Make a meringue by beating egg whites until stiff but not dry; beat in the sugar slowly; beat the gelatine mixture and the meringue mixture together; pour over the chocolate mixture in the pie shell.
5. Decorate with whipped cream and Chocolate Curls (page 579).

Famous Black Bottom Pie.

QUICK BLACK BOTTOM PIE

1. Prepare 1 package of vanilla pudding and pie mix. Save out 1 cup. To the remainder add 1 package melted chocolate (1 ounce); blend and pour into a baked 8-inch pastry shell; chill.
2. To the 1 cup filling saved, add 1 teaspoon rum flavouring and pour carefully over the chocolate layer; chill.
3. Cover with a layer of whipped cream; decorate with Chocolate Curls or Wedges (page 579).

For a larger filling use 1 package of vanilla and 1 of chocolate pudding and pie mix.

APPLESAUCE CHIFFON PIE

1 9-inch gingersnap crumb crust	¼ teaspoon cream of tartar
1 cup sugar	¼ teaspoon salt
1 tablespoon gelatine	½ cup whipping cream
1 cup sweetened applesauce	2 tablespoons finely chopped
3 egg whites	candied ginger

1. Mix ⅔ cup of the sugar and the gelatine in saucepan; stir in applesauce.
2. Heat slowly, stirring constantly until sugar and gelatine are dissolved; chill until mixture begins to mound when dropped from a spoon; beat until foamy.
3. Beat egg whites, cream of tartar and salt together until frothy. Add the remaining sugar gradually, beating constantly until stiff; beat into applesauce mixture.
4. Whip cream until stiff; fold into applesauce mixture along with ginger.
5. Spoon into prepared shell, sprinkle with gingersnap crumbs, decorate with ginger; chill several hours or until set.

PUMPKIN ICE-CREAM PIE

A special for Thanksgiving.

1 9-inch pastry shell, baked	1 cup sugar
1 pint vanilla ice cream	½ teaspoon salt
1 tablespoon finely chopped	½ teaspoon ground ginger
candied ginger	¼ teaspoon nutmeg
1 cup cooked pumpkin	1½ cups miniature marshmellows
	1 cup cream, whipped

1. Stir ice cream just to soften; quickly fold in the candied ginger; spread in pastry shell; freeze.
2. Mix pumpkin with sugar, salt, ground ginger, nutmeg, and chopped marshmallows; fold in whipped cream.
3. Spread over ice cream layer. Return to freezer for several hours or overnight.

FRESH FRUIT PIE

These fillings are cooked with the pastry, which must not be pricked.

Amount of:	Apple	Raspberry	Strawberry	Blueberry
Fruit	6 cups 7-8 apples	4 cups	4 cups	3 cups
Sugar	¾ cup	¾ cup	1 cup	½ cup
Thickener	2 tablespoons flour	2 tablespoons tapioca	4 tablespoons tapioca	2 tablespoons tapioca
Butter	1 tablespoon	1 tablespoon	1 tablespoon	1 tablespoon
Salt	sprinkle	sprinkle	sprinkle	sprinkle
Flavouring	½ teaspoon cinnamon or nutmeg		1 teaspoon lemon juice	½ teaspoon cinnamon

Amount of:	Cherry	Rhubarb	Peach
Fruit	3 cups	4 cups	4 cups 8-9 peaches
Sugar	1-1½ cups	1½ cups	¾ cup
Thickener	4 tablespoons tapioca	4 tablespoons flour	3 tablespoons tapioca
Butter	1 tablespoon	1 tablespoon	1 tablespoon
Salt	sprinkle	sprinkle	sprinkle
Flavouring	¼ teaspoon almond extract	½ tablespoon orange rind	1 tablespoon lemon juice ¼ teaspoon almond extract

1. Prepare the fruit; peel, core and slice the apples or peaches; pick over the raspberries and blueberries; wash strawberries, remove stems and slice; wash and pit cherries; wash rhubarb, cut into 1-inch pieces.
2. Measure the thickener; minute tapioca gives a clear, slightly thickened juice; it may be replaced by an equal amount of flour which seems better for both apple and rhubarb but clouds the fruit filling, or by half the amount of cornstarch.
3. Measure the sugar; part brown sugar adds to flavour in apple, rhubarb or blueberry pie; combine with thickener.
4. Combine sugar, thickener, salt and spice; mix with the fruit.
5. Arrange the fruit in an unbaked, unpricked 9-inch pastry shell (page 472), heaping fruit up a little in the centre; dot with butter; sprinkle flavouring over the fruit.
6. Finish with lattice or upper crust brushed with milk or egg wash. Bake at 425° for 15 minutes, then at 350° for 35 minutes.

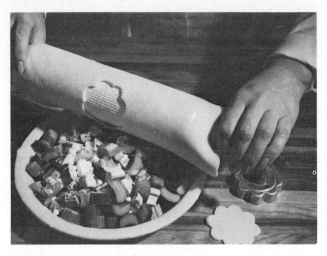

Fresh Rhubarb Pie with topping.

FROZEN FRUIT PIE

1. Substitute 2 15-ounce packages of frozen fruit for the fresh fruit and sugar, if already sweetened.
2. Thaw the fruit; drain and measure the juice.
3. Measure 1½ tablespoons of cornstarch for each cup of juice; Add enough cold juice to make a smooth paste; heat the remaining juice; stir in the cornstarch paste; stir until the mixture thickens.
4. Add fruit, butter and flavouring; taste and sweeten if desired; cool; pour into unbaked pie shell.
5. Finish as Fresh Fruit Pie, step 6.

CANNED FRUIT PIE

Use 2 19-ounce tins of fruit. Follow the recipe for Frozen Fruit Pie.

APPLE CHEESE PIE

Use Cheddar Cheese Pastry (page 474), or cover the apples with processed cheese before adding the top crust.

DEEP APPLE PIE

An easy recipe for beginners, fewer calories too.

1. Wipe, quarter, core, pare and dice 7-8 tart apples.
2. Place in buttered baking dish or deep pie plate; the dish should be very full.

3. Measure 1 teaspoon flour and 2 tablespoons brown or white sugar for each apple.
4. Stir carefully through the apples.
5. Dot over with small pieces of butter; if apples are not juicy, add water, ½ tablespoon to 1 apple.
6. Roll pastry in a circle to fit the dish; make a design in the pastry; Place the crust over the apples; crimp the edge.
7. Bake at 400° for 40 minutes. Serves 6.

Delicious Deep Apple Pie.

APPLE STREUSEL PIE

Spicy crumbs top this mix.

½ cup granulated sugar	7 or 8 juicy, tart apples (6 cups)
1 tablespoon flour	1 9-inch unbaked pastry shell
½ teaspoon cinnamon	½ cup brown sugar
few grains salt	⅓ cup unsifted flour
	¼ cup hard butter

1. Mix together first 4 ingredients; sprinkle over the apples as they are sliced into an unpricked pastry shell.
2. Prepare Streusel Topping by mixing sugar and flour and cutting in butter to make crumbs. Sprinkle over the pie filling.
3. Bake at 425° for 35 to 40 minutes. Serves 6.

APPLESAUCE PIE

Unexpected guests? Use a pastry mix and canned applesauce.

1 9-inch unbaked, unpricked pastry shell
⅓ cup flour
¼ cup sugar
½ teaspoon cinnamon

2½ cups sweetened applesauce
½ cup brown sugar
2 tablespoons flour
¼ cup cream

1. Mix together flour, sugar and cinammon; stir into applesauce; turn into pastry-lined pan (unpricked).
2. Combine brown sugar and flour; add cream; pour over applesauce.
3. Bake at 400° for 30 minutes. Serves 6.

PEACH BERRY PIE

1 9-inch baked pastry shell
1 8-ounce package cream cheese
3 tablespoons sugar
¼ teaspoon salt
1 tablespoon milk

½ teaspoon vanilla
¾ cup sugar
2 tablespoons cornstarch
1½ cups strawberries, crushed
1½ cups strawberries, halved
2 tablespoons lemon juice
1 19-ounce can peaches, drained

1. Beat the cheese, sugar, salt, milk and vanilla together; spread into the baked pastry shell, bringing it up well around the sides.
2. Combine the sugar and cornstarch, mixing until there are no lumps; add the crushed berries; stir over medium heat until clear and no taste of raw starch; add lemon juice and halved berries.
3. Spoon about ½ of the mixture over the cheese; press the peaches cut side up into the cheese; spoon the rest of the strawberry mixture on top. Chill.

OPEN-FACE PEACH PIE

A Mennonite recipe from Kitchener, Ontario.

1 9-inch unbaked pastry shell
¾ cup sugar
¼ cup flour
2 tablespoons butter

14 fresh peach halves or sliced peaches
¼ cup water
2 tablespoons lemon juice
⅛ teaspoon almond flavour

1. Mix the sugar, flour and butter to coarse crumbs; sprinkle ½ in a 9-inch pastry-lined pan (unpricked).
2. Arrange the peaches in an attractive pattern, cut side down.

3. Combine the liquids; pour over the pie.
4. Cover with the rest of the crumbs.
5. Bake at 375° for 40 to 50 minutes.

SOUR CREAM PIE

Another popular recipe from the Kitchener region.

1 9-inch unbaked pastry shell
1 cup sugar
3 tablespoons flour
dash of salt
1 cup sour cream
1 teaspoon cinnamon
2 tablespoons sugar

3 cups tart apples, chopped
or
2½ cups cherries, pitted
or
2½ cups berries
or
12 to 14 peach halves

1. Combine the sugar, flour and salt.
2. Add the sour cream and beat smooth.
3. Pour the mixture over the fruit in a 9-inch unpricked pastry-lined pan.
4. Sprinkle the cinnamon and sugar over the filling.
5. Bake at 425° for 15 minutes; reduce the heat to 350° for 35 minutes.

RAISIN PIE

1 9-inch unbaked pastry shell
and unbaked lattice top
2¼ cups raisins
2 cups boiling water
1 cup brown sugar

3 tablespoons flour
⅓ teaspoon salt
1 tablespoon grated orange rind
½ cup orange juice

1. Wash raisins; add to water; simmer 10 minutes.
2. Combine sugar, flour, salt and orange rind; add some of the liquid from the raisins, stirring until smooth.
3. Pour into the raisins and cook until the mixture thickens and clears and there is no taste of raw starch.
4. Remove from the heat; add orange juice; cool; pour into unpricked shell; finish with lattice top. Bake at 400° for 30 minutes. Serves 6.

For a rich colour and flavour, caramelize the sugar of Raisin Pie; add the liquid from the cooked raisins; simmer until syrupy; add raisins. Substitute 1½ tablespoons cornstarch for flour; mix with a little cold water to a smooth paste. Finish as Raisin Pie.

SCANDINAVIAN "FRUIT" PIE

1 9-inch unbaked pastry shell
  and unbaked lattice top
⅔ cup sugar
3 tablespoons cornstarch
⅛ teaspoon salt
¾ cup orange juice
⅓ cup prune juice

2 tablespoons lemon juice
¾ cup thick applesauce
½ cup currants, washed and
  dried
1½ teaspoons grated orange rind
1 cup cut-up cooked pitted
  prunes
1 tablespoon butter

1. Combine sugar, cornstarch and salt in a saucepan; stir in the orange and prune juices; cook, stirring constantly until thick.
2. Remove from heat, add the remaining ingredients; set aside to cool.
3. Pour into unpricked shell; finish with lattice top. Bake at 400° for 30 to 40 minutes or until nicely browned. Serve warm. Serves 6.

PRUNE PIE

1 9-inch unbaked pastry shell
  and unbaked lattice top
½ pound prunes (cooked)

½ cup sugar
1 tablespoon tapioca
1 tablespoon lemon juice
2 teaspoons butter

1. Remove prune stones, cut prunes in pieces; add sugar, tapioca, lemon juice and ⅓ cup of prune juice.
2. Pour mixture into unpricked shell; dot with butter.
3. Cover with lattice top. Bake at 425° for 30-35 minutes. Serves 6. Reduce sugar if sweetened prunes are used.

APRICOT PIE

Use recipe for Prune Pie; substitute cooked dried apricots for prunes. Increase sugar to 1 cup. Add ¼ cup blanched almonds to the fruit.

MINCEMEAT PIE

1 9-inch unbaked pastry shell   1 28-ounce tin mincemeat (3 cups)

Spoon mincemeat into unpricked shell; cover with plain or lattice crust. Bake at 400° for 30 minutes. Serve very hot, plain or with brandy sauce, or Hard Sauce (page 99).

For mincemeat recipes, see Food Preservation, Chapter 22.

Flame the mincemeat before baking, or for glamour flame the pie at the table before cutting.

ORANGE MINCEMEAT PIE

Section 3 oranges and arrange the pieces over the mincemeat under the top crust. While the pie is warm, brush with Orange Glaze (page 464).

CUSTARD PIES

The high egg content demands a lower cooking temperature for this family of pies. To determine when filling is cooked, slide in the point of a clean table knife; if it comes out free of custard, custard is cooked. An unbaked pie shell is required.

CUSTARD PIE

1 9-inch unbaked pastry shell	¼ teaspoon salt
2 eggs	1½ cups hot milk
¼ cup sugar	1 teaspoon vanilla
	few gratings nutmeg

1. Beat eggs slightly; add sugar and salt.
2. Add milk; strain; cool; add flavouring.
3. Pour into unpricked shell.
4. Place on lowest rack of the oven at 450° to start the cooking of the pastry; turn the indicator to 325°. Bake until custard is firm, for 35 to 40 minutes.

PUMPKIN PIE

2 9-inch unbaked pastry shells	1 teaspoon cinnamon
1½ cups cooked or canned	¼ teaspoon nutmeg
pumpkin	3 eggs
¾ cup brown sugar	1¼ cups milk
½ teaspoon salt	1 6-ounce can (⅔ cup)
½ teaspoon ground ginger	evaporated milk or light
	cream

1. Combine pumpkin, sugar, salt and spices.
2. Beat eggs slightly with an egg beater; add milk and cream and stir into pumpkin mixture.
3. Pour into unpricked shells; bake until the custard is set at 425° for 10 minutes; reduce heat to 325° and bake 30 minutes. Serves 12.

GLAMOUR PUMPKIN PIE

Decorate the top of cooked Pumpkin Pie with pecan halves; glaze by brushing with Caramel Glaze (page 579). Pass bowls of whipped cream, candied orange rind, crystallized ginger, coarsely ground maple sugar.

SOUR CREAM PUMPKIN PIE

Substitute ½ cup sour cream for ¼ cup milk.

ORANGE PUMPKIN PIE

Reduce the 1¼ cups milk in Pumpkin Pie to ½ cup. Add ½ cup orange juice and 1 tablespoon finely grated orange rind.

TARTS

Pastry (Basic Recipe) (2 cups flour) makes 1½ dozen dessert tarts, 2 dozen tea size or 3 dozen hors d'oeuvres.

To cut the pastry for tart pans:

With a piece of string measure the outside of one tart pan from the top down across the bottom and up to the top again. Using that measure find a cookie cutter, jar or saucer that has the same or slightly larger diameter and use it to cut the rolled pastry; or make a cardboard circle the diameter of the string and cut around it with a paring knife or pastry wheel.

Or, shape the dough into a long roll; slice; press evenly into tart tins.

Or, for tiny shallow tarts to be used for hors d'oeuvres roll pastry the size of the whole pan. Place it on the pan and push into each small cup with the fingers. Roll the pin over the pan to cut through the pastry.

1. Prepare the pastry; cut the correct size and fit into the tart tins. If the filling is to be cooked in the tart, do not prick the pastry, but make an attractive edge. If the filling is already cooked, prick the pastry well with a fork, or place a few white beans in each shell until it is baked, to prevent bubbling.

2. Fill the tarts; for fruit tarts, set small circles of pastry on top of the filling to keep it from drying in the oven. Brush the circles with milk.

3. Bake shells at 425° for 8-10 minutes; filled tarts at 400° for 20 minutes. Cool in the pan.

   For a quick variation, cut thin slices from chocolate or plain re-refrigerated cookie roll. Line sides of tart pan with overlapping slices; press one into the bottom; press firmly together.

GLAZED RASPBERRY TARTS

6 large baked tart shells   1½ teaspoons gelatine
1 quart fresh raspberries   2 tablespoons cold water
¼ cup sugar

1. Pick over the berries, filling the shells with the best; save out 1½ cups for the glaze.
2. Combine the 1½ cups of berries and sugar; simmer to extract juice; strain; press gently; there should be ¾ cup juice.
3. Soften gelatine in cold water; dissolve in hot juice syrup; chill; when syrupy, pour glaze over the berries; chill until firm.

GLAZED STRAWBERRY TARTS

6 3-inch tart shells, baked   1 tablespoon orange juice
4 ounces cream cheese   ½ teaspoon grated orange rind
¼ cup sugar   1 pint fresh strawberries
1 tablespoon cream   strawberry glaze (below)

1. Beat the cheese, sugar, cream, orange juice and rind until smooth. Spoon into the 6 tart shells.
2. Wash and hull strawberries; dry on paper towels.
3. Fill tart shells with the whole berries, tips up.
4. Prepare glaze (below); spoon over strawberries; chill well.

STRAWBERRY GLAZE

½ cup strawberries   ¼ cup sugar
½ cup water   2 teaspoons cornstarch

1. Crush strawberries in saucepan; add water and simmer 2 minutes; sieve.
2. Combine sugar, cornstarch; stir in sieved strawberries.
3. Cook, stirring constantly, until thickened and transparent; remove from heat. Add a drop of red colouring if desired. Cool and spoon over berries.

Substitute: red currant or apple jelly, melted and cooled until syrupy. Also can be used for raspberry glaze (above).

MINCEMEAT TARTS

Follow the recipe for Mincemeat Pie (page 492).

GLAZED CREAM TARTS

12 medium baked tart shells   fruit for decoration
1 recipe Cream Pie Filling   glaze
  (page 480)

1. Half-fill the tarts with cooled filling.
2. On top of each arrange a design of fruit, using these suggestions:
   Half an apricot rounded-side up.
   1 small slice of pineapple cut in half. Stand one half up; divide the other half and place at right angles to the first piece.
   A circle of banana slices overlapping, with a cherry in the centre.
   A layer of perfect blueberries, raspberries or halved strawberries.
   A pinwheel of peach slices or peach alternated with orange segments.
   An overlapping circle of green or red grapes, halved.
3. Cover with glaze (below).

GLAZE FOR CREAM TARTS

¼ cup sugar   1 cup syrup from canned fruit
1 tablespoon cornstarch   (peach, pear or pineapple)

1. Combine sugar, cornstarch and enough cold syrup to make a thin paste; heat the remaining syrup.
2. Pour the paste into the hot syrup, stirring until the mixture boils; cool the glaze slightly and spoon over the fruit decoration; let set.

BUTTER TARTS

12 medium unbaked pastry shells   1 cup sugar
1 cup currants or seedless   1 or 2 eggs
  raisins   2 tablespoons lemon juice, or
¼ cup butter   ½ teaspoon vanilla

1. Wash currants or raisins; soften if necessary by placing in a sieve over boiling water; dry on paper towels.
2. Cream the butter; add sugar and mix thoroughly.
3. Add egg well beaten; add fruit and flavouring.
4. Spoon the mixture into unpricked tart shells; bake at 375° 10 to 12 minutes. Makes 1 dozen medium-sized tarts.

   Replace ½ cup sugar with an equal amount of corn syrup for a more syrupy tart.

CHEESE (QUICHE) TARTS

Follow the recipe for Cheese (Quiche) Pie (page 280).

CHEESE TARTS

Reduce sugar to ½ cup; add ¼ cup thick cream; use 2 eggs.

LEMON CHEESE TARTS

Increase butter to ¾ cup; use 6 tablespoons lemon juice, 1 tablespoon grated rind; omit fruit.

MAPLE SYRUP TARTS

8 medium unbaked tart shells	1 cup maple syrup
1 large egg	½ cup chopped pecans

1. Beat the egg with a fork in a 2-cup measuring cup; beat in the syrup; pour syrup into unpricked shells; sprinkle with nuts.
2. Bake at 400° for 20 minutes. This recipe makes 18 to 24 small tarts.

HOLIDAY TARTS

12 small unbaked tart shells	jam (raspberry, black currant,
Almond Tea Cake Filling	apricot)
	candied cherries

1. Roll pastry thin (Galette Pastry page 474 is best for these); line pans.
2. Prepare filling (page 561).
3. Spoon a small amount of jam into each tart shell, fill with chilled filling and top with a cherry.
4. Bake at 325° for 25 minutes.

CHEESE CAKE TARTS

½ recipe Cheese Pastry	1 teaspoon vanilla
2 3-ounce packages cream cheese	½ cup sour cream
2 tablespoons sugar	½ cup cherry jam
1 egg	

1. Prepare small pastry shells from Cottage or Cream Cheese Pastry (page 474); do not prick. Add the filling.
2. Blend cheese, sugar, egg and vanilla thoroughly; spoon into shells.
3. Bake at 350° for 20 minutes; cool.
4. Top with 1 teaspoon sour cream, ½ teaspoon cherry jam. Makes 24.

COOKIES

Cookies are popular because they are easy to make. Those with a crisp texture provide a pleasing contrast to a soft dessert; the softer cookies are good for snacks at any time of the day.

There is an infinite variety of cookies. Some of the categories discussed here are

Drop Cookies
Refrigerator Cookies
Rolled Cookies
Shortbread
Squares and Bars
Unbaked Cookies

TO BAKE

The use of 3 cookie sheets will speed up the baking. Dark pans will brown the cookies more rapidly; they may be lined with aluminum foil. For drop cookies, the pans do not need greasing. Place the first pan in the oven as soon as it is full. Prepare the second pan. Move the first one up in the oven and place the second one on the lower rack. Prepare the third sheet. By this time the first sheet can come out, the second one moves up and the third sheet goes in on the bottom rack. In this way the cookies brown evenly. The sheets should be washed off before more cookies are added. Cookies are done when they may be moved freely on the pan and are an attractive colour, about 10 minutes. Lift the cookies onto a cake rack to cool. They will become crisp as soon as they cool and if left on the sheet will break when they are being removed. If this happens return the pan to the oven for a few minutes.

TO STORE

Store when cool in airtight containers; do not store cookies which contain fruit in the same container with cookies to be kept crisp. To keep soft cookies fresh, leave a slice of bread or a piece of cut apple in the container.

TO SHAPE

Use one of these methods:

Push dough from a teaspoon onto cookie sheets, alternating the cookies to give them more room to spread.

Roll the dough into small balls. Flatten with a glass dipped in cold water; press with the tines of a fork or potato masher, or spread with a knife dipped in cold water.

Mould dough with a pastry bag or cookie press.

Stamp dough with a decorated cookie stamp.

Cut dough with cutter as knife.

TO FREEZE

Baked cookies should be cool before packaging. Bar cookies may be wrapped uncut. Drop cookies should be layered in a freezer container or metal canister (coffee and shortening cans are good, too). Use crumpled saran film to separate layers and protect against breakage. A layer of saran film over the top of the container, directly under the lid, will keep the package air-tight and vapour-proof; or seal the container with freezer tape. Defrost the cookies on a baking sheet in a moderate oven for a few minutes, or on the plate 10-15 minutes.

Unbaked cookie dough is very easy to handle when frozen in rolls or bars, wrapped tightly in foil or plastic film. Allow a generous overlap on all sides of package and seal thoroughly with tape. Or, the dough may be frozen in fruit juice concentrate cans from which both ends have been removed. The dough may be pushed out of the cans when needed with a bottle which is slightly smaller. Allow the unwrapped dough to stand a short time, then slice evenly. Shaped, cut cookie dough may be frozen on the baking sheets and covered with saran film; drop cookie dough can be frozen this way too, if there are pans to spare. To save space, remove frozen cookie dough from pans and package in plastic bags. Defrost at room temperature before baking.

QUICK TRICKS

Prepare a large amount: make 2 or 3 times the basic recipe but before adding the dry ingredients divide the mixture into 3 bowls; make each into a different variation.

Refrigerate the dough: instead of baking all the dough, pack it into a container, cover and refrigerate until wanted. The dough will appear stiffer but should be handled as fresh dough. In this way a pan of cookies may be made whenever the oven is being used.

Quick recipe: press enough cookie dough onto a jelly roll pan or a baking sheet to cover it to a depth of $\frac{1}{2}$ inch. Bake at 375° for 10 minutes or until golden brown. To frost sprinkle evenly with chocolate chips as soon as the pan is removed from the oven; spread the softened chocolate evenly; sprinkle immediately with finely-chopped nuts; cool before cutting into bars, squares or diamonds.

COOKIES MADE FROM CAKE MIX

Start with one of:

1 Applesauce Cake mix	Add:
½ cup chopped walnuts	½ cup soft butter
⅓ cup seedless raisins	1 egg
or	2 tablespoons cold water
1 White Cake mix	
1 cup flaked coconut	
or	
1 Butter Pecan Cake Mix	
¼ cup brown sugar, packed	

1. Combine in a large bowl; beat until well blended.
2. Bake at 350° for 20-25 minutes in a greased 13 by 9 by 2-inch pan and cut into fingers; or drop on a greased pan and bake for 12-15 minutes.
3. Frost while hot with butterscotch morsels. Makes 3½ dozen.

Shaped Cookies: Cookies may be shaped by hand into small balls. Place on greased baking sheet and flatten with floured fork or glass tumbler.

COOKIES MADE FROM PIE CRUST

2 sticks Pie Crust mix	1 egg
½ cup chopped nuts or	¾ cup sugar
sesame seeds	½ teaspoon flavouring

1. Crumble the pastry; add the nuts.
2. Beat egg, sugar and flavouring; add pastry; stir with a fork until well-blended.
3. Shape into a roll 1½ to 2 inches in diameter; chill or freeze the dough. Slice thinly; bake on ungreased sheet at 400° for 8-10 minutes. Makes 4 dozen.

CREAM PUFFS (Basic Recipe)

1 cup boiling water	1 cup sifted all-purpose flour
½ cup butter	4 eggs
¼ teaspoon salt	

1. Add butter to boiling water; heat to boiling; add salt.
2. Add flour, all at once; stir over the heat until smooth; cook until mixture leaves the sides of the pan (about 1 minute); do not overcook.
3. Cool slightly; add unbeaten eggs, one at a time, stirring until smooth after each egg is added; beat until mixture is glossy.
4. Chill (the mixture should be stiff enough to hold its shape).
5. Onto an ungreased baking sheet drop the dough by spoonfuls, leaving a 2-inch space between each puff. Or, force the dough through a piping bag. Use amounts the size of a golf ball for large puffs, the size of a walnut for medium puffs.
6. Bake at 425° for 10 minutes; reduce temperature to 375° and bake until the puffs have turned to a light brown (20-40 minutes). Do not open oven door during the first 20 minutes.
7. Turn off the oven; cut a slit in each puff and return to the oven for 10 minutes. Makes 12 large, 24 medium-sized puffs.

BOUCHÉES

Drop the dough in amounts the size of a marble. Bake at 375° for 30 minutes. Makes 48.

ÉCLAIRS

Shape the dough into 1 by 3-inch strips; bake as Cream Puffs. Makes 20-24.

FILLINGS FOR CREAM PUFFS

Fill Cream Puffs with Cream Filling (page 591), Whipped Cream Filling (page 562), or with ice cream. For fillings for bouchées to be used as hors d'oeuvres see page 72.

CARAMEL GLAZE FOR CREAM PUFFS

¾ cup white sugar	¼ cup butter
⅛ teaspoon salt	¾ cup light cream
½ cup dark corn syrup	vanilla

Combine all ingredients in a heavy saucepan; stir over high heat until mixture comes to a boil; turn heat low and cook to the soft ball stage (page 637), stirring occasionally. Cool and flavour with vanilla. Spoon over each cream puff or dip the top of the puff in the glaze.

CHOCOLATE GLAZE

2 ounces unsweetened chocolate	1 cup icing sugar
2 tablespoons butter	3 tablespoons hot milk

1. Melt chocolate and butter over hot water.
2. Add sugar and gradually stir in hot milk.
3. Using a spoon, pour the warm glaze over the cooled puffs or dip the top of the puff in the glaze.

TO FREEZE CREAM PUFFS

Cream puffs freeze well at three stages.

a. After the batter is shaped on the baking sheet they may be frozen, then removed from the sheet and stored in plastic bags. Bake the frozen puffs as usual, allowing an extra 10-15 minutes. Freezing seems to improve the volume of the baked puff.

b. After the puffs are baked and cooled they may be frozen. To use, allow the puff to defrost at room temperature about 30 minutes.

c. Small puffs may be filled with appetizer mixtures before freezing. Defrost at serving time by placing in a hot oven (400°) for 15 minutes.

DROP COOKIES (Basic Recipe)

½-1 cup soft fat (butter or margarine)	flavouring (see below)
½-1 cup sugar (whlte, brown, or combined)	1½ cups sifted pastry flour or
	1¼ cups sifted all-purpose flour
1 egg	½ teaspoon baking soda
	¼ teaspoon salt

1. Choose the variations from those which follow and prepare the ingredients.. Use pastry flour and the larger amount of fat for rich, tender cookies.
2. In a large bowl, beat the fat, sugar and egg until fluffy; add the flavouring.
3. Sift together the flour, soda, salt and any spices and stir about ⅓ into the first mixture.
4. Add nuts, fruit or colouring if any while the dough is soft.
5. Continue to add the flour mixture, until the dough is not sticky when tested with the knuckles; overmixing will toughen the dough; too much flour makes a dry, tasteless cookie.
6. In oven preheated to 350°, test-bake one cookie before baking the whole sheet. Good drop cookies should flatten as they bake, but should not spread completely flat; add more flour if necessary.
7. Bake at 350° for 10-15 minutes, cool and store (page 498). Makes 5 dozen.

Drop Cookies: Drop batter from a teaspoon about 2 inches apart on a greased baking sheet.

Sukiyaki comes to us from Japan—a traditional communal dish (page 318). Steamed Restigouche Salmon adds elegance to a buffet.

Steaks of Salmon or Arctic Char are broiled to bring out their superior flavour. Stuffed Whitefish makes a fine dinner.

LITTLE BOY COOKIES

To make a less rich, less expensive drop cookie, increase flour to 2½ cups, add ¼ to ½ cup water or milk alternately with flour in the fat-sugar-egg mixture, using the smaller amount of fat. The pan will need to be greased.

BUTTERSCOTCH COOKIES

Use dark brown sugar.

CANDY-CANE COOKIES

Add ½ cup crushed peppermint stick candy.

PEANUT CRISP COOKIES

Add ½ cup crushed peanut brittle to the dough.

PEANUT BUTTER COOKIES

Prepare Drop Cookies (Basic Recipe), using the smaller amount of fat. Add ½ cup peanut butter or peanut butter crunch to the fat.

ORANGE COOKIES

Add 1 tablespoon grated orange rind, 1 teaspoon grated lemon rind and 2 tablespoons frozen orange concentrate undiluted, to fat-sugar-egg mixture. To the orange mixture may be added ½ cup toasted sesame seeds; or add either 4 ounces semi-sweet chocolate coarsely grated or chocolate chips.

CHOCOLATE COOKIES

Use the larger amount of sugar, the smaller amount of fat; add 2 ounces unsweetened chocolate, melted over low heat, to the far-sugar-egg mixture; add ⅔ cup walnuts, chopped, rum flavouring.

Omit nuts, add ¼ teaspoon peppermint flavouring for Chocolate Mint cookies.

SPICE COOKIES

Sift 1 teaspoon ginger, 2 teaspoons cinnamon with the flour; use ½ cup brown sugar and add ½ cup molasses to fat-sugar-egg mixture. ½ cup pecans or ¼ cup candied ginger, finely chopped, may be added.

HONEY SPICE COOKIES

Substitute honey for molasses.

CORIANDER COOKIES

Use the smaller amount of fat and sugar. Omit egg, add ¼ cup commercial sour cream, and to the flour add 3 teaspoons ground coriander.

COCONUT COOKIES

Use white sugar and 2 teaspoons grated lemon or orange rind for flavouring. Sift with flour ¾ teaspoon mace; add ½ cup coconut and if desired ½ cup chopped maraschino or glazed cherries.

PEANUT BRAN COOKIES

Omit salt; add 1 cup bran flakes, ¾ cup salted peanuts, chopped or crushed with a rolling pin.

FRUIT COOKIES

Use brown sugar and ½ teaspoon vanilla. Sift 1 teaspoon cinnamon or allspice with the flour; add 2 cups slivered dates; 2 cups raisins; ½ cup thinly-sliced peel, or a combination.

CHOCOLATE CHIP COOKIES

Use brown sugar and ½ teaspoon vanilla. Add 3 to 4 ounces of chopped semi-sweet chocolate, ½ package chocolate bits or mint chocolate chips. Also add ⅓ cup nuts chopped coarsely.

FRENCH COOKIES

Use white sugar and ½ teaspoon almond flavouring. Add ½ cup chopped maraschino cherries, ½ cup almonds, finely chopped.

SPECIAL OCCASION COOKIES

After 1 cup flour of Drop Cookies is added, bake a test cookie. The cookie should flatten to a 4-inch diameter. Add more flour if necessary. Space widely on the baking sheet to keep the shape and bake until brown around the edge. Remove to a rack and while still warm spoon on semi-sweet chocolate which has been melted over hot water. Leave a 1-inch border. Sprinkle with chopped almonds which have been coloured green. These cookies do not store well.

TURTLES

Arrange split pecan halves (rounded side up) in groups of 3 on greased baking sheets to resemble head and legs of turtle. Shape cookie dough into balls (use one rounded teaspoonful for each). Dip bottom into egg white, slightly beaten, and press onto nuts. Bake in a moderate oven (350°) for 10 to 12 minutes. Cool and frost with chocolate glaze. The frosting is the turtle shell, so a slight edge of cookie should be left showing.

SUGAR CRISPS

Using about 1 teaspoon of dough, shape into small balls; dip into egg white beaten slightly with 1 tablespoon water. Roll in a mixture of ½ cup sugar, 1 teaspoon cinnamon or ¼ teaspoon cardamon, ¼ cup finely ground nuts.

COCONUT SHAGS

Roll the balls of dough in coconut mixed with grated lemon or orange rind.

APRICOT SHAGS

Prepare the cookie dough, using the larger amounts of fat and sugar. Stir in ½ cup apricot pulp; drop the dough by teaspoons into shredded coconut (1½ cups); shape into balls and place 1 inch apart on a greased sheet.

CHERRY WINKS

To the dough add ⅓ cup finely chopped maraschino cherries, 1 cup finely chopped dates, 1 cup nuts. Roll in crushed cornflakes (¾ cup); top each cookie with a bit of cherry.

GINGER CRINKLES

Prepare dough for spice cookies; dip in sugar.

HERMITS

These cookies are better the second day.

1 cup butter	2½ cups sifted pastry flour or
1½ cups brown sugar	2¼ cups sifted all-purpose flour
1 egg	½ teaspoon baking powder
1½ cups raisins	½ teaspoon salt
1½ cups dates (slivered)	1 teaspoon cinnamon
½ cup walnuts (coarsely cut)	¼ teaspoon allspice

Mix as Drop Cookies and bake at 350°. Or bake the mixture in 2 8-inch cake pans; cut in bars. Makes 50-60.

OATMEAL CRISPS

1 cup butter or shortening	½ teaspoon baking soda
1¼ cups brown sugar	½ teaspoon baking powder
1 egg	½ teaspoon salt
1½ cups rolled oats	1 teaspoon vanilla or
1 cup coconut	¼ teaspoon almond extract
1¼ cups sifted pastry flour or	
1 cup sifted all-purpose flour	

Mix as Drop Cookies, bake at 350°. Makes 6 dozen cookies.

½ cup coarsely chopped walnuts may be added. Or add 1 cup glazed red and green cherries, finely chopped.

OATMEAL CRINKLES

1 cup butter or shortening	½ teaspoon salt
1 cup brown sugar	2 cups sifted pastry flour or
1 teaspoon vanilla	1¾ cups sifted all-purpose flour
¼ cup warm water	1 teaspoon baking soda
1 cup rolled oats	

1. Mix as Drop Cookies, adding the water alternately with the dry ingredients.
2. Roll into a ball, then flatten the ball onto the cookie sheet with the fingers or with a fork. The pan should almost show through the cookie.
3. Bake at 375° for 10-12 minutes. Makes 6 dozen.

PEANUT COOKIES

1 pound Spanish Peanuts	1 cup sugar
1 tablespoon flour	1 teaspoon vanilla
2 eggs	

1. Crush the peanuts with a rolling pin; stir in flour.
2. Beat the eggs; beat in sugar; add vanilla; stir in nut-flour mixture.
3. Drop onto greased baking sheets.
4. Bake at 300° until the edges begin to brown (7-10 minutes); do not overcook.
5. Let the pan cool slightly; tap sharply against the table to loosen the cookies; remove to a wire rack. Makes 5 dozen.

REFRIGERATOR COOKIES (Basic Recipe)

¾ cup shortening	2½ cups sifted pastry flour or
1 cup sugar	2¼ cups sifted all-purpose flour
1 egg	½ teaspoon baking powder
½ teaspoon vanilla	¼ teaspoon salt

1. Cream the fat, sugar and egg together until fluffy; add the flavouring.
2. Sift the flour, baking powder and salt together and stir about ⅓ into the first mixture; add nuts or fruit.
3. Add rest of flour mixture until the dough is firm enough to handle; turn the dough out onto a floured sheet of waxed paper; form into a roll 1 to 1¼ inches in diameter or into a rectangle; or pack firmly into a frozen orange juice can open at both ends.
4. Wrap in foil or heavy wax paper and chill overnight.
5. Slice ⅛ to ¼-inch thick; do not let the dough begin to soften.
6. Bake at 350° for 10-12 minutes. Makes 5 dozen.

Use any of the basic variations for Drop Cookies. Chop fruit, chocolate or nuts finely so the cookie will slice without breaking. Roll the rolls in chocolate sprinkles, or in crushed nuts.

Refrigerator Cookies: Slice chilled dough with a very sharp knife and bake slices on an ungreased baking sheet.

OATMEAL SLICES

1 cup fat	¼ teaspoon baking soda
1 cup white sugar	¼ teaspoon salt
1 egg	1 cup rolled oats
½ teaspoon flavouring	½ cup flaked coconut
1⅔ cups pastry flour or	½ cup walnuts
1½ cups all-purpose flour	

1. Mix as Refrigerator Cookies; shape into 3 rolls about 2 inches in diameter; wrap; refrigerate.
2. Cut into ¼-inch thick slices. Bake at 375° for 10-12 minutes. Makes 6 dozen.

OATMEAL MOLASSES COOKIES

1⅛ cups sifted pastry flour or	½ cup granulated sugar
1 cup sifted all-purpose flour	½ cup brown sugar
½ teaspoon baking soda	1 egg
½ teaspoon salt	1½ tablespoons molasses
1½ cups rolled oats	1½ teaspoons grated lemon rind
½ cup fat	½ teaspoon vanilla

1. Sift together flour, baking soda and salt; add rolled oats.
2. Cream butter, sugars, egg and molasses; add lemon rind and vanilla.
3. Combine the 2 mixtures; mix thoroughly with hands. Press and shape dough into a long, smooth roll about 2½ inches in diameter. Wrap in waxed paper.
4. Chill roll until stiff; cut into thin slices. Arrange slices about 1½ inches apart on ungreased baking sheet.
5. Bake at 400° for 8 to 10 minutes or until lightly browned. Makes about 4 dozen.

GINGERSNAP REFRIGERATOR COOKIES

1 cup fat	2¾ cups sifted pastry flour or
½ cup brown sugar	2½ cups sifted all-purpose flour
½ cup molasses	1 teaspoon baking soda
2 tablespoons vinegar	1 tablespoon ginger
½ teaspoon lemon flavouring	1 teaspoon salt
(if desired)	1 teaspoon cinnamon

Combine as Refrigerator Cookies, adding the molasses and vinegar to the fat-sugar mixture. Bake at 400° for 8-10 minutes. Makes 50-60.

ROLLED COOKIES (Basic Recipe)

¾ cup soft fat	2¾ cups sifted pastry flour or
⅔ cup fine sugar	2½ cups sifted all-purpose flour
1 egg	½ teaspoon baking powder
1 teaspoon vanilla flavouring	½ teaspoon salt

1. Beat together the fat, sugar, egg and vanilla.
2. Sift together the dry ingredients.
3. Stir ⅓ of the flour mixture into the fat-sugar-egg mixture; add fruit or nuts as desired while the dough is soft; add rest of flour mixture until the dough is not sticky; chill.
4. Roll ⅓ of the dough at one time on a *lightly* floured board; cut into shapes with cookie cutters dipped in flour.
   (Over-rolling will toughen the dough so that as many cookies as possible should be cut from the dough and the bits of dough collected until all the dough has been rolled once. Then the bits may all be pressed together and rerolled. Too much flour on the board also toughens the cookies.)
5. Bake at 350° for 10-15 minutes. Cool on racks, store in a container with tight lid. Makes 5 dozen.

   Dough may be tinted before baking; spices may be added; the cookies may be decorated with a pastry tube; or they may be spread with a thin butter icing after baking and sprinkled with coloured sugar, decorating candies, shredded coconut or chopped nuts.

CHOCOLATE ROLLED COOKIES

Add 2 ounces of melted unsweetened chocolate to cookie mixture just before adding the flour; reduce fat to ⅔ cup.

ORANGE ROLLED COOKIES

Substitute 1 teaspoon undiluted frozen orange juice for vanilla and add 1 tablespoon finely grated rind.

CHOCOLATE TOPPERS

Melt 1 package chocolate bits over hot water. Put 2 cookies together with chocolate, sandwich fashion. Spread tops with chocolate.

Rolled Cookies: Cut into shapes with cookie cutters dipped in flour.

PLATTER PATTERS

Cut cookies into 5-inch circles, using a coffee can lid as a cutter. Bake. Spread cookies to within ½ inch of the edge with melted semi-sweet chocolate. In the centre of each place a circle of heavy white paper with the name of a popular song written on it.

TOUCHDOWN COOKIES

Bend an empty frozen orange juice or soup can into a football shape; cut cookies with it. Bake. Decorate with frosting to resemble lacings on a football.

BERLINER KRANZ COOKIES

Cut cookies with doughnut cutter; brush with beaten egg white; after baking decorate to resemble Christmas wreaths with green sugar and cinnamon candies.

CHERRY BELLS

Cut rolled cookies into 2½-inch rounds. In the centre place ½ teaspoon of filling made by combining ⅓ cup maraschino cherries, 1½ cups finely chopped nuts. Shape into a bell by folding each side into the centre on a slant. Place ½ a cherry for a clapper.

VALENTINE COOKIES

Roll cookie dough thinly. Using 3 sizes of heart-shaped cutters or cardboard patterns, cut and bake. Ice the small hearts with pink icing and decorate with an arrow; place each decorated heart on top of a medium-size cookie with a spot of icing to hold it, then place both on top of the large one. Using a pastry tube, pipe a scroll or ruffled edge of pink icing lace around the small and medium hearts.

CHOCOLATE PINWHEELS

Divide dough into 2 parts. To ½ add 1 ounce unsweetened chocolate melted over hot water. Chill the dough; roll each colour separately on waxed paper to a 9 by 12-inch rectangle. Invert the chocolate on top of the white dough and pull off the paper. Press gently with the rolling pin. Roll tightly from side; wrap in paper; chill; slice; bake at 350° for 10-15 minutes.

RAINBOW PINWHEELS

Divide the dough into 3 parts. Tint 1 pink, 1 chocolate, using ½ ounce melted unsweetened chocolate. Roll each on waxed paper to rectangles of equal size. Place one on top of the other, removing the waxed paper and pressing gently with a rolling pin. Finish as Chocolate Pinwheels.

DATE PINWHEELS

Divide the dough into 2 parts. Roll each into a rectangle. Cover each with cooled Date Filling (page 564). Roll from the long side to make 2 tight rolls; refrigerate; cut in ¼-inch slices; bake at 350° for 10-15 minutes.

OATMEAL PINWHEELS

See Rolled Oatmeal Cookies (page 516).

CHOCOLATE ROLL

Prepare dough as for Chocolate Pinwheels. Roll and cut the white dough into 2 10 by 4-inch strips. Shape the dark dough into 2 10-inch rolls. Place a dark roll on a light strip and bring the light dough up into a smooth tight covering for the chocolate centre. Finish as Chocolate Pinwheels.

RIBBON COOKIES

Use the Rainbow Pinwheel directions. To pink dough add ½ cup chopped cherries; to the chocolate, add ½ cup nuts. Line a small loaf pan with waxed paper. Press the chocolate dough evenly into it; cover with the white, then the pink dough. Chill until very firm, turn out, remove the paper and slice. Bake at 350° for 10-15 minutes.

SUGAR COOKIES

⅔ cup fat
1¼ cups sugar
1 egg, beaten
2 tablespoons milk
1½ teaspoons vanilla or
lemon extract

2 cups sifted pastry flour or
1¾ cups sifted all-purpose flour
1½ teaspoons baking powder
½ teaspoon salt

Combine as Rolled Cookies (Basic Recipe). Bake at 375° for 10 minutes. Makes 5 dozen.

*Oatmeal wafers, Gingerbread cookies
and Sugar cookies with milk: a filling snack.*

GINGERBREAD COOKIES

Ideal for "gingerbread men" and cookie "cut-outs."

½ cup fat	2 teaspoons baking soda
½ cup molasses	½ teaspoon salt
½ cup sugar	1½ teaspoons ginger
1 egg	1 teaspoon cinnamon
3¼ cups sifted all-purpose flour or	
3½ cups sifted pastry flour	

1. Melt shortening and cool it. Add molasses, sugar and egg, and blend well.
2. Sift in the flour, baking soda, salt and spices. Mix well.
3. Wrap in waxed paper and chill overnight in refrigerator.
4. Roll out on lightly floured board to ¼-inch thickness. Cut into shapes, decorate with raisins and chopped cherries.
5. Bake at 375° for 10-12 minutes.

GINGERBREAD REINDEERS

Make a pattern from cardboard. Decorate reindeers with icing. Gild small match boxes; stick them to the back of 2 animals with frosting; fill with Christmas candies.

SOFT MOLASSES COOKIES

½ cup fat	3 cups sifted pastry flour or
½ cup granulated sugar	2¾ cups all-purpose flour
2 eggs	1 teaspoon baking soda
½ cup molasses	2 teaspoons ground ginger
¼ cup milk	½ teaspoon salt

1. Combine as Rolled Cookies (Basic Recipe).
2. Roll into a square ⅛-inch thick. Sprinkle generously with sugar and cut into 2-inch squares with a knife, or roll and cut with a 4-inch cookie cutter.
3. Bake at 350° for 10 minutes. Makes 5 dozen squares or 1½ dozen 4-inch cookies.

ROLLED OATMEAL COOKIES

1 cup fat	2½ cups sifted pastry flour or
1 cup brown sugar	2¼ cups sifted all-purpose flour
½ cup buttermilk	1 teaspoon baking soda
2½ cups rolled oats or oatmeal	1 teaspoon salt

1. Prepare as Rolled Cookies (page 511).
2. The dough should be very soft; chill several hours to stiffen the mixture. Take out a small amount at a time for rolling.
3. Roll thin; cut with cookie cutter.
4. Bake 12 to 15 minutes at 325°. Makes 5 dozen 2½-inch cookies.

OATMEAL DATE COOKIES

Before serving, put together pairs of baked and cooled cookies with Date Filling (page 564).

OATMEAL PINWHEELS

Roll the dough into 2 rectangles; spread each with date filling or strawberry jam; roll from the long side, sealing the edge under the 2 rolls. Refrigerate; when firm slice in ¼-inch slices. Bake as Rolled Oatmeal Cookies.

OATMEAL TURNOVERS

On each circle of dough place a teaspoon of Date Filling. Fold; press edges together with a fork; prick and bake as Rolled Oatmeal Cookies.

OATMEAL SQUARES

1. Roll the dough on waxed paper into 2 rectangles. Try to have the edges even and the 2 rectangles the same size; turn 1 onto a greased cookie pan.
2. Spread the dough on the baking sheet with Date Filling.
3. Flip the other sheet of dough on top; press the edges together.
4. Bake at 375° for 25 minutes; cut into bars while warm.

SHORTBREAD (Basic Recipe I)

1 cup butter	2¼ cups sifted pastry flour or
½-⅓ cup sugar	2 cups sifted all-purpose flour
(fruit, icing or brown)	

1. Cream the butter; add sugar gradually and cream together thoroughly.
2. Add flour slowly until a stiff dough is formed. Turn out on a floured board; gradually knead in flour until the dough begins to crack.
3. Chill; roll to ¼-inch thickness with as little extra flour as possible; cut into small shapes. *Or,* form into 2 roll 1½ inches in diameter; wrap and refrigerate; cut into ¼-inch slices.

SHORTBREAD (Basic Recipe II)

This is a slightly less rich shortbread which is popular for many of the variations listed below.

¾ cup butter	1 teaspoon vanilla
½ cup sugar	2¼ cups sifted pastry flour or
(fruit, icing or brown)	2 cups sifted all-purpose flour
1 egg yolk	

Combine as above, adding the egg yolk to the fat-sugar mixture. Shape; use as rolled, drop or refrigerator dough. Makes approximately 3 dozen cookies.

2 cups potato or rice flour may replace the wheat flour.

Pat the dough into 2 9-inch pie plates; crimp the edge, and prick the cakes in a pattern with a fork. Sprinkle with candy-coated caraway seed if desired. Silvers of almonds can also be used as a garnish. Cut after baking.

NUT SHORTBREAD

To Shortbread (Basic Recipe) add ½ to 1 cup nuts, finely chopped.

FRUIT SHORTBREAD

To Shortbread (Basic Recipe) add ½ to 1 cup green and red glazed cherries, chopped.

CRESCENTS

Shape dough into pencil-shaped rolls. Cut into finger-length pieces and bend into crescents. After baking, dip the ends into melted semi-sweet chocolate and then into chopped nuts.

PECAN SURPRISES

Shape small pieces of dough around a pecan into a date-like form; bake; while still hot dip several times into a bowl of icing sugar. For added flavour, place a cut vanilla bean in the bowl.

BUTTER RICHES

Shape into small balls; flatten with a glass dipped in sugar; top with a pecan.

CHERRY COOKIES

Shape into small balls; press with a fork to a very thin cookie; top each with half a cherry.

SPRING HATS

From rolled shortbread cut rounds 1 inch and 2 inches in diameter; bake with small rounds on top of large rounds; using a pastry tube or cake decorator, decorate each coated baked hat with a ribbon and flowers made from Coloured Butter Icing (page 569).

SESAME COOKIES

Place ½ cup sesame seeds on a shallow baking sheet and toast in a 400° oven for about 10 minutes, or until golden brown, stirring often; cool. Add half the seeds to the dough before kneading in the flour; shape into rolls; coat with the remaining seeds; chill, slice and bake.

BUTTER BALLS

Shape Nut Shortbread into 1-inch balls; before baking dip into slightly beaten egg white, then into coarsely chopped nuts.

SWEDISH CAKES

Roll into small balls; dip into egg white, then into finely chopped nuts. Place on greased baking sheet, press down centre. Bake 5 minutes at 350°; press down again; bake 10 minutes more. While still warm, fill centres with red jelly. Makes 3 dozen.

THUMB PRINT COOKIES

Form dough into small balls on cookie sheet; with thumb make a dent in each. Bake at 350° for 5 minutes; press down again; bake 10 minutes more. Roll several times while warm in icing sugar. When cool fill the hollow with the filling below.

THUMB PRINT COOKIE FILLING

¾ 6-ounce package (¾ cup) semi-sweet chocolate bits
1 tablespoon shortening
2 tablespoons light corn syrup
1 tablespoon water
1 teaspoon vanilla

1. Melt chocolate and shortening over hot (not boiling) water.
2. Stir in remaining ingredients till smooth.
3. Let cool 5 minutes. Fill cookies. Makes 3 dozen.

ALMOND TEA CAKES

1. Chill the dough made from Shortbread (Basic Recipe II). Butter well 2 dozen tiny tart tins; pat 1 tablespoon of dough into each tin, shaping it with the fingers; smooth the dough off even with the top of each tin.
2. Into the centre of each lined cup put 1 small teaspoon of the filling below.
3. Bake at 350° for 15 minutes. Makes 4 dozen tiny tarts.

ALMOND TEA CAKE FILLING

1 egg white
1 cup brown sugar
1 teaspoon vanilla
⅓ cup chopped nuts
1¾ cups chopped mixed fruit (candied pineapple, cherries, raisins, dates)

1. Beat egg white until just stiff; gradually add brown sugar and beat after each addition.
2. Beat in flavouring; stir in nuts and fruits.

CHEESE DAINTIES

Serve as an appetizer or a cookie.

½ pound processed cheese	½ teaspoon paprika
½ cup butter	½ teaspoon salt
1⅛ cups sifted all-purpose flour	

1. Cream butter and cheese; add sifted dry ingredients gradually and mix well. Roll very thin and cut with a cookie cutter.
2. Place together in pairs with red currant jelly, pineapple jam or orange marmalade.
3. Bake at 325° for 15 minutes. Makes 2 dozen.

CHEESE ONION DAINTIES

Substitute grated Cheddar for the processed cheese; reduce flour by 2 tablespoons; add 3 teaspoons crushed dry onion soup mix; finish as Refrigerator Cookies (page 509).

LEMON THINS

A favourite which uses no egg.

1 cup butter	¼ teaspoon nutmeg
¾ cup brown sugar	¼ teaspoon salt
1 tablespoon lemon juice	cinnamon-sugar mix
2 cups sifted pastry flour or	
1¾ cups sifted all-purpose flour	

Mix as Drop Cookies (Basic Recipe). Press with fork to ⅓-inch thickness. Sprinkle with cinnamon-sugar mix. Bake at 350° for 10 minutes. Makes 3 dozen.

CHOCOLATE BROWNIES

2 ounces unsweetened chocolate	½ cup sifted pastry flour or
⅔ cup butter	⅓ cup sifted all-purpose flour
2 eggs (large)	½ teaspoon baking powder
1 cup brown sugar	⅛ teaspoon salt
½ teaspoon vanilla	½ cup walnuts, coarsely chopped

1. Melt the chocolate and butter together over hot water in a measuring cup.
2. Beat the eggs; add sugar; beat until light and fluffy; add chocolate mixture and vanilla.
3. Combine flour, baking powder and salt; sift into the first mixture; stir well to blend; add nuts.

4. Bake in a buttered 8-inch cake pan 20-30 minutes at 350°. The mixture should be soft in the centre but firm around the edges. Cool before cutting. Makes 25.

FROSTED BROWNIES

When cool, ice Chocolate Brownies with Chocolate Butter Icing (page 570).

RICE FLOUR BROWNIES

Substitute rice flour for pastry flour.

PRALINE BARS

⅓ cup fat	1½ teaspoons vanilla
½ cup sugar	1½ cups pecans, chopped
¼ cup molasses	¾ cup sifted pastry flour or
1 egg	⅔ cup sifted all-purpose flour
¼ teaspoon salt	

1. Melt the fat in a saucepan; blend in sugar and molasses.
2. Add egg, salt and vanilla; beat well; stir in nuts.
3. Stir in sifted flour.
4. Spread in a greased 7 by 11-inch pan; bake at 350° for 30 minutes.

CHINESE CHEWS

2 eggs	⅓ teaspoon salt
⅔ cup sugar	1 teaspoon vanilla
¾ cup sifted pastry flour or	½ cup dates, chopped
⅔ cup sifted all-purpose flour	½ cup raisins
1 teaspoon baking powder	¾ cup chopped walnuts

1. Beat eggs until foamy; add sugar and beat well.
2. Add sifted dry ingredients, flavouring, fruit and nuts; beat thoroughly.
3. Spread in a greased 8-inch cake pan; bake 30 minutes at 350°.
4. Cut in bars while warm; roll in fruit sugar or icing sugar.

FRUIT BALLS

Grease hands and roll baked Chinese Chew bars into balls; ice with thin Butter Icing (page 569) and roll in shaved Brazil nuts. Makes 48.

TUTTI-FRUTTI BARS

To the fruit of Chinese Chews add ¾ cup mixed peel, glazed cherries and pineapple. To the egg-sugar mixture add 2 ounces unsweetened chocolate and 3 tablespoons fat, melted over hot water.

BUTTERSCOTCH SQUARES

½ cup fat	1½ cups sifted pastry flour or
2 cups brown sugar	1⅓ cups sifted all-purpose flour
2 eggs	2 teaspoons baking powder
½ teaspoon vanilla	1 cup chopped walnuts
½ teaspoon salt	or coconut

1. Cream fat, add sugar, eggs and vanilla; beat well.
2. Stir in sifted dry ingredients and chopped nuts or coconut. Bake in 9 by 13 by 2-inch pan at 350° for 25 minutes, until firm to the touch. Makes 48 squares.

PARKIN

An old English favourite.

½ cup fat	1 teaspoon baking soda
2 eggs	1 teaspoon cinnamon
1 cup molasses	½ teaspoon cloves
1⅔ cups sifted pastry flour or	½ cup quick rolled oats
1½ cups sifted all-purpose flour	1 cup raisins
1 teaspoon salt	

1. Heat oven to 375°. Grease a 13 by 9 by 2-inch pan.
2. Cream fat. Add eggs and beat well; beat in molasses.
3. Sift flour, salt, soda and spices; add rolled oats.
4. Blend into the first mixture; add the raisins.
5. Spread batter into pan; bake for 25 minutes, until top springs back when touched lightly in centre. Serve warm, cut in 12 large squares.

CARAMEL SQUARES (Basic Recipe)

These squares are prepared in 2 stages, a base and a topping.

Base:	Topping:
½ cup butter	2 egg whites
½ cup brown sugar	1 cup brown sugar
2 egg yolks	1 cup chopped nuts
1 teaspoon vanilla	
1½ cups sifted pastry flour or	
1⅓ cups sifted all-purpose flour	
1 teaspoon baking powder	
½ teaspoon salt	

1. Cream butter; add sugar, egg yolks and vanilla; beat well.
2. Stir in sifted dry ingredients.
3. Spread mixture evenly in a greased 9-inch cake pan. Bake at 350° until lightly browned, about 25 minutes.
4. Beat the egg whites until stiff but not dry; beat in the sugar slowly; add nuts; spread over the baked mixture; return to oven; bake at 325° until light brown and almost firm, about 30 minutes. Makes 3 dozen.

DREAM CAKE

To the egg white mixture add ½ cup coconut, ¼ cup chopped cherries. When cool, ice with lemon frosting made by adding 1 tablespoon lemon juice to 1 cup Butter Icing (page 569).

CHOCOLATE HALF-WAY SQUARES

Sprinkle chocolate chips on the cooked base, while warm; spread; cover with the egg white mixture; finish as Caramel Squares.

APRICOT BARS

Cover ⅔ cup dried apricots with water; simmer until fruit is tender and thick; cool and chop. Add to the egg white mixture; finish as Caramel Squares, using almonds for the nuts. Frost with Orange or Vanilla Icing (page 570).

BRAZIL ORANGE BARS

To the Caramel Square egg white mixture add 1 cup sliced Brazil nuts; finish as Caramel Squares; frost with Orange Butter Icing (page 570).

CHOCOLATE ORANGE BARS

Spread ¾ package (6-ounce) chocolate chips over the baked layer while warm; finish as Caramel Squares. Frost with Orange Butter Icing (page 570).

Melt remaining ¼ cup chocolate over hot but not boiling water. Remove from heat. With a tooth pick, draw lines of melted chocolate on top of frosting. Draw a fork through the chocolate lines to make a decorative pattern.

CHERRY SQUARES

Add ½ cup well-drained chopped maraschino cherries, 1 cup coconut and ½ cup chopped almonds to the egg white mixture. Finish as Caramel Squares. Frost with Butter Icing (page 569).

OATMEAL DATE SQUARES

1½ pound dates	1 teaspoon salt
¼ cup sugar	½ cup brown sugar
1½ cups boiling water	¼ teaspoon baking soda
juice and rind of 1 lemon	½ cup butter or shortening
1⅓ cups all-purpose flour	1¾ cups rolled oats

1. Cut the dates into small pieces; cook with sugar and water slowly until thick, stirring often to prevent scorching; cool; add lemon.
2. Mix the flour, salt, sugar and soda.
3. Cut in the fat, using pastry blender or 2 knives, until the mixture resembles coarse crumbs; add oats.
4. Pat ½ the crumbs into a buttered 9 by 9-inch pan, making a firm layer. Spread on the date filling.
5. Sprinkle the rest of the crumbs evenly over the mixture; pat gently or cover with a sheet of waxed paper, and pat to compress the crumbs.
6. Bake at 350° about 30 minutes, until golden brown; cool; cut into squares.

KISSES OR MACAROONS (Basic Recipe)

2 egg whites	¼ teaspoon flavouring
salt	½ cup icing sugar
1/16 teaspoon cream of tartar	colouring

1. Beat the egg whites until frothy; add salt and cream of tartar and beat until the mixture forms peaks.
2. Add sugar a tablespoon at a time, beating well after each addition until the mixture is smooth and shiny; add flavouring and a few drops of colour if desired.
3. Spoon onto a foil-lined baking sheet.
4. Bake at 250° for 30 minutes. Pull away the foil. Makes 20.

LEMON MERINGUE KISSES

Put two meringues together with Lemon Cheese Filling (page 566) or Butter Icing (page 569) before serving.

Variations:
Mix with the sugar 1 teaspoon cinnamon, ¼ teaspoon nutmeg, ¼ teaspoon cloves. Fold in ½ cup of any of

shredded coconut	corn flakes and nuts
chocolate chips	drained chopped canned
finely chopped nuts	fruits or glacéed fruits

CHERRY MACAROON PUFFS

1 can (8 ounces) almond paste	1 teaspoon vanilla
3 cups icing sugar	red and green candied
2 egg whites	cherries, halved

1. Line 2 large cookie sheets with aluminum foil.
2. Blend almond paste and sugar thoroughly in a large bowl; beat in unbeaten egg whites and vanilla and mix until smooth.
3. Drop dough by teaspoonfuls onto foil-lined cookie sheets; press half a candied cherry on top of each.
4. Bake at 300° until golden brown, about 20 minutes; cool on cookie sheets. Makes 4 dozen.

CORNUCOPIA COOKIES

6 egg whites	1 cup butter or mixture of butter
1 cup sugar	and fat, melted
⅛ teaspoon salt	1 cup sifted all-purpose flour
	¾ cup finely chopped almonds

1. Mix egg whites, sugar and salt and beat until mixture is just foamy and sugar is dissolved.
2. Add melted butter, flour and almonds and mix well.
3. Drop from a tablespoon onto a greased cookie sheet, leaving about 5 inches between each.
4. Bake only a few cookies at a time at 350° for 8 to 10 minutes.
5. Cool ½ minute; roll cookies around a conical-shaped object such as the tip of a cake decorator in order to produce the cornucopia shape; handle gently and quickly; return to oven if necessary to soften; cool.
6. Fill with icing and dip in chopped nuts.

CALLA LILIES

1 egg white	⅓ cup sifted all-purpose flour
¼ cup sugar	⅓ teaspoon baking powder
¼ teaspoon lemon extract	⅛ teaspoon salt

1. Beat egg white until foamy; beat in sugar until stiff.
2. Add flavouring; fold in sifted dry ingredients.
3. Finish as Cornucopias; cool.
4. Fill with whipped cream and centre with a thin strip of candied orange.

LACE WAFERS

¼ cup brown sugar	¼ teaspoon baking powder
¼ cup corn syrup	½ cup sifted all-purpose flour
¼ cup butter	½ cup flaked coconut
⅛ teaspoon salt	½ teaspoon vanilla

1. Combine sugar, syrup and butter in a saucepan; cook, stirring constantly, until the mixture boils; boil hard 1 minute; remove from heat.
2. Combine dry ingredients.
3. Blend coconut-flour mixture into cooked syrup; add vanilla.
4. Finish as Cornucopias, or curl around a greased wooden spoon handle, or leave flat. Makes 2 dozen.

PORCUPINES

1 cup brown sugar	1½ cups chopped walnuts
2 eggs	1 cup chopped dates
2 tablespoons butter	3 cups coconut

1. Beat the sugar and eggs until frothy; add melted fat.
2. Add nuts, dates and 1 cup of the coconut.
3. Form into small balls. Roll in coconut.
4. Bake at 300° until just beginning to brown. Makes 60.

UNBAKED COOKIES

PEANUT MOUNDS

A good recipe for beginners.

2 cups sugar	2 cups rolled oats
⅓ cup cocoa	½ cup smooth-style peanut butter
¼ teaspoon salt	½ cup coarsely chopped peanuts
½ cup milk	1 teaspoon vanilla
¼ cup butter	

1. Mix sugar, cocoa and salt in a large saucepan; add milk and butter; boil 2 minutes.
2. Remove from heat and stir in remaining ingredients.
3. Drop by rounded teaspoonfuls on waxed paper. Cool. Makes 5 dozen.

PEANUT BUTTER CRISPS

¼ cup sugar	2 cups cornflakes
½ cup peanut butter	1 cup rice krispies or coconut
½ cup corn syrup	

1. Combine the first 3 ingredients in the top of a double boiler, heat until the sugar is dissolved; add the cereals; remove from the heat.
2. Drop from a spoon onto waxed paper, keeping the pan over the boiling water.

PEANUT BUTTER BALLS

1 cup icing sugar	2 cups flake coconut
1 cup peanut butter	½ cup icing sugar
1 tablespoon butter	1 tablespoon milk
½ cup walnuts	vanilla
1 cup rice krispies	

1. Mix first 5 ingredients; shape into balls.
2. Combine icing sugar, vanilla and milk.
3. Coat each ball; roll in coconut. Makes 36.

TOFFEE CLUSTERS

2 packages 3-ounce candy toffee bars	1 tablespoon milk
1 tablespoon butter	2 cups rice krispies or cornflakes

1. Melt toffee; add butter and milk.
2. Fold in rice krispies or cornflakes.
3. Form into clusters with a fork, or butter hands and roll into balls after mixture has cooled slightly; cool on a greased cookie sheet. Chopped nuts, cherries and marshmallows may be added. Makes 1½ to 2 dozen.

BUTTERSCOTCH DROPS

1 6-ounce package (1 cup) butterscotch morsels	½ cup coarsely chopped salted peanuts
1 cup crushed shredded wheat or rice cereal	

Melt butterscotch morsels over hot water. Remove from heat and stir in cereal and nuts. Drop by teaspoonfuls onto waxed paper. Cool. Makes 1½ dozen.

BUTTERSCOTCH PECAN SLICES

1 6-ounce package (1 cup) butterscotch morsels	½ teaspoon vanilla
⅓ cup sweetened condensed milk (½ can)	⅓ cup chopped pecans
	1 slightly beaten egg white pecan halves

1. Melt butterscotch morsels over hot water. Remove from heat and stir in condensed milk and vanilla. Add chopped pecans; mix well. Chill until firm enough to handle.
2. Form into 12-inch roll on waxed paper; roll tightly in the paper to shape evenly. Unroll and mark surface lengthwise with tines of fork; brush with egg white.
3. Press pecan halves into roll to completely cover surface. Wrap in waxed paper. Chill. Cut in ½-inch slices with sharp knife. Makes about 2 dozen.

SCOTCHEROOS

1 6-ounce package (1 cup) butterscotch morsels	3 ounces chow mein noodles (¾ can)
½ cup peanut butter	2 cups miniature marshmallows

1. Melt butterscotch morsels and peanut butter over hot water; stir until smooth.
2. Add the noodles, coarsely crushed, and the marshmallows; stir well.
3. Drop by teaspoonfuls onto waxed paper. Refrigerate. Makes 3 dozen.

CHOCOLATE CLUSTERS

1 milk chocolate bar or 2 ounces semi-sweet chocolate or chocolate chips	2 cups cornflakes, rice krispies, nuts and/or coconut

1. Melt chocolate over hot water.
2. Stir in cereal mixture until well blended.
3. Drop in mounds on waxed paper.

CHOCOLATE MACAROONS

⅔ cup sweetened condensed milk (1 can)	1 cup coconut
1 square (1 ounce) unsweetened chocolate	¼ teaspoon vanilla

1. Heat milk over gently boiling water until thick and caramel coloured, stirring occasionally.
2. Add chocolate and continue heating until chocolate is melted.
3. Remove from heat and stir in coconut and vanilla. Drop by teaspoonfuls onto waxed paper. Chill. Makes 1½ dozen.

SNOWBALL SURPRISES

2¾ cups icing sugar	1 tablespoon cream
⅛ teaspoon cream of tartar	1 egg white
⅛ teaspoon salt	3 ounces unsweetened chocolate
2 teaspoons cold water	1½ cups flake coconut
1 teaspoon lemon juice	

1. Combine first 6 ingredients; add stiffly beaten egg white, enough to make a pliable paste.
2. Dust hands with icing sugar; knead mixture 5 minutes; let stand 1 hour.
3. Form into small balls; chill; dip in melted chocolate; roll in coconut.

RAINBOW SLICES

2 ounces semi-sweet chocolate	⅔ cup rolled walnuts or pecans
1 egg	(chopped)
¾ cup icing sugar	½ cup coconut
30 coloured marshmallows	

1. Melt chocolate over hot water.
2. Beat egg and mix with icing sugar and melted chocolate.
3. Cut marshmallows into quarters with scissors and add with nuts to egg mixture.
4. Shape mixture into a roll; roll in coconut.
5. Chill several hours in the refrigerator. Slice.

OATMEAL PATTY CAKES

2 cups sugar	3 cups quick-cooking oats
½ cup butter or margarine	1 cup coconut
½ cup milk	2 squares unsweetened
1 teaspoon vanilla	chocolate, melted

1. Combine the sugar, butter and milk in a saucepan; bring to a boil.
2. Add the vanilla; stir in the other ingredients at once.
3. Drop by teaspoons onto waxed paper.

COLETTES

6 squares semi-sweet chocolate	2 tablespoons butter
or	
1 6-ounce package (1 cup)	
mint chocolate chips	

1. Heat the chocolate in the top of a double boiler, over hot but not boiling water, until almost melted; remove from the heat, and stir until smooth.
2. With a teaspoon, coat the inside of small paper cups. If the chocolate is too warm, it will run down into the bottom of the cup, instead of coating the sides. Make sure there is a firm edge by adding an extra layer, if necessary, around the top.
3. Chill on a baking sheet or in muffin pans in the refrigerator; peel off the paper; keep in the refrigerator until needed.
4. Fill with Peppermint Cream (page 563) or with any flavoured whipped cream or with ice cream. Makes 24 small; 8 large.

The small colettes may be eaten in the fingers; large ones make an attractive dessert.

LEMON LAYERS

18 graham wafers
⅓ cup sweetened condensed
    milk (½ can)

juice and rind of 1 lemon
Chocolate Butter Icing
    (page 570)

1. Line a greased 9-inch-square cake pan with graham wafers, cutting biscuits when necessary in order to make them fit.
2. In a small bowl, mix condensed milk (not evaporated milk) with lemon juice and rind; allow to stand until thick.
3. Spread mixture on graham wafers evenly; top with another layer of graham wafers, fitting as before; ice with chocolate icing.
4. Chill several hours in the refrigerator; cut into fingers or squares. Makes 25 to 30.

DREAM SQUARES

18 graham wafers
1 cup brown sugar
½ cup butter
½ cup milk
1 cup crushed graham wafer
    crumbs

1 cup chopped walnuts
1 cup flaked coconut
¼ cup chopped candied cherries
Butter Icing (page 569)

1. Line a greased 9-inch square cake pan with graham wafers, cutting biscuits when necessary in order to make them fit.
2. Combine sugar, butter and milk in saucepan; bring to a full boil. Remove from heat and add graham wafer crumbs, nuts, coconut and cherries. Spoon over graham wafers in pan while hot. Top with remaining graham wafers, cutting an extra wafer to fill cracks if necessary. Press them down firmly; cool.
3. Ice top of squares and decorate with finely chopped walnuts, cherries or toasted coconut. Cut in squares to serve. Makes 2-3 dozen.

RUM BALLS

½ pound vanilla wafers
1 cup icing sugar
2 tablespoons cocoa

1 cup pecans, finely chopped
½ cup light corn syrup
¼ cup rum

1. Roll the wafers into very fine crumbs and mix with icing sugar and cocoa; add nuts, syrup and rum.
2. Shape into 1-inch balls. Let stand 1 hour.
3. Roll in icing sugar.
4. Store in tightly covered cookie jar for 4 days before serving.

RAISIN SQUARES

2 cups seeded raisins	½ cup chopped walnuts
¾ cup water	2 cups ginger wafer crumbs
¼ cup sugar	6 tablespoons melted butter

1. Combine raisins, water and sugar in saucepan and cook over low heat, stirring constantly, until thick, about 5 minutes. Remove from heat, stir in nuts. Cool.
2. Blend crumbs and butter. Press half the mixture firmly into a lightly buttered 8-inch-square cake pan. Spread raisin filling evenly over crumbs.
3. Sprinkle remaining crumbs over raisin filling and press firmly. Chill. Cut in squares to serve. Makes 3 dozen.

CHOCOLATE SQUARES

½ cup butter or margarine	1 teaspoon vanilla
3 tablespoons brown sugar	½ cup nuts, coarsely chopped
4 squares semi-sweet chocolate	2 cups broken arrowroot cookies
2 eggs	

1. Combine the butter, sugar and chocolate in a saucepan; stir over medium heat until the mixture bubbles; stir slowly into well-beaten eggs; add vanilla, nuts and broken cookies; mix well.
2. Press firmly into a buttered 8-inch cake pan; refrigerate.

MARGUERITES

Spread chocolate, ginger or vanilla wafers with a meringue mixture. (page 482). Brown at 300°.

MARSHMALLOW SQUARES (Basic Recipe)

32 marshmallows (½ pound)	1 package rice krispies, puffed
¼ cup butter	rice or sugared cereal
½ teaspoon vanilla	

1. Cook marshmallows and butter over hot water until thick and syrupy; add vanilla and beat well.
2. Pour over cereal in a large greased bowl; mix well.
3. Press into a shallow greased pan to a depth of about ¾ inch. Chill and cut into squares. Makes approximately 40.

CHOCOLATE SQUARES

Just before pouring the marshmallow mixture over the cereal, add to it 4 ounces melted semi-sweet or 2 ounces melted unsweetened chocolate.

DATE OR RAISIN SQUARES

Stir 1 cup raisins or chopped dates into the marshmallow mixture just before pouring over the cereal.

PEANUT BUTTER SQUARES

Stir 2 tablespoons peanut butter into the marshmallow mixture before pouring over cereal.

CHRISTMAS SQUARES

Stir ½ cup red and green chopped cherries and ½ cup red cinnamon candies into the marshmallow mixture.

LOGS

Shape the marshmallow mixture into small logs; dip the ends in melted semi-sweet chocolate.

PEPPERMINT STICK SQUARES

Mix ½ cup crushed peppermint stick candy with cereal before adding marshmallow mixture.

QUICK COOKIES

¼ cup butter	⅔ cup cocoa mix
½ cup corn syrup	4½ cups sugar-crisp cereal
1 cup icing sugar	1 cup nuts
salt	⅔ cup coconut

1. Melt the butter; combine with syrup, sugar, salt and cocoa. Mix.
2. Add other ingredients and with a fork stir until cereal is well coated.
3. Pack firmly into greased 9 by 13-inch pan; refrigerate. Cut in squares. Makes 5 dozen.

CAKES

Cakes are examples of drop batters.

Cakes that are fluffy, tender and delicious result from the combination of a good recipe, good ingredients, accurate measurement and correct techniques of mixing and baking.

There are three general types of cakes:

a. those containing some form of shortening, not necessarily butter, called Butter Cakes.

b. those containing no fat, leavened by egg white, called Sponge and Angel Cakes.

c. those containing fat and baking powder, but leavened mainly by egg white, called Chiffon Cakes.

INGREDIENTS

Fat should be of a high grade with good creaming qualities and should always be at room temperature; butter may be used for added flavour. For a predominant butter flavour use butter in the icing. For the quick-mix type of cake an emulsified shortening is necessary.

Sugar should be fine so that it completely dissolves in the batter; coarse sugar results in the formation of dark specks on the surface of the baked cake and in a coarse texture.

Eggs should be medium-sized and fresh, for maximum emulsifying action.

Leavening agents should be as specified in the recipes; unless otherwise stated, baking powder to be used is of the regular (not double-acting) type.

Flour can be all-purpose flour, but pastry and cake flours give the most tender product.

All ingredients should be of high quality and be at room temperature to ensure emulsification of ingredients. This is important if a fine velvety texture is to be obtained.

POINTS TO REMEMBER

Choose a pan of the correct size for the quantity of batter. Oversized pans result in cakes of poor volume, while undersized pans allow batter to overflow with loss of gas bubbles. To determine the volume of an irregular-shaped pan, fill it with water; measure water and use half that quantity of batter; or compare the quantity of water with the amount required to fill a commonly used cake pan and fill accordingly. Paper cups may be set in muffin tins. Or 2 paper cups, one inside the other, may be spaced well apart on the baking sheet.

For butter cakes, place a piece of waxed paper which has been cut to fit the bottom of the pan (by tracing around the outside edge of pan on the paper with a sharp knife) in the bottom of the cake pan. Grease it and the sides of the pan lightly. Do not grease pans for chiffon or sponge cakes.

When filling cake pans, push batter toward the edges and corners of the pans so that it is higher there than in the centre. During baking, the centre area rises highest, reaching the level of the corners, and thus the cake will have an even surface. Do not fill the pan more than half full of batter.

Place pans in the central area of the oven so that no pan touches the sides of the oven or another pan. Racks should be placed so that cakes occupy an area about midway between upper and lower elements; in most ovens this will be the third rack from the bottom. Do not place one pan directly above the other.

In order to determine when the cake is completely baked, insert a toothpick, fine knitting needle or cake tester into the centre area of the cake; if the toothpick comes out free of batter, the cake is baked. Also, the surface of the cake springs back when pressed lightly with the forefinger. Butter cakes come away from the sides of the pan when cooked. Cakes should not be moved nor the door opened during the second and third quarter of the baking time.

When baked, butter cakes should be cooled on a rack for 5 minutes and the sides loosened with a knife. To turn out of pan, invert the rack or cake plate on the pan and invert all, quickly. Remove the waxed paper while the cake is warm. Sponge and chiffon cakes should be cooled by suspending the inverted cake by a funnel, if it is in a tube pan.

2 cups of flour will make:	*Baking Time in minutes:*
one 8 to 9-inch square	40-50
two 8 to 9-inch layers	30-40
one 8 by 4-inch loaf pan	60
12 medium muffins	20
24 medium paper cups	15
50 small paper cups	12

High Altitude Adjustment
For altitudes above 3500 feet increase baking temperature to 375° and bake 35-40 minutes. From 3500 to 6000 feet use recipes especially planned for high altitudes.

To freeze: Butter cake batter may be frozen but a better product results when the cake is first baked then cooled and frozen.

Unbaked batter should not be kept more than one week. Thaw 1½ hours at room temperature; pour into the pan and bake. Frozen cake will dry out quickly after thawing, so should be wrapped and frozen in an amount suitable to the size of the family. Wrap as soon as cool; freeze; protect in heavy carton or metal container. Unfrosted cake will keep 2 to 3 months; frosted 1 to 2 months.

Angel cake is tenderized by freezing but may show a little shrinkage.

Fruit cake shows less tendency to crumble after freezing.

To frost use butter or fudge-type icings. Egg white icings do not freeze well. Uncooked frostings not only freeze more successfully but are easier to handle than cooked frostings. Frost the cake, freeze it unwrapped until firm (2-3 hours), then wrap, re-freeze and protect. Fillings do not freeze successfully.

Defrost cake in the wrapper at room temperature (about 3 hours for a large cake, 1 hour for layer cake, 30 minutes for cup cakes, 20 minutes for an individual portion).

Butter Pecan Cake.

Meringue topping converts this custard into Floating Island. Charlottes or chiffon pie fillings combine with ladyfingers to make this glamorous dessert.

Cool fruit drinks are refreshing to look at and to drink. Colourful fruit both delicious and nutritious served as an appetizer, dessert, a salad or a snack.

BUTTER CAKE (Basic Recipe)

This is the conventional method for mixing butter cakes. Milk, egg and shortening must be at room temperature.

⅔ cup soft fat	¾ cup milk
1 teaspoon vanilla or	2 cups sifted pastry flour or
½ teaspoon almond extract	1¾ cups sifted all-purpose flour
1 cup sugar	3 teaspoons baking powder*
2 eggs	½ teaspoon salt

1. Preheat oven to 350°; grease an 8-inch-square pan or two 8-inch layer pans and line with a piece of waxed paper cut to fit the bottom and lightly greased.
2. Cream shortening and vanilla thoroughly until light and fluffy; add sugar gradually, beating well after each addition. (This thorough emulsifying of the fat and dissolving of the sugar is essential to a fine-textured cake.)
3. Add eggs 1 at a time and beat after each egg is added until the mixture is light and fluffy. (The eggs may be separated, the egg whites beaten and folded in after the last addition of flour. This method gives better volume only if the egg white is folded skilfully and the beating is done by hand.)
4. Add the milk and flour alternately to the fat-sugar mixture, ¼ each time, beginning and ending with flour. This is a drop batter and should be thin.
5. Bake at 350° until the cake is lightly browned, leaves the sides of the pan and springs back when gently pressed. Layer cakes will bake in about 30 minutes, square cakes 50 minutes.
6. Cool about 10 minutes; run a knife around the 4 sides of the cake, place the rack on top, then reverse onto the rack. Peel off the waxed paper.

*If double-acting baking powder is used, use 2 teaspoons.

ORANGE CAKE

Substitute 2 egg yolks for 1 egg. Add 2 tablespoons finely grated orange rind. Frost with Orange Icing (page 570).

SPICE CAKE

Sift in with the dry ingredients 1 teaspoon cinnamon, ¼ teaspoon cloves, ¼ teaspoon nutmeg or mace. Frost with Mountain Frosting (page 572).

NUT CAKE

Chop ½ cup walnuts and add to the batter with the dry ingredients. Frost with Caramel Butter Icing (page 570).

PEPPERMINT STICK CAKE

Add ⅓ cup finely crushed peppermint stick candy to the butter-egg mixture. Frost with Seven Minute or Boiled Frosting (pages 571, 573). Sprinkle with more crushed candy.

CRANBERRY SWIRL

Turn batter into layer pans. With fork, break up 1 cup canned whole-cranberry sauce; sprinkle over batter; with a spatula, make zigzag line through batter (about 2 up and 2 down strokes). Frost with Orange Butter Icing (page 570).

CHOCOLATE FLECK CAKE

Add 1 tablespoon instant coffee to the dry ingredients, and 2 ounces semi-sweet chocolate coarsely grated to the butter-egg mixture. Frost with Coffee Icing (page 570). Decorate with Chocolate Curls (page 579).

SNOW WHITE CAKE

Uses only egg whites.

½ cup shortening	½ cup milk
½ cup fine granulated sugar	1 teaspoon vanilla
1½ cups sifted pastry flour or	½ teaspoon almond extract
1⅓ cups sifted all-purpose flour	3 egg whites
1½ teaspoons baking powder	½ cup fine granulated sugar
¼ teaspoon salt	

Combine as Butter Cake (Basic Recipe) with this exception: beat the egg whites until stiff but not dry; beat in sugar; fold in the egg white mixture with the last addition of flour. Makes 1 9-inch cake.

ONE-EGG CAKE

½ cup shortening
1⅓ cups granulated sugar
1 egg
2¼ cups sifted pastry flour or
2 cups all-purpose flour

½ teaspoon salt
3 teaspoons baking powder
1 teaspoon vanilla
1 cup milk

Combine as Butter Cake (Basic Recipe).

GOLD CAKE

Uses only egg yolks.

2 cups sifted pastry flour or
1¾ cups sifted all-purpose flour
3½ teaspoons baking powder
½ teaspoon salt
1 cup milk

½ cup shortening
1 cup sugar
3 medium egg yolks
1 teaspoon vanilla

Combine as Butter Cake (Basic Recipe). Beat the egg yolks until thick and lemon coloured before adding them. Makes 1 9-inch cake.

CHOCOLATE MOCHA CAKE

A rich dark brown cake.

⅔ cup shortening
1¼ cups sugar
2 eggs
1 teaspoon vanilla
2 cups sifted pastry flour or
1¾ cups sifted all-purpose flour

⅓ cup cocoa
1 teaspoon baking powder
½ teaspoon baking soda
¼ teaspoon salt
½ cup strong hot coffee
⅔ cup sour milk, or buttermilk

1. Stir cocoa and coffee until smooth; cool.
2. Combine as Butter Cake (Basic Recipe), blending the cocoa mixture into the fat sugar-egg mixture.

DEVIL'S FOOD CAKE

Mahogany red in colour.

⅔ cup shortening
1 teaspoon vanilla
1½ cups sugar
3 eggs, well beaten
3 1-ounce squares unsweetened chocolate

2 cups sifted pastry flour or
1¾ cups sifted all-purpose flour
2 teaspoons baking powder
¼ teaspoon baking soda
½ teaspoon salt
1 cup milk

Combine as Butter Cake (Basic Recipe), blending the chocolate mixture into the fat-sugar-egg mixture before adding liquid and dry ingredients.

BURNT SUGAR CAKE

½ cup sugar	2 cups sifted pastry flour or
¾ cup boiling water	1¾ cups sifted all-purpose flour
1 teaspoon vanilla	¾ teaspoon baking powder
½ cup shortening	½ teaspoon baking soda
1 cup sugar	¼ teaspoon salt
2 eggs	⅔ cup milk

1. Caramelize sugar; add water; simmer to make 1 cup syrup; cool completely; add vanilla.
2. Combine as Butter Cake (Basic Recipe), beating the syrup into fat-sugar-egg mixture. Frost with Caramel Butter Icing (page 570).

TOMATO SOUP SPICE CAKE

1 cup fat	4½ cups sifted pastry flour or
2¼ cups light brown sugar	4 cups sifted all-purpose flour
2 eggs	1 tablespoon baking powder
1 can (10-ounce) condensed	1 teaspoon baking soda
tomato soup, undiluted	2 teaspoons cinnamon
2 cups chopped walnuts	1 teaspoon cloves
1 cup dark raisins	½ teaspoon nutmeg

1. Prepare a 9 by 13 by 2-inch pan. Set oven to 350°.
2. Measure soup; add water to make 2 cups; mix well.
3. Combine ingredients as Butter Cake (Basic Recipe), adding soup alternately with flour mixture to the fat-sugar-egg mixture; fold in nuts and raisins. Frost with Snowy Lemon Mountain Frosting (page 572).

Crumb-topped Spice Cake.

QUICK TOMATO SOUP SPICE CAKE

- 1 spice cake mix
- 1 can (10-ounce) tomato soup
- ¼ cup water plus 1 tablespoon
- 1 cup chopped pecans
- 1 cup dark raisins

Combine as directed on the Spice Cake Mix package, using the soup and water as liquid; fold nuts and raisins into the batter.

APPLESAUCE CAKE

- ½ cup shortening
- 1 cup dark brown sugar, firmly packed
- 2 eggs unbeaten
- 1½ cups sifted pastry flour or
- 1¼ cups sifted all-purpose flour
- 2 teaspoons double-acting baking powder
- ¼ teaspoon baking soda
- ½ teaspoon salt
- 1 teaspoon cinnamon
- ½ teaspoon allspice
- ½ teaspoon ground cloves
- ¼ teaspoon nutmeg
- 1 cup canned applesauce
- ⅓ cup walnuts, chopped
- 1 cup raisins

Combine as Butter Cake (Basic Recipe); add applesauce alternately with flour mixture to the fat-sugar-egg mixture. Stir in nuts and raisins. Frost with Orange Butter Icing (page 570).

BANANA CAKE

- ½ cup shortening
- 1 teaspoon vanilla
- 1 cup sugar
- 2 eggs, well beaten
- 2¼ cups sifted pastry flour or
- 2 cups sifted all-purpose flour
- 2 teaspoons baking powder
- ¼ teaspoon soda
- ½ teaspoon salt
- 1 cup mashed ripe bananas (2-3)
- 2 tablespoons milk

Prepare as Butter Cake (Basic Recipe), mashing bananas thoroughly and adding to the milk.

GINGERBREAD

Top gingerbread with thick applesauce and a sprinkling of brown sugar.

- ½ cup shortening
- ½ cup sugar
- 1 egg
- ½ cup molasses
- 2 cups sifted pastry flour or
- 1¾ cups sifted all-purpose flour
- 1 teaspoon baking soda
- 1 teaspoon cinnamon
- 1 teaspoon powdered ginger
- ½ cup sour milk
- ½ cup teaspoon vanilla

Prepare as Butter Cake (Basic Recipe), adding molasses with egg to fat-sugar mixture.

HOT WATER GINGERBREAD

½ cup shortening
½ cup brown sugar
1 egg
⅔ cup molasses
2¾ cups sifted pastry flour or
2½ cups sifted all-purpose flour
2 teaspoons baking powder

½ teaspoon salt
1 teaspoon baking soda
1½ teaspoons ginger
1 teaspoon cinnamon
½ teaspoon cloves
1 cup boiling water

1. Cream the shortening, add sugar.
2. Add egg; beat well; add molasses.
3. Add flour, sifted with baking powder, salt, soda and spices.
4. Add boiling water; mix smooth. (The mixture will be very thin.)
5. Pour into greased baking pan; bake at 325° for 45 to 50 minutes.

A better flavour is obtained if molasses is mixed—½ cup dark and remainder mild flavoured. Strong coffee may replace the water.

QUICK-MIX BUTTER CAKE (Basic Recipe)

This method is designed for the electric mixer.

2 cups sifted pastry flour or
1¾ cups sifted all-purpose flour
1¼ cups sugar
2½ teaspoons double-acting
    baking powder

½ teaspoon salt
⅓ cup shortening
1 teaspoon vanilla
1 cup milk
1 large egg

1. Heat oven to 350°. Line the bottom of a 9-inch square pan or 2 9-inch layer pans. Butter the sides and lining. *Have ingredients at room temperature.*
2. Mix and sift the dry ingredients into a bowl; add the shortening, vanilla and ⅔ cup milk.
3. Beat vigorously with a spoon for 2 minutes by the clock, or mix with an electric mixer at medium speed for 2 minutes.
4. Add the ⅓ cup milk and the egg; continue beating for 2 more minutes, scraping the sides of the bowl down so that all the batter is well beaten. Do not underbeat.
5. Bake at 350°; 30 minutes for layers, 50 minutes for square cakes. Makes 2 9-inch layer cakes.

QUICK WHITE CAKE

2¼ cups sifted pastry flour or
  2 cups sifted all-purpose flour
1½ cups sugar
3½ teaspoons baking powder
  1 teaspoon salt
 ½ cup soft shortening

⅔ cups milk
1 teaspoon vanilla
½ teaspoon lemon extract
⅓ cup milk
4 egg whites

Combine as Quick-Mix Butter Cake (Basic Recipe), adding the unbeaten egg whites with ⅓ cup of milk.

QUICK-MIX GOLD CAKE

1¾ cups sifted pastry flour or
1⅔ cups sifted all-purpose flour
  1 cup sugar
2½ teaspoons double-acting
     baking powder

¾ teaspoon salt
⅓ cup shortening
1 teaspoon lemon flavouring
⅔ cup milk
3 egg yolks

Combine as Quick-Mix Butter Cake (Basic Recipe).

Chocolate Fudge Cake.

QUICK-MIX CHOCOLATE FUDGE CAKE

2 ounces unsweetened chocolate	¼ teaspoon baking soda
¼ cup water	½ teaspoon salt
1 cup sugar	⅓ cup shortening
1¼ cups sifted pastry flour or	½ cup milk
1 cup sifted all-purpose flour	1 teaspoon vanilla
1 teaspoon double-acting	2 eggs
baking powder	

Stir chocolate, water and ¼ cup sugar over hot water until smooth; cool. Complete as Quick-Mix Butter Cake (Basic Recipe), adding chocolate syrup with eggs.

QUICK-MIX DEVIL'S FOOD CAKE

2 cups sifted pastry flour or	1 teaspoon salt
1¾ cups sifted all-purpose flour	¾ cup shortening
1¾ cups sugar	1 teaspoon vanilla
¾ cup cocoa	1¼ cup milk
1¼ teaspoons baking soda	3 medium eggs
½ teaspoon double-acting	
baking powder	

Combine as Quick-Mix Butter Cake (Basic Recipe). Makes 3 9-inch layers.

ONE-EGG CHOCOLATE CAKE

⅓ cup shortening	⅛ teaspoon cream of tartar
1 teaspoon vanilla	⅛ teaspoon salt
¼ cup cocoa	¾ cup sugar
1½ cups sifted pastry flour or	1 egg
1⅔ cup sifted all-purpose flour	milk
1¼ teaspoons baking powder	

Combine as Quick-Mix Butter Cake (Basic Recipe). Makes 1 8-inch square.

QUICK-MIX MARBLE CAKE

1. Prepare ingredients and square plan for Quick-Mix Butter Cake (Basic Recipe); over hot water melt 1 ounce unsweetened chocolate; add to it 2 tablespoons water, ¼ teaspoon baking soda; stir.
2. Prepare the cake; pour about ½ the batter into another bowl; add the chocolate mixture to ½ the batter; beat ½ minute.
3. Place alternate spoonfuls of chocolate and white batter in prepared pan; run a knife up and down in a zigzag fashion; bake at 350° for 35 to 40 minutes.

UPSIDE-DOWN CAKE

The Topping

3 tablespoons butter	OR	3 tablespoons butter
⅔ cup brown sugar		¼ cup corn syrup
		½ cup brown sugar

Melt the fat in a 10-inch frying pan, a 9-inch cake pan or a deep pie pan. (Pyrex, aluminum or stainless steel will not darken fruit, which tin or iron may do.) Sprinkle in the sugar evenly; dribble on the corn syrup if used.

The Fruit

Arrange any one of the following combinations of fruit on the butter-sugar mixture; remember that the fruit will be reversed when the cake is served. Canned fruit should be well drained.

4 slices canned pineapple
6 maraschino cherries

1 19-ounce can drained crushed
   pineapple
½ cup coarsely chopped walnuts
5 maraschino cherries

1 can drained, sliced peaches
10-12 maraschino cherries

6 canned pear halves
½ cup walnut halves

1½ cups mincemeat

1 19-ounce can drained apricot
   halves
½ cup slivered blanched almonds

⅓ cup crushed pineapple
12-15 cooked drained dried
   apricots
13-15 cooked drained pitted
   prunes

1 can whole cranberry sauce
⅓ cup orange juice

2 cups drained canned pitted
   cherries
½ cup halved blanched almonds

The Batter

Use any quick-mix cake, cake mix, the One-Egg Cake (page 539), or use up left-over egg yolks or whites by making Gold Cake or White Cake (page 543).

Prepare the cake batter; pour it over the fruit in the pan; bake at the recommended temperature. The time will be somewhat less because the cake will be in a thinner layer. When the cake is cooked run a knife around the edge invert a serving plate over the pan and quickly invert all together; let stand a few minutes to allow the fruit to loosen.

The Sauce

Serve warm with a sauce made from the fruit juice, thickened with cornstarch or with whipped cream. Serves 8 to 12.

Upside-Down Cake with pineapple.

CRUMB CAKE

This cake keeps well and needs no frosting.

2¼ cups sifted pastry flour or	1 teaspoon ground cinnamon
2 cups sifted all-purpose flour	½ teaspoon nutmeg
1½ cups brown sugar firmly packed	¼ teaspoon cloves
½ cup butter	1 cup buttermilk
2 teaspoons baking powder	2 eggs
1 teaspoon baking soda	1 cup seedless raisins, washed and dried if necessary, or
1 teaspoon salt	½ cup walnuts

1. Grease and flour a 13 by 9 by 2-inch pan.
2. Mix flour and sugar; cut in the fat to size of small peas. Take out ¾ cup of the mixture.
3. To the remainder add the baking powder, soda, spices and ¾ cup of the buttermilk; beat until smooth, 2 minutes at medium speed in electric mixer.
4. Add the eggs and remaining milk; beat 1 minute.
5. Pour into pan; add raisins or walnuts to the reserved sugar mixture. Sprinkle evenly over the batter. Bake at 350° for 25-30 minutes.

SPONGE CAKE I

This is a true sponge cake.

4 egg whites	grated rind of ½ lemon
⅔ cup fine granulated sugar	**⅔** cup sifted pastry or cake flour
4 egg yolks	**⅛** teaspoon salt
½ tablespoon lemon juice	

1. Beat egg whites until foamy; gradually add half of sugar and beat after each addition until very stiff.
2. Beat egg yolks with the other half of the sugar and beat until foamy and light in colour.
3. Add lemon juice and rind to yolk mixture and *fold* all into egg white mixture.
4. Sift in dry ingredients and combine lightly with a folding motion.
5. Spoon into an *ungreased* 9-inch tube pan; cut through the batter gently to break up any large air bubbles.
6. Bake at 350° for 40 minutes, until cake springs back when pressed lightly with finger; invert until cool over a funnel; loosen the cake around the edge and ease out.

If left too long in the pan the crust sticks to it.

Sponge Cake may be served with sliced bananas, sauce and ice cream.

SPONGE CAKE II

Cheaper and bigger than Sponge Cake I.

4 egg whites	1¼ cups sifted pastry or cake flour
¼ cup sugar	½ teaspoon salt
4 egg yolks	1 teaspoon baking powder
¼ cup cold water, scant	2 teaspoons lemon juice
½ cup sugar	

Combine as Sponge Cake I. Bake in a 10-inch tube pan.

HOT WATER SPONGE CAKE

Contains no egg whites.

6 egg yolks	½ cup boiling water
1 cup sugar	1½ cups sifted pastry or cake flour
grated rind of ½ lemon	½ teaspoon salt
2 tablespoons lemon juice	2 teaspoons baking powder

1. Beat egg yolks until foamy; beat in the sugar; add lemon juice and rind.
2. Add the boiling water; sift in the dry ingredients and combine.
3. Finish as Sponge Cake I.

BUTTER SPONGE CAKE

1 cup sifted pastry or cake flour	½ cup milk, scalded
1 teaspoon baking powder	6 egg yolks
¼ cup butter	1 cup sugar
½ teaspoon vanilla	

1. Sift together flour and baking powder.
2. Add butter and vanilla to scalded milk and keep hot.
3. Beat egg yolks till thick and lemon-coloured; gradually beat in sugar.
4. Quickly add flour mixture; stir until just mixed. Gently stir in the hot milk mixture.
5. Pour into greased 9-inch cake pan; bake at 350° for 30-35 minutes.

SPONGE FINGERS

1½ cups sifted pastry or cake flour	½ cup boiling water
2 teaspoons baking powder	1 teaspoon lemon extract
¼ teaspoon salt	Butter Icing (page 569)
6 egg yolks	1 cup ground toasted almonds
1 cup sugar	

1. Grease and flour 15 by 10 by 1-inch jelly roll pan.
2. Sift flour, baking powder and salt together.
3. Beat egg yolks until thick and lemon-coloured; add sugar gradually, beating well after each addition.
4. Blend in water and lemon extract slowly; add dry ingredients and blend quickly.
5. Pour into prepared pan and bake at 375° for 15-20 minutes until top springs back when touched lightly in centre. Cool in pan.
6. Cut into small oblong cakes about 1 inch wide and 2½ inches long.

Ice each cake on top and sides with Almond Butter Icing and sprinkle with ground nuts. Makes 60.

ANGEL CAKE

1 cup sifted pastry or cake flour	1 teaspoon cream of tartar
1¼ cups fine sugar, sifted	½ teaspoon vanilla
1 cup egg whites (8-10)	½ teaspoon almond extract
¼ teaspoon salt	

1. Sift flour and ½ cup of sugar twice.
2. Beat egg whites at room temperature and salt until foamy; sift in the cream of tartar and continue beating until whites will stand up in peaks.
3. Sprinkle the remaining sugar over the egg whites, 4 tablespoons at a time, and beat thoroughly after each addition; beat in flavouring.
4. Sift the flour over egg mixture in 4 separate lots, folding in lightly after each addition.
5. Turn mixture into an ungreased 10-inch tube pan; cut through the batter with a knife; level it; bake at 375° until cake is firm to touch and lightly browned (35-45 minutes).
6. Invert cake pan over a funnel. When cool run a knife around the edge, ease out the cake.

CHERRY NUT ANGEL CAKE

Chop finely ½ cup maraschino cherries; drain. Add ½ cup finely chopped almonds or walnuts. Sprinkle a few tablespoons at a time over the batter; fold in.

CHOCOLATE ANGEL CAKE

¾ cup sifted pastry or cake flour	1½ teaspoons cream of tartar
¾ cup sugar	¼ teaspoon salt
¼ cup cocoa	1½ teaspoons vanilla
1½ cups egg whites (about 11)	

Combine as Angel Cake, sifting the cocoa with the flour and half the sugar. Finish as Angel Cake.

GLAZED ANGEL CAKE

Melt ½ cup apricot jam. Spread over top and drizzle down sides of Angel Cake. Sprinkle with toasted almonds and chopped maraschino cherries. Glaze with more jam.

JELLYROLL (Basic Recipe)

4 egg whites, stiffly beaten	¾ cup sifted pastry or cake flour
¾ cup fine sugar	¾ teaspoon baking powder
4 egg yolks	¼ teaspoon salt
½ teaspoon lemon flavouring	icing sugar

1. Beat egg whites until stiff but not dry; beat in sugar gradually and beat until very stiff.
2. Beat egg yolks until very thick and fold into the beaten whites; add lemon flavouring.
3. Mix and sift flour, baking powder and salt onto egg mixture; fold in.
4. Turn into a greased and lined pan 15 by 10 inches and bake at 400° for 10 minutes. Cover with a damp tea towel and cool.

   To finish preparation, see pictures following.

SPICE ROLL

Using Jellyroll (Basic Recipe) sift flour with 1 teaspoon cinnamon, 1 teaspoon cloves; substitute brown sugar, lightly packed, for white sugar.

Jelly Roll: Turn batter into pan which has been greased and lined with waxed paper.

Bake in a preheated oven until cake springs back when lightly touched. Turn out immediately on towel liberally dusted with icing sugar. Remove waxed paper. Roll up in a towel. Cool.

Unroll and spread with jam, jelly or filling. Using towel to guide the cake, reroll. Roll onto serving plate with seam side down. If necessary dust top with icing sugar.

SUNDAE ROLL

Spread Jellyroll with 1 quart softened ice cream; drizzle with ¼ cup butterscotch or chocolate sauce; sprinkle with ¼ cup chopped nuts. Roll up. Freeze.

APPLESAUCE CAKE ROLL

3 eggs	½ teaspoon soda
¾ cup sugar	¼ teaspoon salt
½ cup sweetened applesauce	½ teaspoon cinnamon
½ cup raisins, washed and dried	¼ teaspoon cloves
1 cup sifted pastry or cake flour	icing sugar
½ teaspoon baking powder	

Prepare as Jellyroll, folding the applesauce and raisins into the beaten egg mixture before adding the dry ingredients.

CHOCOLATE ROLL

¾ cup fine sugar	6 tablespoons sifted pastry or
4 egg whites, stiffly beaten	cake flour
4 egg yolks	6 tablespoons cocoa
1 teaspoon vanilla	½ teaspoon baking powder
	¼ teaspoon salt

Prepare as Jellyroll, combining cocoa with dry ingredients.

ORANGE CHIFFON CAKE

This more recent addition to the cake world combines features of both butter and sponge cakes.

1 cup egg whites (7 or 8)	½ cup cooking oil
¼ teaspoon cream of tartar	5 unbeaten egg yolks
2¼ cups sifted pastry or cake flour	grated rind of 2 oranges
1½ cups sugar	juice of 2 oranges, plus water
3 teaspoons double-acting	to make ¾ cup
baking powder	
1 teaspoon salt	

1. In a large bowl beat egg whites and cream of tartar until *very* stiff.
2. Sift together the flour, sugar, baking powder and salt into a mixing bowl.
3. Make a "well" in the dry ingredients, and add oil, egg yolks, orange juice and rind in that order.
4. Beat with a wooden spoon until perfectly smooth.
5. Pour egg yolk mixture gradually over entire surface of beaten egg whites and gently fold until just blended.

6. Pour into an *ungreased* 10-inch tube pan and bake at 325° for 60 minutes. Invert pan to cool cake, loosen with a spatula.

One third of this recipe using 2 egg yolks makes 2 8-inch layers, 1 8-inch square pan or 1 8-inch tube pan.

VANILLA CHIFFON CAKE

½ cup egg whites
¼ teaspoon cream of tartar
¾ cup sugar
¾ cup sifted pastry or cake flour
1½ teaspoon baking powder
⅓ teaspoon salt
¼ cup salad oil
2 egg yolks
¼ cup water
1 teaspoon vanilla

Follow directions for Orange Chiffon Cake. This amount makes 1 8-inch tube pan, 2 8-inch layers or 24 medium cups.

APRICOT CHIFFON CAKE

Follow Orange Chiffon recipe, replacing orange juice and rind with apricot nectar, and adding 1 teaspoon almond extract.

CHRISTMAS STRAWBERRY CAKE

1 package White Cake Mix
4 eggs
1 cup vegetable oil
1 package strawberry jelly powder
½ cup water
½ cup juice from defrosted frozen strawberries

1. Soften the jelly powder in the ½ cup water.
2. Combine all ingredients and blend together in electric mixer for at least 4 minutes.
3. Bake in 3 9-inch layer pans for 30 minutes at 350° or in 1 9-inch tube pan for 50-60 minutes. Ice with Butter Icing (page 569) and Strawberries.

LEMON CAKE

This moist and tender cake keeps well.

1 large package Lemon Cake Mix
1 package lemon instant pudding
4 eggs
⅔ cup oil
¾ cup water

1. Combine all ingredients, beating for 10 minutes with an electric mixer.
2. Pour into 1 ungreased 9-inch tube pan.
3. Bake at 350° for 50-60 minutes.

CUP CAKES

Cup cakes may be made from the Butter Cake, Sponge Cake or Chiffon Cake batters.

1. For well-shaped cup cakes, grease and flour just the bottoms of the muffin pans to keep the batter from running over the pans; have the batter slightly thicker than for cake.
2. Paper liners in the muffin pans save dish-washing. Peel off when the cakes are cool.
3. Never fill the cups more than half full; to be sure, fill one cup with water, measure, then use half this amount of batter in each cup.
4. To use a baking sheet when many cup cakes are being made, fit one paper inside another and space well apart.

LEMON CUP CAKES

With a paring knife remove a cone from the top centre of the cake; fill the hollow with Lemon Filling (page 564). Replace the cone, pressing gently so the filling comes out around the edge. Sift icing sugar thinly over the surface.

BUTTERFLY CUP CAKES

With paring knife, remove cone-shaped piece from top centre of cup cake. Fill hollow with whipped cream or Snowy Lemon Mountain Frosting (page 572). Cut cake cone in half; press into filling to look like butterfly wings.

JELLY-CREAM CUP CAKES

Spread cup cake with whipped cream; dot centre top with a dollop of red jelly. Or spread top of cup cake with jelly; then spread sides with whipped cream or Seven-Minute Frosting (page 571). Or spread cup cake with jelly; then coat sides with shredded coconut; let stand few minutes.

LACY COCOA CUP CAKES

Cut small cardboard pattern of star, tree, etc. Place on top of cup cake; sift chocolate-milk powder over top; carefully lift off pattern.

SHAMROCK CUP CAKES

Snip green gumdrops to form petals and stem of shamrock. Place on top of frosted cup cake.

COCONUT CUP CAKES

Make Boiled Frosting (page 573). Frost top and sides of about 24 cup cakes; then sprinkle generously with flaked coconut. Tint pink for Valentine Cup Cakes.

CLOWN CUP CAKES

Frost top of cup cake with coloured Butter Icing (page 569). Make eyes, nose and mouth from snipped candied cherries. Turn cup cake on side; add colourful hat made of a conical paper cup.

FRUIT CAKES

DARK FRUIT CAKE

1 pound seedless raisins	1 pound butter
1 pound seeded raisins	1 pound sugar
2 pounds currants	8 eggs
1 pound mixed peel, chopped	¾ tablespoon cinnamon
½ pound glazed red and green cherries	¾ tablespoon cloves
	¾ tablespoon nutmeg
1½ pounds dates, chopped	½ teaspoon baking soda
½ pound blanched almonds, walnuts or pecans	½ lemon, juice and rind
3 cups all-purpose flour	½ cup grape or pineapple juice

To this recipe may be added any or all of the following: ⅛ pound glazed pineapple, ½ cup grape jelly, 1 ounce melted chocolate. Currants may be replaced by raisins; dates by citron peel and cherries.

1. Prepare fruit by washing seedless raisins and currants in several waters; dry thoroughly on paper towels in a slow oven or in a warm place; cut cherries in half; split almonds but leave other nuts whole.
2. Mix fruit, nuts and peel with part of the flour so that each piece is separate and coated with flour.
3. Prepare the pans. (This recipe makes 1 3-tiered cake, or 2 large cakes, or 4 loaf pans, about 12 pounds in all.) Wrap the cake pans with corrugated paper and set them on a sheet of corrugated paper on a baking sheet; check to see that they will fit into the oven without touching. Line with greased brown paper or aluminum foil.
4. Cream butter, add sugar gradually, beating after each addition. This requires a very large mixing bowl; a plastic dish pan is a good size.
5. Beat eggs well and add to butter mixture.
6. Sift remaining flour with spices and soda; add alternately with fruit juice to the butter mixture.
7. Stir in fruit and mix until all ingredients are thoroughly blended.
8. Pour into prepared cake pans. Bake cakes slowly at 250° until cake no longer sizzles and is firm when pressed firmly with finger. A pan of water placed in the oven at the beginning of the baking time should be dry and ready to be removed at half time. This keeps the cake from drying on top. The large cake takes 3 hours, the medium ones 2 hours and the small ones about 1 hour.

9. After baking, the cake should be thoroughly cooled on a rack, then wrapped in aluminum foil and stored in a cake box. Brandy or sherry may be poured on cake from time to time for added flavour. In this case, do not wrap cake tightly. A fine knitting needle may be used to poke a few fine holes into the cake, and the brandy poured down the holes. Another method is to wrap the cake in a piece of flannel and pour the brandy onto the cloth.

LIGHT FRUIT CAKE I

1 pound golden seeded raisins
4½ to 5½-ounce package citron peel
4 to 5-ounce package orange peel
4 to 5-ounce package lemon peel
½ pound glazed red and green pineapple
½ pound glazed red and green cherries
1 cup dessicated coconut
4-ounce package blanched almonds

2¾ cups all-purpose flour
1 teaspoon baking powder
½ teaspoon mace or nutmeg
½ pound butter (1 cup)
1 cup sugar
3 eggs
½ cup warm water
1 teaspoon almond extract
1 teaspoon rose flavouring (if concentrated, use less)

1. Clean raisins, slice peel and pineapple thinly, halve cherries; combine with coconut.
2. Mix and sift flour, baking powder and spice and add half to prepared fruit.
3. In a large bowl, cream shortening and gradually beat in sugar.
4. Add well-beaten eggs and beat well.
5. Fold in other half of the sifted dry ingredients alternately with warm water and beat well.
6. Add fruit to flour mixture and combine mixture until thoroughly blended. Split almonds and add to mixture. Add flavouring.
7. Pour mixture into cake pans which have been lined with 3 thicknesses of newspaper, with a top layer of greased wax paper; or wrap tins as for Dark Fruit Cake.
8. Bake cakes at 275° for approximately 3 hours or until firm and until cake mixture is firm when pressed.
9. Cool on cake rack until thoroughly cold. Wrap in foil and store in a cake tin. Makes 1 large cake, about 6 pounds.

Light Fruit Cake.

LIGHT FRUIT CAKE II

More cake but less fruit.

2 pounds golden seeded raisins	5 cups all-purpose flour
1 pound red and green glazed cherries	1 teaspoon baking powder
½ teaspoon nutmeg	
½ pound red and green glazed pineapples	1 orange (juice and rind)
1 pound butter and shortening	
1 pound almonds, blanched	1 pound sugar
1 teaspoon each of lemon, almond and rose extract	10 eggs

Prepare as Light Fruit Cake I, substituting orange juice for water. Makes 2 large or 1 large and 2 loaf tins.

FRUIT CAKE GLAZE

Used to hold candied fruits in place on top of a fruit cake.

1 cup sugar	½ cup corn syrup
½ cup water	

1. Mix and cook ingredients in a saucepan until mixture forms a soft ball when a little is dropped into cold water or until mixture reaches 230°.
2. Cool slightly; spread on cake when it comes out of the oven.
3. While moist, arrange garnish of candied fruits and nuts; brush with the glaze.

BRAZIL NUT CAKE

3 cups whole brazil nuts	¾ cup sifted all-purpose flour
1 cup glazed red cherries	¾ cup sugar
1 cup glazed green cherries	½ teaspoon baking powder
1 package dates (1 pound pitted whole)	½ teaspoon salt
	1 teaspoon vanilla
3 eggs	

1. Line a 9 by 3 by 2½-inch loaf pan with heavy brown paper; grease it. Heat oven to 300°.
2. Combine the nuts and fruit, uncut. Add the well-beaten eggs.
3. Mix and sift the dry ingredients; combine the two mixtures.
4. Bake in loaf pan 1¾ to 2 hours. Have a pan of water in the oven on the rack below the cake.
5. Cool, wrap in foil; do not cut for several weeks.

LEFTOVER CAKE

LEMON CAKE PUDDING: Crumble cake into crumbs and combine with left-over fruits. Serve with lemon sauce.

TRIFLE: See page 589.

ANGEL DESSERT: Combine broken pieces of chocolate or angel food cake with marshmallow pieces, cubes of pineapple, chopped nuts, maraschino cherries and whipped cream. Chill for 1 hour.

CHOCOLATE REFRIGERATOR CAKE: Melt 2 squares of semi-sweet chocolate and add 1½ cups evaporated milk, stirring until thick. Add ½ cup water. Line a cake pan with waxed paper and place in it a layer of left-over cake, cut in 1-inch squares. Pour half the sauce on this layer; then add another layer of cake and top with remaining sauce. Chill overnight in refrigerator, unmould and serve topped with whipped cream.

CHOCOLATE FONDUE: Arrange cubes of cake, marshmallows, fresh or canned fruit. Guests spear the food with fondue forks and dip into hot Chocolate Sauce (page 98). Twice the recipe serves 6.

BANANA SANDWICH: Place whipped cream or ice cream and sliced bananas between 2 cake slices; top with butterscotch sauce.

TEA TOASTIES: Spread cake slices with butter or margarine; sprinkle with sugar cinnamon mix; broil till bubbly and brown.

FRENCH TOAST DESSERT: Dip cake slices in French toast mixture; sauté in butter or margarine; serve with jelly, maple syrup, or sprinkling of icing sugar.

ENGLISH CRUMB MOLD: Grease 1-quart casserole; fill with alternate layers of cake crumbs and applesauce or stewed fruit. Press down; chill. Serve with hot lemon sauce.

FROZEN CAKE BALLS: Roll balls of ice cream in cake crumbs. Top with chocolate, butterscotch, or fruit sauce.

COOKIE CANDIES: For every cup of cake crumbs, melt 1/3 cup semi-sweet chocolate pieces; add rum flavouring to taste; mix with crumbs. Form into 3/4-inch balls; roll balls in chopped nuts, coconut, or chocolate shot.

CHOCOLATE TIDBITS: With fork, dip 1-inch fruit cake cubes into melted semi-sweet chocolate, covering all sides except bottoms; place on cookie sheet; sprinkle with chopped pecans. Chill until chocolate sets.

STEAMED PUDDING: Wrap *white cake* slices in foil; heat. Serve with coffee ice cream, or hot lemon sauce. *Heat ginerbread*; serve with lemon sauce, or applesauce. Heat *chocolate cake* slices spread with cream cheese, spoon over them canned cherry pie filling.

18 Cake Fillings and Frostings

FILLINGS

LAYER CAKES gain extra richness from fillings: sweetened whipped cream filling or icing made for frosting and filling. Spread generously on cooled cake and allow filling to become firm before applying icing. Cakes baked in deep pans may be split into layers and spread with filling.

CREAM FILLING (Basic Recipe)

For Cream Pie Filling see recipe on page 480.

¾ cup milk	¼ cup milk
⅓ cup sugar	2 eggs or 4 yolks
2 tablespoons cornstarch	1 tablespoon melted butter
⅛ teaspoon salt	½ teaspoon vanilla

1. Heat ¾ cup milk in a saucepan over low heat or in the top of a double boiler over hot water.
2. Mix sugar, cornstarch and salt in a small bowl; add ¼ cup milk and stir until smooth.
3. Add hot milk slowly to the cornstarch mixture, return to heat, stirring constantly until thick; continue to cook, stirring occasionally until there is no flavour of raw starch.
4. Beat the eggs slightly with a fork; add half the cooked mixture; blend and return to pan; add butter. Stir until thick.
5. Remove from heat; cool, stirring occasionally to prevent a skin forming on top; add flavouring; chill in a covered dish before using. This amount fills one 8 or 9-inch layer cake.

Quick Cream Filling: Prepare packaged cornstarch pudding and pie filling as the label directs, reducing the liquid to 1½ cups.

Glamour Touches: Fold into the cooled filling any combination of the following: ½-1 cup whipped cream; ½ cup chopped nuts (walnuts, pecans, toasted almonds); ½ cup fruit (finely cut dates, well-drained crushed pineapple, chopped cherries).

CHOCOLATE FILLING

Reduce cornstarch to 1½ tablespoons, increase sugar to ½ cup, add ¾ ounce bitter chocolate, finely cut, to the heated milk, or 3 tablespoons cocoa to the dry ingredients.

BUTTERSCOTCH FILLING

Substitute brown for white sugar. If the acid in the brown sugar causes the milk to curdle, beating the mixture after the egg is added will overcome this.

WHIPPED CREAM FILLING (Basic Recipe)

This filling may be used to frost a cake; refrigerate iced cake until serving time.

½ pint whipping cream	flavouring:
1 to 2 tablespoons fine sugar	½ teaspoon vanilla or
	1 tablespoon instant coffee or
	¼ cup chocolate syrup or
	coffee and chocolate syrup

Whip cream until fluffy; add sugar and flavouring; continue beating until stiff.

Glamour Touch: squeeze some of the filling through a pastry tube onto waxed paper on a baking sheet, making rosettes.

Freeze and store in plastic bag to use as a decoration on cake and filling.

CHOCOLATE FLECK WHIPPED CREAM

Melt 2 tablespoons semi-sweet chocolate over hot water; cool to room temperature so that it will fleck as it is folded into Whipped Cream Filling.

FRUIT CREAM FILLING (Basic Recipe)

½ tablespoon gelatine
½ cup cold water

1 cup crushed pineapple,
  undrained
1 cup whipping cream (½ pint)

1. Soften gelatine in cold water; dissolve over low heat; stir into fruit; chill until the mixture begins to set.
2. Whip the cream; fold in; chill until almost set.

STRAWBERRY CREAM FILLING

Substitute 1 cup defrosted, drained frozen strawberries for pineapple, or use fresh strawberries, sliced and sweetened.

RASPBERRY CREAM FILLING

Substitute 1 cup defrosted, drained raspberries or sweetened fresh berries for pineapple.

PEPPERMINT CREAM FILLING

Melt ½ pound crushed peppermint stick candy in ½ cup milk; use this to replace the fruit.

ANGEL CREAM FILLING

Add ¼ pound quartered marshmallows, ½ cup blanched toasted almonds, ¼ cup chopped maraschino cherries to the pineapple.

APRICOT CREAM FILLING

Soak 1 cup dried apricots in 1 cup water; cook slowly, uncovered, until soft; purée, blend or beat smooth; add ⅔ cup sugar; substitute 1 cup sweetened purée for pineapple. (Add 1 tablespoon lemon juice if desired.) The baby food variety of puréed apricots could also be used.

CHARLOTTE RECIPES

Charlotte recipes to be found in Desserts, Chapter 19, may also be used to fill and frost cakes.

LEMON FILLING

This recipe is stiff and not sufficient in quantity for a pie. For Lemon Pie Filling, see page 481.

⅔ cup water	⅛ teaspoon salt
grated rind of lemon	2 eggs or 4 yolks
⅓ cup sugar	juice of 1 lemon, or
2 tablespoons cornstarch	⅓ cup frozen lemon juice

Follow the method for Cream Filling (Basic Recipe), adding the lemon juice after the egg has thickened.

Packaged Lemon Pudding and Pie Filling may be substituted, reducing liquid by ¼-⅓ cup; the amount will vary with different brands.

ORANGE FILLING

Follow the recipe for Lemon Filling, reducing the water to ½ cup and substituting orange rind and ½ cup orange juice.

DATE FILLING

This filling keeps well in the refrigerator and may be used between cookies (page 516) or as a Sandwich Filling (page 345).

½ pound dates	¼ cup sugar
1 cup water	

Cut dates into small pieces. Add water; cook over low heat until mixture is quite thick, stirring often to prevent scorching; add sugar; cool.

Use grated rind and juice of 1 orange, or ¼ cup of undiluted frozen orange juice, to replace an equal amount of the water, adding the juice to the cooked fruit.

Add ½ cup chopped walnuts to the cooked mixture.

APRICOT FILLING

½ cup sugar	¼ cup undiluted frozen orange
3 tablespoons cornstarch	juice
	1 cup cooked apricot pulp

1. Combine the sugar and cornstarch; add the orange juice.
2. Heat the sieved or mashed apricots; add the first mixture, stirring constantly.
3. Bring to a boil; boil 1 minute; cool.

PRUNE FILLING

1 package (12 ounces) prunes	¾ teaspoon crushed cardamom
1 cup water	seed
¾ cup sugar	¼ teaspoon salt

1. Add water to prunes; simmer until very tender.
2. Measure ½ cup liquid; add other ingredients.
3. Stone and beat or blend prunes; add liquid; blend well.

MARSHMALLOW CREAM FILLING

¾ cup sugar	16 marshmallows, quartered
¼ cup water	2 egg whites, stiffly beaten
⅓ cup light corn syrup	

1. Cook sugar, water and corn syrup together in a saucepan at 240° until it spins a long thread when dropped from a spoon.
2. Remove from heat immediately; drop in marshmallows.
3. Pour over stiffly beaten egg whites gradually, beating constantly; beat until completely smooth.
   Filling will keep several weeks in a covered jar in the refrigerator.

LEMON CUSTARD FILLING

1 tablespoon (1 envelope)	¾ cup lemon juice
unflavoured gelatine	1½ teaspoons grated lemon rind
¼ cup cold water	6 egg whites
6 beaten egg yolks	¾ cup sugar
¾ cup sugar	few drops yellow colouring

1. Soften gelatine in cold water.
2. Combine egg yolks, ¾ cup sugar, lemon juice and rind; stir over hot water until mixture coats spoon; remove from heat; add gelatine.
3. Cool until partially set.
4. Beat egg whites; beat in the remaining ¾ cup sugar; add yellow food colouring; beat into chilled custard. This amount will fill two 9-inch layers for Cream Pie (page 480).
   If convenient, plan to make up enough Lemon Custard Filling to make an Angel Mould (page 617) for the freezer.

BROILED FILLING

The Oven Frostings recipes (page 577) may be used to make a quick filling and frosting for layer cakes. Spread the filling out to the edges on both layers. Place one layer in the oven and broil until bubbly; leave to cool while the second is broiled. Place this layer on the cake plate and on top of it place the cooled layer.

LEMON BUTTER OR LEMON CHEESE FILLING

¾ cup sugar
    juice of 1 large lemon

1 egg
2 tablespoons butter

1. Combine all the ingredients; cook over low heat, stirring until thick; pour into small jar; cover tightly; refrigerate. This makes about 6 ounces and keeps very well.

2. Use it to fill tiny tart shells; as a filling for layer cake; on a cheese tray. Fold mayonnaise into it for a fruit salad dressing; serve on lengthwise-sliced bananas sprinkled with chopped nuts, as a quick salad.

FROSTINGS, ICINGS AND GLAZES

The frosting is the crowning glory for a cake—and a new frosting can give a new look to the family's favourite cake. Always consider the length of time the cake must stand before serving when choosing the type of frosting to be used.

Icing sugar alone can be used to decorate a baked cake—especially sponge cakes. For a dainty design, place a paper doilie on cake and sift icing sugar over it lightly. Remove doilie carefully and its pattern will be traced on the cake.

FACTS TO CONSIDER WHEN ICING CAKES

1. A cake should be cold before icing. Turn right side up.
2. Ice cake on a rack or cake plate; cake plate should be protected by 4 strips of paper placed so that they overlap; when paper is pulled out after cake has been iced, the cake plate will be free of icing.

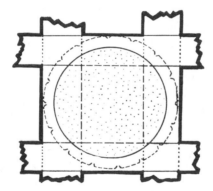

3. To ice the top of a cake only, fasten a strip of glazed paper around the cake, having it extend ¾ inch above the top of cake; pour on the frosting. When it is set, remove the paper, using a knife dipped in boiling water.
4. Heating the knife in hot water from time to time while icing the cake helps to keep icing soft for spreading.
5. Spread with quick, broad strokes. Overworking causes a rough, dull surface.
6. A fruit cake should be brushed over with white of egg, which should be allowed to dry before putting on an icing. This is to prevent the icing from being darkened.

Cakes iced and decorated in a variety of ways.

UNCOOKED ICINGS

BUTTER ICING (Basic Recipe)

3-5 tablespoons butter or
margarine
2 cups icing sugar
(approximately)

3 tablespoons milk
flavouring

1. Cream the butter with 2 tablespoons sugar; add liquid gradually.
2. Sift in remaining sugar to make it thick enough to spread.
3. Add flavouring or colouring.
4. Cover with a damp tea towel if it is not to be used immediately.

FLAVOUR: Vanilla is a popular flavouring but there are many others. Any flavouring should be used sparingly. Drop it onto a teaspoon so that any excess may be returned to the bottle. More can always be added but if too much has been added the only way to save the icing is to make a second recipe omitting the flavouring and then to combine the two. The unused icing, if tightly covered, will keep well in a refrigerator.

COLOUR: Colouring, like flavouring, needs to be used with care. To the basic icing add food colouring a drop at a time. The colour will appear slightly darker in the bowl; too much colour is unattractive. Try a little green fruit colouring with peppermint, cherry juice or red colouring with fruit, raw egg or yellow for a rich creamy colour. For an attractive colour when a pastry tube is being used add a little red and a little yellow colouring but do not thoroughly blend them.

QUICK TRICKS

Double the recipe; refrigerate ½. The next time a cake is baked place a large spoonful of the cold icing on the hot cake. Spread the icing as it begins to melt to give a thin glossy glaze.

Double the recipe before the flavouring or colouring is added; refrigerate ½ in a covered container. Before the icing is needed remove it from the refrigerator; when warm stir in colour and flavour for any of the following variations.

ORANGE OR LEMON BUTTER ICING

Replace the milk with frozen concentrate, thawed but not diluted, or with fresh juice.

CHOCOLATE BUTTER ICING

Sift ¼ cup cocoa with sugar, or melt ½-1 square unsweetened chocolate with the butter over low heat. Try anise, peppermint or maple flavouring to replace vanilla.

Butter Icings.

COFFEE BUTTER ICING

Replace milk with strong, fresh, cold coffee or sift ½ tablespoon instant coffee with the sugar.

MOCHA BUTTER ICING

This is a combination of the chocolate and coffee icings. Use only enough cocoa to give a light colour—1-1½ tablespoons.

RUM BUTTER ICING

Add chopped nuts, dates or raisins to basic recipe. Use rum flavouring to replace vanilla.

CARAMEL BUTTER ICING

Melt 1 cup (6 ounces) caramel chips over low heat; cool; add to butter. Or add Caramel Sauce to replace milk (recipe page 96).

COCONUT BUTTER ICING

Use coconut milk as the liquid; sprinkle icing with fresh, grated coconut.

PEANUT BUTTER ICING

Use 2 tablespoons peanut butter to replace 1 tablespoon butter.

ORNAMENTAL FROSTING

3 egg whites
1 pound icing sugar

1 tablespoon lemon juice or
8 to 9 drops acetic acid

1. Put unbeaten whites into a large bowl; sift in icing sugar; beat vigorously with a wooden spoon.
2. Add lemon juice or acetic acid; beat until stiff Test by cutting through the icing with a knife; if stiff enough, it will hold its shape. More liquid may be required.

   This icing is suitable only for decorating with pastry tubes.

COOKED ICINGS

SEVEN-MINUTE FROSTING (Basic Recipe)

Seven-Minute is a stiff, glossy white frosting made by cooking egg white and sugar while beating constantly until it forms stiff peaks. By hand, this beating takes about 7 minutes, hence its name. Using an electric beater cuts down on both time and effort. The presence of corn syrup, sugar or acid (lemon juice or cream of tartar) is necessary to prevent the formation of large crystals, which results in sugary icing. Cakes iced with Seven-Minute Icing should be used on the day on which they are iced.

1½ cups sugar
2 egg whites
2 tablespoons corn syrup
½ cup cold water

flavouring (vanilla, almond, peppermint, etc.)
¼ teaspoon cream of tartar **may** replace corn syrup

1. Combine all together in top of double boiler; let stand until sugar is partly dissolved. Beat until well mixed.
2. Place over boiling water and beat until the mixture forms peaks which hold their shape (4 to 7 minutes). Stir from bottom and sides with a rubber spatula.
3. Remove from heat; set the top of the double boiler in cool water, and continue to beat until the icing is cool. Spread quickly with as few strokes as possible. This amount will cover sides and top of an 8 or 9-inch layer cake, or 2 dozen small cupcakes. ½ the recipe will frost the top only of an 8-inch cake.

SNOWY LEMON MOUNTAIN FROSTING

Replace corn syrup by 3 tablespoons lemon juice; add ¼ teaspoon grated rind.

MOUNTAIN FROSTING

Replace white sugar with brown sugar; reduce corn syrup by ½.

PRUNE FROSTING

Add 1 cup chopped cooked prunes, sift ¼ teaspoon cinnamon over the frosted cake.

COCONUT FROSTING

Tint icing delicate pink or green, sprinkle 1 cup flaked coconut over the frosting while soft, or leave icing white and tint coconut by combining it with grated orange or lemon rind and 1 tablespoon juice. Let the coloured coconut dry slightly before sprinkling onto the icing.

CANDY CANE FROSTING

Add ¼ cup crushed candy canes. Garnish with bits of crushed candy.

BURNT SUGAR FROSTING

Reduce sugar to 1¼ cups, water to ¼ cup, replace corn syrup with 3-4 tablespoons Burnt Sugar Syrup (see back endpaper).

PASTEL JELLY FROSTING

This frosting does not keep well but it is pretty and easy. Let the children make it.

½ cup tart jelly	⅛ teaspoon salt
1 egg white	

1. Combine the ingredients in the top section of a double boiler. Place over hot, not boiling water.
2. Beat over low heat until the frosting is just smooth; remove from the heat, and continue beating until the frosting stands up in peaks.

BOILED FROSTING (Basic Recipe)

This recipe is worth a little practice. Use the same saucepan each time.

1 cup white sugar	⅓ cup boiling water
⅛ teaspoon cream of tartar or	1 egg white
1 tablespoon corn syrup	flavouring

1. Place sugar, cream of tartar and water in a saucepan; stir, over low heat, until sugar is dissolved.
2. Boil gently at 240° without stirring, until syrup forms a thread about 6 inches long when dropped from a spoon.
3. When syrup is almost ready, beat egg white until foamy, using egg beater.
4. Pour syrup gradually in a pencil-like stream into the mixture, beating constantly with egg-beater until mixture begins to thicken.
5. Beat with a wooden spoon until cool and of spreading consistency. This quantity will frost one 8-inch cake; twice the recipe makes frosting and filling for two 9-inch layers, or about 50 small cup cakes.

See also Seven-Minute Frosting for variations.

CHOCOLATE RIPPLE

Ice cake with Boiled Frosting. Melt 2 squares of unsweetened chocolate with 1 teaspoon butter. Using a spoon, drip the chocolate around top edge of cake and let chocolate run down sides. Or swirl the chocolate over the frosting with a broad spatula.

MARSHMALLOW

Make Boiled Frosting; cut 8 marshmallows in pieces; add to syrup just before beating it into white of egg.

PINEAPPLE

Replace water with pineapple juice. Fold into the cooked icing ¾ cup drained crushed pineapple, cherries, coconut and almonds.

LADY BALTIMORE

Use ½ teaspoon rum flavouring, add ½ cup chopped pecans, raisins and figs to the finished icing.

SEA FOAM

Replace white sugar with brown, reduce corn syrup or cream of tartar by ½.

Clown Cake: A birthday party treat for a little boy. Chocolate layer cake with ice cream cone perched on a cup cake make the outline. Snowy frosting is rippled to make the ruffled collar.

FUDGE FROSTINGS

CHOCOLATE FUDGE FROSTING

2 cups sugar	2 tablespoons corn syrup
1 cup water	¼ teaspoon salt
2 1-ounce squares unsweetened chocolate	2 tablespoons butter
	1 teaspoon vanilla

1. Cook sugar, water, chocolate, corn syrup and salt over low heat. Stir until sugar dissolves.
2. Cook to the soft ball stage (when a drop of syrup forms a soft ball in cold water) or to a temperature of 236°.
3. Remove from heat; add butter and cool to lukewarm.
4. Add vanilla and beat until icing is of spreading consistency. If icing becomes too stiff, add a little boiling water.
   Enough for 2 layers; ½ recipe will frost 1 8-inch cake.

CARAMEL FUDGE ICING

1½ cups brown sugar	3 tablespoons butter
½ cup milk	½ teaspoon vanilla
¼ teaspoon salt	

1. Mix sugar, milk and salt in a saucepan.
2. Boil slowly to soft ball stage or 236° when a little, dropped into cold water, forms a soft ball.
3. Add butter and cool to lukewarm.
4. Add vanilla and beat until mixture is of spreading consistency.
5. Thin icing with a little cream if it becomes too thick.

EASY FROSTINGS

EASY BOILED FROSTING

¾ cup light corn syrup	salt
2 egg whites	1 teaspoon vanilla

1. Heat the syrup in a small saucepan to boiling.
2. Sprinkle salt into the egg whites; beat stiff but not dry.
3. Slowly pour the syrup over the egg whites, beating with the egg beater until the frosting is fluffy and hangs in peaks from the beater.
4. Add vanilla; continue to beat until cool enough to spread.

CHOCOMALLOW FROSTING

6 ounces semi-sweet chocolate	½ cup milk
¼ pound marshmallows (16)	1 cup heavy cream

1. Heat chocolate, marshmallows and milk in a double boiler; heat slowly, stirring occasionally, until blended; chill.
2. Fold in the cream, whipped. Makes 3 cups.

PETIT FOUR FROSTING

This is a quick method. True petit four icing is difficult to prepare in family quantities because it hardens too quickly.

2 tablespoons red currant jelly	red food colouring
sifted icing sugar	small cup cakes or cut squares

1. Heat the jelly in a double boiler over hot water until melted; remove from the heat and add icing sugar to give a thin runny consistency; add food colouring to obtain a pale tint. Keep over hot water while using it.
2. Place the cakes on a wire rack over waxed paper; spoon the icing over 1 at a time, allowing the icing to drip down the sides. If it drips off completely, allowing the cake to show through, add a little more icing sugar. If it thickens, add a few drops of boiling water.
3. When the sides and tops are coated, decorate as desired.
   Other jellies, such as cinnamon apple, mint, black currant or grape may be used to vary the colour and flavour.

Christmas Tree Cake: With a sharp knife, zig-zag cut a 13 by 9-inch cake from corner to corner.

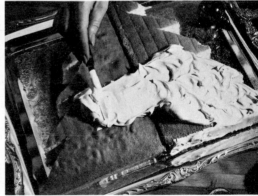

Turn one half top side down, and match long edges to give Christmas Tree. Frost and decorate.

OVEN FROSTINGS

PRALINE GLAZE (BROILED FROSTING) (Basic Recipe)

¼ cup softened butter	¼ chopped nuts
½ cup brown sugar	¾ cup coconut
3 tablespoons cream or rich milk	

1. Cream butter, add sugar and cream. Spread over top of baked cake.
2. Sprinkle coconut and nuts over the cake.
3. Place in the oven about 3 to 4 inches below upper element and broil 3 to 5 minutes. Watch carefully to prevent burning.

LEMON COCONUT

Omit nuts and add 1 teaspoon lemon rind; increase coconut to 1 cup.

PEANUT

Replace nuts and coconut by ¾ cup chopped salted peanuts and 3 tablespoons peanut butter.

HONEY COCONUT

Replace cream and nuts by ⅓ cup honey.

SOUR CREAM

Use sour cream to replace the milk.

PINEAPPLE

Drain pineapple tidbits; dip into the glaze, cover the cake with the remaining glaze, arrange the pineapple in a sunburst effect at least 1 inch from the edge. Broil.

MARSHMALLOW

Replace coconut with 1 cup miniature marshmallows.

ORANGE MARSHMALLOW

Cover with orange marmalade; arrange miniature marshmallows on top. Broil 6 inches from the heat until the marshmallows begin to melt slightly.

MARBLE FROSTING

Leave the cake in the pan. While hot cover the surface evenly with chocolate peppermints. As they meet spread with swirling motions.

CRUNCH TOPPING

This is an upside-down topping.

⅓ cup butter	¼ cup chopped nuts
½ cup graham cracker crumbs	½ cup butterscotch morsels

1. Melt butter in 9-inch square cake pan.
2. Combine crumbs and nuts and sprinkle them over the butter; cover evenly with butterscotch morsels.
3. Pour batter of One-Egg Cake (page 539) over the mixture. Bake at 350° for 40-50 minutes.
4. Remove from oven; let stand 5 minutes; invert onto cake plate and let stand a few minutes before lifting off the pan.

GLAZES

VANILLA GLAZE (Basic Recipe)

Heat 1 tablespoon milk and 1 tablespoon butter in a bowl over hot water; sift in icing sugar to a creamy consistency (about 1 cup); add ½ teaspoon vanilla. The consistency should be a bit thicker if the cake is still warm.

BURNT SUGAR

Substitute burnt sugar syrup for the milk.

COFFEE

Mix 2 teaspoons instant coffee powder with the hot milk.

ALMOND

Add ½ teaspoon almond extract and omit vanilla.

ORANGE OR LEMON

Stir in 1 teaspoon grated orange or lemon rind and use orange juice in place of milk.

BRANDY

Substitute 1 tablespoon brandy for the vanilla.

CHOCOLATE GLAZE

2 tablespoons butter	1 cup icing sugar
2 ounces unsweetened chocolate	3 tablespoons hot milk

1. Melt butter and chocolate over hot water.

2. Add sugar and gradually stir in hot milk.
3. Spoon the warm glaze over the cooled Cream Puff (page 502), or dip the top of the puff into the glaze. Glazes 1 dozen large Cream Puffs, 4 dozen small.

CARAMEL GLAZE

¾ cup white sugar	¼ cup butter
⅛ teaspoon salt	¾ cup light cream
½ cup dark corn syrup	½ teaspoon vanilla

Combine all ingredients in a heavy saucepan; stir over high heat until mixture comes to a boil; turn heat low and cook to the soft ball stage (236°), stirring occasionally. Cool and flavour with vanilla. Spoon over the puff or dip the top of the puff into the glaze. Glazes 1 dozen.

CAKE DECORATING

A variety of attractive garnishes may be made with very little effort.

TRIM WITH COCONUT: Coconut may be used plain, either shredded or flaked, toasted by stirring with a fork over low heat, coloured by shaking a teaspoon of water to which food colour has been added with coconut in a jar, flavoured by shaking with frozen fruit juice, undiluted.

TRIM WITH CANDIES: Cinnamon hearts, crushed candy canes, sliced gum drops moulded into petals, life savers, chocolate bits.

TRIM WITH NUTS: Whole, chopped or slivered nuts, plain or toasted, are always attractive. Brazil nuts dropped into boiling water for a few minutes may be shaved with a potato peeler into loose curls.

TRIM WITH CHOCOLATE: Melted chocolate, either semi-sweet or bitter, may be swirled or dribbled over coloured icing. For Chocolate shadow, arrange in straight lines; dip a knife in hot water; draw through the chocolate at even intervals. For a Spider Web effect, put a little chocolate in the middle to represent the spider. Around it drip 4 concentric circles. Draw a silver knife through these circles from centre to edge, first dividing the surface in 4, then dividing each quarter into 3. Drip a little chocolate around the edge. Melted chocolate brushed onto maple leaves may be peeled off when chilled.

Semi-sweet chocolate melted (always over hot water) and spread in a layer of ⅛ inch on wax paper and allowed to harden in the refrigerator may be cut with tiny truffle cutters and lifted onto the cake.

Semi-sweet chocolate allowed to soften but not melt may be shaved with a potato peeler into curls.

Chocolate Torte decorated with a Spider Web. Napoleons trimmed with Chocolate Shadow (Mille Feuilles). (Bottom) Chocolate Maple Leaves. Eggnog Chiffon Pie trimmed with Chocolate Curls.

TRIM WITH FRUIT: Glazed or maraschino cherries, both red and green, are useful for flowers and leaves. Bits of pineapple, peel, slivered dates or apricots add colour. Angelica, on sale at Christmas, makes realistic leaves.

TRIM WITH A CAKE DECORATOR: If a large cake is to be decorated, a plastic or canvas bag and an assortment of decorating tips will be necessary. With these will come directions for use. Practice will do the rest. However, when several colours are needed in small amounts to add a little glamour, paper tubes will do very well.

Prepare a recipe of Basic Butter Icing (page 569), being sure the sugar is sifted and that nothing is added that would block the tube. The icing must be firm enough to hold its shape. Divide the icing into small bowls and add the colouring. More interesting effects will be obtained if the colour is not evenly blended; avoid either too bright or too pale tints.

To fold a paper tube, use a square of good white writing paper or for larger tubes tracing paper, parchment paper, freezer paper or butcher's wax paper.

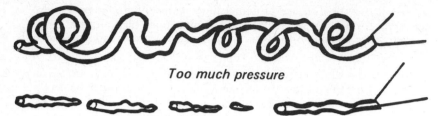

Too much pressure

Too little pressure or moving tip too rapidly

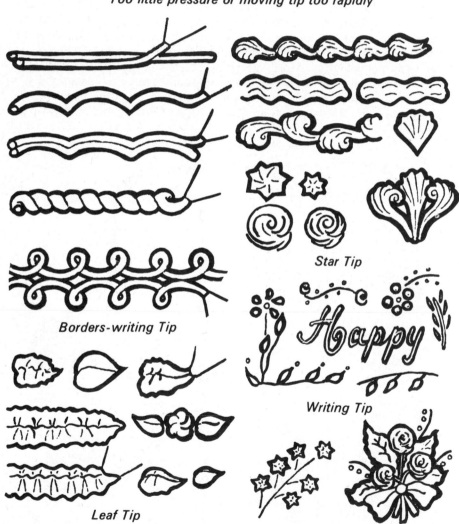

Star Tip

Borders-writing Tip

Writing Tip

Leaf Tip

Two or more tips

Divide the square into 2 triangles. Place 1 triangle with the point to the right and the long edge directly ahead. Place the first finger of the left hand at the centre of the long edge. Pick up point A and roll it away from you over the finger, bringing A to C. Holding A and C firmly between thumb and first finger, lift the tube from the table and roll B forward and over the roll to meet A and C. Slide A, B, and C back and forth until the point D is closed and right. Fasten the 3 points together by rolling the top of the tube forward inside the cone.

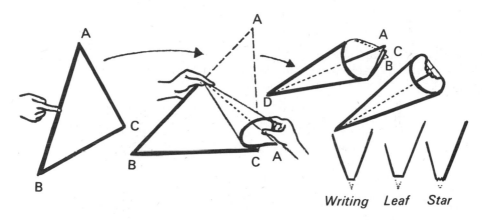

Writing   Leaf   Star

Clip the point of the cone straight off for writing, from the point up each side for a leaf and across in points for a star.

To use the tube, place a teaspoon of icing well down in the tube. Roll the folded points over the top of the cone toward the point, exerting pressure with the right hand and guiding the tip with the fingers of the left. Keep the point close to the surface of the cake and move the tube slowly. Turn the cake rather than trying to move the tube too far.

In this chapter may be found desserts for every occasion, of all degrees of richness, to please every palate. They should be chosen to complement the rest of the meal without repeating either texture or flavour.

Baked Custard in individual dishes. Hot water is placed in the pan halfway up the level of the custard.

BAKED CUSTARD (Basic Recipe)

2 cups milk	⅛ teaspoon salt
3-4 eggs or 5-8 yolks, or	¾ teaspoon vanilla
2 eggs and 4 yolks	¼ teaspoon cinnamon
⅓ to ½ cup sugar	

1. Heat the milk; heat the oven to 300°.
2. Beat the eggs slightly; add the sugar, salt and vanilla.

3. Add the milk slowly, stirring constantly; strain into custard cups or baking dish; if desired, sprinkle with cinnamon.

4. Set dish in a baking pan in the oven; add hot water to the pan half way up to the level of the custard; add cold water if necessary, to keep the water from boiling. After 30 minutes, test by inserting the point of a paring knife; if it comes out clean, the custard is cooked and should be immediately removed from the hot water and set in lukewarm water to prevent curdling the custard by over-cooking. Serves 5.

    Custard can be cooked in the pressure cooker if wrapped with 2 layers of waxed paper, securely tied with a string. Follow the directions for using the pressure cooker, using ½ cup water and 15 pounds pressure for 3 minutes. Cool quickly.

BROWN SUGAR CUSTARD

Replace white sugar with ½ cup dark brown sugar, firmly packed.

MAPLE CUSTARD

Substitute ½ cup maple syrup for the sugar.

LEMON CUSTARD

Add 1 teaspoon grated lemon rind to the strained mixture; replace cinnamon with nutmeg or mace.

CHOCOLATE CUSTARD

Cook 4 ounces semi-sweet chocolate, finely chopped, with ½ cup water until smooth; add to the hot milk.

CARAMEL CUSTARD

In the bottom of each custard cup place 1 tablespoon caramel syrup or thick maple syrup; carefully pour the custard mixture down the side of the cup. Bake as above; refrigerate overnight. To serve, loosen the custard with a knife; invert on serving dish; sprinkle with toasted almonds. In a large baking dish use ½ cup caramel syrup.

CRÈME BRULÉE

1. Replace milk with cereal cream.

2. Bake in a large dish in which the custard is 2-3 inches deep. Cool several hours; just before serving set the custard in a pan of crushed ice; sprinkle a layer ⅛-inch thick of dark brown sugar or crushed maple sugar over the custard; broil until sugar melts, watching carefully that it does not burn. Allow the melted sugar to harden to a glass-like covering; crack with a spoon before serving.

Crème Brulée—an old-fashioned treat.

SABOYAN

A favourite Italian dessert.

6 egg yolks	2 cups dry sherry, Marsala or
½ pound icing sugar	Madeira
	ladyfingers

1. In a large bowl that will fit into a saucepan beat egg yolks with sugar until smooth and lemon coloured; slowly add the wine, beating constantly.
2. Set the bowl over boiling water in a saucepan and beat the mixture with a wire whisk until the sauce rises to 3 or 4 times the original height and thickens.
3. Serve warm in sherbet or champagne glasses; stand ladyfingers around the glass in the pudding.

BREAD PUDDING (Basic Recipe)

Bread Puddings are custards in which 1 cup of bread or cake crumbs may be substituted for 1 of the eggs; they are combined as Baked Custard but are baked; they need not be oven-poached. This recipe serves 4-6.

2 cups milk	⅛ teaspoon salt
1 large egg or 1 egg and 1 yolk	⅓ to ½ cup sugar
2 cups buttered bread, cubed or	1 teaspoon vanilla
cut into strips, or	
1 cup fine dry crumbs and	
1 tablespoon butter	

RAISIN BREAD PUDDING
Add ½ cup washed raisins.

CHOCOLATE BREAD PUDDING
Melt 1 ounce of unsweetened chocolate and 1 tablespoon butter with 2 tablespoons of sugar, and combine slowly with the bread and milk mixture.

LEMON BREAD PUDDING
Slowly add to the uncooked mixture 1 tablespoon lemon juice and a ½ tablespoon of grated lemon rind.

CARAMEL BREAD PUDDING
Reduce sugar to ⅓ cup. Add ⅓ cup Caramel Syrup (see back endpaper.)

JAM OR MARMALADE BREAD PUDDING
Spread 4 slices of bread with butter and jam or marmalade. Cut into strips or cubes.

INDIAN PUDDING
Cornmeal replaces bread in this truly American recipe.

½ cup cornmeal	1 teaspoon salt
4 cups milk	½ cup dark molasses
1 cup brown sugar	2 cups cream
2 teaspoons spice (ginger, cinnamon and nutmeg)	

1. In a large mixing bowl combine the cornmeal and 1 cup of milk.
2. In a double boiler scald the remaining 3 cups of milk; pour into it the cornmeal mixture, stirring constantly; cook until mixture is as thick as cooked cereal (15 minutes).
3. Remove from heat and stir in the sugar, spice and salt; add molasses and cream. Bake in a greased 2-quart casserole dish until set, about 1 hour at 275°. This may be served warm or cool with the cream. Serves 6.

TOMATO SOUP BREAD PUDDING

2 cups buttered bread cubes	¼ cup brown sugar
1 can condensed tomato soup	¼ cup boiling water

Combine soup, sugar and water; pour over the bread in a casserole; bake at 375° for 30 minutes. Serves 6.

SOFT CUSTARD (Basic Recipe)

1. Prepare the mixture for Baked Custard; pour mixture into top of a double boiler or into a heavy saucepan and cook on low heat.
2. Stir constantly until mixture coats a metal spoon; test frequently to avoid overcooking; *immediately* the custard thickens, cool by straining into a bowl; add vanilla. (If the custard begins to curdle, set the pan in cold water and beat it smooth; taste. If there is a raw egg flavour return the pan to the heat and stir carefully again.) The custard should be the thickness of rich cream.

QUICK CUSTARD

Use a vanilla pudding and pie mix; increase milk as required; follow directions on package.

FLOATING ISLAND

1. Make Soft Custard; strain into serving dish.
2. Garnish with Meringue (page 482) dropped in large spoonfuls on the custard. Meringue may be dropped on the surface of hot water in a shallow pan and cooked over medium heat until firm.

ORANGE CUSTARD

Section 4 oranges; place in serving dish, sprinkle with sugar; strain 2 cups chilled custard over oranges. Garnish with meringue or whipped cream.

COCONUT ORANGE CUSTARD

Sprinkle oranges with moist coconut before adding custard.

TRIFLE

Sponge cake makes the best trifle.

2 cups dry cake	2 cups Soft Custard
⅓ cup fruit juice or sherry	garnish (whipped cream, jam
fruit (6 to 8 halves of peaches)	or jelly, cherries, almonds)

1. Cut cake in uniform pieces; arrange in an attractive dish; sprinkle with fruit juice or sherry.
2. Add fresh or cooked fruit, cut in pieces.
3. Make Soft Custard; cool and pour over fruit and cake.
4. Garnish.

ROYAL TRIFLE

rind of ½ orange, ¼ lemon
½ cup Medium Syrup
¼ cup rum
1 sponge cake cut into fingers
1 cup of lightly set lemon jelly

2 cups Soft Custard
2 cups whipped cream
garnish (small macaroons,
  nuts, chocolate curls or fruit)

1. Remove very thin slivers of rind with a vegetable parer.
2. Combine syrup, (rack endpaper), lemon and orange rind; bring to boil, cook for 2 minutes; strain, cool, and add rum.
3. Line a glass bowl with the cake fingers. Gently pour syrup over cake fingers until all are well soaked. (If the cake is stale, it will require more syrup.)
4. Gradually spoon lemon jelly over; sprinkle with nuts and leave until nearly set.
5. Pour over about 1 cup of custard.
6. Fold half the whipped cream into the remaining custard, and spread another layer; top with remaining cream; garnish.

SOUFFLÉS

CHOCOLATE-ORANGE SOUFFLÉ

3 tablespoons butter
3 tablespoons flour
1 cup milk
¼ teaspoon salt
½ cup sugar
2½ teaspoons orange extract
  grated rind of 1 lemon

3 squares unsweetened
  chocolate
4 egg yolks
6 egg whites
¼ cup sugar
whipped cream

1. Melt the fat and blend in the flour; add milk slowly, stirring constantly; add salt, sugar; cook until thick; add flavouring.
2. Heat chocolate over hot water just until melted.
3. Beat egg yolks until thick and light; stir into thickened sauce along with melted chocolate.
4. Beat egg whites until stiff but not dry, gradually add ¼ cup sugar, beating well; fold into the chocolate mixture. Turn into buttered and sugar-dusted 1½-quart soufflé dish. Oven-poach until set (375° for 35 minutes). Serve at once with whipped cream. Serves 4-6.

APRICOT SOUFFLÉ

1½ cups apricot purée	salt
4 egg whites	⅛ teaspoon almond extract
⅛ teaspoon cream of tartar	¼ cup sugar

1. Prepare apricot purée from canned apricots or use the baby food variety.
2. Beat egg whites foamy; add cream of tartar, salt and extract; beat in sugar slowly until whites form stiff peaks.
3. Fold in apricot purée.
4. Turn into 1½-quart casserole greased and sprinkled with sugar; oven-poach at 325° for 40 minutes. Serve with hot brandy sauce and whipped cream. Serves 6.

Substitute ½ pound jar apricot preserves melted over low heat and rind and juice of ½ lemon for the apricot purée.

CORNSTARCH PUDDING (BLANC MANGE) (Basic Recipe)

In these recipes sugar or cold liquid is used to separate the starch grains to prevent lumping.

2 cups hot milk	¼ cup cold milk
½ to ⅔ cup sugar	½ teaspoon vanilla
3½ to 4 tablespoons cornstarch	1 tablespoon butter
⅛ teaspoon salt	

1. Heat milk. The use of a double boiler makes it easier to obtain a smooth product.
2. Mix well the sugar, cornstarch and salt; blend with a little of the cold milk to make a thin paste; be sure there is no unmixed cornstarch.
3. When milk is hot, stir in the smooth cornstarch mixture; continue to stir until there is no taste of raw starch and the mixture has thickened; cover and cook another 5 to 10 minutes. Remove from the heat, add vanilla and butter.
4. Cool by setting the pan in cold water and stirring occasionally, or by pouring the hot pudding into a bowl, covering tightly or placing a sheet of waxed paper on the surface of the pudding. This will prevent a skin forming as the pudding cools.

When the cornstarch has been added to the milk, the pudding may be covered and left *without stirring* in a double boiler over boiling water for 20 minutes, or until it has formed a soft jell.

Use prepared pie and pudding mixes.

CUSTARD BLANC MANGE

The addition of the egg gives a better texture and adds to the nutritive value.

1. Reduce cornstarch to 2½ tablespoons; beat 2 egg yolks or 1 large egg well.
2. When the cornstarch mixture is thick and has no taste of raw starch, pour about 1 cupful into the beaten egg; stir well and return to the rest of the pudding.
3. Stir over low heat or over boiling water until the pudding thickens.
4. Remove from the heat, add butter and vanilla, cool as above.

The variations which follow may be made from either the Basic or the Custard Blanc Mange.

CORNSTARCH SOUFFLÉ

Beat 1 egg white stiff but not dry; beat in 2 tablespoons sugar; fold into hot pudding.

PINEAPPLE SOUFFLÉ

Make as Cornstarch Soufflé, omitting ¼ cup hot milk. Before adding whites of eggs, add ⅓ cup crushed drained pineapple.

CARAMEL PUDDING

Reduce sugar to ¼ cup, milk to 1¾ cups, stir in ⅓ cup Caramel Syrup (back endpaper).

CHOCOLATE BLANC MANGE

Reduce cornstarch by ½ tablespoon, increase sugar to ¾ cup. Mix 3 to 4 tablespoons cocoa with sugar.

or

Melt one square unsweetened chocolate over hot water; add sugar; add milk; reduce cornstarch by ½ tablespoon, combine with salt and cold milk. Finish as Cornstarch Pudding (page 590).

BAKED RICE PUDDING

3 tablespoons rice	½ cup raisins
½ cup sugar	2 cups milk
½ teaspoon salt	1 cup water
½ teaspoon cinnamon	1½ tablespoons butter

1. Wash the rice. Combine all the ingredients in a 1-quart baking dish.
2. Bake at 350° for 2 hours; stir once during cooking. Serves 4-6.

BUTTERSCOTCH PUDDING

Much better flavour than the packaged pudding.

4 tablespoons butter	2 cups milk
3 tablespoons cornstarch	1 egg or 2 yolks
¾ cup brown sugar	1½ tablespoons caramel
½ teaspoon salt	

1. In top of double boiler melt butter. Blend cornstarch, sugar and salt, and add to butter.
2. Heat milk; add milk to the first mixture, stirring constantly until thick; cover and cook 10 minutes.
3. Finish as Custard Blanc Mange.

CREAMY RICE PUDDING

½ cup rice	¾ teaspoon salt
4 cups milk	1 teaspoon grated lemon rind or
2 egg yolks	½ cup raisins
½ cup sugar	

1. Wash rice; cook in double boiler with milk until very soft, about 1 hour.
2. Beat egg yolks; add sugar and salt; add to rice mixture; stir and cook 5 minutes.
3. Add lemon rind and/or raisins. Serve warm with brown sugar and cream. Serves 4-6.

QUICK CREAMY RICE PUDDING

¾ cup quick-cooking rice	¼ cup firmly packed brown sugar
¼ teaspoon salt	1 tablespoon butter
1⅓ cups milk	¼ teaspoon vanilla

1. Combine rice, salt and milk in a saucepan; bring to a full boil.
2. Remove from heat; add sugar and remaining ingredients, cover and let stand 10-15 minutes to thicken. Serves 4-6.

KHEER

To Creamy Rice Pudding add ½ cup mixed nuts (cashews, pistachio, almonds), coconut, sultana raisins. Add 4 flakes saffron (if desired), 2 drops vanilla. Pour into serving bowl and add brown sugar. Sprinkle with nutmeg. Chill before serving.

RICE FRUIT PUDDING

⅔ cup of quick-cooking rice
⅓ cup salt
1⅔ cups of milk
1 tablespoon butter
1 egg yolk
⅓ cup sugar

½ teaspoon vanilla
⅛ teaspoon cinnamon
⅛ teaspoon nutmeg
1 cup diced fruit
   (fruit cocktail, apricots,
   peaches)

1. Combine rice, salt and milk in saucepan and bring to a boil; let stand with the cover on for 5 minutes.
2. Beat egg yolk slightly and add sugar, and gradually add rice mixture and butter.
3. Return to low heat; stir until the mixture thickens (4 minutes).
4. Add vanilla, spices and canned fruit.
5. Serve warm with cream, or chill. Serves 6.

RICE CUSTARD

This pudding uses cooked rice.

1½ cups cooked rice
½ cup brown sugar
2 tablespoons butter
1 egg, beaten

3 cups milk
¾ cup raisins, currants and dates
1 teaspoon vanilla or grated
   lemon rind

1. Combine all ingredients; place in buttered baking dish, stirring once after the pudding has baked about 15 minutes.
2. Oven-poach at 325° for 40 minutes. Serves 6-8.

MAPLE RICE PUDDING

2 cups milk
2½ tablespoons cornstarch
¼ teaspoon salt
¾ cup maple syrup

2 egg yolks
1 cup cooked rice
2 egg whites
2 tablespoons sugar

1. Heat the milk; combine the cornstarch, salt and ½ cup maple syrup.
2. Add syrup slowly to the hot milk, stir until thick; continue to cook until there is no flavour of raw starch.
3. Add the hot mixture to the egg yolks; fold in the rice.
4. Prepare meringue from egg whites, sugar and remaining syrup (page 426).
5. Pour the mixture into a greased baking dish; cover with meringue; bake at 325° until the meringue browns, 20 minutes. Serves 6.

   If not convenient to heat the oven, return the pudding to the heat after the egg yolk is added, and stir until it thickens. Cool slightly and fold in the meringue.

BAVARIAN RICE

A glamour recipe.

1 cup whipping cream
¼ cup sugar
1 teaspoon vanilla

1 cup cooked rice
1 cup mixed fruit and nuts

1. Beat the cream; add sugar and vanilla; save some cream for garnish.
2. Fold rice and fruit into the remaining cream; chill. Serves 6.
   For variety, add any of the following alone or in combination: crushed pineapple, sectioned oranges, slivered apricots, fresh or drained frozen raspberries, marshmallows quartered, slivered blanched almonds, crystallized ginger (chopped), sliced fresh or canned peaches, 1-2 tablespoons brandy or grated maple sugar.

DUTCH PRUNE RIJST

A hot rice dessert of Dutch ancestry.

1 pound prunes, pitted
¼ teaspoon cinnamon
1 tablespoon grated lemon rind
2 cups water
1 cup granulated sugar

1 cup raw, regular or converted white rice
1½ cups juice drained from prunes
heavy cream

1. In saucepan, combine prunes, cinnamon, lemon rind; add enough water to cover; cook until prunes are tender; add sugar.
2. Cook rice until almost tender; drain (page 286).
3. Add juice drained from prunes (if necessary, add rice water to make 1½ cups); cook over low heat until liquid is absorbed.
4. Pile rice in centre of serving plate; ring with border of prunes. Serve with cream. Makes 8 servings.

TAPIOCA CREAM (Basic Recipe)

1½ cups milk
⅛ teaspoon salt
3 tablespoons minute tapioca

¼ cup sugar
2 eggs, separated
½ teaspoon vanilla

1. Heat the milk; add salt, tapioca and ½ of the sugar. Cook, stirring occasionally, until the tapioca becomes transparent and the mixture thickens (about 20 minutes).
2. Beat the egg whites until stiff but not dry; beat in the remaining sugar.
3. Beat the egg yolks; add some of the cooked tapioca; return mixture to remaining tapioca; stir over low heat until the mixture thickens, about 3 minutes.
4. Remove from the heat; fold in the meringue of step 2; place in serving dishes; serve with jam, cooked fruit, fresh berries, or peaches. Serves 4-6.

TAPIOCA PARFAIT

Place teaspoons of fruit against the side of a sherbet or parfait glass alternately with tablespoons of the pudding. Top with a daub of the meringue from step 2 above, decorate with jam.

FRUIT TAPIOCA

1 cup water	½ cup orange juice
½ cup pineapple juice	1 tablespoon lemon juice
¾ cup sugar	1 orange, sectioned
¼ cup minute tapioca	1 cup diced pineapple

Heat the first 4 ingredients slowly, stirring frequently until the tapioca is transparent; add the remaining ingredients; chill. Serve with Custard Sauce (page 98) or cream.

For the pineapple juice and fruit, substitute apricot nectar, and chopped cooked apricots; canned cherry juice and cherries; peach or pear juice and chopped peaches; apple juice and a few cinnamon candies.

TUTTI-FRUTTI TAPIOCA

4 apples	2 cups hot water
4-6 whole cloves	½ cup grapes
3 tablespoons brown sugar	¼ cup walnuts
2 tablespoons water	½ cup dates
3 tablespoons minute tapioca	½ cup sugar
¼ teaspoon salt	

1. Pare, core and quarter apples; place in 2-quart casserole. Stick cloves in apples; pour sugar and water mixture over the fruit. Bake covered at 350° until tender, about 30 minutes.
2. Add tapioca and salt to hot water and cook in a double boiler, stirring occasionally until clear.
3. Cut grapes in half, remove seeds; chop walnuts coarsely; sliver dates with scissors; add sugar, fruit and nuts to tapioca mixture, pour over apples. Bake 5 minutes. Chill and serve with cream.
   Fruit and nuts may be omitted and only apples used.

BATTER AND DOUGH DESSERTS

Strawberry shortcake, cherry cobbler, apple pandowdy and blueberry cottage pudding, formerly summer desserts, can now be made the year round.

SHORTCAKES

1 recipe Sweet Tea Biscuit
Dough (page 440)
fruit (1 quart fresh;
2 15-ounce packages frozen)

2 tablespoons butter
1 cup whipping cream or
ice cream

1. Prepare the Sweet Tea Biscuit Dough; knead slightly on floured board to smooth the dough; roll ⅓-inch thick and shape into large circle, or cut into 3-inch circles.
2. Bake at 425° for 10 to 20 minutes.
3. Prepare the fruit as below.
4. Place the cooked biscuit on a serving plate, split; spread with butter; cover with fruit; top with ice cream or whipped cream. Serves 8.

Strawberry Shortcake with a second layer of biscuit.

STRAWBERRY SHORTCAKE

Wash and hull 1 quart of berries; save a few perfect berries for garnish. Slice the remaining berries and add ⅔ cup sugar; or defrost and drain frozen berries.

PEACH SHORTCAKE

Use 2 pounds fresh, juicy peaches, sliced and sugared. Decorate with blueberries or blue grapes.

RASPBERRY SHORTCAKE

Use raspberries washed, if necessary, and sugared.

RAISIN SHORTCAKE

1 recipe Sweet Tea Biscuit
   Dough (page 440)
½ cup sugar
1 tablespoon cornstarch
   pinch of salt

¾ cup orange juice
2 tablespoons lemon juice
1 cup raisins (washed if
   necessary)
   sour cream

1. Prepare dough; shape into 3-inch circles; bake.
2. Combine sugar, cornstarch, salt; add orange juice, lemon juice, raisins.
3. Stir over low heat until the mixture thickens and there is no taste of raw starch.
4. Spoon warm raisin sauce onto split buttered biscuits; top with sour cream. Serves 4-6.

FRUIT ROLY POLY (Basic Recipe)

1 recipe Sweet Tea Biscuit
   Dough (page 440)
2 tablespoons soft butter

½ cup brown sugar
   fresh or canned fruit

1. Prepare the dough; roll to an 8 by 12-inch rectangle. Spread with butter and sprinkle with sugar.
2. Cover with fruit; roll from the wide side like a jellyroll; seal the edges and ends.
3. Place on a greased pan; cut slits to allow the steam to escape; brush with milk.
4. Bake at 350° until golden brown, about 60 minutes. Serves 6-8.
   Cut the roll into 8 1½-inch slices; place cut side down in a greased 9-inch baking dish; bake at 350° for 45 minutes.

APPLE RAISIN ROLY POLY

1 recipe Sweet Tea Biscuit
   Dough (page 440)
½ cup grated cheese
2 tablespoons soft butter
½ cup brown sugar

2 cups coarsely grated apples
1 cup raisins
1 tablespoon flour
1 teaspoon cinnamon

1. Add the cheese to the dry ingredients of the dough.
2. Prepare the dough; roll and spread with butter and sugar.
3. Combine the remaining ingredients.
4. Finish as Fruit Roly Poly.

CHERRY ROLY POLY

1 recipe Sweet Tea Biscuit
   Dough (page 440)
2 tablespoons soft butter
½ cup brown sugar
1 15-ounce can pitted cherries,
   drained

1 cup cherry juice
1 tablespoon cornstarch
   almond flavouring or
   lemon juice

Prepare as Fruit Roly Poly. Thicken the fruit juice with cornstarch;
add flavouring. Use as sauce on the cherry pinwheels.

BLUEBERRY ROLY POLY

1 recipe Sweet Tea Biscuit
   Dough (page 440)
2 tablespoons soft butter
½ cup brown sugar

2 cups fresh blueberries
¼ cup flour
1 teaspoon cinnamon

Prepare as Fruit Roly Poly, dredging the blueberries with flour-
cinnamon mix. Serve with ice cream or Lemon Sauce (page 94).

FRUIT COBBLER (Basic Recipe)

1 recipe Sweet Tea
   Biscuit Dough (page 440)
1 quart fresh red cherries,
   washed and pitted
¾-1 cup white sugar

2 tablespoons cornstarch or
1 tablespoon minute tapioca
¼ cup water
2 drops almond extract
1 tablespoon butter

1. Place cherries in a large loaf pan, a 9-inch cake or pie pan, or a
   1-quart casserole.
2. Combine the sugar, cornstarch or tapioca, and mix through the
   fruit; add water and flavouring; dot the butter over the mixture.
3. Cover and bake 20 minutes at 400° or until fruit is almost cooked.
4. Prepare the dough; shape to fit the casserole; crimp the dough so
   that it will rest on the fruit; brush with milk and sprinkle with
   sugar.
5. Remove the cherries from the oven; place the dough in position
   and quickly return to the oven (400°) until biscuit is cooked (20
   minutes). Serve warm with ice cream, Brown Sugar Sauce or Lemon
   Sauce (page 94). Serves 4-6.

Quick Variations:

1 19-ounce can cherry pie filling   2 cups packaged biscuit mix

Place the pie filling in the baking dish; cover with the biscuit topping
prepared according to directions; brush with milk; sprinkle with
sugar; bake as directed.

Cherry Cobbler in preparation.

COBBLER VARIATIONS

	replace cherries with	replace white sugar with	replace almond extract with
Apple	4 cups sliced apples	brown sugar	¼ teaspoon cinnamon
Blueberry	2 cups blueberries		¼ teaspoon cinnamon
Peach	4 cups sliced peaches		
Raspberry	2 cups raspberries		omit almond extract
Rhubarb	4 cups sliced rhubarb	brown sugar	1 teaspoon orange or lemon rind
Strawberry	1 pint fresh strawberries		¼ teaspoon vanilla
Canned Fruit	1 19-ounce can	omit or reduce to ¼ cup	1 teaspoon lemon juice
Frozen Fruit	2 12-ounce packages defrosted	omit or reduce to ⅓ cup	follow above

DUTCH APPLE CAKE

1 recipe Sweet Tea Biscuit   2 apples
    Dough (page 440)   cinnamon-sugar mix

1. Prepare the dough; spread in a buttered 8-inch cake pan.
2. Wipe, quarter, core and pare apples; cut in eighths; arrange apples on batter in rows, pressing sharp edges into the batter; sprinkle with cinnamon-sugar mix.
3. Bake at 400° until dough is cooked in the centre (25-30 minutes); serve with brown sugar sauce. Serves 6-9.
   Add ¼ cup chopped nuts to the cinnamon-sugar mix for added flavour.

DUTCH PINEAPPLE CAKE

1 recipe Sweet Tea Biscuit   6 slices canned pineapple,
    Dough (page 440)   drained and halved
                           1 recipe Streusel Topping

Follow directions for Dutch Apple Cake, substituting the pineapple slices for apples and Streusel Topping (p. 489) for cinnamon-sugar mix. Serve with Pineapple Sauce (page 95).

COTTAGE PUDDINGS

Replace the shortcake dough in the cobbler recipes with a cake topping about 1 inch in depth. One-egg cake (page 539), the Quick-mix white or Gold Cake (page 543) or a prepared cake mix make good toppings. Bake at 375° for 30 minutes. Too much cake in proportion to the amount of fruit makes a poor product, so it is well to have a greased muffin tin or a few paper liners for cup cakes ready. These may be filled with excess batter, refrigerated and baked in the last 15 minutes of cooking the pudding. Serves 6-8.

APPLE PANDOWDY

In our modern version of a pandowdy the fruit is folded into a cake batter; another version is similar to a cobbler.

2½ quarts tart apples   ½ teaspoon nutmeg
 1 cup brown sugar   1¼ teaspoons cinnamon
⅓ cup molasses or maple syrup   2 cups shortcake dough
⅓ cup water   (see Shortcakes page 596)
¼ teaspoon salt

1. Wash, pare, core and thinly slice apples. Arrange apples on bottom of baking dish.

2. Mix together the brown sugar, molasses, water and spices; sprinkle over apples.
3. Arrange the shortcake dough, rolled to fit the dish, on top of the apples.
4. Bake at 350° until firm, 35-40 minutes.
5. Remove pudding from baking dish with apple side up. Serve warm and garnish with cream or Lemon Sauce (page 94). Serves 6-8.

WALDORF PUDDING

Fruit:
- 4 medium-sized tart apples
- ½ cup brown sugar
- ½ cup white sugar
- 1 teaspoon cinnamon
- ½ teaspoon nutmeg
- ¾ cup raisins or dates
- ½ cup walnuts

Batter:
- 1½ cups all-purpose flour
- 2 teaspoons baking powder
- 1 teaspoon salt
- ½ cup salad oil
- 1 egg

1. Peel and core apples; chop coarsely into a large bowl; mix in sugar, cinnamon, nutmeg, raisins and walnuts.
2. Sift and measure flour with baking powder and salt; sift over the fruit mixture; add the oil and unbeaten egg; beat for about 2 minutes and spread in 8-inch cake pan.
3. Bake until firm (375° for 40 minutes); serve with vanilla or caramel sauce, whipped cream or ice cream. Serves 6-8.

Quick Trick: Use ½ package of orange muffin mix to replace the batter; add fruit mixture, oil and egg; beat the required length of time.

HUNTER'S DELIGHT

- ¼ cup shortening
- ½ cup granulated sugar
- 1 egg, beaten
- ½ teaspoon soda
- ¾ cup milk
- ½ teaspoon cinnamon
- ¼ teaspoon vanilla
- ½ cup chopped, seedless raisins
- 1 cup bread cubes, packed lightly
- ¼ teaspoon salt
- ¼ cup chopped walnuts

1. Cream shortening, add sugar gradually, cream well.
2. Add beaten egg and mix thoroughly.
3. Add soda to the milk and add to the creamed mixture.
4. Add the remaining ingredients. Blend mixture well.
5. Bake at 350° in a greased casserole for 40 minutes. Serves 6.

APPLE GINGERBREAD

½ cup sugar	½ teaspoon soda
½ cup boiling water	1 teaspoon ginger
3 apples	1 teaspoon cinnamon
¼ cup fat	¼ teaspoon cloves
⅓ cup sugar	½ teaspoon salt
1 egg	⅞ cup all-purpose flour
⅓ cup molasses	⅓ cup sour milk

1. Make a syrup by boiling the sugar in boiling water for 3 minutes.
2. Add the apples which have been pared, cored and quartered; cook until almost tender; pour into a greased baking pan 10 by 6½ inches (not tin); let cool.
3. Make the gingerbread by creaming the fat; add the sugar; cream well.
4. Add the egg; beat well and beat in the molasses.
5. Sift the dry ingredients.
6. Combine the sour milk and dry ingredients with the fat-sugar mixture, stirring as little as possible to have a smooth batter.
7. Pour over the cooled apples in the pan.
8. Bake at 325° for 50 minutes. Serves 4-5.

UPSIDE-DOWN CAKES

Upside-Down Cakes (page 545) make delicious desserts.

Different fruits may be used in Upside-Down Cakes. This is Spiced Peach Upside-Down Cake.

FRUIT CRUMBLE (BASIC RECIPE)

Apple Crumble, Blueberry Crumble, Cherry Crumble, Peach Crumble, Raspberry Crumble and Rhubarb Crumble are all made from the same basic recipe.

Fruit:
- 5 cups rhubarb, cut into 1-inch pieces or
- 4 cups sliced apples or pitted red cherries or
- 2 cups blueberries or raspberries or peaches peeled and sliced or
- 1 19-ounce can cherries or sliced peaches drained or
- 1 19-ounce can applesauce

Syrup:
- 1 tablespoon lemon juice
- ¼-1 cup sugar
- ¼ cup water or fruit juice

Crumb:
- ⅔ cup flour
- ⅛ teaspoon salt
- ½ cup brown sugar
- ⅔ cup rolled oats
- ⅓ cup melted butter or margarine

1. Prepare fruit; place in a 6 by 8-inch baking dish.
2. Prepare syrup by adding sugar and lemon juice to juice drained from the fruit. The amount of sugar will depend upon the sweetness of the fruit, the amount of sugar in the crumb, the sauce being served and one's sweet tooth. For raw fruit the dry sugar may be mixed with the fruit and water added.
3. Combine dry ingredients; add melted fat; mix until crumbly; sprinkle over fruit; bake until fruit is tender (40 minutes).
4. Serve with ice cream or a sauce made by thickening the fruit juice or with Lemon or Brown Sugar Sauce (page 94). Serves 6.

FRUIT BETTY

Apple Betty, Blueberry Betty, Cherry Betty, Peach Betty, Raspberry Betty and Rhubarb Betty may be made by following the directions in Fruit Crumble for the fruit and syrup. Replace the crumb topping as follows:

- 1½ cups dry bread, cubed or crumbed
- ¼ cup butter

1. Melt the fat in a 6 by 8-inch baking dish; stir in the crumbs or bread cubes until slightly browned; empty out all but 1 thin layer of crumbs.
2. Layer fruit and crumbs into the casserole, ending with crumbs.
3. Pour the syrup over the casserole; bake at 350° until fruit is tender (40 minutes); serve with sour cream. Serves 6.

½ cup maple syrup or honey may be used to replace sugar and water. 1 cup crushed oatmeal cookies may replace bread crumbs.

FRUIT CRISP

Apple Crisp, Blueberry Crisp, Cherry Crisp, Peach Crisp, Raspberry Crisp and Rhubarb Crisp may be made by following the directions for Fruit Crumble for the fruit and syrup. Replace the crumb topping as follows:

⅔ cup flour	¼ teaspoon salt
1 cup brown sugar	⅓ cup firm butter

1. Butter a 6 by 8-inch baking dish; prepare fruit and sugar.
2. Combine flour, sugar and salt in a bowl; cut in fat until the texture of coarse crumbs; sprinkle over the fruit.
3. Bake at 350° until topping is brown and crisp (40 minutes). Serves 6. A quick substitute: 1 19-ounce can sweetened applesauce for the fruit. 1 cup packaged biscuit mix, ½ cup brown sugar, ¼ cup fat for the crumbs.

   Variation: Add to the crumb mixture 1 teaspoon cinnamon, ¼ cup finely chopped nuts, ½ cup grated Cheddar cheese or ⅔ cup grated processed cheese. Reduce fat to 1 cup; omit salt.

BUTTERSCOTCH JIFFY PUDDING (Basic Recipe)

2 tablespoons soft butter	¾ cup brown sugar
¼ cup sugar	1 tablespoon butter
1 cup sifted all-purpose flour	1¾ cups boiling water
2 teaspoons baking powder	1 teaspoon vanilla, rum or
⅛ teaspoon salt	maple flavouring
⅔ cup milk	

1. Cream butter and sugar.
2. Measure flour, baking powder and salt; sift; add alternately with the milk to fat-sugar mixture to make a thick batter. Spoon into greased 8 or 9-square inch pan.
3. Sprinkle brown sugar over the batter; combine butter, boiling water and flavouring; pour over batter; *do not stir*.
4. Bake at 350° for 45 minutes. Serves 6.

FRUIT JIFFY PUDDING

Use 2½-3 cups sweetened stewed berries and juice instead of sugar and water.

FUDGE JIFFY PUDDING

Add ½ cup chopped nuts to batter. To brown sugar add ¼ cup cocoa, ¼ teaspoon salt, ¼ cup white sugar.

MAPLE JIFFY PUDDING

Use 1½ cups hot maple syrup with ½ cup hot water for the sauce.

RAISIN JIFFY PUDDING

Add 1 cup raisins to batter; replace flavouring with juice and grated rind of ½ orange.

FOAMY LEMON PUDDING

1⅓ cups milk	⅛ teaspoon salt
3 tablespoons butter	¼ cup sifted all-purpose flour
3 eggs separated	2 lemons, rind and juice (⅓ cup)
1 cup granulated sugar	

1. Heat the butter in the milk until melted.
2. Beat the egg whites stiff but not dry; beat in ¼ of the sugar; add salt.
3. Beat the egg yolks; beat in the remaining sugar; stir in the flour and fruit juice and rind; blend in the milk and butter.
4. Fold in the egg whites; pour into custard cups or a shallow 1-quart casserole.
5. Oven-poach at 325° for 30 minutes for custard cups, 45 minutes for casserole. Serves 6-8.

BUTTERSCOTCH PUFF

Increase milk to 1⅔ cups; substitute brown for white sugar; omit lemon juice and rind; flavour with vanilla; sprinkle with chopped walnuts before baking.

CHRISTMAS PUDDINGS

Christmas Puddings may be too rich for Christmas Day but are welcome throughout the holiday season.

CARROT PUDDING

Less expensive and not as rich as plum pudding.

½ teaspoon baking soda	1 cup grated carrot
½ cup flour	1 cup grated potato
1 teaspoon salt	1¼ cups soft bread crumbs
1 teaspoon cinnamon	1 cup raisins
⅛ teaspoon nutmeg	1 cup currants
½ teaspoon allspice	1 cup brown sugar
cherries, orange peel, almonds	¾ cup suet, finely chopped
finely cut	2 tablespoons sour milk

1. Measure and sift flour and spices; mix ingredients in order given.

2. Fill a well-greased mould not more than ¾ full; cover the mould with a lid or tie on heavy brown paper, greased, or heavy foil.
3. Steam 3 hours; cool covered; refrigerate.
4. Reheat when needed, about 1 hour.
5. Unmould and cut into wedges with a sharp knife.
6. Serve with lemon or caramel sauce. Serves 6-8.

To improvise a steamer, set the bowl on sealer rings in a deep kettle which has a tight-fitting top. Add boiling water until it comes half-way up the mould. Adjust the heat when the water boils so that it will boil gently. As necessary, add more boiling water. If desired, when the pudding is unmoulded it may be dried for a few minutes in the oven. (Pressure cooking is a quick and satisfactory method of steaming a pudding.)

PLUM PUDDING

3 pounds raisins	1 teaspoon cinnamon
¼ pound lemon peel, cut	½ teaspoon nutmeg
¼ pound citron peel, cut	¼ teaspoon cloves
½ pound blanched almonds, chopped	¼ teaspoon allspice
	1 pound brown sugar
½ pound cherries, chopped	4 cups soft bread crumbs
4 tablespoons flour	1 pound suet, finely chopped
1 teaspoon baking soda	½ cup grape juice
½ teaspoon salt	8 eggs

1. Combine fruit and nuts; sprinkle with a little of the flour.
2. Sift flour, baking soda, salt and spices; add sugar, bread crumbs, suet and fruit-nut mixture.
3. Mix well; add grape juice and well-beaten eggs.
4. Finish as Carrot Pudding. Serve with brandy sauce or hard sauce. Makes 4 moulds; each mould serves 6-8.

For glamour, flame the Plum Pudding (page 73).

FRUIT WHIPS

APPLE WHIP

2 egg whites
2 tablespoons fruit sugar
2½ cups thick applesauce

1 teaspoon lemon juice and rind
pinch nutmeg or 1 teaspoon
vanilla

1. Beat white of egg until stiff; gradually beat in sugar; fold in apple-sauce and flavouring.
2. Pile lightly in serving dishes; chill; serve with Custard Sauce (page 98). Or, if desired, sprinkle with a dash of cinnamon or a few red cinnamon candies and serve with whipped cream.

   A quick substitute: omit applesauce, use one of the following: 1 can baby food prunes or apricots, ⅓ cup apricot nectar, juice and pulp of 1 orange. Pour into ice cube tray; chill until the mixture begins to freeze around the edges; finish as Apple Whip.

SEVEN-MINUTE FRUIT WHIP

2 egg whites
1 teaspoon grated lemon rind
2 tablespoons lemon juice
½ cup sugar

3 tablespoons prune juice
dash of salt
½ cup chopped cooked prunes
or apricots

1. Combine first 6 ingredients in the top section of a double boiler.
2. Place over boiling water and beat with an egg beater until stiff enough to stand up in peaks (about 5 to 7 minutes). Remove from heat.
3. Fold in the fruit. Chill. Serve with Custard Sauce. Serves 6.

APRICOTINA

½ pound dried apricots
1 orange, grated rind, juice and
     pulp
1½ cups water

½ cup sugar
3 tablespoons almonds, slivered
1 cup cream, whipped

1. Combine apricots, grated rind, unstrained orange juice and water; allow to stand for 2 hours.
2. Add sugar and simmer 10 minutes; make liquid up to ¾ cup with additional water, if necessary.
3. Reserve 6 apricots for garnish; blend or sieve the rest; chill.
4. Fold whipped cream and nuts into the fruit; taste; add sugar if desired; place in serving dishes; garnish with an apricot.

GELATINE DESSERTS

One envelope of unflavoured gelatine (1 tablespoon), or 1 commercial jelly powder (to which sugar, colour and flavour have been added), will set 2 cups of liquid, if all the gelatine is completely dissolved, and sufficient time is allowed.

When the jelly is to be beaten or much fruit or vegetable is to be added, it is wise to reduce the liquid slightly.

Gelatine dissolves only in hot liquid; it dissolves more quickly if it has first been softened in cold liquid. Boiling gelatine toughens it. Sprinkle the gelatine into cold liquid and leave it while the other ingredients are being prepared; it will absorb the liquid, increasing in bulk and becoming very dry.

To heat all the liquid, only to cool it all down again, is a waste of time; heat only enough to dissolve the gelatine. Gelatine mixtures which have set at room temperature do not soften in a warm room as quickly as those that were set in a refrigerator.

The protein in gelatine is broken down by the enzymes in raw pineapple, so that a jelly containing fresh pineapple will become liquid on standing. Always cook raw pineapple before adding to gelatine mixture. Fruits or vegetables added to a gelatine mixture before it begins to set not only float to the top, but also become limp and soggy. Gelatine added to hot milk curdles the milk; gelatine melted over low heat and added to cold milk does not have this effect. Since most recipes containing milk are beaten after they began to set, this curdling is not usually important but may be disturbing. Beaten egg white is beaten into the jelly but whipped cream should be folded in.

To mould and unmould gelatine mixtures, see Gelatine Salads (page 392).

JELLY DESSERT (Basic Recipe)

1 tablespoon unflavoured gelatine	1½ cups liquid (fruit juice; vegetable or meat stock; carbonated beverage)
¼ cup cold water	sugar, lemon juice or salt

1. Let the gelatine stand in cold water until it absorbs the water and swells.
2. Heat part of the liquid, ½ of it or less; if sugar is needed dissolve it in the hot liquid; add the softened gelatine; dissolve completely.
3. Add the remaining liquid; taste and flavour. Chill several hours.

4. Remove jelly from mould. Serves 4-6.

To save time use a commercial jelly powder; substitute, for the water, juice from canned or fresh fruit, from sweet pickles, or vegetable or meat stock. Follow directions in Basic Recipe.

JELLIED PINK LEMONADE

3 envelopes unflavoured gelatine (3 tablespoons)
½ cup cold water
1 cup hot water

¾ cup sugar
1 6-ounce can frozen lemonade concentrate
3 cups rosé wine

Follow directions for the Basic Recipe; garnish with sweetened whipped cream. Serves 10-12.

FRUIT JELLY

Prepare the Basic Recipe. When it begins to drop rather than pour from a spoon, add any combination of drained, cut fruit (excepting uncooked pineapple). Nuts and marshmallows may be added. Serve with table or whipped cream, sour cream or Custard Sauce (page 98).

Quick Recipe:

1 3-ounce package jelly powder
1 cup boiling water

1 package frozen fruit

1. Dissolve the jelly powder in the water in a 1-quart saucepan.
2. Add the frozen fruit and stir until it separates; remove from the heat.
3. Stir for 1 minute to be sure all fruit is separated; pour into dessert dishes or mould; chill. Serves 6-8.

DANISH FRUIT JELLY

1 19-ounce can pitted red cherries
1 3-ounce package cherry jelly powder

1 15-ounce package frozen raspberries
1 cup sour cream
¼ cup brown sugar

1. Into a 1-quart saucepan measure juice from cherries; to this liquid add water to make 1 cup hot liquid; add jelly powder, stir until dissolved; add frozen raspberries.
2. When mixture begins to thicken stir in the cherries; mould; chill several hours.
3. Serve with sweetened sour cream. Serves 6-8.

RASPBERRY AMBROSIA

1 3-ounce package raspberry jelly powder	½ cup seedless green grapes
½ cup boiling water	½ cup pineapple chunks
1 cup pineapple juice	½ cup flaked coconut
1 package frozen raspberries, thawed	½ cup whipping cream

1. Add jelly powder to boiling water and heat until dissolved; add pineapple juice; set jelly in an 8-inch cake pan (a depth of ½ inch) cut into cubes.
2. At serving time layer fruit and jelly cubes into sherbet glasses or a large fruit bowl; garnish with coconut and whipped cream. Serves 10-12.

SPONGE PUDDING (LEMON SNOW) (Basic Recipe)

Sponges are gelatine desserts to which beaten egg whites are added.

1 tablespoon gelatine (1 envelope)	⅔ cup sugar
	thin shaving of ¼ lemon rind
¼ cup cold water	3 tablespoons lemon juice
⅔ cup boiling water	2 egg whites

1. Soften gelatine in cold water.
2. Make a syrup of water, sugar and lemon rind by boiling 3 minutes; dissolve the gelatine in syrup; add lemon juice.
3. Chill over ice water, stirring frequently until syrupy. Beat egg whites until stiff; beat the gelatine mixture; beat the 2 mixtures together.
4. Pour into a moistened mould or pile lightly in sherbet dishes; chill several hours.
5. Serve with Custard Sauce (page 98). Serves 4-6.

PINEAPPLE SPONGE

Use canned pineapple juice to replace syrup. Use only 1 tablespoon lemon juice; fold in ½ cup well drained, crushed pineapple, just before turning into mould.

GRAPE SPONGE

Use grape juice to replace syrup. Some grape juices need sugar; some lemon juice. Pineapple juice added to grape juice causes a rather unpleasant blue colour. Grape juice set in a tin mould will also show this colour.

Rhubarb juice, raspberry juice or any combination may be used in this way.

APPLE FOAM

1 3-ounce package lemon jelly powder	1 cup cold water
½ cup hot water	2 cups applesauce
	2 stiffly-beaten egg whites

1. Dissolve the jelly powder in the hot water; add cold water; chill.
2. When the jelly begins to set beat it until it is foamy; beat in the applesauce and the egg whites.
3. Pile into dessert dishes or mould, garnish with thin slices of unpeeled apple, dipped in lemon juice to prevent darkening. Serves 6.

Spanish Cream with Strawberries.

SPANISH CREAM (Basic Recipe)

Spanish Cream is a gelatine dessert in which the base is a custard sauce.

1 tablespoon gelatine (1 envelope)	2 egg yolks
¼ cup cold water	⅓ cup sugar
2 eggs separated	⅛ teaspoon salt
1¾ cups hot milk	1 teaspoon vanilla
	2 egg whites, beaten

1. Soften gelatine in cold water.
2. Prepare Custard Sauce from the next 6 ingredients (page 98).

3. Dissolve the gelatine in the sauce; chill.
4. When partly set, beat; beat in egg whites. Mould. Serves 4-6.

For convenience, make a larger quantity of Spanish Cream, saving half for future use in Finnish Torte (page 633).

To save time use 2 cups cold eggnog to replace custard mixture; sweeten as desired. Melt the softened gelatine over low heat and add to the eggnog. Beat when the mixture begins to set; beat in beaten egg whites.

LEMON SPANISH CREAM

Use 1½ cups milk. Increase sugar to ½ cup. Substitute juice and rind of 1 lemon for the vanilla.

COFFEE SPANISH CREAM

Replace ½ of the milk with strong coffee.

PINEAPPLE SPANISH CREAM

Replace milk by crushed pineapple, undrained; replace vanilla by lemon juice.

BISQUE TORTONI

Fold into the beaten Spanish Cream mixture 1 cup cream whipped, ⅔ cup almond macaroon crumbs or ⅔ cup chopped almonds and coconut, toasted. Leave in freezer 2-3 hours. Spoon chopped maraschino cherries and juice over each serving.

ORANGE CHARLOTTE (Basic Recipe)

Charlottes or Bavarians are gelatine desserts into which whipped cream has been folded; sometimes beaten egg whites are added as well. These rich desserts look elegant when moulded or served in parfait glasses or compote dishes; set in crumb crusts these fillings give us chiffon pies; set in a soufflé dish or straight-sided serving dish they become never-fall soufflés.

1 tablespoon gelatine	2 tablespoons lemon juice
(1 envelope)	¾ cup orange juice
¼ cup cold water	2 egg whites
¼ cup boiling water	1 cup cream, whipped
½ cup sugar	orange sections

1. Prepare first 6 ingredients as in Jelly Dessert (Basic Recipe) (page 608).
2. When partly set, beat until foamy; add egg whites, beaten stiff; beat well; fold in whipped cream.
3. Turn into a mould; chill; garnish. Serves 6-8.

APRICOT CHARLOTTE

Substitute 1 12-ounce can of apricot nectar for the boiling water and orange juice in Orange Charlotte.

CHOCOLATE CHARLOTTE

2 tablespoons gelatine (2 envelopes)	5 egg yolks
¼ cup orange juice or light rum	⅔ cup sugar
5 squares semi-sweet chocolate (5 ounces) finely chopped	1 teaspoon vanilla
⅔ cup milk	5 egg whites
	1 cup cream, whipped

1. Soften the gelatine in the ¼ cup of liquid.
2. Melt the chocolate in the milk over hot water; add gelatine and stir until melted; pour into a bowl.
3. Beat egg yolks and sugar; heat in the same double boiler over hot water, heating constantly until thick; chill. Combine the mixtures and refrigerate until they begin to set. Beat in beaten egg whites; fold in whipped cream. Serves 8-10.

CHOCOLATE CHARLOTTE RUSSE

1 recipe Chocolate Charlotte
½ cup cream whipped (additional)
2 3-ounce packages ladyfingers

1. Line an 8½ by 4½ by 2½-inch loaf dish with waxed paper, extending the paper beyond rim; split ladyfingers lengthwise; line the bottom and sides, having the flat side turned in.
2. Pour in ½ of the chocolate mixture; add a layer of ladyfinger halves and the remaining pudding.
3. Top with remaining ladyfinger halves; chill 3 to 4 hours until firm.
4. Using the waxed paper, lift the dessert from the dish and carefully transfer to a serving plate; remove waxed paper; garnish with whipped cream. Serves 8-10.

LEMON VELVET

1 tablespoon gelatine (1 envelope)	½ cup sugar
¼ cup cold water	¼ cup lemon juice
1 cup rich milk or cream	½ cup cream, whipped

1. Soften gelatine in cold water; dissolve over low heat.
2. Heat milk, add sugar, stir till dissolved; cool; add melted gelatine.
3. When partly set, beat until foamy; add lemon juice.
4. Fold in whipped cream; place in serving dish; garnish with fresh or frozen fruit. Serves 6-8.

MAPLE CHARLOTTE

Substitute 1 cup maple syrup for sugar and lemon juice in Lemon Velvet.

CREOLE BAVARIAN

1 tablespoon gelatine (1 envelope)	1 cup cream, whipped
1 19-ounce can crushed pineapple, drained	⅓ cup dark rum
	3 tablespoons flaked coconut

1. Dissolve gelatine in 4 tablespoons of hot pineapple liquid; cool slightly. Fold into the whipped cream and fold cream into drained crushed pineapple.
2. Flame the rum (page 731) and when cool fold into the pineapple cream mixture; spoon into individual sherbet glasses.
3. Simmer remaining pineapple juice until thick, add the coconut, stir and cool slightly. Spoon a little over each serving. Chill and serve. Serves 4-6.

STRAWBERRY-LEMONADE BAVARIAN

1 tablespoon gelatine	1 10-ounce package frozen strawberries, partially thawed
¼ cup cold water	
½ cup boiling water	
1 6-ounce can (⅔ cup) frozen lemonade concentrate, thawed	1 cup cream, whipped

1. Soften gelatine in cold water; dissolve in boiling water.
2. Stir in lemonade and berries; chill.
3. When partly set, fold in whipped cream mould; Serves 6.

BRANDIED COFFEE MOUSSE

2 tablespoons gelatine	¼ cup instant coffee
(2 envelopes)	3 cups water
⅔ cup sugar	¼ cup brandy
¼ teaspoon salt	1 cup heavy cream, whipped

1. Mix together the gelatine, sugar, salt, and instant coffee in a saucepan; add 1 cup of water and place over low heat, stirring constantly, until gelatine and sugar are dissolved. Remove from heat.
2. Stir in 2 cups cold water, and the brandy. Divide mixture in half.
3. Pour ½ into a 6-cup mould; chill. Chill remaining ½ of mixture until consistency of unbeaten egg white; beat; fold into whipped cream. Turn into mould on top of first coffee layer. Chill; garnish with coffee bean candies. Serves 8.

QUICK PINEAPPLE CHARLOTTE

1 19-ounce can crushed	1 tablespoon lemon juice
pineapple	1 pint ice cream
1 3-ounce pineapple jelly powder	

1. Drain crushed pineapple, measure liquid, add water to make 1½ cups, heat.
2. Dissolve jelly powder in this liquid; add lemon juice; chill.
3. When partially set beat until foamy; beat in the ice cream; add crushed pineapple; chill. Serves 6-8.

Variations:

1 3-ounce black cherry jelly powder with 1 10-ounce package frozen raspberries defrosted.
1 3-ounce strawberry jelly powder with 1 10-ounce package frozen strawberries defrosted.
1 3-ounce orange jelly powder with orange juice, mandarin oranges and green grapes.

ORANGE DREAM

1 3-ounce orange jelly powder	¾ cup orange juice
¼ cup sugar	1 package Whipped Topping Mix
¾ cup hot water	

1. Dissolve jelly powder and sugar in hot water; add orange juice; chill until the mixture begins to set.
2. Prepare the Whipped Topping according to the package directions and beat into the jelly; mould. Serves 6-8.

REFRIGERATOR DESSERTS

These desserts need to stand, sometimes for several hours. This means a minimum of last-minute preparation. For other suggestions see Desserts made with Ice Cream (page 623).

COOKIE STACKS

20 chocolate wafer cookies	1 cup Whipped Cream Filling (page 562)

1. Use any whipped cream filling prepared for another dessert, or cake filling, or any pie filling such as lemon, lime or cream. Spread the mixture on 1 cookie; place the next 1 on top, cover with filling and so on to the last 1 of 4 or 5. Do not cover it with filling. A loaf tin is useful for holding these little stacks. Coat each stack smoothly with whipped cream filling and sprinkle with finely chopped nuts or toasted coconut. Chill several hours.
2. Garnish the top with a little whipped cream and a bit of the fruit that is in the filling. Serves 4 or 5.

Variations:
Chocolate wafers with apricot, orange or pineapple cream filling.
Gingersnaps with lemon cream filling.
Vanilla wafers with chocolate, mocha cream filling.
In the same way as above, put together the large-sized chocolate or ginger cookies, placing them in a long roll in a loaf pan or wrapping them with waxed paper or saran wrap to keep them together. Let stand several hours or overnight in the refrigerator. To serve, slice on a diagonal slant.

LEMON REFRIGERATOR PIE

1 small can evaporated milk (⅔ cup)	⅓ cup fresh lemon juice
2 eggs	1 tablespoon grated lemon peel
½ cup sugar	spiced crumbs

1. Pour milk into ice cube tray and chill until crystals start to form.
2. Separate eggs. Mix yolks with sugar, lemon juice and grated peel.
3. Beat egg whites stiff, then lightly mix in yolk mixture.
4. Turn chilled milk into bowl, beat stiff, carefully fold into egg mixture.
5. Press spiced crumbs (see below) firmly into the ice cube tray to line sides and bottom.
6. Swirl top, decorate with lemon peel twists and freeze. Serves 6-8.

TO SPICE CRUMBS

To ¾ cup crisp toast crumbs or graham wafer crumbs, add ½ cup brown sugar, ½ teaspoon nutmeg, ¼ teaspoon allspice, 1 teaspoon cinnamon, ¼ teaspoon ground cloves, ¼ teaspoon ginger. Mix well. Work in 3 tablespoons melted butter.

PUMPKIN PARFAIT SQUARES

To 1½ cups Spiced Crumbs add ½ cup finely chopped pecans. Press against the sides and bottom of a 9-inch cake pan. Fill with Pumpkin Ice Cream Pie Filling (page 486). Decorate with whipped cream. Serves 6.

LEMON COCONUT SQUARES

1 cup sweetened condensed milk	2 cups toasted shredded coconut
6 tablespoons lemon juice	1 19-ounce can (2½ cups) sliced
1 teaspoon grated lemon peel	peaches, drained
1 10 by 5-inch loaf angel cake	mint leaves

1. Combine sweetened condensed milk and lemon juice; stir until thickened; add grated peel.
2. Cut cake into ¾-inch slices; turn each on its side and frost with lemon mixture.
3. Sprinkle squares with coconut; chill. Place 3 canned peach slices on each. Garnish with mint. Serves 10-12.

ANGEL MOULD

1. Tear an angel cake into bite-sized pieces; combine with Lemon Custard Filling (page 565), or with any of the Charlotte Mixtures (page 612).
2. Pour into an angel cake pan; chill until firm.
3. Unmould onto strips of waxed paper on a serving plate; remove the strips.
4. Frost with 1 cup of cream, whipped; garnish with chocolate curls.

MERINGUE SHELLS (Basic Recipe)

Meringue Shells should be kept in a dry, airy place.

4 egg whites	1 teaspoon vanilla
⅛ teaspoon salt	1 cup sugar
¼ teaspoon cream of tartar	

1. Place egg whites in a bowl. Sprinkle with salt and cream of tartar; add some of the vanilla. Beat until foamy. Begin adding sugar, about 1 tablespoon at a time, beating continuously.
2. Add remaining vanilla drop by drop between additions of sugar. The last quarter of the sugar may be folded in.
3. Cover a baking sheet with aluminum foil; spoon on the meringue, making rounds with a hollow in the centre, or force the meringue through a large pastry tip.
4. Preheat oven to 400°. Place the meringues in the oven, turn off the heat and leave without opening the door for at least 2 hours. If the oven is not well enough insulated to hold the heat bake at 275° for 50-60 minutes. Makes 12 meringues 3 inches in diameter or 40 meringues 1 inch in diameter.

Fold in ½ cup (2 ounces) finely-chopped hazel nuts.
Tint the meringues by adding a few drops of red or green colouring.

MERINGUE GLACÉES

Fill meringues with ice cream; add a sauce or fresh or frozen fruit. Here are some suggestions:

Coffee ice cream, chocolate sauce.
French vanilla ice cream, fresh or defrosted frozen berries.
Peppermint stick ice cream, marshmallow sauce.
Lemon Cheese Filling (page 566), fresh blueberries.

ANGEL PIE

1. Prepare the mixture for Meringue Shells.
2. Spread in a deep, lightly greased 8 or 9-inch pie plate so that the mixture is high and thick at the edge, or spoon onto a 9-inch circle.
3. Bake for 1 hour at 275°; cool in the oven which has been turned off.
4. Fill with ½ the recipe of Lemon Custard Filling (page 565) or with any of the Cream Fillings (page 563); cover with whipped cream.
5. Let stand several hours or overnight in the refrigerator. Serves 6-8.

SWISS PEACHES

A good way to use the less-than-perfect meringues.

3 cups soft custard (or
　lemon cheese filling)
1 large can of peach halves
　meringues crushed

2 tablespoons brandy (or
　apricot brandy)
　peach juice
1 cup whipping cream

1. Spoon the soft custard into a sherbet glass.

2. Cover with a layer of broken meringues; top with a peach half, cut side down.

3. Simmer peach juice until thick; flame the brandy, add it to the juice and spread 1 tablespoon over each sherbet.

4. Pipe whipped cream around inside edge of sherbet glass, leaving the glazed peach exposed.

MERINGUE TOWERS

Force uncooked meringue out of a pastry bag through a potato rosette tip, swirling the meringue into cones about 2 inches high. Bake and store until needed.

Push a peach half, rounded side down, into a spoonful of ice cream in a sherbet glass. Set a Meringue Tower over the hollow of the peach; spoon defrosted raspberries over the meringue, leaving the peak uncovered as a garnish.

FROZEN DESSERTS

Frozen Desserts for the Ice Cream Freezer

These recipes are not designed for use in the automatic refrigerator, but for the freezer turned either by hand or electricity. To prepare the freezer, follow directions that come with the equipment.

VANILLA ICE CREAM I (PHILADELPHIA)

1 quart thin cream
¾ cup sugar

1½ tablespoons vanilla

1 pint of the cream can be replaced with 2 cups fruit pulp and juice; vary the sugar to taste. Peach, strawberry or pineapple are popular flavours.

VANILLA ICE CREAM II (FRENCH) (Basic Recipe)

1 cup milk	dash of salt
1 egg	2 cups whipping cream
½ cup sugar	1 tablespoon vanilla

1. Cook first four ingredients as a soft custard (page 584).
2. Strain, cool, add cream whipped just until foamy but not stiff, and vanilla.
3. Freeze.

COFFEE ICE CREAM

Add 2 teaspoons instant coffee to the milk mixture.

CHOCOLATE ICE CREAM

Heat a ½-inch stick of cinnamon with the milk; strain. Chop 2 ounces chocolate; melt in the milk; increase sugar to ¾ cup.

Frozen Desserts for the Refrigerator

To be successful, ice cream made in a refrigerator or freezer, without the beating that is possible in the ice cream freezer, must have some other means of keeping the crystals small. These recipes have been expecially selected for this purpose.

STRAWBERRY ICE CREAM

1 10-ounce package frozen strawberries, thawed	few grains of salt
¼ cup sugar	⅔ cup evaporated milk, chilled
	1 tablespoon lemon juice

1. Add sugar and salt to the berries; let stand.
2. Add the lemon juice to the milk and whip.
3. Beat the berry mixture into the whipped milk; pour into a one-quart ice tray; freeze without stirring at the coldest temperature. Makes 1 quart; serves 10.

Substitute 1 10-ounce package frozen raspberries (thawed)
   or
   1 12-ounce package frozen peaches (thawed and crushed)
   or
   1 19-ounce can crushed pineapple (undrained)
   or
   1¼ cups fresh berries or peaches, mashed, with ¼ cup sugar (additional).

LEMON ICE CREAM

½ cup light corn syrup	½ cup lemon juice
3 egg whites	3 egg yolks
¼ cup sugar	1 cup heavy cream

1. Gradually add corn syrup to beaten egg whites, beating till very stiff.
2. In the top of a double boiler, combine the sugar, lemon juice and egg yolks; stir over hot water until the mixture begins to thicken; remove from the heat; cool.
3. Beat the cream until thick but not stiff.
4. Fold the egg yolk mixture into the egg whites; fold in the cream; add a few drops of yellow colouring. Freeze.

The lemon juice may be replaced with lime or orange juice.

Fruit Marlow with Cherries.

FRUIT MARLOW (Basic Recipe)

30 marshmallows (½ pound)	1½ cups whipping cream
1½ cups hot pineapple juice	fruits or nuts

1. Melt marshmallows in fruit juice, over boiling water.
2. Cool; fold in cream which has been whipped until thick but not stiff.
3. Add fruits or nuts; freeze.

   The cream may be replaced by 1 6-ounce can evaporated milk, chilled and whipped.

COFFEE MARLOW

Use 1½ cups strong clear coffee to replace fruit juice.

APRICOT MARLOW

Replace pineapple juice with apricot nectar; if desired beat in 1 cup canned apricots, drained and chopped.

STRAWBERRY MARLOW

Replace fruit juice with 1 package frozen berries thawed; add 3 tablespoons lemon juice.

CHOCOLATE MINT MARLOW

Heat 2 ounces chocolate and a dash of salt with 2 cups milk over hot water; beat until smooth. Add 30 marshmallows. Cool. Fold in 1 cup cream whipped and ⅛ teaspoon peppermint extract. Freeze.

FRUIT SHERBET (Basic Recipe)

1 teaspoon gelatine	2 cups milk
2 tablespoons cold water	1 egg white
¼ cup hot water	¼ cup sugar
¾ cup sugar	⅛ teaspoon salt
1 cup grapefruit juice	

1. Soften gelatine in cold water; dissolve in hot water; add sugar and sufficient grapefruit juice to dissolve the sugar; reheat if necessary.
2. Add remaining grapefruit juice; chill until syrupy.
3. Add the milk; pour into refrigerator tray; freeze until firm. The mixture will curdle but will be beaten smooth later.
4. Beat egg white until stiff but not dry. Beat in ¼ cup sugar and salt. Break frozen mixture into chunks and beat until smooth. Fold into beaten mixture. Return to tray; freeze firm. Serves 6.

PINEAPPLE SHERBET

Substitute 1 cup undrained crushed pineapple for fruit juice; buttermilk for the milk.

ORANGE CRÈME FREEZE

Use 1 6-ounce can frozen orange juice and ¼ cup lemon juice to replace grapefruit juice.

GRAPE CRÈME FREEZE

Use 1 6-ounce can frozen grape juice and a lemon jelly powder to replace the grapefruit, gelatine and ½ of the sugar.

GLAMOUR LEMON SHERBET

Put lemon sherbet in sherbet glasses. Make a depression in the centre and freeze. Just before serving fill the depression with: green crème de menthe, decorated with a sprig of mint; *or*, frozen raspberries, thawed but still icy; *or* fresh pineapple, shredded and sweetened.

DESSERTS MADE WITH ICE CREAM

LEMON CRÈME ICE CREAM

1 pint French vanilla ice cream	2 to 3 drops yellow food
2 teaspoons grated lemon rind	colouring
2 teaspoons fresh lemon juice	4 tablespoons green crème de
	menthe liqueur

1. Soften ice cream by creaming in a chilled bowl; stir in lemon rind, lemon juice, yellow colouring, working quickly so ice cream does not have time to melt.
2. Cover bowl and refreeze.
3. Spoon into serving dishes. Top each serving with 1 tablespoon green crème de menthe.

MARBLE ICE CREAM

At least an hour before serving time soften the ice cream slightly at room temperature. Marble by stirring into the ice cream:

frozen strawberries which have been slightly thawed and mashed.

4 tablespoons green crème de menthe or other liqueur.

melted chocolate mint or rum wafers stirred with 2 tablespoons hot water.

thawed, undiluted fruit concentrate (orange, lemon, apple).

ICE CREAM MOULD

Chill a ring mould. Fill with alternate scoops of different coloured sherbet or ice cream; pack gently; refreeze. Unmould and fill the centre with fresh fruit. Three pints of ice cream will serve 10.

PEACH MELBA

Arrange a large peach half (or four drained apricot halves) in a sherbet; spoon the ice cream into the centre of the fruit; top with raspberry jam or frozen raspberries which have been thawed.

PEARS HELÈNE

For each serving, place a scoop of vanilla ice cream between two drained pear halves in a sherbet dish. Top with chocolate sauce and garnish with chopped nuts.

QUICK CHERRY TORTONI

1 pint ice cream
¼ cup drained chopped
   maraschino cherries (or
   pineapple or strawberries)

½ cup crushed vanilla wafers
   (12 wafers)
½ teaspoon almond extract

Stir ice cream until slightly soft but not melted; stir into it all ingredients but 2 tablespoons of the wafers; sprinkle the crumbs on top; freeze.

Rum and raisin ice cream is good here.

ICE CREAM CAKE

1. With waxed paper strips line a cake pan the same size as cake layers.
2. Press 1 quart of ice cream into the pan; freeze.
3. Place between two layers of cake; freeze; cut into wedges and serve with sauce.

Try these combinations:

Cake	Ice Cream	Sauce
Angel Cake	Raspberry Sherbet	Crushed Raspberries
Gold Cake	Chocolate	Sliced Peaches
Chiffon Cake	Coffee	Caramel Sauce
Spice Cake	Orange	Chocolate
Sponge	Black Cherry	Lemon
White Cake	Butter Pecan	Butterscotch
Devil's Food	Peach	Chocolate

ICE CREAM ROLL

1. Unroll cooled jelly roll; spread with raspberry jelly, sprinkle with ¼ cup sherry (optional) then 1 pint slightly softened vanilla ice cream.
2. Roll up again; return to freezer. Remove from freezer 10 minutes before slicing. Serves 6.

Variation: Spread a chocolate jelly roll with lime or pistachio ice cream, or vanilla ice cream tinted with green colour and flavoured with peppermint.

ANGEL LAYERS

1 large angel cake or chiffon cake
1 pint chocolate ice cream, slightly softened
1 pint vanilla ice cream, slightly softened
Whipped Cream filling

1. Using a piece of thread divide cake into three layers.
2. Spread vanilla ice cream quickly over bottom layer; cover with second layer of cake, then chocolate ice cream, then third layer of cake; press firmly together; frost if desired with Whipped Cream filling (page 562); garnish with chocolate curls, toasted nuts or cocoanut.

ANGEL RIBBON LOAF

Use a loaf cake cut into layers; put the layers together with any of the marbled ice creams on pages 623, 624.

ANGEL SURPRISE CAKE

1. Cut a half-inch slice from the top of a large angel cake; set aside.
2. Scoop out the centre of the angel cake leaving a shell of ½ to 1 inch on sides and bottom. (A grapefruit knife is useful in cutting and removing the cake.)
3. Fill with 1 quart ice cream of contrasting colour.
4. Replace the top slice; freeze for a half hour to set the ice cream.
5. Frost whole cake with thin Butter Icing (page 569) or with Whipped Cream filling.

Ice cream in these recipes may be replaced by the fillings on page 561 or by the Charlotte recipes on page 612.

BAKED ALASKA

1 8- or 9-inch layer cake (round)	4 egg whites
2 pint containers ice cream	¼ teaspoon salt
(1 vanilla, 1 coloured)	½ cup sugar
15 marshmallows	
1 tablespoon fruit juice	
(orange or pineapple)	

1. Find a bowl which, when inverted on the cake layer, leaves a 1-inch margin of cake; line it with waxed paper strips to extend beyond the bowl.

2. Pack the vanilla ice cream into the bowl, pushing it up on the sides to leave a hollow in the centre; freeze; pack the other colour into the hollow, levelling it off on top; freeze hard.

3. Place the marshmallows and juice in the top of a double boiler; heat over gently boiling water until soft.

4. Beat the egg whites and salt until stiff but not dry in a deep 1-1½ quart bowl; add the sugar slowly, beating constantly to form a very stiff meringue; beat in the marshmallows; continue to beat until cool. (Unless the meringue is standing up in stiff peaks and is sufficient to coat the cake and ice cream thickly, do not continue.)

5. Place the layer of cake on a sheet of heavy white paper on a piece of corrugated paper on a baking sheet; unmould the ice cream onto the cake; peel off the strips of waxed paper; immediately frost the ice cream and the cake with the meringue. It is important to have no thin spots or places where the ice cream or cake is showing. Freeze overnight if desired.

6. Sprinkle with slivered, blanched almonds or coconut; place in a hot oven (425°) to brown. Serve at once. Serves 8 to 10.

   The cake or ice cream may be spread with a thin layer of red jam. Two bricks of ice cream may be placed side by side on a 9-inch square of cake.

ALASKA MARY ANNS

1. Make individual servings by using 6 Mary Ann shells which can be bought from a baker. Divide 1 quart of ice cream among the six little cakes; freeze.

2. Prepare the recipe of meringue; finish as Baked Alaska.

ALASKA PIE

1. Bake a 9-inch pie crust in an oven-glass pie plate; cool.
2. Sprinkle with 1 cup of raspberries; fill with ice cream packed in firmly; sprinkle with more berries; freeze.
3. Prepare half the recipe of meringue; cover the ice cream, bringing the meringue out well to the edge of the crust; finish as Baked Alaska.

DOUGHNUT DELIGHT

Split cake doughnuts; arrange cut side up on baking sheet and heat under the broiler. Spread the bottom half with black currant or strawberry jam. Cover with a scoop of ice cream, cover with the second half; fill the hole with more jam, whipped cream or marshmallow sauce.

Cornstarch Pudding with Pie Filling appears in its many roles with fruit, as a parfait or as a filling for meringues and cream puffs.

PARFAITS

1. Choose a parfait glass with a flaring top, or use an old-fashioned glass.
2. Have ice creams of different colours, fruits and sauces.
3. Arrange in the glass in layers.
4. Return to the freezer; if parfaits are not to be used soon avoid pieces of fruit which will not defrost as quickly as the other ingredients.

The range is endless but here are a few suggestions:

Vanilla ice cream with canned fruit cocktail, or frozen fruit concentrate (thawed); or home made jam or conserve; or liqueur.

Chocolate ice cream with alternate layers of crushed pineapple topped with marshmallow sauce.

Strawberry ice cream with alternate layers of fresh blueberries, raspberries or strawberries, crushed and allowed to stand with sugar. Top with whipped cream and a few perfect berries just before serving.

Combine a 6-ounce can of frozen orange concentrate thawed with 1 cup drained crushed pineapple; layer the fruit with ice cream; garnish with pineapple and a sprig of mint, or with stem-on cherries. Prepare jelly (page 608); cut in fine cubes when set. Layer jelly, ice cream and sauce.

SUNDAE TRAY

1. Set out a bowl of ice cream balls, allowing 1 quart for 8-10 servings.
2. Around it arrange sherbet glasses containing salted nuts; chopped maraschino cherries; ginger marmalade; apricot conserve; crushed peppermint stick candy or peanut brittle.
3. Include small pitchers of chocolate sauce; maple syrup; frozen raspberries thawed, frozen orange juice thawed but undiluted.

ICE CREAM BALLS

Coat ice cream balls with a mixture of sugar-coated rice or wheat cereal and flaked coconut; or with chocolate cake crumbs, or with toasted coconut or chopped nuts; refreeze. Serve with sauce.

FLAMING DESSERTS

CHERRY COUPE

2 cans pitted black cherries	2 pints ice cream
4 tablespoons red currant jelly	½ pint cream, whipped
cherry brandy	toasted sliced almonds

1. Drain cherry juice into a saucepan; add the red current jelly and simmer until syrupy.
2. Pit the cherries; add brandy and let stand for 30 minutes.
3. Drain liquid from the cherries into the syrup; cool.
4. Place a layer of cherries in the bottom of a sherbet glass, cover with vanilla ice cream. Pour some syrup over, top with whipped cream and garnish with almonds. Serves 8-10.

CHERRIES JUBILEE

1 tablespoon cornstarch	3 or 4 strips of orange peel
1 tablespoon sugar	1 teaspoon lemon juice
1 can (12-ounce) pitted black cherries (Bing)	½ cup warm brandy
	1 pint vanilla ice cream

1. Mix cornstarch and sugar together; add liquid from canned cherries (about 1 cup) and the orange peel; stir, cook until the sauce thickens; discard orange peel; add cherries and lemon juice.
2. At the table have the sauce warm in a chafiing dish and ice cream balls in a shallow bowl.
3. Flame (page 731); spoon over vanilla ice cream as it is being served. Serves 6.

Substitute red pie cherries, ¼ cup red currant jelly.

For a sweeter sauce heat together 1 can Bing cherries and 1 cup white corn syrup; flame.

STRAWBERRIES JUBILEE

½ cup sugar	1 tablespoon cold water
½ cup water	1 quart strawberries, washed and hulled
thin slivers lemon rind	
1 tablespoon cornstarch	½ cup Kirsch

1. Dissolve the sugar in water; add lemon rind; simmer 5 minutes.
2. Mix cornstarch and water to a smooth paste; add to the syrup; stir until the syrup is slightly thickened and there is no flavour of raw starch.
3. Add the strawberries; bring to a boil; turn into a serving dish.
4. When ready to serve flame with Kirsch (page 731) and ladle over ice cream.

RASPBERRIES JUBILEE

Substitute 1 pint raspberries for the strawberries.

BANANAS FLAMBÉ

Melt 2 tablespoons butter in a chafing dish and add 6 bananas, peeled and halved lengthwise. Sprinkle them lightly with a little lemon juice, brown sugar, and cinnamon and sauté them until they are lightly browned. Turn the bananas, sprinkle them again with a little lemon juice, brown sugar, and cinnamon, and sauté them until they are tender but not mushy. Flame.

TORTES

MERINGUE TORTE

Tortes are desserts built up of thin layers of cake, pastry or meringue put together with rich fillings.

1. Prepare the mixture for Meringue Shells (page 618).
2. On aluminum foil on two cookie sheets, trace three circles using layer-cake pans as the pattern.
3. Cover two of the circles with a flat layer of the meringue; make a ring 1¼ inches wide and ¾ inch high with most of the remaining meringue; with the last little bit make a swirled "dollop."
4. Sprinkle with chopped almonds; bake at 225° for 1 hour.
5. Criss-cross aluminum foil strips in the layer-cake pans; fill one with a quart of chocolate ice cream, the other with a quart of coffee ice cream (any other combinations may be used); smooth the tops with a spatula; cover with foil and freeze.
6. On top of one circle of cooled, baked meringue place the chocolate ice cream, then the second circle of meringue, the coffee ice cream, and the meringue ring.
7. Fill with a thin layer of chocolate sauce and set the dollop on top.
8. Freeze the torte until serving time; cut with a sharp knife into wedges. Serves 10-12.

Another pleasing combination is vanilla and peppermint ice cream; tint the peppermint a light green colour. These tortes may be made as individual desserts.

NUT TORTE

Try this with black walnuts or butternuts.

4 medium eggs, separated	crumbs
1 cup granulated sugar	1 teaspoon baking powder
1 cup dried, ground bread	1 cup ground nuts

1. Beat egg whites until they stand in soft peaks; gradually add ½ cup sugar, beating until stiff.
2. Beat yolks, gradually adding remaining ½ cup sugar, until very thick and light-coloured.
3. Combine bread crumbs, baking powder and nuts; stir into yolks; fold into whites.
4. Bake 20 minutes at 375° in two buttered, lined, 8-inch layer-cake pans; remove from pans; peel off paper; cool on racks.
5. Fill and frost with Whipped Cream filling (page 562). Serves 8.

ALMOND TORTE

⅞ cup sifted all-purpose flour	½ cup milk
1 teaspoon baking powder	3 egg whites
dash of salt	¼ teaspoon cream of tartar
½ cup shortening	¾ cup sugar
½ cup sugar	1½ tablespoons sugar
3 egg yolks	¾ teaspoon cinnamon
½ teaspoon almond extract	½ cup blanched slivered almonds

1. Combine the first eight ingredients as Butter Cake (page 537).
2. Spread batter in two greased 8-inch layer-cake pans.
3. Prepare a meringue from the next three ingredients (page 482).
4. Spread over unbaked cake mixture in both pans.
5. Mix sugar, cinnamon and almonds and sprinkle over the meringue mixtures.
6. Bake at 350° for about 30 minutes; cool.
7. Put together meringue side up with a filling in between. For filling use recipes on page 561.
8. Garnish with whipped cream and shaved chocolate or brazil nut curls.

DOBOSCH TORTE

⅞ cup sifted all-purpose flour	½ teaspoon cream of tartar
1 teaspoon double-acting baking powder	⅓ cup sugar
	4 egg yolks
¾ cup sugar	¼ cup water
4 egg whites	1 teaspoon vanilla extract
½ teaspoon salt	1 teaspoon orange extract

1. Line 12 by 18-inch jelly roll pans with sheets of heavy-duty aluminum foil.
2. Sift the flour, baking powder and ¾ cup sugar together.
3. Beat egg whites, salt, and cream of tartar until soft peaks form. Slowly add the ⅓ cup sugar, beating until straight stiff peaks form.
4. Combine egg yolks, water and flavouring.
5. Add the dry ingredients sifted together; beat one minute until light and creamy in colour.
6. Fold the batter into the meringue; turn into the two pans, spreading evenly.
7. Bake 10-12 minutes at 350°; cool for 10 minutes; cut each cake crosswise into four; remove the foil; stack and trim.
8. Spread 2-3 tablespoons of frosting between each layer; frost the sides and top.

CHOCOLATE TORTE

2½ cups semi-sweet chocolate bits
⅔ cup butter
4 eggs, separated
1 tablespoon flour

1 tablespoon sugar
apricot jam or apricot filling
chocolate glaze
slivered blanched almonds

1. Melt the chocolate and the butter over hot, but not boiling water; blend. Remove from heat and set aside.
2. Beat the egg yolks until thick and lemon-coloured. Fold into melted chocolate mixture. Mix together the flour and sugar and add to chocolate mixture.
3. Beat the egg whites until stiff but not dry; fold into melted chocolate mixture. Turn into an 8-inch spring-form pan; bake at 425° 15 to 20 minutes; cool.
4. Remove sides of pan. Spread cake top with apricot jam.
5. Frost top and sides with Chocolate Glaze (page 578). Decorate sides with slivered almonds.

PEACH TORTE

This torte is made with pastry.

2½ cups sifted all-purpose flour
½ cup finely chopped toasted almonds
⅓ cup sugar
½ teaspoon salt
¾ cup butter or margarine
⅓ cup cold water

2 cups whipping cream
¼ cup sugar
⅛ teaspoon almond extract
2 19-ounce cans drained sliced peaches
1 cup crushed pineapple drained

1. Prepare pastry from first six ingredients (page 472); divide into 3 balls; roll each to ⅛ inch thickness, trim with pastry wheel to 8-inch circles; bake at 425° until lightly browned (8-10 minutes); cool. These circles may be wrapped and frozen for later use.
2. Whip cream; add sugar and flavouring; set aside 1 cup.
3. Save eight peach slices; chop the rest; combine with pineapple and fold into the remaining cream.
4. To assemble the Torte spread the fruited cream between pastry circles; spread the reserved cream over the top and garnish with peach slices. Chill 2-3 hours. Serves 10-12.

   Make up tiny tart shells from the scraps to fill later with any cake filling, with Quick Cherry Tortoni (p. 624) or with any of the gelatine recipes (pages 608).

Home-made bread and rolls are a treat at any hour.

Versatile cream-puff shells are filled with Chicken à la King. Many varieties of bread may be made.

CHOCOLATE FROSTING

2 ounces unsweetened chocolate	1 teaspoon vanilla extract
	½ teaspoon maple flavouring
1 cup sweet butter	2 cups icing sugar

1. Melt the chocolate in a bowl over hot water.
2. Add the fat and cream until soft but not melted; add the flavourings.
3. Add sifted icing sugar—a small amount at a time creaming after each addition.

ICELANDIC TORTE

Prepare the torte layers from pastry (Peach Torte) from Meringue (Meringue Torte) or from cake (Almond Torte).

Put together with Prune Filling (p. 565); refrigerate at least 24 hours. Serve with a bowl of whipped cream. Serves 8-10.

FINNISH TORTE

3 egg yolks	¼ teaspoon cloves
¼ cup sugar	3 egg whites
½ cup rye crackers crushed	¼ cup sugar
2 squares semi-sweet chocolate (grated)	½ recipe Spanish Cream page (611)
2 tablespoons rolled oats (quick cooking)	1 cup cream, whipped chocolate curls (page 579)
¼ teaspoon cinnamon	

1. Beat egg yolks until thick and lemon-coloured; beat in sugar.
2. Add next 5 ingredients and mix well.
3. Beat egg whites until stiff but not dry; beat in sugar; fold into the batter.
4. Pour into greased pans; bake until cakes are golden brown and spring back when gently pressed; cool.
5. Spread Spanish Cream between layers; cover top and sides with whipped cream; garnish with chocolate curls. Serves 8.

MOCHA BROWNIE TORTE

1 recipe brownies	chocolate curls
1 recipe Mocha Butter Icing (page 520)	

1. Prepare Brownies from recipe on page 520; bake in 2 layers, spread half the cream between the layers; frost the top and sides with the remainder; garnish with chocolate curls.
2. Refrigerate at least one hour. Serves 10-12.

CHEESE CAKE (Basic Recipe)

Crust	Filling
1½ cups graham wafer crumbs	4 eggs
2 tablespoons sugar	¾ cups sugar
¼ cup melted butter	1 cup whipping cream
	⅛ teaspoon salt
Topping	3 tablespoons lemon juice
½ cup whipped cream	(1 lemon)
1 cup sliced sweetened peaches	1 teaspoon vanilla
	2½ tablespoons flour
	2 pounds Cream Cheese

1. Combine the crust ingredients; press most of the crumbs into the sides and bottom of a 9-inch spring-form pan; chill.
2. Beat eggs and sugar until light and fluffy; add cream, salt, lemon juice and vanilla.
3. Sift in flour; add cheese; beat well.
4. Pour into the crumb-lined pan; sprinkle remaining crumbs on top.
5. Bake at 350° until set (about 45 minutes); turn off the heat; open oven door and leave the cake 1 hour or until cool.

Place the cake in the spring-form pan on a decorative plate; run a metal knife around the sides of the pan to loosen the cake; lift off the sides; decorate with topping.

These amounts fill an 8-9 inch spring-form pan and serve 10-12. For family size 5-6 servings use ½ the filling recipe but the full amount of Crust Mixture.

Cherry Cheesecake—a rich and filling dessert.

CRUST

Substitute for graham wafer crumbs and sugar.

1 package rusks	1 teaspoon spice (cinnamon
½ cup sugar	or cinnamon and nutmeg)

TOPPINGS

Cover chilled cake with:

sour cream. Top with fresh ripe strawberries and brush with either melted currant jelly or melted apricot jam. Chill again.

crumbled almond roca or butter crunch.

sour cream; sprinkle with crushed Macadamia nuts.

Add ¼ cup finely-cut preserved ginger to cheese cake mix. Chill. Top with sour cream and sprinkle with chopped preserved ginger and chopped toasted hazelnuts.

Spread with a thick layer of melted apricot jam. Add chopped pistachio nuts and preserved apricots.

Cover with canned Cherry Pie Filling.

REFRIGERATOR CHEESE CAKE

2 tablespoons gelatine	1 teaspoon lemon rind
(2 envelopes)	1 tablespoon lemon juice
½ cup water	3 cups creamed cottage cheese
2 egg yolks	2 egg whites
1 cup sugar	1 teaspoon vanilla
¼ teaspoon salt	1 cup cream, whipped
1 cup milk	

1. Soften gelatine in ½ cup water.
2. Combine yolks slightly beaten with the sugar, salt and milk in the top part of a double boiler; cook over hot water until thick, stirring constantly; remove from heat and stir in gelatine; cool.
3. Add the lemon juice and rind; stir in the sieved cheese; when the jelly begins to set beat in the stiffly beaten egg whites; fold in whipped cream.
4. Turn into the lined spring-form pan; chill until firm.

QUICK CHEESE CAKE

1¾ cups crushed pineapple
1 tablespoon gelatine
   (1 envelope)
1 package (8-ounce) cream
   cheese (softened)

½ tablespoon grated lemon peel
1 package instant vanilla
   pudding mix
1 cup milk
½ pint cream, whipped

1. Drain pineapple; measure softened gelatine into the pineapple syrup. Heat, stirring until dissolved; cool.
2. Beat cream cheese and lemon peel until fluffy; beat in gelatine mixture; add pudding mix and milk, beating until well blended.
3. Fold in crushed pineapple and all but ½ cup whipped cream. Pour into crust; chill in the refrigerator.

CHOCOLATE FONDUE

See page 559.

BABA

See page 468.

CREAM PUFF DESSERTS

See page 502.

20 Candy

HOMEMADE candies can be as delicious, smooth, and professional-looking as those produced in our finest candy shops. Choose a clear, dry day, preferably, and never attempt to double or triple the recipe. The use of a candy thermomcter removes the guesswork from candy-making, but when not available the following cold water test will determine the approximate saturation of the syrup—that is, tell when the candy is cooked sufficiently.

Cold Water Test

Place cold water in a bowl to a depth of 3 inches and allow a few drops of hot syrup to fall off the spoon into the cold water.

Note the appearance of the syrup as soon as it hits the water; it may disperse quickly or settle as a ball in the bottom of the bowl.

If the cooled syrup forms a ball, feel it between the thumb and fore-finger to determine its consistency. Compare results with those given in table below:

Product	Stage	Temperature	Characteristics
	Thread	230-235°	When dropped from a fork, mixture will spin a fine thread about 2 inches in length; when it hits the water it disperses and coats the bottom of bowl.
Fudge; Fondant	Soft Ball	235-240°	Mixture will form a soft ball in water; when rubbed, it gradually melts and disappears.
Caramels	Firm Ball	246-250°	Mixture will form a firm ball in water, which when rubbed will flatten but not disappear.

Product	Stage	Temperature	Characteristics
Divinity	Hard Ball	250-263°	Mixture will form a hard ball in water and will hold its shape when rubbed.
Popcorn Balls; Butterscotch	Soft Crack	270-290°	Mixture will form threads like spun glass when it hits the water; threads will break when rubbed.
Brittles; Glacés	Hard Crack	300-310°	Mixture is very brittle both in the air and water.
Barley Sugar	Clear liquid	330°	Sugar becomes lumpy, then melts to a clear liquid.
Caramel	Brown liquid	338°	Melted liquid sugar turns reddish-brown.

CRYSTALLINE CANDY (FUDGES AND FONDANTS)

FUDGES

Fudges are made up of tiny crystals; the finer the crystals, the smoother the fudge. Beating initiates the growth of crystals and if crystal formation takes place early, they will be large. Avoid excess stirring while cooking, and do not beat or agitate the cooling syrup after cooking until it has reached the correct temperature for beating. The use of brown sugar, syrup, cream of tartar or vinegar in a candy mixture tends to retard crystallization of the syrup; butter and cream also have this effect. Always choose fudge recipes which contain at least 1 of these ingredients.

VANILLA FUDGE

2 cups sugar
⅔ cup heavy cream
1 cup milk
4 tablespoons corn syrup or
2 tablespoons butter
¼ teaspoon salt
1 teaspoon vanilla
colour (optional)

1. Stir sugar, cream, milk, syrup and salt in a saucepan slowly to boiling.
2. Continue boiling over medium heat until the mixture reaches a temperature of 236° or the soft ball stage.
3. Cool without beating to a temperature of 110° or until mixture feels just warm.
4. Add vanilla and colouring (if desired); beat until mixture loses its gloss and thickens; pour into a buttered pan.

MARSHMALLOW FUDGE
Add ¾ cup marshmallow crème and ½ cup chopped candied fruits just before the fudge is ready to be poured; beat in.

PEANUT BUTTER FUDGE
Substitute 3 tablespoons peanut butter for corn syrup.

MAPLE CREAM

2 cups sugar	2 tablespoons butter
2 cups brown sugar	1 cup rich milk
1 tablespoon flour	½ teaspoon vanilla
½ teaspoon salt	

1. Mix first 4 ingredients in a large saucepan, add butter and milk, and bring to the boiling point, stirring until sugar dissolves.
2. Continue cooking mixture until it reaches the soft ball stage or a temperature of 236°; butter an 8-inch cake or pie pan.
3. Cool without stirring to a temperature of 110° or until mixture feels just warm: add vanilla.
4. Beat until mixture loses its gloss; pour quickly.

CREAM GINGER
Cut ¼ pound candied ginger into small chunks. If ginger has sugar crystals attached, soak in milk, then drain, using the milk in the fudge. Add ginger just before the fudge is ready to pour.

BURNT ALMOND
Chop ½ cup blanched almonds finely; spread on a cookie sheet and toast in a slow oven until a rich brown; add to fudge just before it is ready to pour.

PRALINES
Add 2 cups of pecans or 1 cup blanched whole almonds; when mixture begins to thicken drop rapidly from a tablespoon onto a well-buttered baking sheet.

COFFEE CREAM
Substitute ½ cup strong coffee and ½ cup evaporated milk for the milk, or add 3 teaspoons instant coffee to the sugar.

WALNUT LOGS
Melt ½ pound caramels, 1 tablespoon butter and 1 tablespoon water over boiling water, stirring until smooth. Cut Maple Cream when cool into four strips; shape into rolls. Chop 1½ cups walnuts; spread on waxed paper. With spatula, coat fudge rolls with caramel mixture, turning into the walnuts as coated. Slice when cold.

Chocolate Fudge and Maple Cream Fudge with nuts.

CHOCOLATE FUDGE

3 cups sugar
¼ teaspoon salt
½ cup corn syrup
3 squares unsweetened chocolate
1 cup milk

4 tablespoons butter or
  margarine
1 teaspoon vanilla
1 cup chopped nuts

1. In a saucepan, stir sugar, salt, syrup, chocolate and milk until chocolate has melted and sugar dissolved.

2. Butter an 8-inch square pan while mixture is cooking.

3. Cook over medium heat until mixture reaches the soft ball stage (236°), stirring only enough to prevent scorching.

4. Remove from heat, add butter, cool without stirring to 110° or until mixture feels just warm.

5. Add vanilla and beat until mixture loses its gloss; add nuts; pour immediately into 8 or 9-inch buttered pan.

For variety, increase chocolate to 4 squares and decrease butter to 3 tablespoons. Or substitute ½ cup cocoa for the chocolate and increase the butter to 6 tablespoons.

CHOCOLATE MINT FUDGE

Prepare Chocolate Fudge as directed above. Instead of using vanilla, use 2 drops peppermint extract. Mark in squares; top fudge squares with coloured mint wafers if desired. Cool. Cut.

FUDGE ROLLS

Spread 1 cup chopped nuts on a sheet of aluminum foil on a cookie sheet. Pour fudge mixture over nuts; as fudge cools shape into a long roll. When cool, slice.

UNCOOKED CHOCOLATE FUDGE

1 3-ounce package cream cheese	½ teaspoon vanilla
2 cups sifted icing sugar	dash of salt
2 1-ounce squares unsweetened chocolate	½ cup chopped walnuts

1. In a mixing bowl cream the cheese until soft and smooth. Gradually add icing sugar and blend thoroughly.
2. Melt chocolate and then add to cheese mixture. Add remaining ingredients and mix until well blended.
3. Press into a well-buttered shallow pan and chill in refrigerator until firm. Cut into squares. Makes 1½ dozen pieces.

FIVE-MINUTE CHOCOLATE FUDGE

2 tablespoons butter or margarine	1½ package (6-ounce) chocolate bits or
⅔ cup (1 small can) evaporated milk	6 squares semi-sweet or 3 squares unsweetened
1⅔ cups sugar	chocolate
½ teaspoon salt	1 teaspoon vanilla or 2 drops
1½ cups miniature, or cut-up large, marshmallows	peppermint
	½ cup chopped walnuts

1. Butter an 8-inch pie or cake pan.
2. In saucepan, combine butter, milk, sugar, and salt; bring to boil over medium heat.
3. Cook, stirring constantly, for 5 minutes (start timing when mixture begins to bubble around edge of pan); syrup should boil gently.
4. Remove from heat, and stir in marshmallows, chocolate, vanilla and walnuts. Stir vigorously 1 minute, or until marshmallows are completely blended; pour into 8-inch cake or pie pan.

CARAMEL FUDGE

3 cups sugar	¼ cup butter or margarine
1 cup cream or top milk	½ teaspoon vanilla
⅛ teaspoon baking soda	½ to 1 cup pecans

1. Measure 1 cup of sugar into a small heavy saucepan or frying pan and the remaining sugar with cream into a saucepan.

2. Heat both at the same time over very low heat; stir the sugar constantly with a wooden spoon until it is a light brown syrup. Give the other mixture a stir occasionally until it comes to a boil.

3. Add syrup to boiling cream-sugar mixture very slowly, stirring vigorously to keep it from curdling; continue cooking, without stirring, to firm ball (246°).

4. Remove from stove, mix in the soda; add butter, cool to lukewarm.

5. Add vanilla and beat until mixture is thick and heavy and shines like satin; add nuts; pour out onto 2 buttered 8 or 9-inch pie pans.

This recipe is very good with burnt almonds (see Maple Cream). Add 2 teaspoons grated orange rind with vanilla for a different flavour.

DIVINITY FUDGE

1½ cups sugar	¼ teaspoon vanilla
⅓ cup corn syrup	¼ cup chopped nuts
⅜ cup boiling water	⅛ cup chopped maraschino
1 egg white	cherries

1. Put sugar, syrup and water into saucepan.

2. Heat slowly, stir until sugar is dissolved.

3. Boil to firm ball stage (246°); cool slightly.

4. Beat egg white stiff; gradually beat in about ½ the syrup; cook the rest of the syrup to 272°—soft crack.

5. Add to the first mixture, beating until the mixture holds its shape.

6. Add vanilla, nuts and cherries dried on paper towels; pour into 2 8 or 9-inch buttered pans.

Mixture may be dropped from a teaspoon on buttered pan to make bon bons; place bowl over hot water to keep mixture soft.

FONDANTS

Fondants, like Fudges, are crystalline candies and so should be handled as little as possible during the cooking and cooling period. They are used for the fillings for chocolates and are best when allowed to stand for a day before being dipped. Fondant making should be left to the experienced cook! A candy thermometer is essential.

BUTTER FONDANT

2 cups sugar	⅔ cup milk
⅛ teaspoon cream of tartar	2 tablespoons butter

1. Put sugar, cream of tartar and milk into a saucepan over gentle heat.
2. Stir until sugar is dissolved; then boil, not too briskly, to the soft ball stage—236°. Add butter when syrup is almost at this temperature. Syrup should not be stirred during boiling; crystals should be removed from sides of saucepan with a piece of cheesecloth tied around the prongs of a fork and dipped into boiling water; sudden change of temperature causes a hot syrup to crystallize.
3. Remove from heat; let stand a few minutes, then pour carefully on a warm buttered platter.
4. Let stand until almost cold, stir with a flexible metal knife until it becomes opaque.
5. Gather up before it stiffens, knead until very smooth; put into a bowl, cover closely; let stand several hours.
6. Shape: As the fondant ripens it softens. Before using, knead it to a smooth consistency; divide; add colour and flavour as desired to each portion. Shape into centres for dipping or for bon bons; into rolls for slices, or form around bits of candied fruits or nuts or grapes.

CHOCOLATE FONDANT

1. Make Butter Fondant omitting 1 tablespoon butter; pour on buttered platter.
2. Cover syrup, while hot, with grated chocolate.
3. Finish as Butter Fondant.

BON BONS

Melt 1 portion uncoloured fondant in a small container over boiling water; quickly dip coloured shapes in and out. Add a few drops of boiling water if necessary. If temperature is too high or fondant heated too long, the sugar dissolves and fondant loses its creamy consistency.

PECAN ROLL

Use Walnut Logs (page 639) or Caramel Fudge (page 642). Pour over fondant rolls. Roll quickly in pecans.

CHOCOLATE DIPPING

A cooking thermometer is necessary for successful home-made chocolates. Unless a large quantity of chocolate is being used, an even temperature cannot be maintained and the results will not be satisfactory.

1. Arrange fondant centres on rack; wash a coarse darning needle and leave in a convenient place; shape a chocolate dipper out of strong wire by bending a loop at the bottom of a handle.
2. Have other racks convenient for holding dipped candies; cover racks with waxed paper.
3. Put chocolate in top section of double boiler over boiling water and stir until melted.
4. Fasten a thermometer onto the side of the pot or hold so that it does not touch the bottom or sides of the pot; heat mixture with constant stirring until it reaches 130°.
5. Cool the chocolate to 83°; add cold water to the water in the bottom of the double boiler until the water temperature reaches 85°. Maintain this temperature by adding hot water as necessary.
6. Drop the fondant centres, which have been previously cut or rolled into standard sizes, into the chocolate and stir with a fork.
7. Lift out carefully and place on rack; draw the darning needle across the dipped candy to form a thread or "string"—the mark of an expert chocolate dipper.
8. Work rapidly, dropping an uncoated centre into the chocolate as a coated centre is removed.
9. When the chocolate is nearly used up and there is not enough for dipping, add nuts, raisins or puffed cereals to form candy clusters. If the chocolate hardens, it can be melted, cooled to 83° and reused.

NON-CRYSTALLINE CANDY

BUTTER TAFFY

2 cups brown sugar
¼ cup golden syrup
1½ tablespoons vinegar
2½ tablespoons water

¾ teaspoon salt
½ tablespoon butter
2 teaspoons vanilla

1. Mix sugar, syrup, vinegar, water and salt in saucepan.
2. Heat slowly, stirring until sugar is dissolved; add butter; then boil without stirring to hard crack stage—300°. Add vanilla just before turning out.
3. Pour into buttered pan; mark into squares when cool.

SALT WATER TAFFY

Pull taffy which can be tinted a delicate colour.

1 cup sugar
½ teaspoon cornstarch
⅔ cup light corn syrup
⅔ cup water

1 tablespoon butter
1 teaspoon salt
1 teaspoon flavouring
few drops food colouring

1. Mix sugar and cornstarch thoroughly in a large saucepan; add remaining ingredients except flavouring and colouring; heat, with stirring, until the mixture boils.
2. Boil to a temperature of 258°, the hard ball stage; remove from the heat.
3. As soon as bubbling has ceased, pour syrup onto a greased platter.
4. When cool enough to handle, pour flavouring and colouring on the centre of the taffy and fold over, kneading them in without spilling them.
5. Pull quickly until light-coloured, then twist into a rope and cut crosswise with scissors into pieces about 1 inch long; wrap. Yields about 40 pieces of candy 1 inch long.

WHITE TAFFY

2 cups sugar	1 tablespoon butter or margarine
⅔ cup water	⅛ teaspoon salt
½ cup light corn syrup	½ teaspoon baking soda
2 tablespoons white vinegar	few drops mint extract

1. Combine sugar, water, corn syrup, and vinegar in a heavy 2-quart saucepan; stir over low heat until sugar is dissolved.
2. Cover and boil 3 minutes; uncover and boil over moderate heat without stirring to 272° (soft crack stage); remove from heat.
3. Blend in butter or margarine, salt, and soda; pour onto an oiled marble slab or enameled pan.
4. As candy cools, turn edges with a spatula toward centre; sprinkle extract over candy.
5. When cool enough to handle, gather candy into a ball and pull until white and porous; use a little soft butter or margarine on fingers to prevent candy from sticking to hands; pull and twist into a rope about ½ inch in diameter.
6. Cut into ½-inch serving pieces with scissors; wrap each piece in waxed paper for storing. Yield: 1 pound.

TAFFY APPLES

3 cups sugar	12 wooden skewers
½ cup corn syrup	red colouring
⅔ cup water	oil of cinnamon flavouring
12 red apples	(if desired)

1. Cook sugar, corn syrup, and water over low heat to a temperature of 290° or just to the hard crack stage; in the meantime boil water in a large flat pan and put skewers in the washed apples. Line a cookie sheet with foil, lightly buttered.
2. When the correct temperature has been reached, remove the syrup from the heat immediately and set it over hot water to prevent it from hardening.
3. Stir in colouring and flavouring, mix.
4. Hold apple by skewer and plunge it into hot syrup; remove quickly and allow excess to drip off; twirl to spread smoothly.
5. Stand apples upside down on the cookie sheet.
6. Store in a cool place.
   Mild molasses may be used to replace corn syrup if desired.

BE-BOP APPLES

2 pounds light caramels   12 apples
½ cup water

1. Melt caramels with water over hot water. Finish as Taffy Apples.

SPONGE TAFFY

3 cups brown sugar   ¼ teaspoon salt
⅔ cup corn syrup   4 teaspoons baking soda
⅔ cup water

1. Measure sugar, syrup, water and salt into a saucepan.
2. Bring to a boil, stirring until the sugar dissolves; boil, stirring occasionally, until the mixture reaches soft crack stage (about 15 minutes).
3. While syrup is boiling butter the bottom of an 8 by 12-inch pan with deep sides (or 2 8-inch cake pans); place in the refrigerator to chill.
4. Remove syrup; sift the baking soda evenly over the top and stir once to completely combine the soda.
5. Pour, while effervescing, into the chilled pan; let stand undisturbed at room temperature until cold.
6. Loosen the sides, invert the pan and turn out; cut in large squares. Wrap in waxed paper.

PEANUT OR COCONUT BRITTLE

A large, heavy iron frying pan hastens the cooking time.

2 cups sugar   1½ teaspoons baking soda
½ cup water   1-2 cups roasted peanuts or
1 cup corn syrup   flaked or grated coconut
½ teaspoon salt

1. Combine sugar, water and corn syrup and stir frequently until syrup reaches the boiling point.
2. Cover saucepan and boil 3 minutes; cook without stirring, uncovered, to the soft crack stage; add butter and salt.
3. Cook, stirring constantly to 300° or the hard crack stage.
4. Sprinkle baking soda over the entire surface of the candy, add nuts and stir; quickly pour candy onto a greased baking sheet. Work fast or it will get too hard to pour.
5. Cool and break into pieces.

BARLEY SUGAR TWISTS

2 cups sugar	green colouring–peppermint
1 cup water	flavour
1 tablespoon vinegar	red colouring–wintergreen
	flavour

1. Mix sugar, water and vinegar in a saucepan and cook over low heat, stirring constantly, until sugar has dissolved.
2. Increase heat to medium; cover for a few minutes so the steam will wash down crystals; uncover and cook without stirring to hard crack, 300°.
3. When the candy is cooked, pour ½ into another pan; colour ½ with green and flavour with peppermint; colour the other with red and a few drops of oil of wintergreen.
4. Pour each mixture onto lightly greased cookie sheets set on bake-board; cut into strips ½ by 6 inches with a heavy knife; set in a warm oven.
5. Take one strip from each pan and twist into spirals. Makes 24.

VANILLA CARAMELS

2 cups sugar	1 cup milk
1 cup light corn syrup	4 tablespoons butter
1 cup condensed milk	1½ teaspoons vanilla
½ cup 18% cream	

1. Cook all ingredients except the vanilla in a saucepan over low heat and cook to the firm ball stage, 245° for soft caramels and 250° for firmer caramels; stir constantly.
2. Remove from the heat, add vanilla and pour at once into a lightly greased pan, about 9 to 10 inches square.
3. Cut into squares when cold and wrap in waxed paper. Makes 70 to 80 pieces of candy.
   For Chocolate Caramels add 3 ounces of unsweetened chocolate.

BUTTERSCOTCH

2 cups sugar	¼ cup light cream or top milk
⅔ cup dark corn syrup	¼ cup butter or margarine
¼ cup water	

1. Place all ingredients except butter or margarine in saucepan; cook over medium heat, stirring constantly, until mixtures boils.
2. Continue cooking, stirring occasionally, to hard ball stage (258°).

3. Add butter and continue cooking, stirring constantly, to soft crack stage (272°). Pour into buttered 8-inch-square pan. When almost set, cut into squares.

LIGHT POPCORN BALLS

2 tablespoons light corn syrup	½ teaspoon salt
1 cup sugar	1 teaspoon vinegar
½ cup water	1 tablespoon butter
	6 cups popped corn

1. Combine corn syrup, sugar, water, salt and vinegar. Cook without stirring to hard ball stage (258°); add butter.
2. Place the popped corn in a lightly greased bowl and slowly pour on the hot syrup.
3. Mix quickly with forks; cool slightly; grease hands and shape mixture into balls by dropping a spoonful of the mixture into the hands and shaping it lightly. Makes about 3 dozen.

Puffed wheat and salted peanuts make a good replacement for the popcorn. Or melt ¼ pound caramels and 1 tablespoon water, over hot water. Mix with 3 cups popcorn.

Chop red and green glazed cherries or raisins and mix with the popcorn.

POPCORN CATS

Cross 3 cellophane straws for whiskers and stick on with syrup; add a life-saver for a nose and gum drops for eyes. Bend a straw in the centre for each ear.

POPCORN CLOWNS

Add a life-saver mouth, gum drop eyes and nose, and a gay paper hat made from a conical paper cup.

POPCORN CHRISTMAS TREES

1¾ cups icing sugar	8 ice cream cones
1 unbeaten egg white	6 quarts popped corn
¼ teaspoon vinegar	decorettes

1. Combine sugar, egg and vinegar and beat until icing is smooth.
2. Cover cones with icing and roll in the loose popcorn.
3. When dry, decorate with bits of cherries, sugar-coated almonds cinnamon drops stuck on with icing.

POPCORN CARAMEL CRUNCH

6 quarts popped corn	2 pounds icing sugar
1-2 cans mixed salted nuts	16 marshmallows (cut)
2 cups dark corn syrup	

1. Combine corn and nuts in a large greased bowl.
2. Combine syrup and ½ the sugar; stir until the sugar dissolves, over low heat; add the rest of the sugar and stir constantly over medium heat until the mixture comes to a full rolling boil; boil 1 minute.
3. Remove from the heat and add cut-up marshmallows; stir until melted.
4. Pour over the popcorn mixture, stirring with a fork, to coat each piece.
5. Press into 3 baking sheets with sides; cool; break up.

FRUIT MIXTURES

STUFFED DATES

1 tablespoon butter	2 tablespoons orange juice
2 cups icing sugar	1 7-ounce package pitted dates

1. Cream the butter and 2 tablespoons icing sugar; add the orange juice and enough of the icing sugar to make a mixture which can be kneaded.
2. Shape into pencil-like rolls; slice and stuff into dates.
3. Top each date with a bit of green or red cherry, a nut or a sprinkling of grated orange rind or cake decorations.

SHERRIED DATES

1 7-ounce package of pitted dates	nuts
¼ cup dry sherry	tinted flaked coconut

Soak the dates in sherry for 1 hour; stuff with a walnut, almond or pecan; roll in coconut.

FRUIT BARS

¼ cup candied orange peel	4 slices candied pineapple
¼ cup candied lemon peel	1 cup figs
¼ pound dates	1 cup walnuts
½ cup citron peel	rind of 1 orange
1 cup glazed green and red cherries	1½ cups sugar
	½ cup water

1. Cut fruit in large pieces with scissors (dip in hot water frequently); chop nuts.
2. Cut orange rind in thin slivers; cook with sugar and water until syrup forms a 2-inch thread at 230°.
3. Pour syrup over cut fruit mixture; pack into 9-inch cakepan; cool until firm.
4. Cut with sharp knife into small bars; dip in Chocolate Dipping, if desired (page 644), or roll in flaked coconut.

PEANUT BUTTER SQUARES

1 cup pitted dates	1 cup peanut butter
½ cup seedless raisins	¼ cup condensed milk
½ cup currants	

1. Chop all fruits; add peanut butter and condensed milk; mix well.
2. Press into an 8-inch buttered pan which has been sprinkled with icing sugar. Smooth surface of candy and sprinkle with icing sugar, if desired.
3. Chill until firm. Cut into squares.

FRUIT ROLL

½ pound dried apricots	1 cup maraschino cherries
½ pound pitted dates	¾ cup pecans
1 cup shredded coconut	1 cup marshmallows

1. Chop finely apricots, dates, cherries and nuts, or put through food chopper.
2. Cut marshmallows with scissors.
3. Mix all ingredients well; shape into roll 1½ inches in diamater; chill for several hours; slice ¼-inch thick.

   This mixture may be shaped into small balls and dipped in Chocolate Dipping (page 644).

CANDIED ORANGE RIND

rind of 2 oranges	½ cup orange water
1 cup sugar	

1. Remove the rind from oranges.
2. Cook slowly in boiling water till tender, drain; reserve water for syrup. Scrape out white pulp; cut rind into thin strips.
3. Make syrup of sugar and orange water; when boiling add rind, cook slowly until syrup will spin a thread.
4. Lift the rind out; drain; roll in granulated sugar; dry on a wire rack.

EASY-TO-MAKE CANDY

These candy mixtures require little or no cooking and are ideal for young candy-makers.

CHOCOLATE DROPS

6 ounces semi-sweet chocolate	3 tablespoons corn syrup
1 ounce unsweetened chocolate	1 tablespoon water

1. Melt these ingredients together over hot water (not boiling); remove from the heat.
2. Add any of the following ingredients:
   2 cups cereal; ½ cup salted peanuts.
   ½ pound candied fruits chopped.
   1½ cups raisins, washed and dried on paper towels.
   1 package (7 ounces) finely cut, pitted dates.
   1 cup broken nuts.
   1 cup marshmallows cut in pieces.
3. Drop from a spoon onto wax paper on a cookie sheet; chill.

CHOCOLATE BARK

Follow directions above; stir in chopped nuts; pour onto waxed paper on a baking sheet; spread with spatula, refrigerate until firm; break into irregular pieces.

MINT SANDWICHES

Spread melted semi-sweet chocolate between 2 after-dinner mints. Add a dot of chocolate to the top and decorate with a walnut or pecan half.

COCONUT PEAKS

¾ cup cold mashed potato	⅛ teaspoon salt
4 cups icing sugar	flavouring
4 cups flaked coconut	semi-sweet chocolate

1. Combine mashed potato and icing sugar; add coconut and salt.
2. Divide into 4 lots; to 1 add vanilla, to 1 add green colouring and a few drops of peppermint flavouring, to 1 add red colour and cinnamon or wintergreen flavour, to 1 add yellow colouring and lemon flavouring.

3. Form into peaks; allow to stand 20 minutes to dry. Dip the base of each in chocolate melted over hot water and cooled. (If the chocolate runs off to form a base on the candy, allow it to cool before dipping the rest.)

CARAMALLOWS

½ pound caramels
2 tablespoons water

24 large marshmallows

1. Place caramels and water in the top of a small double boiler; heat over boiling water until caramels are melted and sauce is smooth. Remove from the stove.
2. Skewer a marshmallow and dip quickly in and out of the caramel. Drop onto aluminum foil.
3. When cool, cut through once with scissors, making 2 pieces.

CHOCOMALLOWS

½ cup chocolate bits
¼ cup milk
¼ cup icing sugar
16 marshmallows

2 cups flaked or desiccated
    coconut or
1 cup finely chopped nuts

1. In top of a small double boiler (or a small bowl) over hot water, melt chocolate; stir in milk; remove from heat; add icing sugar.
2. Dip marshmallows; roll in coconut or nuts.

CHOCOLATE MINT BALLS

½ pound semi-sweet chocolate
¾ cup evaporated milk
1 teaspoon butter

2 tablespoons icing sugar
1 teaspoon peppermint extract
½ cup chopped walnuts or
    coconut

1. Melt chocolate in top of a double boiler over hot water; add milk, butter, and icing sugar; cook 15 minutes, stirring often.
2. Remove from heat; add flavouring; cool; add nuts; chill in refrigerator.
3. Dip out by teaspoonfuls; shape into balls; roll in chopped nuts or coconut. Chill until firm. Makes 2 dozen small.

QUICK FONDANT

⅔ cup (½ 15-ounce can)
    sweetened condensed milk

1 teaspoon vanilla
4 cups sifted icing sugar

1. Blend together milk and vanilla.
2. Gradually add sugar, mixing until smooth and creamy.

EASY CHOCOLATE FUDGE

2 8-ounce packages semi-sweet
  chocolate
1 15-ounce can sweetened
  condensed milk

1 cup chopped nuts
1 teaspoon vanilla or
¼ teaspoon peppermint
  extract

1. Melt chocolate in top of double boiler; add condensed milk and stir until thick.
2. Remove from the heat; add vanilla and nuts.
3. Pour into a greased 8-inch pie pan and chill until firm.

Pecan Pralines—perfect with after-dinner coffee.

PECAN PRALINES

1 package butterscotch pudding
  and pie mix
1 cup granulated sugar
½ cup brown sugar, firmly
  packed

½ cup evaporated milk
1 tablespoon butter
1½ cups pecans

1. Combine all ingredients except nuts in a saucepan. Cook and stir over low heat until mixture comes to a boil.
2. Boil gently, stirring often to a soft ball (236°).
3. Remove from heat and beat until it begins to thicken; add nuts; drop onto waxed paper. Makes 18-20 pralines 3 inches in diameter.

BUTTERSCOTCH BON BONS

¾ cup chocolate bits
1 package butterscotch instant pudding
¼ cup peanut butter
½ cup chopped nuts
¼ cup light cream

1. Melt the chocolate over hot water; cool.
2. Combine the other ingredients; roll into 1-inch balls; dip in chocolate; chill.

CHOCOLATE CRUNCHIES

3 8-ounce packages semi-sweet chocolate pieces
1 12-ounce jar crunchy peanut butter
1 7-ounce box crisp rice cereal
1 15-ounce box seedless raisins

1. Melt chocolate pieces in top of double boiler over hot but not boiling water; stir in peanut butter.
2. Toss together cereal and raisins in a large bowl.
3. Pour chocolate mixture over cereal and stir until well combined.
4. Drop by spoonfuls onto wax paper or into small foil cups. Makes 8 dozen.

BUTTERSCOTCH CRUNCHIES

1 6-ounce package chocolate chips
1 6-ounce package butterscotch chips
1 cup Chow Mein noodles
1 cup peanuts

1. Melt the 2 packages of chips in a large bowl over hot water.
2. Stir in noodles and peanuts.
3. Drop by spoonfuls onto wax paper or small foil cups; chill until firm. Makes 2 dozen.

NUT TREATS

SUGARED NUTS

1 cup sugar
⅛ teaspoon cream of tartar
¼ cup boiling water
½ teaspoon vanilla
2 cups nuts

1. Combine sugar, cream of tartar and water; cook without stirring to firm ball, 246°.
2. Add vanilla and nuts; stir until nuts are coated.
3. Turn out onto lightly greased cookie sheet; separate with 2 forks; cool.

ORANGE SUGARED PECANS

Add grated rind of 1 orange and 2 cups pecans.

SPICED WALNUTS

Add 4 drops oil of cinnamon, 4 drops oil of cloves, 2 cups walnuts.

SPICED NUTS

1½ teaspoons water	1 cup granulated sugar
1 egg white, slightly beaten	½ teaspoon cinnamon
2 cups nuts	

1. Start heating oven to 350°. Stir water into egg white. Roll nuts in egg white, a few at a time, coating them well. Then roll nuts in sugar mixed with cinnamon.
2. Arrange nuts on well-greased brown paper on cookie sheet. Bake until golden.

GLACÉ NUTS

1 cup boiling water	⅛ cup vinegar or
2 cups granulated sugar	¼ teaspoon cream of tartar

1. Boil water, sugar and vinegar to very brittle stage—310° (syrup begins to change colour).
2. Place over boiling water.
3. Have nuts prepared for dipping—they should be dry and slightly warm.
4. Drop into the syrup, one at a time; lift out with a fork; cool on buttered baking sheet.

FRENCH FRIED FOOD brings to mind crisp, golden brown delicacies. With the right equipment, fat and temperature, this tempting vision is easy to obtain. Fried foods are not indigestible, as we used to believe, nor, with proper care of the fat, need they be expensive. Fats do, however supply more calories than the same amount of protein or carbohydrate.

Fat

CHOICE: Fat with a high smoking temperature is necessary; otherwise there will be decomposition of the fat with fumes, offensive flavour and odour. The smoking point is the temperature at which smoke comes from the kettle of fat. Use a salad oil, high quality lard, or vegetable shortening for best results.

QUANTITY: A small amount of fat will make it difficult to get good results because an even temperature cannot be obtained. 2 to 3 inches must be left between the top of the kettle and the surface of the fat to prevent it boiling over. In a 3-quart kettle, use 1 quart of oil or 2½ pounds of shortening.

TEMPERATURE OF FAT: The longer the food cooks the greater is the absorption of fat. Food should therefore be cooked rapidly, but must be cooked throughout. If a fat thermometer is not available the temperature may be checked by noting the time required to brown a 1-inch cube of bread:

Food	Temperature	Seconds to Brown a 1-inch Cube of Bread
For food already cooked and for oysters	380°-400°	40
For uncooked foods	360°-380°	60
For potatoes—precook at	375°	65
—finish at	390°	40

CARE OF THE FAT: Heat the fat slowly to the temperature required. Each time that the fat smokes there is more decomposition, so be sure the fat is not allowed to overheat.

After using, cool the fat a little; strain through cheesecloth or the cloth-like paper especially prepared for kitchen use.

Small particles left in the fat lower its smoking temperature, and so should be removed. Slicing a raw potato into the fat and heating it, then straining, will help to collect and remove such small bits. Cover and keep cool. Fat which has been used for frying requires a lower temperature for storage.

Equipment

Use a heavy kettle and the amount of fat necessary for the quantity of food to be cooked. Shallow frying is cooking in 2 to 3 inches of fat. Deep fat frying is cooking with the kettle ½-full.

Since the greater the surface the lower the smoking temperature, it is advisable to use a deep, narrow kettle.

The use of a frying basket is best for potatoes, and food which is crumb-coated; for batter-coated food it should *not* be used as the batter cooks onto the wires. An egg lifter or kitchen tongs may then be used.

Have a baking sheet covered with paper towels or unglazed brown paper, to put fried foods on for draining.

If much food is being fried an oven at low heat may be used to keep the food hot until all is finished.

Preparation of Food

Food to be fried should be cut into even-sized portions and should be at room temperature.

In order to prevent food soaking up fat, it is given a coating which cooks quickly and forms an outside protection. This coating may be crumbs or batter.

FOODS COATED WITH CRUMBS

Dry pieces of bread until crisp. Put them through a meat chopper or in a blender, or roll in a paper bag with a rolling pin until fine. Sift; store until needed. Do not save buttered bread or dark toast for crumbs. Packaged crumbs are available and save time, but cost money.

CRUMB COATING

1 cup crumbs or cornmeal	1 egg
2 teaspoons salt	2 tablespoons milk or water

1. Fill 2 plates with sifted crumbs; stir in salt.
2. Prepare egg by beating slightly with water in a shallow dish.
3. Dip the food in crumbs, then in egg and then in the second dish of crumbs; coat thoroughly (any uncovered spot will allow the fat to get in and push the crust off).
4. Let food stand 20 minutes, so the crust will dry and remain on during frying; shake off any loose crumbs.

FISH

Use 1½ pounds fresh fillets or defrost frozen fillets. Cut into serving portions of even thickness (½ inch). Remove scales or bones. Crumb; place in frying basket. Fry at 375° until brown (about 5 minutes); turn and fry. Serves 4-6.

CODFISH BALLS

1 cup salt codfish	½ tablespoon butter
2½ cups potatoes, peeled	⅛ teaspoon pepper
1 egg	salt

1. Wash the codfish, break in small pieces; cover with cold water; heat gradually to simmering; keep at that temperature 30 minutes; drain.
2. Boil potatoes; drain, dry, mash.
3. Add fish, mix thoroughly.
4. Add beaten egg, butter, pepper, and salt if needed.
5. Beat until light; crumb; drop into fat at 390°.
6. Cook to golden brown; drain; garnish and serve with White or Tomato Sauce, or Tartar Sauce (page 79). Serves 6.

SCALLOPS

1 pound scallops (50 small to 25 large)	4 tablespoons lemon juice
2 tablespoons salad oil	½ tablespoon salt

1. Drain the scallops; remove the small muscle.
2. Marinate 1 hour in a mixture of oil, lemon juice and salt.
3. Crumb. Fry a few at a time (365° to 375°). Drain. Serve with lemon or Tartar Sauce (page 91). Serves 6.

OYSTERS

1. Select 1 pint of large oysters; remove pieces of shell; drain from liquid; rinse and dry with paper towels. Season with salt and pepper.
2. Crumb; fry 1 minute at 365-375°.
3. Drain; garnish; serve with Tartar Sauce (page 91) or lemon. Serves 6.

FROG LEGS

2 pounds frog legs	¼ teaspoon pepper
2 teaspoons salt	2 teaspoons lemon juice

1. Cut legs apart at joint if large; remove feet; wipe dry, season.
2. Add lemon juice to egg in the Crumb Coating, and crumb the legs.
3. Fry at 350° for 10 minutes; drain. Serves 6.

FRENCH FRIED ASPARAGUS

1. Choose thick spears of cooked asparagus; crumb.
2. Fry at 380-390°. Drain.

CROQUETTES (Basic Recipe)

1 cup very thick, seasoned White Sauce (page 79)	2 cups finely chopped or ground seasoned foods (variations
2 egg yolks	below)
	1 recipe Crumb Coating

1. Make well-seasoned White Sauce; add to beaten yolks of eggs; stir over low heat until smooth; add the food.
2. Remove from heat, spread on a large plate to chill; spread with melted butter to prevent crust forming; shape as cones, rolls or balls. Roll in crumbs, egg and crumbs. Let stand 1 hour.
3. Fry for 5 minutes at 375°. Makes 12 medium croquettes.

White Sauce replacements:

½ can undiluted chicken, celery or mushroom soup; use less salt.

2 cups hot mashed potatoes.

2 cups cooked rice, heated in 2-3 tablespoons milk; add 2 tablespoons butter; ½ teaspoon salt.

CHICKEN OR TURKEY CROQUETTES

Add 1 chicken cube to the sauce; ½ cup cooked, chopped mushrooms to the finely chopped chicken or turkey. Serve with tomato sauce and chopped fresh parsley.

OYSTER CROQUETTES

½ pint oysters   1 cup cooked chicken

Cook oysters by dropping into hot water until edges curl; drain and cut fine with scissors. Finish as for Croquettes.

Batter-fried shrimp and fish Croquettes.

SHRIMP CROQUETTES

2 cups cooked, chopped shrimp   1 tablespoon Madeira wine

1. In 3 tablespoons oil fry ⅓ cup diced onion, 1 clove garlic and 3 tablespoons minced mushroom; ⅓ cup minced green pepper, 3 tablespoons diced almonds, ½ cup chopped fresh tomato.
2. Mix tomato mixture with shrimp and wine.
3. Finish as for Croquettes.

LOBSTER CROQUETTES

Add 1 teaspoon lemon juice; serve with Tartar Sauce (page 91).

SALMON CROQUETTES

Drain salmon, remove skins, crush bones; add ¼ cup mayonnaise to sauce. Serve with lemon.

VEAL, BEEF OR LAMB CROQUETTES

Substitute brown meat stock or gravy for milk; season with Worcestershire Sauce. Serve with tomato sauce.

ROAST PORK CROQUETTES

Combine diced, cooked pork, minced water chestnuts, green onions and soy sauce.

HAM CROQUETTES

Combine finely chopped cooked ham and grated cheese in Sherry-flavoured sauce.

CHEESE CROQUETTES

Add 1 cup sharp grated Cheddar cheese to the seasoned sauce.

FOODS COATED WITH BATTER

Foods coated with batter should not be placed in a basket because the batter sticks to the wires; kitchen tongs are useful for handling the food.

BATTER (Basic Recipe)

1 cup all-purpose flour	1 tablespoon cooking oil
½ teaspoon salt	1 egg
1 teaspoon baking powder	⅔ cup milk or water

1. Mix and sift dry ingredients; stir in the oil; mix until smooth.
2. Beat the egg and add the milk; add to flour-oil mixture.
3. Beat with rotary beater to a smooth, creamy consistency; do not overbeat.

   For fish, add 1 tablespoon vinegar.

   For fruit, add 2 tablespoons sugar; reduce salt.

   For quick batter, 1 cup biscuit mix may be used with 1 egg and ¼-½ cup liquid.

FISH
Use 1½ pounds fresh fillets (or defrosted frozen fillets). Cut into serving portions of even thickness (½ inch); coat with seasoned flour; dip into batter. Fry 5-10 minutes at 360°. Serves 6.

SHRIMP
1. Wash large raw shrimp; remove the shell; remove the black line; sprinkle with salt; dry on paper towels.
2. Dip in batter; fry at 365° until brown, turning once; drain.
3. Serve with small dishes of soy sauce, Hot Tartar Sauce, Cocktail Sauce (page 64); or with lemon wedges. Serves 6.

CHICKEN
Sprinkle chicken halves or quarters with seasoning; dip into batter; Fry at 350° for 15 minutes until golden brown; drain.

VEGETABLES
A good way to use a little leftover batter.
Slice 3-4 mild onions; separate into rings. Dip into batter; fry at 380° until brown.
Separate cooked cauliflower into flowerets; fry at 380° until brown.

CORN FRITTERS
Drain 1 cup canned kernel corn or cut off the kernels from cooked cobs; stir corn into the batter. Drop from a tablespoon into the fat. Fry 3 minutes at 365°. Makes 8-12 fritters.

APPLE FRITTERS
2 apples	2 tablespoons sugar
¼ cup orange juice	icing sugar

1. Pare, core and slice or cube the apples; dip in orange juice; sprinkle with sugar, let stand 10-15 minutes.
2. Drain; drop into the batter; drop from tablespoon or lift with tongs into hot fat.
3. Fry 3 minutes at 365°; drain; sprinkle with icing sugar. Makes 16 fritters.

PINEAPPLE FRITTERS
Dry sliced pineapple; leave whole or cut into wedges; finish as Apple Fritters. Serve with lemon sauce.

PEACH FRITTERS
Peel peaches, cut in half, remove stone; finish as Apple Fritters.

STRAWBERRY FRITTERS
Wash and hull strawberries; finish as Apple Fritters. Serve with sour cream.

MIXED FRUIT FRITTERS
Combine ½ cup cubed bananas, 1 tin drained mandarin oranges; ¼ teaspoon spice (cinnamon, ginger); finish as Apple Fritters.

SALZBURG APRICOT FRITTERS
¼ cup almond paste	1 cup Orange Sauce
12 fresh ripe apricots	1 tablespoon Orange Curaçao
1 recipe batter	

1. Shape the paste into 12 small balls; halve the fruit; replace the stone with a ball of almond paste, then press the 2 halves firmly together.
2. Dip in batter; fry at 365° for 5 minutes.
3. Drain; sprinkle with icing sugar; serve with Orange Sauce (page 89), to which Orange Curaçao has been added. Serves 4-6.

FRENCH FRIED POTATOES
1. Choose good quality, large potatoes which have been kept in a warm room for a day. 3-4 pounds will serve 6.
2. Allow 1 large potato to each person; pare, cut into strips ½ by ¾ by 3 inches.
3. Soak in cold water 10 minutes to remove the starch particles and to prevent clumping; dry well in a tea towel.
4. Heat the fat gradually to 375°. To fry potatoes for 6 use 2 to 3 pounds of fat which can of course be used again, but should be fresh for the potatoes. This amount will require about 10 minutes to heat. There should be at least 3 inches of melted fat.
5. Place ¼ of the potatoes in the wire basket (or use a sieve) and lower it into the fat. Keep hand to one side of the handle to prevent steam burns but do not let go of the basket until the fat subsides. If it appears to be going to overflow, lift the basket out. Let fry 4 minutes. Shake out of basket into paper towel.
6. It will be necessary to watch the temperature carefully since the cold raw potatoes reduce it greatly. Before adding a new lot of potatoes bring up the temperature each time to 375°.

Softened ice cream is pressed into the sides and bottom of a mould and frozen. Another flavour of ice cream is spooned into the centre and all is frozen. A bottom layer of chopped walnuts adds interest to Butterscotch Cream Pie (page 481).

Pretty, and easier on the calories, is this cake which is only partially glazed. A moist and chewy cookie array includes Oatmeal and Peanut Butter Cookies as well as Bar Cookies.

7. Before serving time heat the fat to 390°; add the potatoes a basketful at a time and complete the frying. Drain the potatoes on unglazed paper, keep hot in the oven; salt just before serving by shaking in a brown paper bag in which has been placed ½ teaspoon salt and ⅛ teaspoon pepper for each potato.

Doughnuts: Drop a few at a time into fat at 375°.

DOUGHNUTS

⅔ cup sugar	1 teaspoon salt
3½ cups all-purpose flour	2 eggs
4 teaspoons baking powder	⅔ cup milk
¼ teaspoon cinnamon	3 tablespoons melted fat
¼ teaspoon cloves	(add from the fryer)
⅛ teaspoon mace or nutmeg	

1. Mix and sift dry ingredients; beat the eggs; add milk and fat.
2. Combine the liquid and dry ingredients, mixing just enough to blend well. The dough should be soft, but if too soft it may break during the cooking. Chill 30 minutes.
3. Roll to ¼-inch thickness; cut with doughnut cutter.
4. Drop a few at a time into fat at 375°; let come to surface and brown on the underside before turning; time 1 doughnut and break open to test cooking time.
5. Remove with a slotted spoon or fork; drain on paper towels.
6. While still warm shake in cinnamon sugar or dip into glaze. Makes 2½ to 3 dozen.

GLAZES FOR DOUGHNUTS

Cinnamon: Mix ½ cup sugar, 1 teaspoon cinnamon, ¼ teaspoon nutmeg.

Sugar: Combine 2 cups icing sugar and 2-3 tablespoons water. Glaze may be flavoured with maple flavouring or instant coffee.

Chocolate: Combine 2 cups icing sugar, 2 tablespoons cocoa and 3 tablespoons water.

Maple Sugar: Roll in powdered maple sugar (may be bought in bags in specialty stores).

DOUGHNUT VARIATIONS

Golden Puffs: Drop batter from a teaspoon into the fat.

Twists: Cut dough into 6 by ½-inch strips. Shape into a circle; press ends together. Twist once; press dough together where it crosses.

22 Food Preservation

Although Nicholas Appert is regarded as the father of the canning industry because he won the prize offered by Napoleon for a more palatable method of preserving food than salting, it was some time until the price of containers was low enough to make canning a popular method of preserving. At first glass was used; the first patent on a tin can was taken out in America in 1825. Since that day food preservation techniques have progressed rapidly.

Today fresh or frozen foods are plentiful in the stores in and out of season. Fewer people grow their own food and fewer still have room to store quantities of preserved foods. Patterns in menu planning are changing; rich preserves are avoided and there is less need of pickles to add flavour to a monotonous diet. There are available, through any provincial Department of Agriculture, excellent booklets on food preservation.

Canning Vegetables

Do not attempt home canning of vegetables, other than tomatoes, or of meats, without a pressure cooker. Since for many people a pressure cooker is not economical either, recipes have not been included in this book. They may be obtained with a pressure canner, or by writing to any provincial Department of Agriculture.

JAM, JELLY, MARMALADE AND CONSERVES

Small quantities made frequently with these easy recipes keep their fresh flavour. They make ideal gifts and have a use beyond the breakfast table; with biscuits and cheese for dessert or a wine party; with fresh muffins or scones for afternoon or morning coffee; as a filling for small tarts, as garnish for salads and desserts.

Success in the making of jellies and jams depends to a great extent upon the proper selection of fruit. Use fruits which are acid and just ripe or slightly underripe; under these conditions the jelly-making principal, pectin, is in its best state for setting the jelly.

Pectin is richest in currants, grapes, lemons, sour and bitter oranges, crabapples, tart apples, cranberries. For other fruits, better results are obtained by adding commercially-prepared pectin.

Never double or triple a recipe when preparing jelly; the additional cooking results in loss of flavour.

When using commercial pectin, remember that the liquid and crystalline pectin are not interchangeable and that recipes prepared for use with the older crystalline pectin may not work as well with the new product on the market.

Preparation of the Fruit

1. Wash large fruits such as apples, cut in pieces, add water according to the table below.
2. Wash small fruits such as grapes or currants, pick from the stems, put into a kettle; break with a potato masher; cook until soft. See the table below for the correct amount of water to add.

   Since much of the pectin is in the skin and core of the fruit it should not be pared.

JELLY: PROPORTIONS OF FRUIT, WATER AND SUGAR

Fruit	Amount of Fruit for 4 Cups Juice (*in quarts*)	Water for Each Quart of Prepared Fruit (*in cups*)	Time of Boiling to Extract Juice (*in minutes*)	Sugar to 1 Cup Juice (*in cups*)
Small Fruits				
HIGH BUSH CRANBERRIES	3	3	15	¾
CURRANTS	4	1	10	1
GRAPES	3	none if ripe	15	¾
Large Fruits				
APPLES	3	3	20	¾
CRABAPPLES	3	3	20	1
QUINCE	3	6	25	¾

Quantities for other fruits have not been given since they are more successfully made with commercial pectin, either liquid or crystal. Follow the directions given with the pectin. One 6-quart basket of grapes or crabapples makes about 6 8-ounce jars.

Preparation of the Jelly Bag

1. Buy ¾ of a yard of 36-inch factory cotton; fold it to make a 27-inch square; double-stitch the open side; wash in boiling water.

2. Turn the single piece at the top over the straight bar of a metal coat hanger; stitch.

3. To hang the bag, detach the handle of a mop; support it between the top rungs of the backs of 2 chairs, or from table to table; hook the coat hanger over the mop handle.

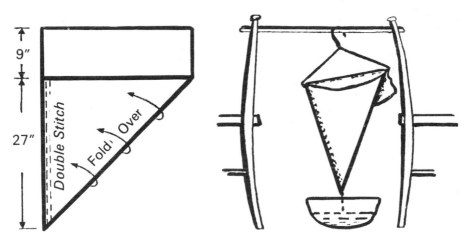

Extraction of Fruit Juice

1. When the fruit is very soft, pour it into a jelly bag which has been rinsed in boiling water.

2. Drip several hours; for the first extraction of juice do not squeeze the bag. The utensil in which the juice is collected may be aluminum, earthenware or plastic; it should not be copper, iron or tin, which may darken the juice.

   The pulp may be emptied into a kettle, covered with cold water, boiled and dripped again. Keep this second extract separate. The first jelly will have more colour and flavour.

Test for Pectin

1. Heat a little of the extracted juice to the boiling point.

2. In a custard cup mix 1 teaspoon fruit juice and 1 tablespoon alcohol. If the juice can be gathered in a thick mass from this mixture there is

sufficient pectin present to form a jelly. If the pectin is stringy and cannot be gathered into a mass the juice should be boiled 10 minutes and retested before adding the sugar; or commercial pectin may be added.

Cooking the Juice

1. Measure the juice; put no more than 4 cups into a saucepan which is at least 3 quarts in size.

2. Measure the sugar; for most fruits ¾ cup sugar to 1 cup of juice is sufficient. Too much sugar makes a thin jelly and one that is too sweet; too little sugar makes a tough jelly and a smaller volume. The table on the previous page indicates the amounts to be used with fruits which do not require commercial pectin; those which do will have a much larger proportion of sugar, as indicated in their own recipes. Warm the sugar in a slow oven so that it will not cool the juice when added.

3. Sterilize the glasses. (4 cups of juice and 3 cups of sugar will fill 6 to 7 jelly glasses of 6-ounce size). Glasses do not have to have a tight seal but should have a wide mouth. Sterilize a measuring cup and a pie plate, with the glasses.

4. Heat the juice rapidly to boiling; add the heated sugar; boil vigorously; remove the scum. The time necessary for cooking varies with the amount of pectin. For acid fruits which showed a good pectin test the time will be about 8 to 10 minutes; with less acid fruits, such as apples, about 15 minutes.

5. *Test* by dipping a large spoon into the syrup; hold up horizontally. When the jellying stage is reached, the drops run together to form a sheet. If a thermometer is used it should register 219°, or 7° higher than the thermometer registers in boiling water.

6. Remove the jelly from the stove; skim.

Bottling and Sealing the Jelly

1. With a metal spoon skim off the foam; pour the jelly into hot sterilized glasses to within ½ inch of the top.

2. Cover with a thin layer of melted paraffin or with circles, cut from heavy waxed paper, ¼ inch smaller than the glass; cool.

3. Add a thin layer of paraffin to cover the space at the edge left when the jelly cooled.

4. Cover with metal tops or with pliofilm; wash the glass and label.

APPLE JELLY (Basic Recipe)

1 box powdered fruit pectin	a few drops red food colour
3 cups canned apple juice	3½ cups (1½ pounds) granulated sugar

1. Scald 5 6-ounce jelly glasses. In large saucepan, mix pectin with apple juice and enough red food colour to tint the mixture light orange.
2. Stir over high heat until mixture comes to hard boil; stir in sugar at once.
3. Bring to full, rolling boil; boil hard 1 minute, stirring constantly. Remove from heat; bottle and seal.

CINNAMON APPLE

Omit colour, dissolve ½ cup cinnamon red candies in the juice.

CRANBERRY APPLE JELLY

Use equal amounts cranberry and apple juice.

GRAPE JELLY

Use bottled grape juice to replace apple juice.

GRAPE AND GRAPEFRUIT JELLY

Use ½ grape juice, ½ freshly squeezed strained grapefruit juice (1-2 grapefruit).

WINE GRAPE JELLY

Use 2¾ cups grape juice; just before removing from the heat add ¼ cup red table wine (Burgundy or Bordeaux type).

WINE JELLY

2 cups sweet wine (port or sherry)	3 cups sugar
	½ bottle liquid pectin

1. Pour the wine into a saucepan, or top of double boiler, add sugar.
2. Heat over boiling water or low heat 2 minutes, or until wine and sugar are heated through; stir constantly, so all the liquid reaches the right temperature at the same time.
3. Add the liquid pectin quickly to the hot, sweetened wine; pour immediately into sterilized glasses; seal with wax. Makes 5 6-ounce glasses.

PINEAPPLE MINT JELLY

¾ cup cider vinegar
¾ cup pineapple juice
crushed pineapple from
19-ounce tin
3¼ cups sugar

½ bottle liquid pectin
green vegetable colouring
⅓ to ½ teaspoon essence of
spearmint

1. Bring the vinegar, juice, pineapple, sugar and pectin to a full rolling boil and boil ½ minute; remove from the heat.
2. Add the colouring a drop at a time to get the desired colour.
3. Add essence of spearmint (this is very strong). Skim.
4. Pour into the glasses; cover with wax. Makes 5 6-ounce glasses.

RED PEPPER JELLY

2 cups ground sweet peppers,
mostly red
5½ cups sugar

1 cup dilute vinegar
⅓ cup lemon juice
1 bottle commercial pectin

1. Wash peppers, remove tongue, seeds and stems.
2. Grind or chop finely; measure pulp and juice.
3. Place peppers, sugar and vinegar in a kettle; heat rapidly to boiling, stirring constantly.
4. Remove from heat; add pectin. Skim and stir occasionally for 5 minutes.
5. Pour into glasses, cover with melted paraffin; let stand 2 weeks before using.

JAM

A jam is usually made from the juice and pulp of 1 fruit. Good jam has a jelly-like consistency without distinct pieces of fruit, a bright colour and fresh fruit flavour.

GRAPE JAM

4 pounds grapes

3 pounds sugar

1. Pick over, wash and remove grapes from stems.
2. Weigh; estimate amount of sugar required.
3. Press pulp from skins; reserve skins.
4. Heat pulp and cook gently until very soft.
5. Press through a sieve to remove seeds.

6. Add skins to pulp and cook 5 minutes.
7. Add sugar; cook gently until thick, about 10 minutes (see test, page 670).
8. Pour into sterile glasses and seal with wax. Makes 10 6-ounce glasses.

BLACK CURRANT JAM

1. Remove stems and blossom from currants.
2. Wash, measure, put into kettle.
3. Add boiling water, 1 cup for each 2 cups of currants.
4. Bring to a boil; boil hard 5 minutes.
5. Weigh and add 1 pound sugar to 1 pound fruit and juice, or measure sugar equal to the original quantity of fruit.
6. Boil 10 minutes or until the juice tests for jelly (see test, page 670).
7. Pour into sterile glasses; seal with wax. 3 quarts makes 12 6-ounce glasses.

RASPBERRY JAM

4 pounds (2 quarts) raspberries   3 pounds sugar

1. Pick over the berries, mash, cook gently 10 minutes, stir frequently.
2. Add sugar, cook 15 minutes or until thick (see test, page 670).
3. Pour into glasses; seal with wax. Makes 6 6-ounce glasses.

STRAWBERRY JAM

1 quart strawberries   ½ cup lemon juice
4 cups sugar   2 tablespoons liquid pectin

1. Wash berries in a sieve; drain; hull.
2. Cut the berries; add sugar; let stand overnight in a glass or plastic bowl.
3. Bring to a boil; boil 8 minutes.
4. Add lemon juice; boil 3 minutes; remove scum.
5. Add 2 tablespoons liquid pectin; stir; bottle; seal with wax. Makes 5 6-ounce glasses.

FREEZER STRAWBERRY JAM

1 quart strawberries	¾ cup water
4 cups sugar	1 package powdered pectin

1. Crush fully ripe fruit; measure 2 cups; add sugar; mix well; stir over low heat until sugar dissolves.
2. Combine water and pectin in small saucepan; bring to a boil and boil hard 1 minute, stirring constantly.
3. Add pectin to fruit mixture; stirring about 3 minutes.
4. Ladle quickly into sterilized glasses; cover jam with tight lids; let stand until set (about 24 hours). Store in freezer, or in refrigerator if the jam will be used within 3 weeks.

FRUIT-CUP JAM

1. Replace ½ the strawberries with 1 medium orange, 1 cup crushed pineapple; reduce sugar to 3¾ cups.
2. Place strawberries in a large kettle and crush well with a fork.
3. Grate ½ teaspoon orange rind and add to berries. Peel and section orange, discarding seeds and membrane. Break up orange sections very finely and add to berries; add pineapple.
4. Finish as Freezer Strawberry Jam.

MARMALADE

This is a form of jelly in which there are thin slices of fruit. The fruit is usually, but not always, citrus fruit.

Use fresh, thick-skinned fruit. Seedless oranges are best. Seville oranges, which are in the stores in February, are bitter, and good for marmalade. Fruit stamped "was treated" or "colour added" should not be used.

Much of the success of the marmalade depends on the thinness of the rind. Quarter the fruit and slice paper thin with a sharp knife. Recipes in which the peel is soaked overnight are more often successful; or in which the peel is cooked in water and left to stand before the sugar is added. This method takes longer but gives soft, delicate pieces of fruit.

Prepare in small quantities for a better result.

To prevent the fruit floating, let the marmalade stand in the saucepan for a few minutes, stirring it occasionally before pouring it into the glasses.

A large open kettle allows greater evaporation and will cook the marmalade quickly, resulting in a bright colour and good flavour.

ORANGE MARMALADE

12 oranges   water
1–2 lemons   sugar

1. Wash the fruit; halve from stem to blossom.
2. Slice thinly; remove the seeds; measure.
3. Add twice the amount of water. Cook slowly uncovered until tender (2 hours). Leave overnight.
4. Measure 2 cups cooked fruit and juice into a broad pan; bring to a boil; add 1½ cups heated sugar.
5. Cook rapidly to the jelly stage (220°) about ¾ hour; bottle.
6. Repeat until all the fruit is used. Makes 35 6-ounce jars.

CITRUS MARMALADE

½ grapefruit   water
2 large sweet oranges   sugar
1 lemon

1. Wash the fruit. Squeeze the juice (measure 1 cup). Cover and leave in the refrigerator to use later.
2. Slice the peel very thinly; measure and add 3 times the amount of water; bring to a boil and simmer uncovered until peel is tender (40 to 50 minutes); let stand overnight.
3. Measure peel mixture; bring to a boil; add an equal amount of heated sugar; boil another 10 minutes.
4. Add the juice and boil until the mixture jells (see test, page 670).
5. Bottle in 10 6-ounce glasses.
   A pressure cooker reduces the time required to soften the rind; consult the manual.

GINGER PEAR MARMALADE

8 pounds pears   ¼ pound ginger
4 pounds sugar   4 lemons

1. Wash, quarter, core, pare and chop pears.
2. Add sugar and ginger and let stand overnight.
3. Add lemons, sliced thinly; cook slowly 3 hours.
4. Bottle.

TOMATO MARMALADE

4 pounds ripe tomatoes	4 oranges sliced very thin
4 pounds sugar	2 lemons sliced very thin

1. Scald and peel the tomatoes. Press each between the hands to extract some of the juice and cut down cooking time. This juice may be seasoned, chilled and served as an appetizer.
2. Cut the squeezed tomatoes into a kettle in quarters, add the fruit; cook 30 minutes, uncovered, until the rind is tender.
3. Add the sugar; boil until the mixture sheets from a spoon (about 20 minutes), stirring frequently.
4. Skim, stir, bottle, seal with wax. Makes 10 6-ounce glasses.

CONSERVES

A conserve is a mixture of fruits to which nuts usually have been added. The consistency is similar to that of jam.

STRAWBERRY AND PINEAPPLE CONSERVE

2 cups strawberries	3 cups sugar
1 cup crushed pineapple, drained	

1. Wash and hull strawberries; crush.
2. Add pineapple and sugar.
3. Cook slowly until thick.
4. Bottle; seal with wax. Makes 4 6-ounce glasses.

DRIED APRICOT CONSERVE

This can be made at any season of the year.

1 pound dried apricots	juice of 1 lemon (3 table-
1 19-ounce tin crushed pineapple	spoons)
sugar	¼ pound almonds (optional)

1. Wash apricots; soak overnight in water to cover; cook.
2. Add pineapple (undrained); measure.
3. Add ⅔ the measure of sugar; cook until thick, stirring.
4. Add lemon juice and almonds, blanched and cut in strips; cook 5 minutes longer.
5. Bottle; seal with wax. Makes 10 6-ounce glasses.

RHUBARB CONSERVE

4 cups rhubarb	3 cups sugar
1 lemon	1 cup raisins
1 orange	1 cup walnuts
1 cup water	

1. Wash the rhubarb and cut into ½-inch pieces.
2. Squeeze the lemon and orange and save the juice; slice rind thinly; chop.
3. Boil the rind in the water, until tender (20 minutes).
4. Combine the juice, rhubarb, cooked rind and sugar. Stir over the heat until the sugar is dissolved.
5. Continue to boil rapidly, stirring constantly until thick (15 minutes).
6. Add the washed raisins and nuts and bring to a boil again. Boil 5 minutes.
7. Bottle; seal with wax. Makes 5 6-ounce glasses.

PEACH CONSERVE

6 quarts peaches (40-50 peaches)	juice of 4 lemons
6 oranges	½ cup maraschino cherries
sugar	¾ pound shelled almonds

1. Blanch, peel and slice peaches.
2. Squeeze juice and pulp of oranges; put rind through a mincer or chop fine.
3. Put peaches in kettle; add orange juice and rind.
4. Weigh; add ¾ pound sugar to 1 pound fruit (about 2 cups chopped).
5. Cook until the mixture sheets from a spoon; stir frequently.
6. Add lemon juice, cherries and chopped, blanched nuts; cook 5 minutes.
7. Bottle; seal with wax. Makes 15 6-ounce glasses.

PICKLES AND SAUCES

With few exceptions, it is necessary that pickles and sauces be carefully sterilized and sealed, as canned foods. Preservatives such as vinegar, sugar and spices are used for flavouring and are not, in all cases, sufficiently concentrated to preserve the food. In the recipes which follow, the sugar and vinegar may be altered slightly to suit individual tastes. Non-iodized salt should be used.

The pickles we have included are easy and economical to make; additional recipes may be obtained from Provincial Department of Agriculture booklets.

INGREDIENTS

White vinegar gives pickles a clear colour.

Cider vinegar is preferred for flavour.

Vinegar, if purchased in gallon quantities, is much cheaper; however, since it loses strength, unused vinegar should be poured into smaller containers and kept tightly covered.

Pickling salt is preferable, to avoid cloudiness.

Whole spice gives a clear liquid, and the strength can be better controlled than when ground spice is used. The spice may be tied loosely in a cheesecloth bag, with a string attached so it can be lifted out.

If ground spice is used, substitute 1 teaspoon ground spice for 1 tablespoon whole spice.

Pickles and relishes will be a fine contribution to any meal.

Spice oil may be used; have a druggist combine ¼ ounce oil of cinnamon, ¼ ounce oil of cloves and ⅛ ounce oil of pimento. Use a few drops up to ½ teaspoon as desired.

EASY DILL PICKLES

This recipe is successful only with really fresh cucumbers.

fresh dill	1 6-quart basket fresh small
small hot red peppers	cucumbers (3 to 4 inches)
pickling spice	2 cups vinegar
garlic	1 cup pickling salt
	10 cups water

1. Wash sealers in hot water; in each put a bunch of dill, a red pepper and 1 teaspoon mixed pickling spice, garlic if desired.
2. Wash the cucumber thoroughly; prick with a fork; pack into the sealer.
3. Combine the vinegar, salt and water; bring to a boil; pour hot over the cucumbers to overflowing; seal; leave 6 weeks. Makes 15 pints.

UNCOOKED GHERKINS

2 weeks to make these, but very easy to do.

3 pounds small fresh gherkins	1 ginger root (broken)
⅓ cup pickling salt	¼ cup mixed pickling spice
boiling water	1 quart cider vinegar
1 teaspoon mustard	3 tablespoons sugar
3 tablespoons salt	2 cups brown sugar

1. Wash gherkins; place in a dry, clean earthenware or plastic bowl.
2. Mix salt well through the gherkins.
3. Pour in boiling water to cover; let stand overnight.
4. Drain the brine from the pickles; wipe dry by rubbing gently with a clean tea towel; wipe out the bowl.
5. Return the gherkins to the bowl; combine the spices, vinegar and 3 tablespoons of sugar; pour over the gherkins; mix well; set in a cool place.
6. Measure the brown sugar; each morning add about 2 tablespoons of sugar to the pickles and stir well; continue each day until the sugar is all used.
7. Remove pickles from the liquid; pack into sterilized jars.
8. Strain the liquid to remove spices; pour over pickles; seal.

MUSTARD DRESSING (Basic Recipe)

½ cup flour	1 quart diluted wine vinegar
¼ cup mustard	1 pound sugar
½ tablespoon turmeric	1 tablespoon mustard seed
1¼ cups water	1 tablespoon celery seed

1. Combine flour, mustard and turmeric; add water; mix to a smooth paste.
2. Combine vinegar, sugar and spices; heat to boiling.
3. Add flour mixture slowly, stirring constantly until the mixture boils again.

QUICK MUSTARD DRESSING

3 tablespoons flour	1 6-ounce jar prepared mustard
2½ pounds sugar	1 quart cider vinegar

Combine flour and sugar; add mustard and vinegar; stir until smooth; heat to boiling, stirring constantly.

CHOPPED MUSTARD PICKLE (INDIAN RELISH)

4 quarts large cucumbers (peel and remove the seeds)	3 red peppers (remove tongue and seeds)
1 quart large onions	2 bunches celery
3 green peppers (remove tongue and seeds)	1 large head cauliflower
	2 recipes Mustard Dressing

1. Chop each vegetable finely; keep separate; cover each with hot brine (1-1½ cups salt to 1 quart water). This quantity requires about 6 quarts of brine.
2. Let stand overnight; drain.
3. Cover with dressing.
4. Mix together and heat to boiling; boil 5 minutes.
5. Seal in sterile bottles.

MUSTARD PICKLES

2 quarts small cucumbers	2 red peppers
2 large cauliflowers	2 recipes Mustard Dressing
2 quarts pickling onions	

1. Wash cucumbers; cut if necessary.
2. Wash cauliflowers; break in small pieces.
3. Wash and peel onions; cut peppers in strips.
4. Put into separate dishes; cover with hot brine (½ cup salt to 1 quart boiling water); let stand overnight; drain.
5. Add vegetables to dressing; cook 5 minutes.
6. Bottle and seal, or keep closely covered in a stone crock. Makes 10 pints.

CHILI RELISH

1 6-quart basket ripe tomatoes, peeled	5 medium onions, chopped
10 green peppers, seeded and chopped	½ cup salt
	1 hot red pepper, chopped
10 sweet red peppers, seeded and chopped	1 recipe Quick Mustard Dressing

1. Combine first 4 ingredients with salt in a large bowl and let stand overnight.
2. Drain vegetables; add hot pepper; add dressing; bring to a boil and simmer about 20 minutes, stirring often.
3. Bottle in sterilized jars; seal tightly. Makes 6 pints.

   The juice which is drained from the vegetables makes a good Tomato Aspic base (page 392) or may be chilled and served as an appetizer. Do not add more salt.

MUSTARD BEANS

4 quarts wax beans	1 recipe Mustard Dressing, using brown sugar

1. Wash young, tender beans, remove tips; cut into 2-inch pieces.
2. Cook in boiling, salted water 15 minutes; drain.
3. Add beans to dressing; cook 5 minutes, mixing well.
4. Bottle in sterilized jars; seal. Makes 4 pints.

RIPE CUCUMBER PICKLE

6 large ripe yellow cucumbers	2 tablespoons mustard seed
9 cups water	1 sweet red pepper, seeded,
1 cup coarse salt	cut into ½-inch strips
6 tablespoons mixed pickling	3 small onions,
spice	thinly sliced
2 quarts vinegar	fresh dill heads
4 cups sugar	bay leaves

1. Peel cucumbers, cut into quarters lengthwise and then into halves; remove seeds.
2. Heat 2 cups of the water and the salt together until salt is dissolved; add the remaining 7 cups water and cool; pour over cucumbers; cover and chill in refrigerator for about 12 hours; drain well.
3. Place mixed pickling spices in a cheesecloth bag.
4. Place vinegar, sugar, mustard seed and bag of spices in a saucepan; heat until sugar is dissolved.
5. Pour ½ inch of the vinegar mixture into a large pan with spice bag; arrange cucumbers in a single layer in pot; bring to a boil and remove from heat as soon as boiling point is reached.
6. Pack cucumbers into sterilized jars.
7. Place red pepper, onion, dill and bay leaves into the pan and heat about 1 minute; place a few pieces of each in jar with cucumbers.
8. Remove spice bag from pan; add remaining vinegar mixture; pour over pickles in jars, leaving ¼-inch head space; work out bubbles.
9. Add more liquid to fill to proper level. Cap. Makes 3 to 4 pints.

RIPE CUCUMBER RELISH

12 large ripe cucumbers	5 cups sugar
8 sweet red peppers	5 cups vinegar
8 large onions	3 tablespoons celery seed
½ cup salt	3 tablespoons mustard seed
	1 tablespoon turmeric

1. Peel cucumbers; halve lengthwise; scoop out seeds.
2. Wash peppers; remove tongue and seeds.
3. Peel onions; cut in quarters.
4. Put all through food chopper using a coarse blade, or chop finely with a sharp knife.
5. Add salt; let stand overnight; drain thoroughly.
6. Add remaining ingredients; cook about 30 minutes, stirring occasionally.
7. Pack in hot sterilized jars; seal. Makes 6 pints.

SWEET PEPPER AND WATERMELON RELISH

2½ cups finely chopped
    watermelon rind
7½ cups finely chopped sweet
    red pepper
1½ cups finely chopped sweet
    green pepper
1½ cups finely chopped onion

½ cup pickling salt
2½ cups white vinegar
4 cups granulated sugar
1 tablespoon mixed pickling
    spices

1. Trim green outer skin and most of the pink flesh from watermelon rind; chop finely.
2. Place peppers, onion, watermelon rind in a large bowl; stir in salt; chill in refrigerator 4 hours; drain; rinse in cold water; drain.
3. Heat vinegar and sugar to boiling point in large kettle. Add drained peppers, onion, watermelon mixture, spices tied in cheesecloth bag.
4. Bring mixture to boiling point; simmer 45 minutes, stirring frequently to prevent sticking; remove spice bag when desired flavour is obtained.
5. Pack into sterilized jars and seal. Makes 2½ pints.

TOMMY'S RELISH

No cooking is required for this delicious relish.

7 pounds ripe tomatoes
2 pounds celery
7 large onions
1 cup pickling salt

6 cups sugar
2 cups white vinegar
2 sweet peppers finely ground
3 ounces mustard seed

1. Peel and chop the tomatoes; chop the celery finely; grind the onions; stir in the salt.
2. Place in a jelly bag and drain overnight.
3. Empty into a large bowl and add other ingredients. Bottle. Makes 10 8-ounce jars.

PLUM KETCHUP

4 pounds plums
1 pint vinegar
2 pounds sugar
1 tablespoon ground cinnamon

½ tablespoon ground cloves
1 teaspoon pepper
1 teaspoon salt

1. Wash plums; prick or cut the skin of each.
2. Add vinegar, cook until the plums are soft.
3. Press through a sieve or food mill or use a blender.
4. Add sugar, spices, pepper and salt; boil until thick.
5. Bottle and seal. Makes 1 quart.

CHINESE PLUM SAUCE

1 8-ounce jar Junior Plums   3 tablespoons vinegar
½ cup sugar

Combine these ingredients; heat until sugar dissolves; bottle.

CHILI SAUCE (Basic Recipe)

16 large ripe tomatoes   2 tablespoons stick cinnamon
   (½ a 6-quart basket)   (broken)
 2 large onions   1 tablespoon whole allspice
 4 green peppers (or 2 green and   1 teaspoon grated nutmeg
   2 sweet red)   1 cup vinegar
⅔ to 1 cup brown sugar   ½ teaspoon cayenne pepper or
 1 tablespoon salt   1 hot red pepper
 1 tablespoon whole cloves

1. Wash and peel tomatoes and onions; remove seeds and tongues from peppers.
2. Cut tomatoes; chop onions and peppers.
3. Place all together in kettle; add other ingredients. Tie spices in a cheesecloth bag.
4. Cook slowly 2 to 2½ hours, or until thick; stir frequently. Remove spice bag when the flavour is the desired strength (about 1-1½ hours).
5. Seal in sterile jars. Makes 4 pints.

   Chili sauce must be stirred frequently. At the last it will scorch very easily. For a really thick sauce, finish it in a shallow pan in the oven to prevent burning.
   White sugar and white vinegar give a lighter colour; brown sugar and cider vinegar give a good flavour.

FRUIT CHILI SAUCE

To the Chili Sauce recipe add 3 ripe pears quartered, cored, pared and cubed; 5 ripe peaches scalded, peeled and cubed; omit cayenne pepper.

CELERY SAUCE

To the Chili Sauce recipe add 1 large bunch chopped celery; omit cayenne pepper.

PEAR CHUTNEY

Chutneys (from the Hindu Catni) are popular with Chinese and Indian dishes.

12 cups pears, pared, cored and diced	1 tablespoon orange rind
2 cups sugar	1 lemon, chopped finely
1 cup white vinegar	2 small dried hot red chilis, crushed
½ teaspoon salt	1 tablespoon candied ginger, chopped
1 teaspoon ground cardamom	
2 cups seedless white sultana raisins	

1. Combine fruit, sugar and vinegar; cook until fruit is just tender.
2. Add the remaining ingredients; stir until well blended.
3. Pour into sterilized jars; seal. Makes 8 pints.

PEACH CHUTNEY

Substitute peaches for pears; cider for white vinegar and dark brown for white sugar.

APPLE CHUTNEY

Substitute 1 pound green apples and 1 19-ounce can blue plums, stoned.

CANTELOUPE CHUTNEY

Substitute 2 limes for lemon, currants for raisins, and diced canteloupe for the pears.

PICKLED PEARS (Basic Recipe)

5 pounds small pears	½ teaspoon allspice
3 cups sugar	½ teaspoon mace or
3 cups vinegar	1 tablespoon crushed stick cinnamon
1 teaspoon whole cloves	1 lemon

1. Peel the pears but do not remove stem (if large, peel, cut in ½, core). If very hard, they may be steamed 8-10 minutes.
2. Place sugar and pears in alternate layers in a large bowl; add vinegar and leave overnight.
3. Drain off the liquid; bring to a boil with spices tied in cheesecloth and lemon thinly sliced; simmer 5 minutes.
4. Add the pears a few at a time and cook until tender. Bottle and keep at least 2 weeks before using. Serve with salads, roast meats.
   Quick trick: Pack fruit into sterilized jars; boil liquid from sweet pickles with spice; strain over fruit; seal; leave in refrigerator at least 2 weeks.

PICKLED CRABAPPLES

Wash fruit, prick skins with a fork, steam; finish as Pickled Pears.

PICKLED PEACHES

Small peaches are peeled and left whole, large peaches halved.

SPICED ORANGE SLICES

Cut washed, unpeeled oranges into ½-inch slices; remove seeds. Cover with water in a shallow saucepan; simmer uncovered ½ hour; drain; continue according to Pickled Pears (Basic Recipe).

SPICED PRUNES

1 cup dried prunes (about 24)	¼ teaspoon dry mustard
¾ cup water	1 teaspoon vinegar
2 tablespoons sugar	1 teaspoon finely grated lemon
¼ teaspoon cinnamon	rind
¼ teaspoon cloves	

1. Place prunes in 1-quart casserole.
2. Combine remaining ingredients and cook until sugar and spices are dissolved; pour over prunes in casserole, cover.
3. Bake in oven (350°) for 1 hour. Bottle. Serve as a garnish with salads and meats. Serves 6.

PICKLED WATERMELON RIND

1 medium watermelon	3 tablespoons whole cloves
5 pounds sugar	3 tablespoons whole allspice
5 cups white vinegar	2 tablespoons whole ginger
5 cups water	2 lemons thinly sliced
4 tablespoons stick cinnamon	

1. Remove almost all the pink from the rind; cut rind in strips, 1 inch squares or small rounds; remove the green skin.
2. Soak overnight in ice water to which salt has been added (4 tablespoons to 1 quart) or soak overnight in limewater made by dissolving 2½ tablespoons slaked lime in 3 quarts of cold water, to crisp the rind.
3. Drain; cover with fresh water; cook until tender, but not soft— about 30 minutes.

4. Make a syrup of sugar, vinegar and water by boiling 5 minutes. Tie spices in cheesecloth and simmer in syrup.
5. Add the fruit; simmer until transparent when a piece is lifted from the syrup; let stand overnight; in the morning drain off the syrup, bring to boil and pour over fruit; repeat.
6. Place in sterile jars; cover with syrup; place a slice of lemon in each jar.

1 cup red maraschino cherries may be added during the last cooking. This gives the rind a delicate rose colour. 1 teaspoon of oil of cloves and 1 teaspoon oil of cinnamon may be used instead of spices.

PICKLED CHERRIES

3 pounds cherries, large	2 cups wine vinegar
2 tablespoons salt	2 cups cold water
2 tablespoons sugar	

1. Leave stems on cherries; pick over and wash.
2. Pack carefully in sterile jars; add salt, sugar, vinegar and water, stirred until well blended; fill to overflowing; seal.
3. Do not use for 2 months. Makes about 4 pints.

MINCEMEAT

2 cups ground beef (1 pound)	1-2 teaspoons mace
1 cup chopped suet (½ pound)	1-2 teaspoons cinnamon
2 cups currants	1-2 teaspoons cloves
2 cups raisins	8 ounces orange peel
6 cups grated apple (6-7)	8 ounces citron peel
2 cups brown sugar	¾ cup cider vinegar or boiled
⅔ cup molasses	cider
1½ teaspoon salt	1 cup brandy

1. Combine all ingredients except brandy; cover and simmer, stirring often, for 2 hours. Add cider if additional liquid is needed.
2. Stir in brandy; pack in sterilized quart jars; seal.
3. Age at least 1 month. Makes 5 quarts.

Quick Trick: Experiment with the many commercial mincemeats available to find one with the flavour that is popular. Add small amounts of fruit juice, maple syrup and brandy as desired.

MOCK MINCEMEAT

1½	cup apples		salt
1	cup seeded raisins	2	teaspoons cinnamon
1	cup cranberries	¾	teaspoon cloves
1	cup currants	¾	teaspoon allspice
½	cup cider vinegar	1½	cups sugar
¾	cup melted butter	1½	cups grape juice

Combine all ingredients; cook, stirring occasionally, for 40 minutes. Bottle. Makes 3 pints.

BEAN RELISH

1	15-ounce can cut green beans	1	green pepper cut in thin strips
1	15-ounce can cut yellow wax beans	1	red pepper (or pimento)
1	15-ounce can kidney beans	1	cup thinly sliced green celery
1	14-ounce can lima beans	1	cup water
½	19-ounce can Ceci peas (garbanzo beans)	2½	cups white vinegar
2	red onions, thinly sliced	3	cups sugar
		1½	teaspoons salt

1. Drain the beans into a sieve and rinse well with cold water.
2. Add the vegetables, cut finely.
3. Combine the water, vinegar, sugar and salt and bring to a boil; cool to lukewarm.
4. Pour over the vegetables.
5. Bottle, cover and store in refrigerator. Makes 4 pints.

FREEZING

Freezing has proven itself to be not only the most popular method of food preservation, but also the means of providing the homemaker with greater flexibility in routines of grocery shopping and preparation of family and party meals. Aside from this convenience, savings of time and money are possible through mass production and mass purchasing when foods are cheap.

The principle involved in freezing fruits, vegetables and meat is to retard the action of enzymes found naturally in food. Many vegetables must be blanched before freezing, otherwise the enzymes continue to ripen the food, causing softening and discolouration. Some fruits must be treated with ascorbic acid to prevent colour change. Meats too are affected by enzyme action, so that their storage period in a freezer is limited.

Suggestions for freezing prepared foods have been given with the basic recipes. For further information on the freezing of foods, provincial Departments of Agriculture provide booklets containing necessary information for successful home freezing. Consult these or freezer manuals.

Included in this chapter are a few general directions which apply to all foods to be frozen.

Select containers that will hold enough food for one meal, with straight sides and flat tops to save space, with wide openings so the food need not be thawed to remove it.

Plastic and metal containers, polyethylene bags, aluminum foil, saran and freezer paper—all these are moisture- and vapour-proof, which is essential for a good result.

The more air that can be excluded the better, so packages should be filled leaving ½ inch head space; bags should be pressed to expel air or it may be sucked out through a straw.

Glass jars may be used for leftovers and small amounts for short storage. A head space to allow for expansion is essential.

Labelling

The correct labelling will greatly assist in efficient use of the freezer.

A label should tell the name of the food; the date of processing; the details of processing; the use for which it is intended; and for locker storage, the name of the packager.

Labelling may be done with a child's crayon, a locker pencil, a china marking pencil, or a label placed between the cellophane and stockinette.

Coloured paper, string or tags may help in finding the food wanted.

Length of Storage

Most foods will keep several months if they are well wrapped and the temperature is at 0°. In the freezer compartment of a refrigerator it is not possible to maintain this low temperature so that foods will not keep as long. Sandwiches, for example, should be used within a week.

Where there is no automatic defrosting, defrost as soon as there is a frost build-up about ⅛-inch thick. Such a layer of frost acts as an insulator and the temperature in a storage compartment rises. During the warm weather when the refrigerator is being opened frequently, the control should be set higher and the baffle flap should be opened. When food is being frozen and fresh packages are to be added, the baffle should be closed and the control set to the coldest position. Later, open the flap and return the control to normal setting.

In a long freezing period certain foods do not freeze well. Synthetic vanilla, pepper, garlic, onions, cloves become strong and bitter; they should be added during the reheating period.

Hard-cooked egg becomes rubbery.

Sauces thickened with flour or starch may separate on thawing.

Many cooked vegetables become soft and mushy.

However, freezing in a refrigerator compartment for a *short* time is usually safe.

Is it safe to refreeze frozen foods? Experts say "it depends" on the food. Use the following as a general guide.

WHAT YOU CAN AND CANNOT REFREEZE

FOODS	Still firm, containing ice	Thawed but still very cold	Completely thawed, almost room temperature	Completely thawed for unknown period
Uncooked meat, beef, lamb, pork, veal	Yes	Yes	Yes	No. If odour is normal cook immediately
Uncooked variety meats, liver, kidney, heart	Yes	Yes	No	No
Uncooked poultry	Yes	Yes	Yes	No
Pies and casseroles of meat, poultry, fish	Yes	Yes	No	No

FOODS	Still firm, containing ice	Thawed but still very cold	Completely thawed, almost room temperature	Completely thawed for unknown period
Soups, sauces, gravy, creamed mixtures	Yes	Yes	No	No
Uncooked and cooked fish, shellfish	Yes	Yes	No	No
Fruit pies, fruits	Yes	Yes, but*	Yes, but*	No, may be fermented
Fruit juices and fruit drinks	Yes	Yes	Yes, but mixture will separate	No
Cream-style pies, cheesecakes	Yes	Yes	No	No
Vegetables	Yes	No — Use immediately	No — Use immediately	No
Baked goods — bread, rolls, cakes	Yes	Yes	Yes	Yes, but**
Ice cream, sherbet, parfait	Yes	Yes, beat during refreezing	No	No
Ice-cream pies or cakes	Yes	No	No	No

*Defrosted fruits quickly lose texture and color, but ferment rather than develop food-poisoning organisms. Use immediately or refreeze and use for fruit sauces, pie fillings, jams, jellies.

**Defrosted baked goods become progressively more stale if refrozen.

Frozen meat and other foods may be cooked, chilled and frozen again. This is not refreezing.

If in doubt about the recognition of spoilage, discard the thawed food rather than taking a chance.

23 Feeding a Crowd

THESE RECIPES are included to help all those who find themselves chairmen of the food committee.

The chairman of the food committee should line up those who will be in charge of the necessary subcommittees. Menu planning and marketing, food preparation, serving and cleaning up are certain to be among the responsibilities, but how will the decorations, publicity, entertainment or hospitality committees affect the plans? Who has arranged for the microphone and lectern? How many are coming?

With these and all other decisions made, the next step is to become acquainted with the kitchen facilities and to learn the possibilities for serving and the arrangements for dishwashing and garbage disposal. Portable electric roasters will hold 50 servings and will keep soups, scalloped potatoes, stew, beans or coffee hot.

The *menu* will be determined by the facilities, the season, the reason for the event, the food budget and the people who will be eating the food. We include in this chapter a few sample menus for which recipes are included in this or other chapters.

Once the menu is decided the *market order* may be planned. Recipes and quantities to serve 50 or 100 are given. Unless large equipment is available and the servers skilled, it is wise to prepare the recipes in smaller amounts or to cook in pans which will control the serving.

A *work plan* and the use of check lists serve as a constant watch on the progress of the project, and provide peace of mind and confidence to those in charge. A *written record* of all facts and figures, along with recommendations for improvement, will provide an invaluable reference for future endeavours.

PROTECTION AGAINST FOOD-BORNE ILLNESS

Food poisoning, which can cause extreme distress to its victims, and embarrassment and loss of reputation to food committees, can be avoided by observing these precautions:

At the Food Market

1. Look for branded meat with government-approved stamp.
2. Keep vacuum-packaged meat refrigerated.
3. When choosing hot barbecue meats, it is best to buy meat hot, right off the spit, or to completely reheat it at home.
4. Select frozen and perishable food last, especially in the hot summer months.

Storage

1. Follow storage directions on the labels of perishable or frozen foods.
2. Promptly refrigerate leftovers from prepared dishes. Do not give bacteria a chance to grow.
3. For safe storage, keep cold food cold (less than 40°) and keep hot food hot (at least at 140°).
4. Refrigerate all dairy and whipped vegetable oil products, e.g. toppings.
5. On a picnic or a trip, take extra care of foods which spoil easily in warm temperatures.

Preparation

1. Good hygiene is always necessary when handling food. Contamination may result from
   a dirty kitchen.
   food handlers with unwashed hands, bad coughs, infected cuts.
   flies, insects and rodents which may carry contamination to the food.
2. Serve prepared food containing eggs, milk or gravy within 2 hours or refrigerate.
3. Refrigerate dishes like potato salad, chicken pies, or chicken salad as soon as they are made, to avoid bacteria growth.
4. Always follow the time and temperatures given on the labels for cooking frozen foods like TV dinners and meat pies.
5. Thoroughly cook all poultry and promptly refrigerate leftovers.
6. Thoroughly clean cutting boards after every use. Cracked or scarred boards are a health hazard.

Courtesy of Department of National Health and Welfare, Ottawa.

SAMPLE MENUS FOR SPECIAL OCCASIONS

THE OUTDOOR BARBECUE

Barbecued Chicken

Savoury Rice   Celery and Carrot Sticks

Tomato Aspic

Rolls

Butter Tarts

Coffee   Fruit Punch

LADIES' LUNCHEON

Chilled Apple Cider

Fruit Chicken Salad

Rolls

Frosted Ice Cream Balls

Spicy Fruit Sauce

Tea   Coffee

PRESIDENT'S DINNER

Sherry Consommé

Spanish Steak

Green Beans   Baked Potatoes
Almondine   with sour cream and chives

Green Salad

Hot Rolls

Cherry Pie   Ice Cream

Coffee

CHOIR COTTAGE PICNIC

Lasagna   Vegetable Relishes

Potato Chips

Chocolate Brownies
à la mode

Coffee   Lemonade

FATHER AND SON BANQUET
Spaghetti and Meat Balls

Green Salad   Crusty Rolls

Deep Dish Apple Pie

Ice Cream

Coffee   Milk   Punch

WORLD AFFAIRS CLUB DINNER
Antipasto

Hungarian Goulash

Spanish Salad

Tapioca Pudding   Parisian Buns

Coffee

QUANTITIES TO SERVE 50

Food	Quantity	Food	Quantity
Punch	2 gallons	Vegetables—	
Coffee	1 pound	potatoes	15 pounds to mash
Tea	¼ pound	any canned	2 No. 10 cans
Cocoa	½ pound	cauliflower	15 pounds
Cream—		carrots	12 pounds
whipping	1 quart	beets	15 pounds
for coffee	1½ quarts 10%	peas	10 pounds (frozen)
for tea	1½ pints 10%	asparagus	15 pounds
Sugar Cubes	1½ to 2 pounds	celery, raw	3 to 4 bunches
Milk	6 quarts	carrot strips	2½ pounds
Ice Cream	7 to 8 bricks	olives	2 quarts
	2 gallons	cabbage	10 pounds
Cake	3 to 4 8 x 8″ cakes	lettuce	8-10 heads for salad plates; 6 for tossed greens
	5 pounds small cakes		
Bread—		tomatoes	10 to 12 pounds
rolls	6½ dozen	Salad Dressings—	
crackers	1 pound	mayonnaise	1-1½ quarts
1½-pound loaf	3 loaves	French	1 quart
Butter—		Salads—	
to serve	1 pound	green salad	7-8 quarts
for bread	1½ pounds	potato	6 quarts
for vegetables	1 pound	chicken	6 quarts
Pickles	2 quarts	fruit	6 quarts
Fruit or Tomato		Fruit—	
Juice	10 19-ounce cans or 2 No. 10 cans	bananas	17 pounds
		raspberries	7 quarts
Macaroni	3 pounds	strawberries	7 quarts
Meat—		peaches	11 pounds
cold sliced	7 pounds	Cheese—	
turkey	40 pounds	Cheddar	3 pounds
chicken	50 pounds	cottage	12 pounds
roast	20-25 pounds depending upon the amount of bone	grated	2 pounds
		Honey	5 pounds
		Jam	2 pounds
haddock		Maple Syrup	½ gallon
fillets	15 pounds	Rice	4 pounds (raw)
ham	2 12-pound hams		

SANDWICHES FOR 100

"Sandwiches" as used here mean 2 slices of bread with filling. Allow 1⅓ to 1½ sandwiches per person; for afternoon tea ½ to 1 sandwich.

BREAD AND BUTTER

10 24-ounce loaves bread   2½ pounds butter

If the filling is to be used generously and is well seasoned, a good quality margarine may replace the butter; 1 pint sour cream beaten into the butter will make spreading easy, and adds flavour.

EGG FILLING

8 dozen hard cooked eggs   1 teaspoon black pepper
1 quart mayonnaise   ¼ cup grated onion, if desired
2 tablespoons salt   ⅛ cup Worcestershire Sauce,
                                       if desired

MEAT FILLING, SLICED

12 pounds boneless roast   ½-1 cup mustard, horseradish or
    sliced by machine   pickle relish
    (ham, beef, butt roast of   salt and pepper
    pork)

MEAT FILLING, CHOPPED

10 pounds chopped meat   1 quart mayonnaise
2 quarts finely sliced celery   2 tablespoons salt
    (2 large bunches)   1 teaspoon pepper

SALMON OR TUNA FILLING

20 cans tuna (7-ounce) or   ½ cup lemon juice
    salmon (8-ounce)   ½ teaspoon pepper
2 quarts sliced celery   ½ cup minced parsley
1 quart sour cream dressing

FOWL FILLING

2 6-pound boiling fowl, sliced, or   2 quarts sliced celery
1 12-pound turkey, sliced, or   1 quart mayonnaise
2 5-pound boiling fowl, chopped,   2 tablespoons salt
    or   1 teaspoon pepper
5 quarts diced cooked fowl

LETTUCE

4 large heads

BEVERAGES FOR 100

These recipes allow two 4-ounce servings for 100 guests.

COFFEE

Electric percolators in many sizes are available today, but it is sometimes necessary to make coffee out of doors when no electricity is available.

2 pounds coarsely ground coffee   5 gallons boiling water
1 teaspoon salt

1. Stitch double seams in a bag made from cotton or porous cloth, twice the size of the bulk of coffee. Soak the bag in cold water before using it.
2. Combine salt and coffee; tie loosely in bag, leaving strings to lift bag out of coffee; drop into boiling water; cover tightly.
3. Simmer below boiling point 15-20 minutes, pushing bag down occasionally with a wooden spoon; remove bag.

TEA

Buy tea bags to make a gallon of tea. If the power supply will support electric tea kettles, 2 kettles and 3 large teapots will keep tea freshly made. Instant Tea made according to the directions is especially good for Iced Tea.

COCOA

Packaged cocoa mix to be added to boiling water will overcome the necessity for a large double boiler in which to heat the milk.

LEMONADE CONCENTRATE

2 pounds sugar   ½ ounce citric acid
1 quart water   ½ ounce tartaric acid
1 tablespoon grated lemon rind   ½ cup fresh lemon juice
1 teaspoon grated orange rind   ¼ cup orange juice

1. Bring sugar and water to a boil; boil 3 minutes.
2. Add rind and fruit juice, stir in acids, strain; bottle.
3. Use 1 tablespoon to 1 8-ounce glass of ice water.

FRUIT PUNCH TO SERVE 100 (Basic Recipe)

Makes 200 4-ounce servings.

6 quarts tea

6 48-ounce cans fruit juice

6 6-ounce cans frozen
    concentrate

6 quarts carbonated beverage

6 trays ice cubes

Make up the punch combining ⅙ of the ingredients at a time to fill the punch bowl or large pitcher.

The tea is used to give body to the punch. It must be fresh tea—not allowed to become bitter. It may be replaced with fruit juice, bottled cranberry juice, lemonade concentrate, lemon jelly powder (dissolved in a little boiling water), white wine, or claret.

Of the carbonated beverages, orange, lemon, collins mix, bitter lemon, tonic water, soda water are better choices than ginger ale.

Combinations of pineapple and grape juice result in an unpleasant blue colour.

Glamour Punch Touches:

Pour enough fruit juice into ice cube trays to fill the tray ⅔ full. Put a pineapple chunk and a maraschino cherry or sliced strawberry in each tray.

Partly fill any liquid-proof cardboard container with fruit juice; add a few sprigs of mint, slices of orange, lemon or lime; freeze. To serve cut away the cardboard and add the block of ice to the punch bowl.

Add sherbet by tablespoons just before serving.

APPETIZERS

FRUIT PUNCH

See preceding recipe.

CONSOMMÉ

2 No. 10 tins consommé
(105 ounces each)

Heat and serve in cups from tea pot or coffee pot. A well-washed electric percolator without the basket, a Silex coffee pot or an electric deep-fat fryer will keep consommé hot for self service. Serves 50.

CONSOMMÉ MADRILENE

Substitute 1 No. 10 tin tomato juice (105 ounces) for 1 tin consommé. Add 1 ounce sherry for each serving to the hot consommé; reheat and serve.

ANTIPASTO

Make up small plates of celery; vegetable sticks; olives; sliced, highly seasoned cold meat; devilled egg. These are colourful and may be arranged at the serving tables to keep the kitchen clear when the main course is being served. It also keeps the guests happy while the head table is being served.

ENTRÉES

BEEF STEW (Basic Recipe)

20 pounds stewing meat	1 teaspoon pepper
6 pounds onions	½ cup fat
3 cups flour	vegetable stock or water
¼ cup salt	2 pounds carrots

1. Cut the fat from the meat; heat the fat in a heavy frying pan; lift out hard bits.
2. Chop and fry half the onions; lift out of the pan.
3. Cut the meat into 1-inch cubes; season; coat the meat with about ½ the flour.
4. Brown the meat in the hot fat, adding a little meat at a time, and extra fat if needed. This step takes time but is necessary for a rich brown colour.
5. Add the cooked onions; simmer in a tightly covered pan on low heat until the juice of the meat begins to thicken; add water or stock to cover the meat; simmer 1 hour or until meat is tender.

6. Add the vegetables; cut remaining onions into quarters or eighths. Carrots may be diced or sliced; cover and cook until the vegetables are tender (about 1 hour).

7. Taste and season; thicken, using the remaining flour. Serve over rice, tea biscuits or potatoes, or make into a meat pie by adding a topping (page 472).

Other vegetables may be added. Many people prefer not to add celery, turnips or potatoes to stew. Serves 50.

HUNGARIAN GOULASH

3 ounces sweet Hungarian paprika	2 green peppers cut in strips
	2 pounds shell macaroni

1. Substitute above ingredients for pepper, carrots and flour of Beef Stew (Basic Recipe).

2. Cut meat into pieces 1 x 2 inches.

3. Melt fat, add sliced onions; cook until light brown; remove onions from pan.

4. Brown the meat; add paprika, onions and salt.

5. Cover and allow to simmer, stirring occasionally until the juice of the meat comes up and begins to thicken.

6. Add water or vegetable stock to cover meat by about two inches; after 1 hour add the peppers; simmer until tender.

7. Boil the macaroni (page 289); drain, add to the goulash just before serving. Serves 50.

Garlic cloves stuck on toothpicks may be simmered in the stew during the last ½-hour, then removed. 1 teaspoon caraway seed may be sprinkled into the goulash before serving.

BEEFSTEAK AND KIDNEY PIE WITH FLAKY CRUST

4 pounds kidneys (lamb, veal or beef)	2-3 cloves garlic

1. Substitute kidneys for an equivalent amount of beef in Beef Stew (Basic Recipe). Pour boiling water over the kidneys and leave 10 minutes; drain, and cut into quarters; remove white tubes, dice meat into ½-inch cubes.

2. Drain and brown kidney with the beef in fat. Complete as Beef Stew. Serve in individual 8-ounce heated casserole or in baking pans with Pastry Crust (page 472). Serves 50.

IRISH STEW

1. Substitute lamb for beef in Beef Stew (Basic Recipe); do not brown it; add onions and simmer until meat is tender.
2. Boil small whole new potatoes, small whole carrots, and frozen green peas in as little water as possible; add to the meat; thicken the stew. Serves 50.

CHICKEN STEW (Basic Recipe)

25 pounds boiling fowl	1 teaspoon pepper
2 bunches celery	butter
4 pounds onions	3 cups flour
¼ cup salt	

1. The day before the stew is to be made disjoint the fowl; cover with water; add celery leaves, 1 pound of onions chopped, salt and pepper; simmer, tightly covered, until chicken is tender (2 hours). Drain off the stock into a bowl; cool and refrigerate. Cool the meat; slice from the bones, keeping the pieces in large slices; discarding skin and bones, refrigerate in plastic bags.
2. The next day cut celery; quarter the remaining onions; boil in water to cover until just tender; save stock.
3. Skim fat from the chicken stock, make up to 3 cups with butter; combine with flour to make a smooth paste. Combine chicken and vegetable stock and make up to 3 gallons with water or boil the stock uncovered to reduce it if too much water has been added.
4. Heat stock; add fat-flour paste and stir until thick; taste and season; strain if lumpy.
5. Add chicken and vegetables and heat; taste again and season. Serve over rice, tea biscuits, or potatoes. Serves 50.

CHICKEN CHOP SUEY

Follow the recipe for Chicken Stew. Dice cooked chicken. Slice celery thin, boil until just tender; add with bean sprouts to thickened sauce and heat. Serves with rice and soya sauce. Serves 50.

CHICKEN CHOW MEIN

Cut the chicken in slivers; serve over chow mein noodles. Serves 50.

CHICKEN À LA KING

1 recipe Chicken Stew	1 4-ounce can pimento
3 pounds mushrooms	1 gallon cereal cream
	(160 ounces)

1. Prepare chicken as for Chicken Stew (page 702). Measure stock into a bowl; refrigerate.
2. Dice chicken. Skim fat from the stock and use it to sauté the mushrooms. Add cereal cream to the stock to make up to 3 gallons; thicken, using the fat to combine with the flour, adding butter as necessary; season.
3. Add diced pimento, mushrooms and chicken.
4. Serve on toast, over biscuits, in tart shells, toast cups, bouchées or puffed pastry shells. Serves 50.

BEEF ROLL (Basic Recipe)

1 recipe Biscuit Crust	1 teaspoon salt (approximately)
1½ cups finely chopped onion	1 cup chili sauce
½ cup chicken fat or shortening	6 quarts ground roast beef
6 quarts cold gravy	1 cup melted butter

1. Prepare the Biscuit Crust as Tea Biscuits (page 437).
2. Roll into a sheet ¼-inch thick and 10 inches wide; brush with melted fat.
3. Sauté the onions in fat; add the meat gravy and salt. Spread the chili sauce on the dough, then the meat mixture; roll as for jelly roll, from the long side; seal the edges by pinching together.
4. Place on a greased sheet; make cuts 2 or 3 inches on top.
5. Cut in 1-inch slices; place cut side down on shallow greased baking sheet.
6. Brush with melted fat; bake at 425° for 20 to 30 minutes. Serve with hot gravy, mushroom or tomato sauce. Serves 50.

Any cooked meat may be used: pork, turkey, chicken or ham. Mushrooms, green pepper celery may be chopped finely and added to the gravy for flavour. Mustard, horseradish or cranberry sauce may replace chili sauce. Canned soups or sauces may be substituted for gravy but may require less seasoning. For Salmon Roll see page 709.

BARBECUED CHICKEN

1 cup fat	½ cup brown sugar
6 onions chopped	8 tablespoons monosodium
4 cloves garlic (optional)	glutamate
1 tablespoon salt	
6 cups ketchup	25 broiler-fryer chickens,
3 cups vinegar (sweet pickle)	quartered

1. Melt fat; add onion; crush garlic with salt; cook until onion is straw coloured; add remaining ingredients and bring to a boil; simmer 20 minutes.
2. Arrange chicken pieces skin-side up on racks set 6 inches from heat. Brush with sauce.
3. Cook until tender, turning and brushing with sauce occasionally. Broil 45-60 minutes. Serves 100.

BISCUIT CRUST TOPPING

3 pounds all-purpose flour (12 cups)	4 teaspoons salt
½ cup baking powder	1 pound shortening
	4 cups milk

1. Mix the dough as for Tea Biscuits (page 437).
2. Roll the dough ½ inch thick.
3. Cut into 2-inch squares, into circles with a doughnut cutter, or into rounds with a fluted cookie cutter.
4. Brush with milk; place on a baking sheet. Bake at 425°.
5. Arrange on top of the pans of hot stew. Serves 50.

PASTRY TOPPING

5 pounds all-purpose flour	5 teaspoons salt
3 pounds shortening	4-5 cups water

1. Prepare as pastry; roll the dough the shape of the container in which the stew will be served; brush with milk.
2. Place on baking sheets; bake at 425° for 10 to 15 minutes.
3. Place on the hot stew just before serving. Serves 50.

MASHED POTATO TOPPING

10 pounds potatoes	2 tablespoons salt
¼ cup margarine or butter	½ cup parsley
2 quarts milk	

1. Cook, drain and mash the potatoes.
2. Add the butter and milk; season to taste.
3. Pour the stew into an oven dish; cover with the topping.
4. Brush with melted butter; brown in a hot oven.
5. Sprinkle with chopped parsley. Serves 50.

CRUMB TOPPING

Use any one of these:

1½ quarts of bread cubes	1 pint potato chips crushed
2 quarts cracker crumbs	1 quart soft bread crumbs

The crumbs may be browned in the oven or fried in garlic butter; allow ¾ cup butter and 2 cloves garlic. (Remove the garlic.)
They are especially good combined with grated cheese. Serves 50.

MEAT SAUCE (Basic Recipe)

2 cups salad oil	1 quart (6 6-ounce cans)
2 pounds chopped onion	tomato paste
2 cups chopped green pepper	¼ cup salt
10-20 pounds ground beef	¼ cup sugar
2 No. 10, or 10 20-ounce cans	⅛ teaspoon cayenne
tomatoes or tomato sauce	10 cloves garlic

1. Put salad oil, onion and green pepper in a large, heavy pan; cook over very slow heat for about 5 minutes; remove vegetables to a bowl.
2. Add meat in small amounts to the hot fat and cook over medium heat, stirring frequently, until meat is well browned; add to the vegetables.
3. Combine canned tomatoes, tomato paste, salt, sugar and cayenne, meat and vegetables. Stir until well mixed. The garlic may be crushed for a highly seasoned sauce or stuck on toothpicks and lifted out later for a milder flavour. Let the sauce simmer, uncovered, over slow heat about 2 hours, stirring frequently, or bake in moderate oven, stirring occasionally. Taste and season. Serves 50.

Meat extract may be added and less meat used for a cheaper sauce. Sweet pickle juice may be used to rinse ketchup bottles and added to sauce to replace part of the tomatoes.

SPAGHETTI WITH MEAT SAUCE

1 recipe Meat Sauce	1 celery stalk
3 packages Spaghetti Sauce Mix	½ pound butter
20 10-ounce packages spaghetti	100 ounces Parmesan or
salt	Romano cheese

1. Prepare the Meat Sauce; add mix and simmer until well blended.
2. Boil the spaghetti until just tender in salted water to which a celery stalk has been added.
3. Drain into a colander; remove celery; add butter; use spaghetti tongs to serve. Serve with sauce and grated cheese. Serves 50.

CHILI CON CARNE

1 recipe Meat Sauce	¼ cup chili powder
6 pounds bacon ends or	3 No. 10 cans kidney beans
2 bacon squares	

1. Prepare the Meat Sauce.
2. Remove rind, slice bacon, fry until crisp; drain; crumble the bacon.
3. Add bacon, Meat Sauce and chili powder to beans. Serves 100.

PORCUPINES

2 pounds regular rice	1 recipe Meat Sauce
	(with 12 pounds meat)

1. Mix lightly washed rice, ground beef, onions; shape into 200 balls by dividing mixture into 20 equal portions and each again into 10 portions; arrange the balls in rows in baking pans.
2. Omit salad oil from Meat Sauce recipe; combine other ingredients, pour over the meat balls. Turn once during cooking. Bake at 350° for 1 hour. Serves 50.

LASAGNA

1 recipe Meat Sauce	4 pounds Mozzarella,
1 pound Lasagna noodles	Romano or Parmesan cheese
4 pounds cottage cheese	minced parsley

1. Prepare meat sauce.
2. Boil, drain and cut noodles into 2-inch pieces. Keep in cold water until required.
3. Arrange sauce, noodles and cheese in layers in casserole, beginning and ending with sauce.

4. Arrange Mozzarella cheese, cut in triangles or strips on top; bake at 350° for 30 minutes.
5. Sprinkle with grated cheese and parsley. Serves 50.

CHICKEN CACCIATORE

25-30 pounds cut-up chicken
    salad oil
1 recipe Tomato Sauce (page 84)

1 quart Chianti (optional)
5 pounds spaghetti

1. Sauté chicken until golden brown; arrange in oven pans.
2. Add sauce mixture to the chicken, simmer covered for 30 minutes or until tender, adding wine at intervals; remove cover if necessary to thicken.
3. Boil and drain spaghetti; arrange chicken on spaghetti; pour sauce over. Serves 50.

SPANISH STEAK

20 pounds bottom round steak,
    cut in portions for serving
3 cups flour
3 tablespoons salt
1 teaspoon pepper

1 cup fat
2 pounds mushrooms
1 bunch celery, chopped
1 Tomato Sauce recipe
    (page 84)

1. Flour and season meat; brown in hot fat using several pans if possible to shorten the time. Arrange meat in baking pans in overlapping rows.
2. Wash mushrooms; drain; remove stems and chop finely; slice caps; fry stems using pans in which meat was browned, adding extra fat as necessary; add caps and fry.
3. Sprinkle mushrooms and celery over meat; add sauce.
4. Bake covered 1 to 1½ hours at 350°; uncover if necessary to allow the sauce to thicken. Serves 50.

MEAT LOAF (Basic Recipe)

30 pounds ground meat*	¼ cup salt
10 cups dry bread crumbs	1 tablespoon pepper
4 quarts milk, water, vegetable stock and tomato juice	3 tablespoons monosodium glutamate
3 cups chopped onion	1 dozen eggs

1. Combine all ingredients; pack tightly into greased bread tins or shape into 2-pound loaves and place in roasting pans.
2. Cover and bake at 325° for 1 hour; uncover to brown.
3. Cut 10 slices per loaf; serve 2 slices to each plate. Serves 100.

*The meat may be beef, a combination of lean pork and smoked ham, or lean pork and veal. 10 pounds pork may be substituted for an equal amount of beef.

8 pounds macaroni may replace bread crumbs; the mixture may be shaped into 6-ounce cakes for hamburgers. Makes 100.

MEAT LOAF WITH CHEESE POTATO TOPPING

1 recipe Meat Loaf	8 cups (2 pounds) grated cheese
8 6-ounce packages instant mashed potatoes	

1. Pack the meat mixture into 8 10 by 15 by 2½-inch baking dishes; bake as above.
2. Uncover, swirl one package instant mashed potato (prepared according to directions) on each dish of meat.
3. Sprinkle 1 cup grated cheese over each pan; bake in the oven until cheese melts and potato browns slightly. Serves 100.

SALMON LOAF

10 1-pound tins salmon (cohoe or pink)	1 tablespoon pepper
16 cups milk and salmon juice	¼ cup grated onion
2 cups fat	1 pound butter, melted
2 cups all-purpose flour	2 quarts crumbs (dry bread or biscuit)
¼ cup salt	1½ dozen eggs

1. Flake the fish; remove the skin; mash bones; drain off and measure juice.
2. Make a thin White Sauce (page 79) from next 3 ingredients; add seasonings and onion.

3. Melt the butter; stir in the crumbs.
4. Beat eggs; combine all ingredients.
5. Pour into 6 loaf tins which have been greased and have a strip of waxed paper on the bottom and ends.
6. Bake in a pan of hot water at 350° for 1 hour. Serves 48-60.

SALMON ROLL

Omit the crumbs and eggs in Salmon Loaf recipe; using other ingredients, prepare as in Beef Roll (page 703). Serve with mushroom or Tomato Sauce (page 84). Serves 50.

TUNA BAKE

1½ cups dried green peppers	48 ounces medium noodles, cooked and drained
6 cups diced celery	
4 medium onions, chopped	6 9½-ounce tins tuna (drained)
½ cup butter	3 cups mayonnaise
6 cans mushroom soup	1½ cups pimento chopped
3 cups milk	2 cups slivered almonds
6 cups shredded process cheese	(optional)

1. Cook peppers, celery and onion in butter.
2. Blend soup and milk and heat; add cheese; heat and stir until cheese melts. Stir in peppers, celery and onion.
3. Combine noodles, tuna, mayonnaise and pimento. Add cheese sauce. Turn into 4 greased 13 x 9 x 2-inch pans; sprinkle almonds on top.
4. Bake at 425° for 30-35 minutes or until bubbling. Serves 50.

MACARONI AND CHEESE

3 pounds macaroni	¼ cup flour
16 quarts boiling water	4 cups milk
8 tablespoons salt	1 cup butter
½ pound butter or margarine	2 quarts crumbs
1½ pounds Cheddar cheese, sliced	½ pound cheese (grated)
4 teaspoons salt	

1. Boil the macaroni in salted water until tender (about 20 minutes); drain.
2. Grease 2 baking pans 10 x 14 x 2½-inches; arrange the macaroni in layers sprinkling each with butter, salt and cheese; pour in the milk, shake in a jar with the flour until smooth.
3. Melt the butter; stir in the crumbs; mix with the 2 cups of grated cheese; sprinkle over the macaroni.
4. Bake at 300° for 50 minutes. Makes 2 pans; serves 50.

VEGETABLES

SCALLOPED CORN AND TOMATOES

6 28-ounce cans tomatoes
½ cup onion, chopped
2 tablespoons sugar
¼ teaspoon pepper

3 tablespoons salt
½ cup butter, melted
10 12-ounce tins whole
    kernel corn
1 quart soft bread crumbs

1. Combine all the ingredients, saving the crumbs to top the dish.
2. Bake at 350° for 30 minutes. Serves 50.

SCALLOPED POTATOES

12 pounds potatoes
1 teaspoon pepper
2 tablespoons salt

½ cup flour
1½ cups butter
2 quarts milk

1. Prepare the potatoes; cut in ¼-inch slices.
2. Arrange in layers, sprinkling each with pepper, salt, flour and butter; top with layer of potatoes.
3. Pour in the milk to come just to the top.
4. Bake covered at 300° for 1 hour, 350° uncovered for 1 hour or until soft and thick. Serves 50.

MASHED POTATOES

12 pounds potatoes, mashed
5 cups milk
½ pound butter or margarine
    (optional)

3 tablespoons salt
½ teaspoon pepper

1. Boil the potatoes; drain and mash.
2. Add heated milk, butter and seasoning; beat until fluffy. Serves 50.

SAVOURY RICE

4 cups chopped onions
1 cup fat
4 cups long-grain rice
2 10-ounce cans consommé

4 cups water
½ cup soya sauce
1 teaspoon salt
¾ teaspoon pepper
¼ teaspoon seasoning salt

1. Cook onions in fat until tender and lightly browned.
2. Combine remaining ingredients with onions.
3. Fill greased baking pans ¼ to ⅓ full. Bake covered at 350° for 1 hour. Serves 50.

GLAZED CARROTS

25 pounds small carrots	1 pound sugar
2 tablespoons monosodium glutamate	2 tablespoons salt
1 pound butter	1 tablespoon ginger

1. Wash and scrape or peel carrots; cut into finger-sized pieces; boil in salted water until almost tender; drain.
2. Arrange carrots in a single layer in shallow baking pans; sprinkle with monosodium glutamate.
3. Melt fat; add sugar and seasoning, pour over the carrots.
4. Bake at 350°, turning several times until lightly glazed (15-20 minutes). Serves 100.

GREEN BEANS ALMONDINE

30 10-ounce packages frozen green beans	1 cup butter
1 tablespoon monosodium glutamate	¼ pound toasted, slivered almonds

1. Boil the beans according to directions.
2. Brown blanched, slivered almonds in a pan in a moderate oven.
3. Add monosodium glutamate, butter and almonds to drained beans with seasoning before serving. Serves 100.

RICE AND BEANS ALMONDINE

Cook 2 cups long-grained rice while preparing half the recipe of Green Beans Almondine. Combine rice, beans and ½ cup chopped pimento. Serves 50.

SALADS AND JELLIES

GREEN SALAD

2 pounds cabbage	3 green peppers (1 cup)
1 pound spinach leaves	2 cups grated carrots
1 pound endive	1 bunch radishes (1-1½ cups)
2 heads lettuce	1 cucumber
½ bunch (2 cups) celery	1-2 pints French dressing
1 bunch green onions	3 pounds tomatoes

1. Wash, crispen and dry all the vegetables; shred cabbage, spinach and endive with scissors; break lettuce in chunks; add chopped celery; add green onions finely sliced (or grate onion later and add to the dressing); slice or dice green peppers, radishes and cucumber.
2. Combine all ingredients except dressing and tomatoes in large containers. Mix lightly by hand and refrigerate in vegetable crispers or plastic bags.
3. At serving time divide into individual servings or into bowls to serve 8-10. Pour salad dressing over each and toss lightly through the salad. Garnish with tomatoes cut in eighths or slices or with cherry tomatoes. Serves 50.

HEAD LETTUCE SALAD

6-8 heads lettuce	1½ quarts bottled dressing

Cut each head of lettuce in 6-8 wedges; serve dressing over each wedge or pass a variety of dressings.

MEAL-IN-ONE SALAD BOWL

4 pounds lettuce, shredded	French dressing as needed to moisten (1-2 pints)
12 eggs, hard cooked, sliced	5 pounds tomatoes
1½ pounds processed cheese, diced	3 pounds crisp bacon slices, or fine strips of cooked ham, turkey or chicken
3 cups beets, cooked, diced	50 stuffed olives
2 cups pickles, diced	
1 cup stuffed olives, sliced	
1½ cups radish slices	

1. Add the French dressing to the mixed vegetables at serving time; fill the salad bowls with salad mixture.
2. Top with tomato wedges and meat; garnish with stuffed olives. Serves 50.

SPANISH SALAD

1 No. 10 can kidney beans	1½ cups pimentos, diced
1 No. 10 can green beans	2 cups salad oil
1 No. 10 can yellow wax beans	2 cups white vinegar
5 large green peppers, cut in strips	1 cup sugar
12 medium Bermuda onions, cut into thin rings	salt and pepper to taste
2½ cups stuffed olives, sliced	stuffed olives, sliced, for garnish

1. Drain all beans thoroughly and place in large bowl; add pepper strips, onion rings, sliced stuffed olives and diced pimentos. Mix lightly.
2. Beat together the oil, vinegar and sugar until thoroughly blended; pour over bean mixture; season.
3. Cover and marinate in refrigerator at least six hours or overnight.
4. Line large buffet bowls with lettuce and fill with salad. Garnish with sliced stuffed olives. Serves 50.

POTATO SALAD

12 pounds potatoes (6 quarts cooked)	1 tablespoon monosodium glutamate
¼ tablespoons salt	½ tablespoon salt
1 large bunch celery (2-3 cups)	½-1 teaspoon black pepper
sprigs of mint	½ bunch parsley (¼ cup)
1 bunch green onions	1 bunch radishes
1 cup sour cream	3 green peppers (1 cup)
3 cups mayonnaise	4-6 heads lettuce

1. Peel the potatoes; add boiling water to which has been added salt, celery tops, a few sprigs of mint if available and the ends of the green onion tops; boil until just tender; drain the water into a container to save for stock; cool the potatoes to lukewarm; dice in half-inch cubes.
2. Combine the cream, mayonnaise and seasonings; mix gently with potatoes; refrigerate at least two hours to absorb dressing.
3. Combine all vegetables, sliced or diced with potatoes, tossing lightly with two large spoons or pancake turners.
4. Taste; season if necessary; serve in lettuce cups. Serves 50.

A potato scoop makes serving easier.

Hard cooked eggs may be added, but they are more attractive when used as a garnish or devilled and placed on a relish tray.

CABBAGE SALAD

10 pounds cabbage, shredded	1 pint mayonnaise
1 quart sour cream	

1. Combine sour cream and mayonnaise; stir through the cabbage. Serves 50.

   2 dozen chopped, red-skinned apples may be added to the salad dressing, or add one 19-ounce can drained pineapple tidbits.

MACARONI SALAD (Basic Recipe)

3 pounds cut macaroni (or shells), cooked	3 cups green onions, chopped
3 cups French dressing	1 bunch radishes, chopped
1½ cups celery, chopped	2 tablespoons monosodium glutamate

1. Chill macaroni in cold water; drain well.
2. Add French dressing; marinate half an hour.
3. Add vegetables and seasoning. Serves 50.

   Add 6 6-ounce cans drained flaked tuna, salmon or cleaned shrimp with ½-1 cup lemon juice or
   Add 4-6 cups diced chicken or
   Add 4-6 cups ham, with ⅔ cup prepared mustard.

JELLIED VEGETABLE SALAD (PERFECTION SALAD) (Basic Recipe)

¾ cup gelatine (12 envelopes)	12 cups diced or shredded vegetables, using 1 of the following combinations:
2 cups cold water	
2 cups sugar	
2 quarts boiling water (10 cups)	a. carrots, cabbage, celery
2 cups mild vinegar	
1 cup lemon juice	b. cabbage, green pepper, celery
4 teaspoons salt	1 6-ounce jar chopped sweet pickle
	1 small can pimento
	c. carrots, cucumber, pineapple

1. Soften the gelatine in cold water; dissolve sugar in boiling water; add gelatine; stir until dissolved; add the vinegar, lemon juice and salt; chill; colour if desired.

2. When the mixture begins to thicken, add the vegetables; pour into pans in which the jelly will be 2 inches deep (2 pans of 20 by 23 by 2 inches).
3. Allow the jelly to set in a cool place but not in the refrigerator, if meal is going to be served in a warm atmosphere.
4. Serve in 2-inch squares. Serves 50.

JELLIED FRUIT SALAD

Replace vinegar of Jellied Vegetable Salad with fruit juice, reducing sugar as necessary; for vegetable substitute grapefruit and orange sections, celery, small green grapes, canned pineapple, canned fruit cocktail.

JELLIED SHRIMP

Usc Jellied Fruit Salad base prepared with grapefruit juice; add finely sliced celery and shrimps cleaned and chopped.

TOMATO ASPIC

Substitute 3 48-ounce cans tomato juice for water, sugar and vinegar in Jellied Vegetable Salad. Add lemon juice, salt and Worcestershire Sauce, to taste. Serve plain or with added vegetables.

For a more highly flavoured aspic, substitute 1 cup tomato juice cocktail, vegetable juice, or tomato sauce for an equal amount of tomato juice. One cup of juice may be heated with a bit of bay leaf, tarragon, oregano, basil, fennel or thyme; strain into the other ingredients.

CARDINAL TOMATO ASPIC

Jelly:	Vegetables:
21 ounces strawberry jelly powder	6 cups carrot (grated), green pepper (diced) and celery (sliced)
1 3-ounce package lemon jelly powder	
13 cups tomato juice	
½ cup vinegar or lemon juice	
¼ cup horseradish	

1. Combine the two jelly powders; prepare according to directions, substituting tomato juice for water; add vinegar and horseradish.
2. When partly set add vegetables; finish as Jellied Vegetable Salad.

JELLIED APPLE SALAD

To 4 6-ounce packages of lime jelly powder, prepared according to directions on the package, add: 6 cups apples, diced; 1½ cups stuffed olive pieces, 6 cups shredded cabbage.

JELLIED GOLDEN SALAD

Drain the juice from 3 19-ounce cans crushed pineapple. Use as part of the liquid required for 4 6-ounce packages lemon jelly powder. When beginning to set, add 7 cups shredded carrots and the drained pineapple.

JELLIED CRANBERRY SALAD

1. Drain the liquid from 2 19-ounce cans sliced pineapple; add to 1 20-ounce can apple juice;
2. Measure; use this liquid as part of the liquid required for 4 6-ounce packages orange jelly powder.
3. When the jelly begins to set add the pineapple finely diced, 4 cups diced celery and 1½ pounds finely chopped cranberries.

CHICKEN SALAD (Basic Recipe)

20 cups chicken, cooked and cut in cubes (4 5-pound fowl)	6 cups cucumber, chopped
3 cups salad dressing	2 cups almonds, sliced and toasted
1 tablespoon salt	3 heads lettuce torn into small chunks
8 cups celery, diced	

Mix the chicken and salad dressing together; season. Just before serving combine all the other ingredients; taste and season. 1 quart pineapple cubes may be added. Serves 50.

FRUIT CHICKEN SALAD

For the cucumbers and almonds in Chicken Salad (Basic Recipe) substitute;

4 cups pineapple cubes	4 cups orange sections
4 cups seedless grapes	3 avocados, sliced

1. Prepare 1 cup of French Dressing (page 398), using juice from oranges and pineapple; marinate the chicken.
2. Toss the fruit together with the chicken and celery; combine with the salad dressing.

TUNA SALAD

Substitute 20 cups (12 13-ounce cans) tuna fish for chicken in Basic Recipe; omit almonds.

SALMON SALAD

Substitute 20 cups (12 13-ounce cans) salmon for chicken in Basic Recipe; omit almonds.

ROAST PORK SALAD

Stuffed shoulder of pork roasted and diced may be substituted for all or part of the chicken; omit almonds.

DESSERTS AND SAUCES

TAPIOCA PUDDING

8 egg yolks	8 egg whites
1½ cups minute tapioca	1 tablespoon salt
1½ cups sugar	1 cup sugar
1 gallon milk	1 tablespoon vanilla

1. Beat the egg yolks; stir in the tapioca and sugar; mix with 2 cups cold milk.
2. Heat the remaining milk; combine with the first mixture and heat to boiling, stirring; cook 3 minutes, or until the tapioca is clear.
3. Make a meringue by beating the egg whites and salt until stiff; add the sugar, slowly, beating until stiff and fine in texture.
4. Pour the hot mixture into the meringue, beating with a wire whip.
5. Add the vanilla; cool, stirring occasionally. Serves 40.

STRAWBERRY SHORTCAKE FILLING

10 quarts strawberries	1 tablespoon gelatine
3 cups sugar	2 tablespoons water
1 quart whipping cream	

1. Prepare the berries; add sugar.
2. Prepare the cream; to keep whipped cream fluffy if it has to stand; dissolve the gelatine in water over low heat. Whip the cooled dissolved gelatine into the cream as it is being beaten.

SHORTCAKE DOUGH

15 cups sifted pastry flour or	1 cup sugar
13 cups all-purpose flour	2½ pounds fat
10 tablespoons baking powder	1 quart milk
1 tablespoon salt	¼ pound butter

1. Combine the dry ingredients; cut in the fat.
2. Add the liquid slowly, stirring until the dough will leave the sides of the bowl.
3. Knead the dough on a lightly flavoured board until smooth.
4. Roll the dough 1 inch thick and cut into 2½-inch rounds or squares.
5. Bake at 425° for 20 minutes.
6. Split each round apart; while still warm place a piece of butter on each half, strawberry filling between and on top.
7. Garnish with whipped cream. Serves 50.
   Allow ½ cup prepared berries for each serving.
   Sliced peaches may be substituted for strawberries.

COFFEE CAKE

1. Prepare Shortcake Dough, adding ½ cup sugar and reducing the fat to 2 pounds; add 6 beaten eggs to milk.
2. Add 1½ cups raisins or blueberries; 1 tablespoon grated orange rind to dry ingredients. Add 6 beaten eggs to milk.
3. Pour batter into 3 greased baking pans, 16 by 10 by 2 inches, making a layer ¾ inch deep.
4. Combine 1 cup brown sugar, 1 teaspoon cinnamon; sprinkle over the batter.
5. Bake at 400° for 20 to 25 minutes. Serves 50.

PARISIAN BUNS

1. Prepare Coffee Cake recipe; add enough flour to work the batter to a smooth dough; knead until elastic.
2. Divide into six pieces; break each piece into 10 to 12 pieces.
3. Round up each piece into a little ball and flatten slightly.
4. Wash each with milk and dip into sugar; place on greased pans. With the finger press a small hole in the centre; fill with a little jam.
5. Bake at 400° for 15 to 20 minutes. Makes 5 to 6 dozen.

PASTRY (Basic Recipe)

10 pounds flour (45 cups pastry
    flour or 40 cups all-purpose
    flour)

½ cup salt
6 pounds shortening
1½ quarts ice water

1. Prepare pastry (page 472).
2. Divide the dough into 10 balls, and each ball in half again. Each of these pieces should make 1 pie with either a full or lattice top (½ pound pastry makes 1 double-crust pie). Makes 20 9-inch double-crust pies.

FROZEN CHERRY PIE

1 22-pound pail frozen cherries
1 pound cornstarch (4¾ cups)
1½ tablespoons salt
9 pounds sugar (18 cups)

1¾ pounds butter (3½ cups)
3 cups lemon juice
2 teaspoons almond flavouring
1 recipe Pastry (Basic Recipe)

1. Thaw the cherries by allowing them to stand overnight at room temperature. Drain; heat almost all the juice in a large kettle.
2. Mix cornstarch, salt, sugar and enough cold cherry juice to make a smooth paste.
3. Heat, stirring until the mixture begins to thicken; add butter, cherries, lemon juice and almond, stir very well.
4. Weigh out 2 pounds of filling and measure it; place this amount in each unbaked shell.
5. Cover with a pierced top or a lattice crust. Bake at 400° for 30 minutes.

    Makes 20 9-inch pies to cut in 5 to 6 servings. Frozen cherries are purchased in a 30-pound or a 22-pound container. To make fewer pies is not economical unless all the cherries can be used.

DEEP DISH APPLE PIE

½ recipe Pastry (Basic Recipe)
10 quarts (18 pounds) sliced,
    peeled apples
1½ cups water
1 teaspoon salt

2½ teaspoons cinnamon
1½ teaspoons nutmeg
6 cups granulated sugar
⅓ cup butter or margarine

1. Prepare ½ Pastry (Basic Recipe); chill.
2. In 2 17 by 11½ by 2-inch pans, arrange apples; pour water over apples; mix next 4 ingredients; sprinkle over apples; dot with butter.

3. On floured surface, roll half of pastry ⅛ inch thick and 1 inch larger than top of pan; cut slits in pastry; place over apples, pressing to pan edges; trim off excess.
4. Bake at 425° until apples are tender (40-50 minutes). Serve topped with whipped cream or soft ice cream. Makes 10 pies to serve 50.

BUTTER TARTS

⅓ recipe Pastry (Basic Recipe)
1 pound (3 cups) raisins or currants
1 dozen eggs
2 pounds (6 cups) brown sugar
2 pounds (2⅔ cups) corn syrup

1⅔ pounds (3⅓ cups) butter and margarine
2 lemons (juice and rind) or ⅓ cup mild vinegar
1 teaspoon salt

1. Prepare pastry; chill; prepare the fruit.
2. Beat eggs; beat in sugar and syrup. Add melted fat and lemon juice; beat well, adding raisins or currants.
3. Roll pastry to fit tart tins; do not prick.
4. Fill each pastry shell about ⅔ full (weigh out 1½ ounces of the mixture in a measuring cup or ladle). Use this measure to fill each shell.
5. Bake at 375° about 20 minutes. Makes 100 medium tarts.

APPLE CRUNCH

2¾ pounds brown sugar
¾ tablespoons cinnamon
1 teaspoon nutmeg
1 teaspoon salt

9 pounds sliced apples (approximately)
3 8-ounce packages corn flakes
½ pound butter, melted

1. Mix brown sugar with cinnamon, nutmeg and salt. Combine half the mixture with sliced apples and spread in 3 buttered pans, 10 by 16 by 2 inches.
2. Crush corn flakes into crumbs, combine with remaining sugar mixture and melted butter. Sprinkle over apples.
3. Bake in moderate oven (375°) 50 to 60 minutes or until apples are tender.
4. Serve warm with thin cream. Serves 50.

If canned apples are used, adjust baking time.

CUSTARD CRUNCH

4 quarts milk (20 cups)	5 teaspoons nutmeg
1 cup butter	2½ teaspoons cloves
20 eggs	2½ teaspoons mace
2½ cups sugar	30 cups puffed cereal
3 tablespoons cinnamon	

1. Heat one quart milk; melt butter in it. Beat eggs, adding in sugar and spices. Add remaining milk.
2. Combine as custard; divide cereal evenly between baking pans and pour custard in. Oven-poach at 325° for 1½ hours. Serves 40.

CHOCOLATE BROWNIES À LA MODE

6 recipes Brownies (page 520)	25 cups chocolate sauce
2½ gallons vanilla ice cream	

1. Bake brownies in 9-inch pans; cool; wrap and freeze.
2. Defrost when needed; cut into 2-3 inch squares.
3. Serve with a slice of ice cream and ¼ cup chocolate sauce. Serves 100.

FUDGE SAUCE

2½ pounds cocoa	4 pounds light corn syrup
10 pounds sugar	2 quarts milk
2 tablespoons salt	¾ pound butter
¾ cup cornstarch	¼ cup vanilla

1. In a double boiler combine the dry ingredients; add corn syrup and milk.
2. Cook over hot water stirring until the mixture thickens.
3. Add butter; cool and add vanilla.

BUTTERSCOTCH SAUCE

4 pounds brown sugar	2 tall tins evaporated milk or
5 cups corn syrup	1 pint cream
½ cup butter	1 tablespoon vanilla
1 teaspoon salt	

1. Cook the first four ingredients until a soft ball forms in cold water, 236°.
2. Remove from the heat; cool.
3. Add the milk and vanilla.
4. Beat until smooth. Allow ⅛ cup to a serving. Serves 50.

SPICY FRUIT SAUCE

4 pounds sugar	1½ cups butter
1 cup cornstarch	1¼ cups lemon juice
2 teaspoons salt	2 teaspoons nutmeg
12 cups pear syrup or other fruit juice	

1. Combine sugar, cornstarch and salt. Mix with a small amount of the pear syrup. Add to remaining syrup.
2. Cook until thickened and clear, stirring frequently.
3. Stir in butter, lemon juice and nutmeg.
4. Serve warm over gingerbread, plain puddings. Serves 100.

Appendix

FOOD DICTIONARY

A

Acidulate. To add an acid, such as vinegar or lemon juice.

À la King. (In a regal style.) Foods served in rich cream sauce usually containing mushrooms, pimento, etc. Chicken à la king is most popular.

À la Mode. (In a manner of fashion.) This term can be applied to almost any food to indicate some popular treatment or addition; pie à la mode means pie served with ice cream.

Angelica. The candied leaf stalk of a European herb; used in decorating cakes, candies and desserts.

Antipasto. An Italian word meaning assorted appetizers of fish, meats, olives etc.; hors d'oeuvres.

Aspic. A highly seasoned jelly made from concentrated meat or vegetable stock to which gelatine has been added; often to mould meats, fish and eggs.

Au gratin. A covering of bread crumbs on meat or vegetables. Often the vegetables are combined with a cheese sauce.

B

Bake. To cook by dry heat in an oven.

Barbecue. To roast meat on a rack, basting it with a highly seasoned sauce. Barbecue can also mean the cooking unit or grill, or the social event at which food is barbecued.

Baste. To moisten food while it is cooking with liquid or fat to keep it from drying out.

Batter. A mixture of flour and liquid which may or may not be combined with other ingredients. It is thinner than a dough.

Beat. To incorporate air into a mixture by means of a wooden spoon or rotary beater. Very rapid beating brings the mixture from the bottom to the top of the bowl quickly and thus incorporates air.

Bisque. 1. A cream soup thickened with bread or cracker crumbs. 2. An ice cream mixture containing finely chopped nuts.

Blanch. 1. To skin fruit or nuts by immersing them in boiling water for 2-3 minutes, then in cold water. 2. To scald fruits or vegetables prior to freezing. Original meaning (French) is to whiten, which probably referred to almonds which are white when skinned.

Blend. To mix thoroughly two or more ingredients.

Boil. To cook in steaming liquid in which bubbles are breaking on the surface.

Borscht. The national soup of the Ukraine, made from beets and other vegetables.

Bouchée. (A mouthful.) A small cream puff containing a savoury mixture.

Bouillon. A clear meat broth.

Bouquet garni. A bouquet of fresh herbs, bay leaf, thyme, parsley and sometimes any of basil, marjoram or celery. They are tied and dropped into simmering food during the last half hour of cooking, to give flavour. Dried herbs, ½ teaspoon of each, and a small bay leaf are tied in a muslin bag and used similarly. The bouquet or muslin bag should be removed before the food is served, and then discarded.

Braise. A method of cooking meats with moisture. See page 128.

Bread. To coat with fine, dried bread crumbs. Foods are often coated in 3 stages—in crumbs, in beaten egg and crumbs again. Used for fish, cutlets, chops and croquettes.

Broil. To cook food by exposing it to a direct source of heat—usually under a heating unit or over a fire. See page 144.

C

Canapé. A small piece of thin, shaped bread, toasted or fried and covered on one side with a mixture of meat, fish, eggs or cheese. Served as an accompaniment to a cocktail, or as an appetizer. See page 66.

Caramelize. To melt sugar slowly over low heat until it becomes brown in colour. The darker the colour, the stronger the flavour.

Caviar. Prepared and salted roe (eggs) of the sturgeon and other large fish. Black or red in colour, they are served on canapés.

Chantilly. A dessert which is decorated with whipped cream.

Charlotte. A gelatine dessert containing whipped cream; often moulded in a shaped mould lined with sponge cake strips or ladyfingers.

Chaud froid. Cold meat, fish or hard cooked eggs, covered with a thick sauce containing gelatine, then coated with aspic.

Chop. To cut in small pieces with a sharp knife or cutter, on a board or chopping bowl.

Chowder. A thick soup made of fish or vegetables containing crushed crackers.

Chutney. A highly spiced relish made from fruits and vegetables; often served with curried dishes; originally from India.

Clarify. To make clear by removing small floating particles, as in soup stock, fat for frying, or in steeped coffee.

Coat. To cover with a fine film as flour, fine crumbs, chopped nuts, etc.

Coddled. Referring to eggs, cooked very gently until lightly set.

Compote. Fruit cooked in syrup so that its shape is retained.

Condensed Milk. Whole milk, commercially concentrated by evaporation, then sweetened; it is thick in consistency. It contains over 50% sugar and is used primarily in the making of cookies and candies.

Condiment. Such mixtures of spices as prepared mustard, chili sauce, meat sauce, etc.

Court bouillon. A highly seasoned vegetable stock in which fish is simmered until cooked.

Cracklings. The crisp residue of the fat of meat, after the fat has been cooked out of it.

Crêpes. Thin dessert pancakes.

Croquette. A mixture of chopped or ground cooked food, cheese, meat, fish, etc., bound together by eggs or a thick sauce, shaped, then dipped into egg and crumbs and fried in deep fat.

Croustade. A case made of dry bread, pastry or potatoes, usually browned and used for serving such foods as creamed meat or fish.

Croutons. Small cubes of dry bread, browned until crisp; usually served with soup.

Curry. A mixture of spices ground and used in a sauce for Indian recipes.

Cut in. To combine solid fat with dry ingredients using two knives, a pastry blender or coarse grater.

D

Dice. To cut into small cubes or equal sized pieces, about ¼-½ inch in cross section. Cut large vegetables into slices and/or strips, cut strips into cubes, with a sharp knife on a board.

Dough. A mixture of flour and liquid in combination with other ingredients, thick enough to roll, knead or drop from a spoon.

Dredge. To coat with flour. This can be achieved by rolling the food in a shallow pan containing flour or by shaking food in a paper bag containing a small quantity of flour.

Drippings. Fat and juice dripped from roasting meat. The fat can be separated from the juices on chilling; it is then referred to as dripping (singular). Some types of dripping may be used in cookery.

E

En brochette. Meat and/or vegetables on a skewer.

Evaporated milk. Whole milk commercially concentrated by evaporation in a vacuum so that it contains twice the amount of minerals, protein, fat and sugar as ordinary whole milk; when very cold it can be whipped to three times its volume. There are some forms of evaporated milk, used primarily in infant feeding, which have been skimmed or partly skimmed prior to evaporation.

F

Fillet. A boneless piece of meat or fish; fillet mignon is a very delectable and tender fillet from the beef tenderloin. Sometimes spelled filet, the French word.

Flake. To break up into smaller pieces with a fork.

Flame (Flambé). To light warmed brandy either during the cooking or as the food is being served.

Fondue. (Melted.) Soft running mixtures into which other foods are dipped, then eaten. Small pieces of French bread are dipped into Cheese Fondue; cake and fruit into Chocolate Sauce. Beef Fondue consists of cubes of tender beef in hot oil.

Forcemeat. Meat, finely chopped and highly seasoned, used for stuffing.

Frappé. A semi-frozen fruit ice, coarse and mushy in texture.

Fricassée. To cook by braising or stewing.

Frost. To apply a sweet topping or icing.

Fry. 1. French fry is to cook in deep fat. 2. Pan fry is to sauté; to cook gently in small amount of fat in a frying pan.

G

Garnish. To decorate with portions of colourful and contrasting food.

Glacé. A clear candy coating, as on fruits or nuts.

Glaze. A shiny coating obtained by brushing foods with sugar, egg or thick fruit syrups.

Grate. To shred food by rubbing it over sharp-edged metal graters.

Grind. To cut or crush in a food grinder or mill.

H-I-J-K-L

Herbs. Leaves and stems of plants used to add flavour.

Hors d'oeuvres. Small portions of food served as appetizers.

Infuse. To extract flavour with boiling water.

Julienne. To cut food, usually vegetables, into match-like strips.

Junket. A dessert of milk, coagulated by rennet, sweetened and flavoured.

Knead. To work and press dough with the palms of the hands, alternately folding and pushing it. See page 452.

Ladyfingers. A sponge cake batter baked in strips; used to decorate moulded desserts.

M

Macedoine. A mixture of vegetables and fruits.

Marinate. To let food stand in an oil and acid mixture such as French dressing for added flavour. The mixture is called a marinade.

Meringue. A stiffly beaten mixture of egg whites and sugar (1) used to cover the top of a pie and usually browned in the oven or (2) made into dessert rings or small cakes and then baked.

Mince. To chop, cut or grind food into very small pieces.

Mincemeat. A seasoned mixture of meat, suet and fruits used as a pie filling.

Monosodium Glutamate (M.S.G.). A chemical substance used in the cooking or serving of foods, to bring out the flavour; it may be bought at some drug stores or in grocery stores under various trade names.

Mousse. 1. A mixture of sweetened whipped cream and other ingredients frozen without stirring. 2. Combinations of cream, fruit, meat, vegetables, etc., thickened with gelatine.

O

Oven poach. To place a baking dish of food usually containing egg or cheese in another dish containing water in which it is baked in the oven. The mixture is thus cooked at a lower temperature, which prevents curdling.

Oxidation. A chemical change brought about by the oxygen of the air; with fats, this is accompanied by an off-flavour (rancidity); with certain fruits—bananas, apples, peaches—oxidation causes discolouration when the cut fruits are exposed to the air. Oxidation of Vitamin C renders it useless, nutritionally.

P

Pan broil. To cook uncovered in a hot frying pan, ungreased or lightly greased, pouring off the fat as it accumulates.

Parboil. To partly cook in boiling water.

Pare. To cut away the outer covering or skin as from apple or potato; to peel.

Parfait. A frozen mixture in which a custard is combined with whipped cream, frozen without stirring. A dessert made by alternating ice cream with sauce in a tall glass. Usually topped with whipped cream.

Pâté. A paste of meat or fish, usually sliced and served for sandwiches or canapés. Pâté de foie gras is a pâté made from goose liver.

Patty. 1. Ground meat which has been shaped into a flat cake before cooking. 2. Patty shells are cases of puff pastry filled with a creamed mixture of chicken, fish, etc.

Petit fours. Tiny cakes with rich icing; often elaborately decorated.

Poach. To cook in simmering liquid below boiling point.

Pot roast. A method of cooking meat which combines stewing and roasting.

Purée. 1. The thick pulp of sieved fruits or vegetables. 2. A soup thickened by the former.

R

Ragout. A stew or braised meat mixture, usually highly seasoned.

Ramekin. Individual baking dishes.

Ravioli. Small shapes of Italian or noodle paste, spread with a meat or vegetable mixture, folded over and poached in a meat stock.

Render. To extract clear fat from the fat parts of meat by low heat.

Rissole. 1. A small pastry, baked or fried, enclosing a fruit or meat filling. 2. To sear or brown food, such as potatoes, with a protective covering.

Roll. 1. To place on a board and spread thin with a rolling pin. 2. A small bread.

Roux. A mixture of flour and melted butter used to thicken sauces. See page 81.

S

Sauté. To brown or cook gently in a small amount of fat in a frying pan; pan fry.

Scald. To pour boiling water over, either draining at once or allowing to stand several minutes.

Scallion. A bulbless onion, shallot, "green onion."

Scallop. 1. To bake a food, usually in a casserole with sauce or other liquid; food and sauce may be mixed together or arranged in alternate layers. Crumbs are often sprinkled over top. 2. A shellfish.

Score. To cut narrow grooves or gashes part way through the outer surface of food as on the skin of ham.

Sear. To brown the surface of a food quickly over high heat.

Sherbet. A fruit ice with egg white added.

Shred. To tear or cut into long narrow pieces.

Sift. To put one or more dry ingredients through a sieve or sifter once or several times. Use 2 paper plates or pieces of paper, sifting from one to the other.

Simmer. To cook below boiling point when small bubbles come slowly to the top and break below the surface of the liquid; at 185°.

Skewer. To fasten meat or poultry to hold its shape during cooking by means of a long metal or wooden pin (a skewer).

Slice. To cut off a thin flat piece from a larger piece, as a roast, a loaf of bread.

Sliver. To cut or shred into long thin pieces, as for almonds.

Soak. To immerse in liquid.

Soufflé. A thickened egg mixture containing any of cheese, fruit, minced meat, fish or vegetables made light by the addition of stiffly beaten egg whites.

Spice. Seasonings derived from roots, bark, stems, leaves, buds, seeds or fruit of certain tropical plants.

Steam. To cook in the steam which arises from a pan of boiling water or other liquids.

Steep. To leave in a liquid just below boiling to extract flavour, colour or other qualities; infuse.

Sterilize. To destroy micro-organisms by boiling in water, by dry heat or by steam.

Stir. To mix ingredients by a rotary motion with a spoon.

Stock. The liquid in which meat or vegetables were cooked.

T

Tamale. A highly seasoned Mexican dish of ground meat, seasonings, cooked cornmeal, beans and fat, rolled up in oiled corn husks and steamed or boiled.

Timbale. A mould of cooked food, meat, fish or vegetables.

Timbale case. A small pastry shell fried on a timbale iron in deep fat and used to hold cooked food.

Toast. 1. To brown lightly by direct heat. 2. Bread which has been toasted.

Torte. A rich cake-like dessert made up of many layers of meringue or cake.

Toss. To lightly mix ingredients with an upward motion, as in green salads.

Truss. To tie a fowl or other meat so that it will hold its shape during cooking.

Tutti-frutti. Mixed fruit.

W-Z

Whip. To incorporate air into a mixture by beating rapidly with a beater or wire whip.

Zwieback. A rusk; dried flavoured bread.

FLAVOURINGS, SEASONINGS, SPICES AND HERBS

"The proof of the pudding is in the eating!" A dish may win honours for its texture, shape, colour and nutritional value; but if it lacks a pleasant flavour, it will be eaten without enjoyment—or perhaps it will not be eaten at all!

Skill in the art of seasoning not only establishes the good cook, but enables her to serve simple, inexpensive foods with style and unlimited variation.

Although these four terms all imply the addition of flavour to food, flavourings are those which we add to cakes and desserts, while seasonings include all the others.

FLAVOURINGS. Include vanilla, maple, peppermint, almond, lemon, etc. Alcoholic extracts and pure oils make up the majority of true essences. Artificial extracts are often synthetic, usually coming from sources other than those for which they are named; some are diluted versions of the original flavourings. Because true flavourings are stronger in flavour than artificial flavourings, less of them is required; 2 or 3 drops of oil of peppermint are equivalent to many of peppermint flavouring.

Maximum flavour is retained when volatile flavouring (those with an alcoholic base) is added after cooking and cooling, thus preventing its loss with the steam. In the making of custard sauce, blanc mange etc., this practice can be followed; however, in baked dishes or those which must be served hot, this is not possible.

Fats retain flavours well, and because they do, flavouring is often added directly to the shortening in the making of butter cakes.

SEASONINGS. Salt, pepper, seasoned salts and monosodium glutamate are included in this category. Celery and onion salts are 2 of the many seasoned salts used in soups, sauces, cheese spreads, on vegetables, etc., made by mixing table salt with ground celery seed in the case of the former, and with dehydrated onion powder in the case of the latter. Blends of seasoned salts are sold under various trade names, and are a convenience for rapid seasoning.

Monosodium glutamate (M.S.G.) appears on the market under many different names. This chemical enhances the natural flavours of food—it does not add flavour of its own! Used chiefly on meats, fish, vegetables, stew and gravies, only a very small quantity of this salt is required. As a general rule, allow approximately ½ teaspoon for a dish which will serve 6.

TO COOK WITH WINE. Add 2 tablespoons of wine to 1 cup of soup, sauce for casseroles, stew and pan gravy for fowl, steak or roast meat. Bring to a boil to evaporate the alcohol.

Use dry white wine for lamb, chicken, veal and fish; dry red wine for stew, game and beef; sherry in consommé.

To flame food the alcohol is evaporated by burning it. This may be done during the cooking to develop flavour, but is more often done at the table for the dramatic effect.

Use dark rum for Christmas pudding, baked bananas and baked apples; light rum for pineapples, fresh or cooked fruit; brandy for crêpes, meat, game, cherries jubilee. Kirsch adds a cheerful flavour to strawberries, crêpes or mixed fruits; Cointreau adds an orange flavour to crêpes.

To warm the liquor, use a small stainless steel or porcelain warmer, or a metal ladle or large tablespoon. Just before serving, pour most of the liquor around the food. Light the rest in the ladle and use it to light that around the food. As the flame dies down spoon the sauce over the food and serve.

Marinate sugared fruit in wine and chill.

Use sweet sauterne or vin rosé for peaches and fruit compote; port for prunes and strawberries.

Replace part of the vinegar in a French Dressing recipe with a dry wine.

Wine left open soon sours. If this happens, remove the cork and cover the bottle loosely. Let it stand in a warm place and slowly the wine will change to vinegar.

SPICES. Spices include the buds, seeds, stems and roots of tropical plants, usually dried and sometimes ground. Spices should be bought in small quantities as their flavour begins to wane after 4-6 months. To retain flavour, they should be kept covered in a cool, dry place.

Used with care, spices should enhance flavour; they should never smother it. With foods that require long cooking, the addition of spices during the last half hour of cooking (when possible) helps to maintain their flavour. For maximum penetration, spices should be added to cold foods well in advance of serving.

Some spices are blended for specific purposes; pickling spice contains about 8 different spices. Chili powder and curry powder, both blends, are used to season Chili Con Carne and Curries, respectively, giving distinctive zest to each.

HERBS. These subtle enhancers of foods are derived from leaves and stems of various plants. Their role in the gourmet's kitchen as well as in everyday family cookery is to impart their characteristic flavour to soups, meats, vegetables, breads and sauces. To the salt-free diet, they are the saving grace!

One should never be conscious of the presence of specific herbs in a mixture—merely aware of a delightful blend of flavours. Herbs should be bought in small containers; once their scent has gone, they should be renewed. A little herb goes a long way. When not following a specific recipe, start with a little herb, and taste to determine if more is needed. About ¼ teaspoon of any dried herb or 1 teaspoon of fresh herb will season a dish serving 5 or 6 people, or will season approximately 1 pound of meat. Those herbs with the most dominant flavours—rosemary, oregano, sage and thyme—should be used with restraint; include only one when blending spices.

As with spices, herbs should be added during the last half hour of cooking for roasts and stews. Chops and steaks should be sprinkled with herbs during broiling or marinated in salad oil with herbs for several hours before cooking. When using herbs in cold dishes—as tomato juice, salad dressing, cheese dips, etc.—add herbs several hours before serving to allow penetration of flavours.

Commercial blends of herbs, such as poultry spice, Italian seasoning and brand-name blends save time and guesswork. The creative cook who likes to experiment with herbs, and who may even grow her own, will with practice convert "guesswork" into skill.

SPICES

DRIED AROMATIC SEASONINGS FROM THE ROOT, BARK, STEM, FLOWER, FRUIT OR SEED

	Caraway Seed	Cardamom	Celery Seed	Cinnamon	Cloves
APPETIZERS AND SOUPS	clam chowder cabbage chowder bean chowder sour cream topping	fruit cups pea and bean soups	on crackers cheese spreads most soups, especially vegetable and tomato soups	fruit drinks and coffee	pea and bean soups
MEAT AND POULTRY	Hungarian goulash kidneys liver pork	liver hamburger sausage	meat loaf stews stuffings marinades	sauerbraten glaze for ham	ham tongue sauerbraten
FISH AND SHELLFISH			fish chowder stuffings		court bouillon
CHEESE AND EGGS	Cheddar cheese blue cheese creamed eggs		scrambled eggs		
VEGETABLES	onions fried potatoes potato cakes sauerkraut turnips	boiled potatoes (in cooking water)	beets lima beans potatoes tomatoes	sweet potatoes	onions sweet potatoes
SALADS	beets cole slaw	orange	aspic potato salad salad dressing	fruit salads	
BREADS AND DESSERTS	breads cakes	coffee cakes yeast breads and rolls	toasted French bread	mincemeat coffee cake cinnamon buns spice cake chocolate cake apple pie, etc.	mincemeat spice cake and buns

SPICES Contd.

Ginger	Mustard	Nutmeg	Poppy Seeds	Sesame Seeds
cheese spreads	potato soup	cream of spinach,	cheese spreads	on buttered
ginger ale	cheese spreads	mushroom and	sprinkled on	crackers
pickles	pickles and relishes	cauliflower soups	crackers	cheese spreads
			garnish for	toppings for
			cream soup	canapés
				garnish for soup
dressing	roast beef	meatballs		coating for
marinades	devilled meats			broiled meats
barbecued meats	meat loaf			croquettes
ham glaze	ham, tongue			cutlets and
pot roasts	cold cuts			chicken
sweet and sour	spare ribs			
sauce	hamburger			
	scalloped fish	creamed lobster	sprinkled on	coating for
		and shrimp	broiled or	broiled fish
			fried fish	
cream cheese	cheese dishes	creamed eggs	in cream cheese	in cheese spreads
	devilled eggs		and cheese	
			spreads	
	dried beans	cauliflower	on noodles	on potatoes and
		eggplant	potatoes	noodles
		onions	spinach	topping for
		potatoes		other vegetables
		rice		
		spinach		
		squash		
		sweet potatoes		
salads	potato salad		fruit salads	chicken and
	cole slaw		salad dressings	fish salads
	salad dressing			
ginger bread		apple pie	rolls	rolls
gingersnaps, etc.		custards	breads	coffee rings
		spice cakes	cookies	
			cakes	

HERBS

SEASONINGS, FRESH OR DRIED, OBTAINED FROM THE LEAVES OF THE PLANT

	Basil	*Chervil*	*Dill*	*Marjoram*	*Mint*
APPETIZERS AND SOUPS	crabmeat, shrimp tuna cocktail tomato juice vegetable soup	garnish for appetizers chicken soup asparagus soup spinach soup	tomato soup tomato juice cheese dips	cheese spread paté tomato and vegetable juice oyster stew onion soup spinach soup	fruit cups and juices melon garnish pea soup
MEAT AND POULTRY	fried or broiled chicken lamb stew duck venison liver	all poultry and game	creamed chicken spaghetti lamb roasts and chops	pork, veal, beef roasts pot roasts goose stuffings	lamb roasts veal stew
FISH AND SHELLFISH	halibut, mackerel in stuffings	all fish	all fish and seafood	stuffing clams crabmeat lobster shrimp	
CHEESE AND EGGS	omelets, any cheese, rice or macaroni dish	scrambled eggs omelets cream cheese	cottage cheese macaroni and cheese	scrambled eggs omelets	creamed cheese
VEGETABLES	asparagus cabbage carrots brussel sprouts squash tomatoes vegetable marrow	asparagus carrots eggplant new potatoes most boiled vegetables	beans beets brussel sprouts cabbage sauerkraut squash tomatoes	dried beans carrots eggplant mushrooms onions peas potatoes spinach squash tomatoes	beets carrots peas new potatoes squash
SALADS	tomato aspic mixed greens French dressing	mixed greens fish salads	tomato potato salad cucumbers	mixed greens chicken salad seafood salad French dressing	fruit salad mixed greens
BREADS	toasted split muffins or rolls herb bread		toast toasted rolls	cheese spread for nut bread	toasted French bread

HERBS Contd.

Oregano	Rosemary	Savoury	Tarragon	Thyme
tomato soup	fruitcup	tomato juice	cheese dips	tomato juice
tomato juice	lamb broth	vegetable cocktail	seafood dips	fish cocktail
vegetable juice	chicken soup	vegetable soup		cheese and
	spinach soup	pea and bean		seafood dips
	pea soup			clam chowder
spaghetti, chili	veal and lamb	gravy	chicken	veal, pork
shish kabobs and	ragouts	stuffing	turkey	meat loaf
marinades	beef steak	stews	game	all poultry and
pork, lamb	partridge and	chicken	beef, veal	game
beef, veal	most game	hamburger	lamb	
broiled and fried		lamb	sweetbreads	
chicken		liver	tongue	
venison, kidney		pork		
stuffing	stuffing	stuffing	all fish and	all fish
baked, broiled	baked, broiled	baked or broiled	shellfish	
fish	fish	fish		
lobster, scallops	salmon	fish chowder		
oysters	all seafood dishes			
crabmeat				
omelets	sparingly in	devilled eggs	omelet	cottage cheese
	scrambled eggs	creamed cheese	all egg and	Cheddar cheese
	omelets	omelets	cheese dishes	egg and cheese dishes
green beans	green beans	dried and green	asparagus	asparagus
lima beans	lima beans	beans	beans	green beans
cauliflower	cauliflower	cabbage	beets	beets
mushrooms	mushrooms	egg plant	chard	carrots
potatoes	potatoes	peas	cucumbers	mushrooms
spinach	spinach	sauerkraut	peas	onions
tomatoes	tomatoes	squash	spinach	peas
turnips	turnips	tomatoes		potatoes
		turnips		spinach
seafood salad	mixed greens	mixed greens	mixed greens	mixed greens
potato salad	fruit salad	tomato salad	tomato aspic	tomato aspic
mixed greens		potato salad	chicken salad	chicken and
salad dressing		vegetable salad	seafood salad	seafood salads
			salad dressing	
pizza	corn bread	in biscuit	in butter	biscuits, corn
	muffins, biscuit	or dumpling		bread popovers
	batter	batter		

TABLE OF WEIGHTS AND MEASURES

The Canadian 40-ounce quart is used throughout the *Canadian Cook Book*

Food	*Weight*	*Measure*
Apples	1 pound	3 cups chopped or sliced
Applesauce	1 pound	2 cups
Asparagus	1 pound	10-12 medium stalks
Bacon	1 pound	20-28 slices (no rind)
		5 cups cooked crumbled
Bananas	1 pound	3-4 cups
Baking Powder	1 pound	2⅓ cups
Blueberries	1 pound	3 cups fresh
Bread Crumbs	1 pound	1 quart dry crumbs
		2 quarts soft cubes
Butter	1 pound	2 cups
	1 ounce	2 tablespoons
Cabbage, head	1 pound	1⅓ quarts, shredded
Carrots	1 pound	3½ cups chopped raw
		4 cups shredded
Celery	1 pound	4 cups diced or sliced
Cheese	1 pound	4 cups shredded
Chicken	5-6 pound hen	1-1¼ pounds meat
	(not drawn)	2 quarts stock
		6 ounces fat
		3 cups cubed cooked meat
Cocoa	1 pound	5 cups
Coconut	1 pound	6-7 cups
Coffee	1 pound	5 cups
Cornstarch	1 pound	3⅛ cups
	1 cup	5 ounces
Cornflakes	1 pound	18 cups
Corn syrup	1 pound	1⅓ cups
Cranberries	1 pound	4 cups uncooked
Cucumbers	1 average	1⅓ cups diced
Dates	1 pound, pitted	2½ cups cut fine
Eggs	1 pound	2 cups (8-10 eggs)
	1 cup	8 whites or 12 yolks

TABLE OF WEIGHTS AND MEASURES Contd.

Food	Weight	Measure
Fish	1 pound	3 cups flaked
Flour	1 pound	4½ cups sifted pastry
		4 cups sifted all-purpose
		3¾ cups graham
	1 ounce	4 tablespoons
Grapes	1 pound	2¾ cups cut and seeded
Green Peppers	1 pound	7 medium
		3½ cups chopped
	1 pepper	9 rings
Ham	1 pound	3 cups cooked ground
		4 cups cooked diced
Lemons	1 pound	4 lemons
juice	1 cup	4-5 lemons
rind	1 ounce	3 tablespoons
	1 lemon	2-3 tablespoons juice
		½- 1 tablespoon rind
Lettuce, head	¾-1 pound	12-16 leaves
		1¼ quarts, shredded
Macaroni	1 pound	4 cups
		8-10 cups cooked
Marshmallows	1 pound	64 whole marshmallows
Meat, cubed	1 pound	2½ cups uncooked
		2 cups cooked
ground	1 pound	3 cups cooked
		2 cups uncooked
Milk, powdered—		
whole	1 pound	4½ cups
skim	1 pound	3¼ cups
Molasses	1 pound	1½ cups
Mushrooms	1 pound	5¾ cups sliced fresh
Nuts	1 pound	4 cups chopped
Olives, stuffed	1 pound	1⅔ cups sliced

TABLE OF WEIGHTS AND MEASURES Contd.

Food	Weight	Measure
Onions	1 pound	3 cups chopped or ground
		4 cups sliced
Oranges	1 pound, 3-4	⅓-½ cup juice
		1-2 tablespoons rind
Parsley	1 ounce	5 tablespoons chopped
Peaches, fresh	1 pound	2 cups sliced
Peanut Butter	1 pound	1⅔ cups
Peas, fresh	1 pound	3 cups
Pickles	1 pound	3 cups chopped
		2¾ cups relish
		16 3″ pieces
Potatoes	1 pound	3-4 unpeeled
		4 cups peeled, diced, raw
		3 cups diced cooked
		2 cups mashed
Prunes	1 pound	4 cups cooked
		2 cups cooked drained pitted
Radishes	1 pound	108 radishes
		4 cups sliced
Raisins	1 pound	2½ cups seeded
		3 cups seedless
Rhubarb	1 pound	4 cups (¾″ pieces)
Rice	1 pound	2¼-2½ cups raw
		6-8 cups cooked
Rolled Oats	1 pound	5½ cups raw
Salmon, canned	1 pound	2 cups
Shrimp	1 pound	½ pound cooked and cleaned
		1⅔ cups cooked and cleaned
		30-33 shrimps
Salt	1 ounce	5 teaspoons

TABLE OF WEIGHTS AND MEASURES Contd.

Food	Weight	Measure
Spaghetti	1 pound	2 quarts cooked serves 18 (½ cup portions)
Spices	1 ounce	4 tablespoons ground 4-5 tablespoons whole
Strawberries	1 quart box	3 cups crushed
Sugar, brown	1 pound	2¾ cups (2¼ firmly packed)
white		2 cups
loaf		80-90 pieces
icing		3½ cups
Tomatoes	1 pound	4 (2½ inch diameter) 20-25 ¼-inch slices 3 cups cut in eighths
Tuna, canned	1 pound	2 cups
Turkey	20 pounds drawn	7½ pounds meat
	24-26 pounds (market dressed)	6 pounds sliced meat

TABLE OF CALORIE VALUES

Food	Quantity	Calories	Food	Quantity	Calories
BEVERAGES			**BEVERAGES**		
Beer	12 oz.	150	Tea, clear	1 cup	120
Carbonated			1 tbsp. milk	1 cup	20
beverages	8 oz.	100	lemon	1 cup	20
Cocoa, Whole milk	1 cup	235			
Coffee, clear	1 cup		**BREADS**		
1 tbsp. cream	1 cup	30	Bread, white	½″ slice	75
1 lump sugar	1 cup	25	whole wheat	½″ slice	85
Juice, apple	4 oz.	50	Cinnamon toast	½″ slice	125
grapefruit			Hamburger roll		150
(canned)	4 oz.	51	Melba toast	1 piece	20
orange (fresh)	4 oz.	50	Muffin, bran	1 large	125
(frozen)	4 oz.	35	Sandwich, meat or		
tomato	4 oz.	50	cheese		200-300
Sherry	3½ oz.	120	Wiener bun		155

TABLE OF CALORIE VALUES Contd.

Food	Quantity	Calories	Food	Quantity	Calories
BISCUITS, PACKAGED			**FRUIT, CANNED**		
Chocolate chips	1 biscuit	50	Apple sauce	1 cup	200
Chocolate marshmallow		60	Grapefruit	½ cup	85
Crème sandwich		50	Peaches	2 halves in syrup	100
Ginger snap		15	Pears	2 halves in syrup	100
Graham cracker		30	Pineapple	1 slice in syrup	100
Macaroon		20	Rhubarb, stewed	1 cup	380
Ritz cracker		16	**FRUIT, FRESH**		
Soda cracker		30	Apple	1 medium	75
Triangle thin		9	Avocado	1 half	280
			Banana	1 small	80
CEREALS			Blueberries	¾ cup	60
Corn flakes	1 cup	100	Cantaloupe	1 half	40
Shredded wheat	1 biscuit	75	Grapefruit	½ medium	75
Oatmeal, cooked	1 cup	150	Orange	1 medium	75
			Peach	1 medium	50
			Pear	1 medium	100
DESSERTS			Raspberries	¾ cup	60
Cake, angel,			Strawberries	1 cup	55
unfrosted	1 serving	125	Watermelon,		
butter, frosted	2″ square	250-350	wedge	4 x 5″	120
cupcake, iced	medium	170	**FRUIT, FROZEN**		
fruit	3 x 3 x 1	225	Blueberries	¼ package	40
jelly roll	1″ slice	250	Raspberries	¼ package	75
strawberry			Strawberries	¼ package	80
shortcake	1 serving	300	**MEAT, FISH AND POULTRY**		
Chocolate éclair	1 small	250	Bacon, side	2-4 slices	100
Ice Cream, rich	½ cup	300-500	back	1 slice	60
less expensive	½ cup	150-300	Beef, stew	1 cup	200
sherbet	½ cup	75	sirloin steak	4 oz.	300
Pie, cream	4″ slice	300	Chicken, fried	1 piece	150
fruit	4″ slice	300-400	broiled	½ medium	125
Mince	4″ slice	500	stew and		
Puddings,			dumpling	1 cup	190
cornstarch	½ cup	200	Ham, smoked	4 oz.	420
cottage	½ cup	100	Hamburger on a bun		300
custard	½ cup	100	Hot dog on a bun		300
tapioca	½ cup	200	Fish, white	3 oz.	100
			salmon, canned	½ cup	170
EGGS			Lamb, stew	1 cup	250
Boiled or poached	1 egg	75	chop, broiled	1 small	100
French toast	1 slice	200	roast, leg	1 thin slice	100
Fried	1 egg	100	Liver	4 oz.	160
Scrambled	1 egg	200	Oyster stew	6 oz.	200

TABLE OF CALORIE VALUES Contd.

Food	Quantity	Calories	Food	Quantity	Calories
MILK AND MILK PRODUCTS			**VEGETABLES**		
Butter or margarine ¼″ pat		50	Asparagus	½ cup	15
	1 tbsp.	100	Beans, green	½ cup	15
Cheese, cheddar	1 oz.	100	Cabbage, cooked	1 cup	40
cottage, skim milk	1 oz.	25	raw	1 cup	25
processed	1 oz.	100	Carrots, cooked	½ cup	30
Cream, top milk	1 tbsp.	30	raw	1	20
sour	1 tbsp.	30	Celery	1 stalk	6
whipping cream	1 tbsp.	50	Corn	1 ear	100
Milk, buttermilk	1 cup	85	Lettuce	1 large leaf	3
skim	1 cup	85	Peas, cooked	½ cup	55
whole	1 cup	165	Potatoes, baked	1 large	150
Milkshake		300-500	chips	10	100
chocolate malted with ice cream		625	mashed with butter	½ cup	80-120
			with gravy	½ cup	150
SALAD DRESSINGS			sweet	1	190
Salad dressing	1 tbsp.	75	Rice, boiled	1 cup	200
mayonnaise	1 tbsp.	100	Spinach, cooked	½ cup	25
French dressing	1 tbsp.	75	Tomatoes, raw	1 medium	20
			cooked	1 cup	40
SALADS			Turnips, mashed	1 cup	40
Salad, cabbage, with dressing	½ tbsp. Fr.	50			
chef's, with dressing	½ tbps. Fr.	75	**OTHER FOODS**		
Waldorf	½ cup	100	Gravy	1 tbsp.	50
			Macaroni and cheese	1 cup	210
SOUP			Spaghetti and tomato sauce	1 cup	210
Bean and bacon	1 cup	435	with meat and cheese	1 cup	400
Beef and vegetable	1 cup	200	Candy bar		300-500
Consommé	1 cup	25	Chocolate	1 oz.	140
Cream of chicken	1 cup	220	Jam or Jelly	1 tbsp.	50
mushroom	1 cup	340	Nuts	¼ cup	200
pea	1 cup	340	Peanut butter	1 tbsp.	100
Tomato	1 cup	205	Syrup	1 tbsp.	75
Vegetable	1 cup	205			

INDEX

NOTES

NOTES

NOTES

NOTES

NOTES

1 2 3 4 5 6 7   75 74 73 72 71 70 69

MILK AND CREAM

to sour milk	Measure vinegar or lemon juice into measuring cup (1 tablespoon per cup); add milk. Let stand to thicken.
to whip cream	Chill the bowl, beater and whipping cream (35% butter fat). Beat rapidly until the cream thickens and will hold its shape. Overbeating breaks the foam and forms butter.
to flavour whipped cream	Add 1 teaspoon sugar, 2 drops vanilla to each cup of cream when partly whipped.
to whip evaporated milk	Chill milk in a freezing tray until crystals appear at the edges (about 30 minutes); whip rapidly in cold bowl.
to whip skim milk powder	Sprinkle milk powder into an equal amount of cold water; beat until fluffy.

SUGAR

to caramelize	Stir 1 cup white sugar in a heavy pan over high heat. It will become lumpy and will then melt to a clear liquid (barley sugar). Reduce the heat and push the larger lumps to the centre until the syrup is reddish brown. Immediately, without stirring, add 1 cup boiling water, standing well back to avoid the sudden formation of steam. Simmer until smooth and syrupy. Bottle for later use.
for burnt sugar	Continue to cook caramelized sugar until it foams up into a dark orange colour. Then add the water.
to flavour icing sugar	Add 1 vanilla bean, cut into pieces, to 1 pound of icing sugar. Cover tightly. Use to sugar doughnuts, shortbread or for glazes.
to soften brown sugar	Place a slice of apple or bread on a piece of waxed paper on top of the sugar in a tightly covered container. Leave overnight. Replace if necessary.

TABLE OF SYRUPS FOR CANNING, FREEZING AND BEVERAGES

Type of Syrup		Sugar (in cups)	Water (in cups)	Approximate Quantity of Syrup (in cups)
Thin	20%	1	4	4½
	30%	2	4	5
Medium	40%	3	4	5½
	50%	4	4	6
Thick	60%	6	4	7
	65%	6½	4	7½

Combine sugar and water; stir until the sugar dissolves; bring to a boil; boil 2-3 minutes. A thin shaving of lemon rind is often added for flavour. Since syrup is most often used for fruit punch, for canning or for freezing fruits, it is usually made ahead of time and refrigerated.
Ascorbic Acid may be added to the syrup for peaches or apricots to prevent darkening. Use 200 milligrams to 1 cup syrup. Crush the tablet with 2 tablespoons syrup, then mix into the total amount, or use ¼ teaspoon powdered ascorbic acid to 1 quart sealer.